THE
COLLECTED ESSAYS
OF

John Peale Bishop

JOHN PEALE BISHOP
About 1922

THE
COLLECTED ESSAYS
OF

John Peale Bishop

EDITED WITH AN INTRODUCTION

BY

EDMUND WILSON

OCTAGON BOOKS

A DIVISION OF FARRAR, STRAUS AND GIROUX

New York   1975

Reprinted 1975
by special arrangement with Charles Scribner's Sons

OCTAGON BOOKS
A DIVISION OF FARRAR, STRAUS & GIROUX, INC.
19 Union Square West
New York, N.Y. 10003

814. B622c

Library of Congress Cataloging in Publication Data

Bishop, John Peale, 1892-1944.
  The collected essays of John Peale Bishop.

  Reprint of the ed. published by Scribner, New York.

[PS3503.I79A16   1975]   814'.5'2   75-25780
ISBN 0-374-90643-2

D 340

COPYRIGHT NOTICES AND
⤳ ACKNOWLEDGMENTS ⤶

ᴇᶠ INTRODUCTION ᶳᵛ

JOHN PEALE BISHOP at the time of his death had been contemplating bringing out a volume of his selected essays, and some notes among his papers show that he had meant to include at least nine of the pieces here reprinted. I have added a number of others which seem to me of equal importance. The result is not a series of literary critiques—though there are some admirable studies of literary subjects—but a set of discourses on various aspects of contemporary civilization: literature, painting, moving pictures, architecture, manners, religion. In painting Bishop had a special interest, for his father had studied art before he had studied medicine and had taught the son to paint when he was still a child of four. Later on, during a boyhood illness which had prevented him from using his eyes, so that his attention was diverted to the books read him, he gave up painting for poetry; but there was always in his poetry a large element of color and plastic form, and he occasionally in after-life went back to the brush again. Of the problems of the moving pictures he had acquired some special knowledge through working for a time, in 1924, in the titling department of Famous Players-Lasky. I have not reprinted here any of his papers on costume and cooking, though he occasionally wrote on these subjects. His interest in ornithology, which had also been stimulated in childhood by his father and which was revived in his later years when he went to live on Cape Cod, that great natural laboratory for bird-watchers, played a considerable part in his poetry but is represented here only by his review of *Audubon's America*.

Along with his more elaborate essays, I have included a selection from his reviews. The notes on the young novelists of the twenties have seemed to me worth preserving as conveying the spirit of that era and bringing to bear on it a sounder taste than its exponents were always able to exercise. The discussions of Southern novelists show the same kind of discrimination in a field in which Bishop worked himself. I have reprinted all his reviews of poetry written after his college days. We have been fortunate in this country during the last twenty-five years in having had at one time or another several poets of distinction regularly reviewing poetry. Bishop was one of these: from the beginning of December, 1939, to the middle of February, 1941, he had first choice of all the poetry at the *Nation*, and he contributed a number of other reviews to *Vanity Fair*, the *New Republic* and *Poetry*. I have not hesitated to put in, also, some of his aphorisms and notes on literature—especially since Bishop was aware that he often wrote more effectively in coining his thoughts into epigrams and paragraphs than in developing them as organized essays, and not long before his death had spoken to me of publishing some of his ideas in this form. I have added, at the end, four pieces from his unpublished or uncollected fiction—the first two of these characteristic of the more sensuous vein of his youth, with its fantasy and its dandiacal elegance; the two others, of the mood of his later years, more sober and sometimes macabre. The second piece—*How Brakespeare Fell In Love With a Lady Who Had Been Dead For Some Time*—is an episode from an unpublished novel on which Bishop spent a good deal of work. This book—*The Huntsmen Are Up In America*—was finished in 1926. It deals with the childhood and youth of a boy named Brakespeare More-O'Brien, the son of a Virginia lady and a rich Irish-American businessman, who—as the result of the infidelity and elopement of his mother—is brought up by his father, in Virginia, in an exclusively male household, under the influence of an eighteenth-century grandfather, so that he has to discover late for himself both women and modern America. The criticisms of F. Scott Fitzgerald and of the publisher to whom Bishop sent the novel had the effect of discouraging him with it; but, though the book does have serious weaknesses—he does not seem ever to have been very clear as to what destiny he intended for his hero, and the last chapters suffer from this—he put into it so much charming description and so much amusing commentary that one regrets that he should not have worked longer on it and given the ending more drama or point. The story has also an autobiographical interest—not, so far as I know, from recording any actual facts of Bishop's life, but from its reflection of the various elements which had gone to form his tastes and his tempera-ment, its locating on a Virginia estate and in the culture of an earlier time the rather special intellectual dwelling from which he first looked at the American world.

John Peale Bishop was born May 21, 1892, in Charles Town, West Virginia, in the Shenandoah Valley, and his people were mainly Virginian, though the family of his paternal grandfather had come from New London, Connecticut. A little treatise called *Colonel Cameron: His Ancestors and Descendants*, composed by John in his boyhood and carefully written out in a blank-book, shows how proud he was of his mother's lineage, full of ancient and noble Scotch names. He went to day school at Hagerstown, Maryland, which is not very far from Charles Town, to boarding school at Mercersburg, just across the boundary in Pennsylvania, and to college, in 1913–17, at Princeton —so that the whole of his youth was passed within a very small area of the East, where the South shades into the North, and in old-fashioned and countrified places, where one was little aware of modern industry. In a note on Bishop's literary generation at Princeton in the *Princeton University Library Chronicle*, Mr. Christian Gauss has written that "even as a freshman John had a self-possession and self-mastery which gave him the poise and bearing of a young English lord." Yet he was also sometimes shy and sometimes crude amid the monied proprieties of Princeton. Later on, in the days after the first world war, when one saw him in his handsome dressing-gown amid the Japanese screens and Renaissance beds of his friend Townsend Martin's apartment, which he inhabited during the latter's long absences, one felt about him that he was something like a Wycherley who had adapted himself to the nineties. What was not at all *fin de siècle* was the touch of eighteenth-century coarseness that was still country-bred and Southern and that was not in the least inimical to his fastidious taste and intellect but the soil out of which they grew and which gave them a solid base such as one did not ordinarily find in the Puritanical Northern aesthete. It was a type, too, that sometimes had facets of the fabulous bucks of the Regency of whom he delighted to read at that time and about whom, in *The Death of a Dandy*, he wrote one of the most brilliant of his longer poems; but he was also a romantic poet, not of the feverish or the ethereal kind, but in a vein in which purity of style gave refinement to emotions strongly sensual. And it was for poetry that he chiefly lived. He had no interest at all in politics, little in personalities; he very rarely read history or fiction and did not care to discuss general ideas. To quote Mr. Gauss again: he had at twenty-one come to Princeton "with a more carefully thought out and more accomplished mastery of the technique of English verse than any other undergraduate." Later, when he lived in New York and had a job on *Vanity Fair*, of which he eventually became managing editor, his poetry made heavy demands on him, and he would exhaust himself working through the weekends or in the evenings after returning from the office, and would try out, the first thing in the morning, reciting them while he made his toilet, the lines he had produced the night before, with an enthusiasm which to some of his college friends seemed almost Elizabethan, to others quite outlandish, but which, in any case, was perfectly spontaneous. At this time, he used to like to quote a poem of Yeats's called *Adam's Curse* (the passage occurs twice in the essays that follow):

> "Better go down upon your marrow bones
> And scrub a kitchen pavement, or break stones
> Like an old pauper, in all kinds of weather;
> For to articulate sweet sounds together
> Is to work harder than all these". . .

He had in common with Yeats a quality of feeling and phrasing that was noble not by convention but naturally. His verse was neither, like Wallace Stevens', the voice of a helpless pierrot imprisoned in a functioning businessman; nor, like Eliot's, a halting strain that was constantly being turned self-conscious by interruptions from an ignoble actuality. It was Bishop's native mode of speech, that was as much in evidence in the letters that one had had from him during the war and in the frivolous unsigned sketches that he wrote to order for *Vanity Fair* as in the poetry that he wrote for himself.

Bishop's weakness was in allowing himself to be influenced by the idioms of others. At college it had been Shelley and Swinburne; in New York it was Yeats and Pound. But during these years he had every appearance of progressing with the normal growth of a writer of first-rate talent: one felt that he was already commanding an idiom of his own. When, after his marriage to Margaret Hutchins, he went to Europe, in the summer of 1922, this development seemed somewhat slowed-up. He chastened and tightened his romantic style, but, now echoing Pound and Eliot, he lost much of his early élan. He improved his Italian and French; he studied ancient Provençal and took to translating the troubadours. He had never lived in Europe—had had, in his army days, only a glimpse of France; and he came to it with a lively appetite. Yet one regretted his absence from America, where one imagined that the literary revival would have continued to be stimulating for him. When, however, he returned to New York in 1924, he seems to have found America intolerable. He had no gift for advancing himself; he did not much enjoy the excitement of the twenties. The whole environment seemed a great deal more alien to him than Italy and France had been. And his failure in adapting himself prevented him from finishing his novel—since he had planned to bring his hero back from abroad—in any effective way. Brakespeare was to have hailed America—to have celebrated and revelled in it; John Bishop, in fact, rejected it. The Bishops went back to France in 1927 and bought the Château de Tressancourt at Orgeval, Seine-et-Oise, forty minutes out of Paris, supposed to have been built as a hunting-lodge by Henry of Navarre and enlarged in the eighteenth century, where they lived until 1933. Here Bishop tried again to do somethings in prose fiction with the country where he had been born and toward which he still turned, and worked on his two books of Southern fiction, *Many Thousands Gone* and *Act of Darkness*, which were published in 1931 and 1935. They were quite different from the early novel: more realistic and much better thought-out, but quite without the kind of brilliance that the latter had shared with his poetry.

When Bishop brought his family back to America—he now had three sons—in October of 1933, he went at first to live in Westport, Connecticut, and then in South Harwich on Cape Cod, and he began to occupy himself with the history of the New England branch of his family, about whom he wrote his poem *Beyond Connecticut, Beyond the Sea*. He had changed much since his first years in New York. In some ways his horizons had widened. He now read fiction, biography and history, and he reflected on historical problems. He had begun writing the thoughtful essays included in this volume, in which he tried to trace the effects on culture of the rise of the middle class—a phenomenon of which in his youth I do not believe he was even aware—and to expound, as an antidote to these, the virtues of the Southern tradition, as well as to justify the practice of the arts as activities respectable in themselves against what seemed to him a dangerous pressure in the direction of propaganda. And he resisted not only propaganda but journalism. No one was ever less of a journalist than Bishop, and his essays are seldom polemical. They illustrate themselves what they preach; and though he was less a master in prose than in verse, a little lacking the same sense of the prose unit that he had of the stanza and the poem, one finds in these papers the purity of tone, the intellectual elegance—as well as sometimes the sensuous images—that are characteristic of his poetry. They flash, besides, at their most inspired, with a rare kind of imaginative fire, when the felicitous or witty phrases keep pace with rapid spurts of insight. Brought together, they will, I believe, like his poetry, make an immeasurably stronger impression than—scattered, many of them, in periodicals of limited circulation—they ever did when he was alive. Some—like so much of his verse—have never before been published. He had a queer way of hiding his work or of preventing it from being well known. It was partly that he never thought it good enough and was always holding it back for improvements, partly that he had not the same boldness that had distinguished his early career, when, as at Princeton, he had not hesitated to publish and defend poems that shocked philistine opinion. He was now shy about exposing his writing. His first collection of poems since a book, published in 1922, in which I had collaborated with him, came out only in 1933, and his next, in 1935, was published in a limited edition of one hundred and fifty copies, so that few people except his friends ever saw it. Besides these, he had published only *Green Fruit*, in 1917, when he had just got out of college.

In the meantime, along with the broadening of his intellectual life, he had been growing somewhat more conventional at the same time as more "sophisticated" in the then current sense. His years in France had given him something of the detachment and the addiction to the amenities that are characteristic of American expatriates. His health, which had been frail in his boyhood, failed him also in later life, and he was incapable of the nervous effort, which even at the time had taxed him, of his days at *Vanity Fair*. One tended to assume with sorrow that his passion for poetry had also lapsed; yet, as one gradually saw more of his work—a volume of *Selected Poems* came out in 1941—one realized that this was not the case. His vein had gone partially underground, but it was still living and still uncorrupted. His echoings of other poets now seemed no more important than catchphrases and intonations picked up in conversation that do not affect one's opinions or the quality of one's personality. Though he had dressed in a variety of fashions, like the dandy that he always was, he now stood out unmistakably in his generation as a writer who had been something in himself and who had succeeded in holding on to what he had. He had never exploited his gifts or abused them in any way. At most, his Muse had sometimes been daunted, sometimes discouraged, sometimes bored; but she had gone on expressing in her beautiful speech discouragement, dismay or ennui—as well as her persistent delight in colors, textures and shapes. And she had laid up for her poet a treasure.

The Bishops in 1937 built a house at South Chatham on Cape Cod, where Bishop lived, with occasional absences for visits or lecture-trips, all the year around. His place, to which he gave the name Sea Change, looked out on a stretch of salt-marshes and the quiet coast of the bay. The house itself, a special creation of Bishop's old Princeton friend, the architect William Bowman, had something of that lofty splendor which John always managed to summon.

You ate on Dutch marquetry chairs at a long Louis Treize table in a high coral-pink room with Venetian cupboards in the corners and windows on three sides that opened on the white-wicketed lawn and gave a view of the pale blue water. At that time he liked to play on the phonograph Mozart's flute and harp concerto and the medieval plain-chants of the monks of Solesmes Abbey (both invoked, I find, in these essays); but when he spoke to me of the sadness with which the joyousness of Mozart was tinged and of the thin resignation of the plain-chant—as if life at that low point in the Middle Ages had been almost about to stop—I did not realize that it was anything but a mood. Yet he had sunk so far below his old self, his old responses even to the things that were still most important to him, that I remember being startled one day, when I had said something approving about Robert Frost—about whom, except for a few short poems, I did not myself much care—to see him brusquely aroused for a moment into something of his old interest and insolence and to hear him treat Frost de haut en bas in the tone of Byron on Wordsworth. In 1941 and 42 Bishop spent almost a year in New York as Director of Publications of the Bureau of Cultural Relations of the Council of National Defense. He studied Spanish and translated some Spanish poems. The fall of France was a terrible shock to him: one was astonished at the violence of his reaction to it. It was as if he had located in France the "good society" which he liked to imagine and which had faded from modern Virginia. His friend F. Scott Fitzgerald had died suddenly of a heart-attack on December 21, 1940, and John, while still in New York, wrote the elegy called The Hours, which set him off, when he returned to the Cape in the spring after his months of office-work, on a whole burst of creative activity that—flowing on into his Phi Beta Kappa poem and others of his later pieces—seemed to commence a new phase of his poetry. He went to Washington in November, 1943, to take a post in the Library of Congress which had been offered him by Archibald MacLeish, but he had already a leaking heart complicated with other disorders, and he was obliged to return to Cape Cod, where he died in the Hyannis Hospital on April 4, 1944. Even through these last days, when his life was running low, he had continued to work on his unfinished poems.

EDMUND WILSON

⋖§ CONTENTS §⋗

xv

THE
COLLECTED ESSAYS
OF
John Peale Bishop

ESSAYS

THE SOUTH AND TRADITION

I T REQUIRES a certain temerity to approach the Southern tradition. And yet I do not think that many persons, except a few old ladies and Mr. Joseph Hergesheimer, are likely to lose themselves in moonlight on the wet lawns, lamenting the lost valor, or wandering among the neglected box-trees to let themselves assume romance under the vanished colonnades. On the contrary, we suspect the past. We do not want a history of the South that points up the gallant Confederates and forgets the Colonel's mulatto daughter. Ours is a generation that, having been through a later than the Civil War, likes to believe the worst of everybody. So that when we search old closets it is more often to come out with a skeleton than carrying the remnants of grandmother's wedding gown.

Yet when we really begin to think about the closet and its contents, we know that the skeleton was once a man and that grandmother's wedding dress, for all the quaint cut of the sleeves and the yellowing color of the satin, belonged to a woman. We see that bed to which she came as a bride: there she was to suffer childbirth, and when she was carried from it she went feet first. And grandfather, too, though he had his faults, was once alive. His economy may have been worse than his morals; he may, if he were a Virginian, have come to the conclusion about the time of his marriage, that is to say, somewhere around 1850, that the only way he could make both ends meet was to encourage the breeding of the blacks. Yet, when we have listened to the scholars who have lately been at the records and have examined the account-books, not passing the papers in the secret drawer or omitting to uproot the family tree—even when we have heard the full scandal of statistics relating to grandfather, we still know, not only that he was alive, but that he had arrived at a manner of living somewhat more amiable than any other that has ever been known on this continent.

This life continued the English social tradition, and was in many aspects as crude as country existence under Queen Anne. It had been adapted to the climate, which was warm and republican; but it kept a provincial look. The White Sulphur Springs may be made to do duty for Bath, but there was no city to take the place of London. The roads were bad. Yet there was ease, and, as in eighteenth-century England, a surprising policy. When in her carriage grandmother passed an acquaintance, she knew that her bow must be a bend of her whole haughty back and not a mere nod of the head. And in her kitchen, where so many concessions had to be made to the African fondness for grease, the hand-copied recipes were many, varied and elaborate. For the South, whatever may be said, had at least passed those two tests which the French have devised for a civilization and to which they admit only themselves and the Chinese. It had devised a code of etiquette and created a native cookery.

There could have been neither, had grandfather been, as most of his compatriots were, forever on the move. But he was attached to the land, and from it and the remembered experience of the past he had arranged his living in quite another fashion than the industrial East and the wandering West. And he was quite aware of the difference. So much so that, when circumstances pressed to war, he could, along with General Lee, refer to the opposing Americans simply as "those people." No phrase could show a greater alienation. However, his own way satisfied him, and he was quite prepared to fight for it. Since slavery was a part of his system, he could defend slavery. And so he did, with what effort is known.

That is, of course, our fictional grandfather did. But to keep the record straight and not run away from the unforgivable fact, I must put it down that my own Virginian progenitor did not fight. He was, in 1861, though still comparatively young, so far advanced in corpulency that he could only with the greatest difficulty move from the front porch. He saw a neighbor of his, quite as fat as he, drive off one morning, whipping down the road, to join the cavalry in a one-horse buggy. But he did not emulate him.

Yet, combatant or not, he held to his tradition. We are so accustomed to take it for granted that this is what the Southerner would do, that we forget how strange this was in America. For though for the country as a whole there are traditions of a sort (as in our foreign policy, for example) they are not there as aids to living. And this is the use of customs, courteous manners, and inherited wisdom. While there is always much that a young man must, of necessity, face in complete nakedness without so much as a tatter from the past, it is not a very profitable way to go through life. It means an emotional impoverishment. To have to learn everything for one's self is, as Ben Jonson remarked, to have a fool for a master.

4

And yet nothing is more common for Americans. It is constantly said that America is too young to have acquired traditions. But this is not exactly true. It is because we are continually beginning the world again, every ten or fifteen years, that we wear that desperate look of youth. Ours is a mechanic's conviction that history is all bunk. There was never before, I suppose, a generation sent out so thinly prepared by its parents as that which went to make the Great War. The first wind from a shell shook the last metaphysical rag from our backs. We had no tradition of bravery, none of endurance; we only said, "What anybody else can do, we can do." In consequence, having stomached the war as best we could, we were presently found glorifying cowardice. A little later, we were quite as ready to cover the Chicago bandits with glory because we had heard from the newspapers that they at least were brave. Ten years' experiment taught confusion. But there is no need to repeat that tale. Let us remember grandfather sitting on his front porch; or his brothers, spurred and slender in their sashes, riding off toward a battle, which may have been Bull Run and was ultimately Appomattox. They, at all events, had a tradition, which they carried with them and found as useful as a bodyservant. And yet they were, as Americans, far younger than those who tell us we are still too young.

For it is to be noted that the Confederacy, for all the brevity of its formal existence, achieved more surely the qualities of a nation than the enduring Republic has been able to do. There were more emotions shared; its soldiers knew how to speak to one another or without speaking to arrive at a common understanding. Their attitude toward life was alike, and when they faced death it was in the same way. This makes for integrity, as it certainly also makes for a sounder emotional life.

II

It is not simple to say why this was so. But for one thing, Jamestown was not settled by Pilgrim Fathers. Now, I know it has been recently discovered that very few gentlemen came to Virginia, and I dare say another scholar will soon say that almost none of those who made New England were Puritans. Already we are told that more came for cod than for conscience' sake. But it will not do to let our modern obsession with numbers construe the seventeenth century; nor, because our contemporary intellectuals are ineffectual, must we suppose that the early New England theologians were anything of the sort. It required only a few men of character to set whatever thought there was, just as in Virginia we may be sure that, small though the number of gentlemen was, it was they who determined the colony's complexion.

True, Puritanism in its fine strictness and rigor did not outlast a generation; it was too uncompromising a creed for respectability, and when Jonathan Edwards tried to revive it a century later, he was cast out as a social menace. But the trick had been done, and a cast given the mind; that conscience was not henceforth to be silenced. But in the place of the old dependence on the arbitrarians of God, the younger men had begun to devise a doctrine which was later to be called self-reliance. It was they who have determined America, and they were, no less than their uncompromising fathers before them, enemies of custom.

The Puritan set out to destroy tradition; how much he made away with in England is only beginning to be understood. And on the rocks of New England, where he had nothing but hardship to oppose him, he was relentless. On the other hand, there were not so many who came South who did not hope to live as well as their plantations would allow them. And with tobacco that was very well.

This is the significance of their loyalty to the Stuarts: it may well be that they thought no more about the Divine Right of Kings than the Cape Cod fishermen did of the Divine, *tout court*; but they did subscribe to an ancient and aristocratic ordering of society. Sailing from England, they had not, like the Puritans, consciously cut from the past. They imported customs when their pockets were empty; they made an effort after gentility, even when the wilderness decided for simplicity. And though later, using their intelligences, they, along with the other colonists, rejected the past politically, the best of them continued, as far as their purses would let them, to live traditionally, unbending in manners only so far as was necessary to fit the times. In short, they lived as well as their plantations would allow them.

So much would seem to be the fact of the Cavalier South. The myth is something else again; possibly it is more important. For when all is said and done, a myth is far more exciting to the mind than most discoveries of mere things. So long as Rome was a myth, a matter for the imagination, stirred only by a few battered columns and a dismantled Forum, Europe was able to produce an architecture from its forms, through three centuries incomparable for fecundity. But as soon as Pompeii and Herculaneum were unearthed, the facts of the Roman world uncovered, classical architecture died and in its place succeeded only the lifeless excellence of archaeology.

Just when Southerners first began to find ancestors among the adherents of the Stuarts I do not know. But I suspect that Sir Walter Scott put them on that trace. Scott was enormously read throughout the South, and he undoubtedly made more conscious a romantic disposition that was already there. For if the Cavaliers were not ancestors, they could at least be seen as antecedents. Call it a myth: grandfather's parentage was all Scotch-Irish and grandmother could name only a Jacobite great-grandfather who had come scurrying from the battle of Culloden. There still remains that assumption of charm, that very real desire to please, a high-heartedness with hope, a recklessness against odds; all of which qualities may be seen riding and fighting in Jeb Stuart's cavalry. One Stuart at least is ours authentically. No one can deny those young men their horses, their hard riding and hard drinking, and a strange and not very thoughtful capacity for despair. They were not, if you will, very much like the pretty nobles who rode with Prince Rupert, but neither were they like those clear-eyed, stern young men who came down from Massachusetts and wrote letters home full of moral observations on the inhabitants of the Peninsula. The type persists. It has been finely portrayed by Mr. Faulkner in his *Sartoris*. In the conclusion of his novel, meditating on his pilot of the last war, he suggests that his qualities are now anachronistic. Certainly, they seem to have small place in modern life. And yet it is to be wondered whether they ever made for anything more telling than admirable failure. Even at Roncevaux.

In the same way we may assume that there was in the South an aristocracy, that is to say a class which, having the wealth, also took on the power and the responsibility of rule. Everywhere—at least this is true of the past, and the past is all we know that is true—the rich, as Lorenzo de' Medici has said, must have the state. But what distinguishes an aristocracy is that the government is directed in the interests of a class which acts together and whose individuals do not, as plutocrats do, destroy one another—and eventually the state—in a mean competition for privileges. It is this which gives it stability. A government by businessmen, as we have seen, not only corrupts government, but, being a cut-throat affair, frequently ends by destroying business.

An aristocratic class arises from wealth; descent has nothing to do with it at the start, though later the qualities of breeding begin to count and in the long run an aristocracy serves powerfully to mitigate the pure influence of money. Mr. Jefferson could not find any particular information on his paternal ancestors back of his grandfather; he was, however, to the curve of his calves an aristocrat; no man ever lived in more civilized elegance than the doctrinaire of Monticello. Nor did he shirk the responsibilities of rule. Manners must be acquired young. But it is not necessary to inherit them from forbears who, like those of Orlando, came out of the mists of the North wearing coronets on their heads. A grandfather will do, if the servants are good.

What is necessary, if a tradition is to be carried on, is that it should be inculcated in children before they have acquired minds of their own. It is too late to teach a child morality at seven. And in modern America, where the parents have given up all hope of controlling their progeny and have thrust the moral task on the school— which, in the more modern classes, is now passing it on to the children themselves—we have not only a great number of unmannerly brats, but a constantly increasing host of youthful criminals. That was where, in the South, the Negroes came in. They have, as someone said of cats and children, an "ancient and complicated culture of their own." But what they taught the young put in their charge was not their own, but their masters' morality. Of that they had acquired quite enough for the purpose; profoundly conservative, and possessed even as Africans of an instinct for courtesy and great tact, they were no small factor in enriching the Southern tradition. What they had to impart was of value, since they had lived always under that society to which later their charges would belong. Whereas, there is nothing, or next to nothing, that an immigrant nursemaid can pass on to an American child; she herself has been displaced, and whatever she knew in Scandinavia or Ireland has already lost much of its meaning; to the child it will be of no use whatsoever.

III

Tradition is all the learning life which men receive from their fathers and which, having tried it in their own experience, they consent to pass on to their sons. What remains is, if you will, a technique. Like anything else that is living, a tradition is in constant change. Not only does each generation have to face and survive new conditions; but what is more significant, it must, in civilized societies, come to a new conception even of what is least changeable in human nature, its fears and appetites. Thus we find our ways of making love, eating and drinking, facing war and approaching death, subject to fashion. And in high civilizations there is a continuous succession of manners, which apply not only to the fine arts but, perhaps more essentially, to the arts of living.

THE SOUTH AND TRADITION

Tradition is not therefore discarded; for not only is there a return after each youthful mutiny, but the change itself takes place within limits traditionally defined. Thus, a recent American writer, describing the generation of French writers who have come to maturity since the war, says of them that they are in full reaction against the *esprit français*. *Ils ne veulent pas êtres dupes.* This is accurate enough; it only remains to be added that the desire not to be taken in is the *esprit français* and the very essence of it. Of those whom I have myself known, and they include at least two of the most violent, I should, speaking as an American, say that they were French to the bone. They are not like the generation of Anatole France, but they differ from all that one thinks of as traditionally French only in being more brilliantly alive.

The use of tradition is, as the French abundantly prove, to provide a technique of living and offer a discipline and a pride. We must live from the instincts, for the mind unsupported not only cannot tell us how to behave, it cannot give us any very satisfactory reasons for living at all. It is to be recalled that the eighteenth century, which thought itself very rational and was intelligently curious as to man's nature, soon found itself faced by a boredom with existence so profound that it had to invent a new word for it—*le néant*, which I suppose could be translated as the blind abyss of nothingness. And there was in Mr. Shaw's intellectual Ancients nothing to make us think that their existence in any way justified all the time they had spent about it. They lived from the mind, at least from Mr. Shaw's mind, which is quite adequate for Mr. Shaw; but there was no doubt about their deficiencies the moment he compared them with the prophets and sybils of the Sistine Roof, those men and women of Michelangelo's who have grown old in passion and whose painted limbs are still tumultously strained.

But if the instinctive life is the only one available, the time given us who are not Ancients to explore its possibilities is very short. It is in fact too short to spend trying to find out everything for ourselves with no dependence on what has been tried and approved by men and centuries. The assumption commonly made in America is that the machine has so altered the present from the past that nothing our parents knew is of any use to us. The answer to that, which may be a futile one, is that had we retained our integrity as men, we should never have allowed mechanization to proceed so rapidly as to destroy all that accumulated wisdom. How meagre life is without it, needs no demonstration by me. For one objection to the machine is this, that it constantly tends to force the economic problem foremost.

9

Indeed, it may, particularly in times of crisis, make it so insistent that there is neither thought nor strength to deal with any other. And all those subtler and more passionate problems, which should engage our first attention, are left to one side, or receive only the most hurried attention. Behavior, our relations to others, men and women, our attitude towards ourselves, living in its extremest definition and in that sense which means only proper exercise of the body—all these, as Mr. John Maynard Keynes, himself no mean economist, has pointed out, are the proper studies of mankind. But so long as man is regarded simply as an economic unit, as he will be while we are content to overconsider the machine, then the only ideal that can be proposed is one of scientific efficiency. Man in the grander sense does not exist, and the human animal is atrophied. It does not seem to me to matter a great deal whether one is led to this state by Ford or Lenin, or it matters only as a choice of doctors might if we had decided that all our problems would be simplified (as no doubt they would be) if we were made sterile.

This the poets and novelists have always known. Hence their predilection for exalted personages, or at least for those who are beyond economic necessity, either because they are well-off and, as Mr. Edmund Wilson says of Proust's characters, can afford to be neurotic, or because as vagabonds they have decided to ignore it. This also explains why serious sociological novels, unless satirical, are so profoundly unsatisfactory from the literary point of view. They displace the novelist's problem. The recent novels of John Dos Passos are in this respect instructive.

But the instincts demand a discipline. Else they are distrusted. The Yahoos never existed except in Swift's imagination, and the attempt to revive them after the war was, on the whole, a failure. A number of charming people tried their best, but their Yahooism was more apparent than real, and even the momentary pretense was more than most of them could make without recourse to gin or some other stupifier. No, the danger is not that, without some form of inherited control, we shall be in for debauchery, but rather that we shall succumb to a spurious refinement, as debilitating as it is unreal, being based not on a fine sensibility but on fear. At all events that is what seems to happen in America, where the desire to be correct and to live by the advertisements tends to obliterate anything that can properly be called desire.

But their discipline should be something quite different from that recently recommended by the Humanists. For theirs was in part a counsel of exhaustion and in part a pathetic nostalgia for the small-town morality of an older America, dominated by the thin spire of the white meeting house. The art of living also has its academicians, and they are of them. Their references to the Greeks were intended only for those who would not take the trouble to look up the sources and see how far apart their counsel was from Aristotle and others of that violent race, who never, in their clear-sightedness, supposed, as Mr. Babbitt plainly does, that a mild happiness was the end of life. What we ask is not repression of passion, but a discipline that will in controlling it also conserve it. For this is, I take it, the secret of classical morality, in which it is opposed to romantic morality, which directs us on the road to excess in order that we may arrive at the palace of wisdom. They are opposed, but there is probably no reason why a man should not successively follow both, for even Aristotle thought it was impossible to expect moderation from the young. Drunkenness is good for youth, for they need to learn the limits of their own nature; but after a certain age it becomes necessary to know how to drink, that is to say, how to extract the utmost in pleasure from liquor without becoming either a drunkard or a boor.

Something of this inherited wisdom was certainly in the South, where the young men were allowed to be libertine and wild, and the old men were expected to lay their Horace beside the bottle of Bourbon. For theirs was a civilization of manners, and it is only through that unconscious instruction which we appropriately call being well-bred that the discipline of which I speak can be imposed. The sense of the earth was strong in them, so that they could not cultivate many illusions as to the ultimate improvement of mankind. But in the meantime, their manners gave them assurance and, because they knew that the use of civilities is to keep others at a distance, they preserved integrity. There is even today among the poorest Southerners a self-respect, a sense of their worth as men, regardless of what they have done or accumulated, that sets them apart from the more successful American who is lost without his bankbook and recognizes no pride but that of achievement.

IV

I have possibly, in insisting on the Southern tradition, represented it as being richer than it ever actually was. I have indeed meant to put it at its best; and though I have been accused of having elsewhere shown it as already in decline before the Civil War, I had rather accept that accusation than try to prove the contrary. What is true is that of the several social revolutions which America has undergone, the South escaped the effects of the first two. The separation of the colonies from England left her with the upper classes secure on their plantations. Jefferson seems to have affected his Virginia neighbors more by his example as a highly civilized country gentleman with a taste for architecture and gardening than by his writings as a democratic doctrinaire. Jackson and his followers certainly did attaint the tradition; but the full effects of the backwoods rebellion were not greatly evident before the divisions of armed conflict in the sixties revealed them. Of the Civil War and the Populist Revolt it is not necessary to speak. That they were disastrous to the traditional manner of living is tragically evident.

The South developed the virtues of an agrarian civilization. In some respects that civilization was poor. How account for that poverty, in literature let us say, as well as for a decline in the quality of Southern thought even where it had been most vigorous, in politics? It sprang, I should say, less from the exasperating presence of slavery in an age which could not well defend it, than from the South's rapid increase in size without a corresponding increase in means of communication. There were no cities to serve as centres of attraction. We cannot read the contemporary records of those marvellously talented Virginians who declared for independence and set the Republic on its foundations without being struck by the intense realism of their minds. They were critical as the statesmen of the Confederacy did not dare to be. And no small part of this vigor and alertness is to be traced to their conversations. They were, it appears, in constant contact with one another. Their wits were edged by talk, their idiosyncrasies corrected, their courage confirmed. In a word, they were worldly men, which is what statesmen ought to be. Williamsburg was a capital such as Richmond never was, and Alexandria heard more sound sense than has since been talked beside the Potomac.

So it is that we return to this tradition, not because it was romantic, but because it was, in so many ways, right. Grandfather as he sits on the front porch in the hazy heat of a summer afternoon is not an heroic figure. But he is a solid one and that not only in the sense of those too, too many pounds of flesh. He was clear as to his political position. And though there were many even then who saw him as out of his times, pathetic in the stubbornness of his eighteenth-century opinions, a late time has confounded his opponents. He saw that there must be a symmetry between agriculture and industry; that if you import labor for exploitation you must let it breed but not govern; while a Republic was doubtless the most propitious form of government for Americans, it would last and hold its integrity only so long as you did not let it become a real democracy. His opinions were sound; only one wishes he had not been so nervous about them. He mixed his juleps and pointed his country manners; he had, alas, only a realistic conception of justice, so that, unlike our present state, with its noble experiments and its perfectly moral laws, his jails were empty.

So it is, when we discover that without a past we are living not in the present, but in a vague and rather unsatisfactory future, we turn back to him. And suddenly even his fat becomes eloquent, for it speaks of imperfection. His day was simpler than ours. That is not to say it cannot instruct us. And we have this for our encouragement, that if there is anything profitable we can learn from him, it will have come from a man who had not only his social attachments but also his lonely being. That is a start, and a good one, in these days when everyone is ready to make a civilization in which nothing so fallible as grandfather will be left, but all will be ordered for the best in the best of dehumanized worlds.

Virginia Quarterly Review: April, 1933

THE INFANTA'S RIBBON

I

A POEM HAS this in common with a living substance: it is not readily exhausted by the intelligence. Analyze it we may, but in the process we are all too often aware that what was most essential to its being has eluded us. Decorticate a stem, split it into its fibres—it can no longer bear a flower. We cannot with the knife reveal its life; we can but sever it. And yet by the dissection, if we have skill and previous knowledge enough, we may discover something of how the plant achieved its purpose, coming to flower and preparing to seed.

In criticism of the arts, the technical approach is often the most profitable. It would seem that in this, as in other serious inquiries, the proper question is How? By asking it, we may miss something, and that the very secret and essence of the art; but pursuing it, we are much more likely to have something to show for our pains.

It is not a popular approach. For it has no anecdotes to offer, showing up the artist in his wilful and often deplorable incapacity in everything but his craft. It has none of those charming and provocative comparisons to make between, say, Proust's vision of the young girls at the seashore (adding, it may be, the suggestion that those were not girls at all that the living Marcel looked on with such constant inconstancy of longing) and the philosophy of Bergson, which the author of A l'Ombre des Jeunes Filles en Fleurs knew, or the theories of relativity of Einstein, which he almost certainly did not. It does not frisk the poet's empty pockets in the hopes of finding there an economic explanation of his immaterial possessions. So that, when its findings do not seem deadly dull, they are apt to strike the layman as incorrigibly frivolous.

"All painting," said Renoir, "is in the pink ribbon on the dress of the Infanta." What a remark! How expect a man seriously concerned with all that is most important in a world in turmoil to pay any attention to so trivial a pronouncement. Either, he must feel, painting is something more than this, or it is not worth bothering about. And surely there is more to the painter's art than a transference of pigment to canvas that leaves us staring at the Spanish princess's

14

stupid face and her incorruptible ribbons. Is it not possible that in the long blank Hapsburg lineaments there is a secret criticism of the principle of dynastic rule? Are there not there, already foreseen, the far causes of actual civil war? And what of the peasants, downtrodden and deluded, desperate at their toil? Did Velasquez never have to hide their sufferings in his heart while he stood in the palace painting the royal buffoons and dwarfs? Alas, there is no evidence on the canvas that he did. He painted what he saw before him, including the Infanta in her farthingale. What, then, is art? The seriousminded man will, like Pilate, begin his questions with a *What*? And unlike the wiser Roman, he frequently stays for an answer.

What is poetry? We may ask, and have no lack of responses. But definitions of poetry are notoriously unsatisfactory. Suppose on the other hand we ask how some particular poem is made. We may get something not too indefinite, though it may well turn out to be only a tag of the Infanta's ribbon.

II

I should like for the present purpose to take *Clair de Lune* by Paul Verlaine. It is short and comparatively simple; its complications are those of the art. It is in order to concentrate on them that I have chosen a French rather than an English poem.

> Votre âme est un paysage choisi
> Que vont charmant masques et bergamasques,
> Jouant du luth, et dansant, et quasi
> Tristes sous leurs déguisements fantasques.
>
> Tout en chantant sur le mode mineur
> L'amour vainqueur et la vie opportune,
> Ils n'ont pas l'air de croire à leur bonheur
> Et leur chanson se mêle au clair de lune,
>
> Au calme clair de lune triste et beau,
> Qui fait rêver les oiseaux dans les arbres
> Et sangloter d'extase les jets d'eau,
> Les grands jets d'eau sveltes parmi les marbres.

The emotion is apparent. But it is not clear that any interest can be attached to this improper to poetry. Verlaine extraordinarily

15

combined spontaneity with an expert skill; what his stature was need not concern us; it is enough if we can say, as in this instance we must, that he was an authentic poet.

Now the first thing to be noticed is that the poet attains his effects, whatever they may be, through words. The point has been made positively by Mallarmé. I shall go on to say that the poet's is the only art that will allow one to do so. For a little observation will make it clear that the novelist deals, not in words, but in incidents. They are his medium; it is upon them and their arrangement that he must count to convey whatever impression he wishes to the reader. And the purer his craft, the less consciousness of his words. That Stendhal read every morning in the *Code Napoléon*, in order to remind himself from that colorless style how transparent his own prose should be, may be only a literary legend; it represents, nevertheless, a practise in perfection. *Le Rouge et Le Noir* is unforgettable; but I doubt very much if anyone without special effort ever remembers a single word Stendhal wrote. Of course, the novelist has to write down his incidents, and even the most practised craftsman may daily experience difficulty in bringing his imaginary actions to the page and so become conscious that he is writing. But even in his transcription of incident, his unit is not the word, nor the phrase; it is nothing less than the paragraph. And the author's consciousness is not that of the reader.

But most novelists have something less than Stendhal's austerity and among them some will be found who depend upon words almost as much as the poets. They may even, on occasion, manipulate their prose as though it were, in everything but metre, poetry. The later Joyce is of these, as the author of *Dubliners* was not. In his *Anna Livia Plurabelle*, incidents do exist, but they are submerged in the consciousness, so completely is the attention dominated by the harmonious progressions of amazing words, arranged in rhythms that are extremely complicated and yet have all the vividness of actual speech. The words have been so often dismembered, that we would be inclined to call the whole work a case of philological matricide, were it not that, as it progresses, we are left in something of the same doubt as the great Irishman himself as to whether English is, or is not, his mother tongue. Ernest Hemingway can employ incident, and, perhaps for that very reason, can write pure prose. And yet we find him opening the story called *In Another Country* with this sentence: "In the fall the war was always there, but we did not go to it any more." This in its way is very fine; but it is the way of poetry.

III

Now, as Cocteau has remarked, there are always for the poet too many words in the dictionary. A poem demands that a comparatively small number be selected. And these, following the normal order of the language, more or less, will occur in statements, more or less intelligible. So far the ground seems to be sure; the advance has been slight. However, at this point, I believe, it is possible to generalize further and, tentatively at least, to set up two "laws" for the structure of poetry.

Poetry is such an arrangement of words that their real qualities take precedence over their arbitrary ones.

Poetry is such an arrangement of statements that their arbitrary pauses take precedence over the real ones.

As used here, the arbitrary qualities of a word are those which will be found assigned to it in the dictionary, where it has a meaning more or less close to a "root" and one or more meanings which it has kept or acquired in the course of its history. But all these meanings, whether they belong to the past or the present, have been arbitrarily attached to it. They hold only within a given language group and there only by common consent. The real qualities of a word are those which are perceptible to the senses, with all that implies of accent, quantity, consonantal and vowel conjunctions. These, too, vary with the tongue that speaks them; they are inalienable. Therefore, they are called real. And to these must, for the art, be added—for they also have an imaginative reality to the artificer—all the sensuous and emotional associations which the word may carry for him. He may choose among them, but he cannot avoid them. These last belong rather to the poet's history than to the history of the word. They distinguish his style from that of another poet and upon their richness and intimacy much of his merit will ultimately depend.

The real pauses are presumably those which are dictated by the structure of the poet's sentences. But upon these he superimposes other pauses, which are placed where they are simply by the poetic will. And they take precedence over the logical pauses.

Let us return now to the poem of Verlaine. A first glance reveals that it is composed of three quatrains, alternating masculine and feminine rhymes. The very fact that the composition is in verse presupposes a pause at the end of each line. This the rhymes insist on. The solution of the simple rhyme scheme at the end of each stanza increases the pause. In other words, there are throughout the poem alternations of silence as well as of sound.

These occur at regular intervals in *Clair de Lune;* and yet their position is arbitrary. They may, as in the fourth line, coincide with a logical end; they may come, as in the third line, in conscious contrast to it. It is in his ability to vary his pauses, and to play one sort against the other, that the interest of Verlaine's verse lies. And as long as we can follow it, our pleasure is increased by the intricacy of the play. For in such poems as the narratives of Sir Walter Scott, the pleasure is primary. And in such free-verse poems as those of Miss Amy Lowell, written as she said in cadence, which means simply that she allowed the phrases of her sense to determine the phrasing of her sound, the gratification is small; now that the charm of their irregularity is gone, her compositions have only a slight interest and that not inconsistent with prose. Verlaine's verse is superior; but the sources of our pleasure in it have yet to be disclosed.

It is to be noticed that the very first word with which Verlaine intends to rhyme, *choisi,* is reinforced by the preceding word *paysage,* in which the sounds of the rhyming syllable occur in reversed order and with a lengthening of the vowel. *Si* follows *ys.* And not only is this sound repeated, as would be expected, in the rhyme word *quasi,* but it occurs in the next line twice, again in reversed order, in *triste* and *déguisements,* where the sound of the following *s* changes slightly. The initial vowel of *votre* leads in the next line to *vont,* and *vont* by its concluding nasal sound is in turn linked at once with *charmant,* and after some delay, with *jouant, dansant,* and *déguisements.* Not only is the preceding vowel varied in both the first and last members of this series, but in *fantasques* we are given another variant on this sound by being allowed to hear the final *t.* Now going back to the second word of the poem, *âme,* we find that with it we are introduced to another sound sequence, since the *a* and the *m* will occur in reversed order in *masques,* a syllable which is itself repeated in *bergamasques.* In the third line, there is a very fine progression of vowels in the phrase *jouant du luth,* which, interrupting the longer harmonies, increases our pleasure when they return. In the fourth line, *leurs* prepares us for the rhyme in the first line of the second quatrain, *mineur,* a line which with the word *chantant* links this stanza with the dominant sequence of the one which precedes it. I should also like to point out that the word *triste* in the last line, in which for the fourth time is heard the combination *i* and *s,* is to be repeated in the opening line of the third stanza.

It would be tedious to go on here to analyze the remaining stanzas; it is enough to say that they display the same awareness of means directed toward an end, that every linking of sound leads resolutely toward a close, and that the last line perfectly concludes the poem. *Clair de Lune* is a composition in words, how deliberately done, we need not inquire. Though the ultimate impression it makes is single, yet the words may be conceived as existing on three levels. They are arranged, first, to attain the ear in a complicated harmony of sounds; they are set in a sequence of statements, in which no word departs from a meaning ordinarily accepted by the conventions of French speech; and as they come to the poem they bring with them sensuous and emotional associations as imprecise as the moonlight which they celebrate and as personal to the poet as the sighs of his body. These do not fail of communication, because Verlaine, while neglecting none of their other functions, has combined them to effect images of a rather startling clarity. We have already seen something of the employment of the word *masques* in the harmonious development of his verse. It has, when first encountered in his lines, a meaning that will be found in any dictionary, that of false faces of painted cardboard, worn as a disguise. It at once becomes personages wearing such disguises, and as soon as it is followed by the word *bergamasques*, these are seen to be figures in the costumes of the Italian comedy, looking much as they do in the French paintings of the eighteenth century; so that the masks themselves, if we are at all familiar with the pictures of Watteau and his followers, acquire a definite shape and color, though nothing has been said about either. For in enlarging the word, Verlaine has not made it more vague. On the contrary, as it merges with the other words of his verse, the images become clearer; and it is upon their evocation that the poet very largely depends to convey an emotion, possibly strong, but which, even to him, must have remained without precision until his art found for it this ordered expression. For what is left of personal emotion in this poem is no more than a trembling premonition.

A poem could hardly come closer than this to the condition of music. And the means by which Verlaine secures this impression approximate, as nearly as words will allow, the methods of the musician.

Ils n'ont pas l'air de croire à leur bonheur shows a progression through harmoniously related, yet never identical, sounds. But the sounds are those of words which, forming statements, do not depart from the utmost simplicity of speech. For this is a poem. In the first two lines the assertion is made that the soul of a certain person (whether the poet or another, need not now concern us) resembles one of those landscapes in which Watteau and some succeeding French painters were accustomed to show the personages of the contemporary Italian comedy. The possibilities of the comparison are developed: dancers and musicians appear with their appropriate actions; fountains rise and the waters fall into the basins of marble. Image is added to image, but there is no progress unless through the verse. It is as music that the poem moves and like music comes to its close.

At this point we may well ask the use of this complication. It has long been noted that all the arts employ the device of return with a difference. There is pleasure in the recognition of an element that returns; but, for the gratification to be complete, it is necessary that the return be retarded and accompanied by surprise. So we commonly explain the employment of rhyme, assonance and alliteration. The adroit use of such devices does procure pleasure, a pleasure that is ultimately the reader's; but it may be seriously questioned whether enjoyment in poetry, as in love, does not mask a profounder purpose. The purpose of the poet, as of the race, is to assure a progress in time. What we call the living quality of a work of art is precisely this: that it endures, continually changing, without ceasing to be itself.

The aim of such a poem as *Clair de Lune* has been defined by M. Paul Valéry: it is meant to produce in us who read it a state. It is an aim which, within the strict limits of M. Valéry's definition, probably no contemporary poet would admit. But I think we may go further and say that the state which this poetry produces, in so far as we are subject to its influence, is one in which we escape the limitations of actual time. Hence the release which accompanies it. The progress in Verlaine's poem, as has been said, is through the verse; the verse proceeds in time, measures and controls it, so that we conclude in the end that the poet has substituted another time for that in which we live and are destroyed.

This is not to assume that Verlaine has transported us to the eighteenth century. That is not in his power; and besides, the creatures he presents were even then fantasies. He has created another time, and one not measured by the calendar. It is in this sense, possibly in this sense alone, that the poem can be called a creation. To achieve it has required the full resources of an art.

IV

In so far as Verlaine's poem may be said to belong to an actual epoch, it is to the nineteenth century. A work of art cannot be of another age than that which produced it. It is perhaps necessary to labor this point, first, in order to make clear just what happens in the poem under discussion, second, to be rid of those critics who so easily declare that, because an artist chooses his images out of the past, he is preparing an escape to the past. The date of composition of *Clair de Lune* may, with reasonableness, be assigned to the period when Verlaine was engaged to the young girl he was afterwards to marry. Even then he knew something of his divided character, and though love is triumphant and life favorable, he cannot believe in his happiness. It appears that the poet's forebodings were only too well borne out by later events. The immediate occasion, then, of the poem is an emotion arising out of an episode in the poet's own life. Verlaine is not looking vaguely for an escape into the past; it would be more nearly true to say that he is looking with appalling clarity into the future. As a matter of fact, what he was looking at was the present of his own heart, in which both past and future were contained. What led him to lift these images from French painters of the preceding century we can only conjecture; it was not inability to consider the contemporary scene. For what is manifest in the poem is a relation between himself and the outer world. It was one not to be traced by logic, nor could it even be apprehended by the senses until these imaginary Italian comedians had been found. The poem came into being only when this abstract relation had been made palpable through the relations, both logical and sensuous, of the words of which it is composed.

What I have described as being behind the poem assuredly is not in it. I am using knowledge which I have derived from other sources, notably from M. François Porcher's biography of Verlaine. For once the poet has chosen these images, apparently so remote from the life of a *petit bourgeois* of the Second Empire, they begin to acquire an objective reality and become, I know not how consciously, a comment on the time in which he wrote. What Verlaine is saying is, in effect, very much what Talleyrand had said earlier: No one can know what happiness is who did not live before 1789. Talleyrand had. He had been young then, and highly placed, surrounded from birth with privilege. Presumably he knew what he was talking about. It goes without saying that there were many contemporaries of his in the France before the Revolution who knew nothing whatever about being happy. But by the time Verlaine came along, no one, not even a young poet, could any longer believe in happiness. It had become the dream of a dream, and of the figures that inhabit it, masked though they are, and wearing the fantastical dress of the eighteenth century, he can only declare with a sigh:

> Ils n'ont pas l'air de croire à leur bonheur.

It is perhaps the most significant comment that could have been made on the nineteenth century. It is in no one line; the comment is the complete poem.

In attempting to discover how a poem is made, in practise it has proved impossible to ignore the meaning. And if the analysis of *Clair de Lune* is just, it should go a little way toward making it clearer why the effort to distinguish between form and content is futile. The poem cannot be disassociated from the words in which it is written, poetry from verse.

All painting is in the Infanta's ribbon.

1934

THE GOLDEN BOUGH

I

AYEAR OR SO after the war, there appeared in the *New Republic* a critical appraisal by Sir Gilbert Murray of *The Golden Bough*. Quite rightly the distinguished Greek scholar declared it one of the finest creations among contemporary letters. He then went on to give it as his opinion that these twelve volumes of Sir James Frazer on magic and primitive religion represented the most devastating attack anyone had made on Christianity since William Godwin.

I have had to sum up Professor Murray's review from memory, for I no longer have it by me; but I do not believe I misrepresent him. His opinion was one which might readily be shared by any liberal mind of his generation. Nor can it be said that the statement I have attributed to him belies *The Golden Bough*, for it is a possible, indeed I think the proper, interpretation to put upon the author's purpose.

But if the purpose of Sir James Frazer was to deny to Christianity any special privilege over those other mythical cults which to the anthropologist are strictly comparable to it—unless it be the somewhat dubious one of being the closest to us in time—it is nowhere clearly avowed. It is the reader himself who is allowed to come to that conclusion; but the material is assembled in such a way that he can scarcely come to any other.

The plan of *The Golden Bough* is immense. The author's strategy is conceived with great cunning and carried out with great art. The direction of the attack is for a long time concealed. Sir James Frazer's announced intention is to study, and as far as may be explain, an obscure rite that is known to have been practiced in a grove of Diana near Nemi well into historical times. There grew a certain tree, by night and day guarded by a man who was both priest and murderer. For he had killed his predecessor and would in turn be killed whenever a stronger or craftier than he arrived. The office of King of the Wood, for so he was called, was thus perilously held. But his assailant could only be a runaway slave and before advancing to his attack he must have torn a branch from the sacred tree. It was the belief of the ancient writers whose word has come to us that this branch, in some way, represented the Golden Bough which Aeneas, at the Sybil's bidding, plucked before venturing into the dim underworld of the dead. Such was the condition of the culprit's attack on one who was both priest and king; if able to slay him, he reigned in his stead.

Why was the succession to the priesthood at Nemi by mortal combat? Why must the aspirant advance bearing not only the sword, but a bough from the sacred tree? These are the two questions which Sir James purports to set himself to answer. There was, apparently, no other cult in the classical world which resembled this; and the explanations which writers of the imperial age pretended to give of it, Sir James at once dismisses as unhistorical. The deadly renewal of the guardian of the tree is clearly a survival of the utmost antiquity. Though in the dark grove of Diana it was still being enacted in their lifetime, the civilized minds of Plutarch and Servius were incapable of understanding it. It may well be that the participants in the rite were without any clear conception of what they were doing. For the custom remains when the myth that gave it meaning has long disappeared. It is with this incident that Sir James Frazer opens *The Golden Bough*. We are invited to gaze at the lovely landscape about Nemi, the terraced gardens, the azure lake. But it is only a moment before we find ourselves looking, terribly, into the backward and most distant stretch of time.

The King of the Wood stood for a god, Virbius, who, dying as a man, at once came to life in the person of another man. So much is known; but the records are fragmentary. The cult at Nemi can be explained, if at all, only by seeking counterparts in other cults on which we possess fuller information. The search will be long and laborious. We shall visit, Sir James warns us, many strange foreign lands, with strange foreign peoples and still stranger customs. We shall indeed. For before we have done with the Golden Bough, we have ranged from Egypt to the Mexico of the Montezumas, from the Creek Indians of our own Northwest to the mild rice-farmers of the island of Bali; and the customs, though often strange beyond all imagining, are even stranger in their familiarity. For however wide we wander, however deep we delve into the records of the past, we are always coming up against one being, the Vegetable God, who as the decapitated Texcatlipoca or the dismembered Osiris is strange, but who is not strange at all, once our astonished gaze has recognized the likeness, as Jesus.

Christianity is seldom mentioned; there is no need it should be, for Sir James naturally assumes that the main articles of the Christian faith are known to his readers. The argument of *The Golden Bough* is by analogy; one term of the comparison is always the strange rite at Nemi; and one cannot too highly praise the scrupulous care and skill with which cult after cult, the world over, is related to it. One obscure superstition is illumined by comparison with another, until at long last the secret of the sacred grove is disclosed. The culprit who stalks with drawn sword about the tree is none other than the mortal image of that being on whom primitive man sees all life, his own life and fecundity, the fertility of his flocks, and the fruitfulness of grain, fruit-trees, and vines, depending. He is the god that must die that his vigor be renewed. He is the god that must die in the person of man and come to life again in another man. With Attis, Adonis and Thammuz, we begin to close about the Christian altar. Behind them, as behind the slave who was King of the Wood, there looms, scarcely named, yet continuously present, the shadow of that other God, who as Son of Man, mocked as King of the Jews, died on the tree. And inescapably we are brought to conclude that Jesus the Christ acquired divinity by assuming the attributes of another deity. He has come violently to death many times before Golgotha, the Son of God, himself very God, dying to appease the God. He has been, like Odin in the mists of the Northern forest, sacrificed to Himself. He has been wounded by the boar as Adonis, been emasculated as Attis, been decapitated and His bloody head spitted on a spike as the Maize-God, Texcatlipoca. Always His sufferings, death, and resurrection have been celebrated in appropriate rites.

The lineage of Christ is thus seen to have been very different to what we have hitherto assumed to be His. And it is not only His death and His resurrection that conform to the pattern of the Vegetable God. Jesus was born in Bethlehem, the House of Bread, not because the town was associated with David, but because the place had been from time immemorial a seat of Adonis worship. We have come very far from "that distant and domestic prodigy" of which the great Gibbon was, as historian, so rightfully disdainful. And all the attendant circumstances of the virgin birth, the sudden shining star, the gift of myrrh, even the straw on which the Holy Child was laid, are now seen to have been determined, not as the gospelers in their ignorance and innocence supposed, by Hebraic predictions, but by other more remote and divine precedents. Incidentally, the Magi's star, whose identity has been sought, with a curious mixture of piety and skepticism, in some extraordinary but not miraculous conjunction of planets, was in all probability, if we may trust Egyptian and

Babylonian parallels, merely a star whose reappearance in the sky was eagerly watched for each year. It was not a portent of disturbed nature but a reassuring sign of returning seasons and the natural rebirth of vegetation, no miracle but a shining manifestation of the mysterious order in the heavens.

Much of this is not new. The early Fathers of the Church could not ignore the strong resemblances of their faith to some others which, for a time, were even more popular in the late Roman Empire. Even had they wanted to do so, they could not overlook the remarkable coincidences in the deaths and resurrections of these multiple deities. For as late as the fourth century worshipers of Attis were still extant and contemptuously contending that since their god was the older, it was obvious that he was the original and the god of the Christians the counterfeit. The good Christians, says Frazer, easily rebutted this argument by "falling back on the subtlety of Satan, who on so important an occasion has surpassed himself by reversing the usual order of nature." Gibbon was troubled to discover that the patron saint of England, Saint George of Cappadocia, had been in life an unscrupulous scoundrel, of more than ordinary capabilities, but, as far as the record goes, of no morals of any kind. The anthropologist suggests that the true Saint George is not the historical bishop who, as we would say today, turned his office into a racket, but a spirit of vegetation who at some time which we do not know acquired the name of George, sometimes with the appellation Green; his festival carries on, among others, the Roman feast of the Parila. The Blessed Jacques de Voragine, writing his *Golden Legend* in the thirteenth century, was well aware that many of the saints in his calendar were only lesser pagan deities who somehow had acquired aureoles. But he is not disconcerted by the slightness of their disguise. The old historians of the Church did not find it necessary to hide that it had survived less through the stubbornness of the martyrs than through the suppleness of the bishops, who were more than willing that pagan practices should continue, if only their followers were attached to the true faith. And continue they did. I have myself seen in the streets of Sorrento, since the coming to power of the Fascists, processions which undoubtedly honored the Great Mother of the Gods, though the image borne by her worshipers was simply known as Our Lady.

But *The Golden Bough* does much more than multiply instances of the correspondence between Christianity and the rival religions by which it was surrounded in its infancy. For gradually, in Sir James Frazer's pages, there is revealed what one may in all simplicity call the true religion of mankind. It is older than mankind, but not, as it happens, as old as the race; for though it is possible to trace it very far back, until we come on shapes of gods as rude, terrible, and intricate as Mayan sculptures, beyond these there is still a savage jungle of fear, where every man is a magician and there are no gods and no time. For this religion is, I think we may say, coeval with the conception of time. The gods cannot come to birth until there is knowledge of the revolving year and a memory of the seasons' return. It is to them that all legends quite rightly assign the first gifts of civilization, corn and wine. As civilization advances, their spirituality increases. Yet something of this earlier timelessness clings to them in their latest aspect, just as in the minds of their worshipers belief in magic is never entirely abandoned. This religion is not confined to the shores of the Mediterranean; it has been honored everywhere, changing to conform to climate, but much less than a materialist would have conjectured. Amazed, the Spanish conquerors marching through Mexico found it there, all its essential mysteries and ceremonies preserved. It had scarcely changed in that tropic air. Only the sacrifices were not, as they had long since become in Europe, symbolical. When the gods periodically died, it was in human shapes, and though a certain skepticism seems to have crept in among the Aztec nobles, the altars were still drenched in divine blood. The soldiers of His Catholic Majesty could only regard this religion as a sanguinary and cruel parody on their own.

It is possible to take *The Golden Bough* as a long record of human error and folly. It is so that the author, as he approaches the end, with melancholy regards it. He does not often mention Christianity, but there is at least one occasion when he makes clear what he thinks of it. It was, to begin with, a moral reform, noble in its aspirations, but for the many impossible in practice. Its Founder was scarcely dead before it began, wisely, to modify the faith which, whatever bliss it may have promised its followers in the next world, most effectively destroyed their usefulness in this. Then the Church, as it became more popular, became more debased, acquiring their superstitions with the ignorant, consoling the low and the weak with the same old magic formulas in which they had always believed. In a few years its purity was lost; with the centuries it became a fusion and confusion of cults, some as old as memory on the nearer Asiatic shores, some as ancient and dark as the Northern forests out of which they came.

Certainly one can with no great difficulty believe that *The Golden Bough* was intended by the author as an onslaught on the assumptions of traditional Christianity. And his compatriot, whom I cited at the beginning of this article, at once seized this and with perfect propriety presented it in his criticism. Such a conception was probably inevitable for an informed and liberal mind of the late nineteenth century. It is not necessarily ours.

II

The preface to the first edition of *The Golden Bough* is dated from London, 1890. Since then another generation has been born, grown up, come to maturity; its approach to the material assembled with such mastery by Sir James Frazer, and added to by his followers and rival anthropologists, must be different from his. There are, to be sure, many who would still follow him to the letter; but their reactions are too like his to demand further comment. It is of the others I wish to speak.

For it is also possible for us, regarding Christianity in the light cast from the sacred tree at Nemi, to find that it has gained as much as it has lost. Since it had already forfeited in our minds any special claims it may once have had as a supernatural revelation, these should be counted an inconsiderable loss. By extending its existence into the dark backward and abysm of time, it has gained, not only the respectability of age, but another authenticity. A religion less than two thousand years old had always troubled us; but now its tradition stretches as far as any imaginable race of man. It is shown as a heritage, not from Judea and Greece only, but from the earth. In uncovering the depth and richness of the past, the anthropologist had disclosed the fears and desires common to mankind. And as in post-Renaissance astronomy the earth became a star among other stars, so now in this knowledge Christ was become a god among other gods. But taking religion as a revelation of human destiny, we must see that He is not less divine because of the company of Adonis, Osiris and Thammuz. His divinity is to be found in precisely those attributes which He shares with these and other older incarnate gods.

Christianity has been many things at many times. Yet it is possible, when informed by the anthropological curiosities of *The Golden Bough*, to see that its central mystery is the Mass. This, in the last analysis, turns out to be a symbolic presentation of the eternal relation of man to a living and sustaining earth. His dependence is not passive; for, just as the consecrated priest has power to draw the god to the altar, so does the fertility of the earth, its power to bear abundantly in flock and field, demand man's intervention. The French peasant, in a perfectly profane way, has this sense of the land's desire for cultivation, and can eloquently describe the ruin that comes to it when too long allowed to lie fallow; and it is worth remarking that his land, protected by portions of the original forest of northern Europe, is still, after two thousand known years of tillage, productive. This conception comes relatively late; it is an essential condition of man's emergence from savagery. But religion—and this is an important point in its opposition to magic and science, as the latter is commonly accepted in the contemporary world—supposes that the sources of life are ultimately beyond man's control.

To eat the body of the God, to drink His blood, relic though such a communion be of the savage rite, is still to celebrate life. The Mass is a ceremony derived from the immemorial worship of the Vegetable God; but on other occasions we have seen men turn what was originally a form for expressing physical concerns to spiritual ends. If it was fear that first created the gods, as the ancients said, thanks to Frazer that fear could now be particularized: it was fear that life might cease. The Catholic Church has always insisted that the Scriptures were not enough, that the traditions of the Church carried down from its first two centuries were an important part of its teachings. We see now how right that claim was. It was in these years that the man was made God.

Yet the Church also celebrates death. This is an extremely difficult subject, and though The Golden Bough indicates why the worshippers of the God must at certain periods ceremoniously mourn his sufferings and death, concluding, of course, with joy at His resurrection, we must, I believe, go beyond anthropology to explain that peculiar taint of death which clings to Christianity.

There is an acceptance of death as fulfillment which comes to strong men when life is at the full. It is in Othello's

> If it were now to die,
> 'Twere now to be most happy.

It is in Mozart's most triumphant music, where the consciousness of being close to ceasing is a constant accompaniment to joy. Such an emotion is wholesome and humane. But there is a death-longing which all too often afflicts Christianity and in some centuries seems to pervade it to the exclusion of all else. Asceticism has a long and complicated history. I can here only hazard the opinion that its association is closer to the collapse of the State than to the rise of the

Church. The belief in dying as an escape from time and change into the unchanging and timeless has a respectable background in Greek thought; but before this could influence the Fathers of the Church, Greek philosophy had followed the Greek state into decay. It was in this late form that it was received by Christianity, just as the music which the Church made its own, as Gregorian and Ambrosian chant, appears to have been an adaptation of the modal music of the Greeks in a last and most decadent stage. We do not know much about it; but certainly what speaks from that music is nothing so strong as the will to die, but merely a desire not to be. It is this desire and no other which looks out at us from the will-less and indeed to me the soulless eyes of Byzantine saints. Into the stones of the Romanesque churches of France was carved the desperation that overtook men at the falling apart of the Carolingian Empire. But in the earliest Gothic churches, life reawakens with fear, but with that fear which recreates the gods. The Last Judgment is over the portals, Christ awfully fulfilling a dream of justice; it is upon that imagined scene that are fixed the dreadful eyes of the prophets who stand in the porches of Chartres. Then, quite suddenly, in the second half of the thirteenth century, all the churches began to blossom in stone. The fearful gaze of the gaunt statues at Chartres becomes the radiant look of the smiling angels at Rheims. And that change is accomplished with the recovery of the active will and the beginnings of a more stable society. From then on, and until the springtide is past, the Mother of God lifts for adoration the body of a child, reborn as god; laments over the body of the god, dying as man.

> King Abundance got Him on
> Innocence; and Wisdom He.
> That cognomen sounded best
> Considering what wild infancy
> Drove horror from His Mother's breast.

III

What we sought, the generation of which I speak, was what men have always sought, to have life and to have it more abundantly. And for those of us who had emerged from the war, that search was made more acute by our recent escape from annihilation in youth. But living means not merely engaging in action, or—what is more likely, as we had learned to our cost—having a number of things happen to one, but an increased awareness of being. And for that a new consciousness was necessary; for in the midst of an almost intolerable confusion, it was at last clear that the old consciousness would no longer serve.

It may be said that what we sought was a religious consciousness, if religion may be understood to be a lively and communicable sense of the powers superior to man which control the course of nature and of human life. That these powers exist, there is not and has never been a denial. We no longer regard them as supernatural, but they are precisely those to which our ancestors gave names and which they worshiped as divinities. We could hardly escape a scientific account of them as natural forces, which, though we might think it partial, was the best available. What was not so satisfactory was the definition science gave to the relation between them and us.

America was a creation of the Protestant mind. And as Americans we had, regardless of religious convictions, received its impress. Now it can be seen that Protestantism very early exhausted its interest in religion; whatever it had to say on the relation of God to man was soon said. After the great theological controversies of the sixteenth and seventeenth centuries, there is little but repetition, and soon not even that. From the very start, it would appear that the partisans of the Reformation had all they wanted to carry on in the practical world. And it was there, one suspects, that the Protestant treasure lay. Mean as may seem the morals of the Protestants, they undoubtedly conduced to commercial conquest; they steadied the pioneer in his advance into the New World.

But from the vantage of the Golden Bough, it will be seen that the Protestants rejected the essential mystery of Christianity. In discarding the Mass, they were depriving Christ of His powers as a God. Without them, He must lose His divinity. And this, as a matter of history, is exactly what did happen. What is left to the Protestant churches today is not much, and that little is scarcely remarkable as religion; it is, in fact, only with the greatest difficulty to be distinguished from the secular ideals of humanitarianism and social service. Were it not that we can still read seventeenth-century sermons and hear the music of Johann Sebastian Bach, it would be almost impossible to conceive that the Protestant churches had ever been repositories of spiritual wisdom. And it is worth noting that we have in Bach an awareness of all the inquiries which the Counter-Reformation had proposed to the Protestant soul, very powerfully combined with the baroque conception of time. It was still not too late for the musician to reconcile the opposing tendencies of Protestantism.

For there is another sphere, comparable to theology, in which the Protestant mind has been continuously brilliant. I mean that of science. Copernicus could dedicate *De Revolutionibus Orbium Celestium* to the Pope, but it was of necessity a Protestant mind that first analyzed the motions of the stars, devised a cosmogony to replace that which the Catholic Church had inherited from the classical astronomers, and, after a century or two, substituted natural forces for the Deity. John Napier, the mathematician, was devout; and Kepler, having discovered that the squares of the times of the revolutions of any two planets, including the earth, about the sun are proportional to the cubes of their mean distances from the sun, could still exultantly cry: "I will triumph over mankind by honest confession that I have stolen the golden vases of the Egyptians to build a tabernacle for my God, far from the confines of Egypt." The boldest intellectual may fail to perceive the implications of its findings. But to us, looking back, this diversion of interest is apparent in the Protestant mind from the moment it casts off the authority of a Church whose majesty and wisdom ultimately reposed on a myth. The two factions are, and have long been, irreconcilable.

Yet it must not be forgotten that the scientific universe rose in opposition to the older Church and was the creation of profoundly religious men. And it is now a commonplace to say that their dogmas were influenced, however contrarily or unconsciously, by the very dogmas which they sought to displace.

The Golden Bough reveals a profound continuity in the human mind. The desire of the body is to continue, the deepest need of the mind is for order. For it is only by perceiving order in those external forces upon which his continuance depends, that man can hope to bring his own being into accord with them. Without that harmony, he suffers, and, so quickly does a carnal predicament become a spiritual distress, his suffering is not limited to his body. He may not only find living difficult; he may even cease to want to live.

After magic, religion; after religion, science: each is a mode of thought; each presents us with its own world of reality. The first two were discarded, as Sir James Frazer tells us, because the control which they pretended to exercise over the more human powers who determine whether we live or die was incomplete. The conception of order upon which each of them is based is ultimately remote from the multitude; their common method of persuasion is miraculous. And this is no less true of science than of its predecessors, for more people could read Saint Thomas Aquinas in the Latin in the

Middle Ages than today can follow the physicists into that mathematical empyrean where their true secrets are disclosed.

"All sciences which have for their end investigations concerning order and measure are related to mathematics. And a proof that it far surpasses in facility and importance the sciences which depend upon it is that it embraces at once all the objects to which they are devoted and a great many more besides." So Descartes; the universe, though complicated since his day, is still a creation of the mathematical mind. But its high wisdom is inaccessible. We accept the world of the scientist, just as the savage accepted the world of the magician, because each proclaims his power to bend the forces of nature to his will and to our advantage. We believe because we see, and we see that it works. There is this difference, that magic pretends to divert the courses of nature, science only to utilize them. Religion asks not to control, but to placate the heavenly powers. It is easy to see, without the special information which Sir James Frazer has given us on the role of king as god, why religion is associated with an arbitrary rule, with a royal or an aristocratic society. Science and magic both favor democracy. In savages of the lowest scale, like the Australian aborigines, every man makes his own miracles. In the ideal scientific state, all classes will be leveled, since each is deprived of any special function. The beginnings of savagery and the end of civilization thus come extraordinarily to resemble one another.

Our faith was given to science in the first instance because, having accepted mathematics as an instrument of exact inquiry, it was able to project a superior order upon the heavens. Its first great triumph was to simplify the movements of the planet Mars, that *inobservabile sidus* of the classical astronomers. It did not, of course, actually simplify them; Mars still pursued its course about the sun exactly as it had done when the Chaldeans first peered at the ruddy wanderer of the skies from their terraces; it merely made them simpler for the mind. It was in that relative simplicity, that more readily appreciable order, that the superiority of science lay. So far from the common tribulations of mankind was the direction of its concern. Science has since increased its observations, improved its instruments. But it does not relate man to these ampler heavens; nor can it properly do so; for its perfect instruments are not adapted to this use. Measured on astronomical scales, man's life is inconsiderably brief and small. The greatness of his heart it cannot measure; it can only deny it. What compass can circumscribe Hamlet? What equation, one may ask, corresponds to Coriolanus before Rome? We have reached the skeptical point where we see the scientific universe as a projection of our own immortal desire for order, yet realize that it leaves all our desires, even that desire, unsatisfied.

"The abundance, the solidity, and the splendor of the results already achieved by science are well fitted to inspire us with a cheerful confidence in the soundness of its method." So Sir James Frazer could write before the last war, and add: "It is not too much to say that the hope of progress—moral and intellectual as well as material— in the future is bound up with the fortunes of science, and that every obstacle placed in the way of scientific discovery is a wrong to humanity."

Yet soon after this had been written, it began to be suspected that the great period of activity which began with the Renaissance had come to a close. Its glory had been a conquest of space; for the first man was able to conceive his earth as one sphere; he had mapped its seas and measured its continents. His heaven was infinitely more vast than any his ancestors had known and he had filled it, not with hierarchies of angels, but with his own knowledge. But for some reason, that knowledge no longer availed him.

After such knowledge, what forgiveness?

The question was asked and not answered.

In the decade after the war, we saw the capitalists endlessly scheme, and fail, to bring back world trade; we saw the communists endlessly agitate to bring on world revolution, and fail. That conquest of space was accomplished; yet the forces that had brought it about could not come to a stop. We heard as it were a victorious general proclaiming that order was being established everywhere. But we were like a poor and vanquished people, returning to burnt homes and devastated fields. Everywhere we looked was disorder.

For this was the paradox by which we were faced: that pure science has introduced into the world of thought we call the universe a never before known order, but the applications and derivations of scientific thought, not all of them material, have brought into our lives an unparalleled disorder.

Sir James Frazer, writing before the war of 1914–1918 was aware as were few living men of the primitive substructure of modern civilization. But what was frightening in the aftermath of the war was not that the conflict shattering the walls had revealed old and almost forgotten foundations; it was that an advancing civilization should so terribly emulate savagery. It was society in its most modern form that had insisted on returning to that democracy in arms of savage tribes. It was the advance in technics that had made troglodytes of armies. If we were dying, it was not from our vices but from an excess of our virtues. If there was a revolt from reason, it was not against reasoning as an instrument of living, but against the rationalism of the eighteenth century which, after being transformed into the materialism of the nineteenth century, had in our own become dynamism. A faith in progress had become a most unreasonable faith in motion for its own sake. And its works were not good.

The cure, it has been maintained, is more science: if only the methods which the astronomer, the physicist, and their more practical brother, the engineer, have so successfully employed, each in his special field, could be applied to ourselves and the society in which we precariously survive, all would be for the best in the bravest of new worlds. There are two serious objections to this proposal. Order in a living society cannot conceivably be of the mechanic kind. Methods which ultimately derive from the contemplation and measurement of space cannot without peril be applied to beings whose meaning can only be disclosed in time.

Science is not without a concept of time; but it is, as far as one not a mathematician can discern, a corollary of the original conception of order in space. It is not one by which men and women, subject to decay, can live.

It was the triumph of the European mind, in its youth and springtime of thought, that it was able to adapt the Christian myth to its needs and, extending the human drama to include, not merely lives, but conceivable centuries, to endow it with shape and meaning. (May I point out that there is no time in primitive Christianity? The Kingdom of Heaven is at hand.) We are still under a tremendous debt to this conception of a higher order dominating and informing the world; it was made possible only through an increase in time. But we must remind ourselves that the order thus introduced into history was expressed in symbols and is therefore one not readily appreciated by the abstract and reasoning mind, and that the divine comedy could not come to completion until eternity had been added to time. Yet the present theory which attempts to impose a rational order upon human history has also found it necessary to add to the drama an act which as yet has taken place on no earthly stage, an apocalyptic scene, in which Capitalism is transformed into Socialism, Prehistory ends and History begins.

We are now, I think, in a position to see why myths have suddenly become so important to us. It is because through them we see mankind in time. That enormous impetus imparted to the human spirit at the Renaissance to face the unknown with no comfort but its own courage and despair resulted in an unprecedented conquest of space. If this advance produced a mysticism of its own, to which even the humblest could respond, as is shown, I believe, by the American pioneer, that movement has now spent itself. It lies gasping with its own success, like Alexander when he had trampled Europe, Asia, and Africa. And as Aristotle's one-time pupil, as he went, put the likeliest barbarian youths under Greek pedagogues, so the scientists have converted the earth to their instructions.

I have so far used Sir James Frazer's definition of religion. And it is worth remarking that in his view religion is no intoxicant distilled for the masses, which priestly cunning and their own folly lead them to drain, in order to support their oppressions, dull their pain and defer their hopes. On the contrary, it is a conceit of the world so high, so difficult, that few are able to keep it continuously before them. The many, of whatever class, can at best be constrained to conform outwardly to its customs and ceremonies. But religion, it seems to me, may attain an even nobler form than any Frazer has set down—an omission proper enough in a work devoted to its more primitive aspects. There is the religion of Saint Augustine and Dante, in which the gods are no longer to be propitiated save by conformity to their will. Call the gods what you like, provided you believe in them. And you cannot seriously refuse to believe that our lives are at long last dependent upon forces beyond our brief volition. In an age committed to determinism, it is difficult to understand completely what is meant by Saint Augustine's, "My will purified is God's will, and in God's will is our peace." But even in a deterministic age, we are plagued by the necessity of conforming to our destiny, and the problem remains of according desires with fate.

Virginia Quarterly Review: July, 1936

HOMAGE TO HEMINGWAY

I

ERNEST HEMINGWAY had the chance to become the spokesman of the war generation, or, more particularly, he came to be regarded as the spokesman of that generation by those who had not, in their own persons, known the experience of war. The phrase which he had culled from one of his many conversations with Gertrude Stein and printed opposite the title page of *The Sun Also Rises*—"You are all a lost generation"—was destined to *faire fortune*. And to this he appended another quotation from the aged and charming cynic of *Ecclesiastes*, which not only pointed the title of his book, but linked its own disillusionment with another so old and remote in time as to seem a permanent proclamation of the vanity of things.

His own generation admired him, but could also appraise how special his experience had been. It was a still younger generation, those who were schoolboys at the time of the War, who were infatuated with him. Hemingway not only supplied them with the adventures they had missed; he offered them an attitude with which to meet the disorders of the post-war decade. It was they who accepted the Hemingway legend and by their acceptance gave it a reality it had not had.

It is as one who dictated the emotions to contemporary youth that Hemingway has been compared to Lord Byron. The comparison is in many ways an apt one. The years of Byron's fame were not unlike the decade after the last war. The hopes raised by the French Revolution had then been frustrated and all possibilities of action were being rapidly destroyed by those in power. In the 1920's, the disintegration of the social fabric which began before the War became apparent to almost anyone. Here and there were new faces in politics, but Hemingway, who had worked on a Midwestern paper in his youth, gone abroad shortly after the War as correspondent to a Canadian newspaper, come into contact with the literary diplomats at the Quai d'Orsay, followed the French troops of M. Poincaré into the Ruhr, known Mussolini when he too was a journalist, seen war and government from both sides in the

Turkish-Greek conflict, was not likely to rate the new gangsters above the old gangs. It should have been obvious to a disinterested observer in 1922 that there was no longer much prospect of immediate revolution in the countries of Europe. It was in 1922 that Hemingway seriously began his career as a writer.

He was to become, like Byron, a legend while he was still in his twenties. But when I first met him in the summer of 1922 there could be no possibility of a legend. I had just come abroad and, calling on Ezra Pound, had asked him about American writers of talent then in Paris. Pound's answer was a taxi, which carried us with decrepit rapidity across the Left Bank, through the steep streets rising toward Mont Saint-Geneviève, and brought us to the Rue du Cardinal Lemoine. There we climbed four flights of stairs to find Ernest Hemingway. He had then published nothing except his newspaper work, none of which I had ever seen; so that my impressions could be only personal. From that time until 1930 I saw Hemingway fairly constantly. Since then he has retired to Florida, and I have seen him but once. Any later impressions I have are gathered entirely from his books. I say this to make clear what I shall have to say about the legendary figure.

The legend is, in some ways, astounding. Nothing is more natural than that the imaginative man should at times envy the active one. Stendhal would have liked to be a handsome lieutenant of hussars. But the born writer is, by his very imagination, cut off from the satisfactions of the man of action; he can emulate him only by a process of deliberate stultification. Hemingway, as he then appeared to me, had many of the faults of the artist, some, such as vanity, to an exaggerated degree. But these are faults which from long custom I easily tolerate. And in his case they were compensated for by extraordinary literary virtues. He was instinctively intelligent, disinterested and not given to talking nonsense. Toward his craft, he was humble, and had, moreover, the most complete literary integrity it has ever been my lot to encounter. I say the most complete, for while I have known others who were not to be corrupted, none of them was presented with the opportunities for corruption that assailed Hemingway. His was that innate and genial honesty which is the very chastity of talent; he knew that to be preserved it must constantly be protected. He could not be bought. I happened to be with him on the day he turned down an offer from one of Mr. Hearst's editors, which, had he accepted it, would have supported him handsomely for years. He was at the time living back of the Montparnasse cemetery, over the studio of a friend, in a room small and bare except for a bed and table, and buying his midday meal for five sous from street vendors of fried potatoes.

The relation of a living writer to his legend may become curiously complicated. If we take the account that Mr. Peter Quennell has recently given us in *Byron: the Years of Fame*, it would seem that superficially the poet had at twenty-two only a very slight resemblance to the picture which the public presently began to compose of him. On the contrary, he seemed to his friends a personable, gay young man, an excellent drinking companion; there was, of course, the limp; and he had, as they may not have known, the consciousness of a bad heredity. Childe Harold was made of emotions only latent in Byron. It was a corollary of his fame that the poet should be identified with Childe Harold in the minds of his admirers. But it was not long before in his own imagination he became Childe Harold. And presently Lord Byron is committing incest with his sister. His conscience required that he complete the fiction by a private action. Byron's public stood as panders beside Augusta's bed.

In attempting to say what has happened to Hemingway, I might suggest that, for one thing, he has become the legendary Hemingway. He appears to have turned into a composite of all those photographs he has been sending out for years: sunburned from snows, on skis; in fishing get-up, burned dark from the hot Caribbean; the handsome, stalwart hunter crouched smiling over the carcass of some dead beast. Such a man could not have written Hemingway's early books; he might have written most of *Green Hills of Africa*. He is proud to have killed the great kudu. It is hard not to wonder whether he has not, hunting, brought down an even greater victim.

Byron's legend is sinister and romantic, Hemingway's manly and low-brow. One thing is certain. This last book is hard-boiled. If that word is to mean anything, it must mean indifference to suffering and, since we are what we are, can but signify a callousness to others' pain. When I say that the young Hemingway was among the tenderest of mortals, I do not speak out of private knowledge, but from the evidence of his writings. He could be, as any artist must in this world, if he is to get his work done, ruthless. He wrote courageously, but out of pity; having been hurt, and badly hurt, he could understand the pain of others. His heart was worn, as was the fashion of the times, up his sleeve and not on it. It was always there and his best tricks were won with it. Now, according to the little preface to *Green Hills of Africa*, he seems to think that, having discarded that half-concealed card, he plays more honestly. He does not. For with the heart the innate honesty of the artist is gone. And he loses the game.

II

The problem of style is always a primary one, for to each generation it is presented anew. It is desirable, certainly, that literature reflect the common speech; it is even more necessary that it set forth a changed sensibility, since that is the only living change from one generation to another. But to an American who, like Hemingway, was learning the craft of prose in the years that followed the War, that problem was present in a somewhat special way. He must achieve a style that could record an American experience, and neither falsify the world without nor betray the world within.

How difficult that might be, he could see from his immediate predecessors; they had not much else to teach. On the one side there was Mr. Hergesheimer, whose style falsified every fact he touched. On the other was Mr. Dreiser, a worthy, lumbering workman who could deliver the facts of American existence, all of them, without selection, as a drayman might deliver trunks. Where, then, to start? To anyone who felt there was an American tradition to be carried on, there was but one writer who was on the right track: Sherwood Anderson. When he was in his stride, there was no doubt about it, he was good. The trouble with Anderson was there was never any telling just how long he could keep up his pace. He had a bad way of stumbling. And when he stumbled he fell flat.

So did Mark Twain, who loomed out of the American past. All authentic American writing, Hemingway has said, stems from one book: *Huckleberry Finn*. How much he was prepared to learn from it may be ascertained by comparing the progress of the boys' raft down the Mississippi with the journey of Jake and his friend from France to Spain in *The Sun Also Rises*. Mark Twain is the one literary ancestor whom Hemingway has openly acknowledged; but what neither he nor Sherwood Anderson, who was Hemingway's first master, could supply was a training in discipline.

It was here that chance served. But it was a chance from which Hemingway carefully profited. There was one school which for discipline surpassed all others: that of Flaubert. It still had many living proponents, but none more passionate than Ezra Pound. In Paris, Hemingway submitted much of his apprentice work in fiction to Pound. It came back to him blue-penciled, most of the adjectives gone. The comments were unsparing. Writing for a newspaper was not at all the same as writing for a poet.

Pound was not the young American's only critical instructor. If Hemingway went often to 70, bis, Rue Nôtre Dame des Champs, he was presently to be found also at 12, Rue de Fleurus. There he submitted his writings to the formidable scrutiny of Gertrude Stein. It was of this period that Hemingway said to me later: "Ezra was right half the time, and when he was wrong, he was so wrong you were never in doubt about it. Gertrude was always right."

Miss Stein, for all her long residence abroad, was American. As she sat in one of the low chairs in the pavilion of the Rue de Fleurus, she was as unmistakably American as Mark Hanna; the walls were covered with Picassos; but with her closely clipped masculine head and old-fashioned dress, she might have been an adornment to the McKinley era. And if the problem was to combine Mark Twain and Gustave Flaubert—to convert a common American speech to the uses of the French tradition—it could hardly be doubted that Miss Stein had done it. She had taken up, in her *Three Lives*, where Flaubert left off. In *Un Coeur Simple*, he had presented the world through the eyes of a servant girl; but the words through which her vision is conveyed are not her own, but Flaubert's. Miss Stein had rendered her servant girls in an idiom which, if not exactly theirs, is supposed to be appropriate to their mentality. It is, so to speak, a transcript of dumb emotions. Having made it, Miss Stein discovered that she had arrived at a curious formalization of the common speech, which, she presently decided, might be put to other uses than the one for which it was originally intended.

If Gertrude Stein is always interesting in what she sets out to do, the result, once her writing is done, is all too often unsurpassed for boredom. She has told us in her *Autobiography of Alice B. Toklas* that she is a genius. We would have preferred that the statement had been made by someone else, but it happens to be true. Miss Stein has a mature intelligence; her genius, unfortunately, has not yet arrived at the age of three years. Ernest Hemingway, at the time he came under her influence, was a young man of twenty-four. But he was all of that. Miss Stein had developed a literary medium; but she had no material, at least none that was available to that strangely infantile genius of hers. She had at last realized that proud jest of Villiers de l'Isle-Adam; she had had, quite literally, to let her servants live for her. The relation between a writer and his material is much more mysterious than most critics would like to admit. Miss Stein had led, in Paris and elsewhere, what anyone would call an interesting life. She could never write of it until, leaving the genial baby behind, she assumed the proportions of Miss Alice B. Toklas, her companion, and began writing as an intelligent being of her own years.

Hemingway had an abundance of material. There was a boyhood in the Midwest, with summers in the forests of Michigan, where he had come in contact with the earliest American way of life. There were the love affairs of a young man. There was not one war, but two. He had known in his own person an experience for which Gertrude Stein had vainly sought a substitute in words.

What she taught Hemingway must be in part left to conjecture. Like Pound, she undoubtedly did much for him simply by telling him what he must not do, for a young writer perhaps the most valuable aid he can receive. More positively, it was from her prose he learned to employ the repetitions of American speech without monotony. (I say this quite aware that Miss Stein's repetitions are monotonous in the extreme.) She also taught him how to adapt its sentence structure, inciting in him a desire to do what Hemingway calls "loosening up the language." She did not teach him dialogue. The Hemingway dialogue is pure invention. He does not talk like his characters and neither does Miss Stein. And it was not until they had read Hemingway's books that the two ladies of the Rue de Fleurus acquired those dramatic tricks of speech.

They are brilliant. But they have deafened Hemingway to the way people talk. In *The Sun Also Rises*, each of the characters has his own particular speech, but by the time we reach *Death in the Afternoon* and the extraordinary conversations with the Old Lady, there is no longer even the illusion that there is more than one way of talking. It is a formula, in that book employed with great dexterity and no small power; but it is dramatic only in words; in terms of character it is not dramatic at all.

There is no space here to appraise Hemingway's style with accuracy. It is enough to say that, as no one before him had done, he made Midwestern speech into a prose, living and alert, capable of saying at all times exactly what he wanted it to say. It is no longer the lean unlovely thing it was. Just as Eliot, in such a poem as *Sweeney Among the Nightingales*, had shown how by controlling the sound apart from the sense the most prosaic statements could be turned to poetry, Hemingway made this American speech into prose by endowing it with a beauty of accurate motion. It is changed, as a gawky boy may change in a few years to an accomplished athlete; its identity is not destroyed. And here I am reminded of a remark of Hemingway's that it was Napoleon who taught Stendhal how to write. It may be that more than one of the best qualities of this prose were acquired from a careful watching of Spanish bullfighters.

III

We were in the garden at Mons. Young Buckley came in with his patrol from across the river. The first German I saw climbed up over the garden wall. We waited until he got one leg over and then potted him. He had so much equipment on and looked awfully surprised and fell down in the garden. Then three more came over further down the wall. We shot them. They all came just like that.

It is easy to see how a story like this could convey the impression that Hemingway is indifferent alike to cruelty and suffering. And yet this tale is a precise record of emotion. What we have here is not callousness, but the Flaubertian discipline carried to a point Flaubert never knew—just as in the late war military control was brought to such perfection that dumb cowed civilians in uniform, who cared nothing for fighting and little for the issues of battle, could be held to positions that the professional soldiers of the nineteenth century would have abandoned without the slightest shame. Flaubert describing an incident, despite his pretending to be aloof, or even absent throughout, is continually intent on keeping his emotions implicit within the scene. The reader is never left in the slightest doubt as to what he is supposed to feel from the fiction. But in this account of the Germans coming over the wall and being shot, one by one, all emotion is kept out, unless it is the completely inadequate surprise of the victims. The men who kill feel nothing. And yet what Hemingway was doing in the summer of 1922, lying on a bed in a room where the old Verlaine had once had lodging, was first remembering that he had been moved, and then trying to find out what had happened to cause the emotion. It is the bare happening that is set down, and only the happening that must arouse in the reader whatever emotion he is capable of according to his nature: pity, horror, disgust.

But this was a point beyond which Hemingway himself could not go. And in the stories that follow the first little volume, published in Paris and called *In Our Times*, he is almost always present in one guise or another. That is not to say, as might be assumed, that these stories are necessarily autobiographical. Wounded in the War, Hemingway was a very apprehensive young man. Indeed, his imagination could hardly be said to exist apart from his apprehension. I should not call this fear. And yet he could hardly hear of something untoward happening to another that he did not instantly, and without thought, attach this event to himself, or to the woman he loved. The narration is still remarkably pure. But there is always someone subject to the action.

For this is another distinction. In Flaubert, people are always planning things that somehow fail to come off—love affairs, assignations, revolutions, schemes for universal knowledge. But in Hemingway, men and women do not plan; it is to them that things happen. In the telling phrase of Wyndham Lewis, the "I" in Hemingway's stories is "the man that things are done to." Flaubert already represents a deterioration of the romantic will, in which both Stendhal and Byron, with the prodigious example of Napoleon before them, could not but believe. Waterloo might come, but before the last battle there was still time for a vast, however destructive, accomplishment of the will. Flaubert had before him Louis Philippe, whose green umbrella and thrifty bourgeois mind would not save him from flight; Louis Napoleon, whose plans were always going astray. But even Sedan was a better end than Woodrow Wilson had, with his paralytic chair and his closed room on a side street in Washington. And in Hemingway, the will is lost to action. There are actions, no lack of them but, as when the American lieutenant shoots the sergeant in A Farewell to Arms, they have only the significance of chance. Their violence does not make up for their futility. They may be, as this casual murder is, shocking; they are not incredible; but they are quite without meaning. There is no destiny but death.

It is because they have no will and not because they are without intelligence that the men and women in Hemingway are devoid of spiritual being. Their world is one in time with the War and the following confusion, and is a world without traditional values. That loss has been consciously set down.

IV

It is the privilege of literature to propose its own formal solutions for problems which in life have none. In many of the early stories of Hemingway the dramatic choice is between death and a primitive sense of male honor. The nineteen-year-old Italian orderly in A Simple Enquiry is given to choose between acceding to his major's

44

corrupt desires and being sent back to his platoon. Dishonor provides no escape, for in *The Killers* the old heavyweight prizefighter who has taken that course must at last lie in his room, trying to find the courage to go out and take what is coming to him from the two men who are also waiting in tight black overcoats, wearing gloves that leave no fingerprints. One can make a good end, or a bad end, and there are many deaths besides the final one. In *Hills Like White Elephants*, love is dead no matter what the lovers decide. "I don't feel any way," the girl says. "I just know things." And what she knows is her own predicament.

The Spaniards stand apart, and particularly the bullfighters, not so much because they risk their lives in a spectacular way, with beauty and skill and discipline, but because as members of a race still largely, though unconsciously, savage, they retain the tragic sense of life. In *The Sun Also Rises*, the young Romero, courteous, courageous, born knowing all the things that the others—wise-cracking Americans, upper-class British or intellectual Jews—will never learn, is a concentration of contrast. And yet the character in that novel who most nearly represents the author is aware, as soon as he has crossed the border back into France, that it is here that he belongs, in the contemporary world. He is comfortable only where all things have a value that can be expressed and paid for in paper money.

The best one can do is to desert the scene, as every man and woman must do sooner or later, to make, while the light is still in the eyes, a separate peace. And is this not just what Hemingway has done? Is there a further point to which he can retire than Key West? There he is still in political America, but on its uttermost island, no longer attached to his native continent.

His vision of life is one of perpetual annihilation. Since the will can do nothing against circumstance, choice is precluded; those things are good which the senses report good; and beyond their brief record there is only the remorseless devaluation of nature, which, like the vast blue flowing of the Gulf Stream beyond Havana, bears away of our great hopes, emotions and ambitions only a few and soon disintegrating trifles. Eternity—horribly to paraphrase Blake—is in love with the garbage of time.

What is there left? Of all man's activities, the work of art lasts longest. And in this morality there is little to be discerned beyond the discipline of the craft. This is what the French call the sense of the *métier* and their conduct in peace and war has shown that it may be a powerful impulse to the right action; if I am not mistaken, it is the main prop of French society. In *The Undefeated*, the old bullfighter, corrupt though he is with age, makes a good and courageous end, and yet it is not so much courage that carries him as a proud professional skill. It is this discipline, which Flaubert acquired from the traditions of his people and which Pound transmitted to the young Hemingway, that now, as he approaches forty, alone sustains him. He has mastered his *métier* as has no American among his contemporaries. That is his pride and his distinction.

The New Republic: November 11, 1936*

* Included, in 1937, in *After the Genteel Tradition: American Writers Since 1910*, edited by Malcolm Cowley, in the somewhat expanded form in which it appears here.

MOLL FLANDERS' WAY

WHEN, IN 1668, Daniel Defoe wrote a preface to his history of Moll Flanders, he sent forth his fear that with so many novels and memoirs then coming from the press, his own, which was a novel in the form of a memoir, would find favor among only a few. For it was drawn from the confessions of a notorious character lately confined in Newgate prison. He implies that those familiar with the criminal annals of the poor in London would soon surmise who was the original of his portrait. Her real name remains concealed from his readers; it is enough for them to know that it was as Mrs. Flanders that she was known in her more prosperous pickpocketing days.

It was shoplifting, or rather an attempt at shoplifting which failed, that landed her in prison; for Moll was surprised by the door's opening and someone's coming in from the back of the shop before she was able to make her getaway with the goods she was on the point of stealing. The two necessary witnesses are produced in court to swear not only to her breaking and entering the shop, but, falsely, to her having been discovered with the stolen goods on her person. She is condemned for one of the few crimes she did not commit; the incident has only a mild irony; since this is England of the seventeenth century, she is sentenced to be hanged by the neck until she is dead.

Moll Flanders is only saved from an end, which at the time was all too common a one for the English poor, first by a repentance apparently so profound that she convinces even the hardened and cynical prison chaplain that, though born and nurtured in crime, she is no longer at heart a criminal, and secondly, by a wise dispensing of money in such proper places and in such sound proportions as to convince those responsible for the safety of property and the punishment of all offenders against it, that she is not poor. Since she is not impoverished, she need not hang. Her sentence is commuted to deportation, and she ships, with one of her many husbands, a highwayman, to America. By the sincerity of her repentance we are not altogether convinced; we cannot but suspect that if Moll had not been so skillful as a thief and so foresighted as to have laid by a convenient sum, she would never have escaped the hangman. She repents, but only when she is uncomfortably close to the gallows' stairs and the hangman's neckcord. But Defoe assures us that Moll Flanders is constant in her repentance and that for the reader the last years of her life are alone likely to be profitable.

"Twelve years a whore, five times a wife (whereof once to her own brother), twelve years a thief, eight years a transported felon in Virginia—" Could any record be more deplorable? And with so many novels and memoirs pouring from the press, memoirs and novels, with which Moll and her confessions would have to compete, Defoe puts himself to some pains in his Preface to insist that, however immoral his novel may appear, the reader has only to look at it aright, and he cannot fail to find it to his moral advantage. And, in the novel itself, he allows Moll in her old age abundantly to profit by her honest way of life. Her husband, though once a highwayman, is a gentleman, and though not much use to her in America, affords her considerable satisfaction as a spectacle. Her plantation prospers; she comes into an inheritance; and at last she returns to her native land to live out her old age in a state at once complacent and repentant; through her own efforts and some luck, she is provided with every creature comfort; her reputation is forgotten, while her mind is agreeably enlivened by recollection of her former crimes. All that Moll needed was a chance. Her creator does not allow it to her until she is past sixty; but it is not too late; if Moll Flanders does not come out on top, she emerges somewhere near the middle in the utmost respectability.

Daniel Defoe in his Preface, as Moll Flanders in her history, impresses us as being both honest and hypocritical. But it is because their honesty constantly gains on their hypocrisy that in the end we are won by them. Defoe was one of the truly great narrators in the English tradition; he constantly imposed on his readers as true accounts that which he knew to be false; he represented himself as an eyewitness of events which not only he had not seen, but no one else had. He could describe a journey across Africa in such a way that we are quite ready to believe that he had actually traversed that darkest of continents; and it is only because we now have outside knowledge to prove him false that we know not only that Defoe had never made that trip, but that neither his Captain Singleton nor, at the time, anyone else had. Moll Flanders is a professional thief, and is no more honest in the Shakespearean sense of the word than in ours. And yet there is no quality by which she so profoundly impresses us as by her honesty. She does not deceive herself; she deceives us only in so far as we want to be deceived. Her hypocrisy is a concession to the society in which she found herself in the England of the seventeenth century. It is perhaps also a concession to existence.

What the novels and memoirs were which Defoe feared would distract his public from his narrative of the famous woman of Newgate, I do not know, nor what their merits. They are gone. So far as the common reader is concerned, there is no novelist in English before Defoe; there is none certainly that any but a special scholar or a peculiarly industrious seeker after literary curiosities will ever read much beyond the title. Or if he tries it, he will find he must make strange allowances for the taste of the period. Congreve's *Incognita*, for example, is apparently a reminiscence of an escapade in his youth, told as though it were intended to be offered as a plot for one of Shakespeare's youthful comedies. When certain English publishers reprinted it some years ago, they called it on the dustcover the first English novel. *Incognita* has charm; but it is only by the loosest definition that it can be called a novel.

But in reading Defoe, no allowances are necessary; and however strictly we may define the novel, we cannot deny the title to *Moll Flanders*. Not only is it a novel of great excellence, but as I reread it, it seems to me to possess not only the essential qualities of that form, but to suggest, if only by the slightest hint, all that the particular mould of experience was to be capable of containing.

If Defoe feared that *Moll Flanders* would fail to find readers, it was not on account of the form in which he had cast her tale. That he never doubted, any more than he doubted that he, a man, could charge every passage with the conviction that a woman is speaking; her voice he takes as he finds it, for it was not too impolite; he only avoids some of the viler words which in sixty years, varied by vice, she had picked up. That again is a concession to the reader. But the novel he accepts apparently without the slightest consciousness that he himself was one of its creators. For Defoe, it already exists; it needs only to be brought into being by calling up characters, each of whom was committed, through their own fault or fortune's, to a certain course of action.

Not only *Moll Flanders* remains, but the form of Defoe's narrative. Wherever the common reader is to be found—I find Mrs. Woolf's, or rather Dr. Johnson's, phrase convenient—he is so held by the novel that no other form of creative literature can possibly hope to compete with it. It is hard for us to remember that this was not always so. If we have a story to tell and it is one which requires any considerable stretch of time to be carried to completeness, it will almost certainly take shape as a novel. The novel is that form of literary expression which belongs to the middle class, and is the only one which that class has created. It did not, and doubtless could not, come into existence until the middle class had so increased in importance that it demanded a means of projecting into imaginary realms its own conception of the morals and meaning of the world.

Men have always loved telling tales and listening to them, and they have, since they could do so, on occasion written down any that seemed worth conserving. So long as the court dominated the consciousness of society, romances were read, pastorals, six thousand pages long, so preposterous and in their later days so precious, that not only is it impossible for us to read them, but it is even incredible to us that anyone should have considered it worth his while to waste his sight, and by candles at that, over the interminable volumes of Mlle. de Scudéry. In them the loved ladies are inaccessible, the sentiments of the lovers impossibly high flown, the incidents astonishing, lofty, cold and conventional. Nothing is so perpetually subtle as reality, nothing so quickly tiresome as the imaginary.

The French will say that the *Princesse de Clèves* is their first novel, and say it because, for the first time in their letters, through Mme. de Clèves and M. de Nemours, real lovers speak from the printed pages. But Mme. de La Fayette's book is rather a condensed and slightly disguised memoir. "Ce n'est pas un roman," she said. And it was to memoirs that reality was confined in the literature of the court. Saint-Simon's *Memoirs* are just what they pretend to be: begun in 1691 at the age of sixteen, a record of conspicuous men and women about the King Louis XIV, seen through the eyes of a courtier, uncommonly gifted, proud, without prejudices, but superbly conscious of the prerogatives of his recently acquired rank. If Saint-Simon has the gift of sight, which is the greatest an artist can possess, he looks out always from under a full-bottom wig. He sees life a *Duc et Pair*.

But when we come to the *Memoirs* of Casanova, we are not sure, in spite of the authenticity of such names as the Abbé de Bernis, whether we are dealing with a superb work of the imagination or with a record of observed reality. The middle class had long since begun to make its power felt in politics, but it was not until life in France had been profoundly influenced by the thinking and the sensibility of the bourgeoisie that we find a small, but nevertheless authentic, novel. And *Manon Lescaut* is in many ways not unlike *Moll Flanders*. For, if we make full allowance for the difference in national and personal qualities of the Abbé Prévost and Daniel Defoe, we shall find that they have much in common. And what they share is the middle-class conception of life.

If, as I have assumed, the novel is the literary expression of the middle class, it should be expected to appear at the very moment when the middle class is preparing to play its rôle in history; and that, as a matter of fact, is what, in every country, happened; its great period coincides with that in which the middle class is rising to a place of power; and as the nineteenth century proceeds and the middle class continues to maintain and even to increase its dominance until it controls the commerce of the entire world, the novel becomes so much the dominant form of literary expression that all other forms, the poem and the play, even historical writings, only exist as its envious rivals, attempting, not always with success, to imitate its methods.

But as that century proceeds, the dominant class is subjected to more and more searching criticism and is shaken in its assurance. For if, in the eighteenth century, the best of the middle class could regard themselves, and rightly, as carriers of the Enlightenment, it was obvious by the middle of the nineteenth that only the speculative mind could still move in expanding realms of light. On earth, Prometheus had become as grimy as Pluto; industrialism had covered a green and pleasant land with heaps of slag and hideous agglomerations of slums. The streams were poisoned by corrosives, and the air darkened by smoke. That day in whose dawn it had been a very joy to be alive grew so dark now that even the hope of happiness disappeared. Love itself gleamed no more brightly than a straw in a stable.

It was in the midst of this disastrous triumph that the novelists began to grow self-conscious. The old easy assurance, which allowed the plot to serve as skeleton and depended upon it to give strength and articulation, was gone. With Flaubert all innocence is lost; he must know what he is doing, as he places each word; he is condemned, like Adam after the Fall, to sweat and unremitting toil, and like Eve he can bring his conceptions to birth only after long and excruciating labor. Henry James explores the technique of his chosen craft with a conscience as delicate as though he were probing a course of conduct by which he would be forever saved or damned. And as for those who pretend to ignore such distinctions and to do without this inner discipline, their novels fell into formlessness and indeed, as in the case of H. G. Wells, ceased to be novels at all.

Since the novelist aims at creating a complete credibility, he is largely confined to that portion of society which, through the chances of his life, he has come profoundly to know. The novel is itself a product of the middle class; it is probably not altogether chance that most successful novels have dealt with that class. Virginia Woolf has pointed out how rare in all the course of the English novel are accurate portraits of the aristocracy, and even D. H. Lawrence—who down to the present is the only English novelist who has been competent alike through genius and a proletarian birth to record the laboring class—as a matter of fact, once he had finished with his miner father in *Sons and Lovers*, concerned himself with them scarcely at all.

We have heard a great deal in the last few years about the proletarian novel. I am not sure that the term has meaning, if we apply both words strictly; but as commonly used, what is meant is that an invention of the middle class shall be appropriated and, with whatever violence is necessary, made to promote the interests of those whom the middle class has exploited and humiliated, sometimes starved, and on occasion murdered in the interests of property. Moll Flanders belongs to the predatory, not the oppressed poor, and yet there are indubitably certain points at which Defoe's novel does what the proletarian novel would do. Moll is born in a prison of a mother, condemned to death as a thief, who has only escaped the gallows by pleading that she is with child. Moll is not one of the people of property; it is the peculiar irony of her history that, having been brought up as though she were, she has absorbed most of their preconceptions. Down to the last decade of her career, her property is come by, for the most part, frankly through theft or trickery. She commits every crime and is guilty of only one, that of being poor. She is, if you will, a creature of heredity and environment. She comes within a few days of the gallows, in order to expiate, not her own, but the sins of the society into which she has been so unhappy as to be born without position, without privilege, and above all without a competence. Moll comes from the bottom of the pile. Conceived upon a condemned mother by a chance father, born in prison, soon corrupted by a son of the comfortable house in which charity has placed her, again and again a seeming chance casts her into a disreputable choice; actually she has no choice, and the slightest consideration will say that it is not chance, but a society in which she has the lot to belong to an oppressed class that is to blame for all her shortcomings. For Moll is fundamentally decent, and all she needs at any time in her career to put on the outward show and apparel of decency is a little more money, a little less dubiously acquired.

This, as I recount it, is not quite the story as Defoe tells it; for Defoe was writing in the seventeenth century. But the conscious moral which he draws in his preface to *Moll Flanders* is not the one which is carried, at least for us, by her imagined confessions. But even when he wrote, the essential character of the middle classes had been displayed in England, and it was already possible to criticize their morality. Like all the great novelists who were to follow him, Defoe both partakes of the middle-class view of conduct and surpasses it. And he opposes it in the only way that is open to the artist to oppose any set of abstract principles: not, as our own proletarian novelists would do, by offering in their stead another, and supposedly better, set of abstract principles, but by confronting them with the passions of life and the consequences of action.

The aristocratic conception of what is right conduct was not the same. It, too, showed an inner conflict. The nobles were in the first instance those who had won their power by the force of arms, and as long as they were dominant, the morals of the fighter influenced society. Now, on the battlefield, only deeds are of avail and acts are good or bad according to their consequences. Man is a responsible creature: he may fail and yet fail nobly. Good intentions are nothing; what counts is what he does, how he does it, and its final cost. Superimposed upon this code, and often in conflict with it, were the teachings of the Church; but it must not be forgotten that for some centuries preceding the rise of the middle class, the Church had taken over much from the Aristotelian ethics. Of all sins, the most displeasing, the most abject, the one which could look forward to the coldest punishment in the deepest Hell was treachery. That a soldier could understand.

I need hardly say that almost the whole of this morality was reversed by the middle class. Trickery was the life of trade, and without a whole bag of the liveliest tricks Moll Flanders would never have lived to cheat the hangman. In the classical morality, when everything went against him, a man could still die grandly. It was his choice, when all was lost to fortune, not to lose his honor. Moll Flanders is a whore, a thief, a felon. And yet throughout we are convinced that she is a genuinely decent person, and that it is only outward circumstances which prevent her from being an entirely respectable one.

It is Defoe's greatness that he never lets us doubt this. And who will say that no small part of the success of the novel is due to just this, that it can show so much better than the play, not only what the characters do and say, but all the inner promptings, so often obscure, velleities not voiced, and intentions corrupted as soon as they pass into actions.

It is in the disparity between what was meant and what was actually achieved that there is scope for the novelist's irony, and without irony the novel has neither conviction nor force. That is why obvious virtue is so dull in the novel; a good person who goes straight toward good deeds always fails to convince us, not because goodness does not exist, but because in such a case the novelist has no means of granting it a third dimension. We believe, for instance, in Mme. Verdurin's virtuous act, when she retires to her bedroom with her husband, after the party at which she has so humiliated M. de Charlus and so meanly separated him from Morel. We believe Proust when he tells us that she then decides, with a generosity which is increased by its proposed secrecy, to endow Cottard. But we are not asked to believe in Mme. Verdurin's virtue. In the same way we believe Baron de Charlus is not without a moral grandeur, though we are constantly seeing him exposed by his vices to the lowest and most ignominious performances.

In a state dominated by a class destined to combat, the deed itself is felt to hold all tragic possibilities. The Church did not deny this, but merely added that, once committed, the consequences of an act might redound to all eternity. But whether immorality was believed in or not, a man might suffer after death through his fame. It was important, therefore, that what he had done on this living earth should be truly recounted.

"Absent thee from felicity awhile," the dying Hamlet implores Horatio, and for no other reason than that he fears that his cause will not be reported aright to the world.

"When you shall these unlucky deeds relate," Othello asks the Venetian ambassadors, when he is on the point of suicide, "Speak of me as I am; nothing extenuate, nor set down aught in malice."

But, with the rise of the middle class, what is felt is, as I have said, the disparity between what is willed and what is done. There is scarcely a heroine of the novel, from Moll Flanders on, who is not in need of a great deal of extenuation. Occupations have become mean, and it is ignominy not ambition that leads to crime. Tess of the d'Urbervilles kills her child and Raskolnikov murders the two old women, the money lender and her companion. Yet Hardy distinctly tells us that Tess was a good woman and Dostoevsky so leads us that all our sympathies are with the tortured student and not with his tormentors, who are the rightful protectors of society. It is precisely the greatness of the novel that it has been able to do this: that, in circumstances so small that they have lost the potentiality of tragedy, it has been able to find tragic possibilities, not in what was done, but in the failure of accomplishment, that, working with minor scale, it has yet been able to measure simultaneously the meanness of action and the essential greatness of the human soul.

Story: November, 1937

THE STRANGE CASE OF VARDIS FISHER

I

VARDIS FISHER has written three novels of pioneering life in the Idaho benchland: *Toilers of the Hills* (1928), *Dark Bridwell* (1931), and *In Tragic Life* (1932). All are laid in the years between the turn of the century and the end of the World War. *In Tragic Life* is also the first of four novels, all with titles taken from one poem of Meredith's, which, despite their having been published separately, may best be regarded as a single work. Together they compose the history of Vridar Hunter, from birth through young manhood; the name is a most transparent disguise for Vardis Fisher. And there are, scattered throughout the work, other even more definite indications that it is strongly autobiographical in character. The form of fiction is carefully preserved through the first volume; in those that follow, *Passions Spin the Plot* and *We Are Betrayed*, it tends constantly to break down; and in the last volume, *No Villain Need Be*, it frequently disappears altogether to leave nothing behind but Mr. Fisher's opinions on a great variety of topics, including communism and the impulse to rape among married men of middle age.

In Tragic Life opens with the arrival in Idaho of the first of the clan. Joe Hunter is a young man, stout of heart and body, who paces West in 1869 with no heavier provision than his gun, a knife and a bag of ammunition. His wanderings end only when he has found a wife, an Irish girl of sixteen, whose parents had come out with Brigham Young. With her he enters the Snake River Valley and, being one of the first white men there, is able to choose the richest land. He prospers and grows fat. His wife is as robust and even more earthy than he; on her, he begets four daughters and eight sons, all of whom in time grow to be, like himself, tall, handsome and strong.

The eldest of them, another Joe, marries Prudence Branton, of mixed stock, Pennsylvania Dutch and English. One of her ancestors fought at Concord, another signed the Declaration of Independence. Stern, ambitious, puritanical, and more than a little mean, she holds herself, as do all her family, above the Hunters and their unruly connections. Assuming a social as well as a moral superiority, she has nothing but contempt for tillers of the soil. As a matter of fact, Prudence's father is a small-town cobbler, and her strain is decidedly queer. From such vigorous seed cast on such starved ground, Vridar Hunter is sprung.

But before his birth, the rich valley to which his grandfather had come had long since been homesteaded from end to end. The second Joe works barren fields. After seven years of marriage, seven years of desperate and starving toil, he finds himself hopelessly in debt. In 1901, Vridar being then a small boy and his brother Mertyl a baby, Joe packs his few belongings on a wagon, ties a cow behind and sets off for a fresh start. For seven dollars and a worn-out horse, he acquires land on the boundary of the Antelope Hills. "It was bottomland, a great hole sunk in the earth, river-haunted and mountain-walled. A third of it was cottonwood island, a third was swamp and meadow, and a third was dry and hot and brush-covered earth." And to the growing Vridar, a weakling at birth and morbidly sensitive always, it is an abode of loneliness, desperation and fear.

But it is his homeland and he cannot escape it. Though the accidents of his story carry Vridar to many places, the determining background is always the Idaho benchland.

His struggle might have been less intense and bitter, it might not have been violently insane, as in time it came to be, if two facts in his life had been different. One of these was his father, that powerful and silent man who never knew fear and had for it only contempt. The other was this wild and unpitying outpost that was to be his home.

To it in the end he returns. His parents are aged, his two sons almost half-grown. His own youth is past and his fears allayed, in part subdued. For the story of Vridar is essentially one of fear and the struggle against a fear of life, whose first causes, he would have us believe, lie back of his birth. It is increased in his poverty-bitten boyhood by a pioneer upbringing, at once brutal and idealistic, undisciplined and repressed. With the advent of adolescence, it becomes a nightmare of terror, from which he wakes, impotent, shattered and shamed. So far *In Tragic Life* takes him; the remaining volumes are an account of his attempts to overcome this fear and the consequences of having been shaped by this land of buck-brush and wolves.

ESSAYS

II

A novelist can make no more serious demand on his art than that it tell us this: Granted such and such circumstances—and they will probably be those which the unsought experience of his own life has led him to consider—how shall a man conduct himself so that his soul may not sicken and die? It is because Vardis Fisher makes this demand that he commends himself to our interest. His resources as an artist are limited, his taste is uncertain and his sense of form is not strong enough to allow him with impunity to discard the common conventions of the novel. But no one could doubt the earnestness of his moral purpose. His effort has been extreme to set down his conclusions honestly. Moreover, the circumstances into which his characters are cast concern us all, though it may be remotely. They are those of the frontier. As it happens, this is a very late frontier. We are conscious, in those three novels of Vardis Fisher that are laid entirely in the Idaho benchland, that the whole pioneer movement has come to a dead end; its exhaustion has left these people depleted; morally and emotionally, it still runs its course. The space of the American continent has been conquered; but these Idahoans are still held by the example of their fathers; they cannot stop, but must forever be making a fresh start. The heroic age is past. Courage and hope, those two most admirable virtues of the frontiersman, have become in this late and unpromising land, cruelly meaningless.

But it is precisely because this late frontier has been observed by a contemporary and, it is scarcely to be doubted, accurately observed, that Vardis Fisher's account has value. As Turner has pointed out in his classic work on the significance of the frontier in American history, there is a strong continuity in the influence of the frontier, constantly changing though it was, on those who confronted it. They must pass through the same experiences. Decade follows decade, yet those who fell the tall forest and lay low the wilderness, whether in the Old West along the Appalachians or in this more recent West under the Antelope Hills, come after a time roughly to resemble one another. Their hearts have been put in hostage to the same forces. Plymouth goes in debt to pay for King Philip's War, and the farmers of the Dakotas mortgage their farms to buy more land in order to raise wheat for the soldiers of the World War. We are all inheritors, variously remote, of conditions that may well have been like those which so closely affect the Hunters in Idaho, their kinsmen and neighbors.

There have never been lacking, even from the beginning, men

58

who refused to take the frontiersman at his own high moral appraisal. William Byrd travelled in North Carolina in the early years of the eighteenth century and came back to say just what he thought of the settlers there. And it was nothing good. But these critics, for the most part, have come from the seaboard; and their opinion has been discounted. Americans have preferred to take a romantic view of the pioneer; it has been enough that they could speak of the dangers he has passed and vaunt the heroic endurance of hardship. They have concentrated on the advance and not until lately minded its ruthlessness. Mr. Fisher has taken another turn. His writings are not pleasant, and I doubt if as writing they please even himself; but he has explored the possibilities that open to the pioneer once he has stopped. And whatever the choice, he has counted the cost, not only to the men, but to the women and children.

Something of the romantic view is left in Vardis Fisher's regard for Dock Hunter in *Toilers of the Hills*. And yet this story of Vridar's uncle and his attempts, dim-witted, and all the same successful, to find out for himself the secrets of dry farming reminds us of Ty Ty Walden and his digging for gold in *God's Little Acre*. The Georgian and the Idahoan are brothers under the skin and also under the scalp. It has long occurred to me that Erskine Caldwell's red clay countryside, on the subject of which some Southerners are so sensitive, represents not so much a condition peculiar to the South as a deplorable case of arrested and decadent frontier.

Dock Hunter's life finds its meaning in toil. He is determined to convert a waste land into wheatfields. His land when he first encounters it is all a dry desolation, sagebrush, dwarf mahogany, serviceberry and smaller weeds and grasses. He must work not only against nature in its most inclement form—against drouth, snowstorms that come with thunder and lightning, wild mustard that springs in his wheat and grasshoppers that fall on his fields—but against the indifference and derision of his wife. "Things," he declares morosely, "have got out of God's control."

That he is saved in the end is due less to his own efforts, though these are prodigious, than to a distant and unforeseen disaster. He does indeed learn something about dry farming. But it is the War in Europe that advances the price of his hard-grown wheat.

All this sounds commonplace enough in a novel of pioneering life. What is not commonplace are the emotions Mr. Fisher manages to derive from his material. He makes us admire Dock for his persistence, and at the same time we are made to feel that his will is not quite human, that his toil all along has been completely witless.

Dark Bridwell is the story of the Bridwells: Charley, his wife Lela and his eldest son Jed. This is the family which Joe Hunter, when he arrives on the slopes of the Antelope Hills, finds living in a one-room cabin of cottonwood logs, built long since and abandoned by an early settler. Charley is no toiler of the hills. Those who know him declare, not without joy, that he is the laziest man who ever drew the breath of life. He has come late on the wild scene, but is one with the earliest adventurers of the West, with those *voyageurs* and trappers whom Catlin met on his travels, a hundred years ago, at the juncture of the Missouri and the Yellowstone, washing down choice beaver tails and buffalo tongues with three kinds of French and Spanish wine. He is of those lonely men who precede the true settlers and make them, when they appear, seem sluggish of mind and body. Given the need, he bestirs himself. Charley is fond of the good things of life and, thief and vagabond, knows how to get them. He is full of devilish fun. More than any other in these books, he has been assimilated to savagery; he has the savage skills, can shoot, ride, trap and swim, make his fragrant bed of soft pine boughs and imitate the cries of wild beasts until they themselves are deceived. And a small point, but important: he keeps himself clean, bathing in winter like an Indian in the piled snow. The filthy Hunters live in filth, unwashed from one year's end to another.

Charley Bridwell is a generation too late. Hence he is frustrated. And yet it is precisely because he has deliberately deserted civilization and willfully adopted savagery that he is superior to those round him. His will is active. His manhood is saved. He knows that he needs to know. Too many of the rest have lapsed into a primitive state where nothing is known and all is once more a subject for primal speculation. When Dock Hunter and his friend Lem Higley spin their yarns, we might almost as well be listening to conversations in the Dordogne caves. To Dock, the moon is flame; but to Lem, who has pondered deeply on the subject, the moon is a chunk of ice. When it floats north, there are cold spells; when it retreats, we have summer. "All my reason," Dock declares, "is set against what science says." But on the other hand, Dock says, "I ain't had no mind for church." He has heard certain things from the Bible and is under the impression he owns one; as a matter of fact, he does not. He is an animist, to whom his binder and the wild mustard weed, the hills and the sky are all equally alive, malignant and aware. One cannot but feel that he has mislaid a thousand years or more of history without knowing that they, too, are not there.

But if Charley Bridwell is able to fulfill the deepest needs of his being in this remote wilderness—himself turned wild and his desires sagely held to those the lonely hills can gratify—he is defeated in the long run by those whom he has forced to follow and share his loneliness: his wife and his children. It has been Charley's intention that his two sons and daughter should grow up lovely and fresh and clean as trees in the simplicity of nature. But Jed, the oldest boy, who has inherited his father's violence and his mother's restlessness, grows up, not like a sapling, but like a wolf cub. He is a child of nature indeed, implacably cruel, maliciously cunning, secret, sturdy and lewd. He runs away in his first teens and returns only when his man's strength is attained, and then it is, after an ancient and apparently natural precedent, to try to kill his father and carry off his mother. The other boy and the girl turn out no better; they only prove, as the bawd in Sanctuary observed, that children can learn meanness anywhere.

Joe Hunter, of the autobiographical novels, has the industry of Dock; but he has, as his brother has not, an ambitious wife. They struggle and starve and save, not for themselves but their children. They live by hope. The remote end they foresee for their labors is that their children may not, as they do, till the soil. Their determination forces them also to half-starve the children. They grow up underfed, unkempt, unfit for life in these hills, and at the same time unprepared for any life in the world beyond them.

Exploitation of the soil, a savage return to nature and a hope for their children's future, these are the three solutions offered by these pioneers. None of them, save possibly Dock Hunter, has any conception of living with the land. And Dock, as we have seen, has fallen almost below the human level. In the rest, as in all too many of the Western pioneers, is implicit one or another way of life, derived from the eighteenth, or it may be an even earlier century—still pursued, though it has faded from the consciousness and is no longer appropriate to the time. Because the first Americans were really colonists, they had quite naturally the colonial point of view of the new continent as a land to be explored, exploited and if need be exhausted; then they would move on. No use to conserve for posterity; the posterity of the exploiters would be taken care of out of the profits. Joe and Prudence Hunter, the moment they have made any money out of their farm, escape and buy first a small-town garage and then a grocery store in Salt Lake City. It is only because they are failures there that they come back to the Antelope Hills. Charley Bridwell still carries on the romantic heresy that man has fallen from a state of nature and needs only to leave civilization behind to recover his native grace and innocence. He does for a time act out his savage play; it is his children who seize on his fantasy and ferociously give him the lie.

For the rest, Mr. Fisher's characters seem to be living with a few odds and ends which their fathers carried with them from the East, as occasionally some fine old New England secretary was borne precariously across the prairies in a covered wagon to be set up at last incongruously in a sod hut, more an encumbrance than an ornament, its purpose lost, its use doubtful. It is interesting that Vridar, when in his mid-thirties he reaches Europe, feels more at home in England, of which he has had a long, if somewhat abstract, knowledge from his reading, than he has ever done in the East. He looks upon all traditions and traditional forces as his enemies, since he attributes, and perhaps rightly, his incompetence for life to the spiritless Puritanism which his mother imposed on him as a child. For in Prudence's hard worn hand all the flowering of New England has become a dry and bitter nosegay, fit only to be thrown away as soon as possible.

But the unfailing Prudence, though she can be seen as a last Puritan, lost in this desert of sagebrush and dust, but still in the bright brittle sunlight standing upright, thin and bloodless, with no desire but to be out of the human heat, bringing to life only distrust, taking from love only disgust, is, as it happens, a figure that regularly recurs on the frontier and always at the same moment in its history. The first generation of pioneer women are not usually as bawdy as Vridar's grandmother Rose; but they are commonly not behind her in sturdiness, competence and downright sense. It is in the second generation that we are apt to get, on the one hand, slatterns like Opal Hunter; on the other, the overrefined, prudish and fastidious women. The contrast between generations has been perfectly brought out by Glenway Westcott in *The Grandmothers*, where the mother is of the last kind. It was not confined to the West. Little Eva also had a mother.

III

Toilers of the Hills and *Dark Bridwell* are honestly conceived and sensitively written. Without being great, or anything like it, they are good books which deserve more recognition than they have hitherto received. Though Mr. Fisher lacks Erskine Caldwell's amazing comic gift and his facility for inventing fables, his first novel can stand being compared with *God's Little Acre*. He has not the depth of pity that is brought to the portrayal of Southern poor whites in *As I Lay Dying*, nor has he William Faulkner's admirable control of his material. Nevertheless, in his first two novels and in the earlier portions of *In Tragic Life*, Mr. Fisher has given us a comparable record, if it be considered solely as record, of the privations, humiliations and aspirations of the agricultural poor. He is a lesser artist than either Mr. Caldwell or Mr. Faulkner. Like another Hamlet, pioneer and not prince, he has eaten air promise-crammed; he has breathed an atmosphere less dense, less saturated, than the Southerners. The poor whites of Mississippi and Georgia are still a part of a social situation which, however impoverished, is still much more complicated than any Idahoan can know. I am unfamiliar with the region Mr. Fisher describes; whatever impressions I have been able to form of its people are entirely derived from his writings. (The only native of Idaho I know is Ezra Pound, and he is quite unlike anything recognized by Mr. Fisher in his pages.) I can only say that his poor farmers seem to me as abject as those in *As I Lay Dying* and depleted, as they are not, of human dignity. In cruelty and unabashed lewdness, they surpass the characters of *Tobacco Road*—if not in performance, certainly in precocity. Where they really exceed the Southerners is in hope. They still think of themselves as pioneers and are not easily defeated.

That naturalism is not an alternative to romanticism but rather a derivative from it, has long been recognized. And as Mr. Fisher's method in the later portions of *In Tragic Life* and the volumes that follow attains an extreme of naturalism, so his matter becomes an exasperated romanticism. The chapters in which the adolescent Vridar goes through the usual autoerotic struggle of his age are like nothing so much as certain passages in Octave Mirbeau's *Sébastien Roch*. We are still for a time in the Idaho benchland; but from the moment Mr. Fisher begins to concentrate on Vridar Hunter, the surroundings, while remaining as sordid as ever, become dim. And we are left looking on the one reflected face, seen as in a mirror darkened at twilight, of the romantic sentimental hero, as yet a boy but already incapacitated for adaptation to this or indeed any later environment, morbid and overwrought, a prey to impulses, yet determined with a strange pertinacity to assert his unruly and unmannered ego.

IV

Mr. Fisher's tetralogy, as he rather impressively calls it, carries Vridar from his native farmland to the small town of Annis, thence to Salt Lake City, Chicago, New York, and even, though briefly, to Europe. Thus, among the potential themes is one which Henry James, along with others, has magnificently employed: the approach to the capital. It is one of the great themes of the novel. There is an account of the education of Vridar and his younger brother Mertyl, for which both they and their impoverished parents are called on to make consuming sacrifices. Vridar's part in it is narrated in no inconsiderable detail, from his first appearance in school to his acquisition of his degree as a Doctor of Philosophy. And it is told so that it becomes not only an academic but a sentimental education. And that, too, is one of the great themes of the novel. And last we have, marking the sentimental advance, his relations with three women: his stern and forbidding mother, his childhood sweetheart, Neloa, whom he marries extremely young, and Athene, whom he meets in Chicago and for whose sake he prepares to abandon his wife and the two children she has borne him. Neloa, in a final act of renunciation and despair, commits suicide. Each of these women dominates one or another phase of his long struggle against the morbid fears with which an unwholesome heredity and the cruel loneliness of his childhood have endowed him.

At first glance, we would seem to have here the material for a novel of the massive sort of *Le Rouge et le Noir*. But we have only to go a little way into Mr. Fisher's protracted narrative to find that this is not so at all. The mastering emotion of Julien Sorel's life is that ambition which a childhood under Napoleon so readily engendered and which young manhood under the Restoration found all but impossible to fulfil. Julien's story, presented in all its personal intensity, becomes the moral history of his generation in France. From being a telling record of its time, it has acquired the timelessness of art. And because Julien's passion is active, male and full of pride, Stendhal, in spite of chance, has been able to bring his history to a tragic conclusion. But Vridar Hunter, though he achieves the ambition of his parents and becomes a college professor, though he overcomes the worst of his fears and, after his marriage to Athene, subdues remorse and so far escapes reproach as to appear relatively calm, is never a tragic personage. The approach to the capital fails to attain any but the slightest significance, for Vridar is incapable of understanding a complicated social background. Then, too, neither in Chicago nor in New York do we ever see much beyond those academic circles which seem closed to the life around them. The sentimental education does not get very far, since Vridar is as evasive as he is irritable. He will take no responsibility for his acts. That his suffering should be passive, we can endure well enough so long as he is very young, for no one expects a boy to put up any tremendous show against the cruelty of circumstance. We can admire his stout support of poverty and share with sympathy the agonized bewilderment of his adolescent years. But as a man, Vridar, with his lack of pride and his even worse lack of sense, is harder to put up with. He moves from self-pity to self-complacency. And Mr. Fisher's art eventually becomes as self-indulgent as his hero. Vridar's sickliness never becomes the sickness of his time. His remains a personal record.

"It is not possible today to imagine, even to imagine vaguely, what an honest book, a completely honest book, would be like," Vridar says at one point. And again, in announcing his intention to write such an honest book, he gives as his reason, "Because every other kind has been written."

The profession of such an aim implies a certain naïveté. It should be obvious to anyone that every writer worth his salt is as honest as he knows how to be, and that his honesty, such as it is, is not a matter of intention, but first of sight and insight, and then of literary skill. An honest writer will not suppress any fact about a character that is essential to its presentation, nor if he is skillful enough need he, no matter how delicate the taste of his age. Dickens, when in the reign of Victoria he wrote *Oliver Twist*, could make it quite clear to anybody who wants to understand Fagin that his vices with young boys are not limited to teaching them to steal. But literary integrity will also demand that the writer ruthlessly suppress any fact that will not fit into the design of his composition; it will equally demand that anything that life has failed to supply and which is needed to fill in his book's design, he must invent. Honesty does not consist in telling all. And that is just what Mr. Fisher does. He tells all.

We ask of the novel that it give us, not the illusion of real life, but the reality of the imagination. When it does this, it is a subject for literary criticism. But only *In Tragic Life* of the four volumes which Mr. Fisher has devoted to Vridar Hunter can properly be called a novel. It is one which, without unfairness either way, might well be compared with Thomas Wolfe's *Look Homeward, Angel*. After that Mr. Fisher's honest work steadily deteriorates. It becomes a confession. And since it is a confession, it would be wrong to leave anything out, for any omission might endanger, or indeed destroy, that hope of expiation in which it is set down. That Vridar, wanting to desert Neloa for Athene, is able to see himself as another Shelley forced to choose between a Harriet and a Mary, does not help at all. This is no place for literary precedents. It is a situation that one is ready to believe actually came about, and one is ready to believe that it has been set down by one of the participants with all the conscience he can bring to bear on it. It is painful. But it is not literature. And hence it is not a subject for literary criticism. *The Southern Review: Autumn, 1937*

THE MISSING ALL

I

ALLEN TATE, in the first of his recent *Reactionary Essays*, speaking of the tradition of Puritan theocracy as it was finally reflected in the poetry of Emily Dickinson, has this to say: "Socially, we may not like the New England idea. Yet it had an immense, incalculable value for literature: it dramatized the human soul."

This is quite true. In those allegories which we call his novels, Hawthorne is concerned only with spiritual conflicts. But Hawthorne came late; before the Civil War his New England was already on the decline. Salem harbor was not empty: the clipper ships, still increasing in speed, scudded, all whiteness, on the farthest oceans; brigantines called with a Yankee twang among the Malayan islands; and captains from Bristol still occasionally caught a profitable black cargo on the Gold Coast of Africa. But the land, once neglected for the sea, was being abandoned for a Western promise. The mecantile class was destined to go down before the mill-owners, for they, no more than the farmers, could withstand the necessities of the time. *The Scarlet Letter* is fine, intense, austere, but already a little strangely so. Hawthorne is at his best looking backward.

The great seventeenth-century certitude of God is gone. Emily Dickinson seldom came down to the parlor when there were guests in the house at Amherst.

> The missing All prevented me
> From missing minor things.
> If nothing larger than a World's
> Departure from a hinge,
> Or Sun's extinction be observed,
> 'Twas not so large that I
> Could lift my forehead from my work
> For curiosity.

This is magnificent. And it is New England. There the summer is brief, and after, the bedrooms are chilly. They admitted, however, "a polar privacy." Upstairs, in New England, the soul was still intact.

66

But already Ohio had been settled with white villages dominated by a spire. New England moved westward; men and women followed the course of the rivers into Illinois and mounted the currents, flooded yellow in spring, into the forests of Michigan. With them went the New England idea.

II

In the summer of 1922, in Paris, Ezra Pound told me about a young newspaper correspondent who had written some stories. Pound had not then renounced discovery; he had a restless passion for literature which led him to seek it out wherever it might be. And presently he took me to the rue Cardinal Lemoine, where I followed him up five flights of narrow winding stairs. At the top, answering the poet's knock against a door under the roof, came a stalwart, smiling, good-looking young man. It was he, Pound said, who had written the stories. His name was Ernest Hemingway. As he led us into his apartment, I saw that he limped badly.

We did not stay long. On the way back across the Left Bank, Pound told me that the limping young man had been with the Italians during the War and, when his trench was blown up, wounded and, covered by falling dirt, left four days for dead.

III

Just how old Scott Fitzgerald was when I first met him is a question. He afterwards said that he had lied so often about his age that he had to bring his old nurse on from St. Paul in order himself to know in just what year he had been born. He was, as nearly as I can make out, seventeen; but even then he was determined to be a genius, and since one of the most obvious characteristics of genius was precocity, he must produce from an early age. He did, but wanted through vanity to make it even earlier.

Long afterwards, I complained to him that I thought he took seventeen as his norm, making everything later a falling off. For a moment he demurred, then said, "If you make it fifteen, I will agree with you."

He had, like myself, only arrived in Princeton; the Commons for Freshmen was not yet open; we sat side by side at a large round table in a corner at the Peacock Inn. It was the first time I had gone out alone, for in those opening days we stuck very close to the boys who had come down from school with us. It was by chance that I sat next to this youth, so quick to conversation; we stayed on when the others had gone. In the leafy street outside the September twilight faded; the lights came on against the paper walls, where tiny peacocks strode and trailed their tails among the gayer foliations. I learned that Fitzgerald had written a play which had been performed at school. Places were cleared; other students sat down at the tables around us. We talked of books: those I had read, which were not many; those Fitzgerald had read, which were even less; those he said he had read, which were many, many more. It was the age at which we were discovering Meredith and the writers of *The Yellow Book*. Wells had not yet come, but to the youth from St. Paul it was soon clear that Compton Mackenzie had.

Fitzgerald was pert and fresh and blond, and looked, as someone said, like a jonquil. He scribbled in class, or sat in an apparent dreaming drowse from which he was startled from time to time by a question which he had only half heard. Though he arrived at what seemed a clever way of stalling until he could at least guess what had been asked him ("It all depends on how you look at it. There is the subjective and the objective point of view"), it did not prevent his being dropped from the class. He had an ailment, which served as excuse for his departure. Like so many precocious literary talents, he had, I believe, a tendency to tuberculosis. When he returned, it was, so far as the registrar of Princeton was concerned, to take his place in another class. I saw as much of him as ever, perhaps more, for his ambitious political career on the campus had been damaged by his absence.

He left Princeton without a degree and without much of an education; but he had with him the material for two novels. The first, *The Romantic Egoist*, not many have seen in its entirety besides myself, a few old school friends who appeared in it, and the unwilling publishers. It was written on Saturday nights and Sunday afternoons at the Officers' Club at Fort Leavenworth, Kansas, where he was stationed during a period of training as Second Lieutenant in the regular Army. Scraps of it were saved, trimmed and refurbished to appear here and there as patches in *This Side of Paradise*, a book which, when it appeared, was reviewed by one of the author's Princeton friends, T. K. Whipple, as *The Collected Works of F. Scott Fitzgerald*. So it was, for the time being, for not a line from any of those poems scribbled in lecture halls, if it chanced to be good, had been wasted.

THE MISSING ALL

IV

Some of his earliest stories Hemingway wrote lying on a bed in a roof-sharpened room which once had provided shelter for Verlaine in his last decrepit and drunken years. After the war, which Hemingway had seen fought with terrible retreats, on the Italian front, he passed as newspaper correspondent from line to line of the Turkish-Greek War; talked to the Greek King; heard at the Quai d'Orsay what the French Foreign Office wanted the reporters to hear; saw in the Ruhr a good deal that Poincaré did not want him to see. Between times, he drank with the other reporters in the bars of the rue Daunou. He ranged with Pamplona to Kansas City, but always came back to Paris. Much of his writing was done there, and perhaps only there could he have developed a perfect consciousness of his craft. From Pound, he learned the lesson of Flaubert, profiting by it only because of his innate honesty, his incorruptible subjection to his art. He dislikes, with strange intensity for a writer who has successfully surmounted every one he has undergone, to admit influence. Mark Twain apart, there is none that he freely owns. Yet in those years he read Turgenev and Defoe, masters both of straight narrative, and Marryat, and showed his sound instinct by learning from the Joyce of *Dubliners* and discarding, with immense admiration, the Joyce of *Ulysses*. Yet it was Sherwood Anderson of the Ohio Valley, and Gertrude Stein, who sat among the Picassos like a monument of home, who taught the young Hemingway to write as an American. It was from his own speech that he made his admirable prose.

Fitzgerald came over for the second time in 1924. We had a late and confused lunch at Armenonville in the Bois, the green of early summer making a calm background for the disturbed waiters. His wife and child were with him, and it was very hard to order satisfactorily for a little girl in so expensive a restaurant. Fitzgerald, to quiet her, took out his shoestring and gave it to her with a handful of French coins to play with on the gravel under the tables.

He was on his way to the Riviera, which was not then, as it soon became, a summer resort. *The Great Gatsby* was written at St. Raphaël, and that other novel, which was to consume nine years in the writing and accumulate as a trunkful of manuscript before he called it *Tender Is the Night*, was started at Juan-les-Pins. It is an uneven and at times unnecessarily romantic book; yet, crowded with incident, it is as complete a record as any yet written of the discordant doings of Americans abroad in that decade.

V

"All modern American literature comes out of one book by Mark Twain called *Huckleberry Finn*," Hemingway allows himself to say in a conversation in *The Green Hills of Africa*. And to insist upon it he adds: "All American writing comes from that. There was nothing before. There has been nothing as good since."

And Fitzgerald, toward the end of *The Great Gatsby*, has his narrator meditate on the tragedy which has just occurred and remark that all the principals have come out of the Middle West. The body of Gatsby, after the bullet, floats on the bathing mattress around the artificial pool on his Long Island estate. But all that had made the life of Gatsby had come out of the Midwest. This return toward the East was one of the factors that made the time. The Midwesterner had become the American. He was ready to deny the authenticity of any compatriot not of his kind. Sinclair Lewis's Babbitt had superseded an older conception which Henry James had dared call "The American."

Fitzgerald and Hemingway belong to what was in its day the Younger Generation. It was certainly not the first to be called so, but it was the first to gain capitals from the press. And, as Malcolm Cowley has pointed out, it was really the first literary generation in America. There had been groups before, but they were not united by a communion of youth, a sense of experiences shared and enemies encountered simply because they happened to have been born within certain years. They were those who were of an age to be combatants when America declared war on the Central Powers.

Not all of them fought; but most of them had of their own choice supported a uniform of some sort. When they returned from arms, it was in revolt. What they protested against was called Puritanism, which is a fairer name than it deserves; for the enemy was the New England idea, not in its original purity, but in that corrupt state to which it had arrived through the hundred and more years in which the West was settled.

The pioneer had not gone into the wilderness empty-handed. For beyond those two instruments of the Puritan condemnation of nature, the rifle and the axe, he carried the New England idea. In the shadow of the forest, something of his intellectual toughness was shed. When at last the pioneer strode out on the prairies, his skin was toughened by the sun and the rain; he was hardened to the bone; his distrust of nature had not lessened. That hatred of death which is behind the Puritan hatred of life was still with him, but through varying vicissitudes was lost. The meaning of Puritanism is a contempt for mortality; in the Midwest it was forgotten.

The New England idea had never provided the new country with a particularly satisfactory morality. Along the seaboard, it was counterbalanced by other forces, inherited decencies, values transmitted and transmuted, some brought by sailing vessels, all altered by these shores. There was, in brief, a culture, rather cold, but flowering nevertheless in a lovely and inclement air. But across the Appalachians, New England began to go bad. It needed the strictness of the village, it demanded the sense of the community. Else it was disembodied. Beyond the mountains, in the limitless expanse of the West, it was not all wrong. But it certainly was not so good.

Mark Twain has shown its shortcomings. To him, it was all meanness and hypocrisy, so that his serious work is one long protest against a morality that neither aided goodness nor sustained honesty. Huckleberry Finn, who is his creator's exponent of natural morality, becomes in Missouri a notoriously bad boy. All is reversed, so that Huck himself is almost convinced that he is lost.

So long ago did the Midwesterner decide that New England morality was inadequate. But with what could he oppose it, unless with conceptions which had been shaped for him, as for all Americans, in Concord and by Walden Pond? The Midwesterner was self-reliant, he had a profound trust in the natural goodness, the sanctity almost, of unrestricted man. If we look closely, we shall see his beliefs return, altered but recognizable, not only in the Green Hills of Africa, but in all of Hemingway. We shall find them as well in Fitzgerald.

They came from all over, those who made up the Younger Generation, but it is scarcely an accident that those I consider here as its spokesmen had their origin in the Middle West. There were others, no doubt, who equalled them in talent. But the time was favorable to Hemingway and Fitzgerald. They had, as Hemingway was to say later of the garbage men of Havana, the viewpoint. And more than any others who wrote in prose, they succeeded in communicating their emotional attitudes to their contemporaries. They were never consciously regional, as a somewhat older lot of Middle Western writers were: Masters, Sandburg and the Anderson of those years when Mr. Mencken was proclaiming that Chicago was the literary capital of America. They had no need to be. They could, as Middle Westerners, assume that they were the country. And in many ways they were right. "Wait and see," Masters had written, not all ironically, in 1918, "Spoon River shall be Americee." And now Middletown was spreading from coast to coast its monstrous and monotonous regimentation of mediocrity. Besides, the Younger Generation were conscious of belonging nowhere. How could they have a place in space, whose roots, whether deliberately or through the uncontrolled accident of war, had been destroyed in time?

They converged on Chicago, and one or two, I believe, stayed there. They came to New York and, once so far, found it as simple to cross the Atlantic as to survive in that costly city. From Land's End to the Golden Horn they scattered; carried, as it were a knapsack, their childhood through the Alps; saw girls with print dresses over their starving nakedness throw themselves from bridges of Vienna; saw the hungry eyes of boys, ready for depravity, in the underworld of Berlin; saw the collapse of empires. Some sought the more than sunny warmth of the Mediterranean; some reached Persia; a few, even in those years, penetrated Russia. The world was in throes, but, like the Magi in Eliot's poem, when they had come to the end of their journey, they did not know whether it was a birth or a death they had come for. But most Paris attracted them. In the international intellectual ferment there, they were variously aware of their century, increasingly conscious that they were creatures of its catastrophes. There it seemed possible to know what was happening: not that the event was likely to take place there—Paris was too old; but because it was old and sensitive with a very long memory, it seemed possible that the import of the event would be known there sooner than elsewhere. The collapse of the New England idea was only one more loss in the spiritual débâcle of the times. Meanwhile, one could eat on the sidewalks of Paris, drink at every corner, make love in the streets, under the trees.

VI

In Fitzgerald the romantic will is strong, all its pursuits subject to disillusionment. In his novels, these pursuits are many, and love is among them, particularly the first loves of endowed youth, prolonging anticipation, delaying those satisfactions which are of the feelings rather than the senses. For his young men are assuaged by what stirs them, the scents, dresses, the slippers of silver and gold. He lingers with knowledge over these adolescent sentiments, confined, like those nostalgic dance tunes which recur through his pages, to the shortest of seasons. Obviously he prefers these young attachments, in which the emotion, part vanity, part desire, has been just felt and is not yet proved by performance. He has not, however, evaded his responsibilities as a novelist; he has seen his lovers through, to tell what becomes of them later. Afterwards come the broker's office, the bank, the racket; the sad young men take to drink; successful or failures, they know the discouragement of a predatory civilization. For let no one be mistaken: though love is always in the foreground in the sentimental world of Fitzgerald, no allure is so potent as money.

"The rich are not as we are." So he began one of his early stories. "No," Hemingway once said to him, "they have more money."

This belief, continually destroyed, constantly reasserted, underlies all that Fitzgerald has written. It made him peculiarly apt to be the historian of the period. Those who have wealth have an assurance that those without cannot hope to have; they dance, they play, they marry none but the loveliest girls; they beget their own kind. They dare where others falter. Pretty much anything goes, so long as there is money. At their worst, the successful will still have the air "of having known the best of this world." They must have spiritual possessions to match their material accumulations.

That the rich are a race apart is a current and not always complimentary assumption. In the Midwest where Fitzgerald grew up, it was the common dream that riches made the superior person. To the acquisitive powers all others would be added. His America, at least in recollection, was that country which, with a sort of ignorant corruption, could profess its love for Lincoln while completely satisfying the appetites of James K. Hill. And worse than Hill. The Great Gatsby is the Emersonian man brought to completion and eventually to failure; he has returned to the East; the conditions which could tolerate his self-reliant romanticism no longer exist.

Fitzgerald partakes of that dream and is too intelligent not to know it for what it is worth. One can scarcely say that he thinks; like the Rosemary of Tender Is the Night, his "real depths are Irish and romantic and illogical." He has an uncanny touch for probing his own or another's weakness; politically ignorant, he can see much that ails society. He gave as no other American writer the expensive charm, the sensational display of the post-war decade, but began counting the cost long before the bills came in. He made money and, like Gatsby, remained an intruder in the moneyed world; he admired it and would have liked to be a part of it; and yet with every passing year it becomes more difficult for him to face it. He has learned the price of everything, and is not a cynic, but a moody sentimentalist who gives himself a very bad time. At heart, he is a prude and suffers from remorse. For Fitzgerald, brought up as a Catholic, cannot but recognize damnation when he see it. His Nicole, irresponsible, heartless, beautiful and mad, crosses herself reverently with Chanel Number 5.

VII

The story that Ezra Pound told me in the taxicab was that Ernest Hemingway, at nineteen, had been dead and brought to life again. He had lain four days under the débris of the trench, which is one day longer underground than Lazarus. I do not doubt Pound's word, but I have never asked Hemingway to substantiate the story and it is not in his writings, as almost everything else from his youth is. Even if it should not conform to fact, it would still be true. It was true for a great part of Hemingway's generation.

It was his awareness of death that separated Hemingway from the Middle West. The West had never known what the war was about; Hemingway returned from it like Krebs in that story which is the best account written by an American of the returned soldier. Krebs found all communication with his family impossible. He sat on the front porch and saw the girls that walked on the other side of the street. "He liked the look of them much better than the French or the German girls. But the world they were in was not the world he was in." He could not talk to any of them. The Midwest had never, like the lady in Amherst, known what it was to die every day it lived. Behind the Puritan hatred of life was always the hatred of death. That alone gave it excuse and dignity.

It was in a Midwestern town that the old prizefighter of *The Killers* merely waited for death. Lying on a slovenly bed, he waits for nothing but the courage to get up and go downstairs to take what is coming to him in the street from the two men who also wait, with black gloves and hands in the bulging pockets of their tight black overcoats. It was the first of the gangster stories, and was never bettered. Hemingway concentrates not on the killing, but on the apprehension of the old double-crosser on the bed.

Presently, Hemingway was to be found in Spain, seeking to learn from the bullfighters how it is a man confronts death on the sunny sand with skill and beauty and discipline. For in the *corrida* he saw his own apprehension reduced to a ritual, publicly performed, more violent than any ritual of the Church, and more immediate, since it was concerned only with the body, its courage and control. It was because of their tragic sense that the bullfighters were utterly alive; Hemingway's famous remark about them has been misinterpreted as an admiration for mere toughness. But his real meaning is made clear if we see how, in *The Sun Also Rises*, he plays his own characters— Americans, British, Jews—of the contemporary world against his Spaniards. Plenty of things can happen to his drunken expatriates, but nothing they do, nothing that is done to them, can have any significance. For they are all of them, amusing as they are, aimless and will-less; they are so completely devoid of spiritual life that neither stupefying drink nor the aware intelligence can save them. The Spanish Romero, young and courteous, is there for lively contrast. He is as far as anyone could be from a tough guy.

The most tragic thing about the war was not that it made so many dead men, but that it destroyed the tragedy of death. Not only did the young suffer in the war, but every abstraction that would have sustained and given dignity to their suffering. The war made the traditional morality inacceptable; it did not annihilate it; it revealed its immediate inadequacy. So that at its end the survivors were left to face, as they could, a world without values.

Conscious of this as he is, Hemingway is, among his contemporaries, incomparably conscious of the art of prose. He seems to have known throughout what he had to do; and that was, as he discovered on the bed in Verlaine's old room, to find out in any given incident what really had happened. It is the mark of the true novelist that in searching the meaning of his own unsought experience, he comes on the moral history of his time. It is a hard task, and one that requires great scrupulousness; it is not one that can be generously undertaken while serving a cause.

Hemingway's accomplishment will, I think, stand. It has an historical, as it has a literary importance. It is idle to predict for posterity, but what he has done should give him a place in American literature as sure as that of—to name a writer he admires not at all—the New England Nathaniel Hawthorne. For it was given to Hawthorne to dramatize the human soul. In our time, Hemingway wrote the drama of its disappearance.

VIII

To those returning from the war, the New England idea appeared no more favorable than it had to Mark Twain. It showed as meanness and hypocrisy and repression; it had crossed the continent and was everywhere. So now, to every revolt that had been started against it, intensity was added. The war had removed young men from families and all the ordinary restraints of society, and had given them to the army, which imposed strange new restrictions of its own. It left them impatient of all discipline and profoundly distrustful of the very words which had once been used to signify virtue. They returned from whatever danger they had been in to find the country made safe, remarkably safe, for complacency. Their lives had been salted by the taste of death. They thought they had now a right to lead them. Returning, they found an opposition in control, decidedly prepared to deny this. For neither had their opponents come unchanged through the war. They had discovered, or so they thought, better means and more competent to prohibit, to cast out, our corruptible nature. Intolerance had new screws, and they would twist them. Never had the old Puritanism looked so strong. It was about to collapse.

It was precisely because all spirit had gone out of it that Puritanism had now resorted to laws, depending on the police to enforce what the conscience would no longer command.

Against all this, then in his earliest twenties, Fitzgerald appeared, proclaiming anew the inalienable rights to liberty and the pursuit of happiness. Handsome, gifted, fortunate, he made himself for a time the embodiment of youth's protest against the inhibitions and conventions of an outworn morality. He had allies, and quickly found followers. Sincerity for hypocrisy, spontaneity in the place of control, freedom for repression—who could resist such a program? The response was prodigious. Success, as we know, was only less immediate. The faults in that program were not so soon apparent.

Only one of them can I comment on here. With all respect for the original author of the phrase, happiness cannot be pursued. At least not so rapidly as the Younger Generation demanded. Sensation came. No man can say, I will be happy at such an hour. He can perfectly well say, I intend to get drunk tonight, and if only he has money, r friends, to pay for his drinks, by midnight be as drunk as he pleases, in spite of all prohibitions. In this discrepancy between happiness and dissipation lies, I should say, something of the history of the 1920's in America.

The decade was over when Fitzgerald wrote an essay which was a sort of farewell to it.

"Contemporaries of mine," he wrote of those years, "had begun to disappear into the dark maw of violence. A classmate killed his wife and himself on Long Island, another tumbled 'accidentally' from a skyscraper in Philadelphia, another purposely from a skyscraper in New York. One was killed in a speakeasy in Chicago; another was beaten to death in a speakeasy in New York and crawled home to the Princeton Club to die; still another had his skull crushed by a maniac in an asylum where he was confined. These are not catastrophes that I went out of my way to look for—these were my friends; moreover, these things happened not during the depression but during the boom."

THE MISSING ALL

This is not exaggerated: I could put names to most of these catastrophes, and for every one I cannot name I could offer three out of my acquaintances. All these were excellent people; personable companions. Morally, they were, perhaps, the last romantics, and it may be that the worst enemy the romantic has to fear is time. Or it may be that, like the earlier Romantics, they did not know enough. But at least they knew their own predicament.

Virginia Quarterly Review: Winter, 1937

O UTSIDE HIS ART, the pressing problem
of the poet is how to keep alive. That is, of course, not a problem
peculiar to the poet, but what has always made its solution difficult
for him in the extreme is that he must contrive some way to keep
body and soul together which will not cause him to lose too much of
the energy that should go into his poetry.

Poetry cannot be counted on to make a profit for anybody else,
and consequently will not support the man who makes it. An actor
may, as he thinks, be poorly paid; but at least he will be paid for
acting, for the simple reason that plays, which have been known to
make money for the producers, cannot be put on a stage without
actors. But the greatest poet of our time, one who is not less read
because he is great, William Butler Yeats, has told us that it was not
until he had passed the age of fifty and had been continuously in
print for more than thirty years, producing plays, writing not only
poetry but prose, could he hope to support himself. For a poet is paid.
But if we consider the expense of time in proportion to the pay, we
must come to the conclusion that he is, beyond the worst exploited
worker in the country, poorly paid. He is not, however, exploited.

> Better go down upon your marrow bones
> And scrub a kitchen pavement, or break stones
> Like an old pauper, in all kinds of weather;
> For to articulate sweet sounds together
> Is to work harder than all these, and yet
> Be thought an idler by the noisy set
> Of bankers, schoolmasters, and clergymen
> The martyrs call the world.

What then? If a poet cannot look to his art to support him, he
must find something that will. What they have found, the ways the

---

* This essay was evidently written for the Federal Poets' number of
Poetry, July, 1938, but it did not appear in that issue and does not seem to have
been printed at all.

poets have chosen to keep themselves alive, have sometimes been very strange. Some have been ignominious, some have come close to crime. Most have been respectable, but this cannot be said to be all to the good, for being respectable, like being a revolutionist, brings with it responsibilities which a poet, perhaps, would do well not to assume. Matthew Arnold was one of His Majesty's inspectors of schools and in this capacity acted for thirty-five years with constant conscientiousness. His purpose, which was consistent, was nothing less than to convince the English people that education was a national concern. The importance of what he accomplished measures, we can hardly doubt, an immense loss to poetry. Paul Verlaine began making his living as clerk in an insurance company, tried other things, teaching among them, then sank, in his later years, to lower and lower expedients to keep breath in a body that was as diseased as it was vicious. In his extreme squalor, he lived, at least for a time, on what was brought to him in the bed and room they both shared by a slattern, no longer young, who walked the streets for him. It is true that the last of his verses are hardly up to the first, but who can say that the successive choices of poor Verlaine were wrong for poetry? In his particular case, I think the most repulsive actions arise not from the demands of the poet, but from desires, never overcome, cunning as they were ineffective, to recover middle-class respectability. At all events, it can be said that, once the middle class began to dominate society and down to our time, poets, even if they were of the stature of these two, had to find some work outside their own—or, if that failed, somebody—to support them.

The choices they made, strange as some of them may seem, were doubtless in most cases right. For as long as there was a choice, the poets' instinct would serve them. But in times like the present, when work is for many so exceedingly difficult to come at, there is, perhaps, no longer a choice.

With the decline of the middle class, the State has appeared as a possible patron.

Private patrons of the arts are commonly supposed to have gone out with the eighteenth century. As a matter of fact, here and there they have survived into our own day. Lady Gregory at once comes to mind; she is but recently dead, and yet it is possible that so perfect a heartener of poets could only have been found in a country where so much of the eighteenth century lingered on. Her class is now, even in Ireland, disappearing. In the past, patronage accounted for much that was greatest in the arts. But when I speak of patrons, I do not mean those who call themselves so, sometimes from vanity and sometimes from acquisitiveness—though even their support has not always been to be despised. For it has been at times the only support the arts could count on and, once work had been produced, was often generous enough. But what I am concerned with is that sort of patron, and Lady Gregory was one, without whom certain works of art would never have come into existence at all. They not only keep the artist alive; they may aid him also by clarifying his problems. In fact, they will almost surely influence all that he does. And in order that that influence should be good, not bad, it is necessary that there should not be too great a disparity between the sensibility of the patron who commands the work and the artist who produces it. The patrons of the past to whom we now look back with such gratitude—like that German nobleman who could not sleep and, having in his household a young boy who played the harpsichord and welcomed difficulties, commanded from Johann Sebastian Bach music against his insomnia and thereby brought into being the *Goldberg Variations*—must have been, more often than not, pretty intolerable persons. Their manners, I think we may take it, were overbearing; their remunerations, we know, were often mean. There was the enormous consideration to be given to rank and station—and that we find difficult to comprehend, much more to acquiesce in. But down to the end of the eighteenth century, it had to be forthcoming, no matter who the artist, what his accomplishments. Yet there was one thing the noble patron had, which his successor was not to have, and that was the feeling for the thing well done. Between him and the artist was the tremendous distinction of class; but between their taste and judgment the difference would seem to have been as slight as it ever can be between those who are worldly and those who are not.

But after the revolutionary disturbances of the late eighteenth century, all the poets whose names are worthy to be recalled were, as far as I know, themselves of the middle class. There was no longer between them and those to whom their poems were addressed any but minor differences of caste. But between them and their middle-class audience there was nevertheless a gap, and a gap that was destined to widen immeasurably. For nothing was further from the top class of society than disinterested contemplation and useless joy. The members of the middle class had their virtues, but they were not the "wasteful virtues" of the poet. They affected poetry, as they affected the other arts. But it was difficult, not to say impossible, to find a patron in that class, not because they were any more heartless than the aristocrats had been, but because, so far as the arts were concerned, their sensibilities were deplorably deficient.

LIVING HOMER BEGGED HIS BREAD

Down to the time of their dominance, the poet depended mostly on private patronage, unless, as not infrequently happened, he himself belonged to the class that bestowed patronage and need not look beyond his own for support. But if he did not and that support was withheld, the poet might starve or take a shorter way to suicide. Not all the ways of bestowing support were desperate to pride.

But with the rise of the middle class, except when, in their first period of uncertainty, they still, as far as they could, followed the forms of life set them by the class they were displacing, this could no longer be. Once they were completely sure of themselves, they were slow to recognize talent. And this lag in recognition meant that the artist might starve before he was rewarded, unless he could find, outside his art, some means of support.

What it cost poetry to have the poets support themselves, I have tried to indicate in the case of Arnold. It would be easy to come closer to our own day and discuss living poets; but it would scarcely be politic. It is enough to say that it has been, until recently, relatively easy to find work that would keep a man alive. It has always been extremely hard to get a job that was not so exacting as to consume most of one's energies.

The present administration at Washington has recognized the existence of artists in America. Having scanned the numbers of the destitute, it could hardly avoid recognizing that there were among them some who had other claims to attention than the fact that they were without means of support.

This patronage of the arts, if it can be called that, has, so far, been wholly justified by what has been accomplished under it. To speak only of poetry, much has been written which could not have been written without it. To show something of what has been written under the Federal Projects is the purpose of the present number of *Poetry.*

It is now very hard to get a job. It is hard to keep alive. "When you realize that these poets were completely destitute before going on the Federal Projects"—I quote from a letter written to me by one of them—"you can see matters were helped a great deal when they were assured of their $23.86 a week. . . . The *Guide Book* work helps little, but it does give many of them a certain amount of economic security, and that, it must be admitted, is essential." From the standpoint of the relieved poets, it is no small thing the government has done for them. But from the standpoint of the government, with millions of unemployed to succor, it was a very small thing. And it was done, from what I gather, rather shamefacedly.

81

But because it was small the poets were left in comparative freedom. There has been some set hackwork, such as the Guide Books. But what has been written as poetry has been freely written.

It is no wonder that under the circumstances the notion of permanent support by the government of poets is an attractive one. But make no mistake about it—if the government should really take these poets under its care, it would at once set about taking control of their poetry. It would censure and suppress; it would command what it wanted. We need not, I hope, have to learn from Germany and Russia what can happen to art and to artists when the government takes complete control of them. But our own government would still get what it wanted, and what it wanted might not be so much what would please the official sensibilities as what would not offend them. I do not know, but I hardly think I would like to see Mr. Farley set up as arbiter of the arts. You may say that Mr. Farley is far too important a man politically to have such an assignment. But who knows that the man who does take the job will have finer sensibilities than the Postmaster General? And he will not get even, perhaps, what he himself thinks good; he will get what he thinks fit for the public. He will get official art. And while official art might do much to keep poets alive, it would not do so much for poetry.

1938

THE POEMS AND PROSE OF
E. E. CUMMINGS

I

I T IS IMPOSSIBLE for me as I reread the poems of E. E. Cummings not to recall the emotion with which I first read *Tulips and Chimneys*. Their freshness and grace have not been lost, but to these qualities there was then added a rare excitement of discovery. This was early in the summer of 1922; John Dos Passos had loaned me a copy of the manuscript which Cummings on going abroad had left in his hands that he might arrange, if he could, for its publication. The following year, Thomas Seltzer was persuaded to bring out *Tulips and Chimneys*, but only in a much shortened form. About half the poems I had read in manuscript did not appear in print until much later and then scattered through volumes which wore other titles.

The *Collected Poems* contains whatever from earlier books the poet "wishes to preserve." A number of the most youthful poems have been dropped; some twenty recent compositions have been added.

No one can quarrel with a poet's selection from his own work. Still, I cannot but regret that since the manuscript of which I have just spoken was scattered, it has not been possible for anyone to trace the development of Cummings from poem to poem. The order in which the poems have now been arranged still represents little more than the accidents of publication. In the pages that follow I shall not hesitate to take into consideration some of the poems which have disappeared from *Tulips and Chimneys*. And though it is too early to take a historical view of Cummings, it may aid in "placing" him if I return to my first encounter with his poetry. I cannot do otherwise.

He appeared as a young and romantic poet. But he was one unmistakably of his time. That he derived from Keats and had been instructed by the poets of the last century was obvious; but even in the earliest poems, where their trace is most strong, the movement of Cummings' verse is already his own. His charm, at once, is his rapidity.

The influence of the romantic tradition was soon left behind; but not the romantic attitude. That was authentic and not taught—at least, not by the English poets. It stood no more in critical favor than it does now, however the cry against it in some quarters has changed. This poetry was aware, as only poetry can be, of what was going on. The sensibility of the poet was singularly uncontaminated. He defied, indeed, every principle which Ezra Pound had taught us was right for poetry; and there was none of us then who had not listened with attention to Pound. Here was no effort for the one precise word; instead, adjectives, which were Pound's abhorrence, were piled one on another in a sort of luminous accumulation. If Cummings, in writing, had kept his eye on the object, it was of no avail, for the objects had their outlines distorted, or else they dissolved, leaving behind only an impression of their qualities. Here was a poetry as shining and as elusive as quicksilver. If there was anything precise about it, it was, as Cummings was to note later, that precision which aims at creating movement. Yet none but a poet could have been so preoccupied with words; nor could anyone not a poet have so enlivened them with his presence.

Here was no Prince Hamlet nor was meant to be; here was quite another figure, fine, impertinent, full of shocks and capers, in the midst of some absurd mockery suddenly turning surpassingly lyrical. Here was Mercutio.

The impulse which the romantics of the early nineteenth century had given poetry had long been exhausted. By the turn of the century, it had so definitely expired that when Francis Thompson came along, it was scarcely possible for him, a belated romantic, to create poetry. He could only make elaborate garlands for its corpse.

When romanticism reappeared, it was not at once recognized. It had changed its aspect. It appeared as the reverse of itself. But a coin has the same value, whether it falls heads or tails. And though we may prefer to call the poetry that was written in the years close to the War, and for some time after it, anti-romantic, its ultimate value is romantic. And this was so, even though almost every critical opinion, including that of the poets themselves, was against anything of the sort. For no other poetry was possible.

Classical poetry is necessarily moral. It can come into existence only when there is a moral order which both society and the poet can accept. The *grand siècle* produced such a poetry in France. When T. S. Eliot espoused the cause of classicism in literature, it is to be noted that he came out for Catholicism. He had to have some sort of authority in morals, even though the only one available should be his collection of English Bishops, some living and some dead. Mr. Eliot is not so much a classicist as a poet who at times is like Flaubert in trying to strip romanticism from his soul and at times is like the saints who would rid themselves while still in the flesh of every accident of birth and change.

A romantic immorality must return whenever civilization is found no longer an aid but a hindrance to the accomplishment of desires. The alternative is asceticism. A protest was bound to be made by a generation in which the individual had suffered so much from society and suffered, as he felt, under the most false pretenses. The armies and the governments of this world had ignored the lonely man; but death had not ignored him. It was only to the individual that death paid any attention. It was this contrast between the death of a man—I have seen them dug up out of the earth of France at Montfaucon—this death known in the flesh that lives and rots, and the impersonal casualty lists put out by the governments that gave everyone who went through the War a permanent distrust and horror of abstract forms of information. The gap was too great. Death was not forgotten. For death was an enemy of the individual even more redoubtable than society, for he was inescapable. Nevertheless, awareness of his imminence had its compensations. He was a silence increasing the intensity of every sound. Romantic emotions reappear in every generation and always at that moment when the young first conceive their own annihilation. At that moment, regardless of the state of society in which they find themselves, there follows an assertion of whatever they conceive themselves to be in their own right. This consciousness is enhanced for the young to whom death is continuously present, as in war. In Cummings there is an untiring protest against everything that stands in the way of a man's knowing himself alive and a praise and exaltation, which otherwise would be excessive, for whatever comes to the aid of that awareness.

            Among
                 these
                      red pieces of
            day (against which and
            quite silently hills
            made of blueandgreen paper

            scorchbend ingthem
            -selves-U

pcurv E, into:
>anguish (clim
b)ing
s-p-i-r-a-
l
and, disappear)
>Satanic and blasé

a black goat lookingly wanders

There is nothing left of the world but
into this noth
ing il treno per
Roma si-gnori?
jerk.
ilyr, ushes

This is an example, and by no means an extreme one, of Cummings' method. A momentary relationship is established between the poet and a black goat wandering at twilight among the Italian hills. Then the train departs, and this particular landscape is gone. Presumably the goat continues to wander, to browse, or whatever it is a goat must do to pursue its life. The sky has darkened, and into a dimness in which nothing can be seen, the train, after a pause, proceeds. The goat is not a symbol of anything. He is what Cummings would call an actual miracle. He is a creature of the outer world who is capable of becoming a creation of the mind. It now becomes the poet's task to set down, without falsification, this fragment of time, which is not so insignificant as it seems, for it is like no other since the beginning of the world. And in that instant something has happened to the poet to assure him that he is alive. And Cummings belongs to a generation which for years after the War, and not only because of the War, needed constantly to be assured that it was among the living.

The world can be known only in its momentary aspects; for once the moment has passed, whatever has been known must change. The importance of the moment increases, once we have admitted the discontinuity of the mind. The mind in Cummings has become its own material. The center no longer holds, and he ends by becoming fascinated by the speed of its fragments. By sticking strictly as may be to what he knows, by staying within the record of sensations, Cummings has been able to do what a generation of poets in Europe, with considerably less success, attempted to do. Whether they were called Futurists in Italy, or Dadaists in France, or by other names in other countries, their aims have been more completely accomplished by Cummings than by any poet on the Continent. He has the advantage of being an American, with whatever that implies in the way of a natural appetite for disorder. He has, too, in a degree that none of the others had, the sensibilities and the wit of a poet.

II

At the time when Cummings' manner was formed, it seemed not only possible, but imperative, that every element of technique should be recreated. He was aware of Joyce's experiments in prose in *Ulysses;* some of them he has repeated, concentrating them, as he might well do in the smaller space of a poem; in his own prose he has carried them still further, especially in *Eimi,* by accelerating their performance. He had before him the example of Picasso, who had already passed through three or four periods, each representing a progress in emotion and a prodigious renewal of technique. What could be more natural than that Cummings, who is painter as well as poet, should attempt to emulate in literature the innovations of his contemporaries in painting? In Picasso, as in some others who were renewing the painter's art, he saw what intensity might follow distortion of line and immensity of form. And Cummings has taught himself to see somewhat as they see, but without losing his personal vision. He juxtaposes words as they do pigments. The effect is not altogether a happy one, for what is gained in intensity may be lost in meaning. When a painter distorts a line, he may increase its functional value; but a sentence can easily be so dislocated that it will no longer work. The impressionist method, so apt to seize the aspect of a momentary world, permits Cummings to rely on the vaguest associations. It has led him as a poet, not to weight, but merely to touch his words with meaning. In fact, the significance of his words is often in their position. Then, too, it is probably the example of the Post-Impressionists and the Picasso of the *papier collé* period that has persuaded him to admit to his poetry much that was tawdry, trivial, and lewd—material whose advantage to him is certainly in part that it has hitherto been considered inadmissible.

Cummings has his own punctuation, his own typography and not only his own speech and prosody but his own grammar. What he has aimed to do is to set down all that his mind, prompted by the sensations of the body, inevitably and spontaneously knows. His art is personal. It could not well be anything else; for it reposes upon a conviction that each man's world is his own and that no other can be known. "Regarded as an existence which appears in a soul, the whole world for each is peculiar and private to that soul." * Other poets have professed some such philosophy, but, so far as I know, Cummings is the first actually to carry it into his writing. He does not write as a common-sense dualist. He was born and brought up in Cambridge, Massachusetts; and though he has constantly cried his repudiation of his birthplace and all its academic works, including the late Josiah Royce, it is only as a child of Cambridge that he can be so passionately private and peculiar. In Russia, he met a compatriot, a young woman reporter, who told him he was not part of the world. Their conversation is related in *Eimi*. Cummings' reply is unhesitating: "Quite so. Actually the world is part of me. And— I'll egocentrically tell the world—a very small part."

Ever since T. S. Eliot published his essay on *Tradition and the Individual Talent* the personal in poetry has been suspect. Mr. Eliot in that essay quotes Remy de Gourmont on Flaubert, and it is, of course, very largely from admiration of the incomparable display of impersonal art in *Madame Bovary* that this opposition to the personal in literature has risen. Now one can share that admiration without being sure that what was not impossible for a practitioner in the art of prose narration is also practicable for the poet, particularly the lyric poet. Mr. Eliot has held up to us *The Phoenix and the Turtle*, and he was, at the time he did it, right to do so, for it was then a neglected poem. But there is in all Shakespeare only one *Phoenix and the Turtle*, and against it may be placed one hundred and fifty-odd sonnets. They, to be sure, represent a disciplined art. And all must in the end come back to a question of discipline and not of personality. The objections which may properly be brought against Cummings are not that his art is personal and that therefore it is unintelligible, because on such grounds we should also have to declare there is no knowing Proust or any number of other writers whose worlds are not less private than that of Cummings. Rather it may be said of him that he is constantly trying to affect us by other than purely literary means. He attempts to seduce us without departing from his solitude. Cummings' faults are those of the sensitive writer, and the interest of his poetry is that it is a product of his sensibility. No one poem is unintelligible. On the contrary, it is much more likely that if we try to take it as complete, its meaning will be too soon

* It is not Cummings, but T. S. Eliot, who, in his notes to *The Waste Land*, quotes this remark from F. H. Bradley.

exhausted. For its concern is with the immediate and with the moment. It may charm or amuse; but it is only by Cummings' poetry as a whole that we are profoundly impressed. It is not unattached to his personality; but the interest of that personality is in its singular capacity to report the age.

The problem is not one of escaping personality (for that way impotence lies) but of transcending it. And that a poet may do in one of two ways: he may dramatize his personal desires directly or he may find in the outer world some drama, into whose actors he can fuse his own desires and in whose catastrophe he can, though only on an imaginative plane, resolve his personal conflict. The one method is that of *La Vita Nuova*, the other is that of *The Divine Comedy*. It is the more mature work which, in Dante's case, is the more profoundly personal. But Cummings has almost no imagination. He is said to be confined in his own world; but it is a world which has too much in common with ours to make communication impossible. He is subject there to a conflict of contrary desires: he would be like others and yet utterly unlike; he would be like the man who suffers, but not like the man who dies. He has taken the only known way to immortality. Out of this conflict he has made his poems, both lyrical and satirical. But nothing has made him a dramatic poet.

III

Cummings' prose has never had anything like the attention it deserves. *The Enormous Room* came out in 1921, when a reaction had set in against almost all that had then been written about the War. It did not exploit that reaction and failed, as so many later books did not, to profit from it. *Eimi*, which is an account of a journey made through the U.S.S.R. in 1931, appeared the following year, in the midst of the depression communism. It was derided or ignored. And yet *The Enormous Room* has the effect of making all but a very few comparable books that came out of the War look shoddy and worn. It has been possible to read it, as I have done, at intervals over the seventeen years since its publication, and always to find it undiminished. So it has slowly found readers. But those who were attracted to *The Enormous Room*, because of the compassion Cummings showed there for the lowly and despised, were repulsed by *Eimi*, which makes it clear that he will have nothing to do with the communist effort to improve the condition of mankind. The one book is, nevertheless, the complement of the other, and the only change in Cummings to be marked between them is the change from youth to maturity. And in *Eimi*, he makes every other writer on Russia appear dishonest or credulous.

These books have behind them what must be regarded as the two most important events of our time. And the backgrounds, in so far as they affect his narratives, are set before us with great vividness. The incidental characters are presented with an admirable skill and they remain convincing, even though in the parts they play there is almost always some exaggeration, comic or pathetic. For again and again, as Cummings produces a character, we are reminded of Dickens. But the center of *The Enormous Room* is not the War, nor that of *Eimi* the Russian Revolution. At the core of each is a spiritual crisis.

In 1917, Cummings was confined for some months, at the behest of the French government, in a detention camp, along with a number of others, whom, for reasons of their own, the French officials suspected of being spies. Cummings, who until his arrest had been an ambulance driver in an American unit, encountered, in that huge barracks at La Ferté-Macé which he calls the Enormous Room, a sad assortment of men. They from being his companions in misery become, whether they speak or not—and the most eloquent are those who have the smallest command of words—his counselors in compassion. He was here in the backwash of the War. Some of these men were its wrecks; more of them, war or no war, the common scum of humanity. Among them the narrator met a problem much older than the War. In his own soul he met it: the significance of human suffering. He met it with the intensity of youth and knowing that upon some solution of it depended his sanity. It is a problem much greater than that of injustice, for it includes it. And it is worth noting that it is not with its injustice that Cummings reproaches the French government, but with its stupidity, in confining to the Enormous Room specimens of humanity as small as these.

The mind provides no answer to the problem of suffering. The answer must come from elsewhere. There are good men and bad in the Enormous Room, there are brave men and cowards. There is that truculent bullying pimp called the Fighting Sheeney, there is that grave and handsome Gypsy known as the Wanderer. Men come and go in this imprisonment, which they are not allowed to call a prison. They are made very real to us in their great variety; they reveal themselves and none is like another. They have, nevertheless, something in common. Their pain is real and they share their misery. They are, in a way, like those mountebanks painted by the young Picasso, those starved and wandering Spaniards, whose long-drawn skulls seem not made for any thought, but only to contain the burden of suffering humanity. There are eyes which meet Cummings in prison which are very like those in the Picasso paintings; they have been beyond the blue of the horizon and they know there is nothing there that is not also here.

The answer, even for a poet, is not in words. The climax of *The Enormous Room* is reached in the episode of Supplice. Supplice is a Pole, and what he speaks of anybody else's language is very little; there is one of his compatriots in prison, but even he says he cannot understand Supplice's Polish. He is the most abject of men; below him is nothing conceivable, and he is tortured by those who, but for him, would know themselves on the bottom. He is attracted to excrement; it is he who every morning, without being ordered, bears away from the Enormous Room the refuse from so many human bodies. What Supplice has to say is only pathetically little more than nothing. What he has to impart is as tremendous as humility.

When Cummings has done with Supplice, he has only one portrait to follow, drawn on a comparable scale: Jean le Nègre. Jean is black, swaggering, immense. He has been arrested in Paris for impersonating an English officer. In prison he is far from silent; but what is remarkable about his speech is not its amazing mixture of childish French and pidgin English, nor even his capacity for lying. It is that Jean does not know himself when he is lying and when he is not. His is the mind of a child, an utterly timeless mind, without memory; what is true today may be false tomorrow. He is at one time the child of a sixteen-year-old father and a mother who died before he was born; at another he is the son of the Lord Mayor of London and the Queen. Only laughter could resolve these contradictions. But wherever he came from, Jean is the only person in this gallery who could follow Supplice and make a proper contrast. For what can oppose the poverty of the spirit, but the pride of the body? Jean is all laughter, sinew and sensuality.

Here, at the very start, we have in Cummings what has been called his cult of unintelligence. He was one who could not but seek a wholesome being. He emerged from imprisonment profoundly shaken. Where else was he to look for what he sought in a world dead at the top, if not below? And in Cummings there is from now on, in all he writes, an exaltation of the lowly and the lively. He is himself, and he accepts his common lot. With the others, he suffers; he exults alone, and in a world of his own. But something happens to alter this attitude shortly after he crosses the Polish border into the Soviet

Union and in the customs house encounters upon one wall, framed in bunting, the colored photograph of Nicolai Lenin.

IV

The style which Cummings began in poetry reaches its most complete development in the prose of *Eimi*. Indeed, one might almost say that, without knowing it, Cummings had been acquiring a certain skill over years, in order that, when occasion arose, he might set down in words the full horror of Lenin's tomb. It is brought to us through every sense: the solid stench of numberless multitudes endlessly waiting, endlessly treading downward into the darkness to look on the maker of their world, the corpse of the man with the small, not intense, face and the reddish beard, secret, being dead, as when alive, intransigent even in mortality. For in Russia Cummings was not only in a new country; he was in a new world. Impressions pressed, one on another, in such confusing rapidity that no one with less than his skill could possibly have caught and recorded them. Sensations are transformed into words at the moment they arrive in the consciousness; there they confront other words and are confused with recollections from the world beyond Russia and the instantaneous reactions of Cummings' spirit. All these are given as they occurred, or at least we have the illusion that they are, so that they must be read as rapidly as they are recorded. *Eimi* demands much the sort of attention, prompt and yet easily scattered, with which we discover from a few pages of the morning newspaper what went on in the world the day before. Not the least of its interest is what it has to show of the workings of a contemporary mind. It is more or less incidental that the mind happens to be Cummings'.

Russia no doubt has changed since 1931, but mostly in such a way as to make apparent to everyone of good will what Cummings was almost alone in seeing when he went there seven years ago. He had been warned, before going, that because of his lack of political and economic training he was not at all prepared to understand Russia. He was peculiarly prepared to see the Russians.

It was precisely because he did not approach them through theories that he saw through their pretenses with such astonishing honesty of vision. He was the child who saw, not the King, but the Kremlin, naked.

He was certainly not interested in discovering for himself how far Comrade Stalin had been able to carry out the predictions of the

Communist Manifesto. He did not care how many motors had been turned out under the Five Year Plan. He had come from the land of Detroit. He had never, I am almost sure, read the *Communist Manifesto.* If there were words from any political document in his head, they were from a much older one, which had been drawn up and signed by none but Americans. And if the Declaration of Independence had not existed, Cummings in Russia, I dare say, would have invented it. His sole interest in government was the effect on the governed. What he wanted to know was not what material progress had been made by the workers since the Revolution. What he wanted to know about the socialist experiment was whether it was better prepared than the democracy he had left to assure to those under it the rights to life, liberty and the pursuit of happiness. The rights of man were not inalienable in the America of 1931. Least of all, in the cities where were most machines.

He found in Russia not liberty but a joyless experiment in force and fear. He found not life, but in men and women a willingness not to live, if only they were allowed not to die. Apathy made possible the Stalin régime. Apathy supported it, and it was this same apathy which accounted as no native lack of ability could do for the drabness, the ineffectiveness, the filth of all the Russians were supposed to do. A lack of comfort might mean many things and not be serious; it might even be admirable; only if it meant a dearth of spirit was it appalling. The country was in a state of civil war, which had, perhaps, been deliberately protracted. But it had been much worse. Anything was better, as one Russian woman explained to Cummings, than the time when "they made us lie down at the point of the bayonet." The Russians had long been unhappy; they were now, it might be, somewhat less so; but their suffering, whatever it was, was suffering in silence. Cummings understands that the despair of the individual may become the enthusiasm of the masses. For what else is propaganda for? But as for the efforts of the Soviet Government to increase the happiness of the Russians, he sums them up in one succinct phrase—"Pippa passes the buck!"

The Red Dawn has faded into the most depressing of days. But Cummings does not, as so many of the later commentators do, attribute the failure of the Russian Revolution to Stalin. No revolution can do more for a people than restore it to itself, and not much more could be done for the Russians than to massacre their former masters. For every one of them looks over his shoulder before he speaks—and that not only on account of the political police; every man is suspect where no man trusts himself. But in so far as any man is responsible for this world in which the Russians do not live, it is Lenin. Stalin is an idea become action. It was Lenin who first converted the idea into an act.

Lenin inherited a doctrine, which he attempted to impose upon the Russians. And this, to Cummings, is among all others the unforgivable crime. A poet may be as violent as he wants with words and make them obey his will. But for a man to do likewise with living men and women, he must be more than a man. And that Lenin was not. He was not a source of power, however much power he acquired. He was a secondary figure like Cromwell, like Saint Paul. The poet works with form as his end. The reformer starts with a formula. The distance between them is as great as the distance between life and nonexistence, between the life of the spirit and the suicide of the soul known as dialectical materialism. Lenin probably believed that he had come into the world that men might have life and have it more abundantly. But the almost immediate effect on whoever accepted his doctrines was an acceptance of lifelessness. He took away from his followers the little life they had.

Cummings seems to have gone to Russia very much as he went to imprisonment, not altogether unwillingly, knowing that an important experience awaited him there, without in the least knowing what the experience would be. In Russia he was not granted his experience; he was prepared for it. In prison he had accepted suffering as inseparable from the life of man. But in Russia he was repulsed by the spectacle of untold multitudes suffering and willing to suffer in silence. He was appalled. In the Enormous Room he had been taught to know himself a man among others. But in the Soviet Union he saw that something more than patience, something more than compassion, was needed to make a man.

Throughout *Eimi*, Cummings maintains an analogy, never too hard pressed, between his own progress from circle to circle of Soviet society and Dante's passage through Hell. The moment at which he emerges to see the stars is when he returns to Europe, where it is once more possible for him to assume the full responsibility of being a man. In prison he had learned a passive acceptance of his lot. It was on his return to freedom (his ticket was sold him in Constantinople by a pleasant young Englishman to travel towards Paris by International Express) that he experiences that sense of the wholeness of life—that complete vision which includes both divinity and depravity—that allows him, as he approaches the borders of Italy, without presumption, to call upon the name of Dante. For now he knows there is but one freedom, a freedom active and acquiescent in the vision, the freedom of the will, responsive and responsible; and that from it all other freedoms take their course.

"He that knoweth the eternal is comprehensive; comprehensive, therefore just; just, therefore a king; a king, therefore celestial; celestial, therefore in Tao; in Tao, therefore enduring."

And with that quotation he knows he is forever beyond the U.S.S.R.

The Southern Review: Summer, 1938

THE DISCIPLINE OF POETRY

WHAT IS THE relation of verse to poetry? What advantages can a poet at present hope to gain by accepting constraints which, however useful they may have proved in the past, are now mere conventions? Arbitrary they have always been; suddenly—though not perhaps for the first time—they appear futile. Why should anyone whose aim is communication impose upon himself conditions which the enormously increased range and power of prose have shown to be not only unnecessary, but even, if they are truly as outworn as they seem to be, a little ludicrous?

These are questions that have been put; and they have had their answers. Some of them are rewarding. I should mention, first, that of Paul Valéry in his essay *Au Sujet d'Adonis*, where, in certain passages, seeming to praise La Fontaine, he is examining those forms which so felicitously served the seventeenth-century poet in an endeavor to discover a beauty which belongs to verse in its own right, a permanent value and a virtue that cannot be alienated by prose.

M. Valéry is a poet, and one who, perhaps more than any other now living, assures the continuity of the French tradition; it may be said, indeed, that his most notable achievement has been to bring back into the tradition the somewhat aberrant poetry of such symbolists as Mallarmé. It is not astonishing that, as a disciple of Mallarmé and an admirer of La Fontaine, he should find the virtue that puts verse over prose in its more perfect artifice. To control nature—nothing is more superbly human. And it is the part of the poet to impose upon our natural speech the utmost possible control. The laws to which La Fontaine submitted were actually the instruments of his power; under these constraints, his sensuousness was not crushed nor did his emotions perish; on the contrary, they combined, they increased, they multiplied. But we are far, as even M. Valéry must admit, from La Fontaine. His laws are no longer enforced nor are they likely to be. To ask now of a reader that he take pleasure in their observance would be to transport him to a baroque court and expect him to move at ease among its forgotten formalities. The question now is not whether the poet can accept these laws. The only laws which a poet can find to obey are those of his own devising or those which, inherited, he accepts solely because they are among his possible choices. Under the circumstances, there is some doubt as to their validity.

It will be noticed, however, that in M. Valéry's opinion poetry is a force making for civilization. But an opposite view has been expressed, and with no less force, by Edmund Wilson in *Axel's Castle*. Three of the men whom he, as critic, considers in that volume are poets, Eliot, Yeats, and Valéry; and they have their place there only because of his enormous admiration for their work, which is certainly as important to our time as that of any of the prose writers he puts beside them. However, Mr. Wilson seems to feel that poetry is no longer entitled to that prestige which he among others—though unwillingly, it appears—grants it. "Are not prose and verse, after all," he asks in his essay on Valéry, "merely techniques of human intercommunication, and techniques which have played various roles, have been used for various purposes, in different periods and civilizations?" This sounds like common sense. But the period of poetry is the past. For on another page, and after quoting two modest remarks by contemporary poets on the function of their art, he declares: "It is much more likely that, for some reason or other, verse as a technique of literary expression is being abandoned by humanity altogether." The reason at once comes out—"because it is a more primitive and hence a more barbarous technique than prose."

It is not always easy, reading the reports the papers bring us, to see in what respect the grand *siècle* was a more barbarous age than our own. But the answer is, it did not have our prose. It had Bossuet and Fenélon; it had Saint-Simon and Madame de La Fayette. But it did not have that prose which came into being with Flaubert and which in the last eighty years has so consistently encroached on the province of poetry that it is possible for Mr. Wilson to suppose that it will end by displacing it altogether.

The positions of M. Valéry and Mr. Wilson are so far apart as to seem irreconcilable. They measure, not so much the distance between France and America, between poet and critic, as the extent of the uncertainty which our civilization, as opposed to the seventeenth century, allows as to both the function and the status of verse.

II

I have taken these two men as examples of the widely divergent views that can be held on the relation of verse to poetry. I have, no doubt, made their positions appear more extreme than they really are. Both are intelligent men, and both, knowing that they might be called on to defend these positions, have made modifications to secure themselves against too easy an attack. We should be grateful that they have advanced their salients so far; whether they are tenable is another matter. At the moment what is most important is to understand how they got there; for each has come to the place where he now stands as the result of one or the other of two movements, both of which have profoundly affected the history of poetry.

From the time of Poe and Baudelaire on, poets have sought to bring their art closer to the condition of music. The music of the mid-nineteenth century no longer impresses us as it did those who first heard it, for to us more seems to happen musically in almost any concerto by Mozart, composed though it may have been for a small orchestra, than in an opera by Wagner. The music of Mozart is unconfused by literature. It was in fact the very confusion of music and literature in Wagner that made him accessible to the poets of his time. Wagner was himself a minor poet, but one who, by an extraordinary chance, was coupled with a composer. He succeeded prodigiously in doing what the romantic poets, with only the modest sound of words at their disposal, had only despairingly dreamed of doing. Their most sonorous phrases seemed no more than the scraping of shells against the sea, when compared to this huge welter of orchestral sound. What was worse, Wagner could be impressive where the man of words with the same aim would have been simply absurd. Those who first heard this music were crushed. They were envious. And they were proud. Out of this pride and envy was conceived a poetry which should attain its ends by the perfection of its form.

Philosophy might precede a poem, but its reflections could have no place in it; for how could a composition in words, which was designed to act directly on the sensibilities, as music did, include, as poets of the past had often done, the formulations of abstract thought? Poetry had already been declared to stand outside contemporary morality; it would now show itself proof against the seductions of rhetoric and sentiment. It was, in short, to be pure. A poem was that which was not translatable, which lost, as prose did not, all the significance of its meaning when translated into another language, into other terms. Its significance was in its form, where, as in the God the saints adored, desire and its embodiment were one, the idea and its realization indissoluble.

The ambition to write pure poetry lasted a long time and was known in more countries than one. But the program was worked out in France. And French is, for some reason, a language which has never supported a great philosophical poet; on the other hand, it is peculiarly liable to the abuses of a sort of rhetoric which sounds very well, but whose grandeur ends in inanity. When the first symbolists shoved philosophy out of the door, what they were really doing was locking it against poor Alfred de Musset. And when they spoke, as Verlaine did, of taking eloquence and wringing its neck, what they really wanted to do was to choke Victor Hugo. They were doing, in other words, what every generation of poets has to do: getting rid of their predecessors.

Now, pure poetry can exist, but when it comes into being, it is almost found to rise as statues do from some Renaissance buildings, in such splendor that the walls below seem to have no other purpose than to support them. Actually, they are what they appear to be only because of the surrounding structure; they have that look of perfection only because of where they stand. To aim at pure poetry was to endeavor to create these lofty statues and yet to have no place to put them. It was an attempt to write *Full Fathom Five* without having written *The Tempest*.

That pursuit, as Valéry himself has confessed, led away from poetry. It led at last into a region as remote as it was deserted, for it lay beyond the confines of human experience. The air there was very pure indeed; but it could not be breathed. The poets who pursued purity found that another danger waited for them, the same that lies in wait for everyone who undertakes, whether in morals or art, to follow the cult of perfection: sterility. The poet Mallarmé was his life long haunted by a horrible fear of impotence. He even managed to write a very good poem about it.

The Symboliste movement—as it has come to be called—did, as a matter of fact, produce an extraordinary amount of poetry, much of it, even today, admirable, and some of it indubitably great. It did so because the poets who followed it wrote as they could and not always as they would. Their muse was not so pure as her reputation: the best that can be said of her is that she had been effectively warned of the seriousness of certain vices. She did not always avoid the dust and heat.

III

The reaction from a poetry which aimed at the condition of music was a poetry which approached the confines of prose. The writing of prose had acquired a new consciousness with Flaubert, who expended on his novels such scrupulous care as to excite not only the admiration but the envy of the poets. Baudelaire, who was one of the first to understand exactly what Flaubert had accomplished in *Madame Bovary*, had no need to be told by him that the bourgeois were now all mankind. *Les Fleurs du Mal* was published in the same year as *Madame Bovary*, so that it was not the direct example of the novelist so much as similar influences, working through the same atmosphere, that had brought upon the poet the necessity of having his own art conform more closely to the age. He saw that poetry must be forced to include, as it had so far done only imperfectly in France, the circumstances, however sordid, of contemporary life.

Baudelaire looked about him in the streets of Paris, in the poor streets, along the quays, even in the common ditch of the dead who have died poor. He looked for poetry there, and before the mirror in his own room. And he found poetry where it is most likely to be found: among the damned.

He was not the first, even in France, to bring into poetry the common man and his misfortunes; but he was the first to know what to do with him when he got him there. Baudelaire, to whom must also be traced the beginnings of the pursuit of pure poetry, was prosecuted in the courts for obscenity and in the schools reproached with being a *prosateur froid et alembiqué*. In giving him credit for having started the two most important developments of poetry in the nineteenth century, I am only saying what is true: that he was the greatest poet of the century and that in him all its poetic tendencies were present, certainly in their beginnings, and perhaps also in their end. For neither T. S. Eliot nor Allen Tate would be today what they arc had it not been for Baudelaire.

From his time on a certain realism was cultivated, sometimes in opposition to symbolism, but quite as often in the same house with it, sometimes in the same poem. The two tendencies are quite easy to separate critically; it cannot always be done in practice. But a new direction was given this movement toward prose in the first decade of the present century. Flaubert was now dead and had been made a saint by the novelists. Ezra Pound around 1912 began declaring that those principles which Flaubert had laid down for the proper conduct of the novel should be applied to poetry. Baudelaire had carefully excluded from his poetry everything which might just as well be expressed in prose; he had laid his hands often enough on material which might have been thought more appropriate to prose, but he had rigorously held aloof from its methods. But Pound now cried from the housetops that poetry must catch up with prose. And to the generation that heard him, their heads full of Remy de Gourmont, such an aim inevitably brought about a disassociation of verse from poetry.

I do not wish to disparage the poetry of Ezra Pound, which had other sources of power and was subjected to other influences than that of Flaubert, nor do I deny that much that was done under his instigation had at least the beauty of necessity. Various means are available to the poet who must renew his form, but he can hardly renew his substance without coming into contact with contemporary prose. If he falls into its debt, the writers of prose have their own way of collecting. For while he picks up without asking whatever he can use from their store, they retaliate by taking over whatever tools of his craft they can find to fit their hands. Poetry in England may have been in 1912 as far behind the prose of France as Pound said it was; but in general, wherever there is a living prose and a poetry that is alive, their development proceeds together. Nothing can happen in one art without its presently affecting the other.

It is the existence of works like the *Anabase* of St.-J. Perse, which is a poem not written in verse, and the *Anna Livia Plurabelle* passage in the *Finnegans Wake* of James Joyce, in which prose has adopted all the devices of poetry except meter, that makes it possible for a critic like Mr. Wilson to say there is no absolute difference between poetry and prose, and that since this is so they might just as well be judged on the same basis. There is no absolute difference. There never has been. Mr. Wilson's mistake is in supposing that this difficulty of distinction is something new. Aristotle was aware of it. The difficulty need not force us into confusion. There is a border line where poetry and prose merge into one. But the fact that there is a province called Alsace should not lead us into saying that France is the same country as Germany.

IV

We constantly use the word *verse* to cover writing which aims at the state of poetry, but somehow fails to come off. A versifier, in this pejorative sense, is simply a bad poet. But upon examination it is almost certain to be found that he has not only failed to write poetry, he has written bad verses.

Je suis belle, ô mortels! comme un rêve de pierre.

How, in such a line, segregate the verse from the poetry? It cannot be done, for in this opening verse of one of Baudelaire's sonnets, as in any other superbly successful work of art, the conviction is carried that in the writing of the line the desire to do and the doing are one. But if we listen to this line so as to be conscious of every sound of which it is composed, their sequence and order, to say nothing of the movement, so startlingly discontinuous, of the whole line, we can hardly escape the conclusion that it is great poetry only because it is at the same time the most expert possible verse. But the contrary will not be found.

The poet is attracted to verse because of the resistance it offers him. This prose writers find hard to believe, particularly if they happen to be among those who occasionally take time off from the responsibilities of their own craft to write a little verse. To them it is play; and the only trouble, they say, is that the words come too docilely to their call. Ford Madox Ford, Remy de Gourmont and Bernard Shaw have all, before Edmund Wilson, derided the hardships which the poets pretend to encounter in the exercise of their art. The evidence of the poets, from Dante to Yeats, is quite otherwise:

> Better go down upon your marrow bones
> And scrub a kitchen pavement, or break stones
> Like an old pauper, in all kinds of weather;
> For to articulate sweet sounds together
> Is to work harder than all these, and yet
> Be thought an idler by the noisy set
> Of bankers, schoolmasters, and clergymen
> The martyrs call the world.

And the poets are right. For just as one of the masters of modern prose has defined a writer as one to whom writing comes with more difficulty than to ordinary people, so a poet may perhaps be defined as one to whom verse comes hard.

If we can call poetry what is striving to be said, it will have its own demands, and these should be strong and more often than not conflict with the requirements of the verse. In the line I have quoted from Baudelaire, the conflict is no longer felt, for it has been resolved, and nothing of it remains—since this is but a single line—but an air of intensity and that rather startling caesura. But in a long poem, the struggle is more difficult to conceal; nor is there any reason why it should not be, for the poem can only gain by having it continually present. It remains in magnificent suspense in the mature Shakespeare, where the rhythmical forces beat against a not impregnable line, a line which is always about to break, which does break, which holds and is again assaulted. We listen to that insistent dissonance with excitement, as to constant warfare. There is a struggle here between what is man and not man, between the pulse and the passions of man and time, for the verse, having duration and measure, creates the sensation of time. And in that struggle we cannot but be involved.

But Shakespeare's force is rare and so is his skill; and even he grew old and in the end was content with his skill. Toward the end he wrote the most beautiful verses anyone has ever written in English—the most beautiful, not the best. By that time he had made a habit of it and against the beat of the verse could thrust the throb of a passion which he felt more in imagination than in heat, on behalf of others much younger than he, or corrupt as he had never been, or jealous as he once had been, or wise as he was now.

The contest is not always so even. For when the requirements of the verse are met at the expense of the poetry, the result is apt to be precious. It may be superficial and false. Such poetry—for where there is craft enough it will come so near to poetry that there is no other name for it—is never of the greatest, but it is capable of affording great pleasure and within its range complete satisfaction. Much of Valéry is of this kind, the best of Pope, and some of Poe.

> Onde déserte, et digne
> Sur son lustre, du lisse effacement d'un cygne.

I do not see how anyone could deny that such lines have the integrity and the radiance of poetry. They are perfect in their artifice.

But where the poetry overcomes the resistance of the verse, what we get is Whitman or something not nearly so good as Whitman. Where the importance of what is to be said surpasses everything else, we get the later poems of D. H. Lawrence. It would be hard to find a case in which the value of craft is more clearly shown by its absence. Lawrence to every appearance was born to be a poet; he had every gift and only lacked the knowledge. He is the perfect instance of the bitter fact that the man who looks only for expression never succeeds in finding it. When his spirit was with him, he could accomplish a prose as beautiful and moving as any our time has known; but Lawrence died as he had lived, a poet thwarted in what he had to say. "Any poet who does not know exactly what rhymes each word allows," said Baudelaire, "is incapable of expressing any idea whatever." He knew. And Lawrence did not. It was a knowledge of which he was, I should guess, contemptuous. All he knew was that he had not at his death succeeded in saying what he was born to say.

Where there is no conflict between the poet and his verse, we get neither verse nor poetry. We get *The People, Yes,* which claims our attention only as communication.

V

The aim of all the arts is to present the conflict of man with time. This is as true for those arts, like architecture, which we ordinarily call spatial, as it is for those arts which, like music, are strictly temporal. And the famous release which the arts afford is essentially a release from time. In the Western world this is brought about by an assertion of control, in the East, apparently, by providing an escape from the inescapable; for there the arts aim to bring the listener or the beholder into a state of beatitude in which there is no longer an awareness of time and its duration.

Now obviously man cannot control time; what he controls, if he is an artist, is the consciousness of it. That he can order, that he can measure, that he can cause to come to a definite close—but only within the limits of his art. The means which the poet uses to that end is verse. For this it was devised, and for this it will doubtless continue to be used as long as time remains for man a living condition of his thought and not merely an abstract or mechanical conception.

The function of rhythm is to convey to us a sense of duration, which in itself is a frightening thing; in order that it should also be a source of delight, it is necessary, not only that it should be controlled at every point, but that it should come to an end. Hence, rather strangely, we rejoice when we see the Shakespearean stage littered with corpses and no one left alive save those who, like Horatio, survive only to prolong the tragedy in report and those who, like Fortinbras, are capable of starting a new tragic action outside the limits which the poet has laid down for this one.

But the creator of rhythm must work within even closer limits in order to feel a more immediate resistance. Though one form may offer a greater freedom than another—that is to say, a greater range of choice—there is no such thing as free verse. The one freedom which is allowed the poet is the possibility of expanding or contracting these limits. To do away with them entirely is to lose, not only the chief advantage his craft allows him, but his fecundity. In art, as in love, nothing is more sterile than limitless desire. The pauses which the verse introduces into the text, against the sense, will now perhaps no longer seem to us arbitrary. For they bring to the passage of poetic time a seeming necessity. They give it an objective reality, in which we can, as long as we are willing to accept the convention, believe. Only a rhythm marked by recurrent accents or their equivalent can give us this immediate perception of time. All the other devices which poets use and which make for a continual charm of complicated sound, serve to increase this perception. They make more happen, poetically speaking, within a given measure of time.

What is controlled in verse is not so much natural speech, as Valéry suggests, for in some very great poetry the speech is so close to nature that if it departs from it, it is not easy to say where; what is controlled is not so much the words as their movement. That movement is not simply measured and made to pause at predetermined but completely arbitrary intervals; meter does that much, and so much anybody can learn to do. But in good poetry, as I have earlier pointed out, there is a contest between the rhythm and the meter, and upon its complication a great deal of the quality of the poetry depends; but, more than this, there must also be assured an artifice of harmonious sound. This is not merely to allow the speech to come agreeably to the ear, to provide a musical accompaniment to whatever is being said, but even more to convey an impression of continuity in the midst of change. Only in this way can words be given a life of their own, apart from whatever life they may have simply because they are derived from a living speech. The line I have already quoted from Baudelaire, "Je suis belle, ô mortels! comme un rêve de pierre," has an identity of its own, which depends as much on the repetition of certain sounds as it does on the importance of the statement. It is precisely the quality of a living thing that it can change without its identity being destroyed.

Now the novelist, if he aspires to the status of an artist, has also to create a sense of duration. It is notorious that one of the most difficult technical problems which the writer of fiction has to face is to produce the illusion of a passage of time. But he cannot do it with words. The "Three years passed in this manner" which Balzac used is one of the most derided sentences in the history of the novel.

The means at the disposal of the poet are words, and he has no other; if he is sufficiently their master, he needs no other to create and control time. But the novelist can only do this by a proper ordering of his incidents; though he must write in words, they are important only as they contribute to the credibility and significance of the events he narrates. Yet it is quite possible to write in prose and have quite other aims than those we associate with the novelist. What Joyce is after in that fragment of Finnegans Wake to which I have already referred is by no means to record men and women and the many changes time works in them, as Tolstoy does in *War and Peace*. What he wishes to do in *Anna Livia Plurabelle* is to communicate directly to us the passage of time. He is not here concerned with a few hours in the life of Earwicker; what he wants us to feel is a thousand years, with all the complications for Ireland carried in their flow. Once this aim is granted, for an artist like Joyce there was really no choice; in writing what is ostensibly prose, he employs the methods of poetry.

But suppose, on the other hand, the aim of a poet was to prepare us for images of space, to show us an Asiatic people, a wandering barbarous tribe, forever moving about, in whom there is an awareness of the manifestations of time in nature and in men and women; they know youth and age, growth and decay; but there is in them no consciousness of time as we in the West know it—only a sense of endlessness in which one century passes very much like another. If he were wise, he would drop verse. And that, in order to write *Anabase*, is just what M. Perse has done.

That the position of the poet in the world at present is anything but reassuring, I should be the last to deny. But who can suppose that, when enormous floods of words pour daily from the press, conveying information that may be temporarily true or permanently false, persuading the vast numbers of the literate to opinions whose only significance is that they may one day lead to action, it is the art of prose that is being practiced? Every force in the world which today presses with threats against poetry, tomorrow threatens any prose which, by reasons of intensity and integrity, is comparable to it.

It is not humanity that abandons its arts. It is the arts which desert mankind, because of what it has become, or rather because of what it has ceased to be. Poetry has disappeared, and for centuries at a time; but those centuries have not been periods in which man could be proud of the course of his civilization.

Virginia Quarterly Review: Summer, 1938

THE POETRY OF JOHN MASEFIELD *

T HOUGH HE HAD already published his *Salt Water Ballads*, the first book of John Masefield to make a stir was *The Everlasting Mercy*. That was in 1911. The next year came *The Widow in the Bye Street; Dauber* and *The Daffodil Fields* both appeared in 1913. No narratives quite so rapid as these had been written in English verse for a long time. They were moving because of their compassion for the men and women of whose sad lot they told. Though Masefield was close to his characters, in his comments on their actions, their wrongs, there was nothing of self-commiseration. He wrote about outcasts, but celebrated only those who were "too strong to die," or who, if they must find death, could front it, outfacing defeat. He was at once familiar and heroic. Masefield's reputation was made.

In Paris, the Spanish painter Pablo Picasso in the year 1911 for the first time introduced letters into his composition in the *Souvenir du Havre*. The title was actually painted into the picture, as were also bits of heavily grained wood, the stripes from a French sailor's tricot, pieces of brick wall, and glasses of red wine from water-front bars. From painting such commonplace things, it was logical for Picasso to pass to devising a composition in which sandpaper, wallpaper from wrecked buildings, newspapers, should be glued to the canvas and take the same value as those parts of it which were still colored with pigment. The aim was to create an art which should have a movement of its own, out of whatever came most readily to the hand. On the slopes of Montmartre Picasso found an abundance of humble objects which no one had thought it worth while to paint before: the hideous luxuries of the Parisian poor, zinc made to look like wood, wood painted to imitate marble, oil cloth; these and the things that made the pleasures of the poor, playing cards, sacks of tobacco, labels from bottles of Anis del Oso were attached to the

* Written on the occasion of the publication of Masefield's *Selected Poems*.

canvas and deliberately brought into relation with paint, which was the same medium with which had been performed the miracles of El Greco. The *papier collé* period of Picasso coincides with that in which Masefield was producing his narrative poems.

At first sight, there may seem to be nothing in common between them but the dates. But that, after all, is a great deal for a poet and a painter to have in common. For if there is anything we want to know about a work of art, aside from what it is in itself, it is when it was done. Of course, if outside knowledge is lacking, we can usually contrive to find out from the work itself when it was composed. But in a period so portentous with change as the decade from 1904 to 1914, it is convenient, as well as wise, to have each work carefully dated. For in the arts, this, and not the decade after the war, was the time of great change.

But this much more can be said: that in both Masefield's narratives and Picasso's *papiers collés*, the immediate interest was attached more to what they were made of than to what was made. Masefield's early poems were made of sailors and ships and the sea, of the poor and daffodils and the countryside of England; they were made of simple things which ought not to age, of common things that ought not to change. Yet they have both changed and aged. Both Picasso and Masefield have lost something since the present for which their work was done has become a past that is, beyond all count of years, remote from us.

I happened to see, not too long ago, but almost exactly twenty years after they had been painted, a number of Picassos of this period. The old newspapers had yellowed. But what must have struck any observer was not the commonness of the details, but the elegance of their composition. Neither the cubist paintings nor the *papiers collés* were any longer outrageous. They had qualities that were not all on the surface, but their charm seemed to rise from a deliberate superficiality. It is not altogether fair to Masefield to attempt to criticize his long narrative poems through the detached passages in the *Selected Poems*. But it is the poet who has detached them, and it must be he supposes that these are fair selections by which to judge him. Besides, they remind us of the complete poems. There is little doubt that they have changed, just as the Picasso paintings have changed. But there is an important difference, which is the point of this comparison. Picasso, painting before the war, was one of those who helped to create the sensibility of the age that was to follow. The sensibility out of which Masefield wrote was his own and yet was in part a reflection of his age, and perhaps even

more of the age that preceded him. He is without the vulgarity of
Kipling, he is not so complicated as Meredith nor so mature as
Arnold. He has something in common with all of them. This may
explain why he is less impressive than he once was. While Picasso
has both lost and gained through the changes of time, Masefield has
only lost.

How grand he looked upon our wedding day.
"I wish we'd had the bells," he said to me;
And we'd the moon that evening, I and he,
And dew come wet, oh, I remember how,
And we'd come home to where I'm sitting now.

And he lay dead here, and his son was born here;
He never saw his son, his little Jim.
And now I'm all alone here, left to mourn here,
And there are all his clothes, but never him.
He's down under the prison in the dim,
With quicklime working on him to the bone,
The flesh I made with many and many a groan.

Here, in *The Widow in the Bye Street*, we find again vigor and
a happy precision, the ease of rhythm and the facility in rhyme
which made Masefield so rapid in narration. But the sordidness of
detail, which was once associated with Masefield, seems rather hard
to find.

Dull Bloomsbury streets of dull brick mansions old,
With stinking doors where women stood to scold,
And drunken waits at Christmas with their horn,
Droning the news, in snow, that Christ was born.

And the "stern realism" is more a matter of the spirit than of the
facts. He is a very sad poet, Masefield; he is not an indignant one.

He sees man against nature—against the delightful and indifferent earth, the enticing and disastrous sea. He has seen him, too,
struggling against his own malign brutality. And it is always by natural, not by social, forces that he is struck down. There is no more
social consciousness in Masefield's poems than there is in the early
work of Picasso, when he painted and drew Spanish starvelings and
the lost people of Montmartre.

There is compassion. But that is quite another thing. It was not that the age could not have supplied a social consciousness. It was that the interest of both, as artists, was elsewhere. They were drawn toward outcasts, for whom neither their society, nor any other conceivable, could do much.

For Masefield, no more than Yeats, thought that the poet had any gift to set the statesman straight. And this, in the domain of power, is undoubtedly true. But where the poet can put the statesman right—if the latter should ever take the trouble to listen to him —is by reminding him what men are, what they truly want, what they truly suffer. And if a Cabinet Minister could really read Masefield, he might at least acquire modesty.

At the beginning of the war, Masefield wrote one of his best poems: *August 1914.* In *Gallipoli* he wrote in prose a moving account of one of the bravest and most disastrous episodes in the history of British arms. The quatrain which he set as epilogue to that volume is here included:

> Even so was wisdom proven blind,
> So courage failed, so strength was chained;
> Even so the gods, whose seeing mind
> Is not as ours, ordained.

August 1914 celebrates not so much the armies of England as the countryside they are leaving behind. And indeed, however much Masefield may have felt the war as a man, he was not affected by it as a poet. Why should he have been? He had already praised the virtues the English were to show between 1914 and 1918; he had declared the humiliation in the command, the stoutness in defeat. He had already deserved, if not won, laurels from his King.

After the War came *Reynard the Fox*, which is the best because it is the liveliest of his narratives, and *Lollingdon Downs*, a series of sonnets, which, with those which were soon to follow *On Growing Old*, are the noblest expression of his meditations on life. Though these added to his reputation, they did not show any significant change in manner, none but the slightest increase in stature. Nor have any of his later books done so, as far as excerpts from them in the *Selected Poems* show. What Masefield had, he had from the beginning. He was mature before the War.

He was left an orphan as a very young boy and at twelve sent to sea on a sailing vessel; at seventeen he washed dishes in a New York saloon, worked in an American factory, did any sort of odd job to keep alive. He had known the worst vicissitudes his life could offer when, still under thirty, he landed in Fleet Street. He had made his strength; his sadness is constant. He was not unaffected by literary experiences that had immediately preceded him and he had, of course, read Shakespeare and Chaucer. But the meaning he gives to life is essentially that of the Anglo-Saxon poets. He is like no other so much as the lonely poet of *The Seafarer*. They are alike in what they praise and what they lament. They have the same manly melancholy, the same salt taste and the same serious steady sea-eyes.

Poetry: December, 1938

MATTHEW ARNOLD: STRUGGLE
AND FLIGHT*

I

MR. LIONEL TRILLING'S book on Matthew Arnold is not precisely the study one had been led to hope it might be from his introductory note. He is not much concerned with the misconception of Arnold which reduces his subtle and elaborate thought to a few phrases, such as those about "culture" and "sweetness and light," which, often repeated and not always understood, have ended by acquiring a pious and rather silly sound. His critical intention, Mr. Trilling says, "has been to make clear what, in my opinion, Arnold as a poet and as a critic of literature, politics and religion actually meant and said."

Mr. Trilling's scholarship is sound; he has gathered together for his study all the available published material on Matthew Arnold. His intentions are admirable. And though he makes clear what his opinions are on a great variety of topics as he goes along, I find, when he has done, that I am left in great doubt as to his opinion of Matthew Arnold. Point by point the portrait is built up, and as this stroke or that is applied it seems skillful enough; and yet when we look at the product as a whole we are not convinced. It is not composed. We are not sure which is man and which is background. Mr. Trilling is a professional scholar; his mind is open, so open that almost any liberal notion can find its way in; but it is still an academic mind. He lacks that clarity, that willingness to try for the most difficult definitions which so distinguished Arnold the critic among his contemporaries.

I have no intention of quarreling with Mr. Trilling's commentary. To do so would be futile. In these days, we get far too many comments on commentaries. I speak only for myself when I say that the value of his book, with its wealth of material, much of which was new to me, has been to call my mind once more to Matthew Arnold. I shall not, I hasten to add, attempt a completely new estimate of

* This essay, evidently unfinished, was stimulated by Lionel Trilling's *Matthew Arnold*, of which a review will be found further on.

him, for I can hardly hope briefly to succeed where the scholar at long length has failed. I would like merely to consider him as an English poet of the mid-nineteenth century who was peculiarly aware of his position. Arnold's poetic predicament was not the same as ours, but it has enough in common with ours so that I cannot but think that a consideration of what he did about it, of his struggle and flight, may have a point for us.

Of all the Victorian poets, Arnold was the most passionate. Emily Brontë may be more intense—Arnold thought her so, for it is of her that he speaks in *Haworth Churchyard*:

> (How shall I sing her?)—whose soul
> Knew no fellow for might,
> Passion, vehemence, grief,
> Daring, since Byron died . . .

But Emily, dying young, had scarcely looked beyond herself; her gaze had hardly gone into the world beyond the moorland town, the church at the crest of the hill, the lonely bleak churchyard where the poet was later to celebrate her repose. Matthew Arnold was in the world. He had looked at it unamazed. The son of the great Dr. Arnold of Rugby, he served as secretary to Lord Lansdowne when young, and it was from the hands of that liberal peer that he received his post as Inspector of Schools. He became Professor of Poetry at Oxford—a chair which until he came might as well have been occupied by a ghost as a man, so silent it had long seemed, so indifferent to anything but the past. Arnold made it a place of power, from which to speak to all England. It is worth while, in considering him, to remember that he was the only poet of his period to match himself, as Byron a generation before had done, with the world.

There are certain qualities which we have a right to expect of the poet in the world, qualities which Byron almost continuously displays. There are others, only nurtured in solitude, which we must not look for in their poetry. Their rhythm will never shudder, as another poet, solitary in his youth, has put it, because of their uncertainty. They will have a confidence in their poetic bearing which will show itself whenever they move; but they will neither exasperate nor delight as do the others. They will be manly always, but somewhat coarse.

Arnold in the common run of his poetical work is coarse—just how coarse we may readily discern by comparing the poem from which I have just quoted with poems of Yeats which happen to be quite similar in content. The earlier portion of *Haworth Churchyard*, addressed as it is to Harriet Martineau, might very well be compared to the famous tribute to Lady Gregory beginning

> Now all the truth is out
> Be secret and take defeat,

while the latter part might well be put alongside *In Memory of Eva Gore-Booth and Con Markiewicz*, which is so like it in everything but art. But that is not to say that *Haworth Churchyard* is a failure. Fine it is not, but moving it is; for Arnold's emotion is strong and even when his skill in verse is least he still knows how to write. When what should be poetry drops into prose, it is a readable, it may be even a strong prose. It is impossible when reading the common run of his verse not to be reminded of what he said of the poetry of Dryden—a man whom Arnold cannot be said to have taken at less than his true worth—that it was "admirable for the purposes of an inaugurator of an age of prose and reason." But Arnold was not of Dryden's age; he was heir to the revolution of reason which the eighteenth century had brought about. His was not an age of prose. It was a prosaic age—a very different thing. When Arnold drops, it may be below Dryden's level; but it is not so far down at that. When he declines, it is to a prose in the Oxford manner, which in his day was not so old as it now is, not so made—above all, not so academic. He wrote prose like a master; it must be admitted that he sometimes wrote a poetry as awkward as an undergraduate's.

Arnold is something more: he is that Victorian poet who was most completely aware of his time. He is seldom the complete poet, but when he is, he moves us as no other among his English contemporaries can. And it is because of his awareness that he moves us; it is because of what he knows that he gives us the sense of what it was to live, of how little, even with Arnold's passion, it was possible to live, in England in the mounting years of the nineteenth century. Arnold is in England, as Baudelaire was in France, the poet of the triumph of the middle class, the poet who comes at the moment when the triumph has turned to agony.

II

Baudelaire was born in 1821; Matthew Arnold in 1822—so that both were young men in 1848, the year that brought revolution to

France and to England grave riots and the threat of revolution. Baudelaire even made a not very convincing appearance on the barricades. Arnold wrote sonnets to a republican friend to say that he was with him, but prompted more to patience than to that prospect of hope which was then being proclaimed in France. And after that year both saw the consolidation of the power which the middle class had been so long in winning. The stroke to the right had been won with the help of the workers; and now the workers had been put down. After so great an achievement great pride might have been shown, had it not long been contrary to the middle class ever to be proud. "Can any life," Arnold was to ask, "be imagined more hideous, more dismal, more unenviable?" It might be supposed that he was speaking of failure. He was not. He was speaking of the middle class in the might of success and the fullness of acquisition.

A prosaic age is one that has lost coherence. The eighteenth century had hideousness and drabness to show no less than the nineteenth, as Arnold, who had looked into the English caricaturists, well knew. But the age which Hogarth sets before us in such unenviable brutality had not lost the power to make beautiful things, and not only had their beauty a social use, but more than a little of their significance depended upon an assertion of a social order. Men still knew where their loyalties were and where they owed allegiance; they knew to whom respect was due and from whom obedience could be exacted. In a society where every man knows his place, he may have much injustice and discomfort to put up with, he may know all sorts of hungers and privations; he will still know the ground sound beneath his feet. Distress he may know, but not disintegration. His soul has still its mask of union on. He will not be, as the young Matthew Arnold knew himself to be, in fragments.

The age of reason had greatly increased man's confidence in himself. Mankind, said Voltaire, had lost its civil status and must find it again. But that was to prove much more difficult than the eighteenth-century philosophers had expected. The reign of reason had no more than been inaugurated before it was being called a reign of terror. It was found that a philosopher could cut off people's heads as well as anybody else and with even less than common piteousness. A state could not exist without authority. And what authority other than reason itself could be found? Robespierre had stood by the guillotine until he fell by it. And it was decided that Louis XVIII, returning with troops to Paris to be restored to his ancestral throne, could also apply to reason as the final authority for his power. "What bores me in France," said Baudelaire, "is that everybody is like

115

Voltaire." It was seventy years since the sage of Ferney had been buried with honors like a god. In the course of the reaction, his corpse had been disentombed. It is fitting, perhaps, that the man who more than any other came to represent to those that followed him the corrosive powers of the disembodied mind should have had, somewhere between tomb and tomb, his body lost.

The advent of the middle class to power had produced a great sense of liberation. But Liberalism, as it was known in England, made for a great sense of confusion. And Matthew Arnold is, above all others, the poet of that confusion.

> Ah, love, let us be true
> To one another! for the world which seems
> To lie before us like a land of dreams,
> So various, so beautiful, so new,
> Hath really neither joy, nor love, nor light,
> Nor certitude, nor peace, nor help for pain;
> And we are here as on a darkling plain
> Swept with confused alarms of struggle and flight,
> Where ignorant armies clash by night.

In spite of the long time it had been coming to power, the middle class had scarcely known what it was to secure men's loyalties. An aristocracy could oppress and could afford to ignore the results of its oppressions. At worst, it could only ask men to die for it and many and long wars had shown how secure was their consent. For in the dying, in both leader and led, moral qualities might be displayed which all men could admire and admire without being told. But the choice which the manufacturer gave was to work at his will or else to starve to death, an ignoble choice which aroused no one's honest enthusiasm. The middle class insisted upon morality, and we need not wonder that it did, for who, without special instruction, would ever have been persuaded that Mr. Murdstone was morally admirable?

The middle class had acquired the power, but had neither the knowledge nor the experience to use it; its members having themselves in their middle capacity always identified power with money could not conceive that the ultimate sourse of power in this world is force. A fine war, Louis XIV is said to have remarked, is costly. The mistake of the nineteenth century was to identify war and money. Abroad it saw every conquest end in exploitation and at home created that confusion which it called class warfare. We are shocked, for instance, by the wars which England waged in China to secure the opium trade, as we are not by the War of the Spanish Succession, which, though it has been called a dynastic war, was fought for no family advantage but in a large dispute of power. Men died in both, and most, no doubt, unwillingly. Nevertheless, we must distinguish between wars and see that it is the later sort of war that had rendered all wars senseless, cruel and immoral.

The middle class was in power and after 1848 appeared more solidly ensconced than ever. It had the power, but, as Arnold soon discerned, it did not have the authority.

The old governing classes had been sustained by tradition, and tradition had sufficed until men of a levelling rational turn of mind began to look into its origins and find there nothing but ignorance and injustice. The new governing classes depended ultimately, not upon reason, but upon revolution, and revolution, as the year 1848 had shown, was a reason that could be invoked from below, not to uphold but to displace them. Marx was not the first to perceive that society was now committed to a perpetual revolution. It had been claimed for the commercial and industrial classes in England that theirs was a revolution by due process of law. They made their way by a promise of progress. And more and more they made the law.

III

Matthew Arnold from the very start knew that his struggle would be with the whole contemporary world. That world came to him first wearing the countenance of Dr. Arnold of Rugby. The youth recognized the enemy in his own father.

Dr. Arnold had that sort of moral authority which, though it asks many questions of others, never questions itself. God might abdicate the heavens, and the next day Dr. Arnold would have been found in his master's chair, acting with all the certainty of a god and the assurance of a physical force. (Behind this chair, Matt, when a disgraced schoolboy, had made faces.) It was indeed to be suspected that there had been an abdication in the heavens; if it were so, then God had let him down rather badly; but that was no reason why he, Thomas Arnold, should ever let anybody down. He promptly decreed a rôle of social usefulness for the Church and told it plainly that unless it did as he said, it had no chance for survival. With authority gone from the Church, there was still the State. "The state is sovereign over human life," he declared, "controlling everything and itself subject to no earthly control." He was more than a schoolmaster: he was an example to all England, for he ruled his school precisely as he would have governed an Empire. It is more than surmise to see in him an ancestor of certain contemporary Britishers who look with complacent admiration toward the totalitarian dictators of Berlin and Rome. But what is important at the moment is to remember that he was Matthew Arnold's father. It would seem that General Aupick himself could not more promptly have aroused the impulses of a young poet to rebel.

A poet is always on the side of the angels, but seldom on the side of the good angels. How profound was Matthew Arnold's rebellion must be a matter of opinion. It was not prolonged. He was only twenty when his father died. For another ten years he held out; he was everything that his father was not; and for that time he was a poet.

He was not alone in his search for authority; others beside Arnold in that age craved certainty and consolation. But the loss of his father while still so young—and of a father made of so much that a poet must oppose, if he is not to compound his own betrayal —made his search singularly passionate, persistent and painful. He sought the laws of his own being. If he is to be considered as a poet, there can be but one conclusion, that he sought them in vain. It can scarcely be doubted that, given the choice, he would rather have been saved as a man than as a poet. But when had ever a poet that choice? And even as a man it is easy for us to see where Arnold went astray.

He became in time his own father, while remaining his father's son. He was both Sohrab and Rustum. He was Sohrab, who knowingly sought his father and unwittingly found him, and by his own famed father, on the sand, was slain.

Dr. Arnold had while a very young man engendered a poet; mature, he had formed him; then when he was little more than a boy, left him to become the foiled circuitous wanderer. In the end he destroyed him.

He destroyed him as a poet. He did not destroy him as a disinterested mind. And now that the middle class, which in the England of the Arnolds was so strong, has been in many countries overcome, and in no country survives unchallenged, now that all over the world men without unwillingness, without even a look, are leaving that liberty which was once so esteemed, it is well to recall that freedom of contemplation, freedom of thought and freedom to utter what thought has found, belong to a world in which men of the middle sort are dominant. All that knowledge which for us takes shape as science could not have come into existence had there not been to nurture it a number of men whose interests were opposed to dogmatic authority. And these were men of the middle condition in society. Though the bourgeoisie are supposed, and rightly supposed, seldom to act contrary to its material interests, it is from that class as from no other that has risen the disinterested mind. For in that class the sons constantly rise in opposition to the fathers.

The first great discoveries had been made, every search starting in the assurance of the excellence of God. The intellect shrank with horror, so Copernicus said, from the possibility that He had constituted the heavenly bodies in any but a perfect order. The intellect had its way, the order it demanded had been made apparent, but in an indifferent heaven. The stars made sense, as they had not done before; they no longer made music. It was the silences of the eternal spaces which affrighted the seventeenth-century mind of Pascal, as it was the silence within him that set his body round with spikes. The nineteenth-century Arnold is afflicted that he has only silence to counsel him on his conduct; he complains when he is just past thirty that he is already three parts frozen over; and from then on he seems to be trying to lead the good life as his father understood it, with none of the peculiarly personal convictions of his father to sustain him. The silence had come down from heaven to earth.

The mind was restless with contemplation and, delighted by its own curiosity, was never tired. But of moral certainty there was none. What assurance was there that man was happier for not being a brute? And the solitude which had once been an absence of God had now become a human separation. "I desire with all my heart," Baudelaire wrote to his mother, "(with what sincerity none but me can know!) to believe that an exterior and invisible being is interested in my fate; but what shall I do to believe?" Baudelaire declares his irremediable loneliness, as Matthew Arnold complains of an "isolation without end prolonged." It is indeed the cry of the century. And if I cite Baudelaire it is because I believe that he was clearer than the English poet as to the cause of that loneliness. When communion with God ceases, it is perhaps only a matter of time before communication between men and women comes to an end and between them spreads only

> The unplumb'd, salt, estranging sea.

We can make any number of explanations of this sense of isolation, but when they have all been made, we can only come back to the fact that these men felt themselves irremediably alone. Now, so far as the poets are concerned, one of the explanations that has constantly been made for them is that they deliberately cut themselves off from the common experience of their time. It has been said that in order to pursue their poetic calling in a prosaic age, they retreated from it. There is something in this accusation, which, if I am not mistaken, was first brought against the romantic poets by De Musset, who was one of them. But Matthew Arnold was never out of the world of his contemporaries, and if he failed to share the common experience, it was because he knew there was no longer a common experience to be shared. Baudelaire was not exaggerating when he said that he fed his remorse in the same way as the old bums under the bridges he could see from his house in the Ile Saint-Louis nourished their lice. The life of a poet has necessarily much in common with a life of contemplation, and he will suffer many of the ills of that life. He will know the hopeless inertia with which monks are so familiar, and like them he will know the distress of spiritual drouth. But in addition he must suffer as do ordinary men. Had not the young Arnold, in one of his earliest poems, declared that the poet must know their labor and pain? And in that century he could not but know their isolation, which was one of the consequences of the assertion of the individual. If he stands out against society, he must not merely stand alone among men: he must lie down in the bed of his love alone.

IV

Arnold did not become a critic; he was a critic; but in ceasing to be a poet, he became nothing else unless it was a moralist. It was precisely his critical faculties that gave substance to his poetry, but it was the moralist who gave it its aim.

The critic always worked with the poet; it was the moralist who for so long suppressed the young *Empedocles on Etna*, because it was so pessimistic and offered little to men whose need was for "something to animate and ennoble them—not merely to add zest to their melancholy or grace to their dreams." And it was the moralist in Arnold who was not content merely to remove this early poem; he must in the end repress the poet who wrote it.

Now a poet is naturally a moralist, for men do not only feel but act; they do not merely dream but do; and all have their consequences, the consequences of emotions being only a little more remote than those of actions. It is literally true that in dreams begins responsibility. And out of the fullness and abundance of his nature the poet must assume the responsibility and consider the actions. If he does not, he will cease to be the whole poet. He cannot avoid moral judgments, because he is a man; he will rarely state them directly, because he is a poet and knows that such statements carry no conviction unless they come merely as words which declare what has already in the poem been present to the imagination. And what those words declare will not accord with any moral system; on the contrary, they will commonly oppose the current morality. And in the nineteenth century the artist had no choice but on every occasion and by whatever means were his to declare his immorality.

It is significant that among the first cares of the French Revolutionists, once they had come to power, was to establish a system of weights and measures which should be as satisfactory to logic as it was convenient in use. The traditional *aunes* and *livres* with their changing and uncertain values were discarded, and for them substituted the precise and unchanging standards of the metric system. A similar reform was undertaken in morals. But how was one to measure the forces for good, for ill, in man's heart. If only a natural order could be presupposed for man, to find it would be to discover a moral order. But that was not what happened. Man's lost and noble innocence was not recovered. What came into effect as the result of the French Revolution was middle-class morality. It had always taken a limited view of man, but that had not much mattered so long as it was kept in the strict place assigned it under the older society. Now that most of the limitations had been removed, what had been virtues of the middle class became by their very excess vicious, whereas one of the oldest and most dangerous of vices, avarice, was allowed play as unlimited as the wind.

The basis of practical morality is society. The French understand this when they say of a man who behaves badly, not that he is bad, but that he is *mal élevé*, badly brought up. What is good in any society is what at the moment seems to contribute to the continuance of that society, just as what is bad is what appears to threaten its existence. Thus, when a country is in the throes of a revolution, assassination may come to be considered a virtue, if it seems necessary to assure the continuity of what has been started. . . .

1939

THE MYTH AND MODERN LITERATURE

W HY HAVE SO MANY good writers recently come out of the South? Why has that part of the country which, not so long ago, meant little or nothing when literature was considered, why has it, after a silence so prolonged, suddenly found so many writers to call its own? The South has not prospered lately. It was with the depression that most of its writers, some of whom had been working unregarded for years, began to acquire an audience. Their books had not been built out of low-price cotton. Not all Southerners who are read are to be taken seriously. But there are some who would have to be included in any serious reckoning of American writers today, a saving remnant that is, perhaps, not so small. Certainly, it will not seem small to anyone who can remember when Mr. Mencken was a literary critic and the South was his particular literary desert, to which he was never tired of returning in order to declaim that it was, apart from Mr. James Branch Cabell, all an arid vacancy.

Why has the South, in so short a time, produced so many writers of its own? The question can be put in a more general form. What conditions are necessary that a body of literature come into being in a country, in a region, which hitherto has had little or none that was of more than local interest? It would be convenient if we could say that it comes with prosperity. But we cannot say of literature, as we well might of architecture, even that it perishes from poverty. The use of prosperity, so far as the writer is concerned, for he is not likely to share in it personally, is that he may, through his work, reflect some of the surrounding confidence. The apparent and prodigious wealth of America in the ten years after the war, the prestige that followed the disposal of so much power, did leave its mark on American writing. But the Southern writer, unless he happened to be Thomas Wolfe, did not have much to do with that prodigality. He did not believe in its premises; how, then, was he to believe in its promises? The moral collapse that came with the crash of 1929 restored his own moral confidence. And like the French in those years, before they themselves became involved, he was not above experiencing a certain pleasure in the fact that events had proved him right.

Men and women no longer knew what to do. And so they read, as they had not read the novels of Stark Young before, *So Red the Rose*, in which women and men, at every hour of the day, knew just what to do. Subject to reverses no less serious, since they, too, had to see their world fallen about them, Stark Young's characters had not fallen into moral uncertainty. What Americans were later involved in was not merely an economic but a moral crisis. What was lost was more than money, more certainly than paper profits. What was gone was the myth of progress.

It is by such myths that men live. Throughout the nineteenth century they had been carried forward, at a pace that never diminished, by the myth of progress. This was true in Europe, as well as in America, but because this was a country for pioneers, Americans were carried much faster and further.

Before considering the Southern writers more closely, it may be well to look at another literature, which, like theirs, came out of nothing, or next to nothing, and which, though it thought of itself as national, may as well be called regional. For when the Irish Renaissance began, though the Irish were a people who could claim a past, and hence a consciousness which was not that of their conquerors, they could not call themselves a nation. They did not—they do not yet—possess the whole of their small island. Their relation to England is not exactly that of the South to the East, but the two have enough in common to make comparison possible.

Their literature, Yeats tells us in his *Ireland after the Fall of Parnell*, had fallen into contempt. "No educated man ever bought an Irish book." And the one scholar of Dublin who had anything of a reputation outside his own country, Edward Dowden, used to say that he could recognize an Irish book by the smell, even the glue that held the pages together within, the binding being inferior. And yet, in a space of time which, when we look back on it, must seem incredibly short, a literature was created which, though it excited the liveliest opposition in Ireland, was soon recognized as having importance by those who had no patriotic reasons either to condemn or to praise. Many men, and at least one woman, contributed to that movement, and even the failures among them may have been in a measure indispensable to it; for every movement in the arts demands a mass of workers whose endeavors will never come to much. The Irish Renaissance created a considerable literature; while it was first addressed to the Irish, it by no means limited its appeal to them.

Now the Irish had, at the time the generation of Yeats began writing, a myth to work against: the myth of Young Ireland. They also had, which was of importance to some of them, an heroic past, a world so misty and remote that, when recovered either from popular or scholarly memory, whatever happened there appeared to have mythological proportions. Personally, I have never been able to work up much interest in the Irish myths. I can appreciate the words into which the modern poets have put them, but the myths themselves seem to me to have very little to say. Whether in Synge's cloak or Yeats's embroidered coat, Deirdre remains no more tangible to me than so much Celtic twilight; she is not another Helen. And it is worth remarking that Yeats as he grew older more and more abandoned the world of Irish mythology and if he wanted a myth took one, like that of Leda and the Swan, which is accessible to anyone of European mind.

For if I am to speak of literature and the myth, I must make it clear that this is not the sort of myth with which I am now concerned. Because we all carry around with us, below the mind that is conscious of modernity, a primitive mind—to which at times we have access, if only in sleep—myths which are the true creations of that mind have an endless power to stir us. And since the conscious mind, working over these myths, can through them express relations which, if put into a more abstract form, would suffer a loss both in complication and profundity, they are of great use to the poet. But when they are used—and this is my point—they must be used directly, which is exactly what Yeats does in his great sonnet on Leda. Whereas, in the case of what I shall call the contemporary myths, which are created not by the unconscious but by the conscious mind, he must work in opposition.

The myth of Young Ireland was of this latter sort; and so was the myth of the Old South. Both were romantic. And when Synge put his *Playboy of the Western World* against the romantic popular conception of Ireland, he was assailed with the same cries of rage and hurt as resounded all over Georgia toward Erskine Caldwell when he set down his truth about *Tobacco Road*.

These myths came into being in part to compensate a proud people who, for all they had been conquered, had by no means foregone their contempt for those who had overcome them. To be held subject by those whom you feel to be your inferiors in everything but wealth and numbers, in time makes for a romantic conceit, which may well mask a profound conviction of inferiority. It precludes criticism, and any people who will allow no criticism can scarcely avoid becoming less than their former selves. Allen Tate has analyzed the part that slavery played in this avoidance of criticism. While it lasted, it made the Southerners very touchy to outside comment; when it was gone, they felt they had lost their only imperfection.

"All the past," Yeats says of the prose of Young Ireland, "had been turned into a melodrama with Ireland for blameless hero." And the poetry differed from the prose in being not less occupied with Irish virtue, but only in being a little less taken up with the invader's vices. The parallel literature in the South is to be found in the novels of Thomas Nelson Page. But the Old South was no invention of Page's, and still less of his followers; it was a spontaneous creation of defeat and despair. It found its heroic Danaans in the ragged armies of Lee.

A myth is of great use to a writer, since through it he comes in contact, as he might not otherwise do, with the common mind and makes its resources of feeling and sentiment, its depths of desire, his own. But in his employment of the myth, he must complicate and correct it, according to his own sense of the fatal abundance of life, its excess and its cruelty. For in order to form any conception of life that will make a consistent whole, something must be left out; and the common man, who is more intent on conserving the sources of his life than on contemplating them, will almost always begin by leaving out the essential cruelty of living things. This is so in any society. In the myth, Ireland is Kathleen ni Houlihan, an old hag, whose love is strong enough to draw the young man from his bride; but it is her attraction and not the death towards which she draws him that is dwelt on. And as long as young men must die for her, it is perhaps just as well that they look on her in this way. But to Stephen Dedalus, Ireland is the old sow that eats her farrow.

One of the first things a creative artist will do, then, is to restore cruelty in his aspect of things. Mr. Caldwell runs an automobile over the old grandmother in *Tobacco Road* and leaves her to rot indifferently on the ground, while what is perhaps his most famous story, *Kneel to the Rising Sun*, is piled with purposeful and meaningless cruelty. Mr. Faulkner, who is a more sensitive person than Mr. Caldwell, and apparently even more vulnerable to pain, has spared his readers no horror that either local tales of his part of the country or his own hurt imagination could suggest. It is not that Southerners are more cruel than other Americans, though poverty is a great encourager of cruelty and parts of the South have long been poor. It is rather that when men are cruel there, it will be in a more personal and eccentric way than in the environs of Detroit and Red River, where murder, like everything else, is mechanized. Cruelty is one of the ways in which life in the South exceeds the myth. Perhaps because of an old recollection of slavery, perhaps, too, because of a deep instinct for social order, it was necessary in the Southern myth that as much as possible cruelty should be left out. In the Irish myth, incompetence was accounted charm, truculence became bravery, bigotry was a finer faith, and treachery a nobler loyalty.

The Southern myth was romantic. Considering the time in which it took form, it would be foolish to expect it to be anything else. But the mood of the present generation of Southern writers is not romantic. And when they began to work among the mythical remnants of the Old South and got down to facts, what they discovered was a society which, though it constantly entertained romance, was severely classical. What they found was a social order which, though colored by the presence of African slaves, was very close to European society in the eighteenth century. It was not English, it was not French; it was, in fact, like nothing but itself. It had few cities. But as in provincial France before 1789, as in countrified England before the industrial revolution, society was still based on the family. Its structure was regulated by custom, as, though affected by climate, its speech and manners were maintained by tradition. It was not everywhere established: the wilderness constantly encroached on cultivation. And in the mountains, it was displaced by an even older order of living—one which, late as it may have come to America, was scarcely to be found in Western Europe, except in its wilder and more remote regions, much after the seventeenth century. One of these regions was the Scotch Highlands, where change was so slow that it is said that, as late as 1745, after the battle of Culloden, the Scotch dead were buried as clansmen, all of one name in a common earth, while the English dead were accorded each his separate grave. The Scotch came to America about this time in some numbers, and it may be it was they who taught their ways to the Appalachians. At all events, the Southern mountaineer was tribal. And unless Mr. Jesse Stuart in *Head of W-Hollow* is writing about the past, he remains so.

When I say that insofar as there was a social order in the Old South, its source was in the family, I may seem to be saying something that is as true anywhere as there. For we assume that no other source is possible for society. But it is not so where industrialism has reached a sufficiently advanced state: then only the individual counts. The political man presupposes a social order and the old Southerner was if anything too exclusively concerned with politics. The economic man cannot but hasten the arrival of anarchy. This contrast is at the core of Allen Tate's *The Fathers*, as it underlies nearly everything that poet has written in prose.

Southern writers, having a myth to work with, could oppose to it the "minute particulars of mankind." In the Old South they discovered a past which they could by no means altogether praise, but which was not without its power for truth. It could be used, not merely in contrast to the present—both as that present belongs to the South and to other parts of the country which have no such past—but in criticism of it. The Old South was a possible, a proved, form of life. It is because he is aware of what a Sartoris once stood for that Mr. Faulkner can recount to such bitter effect the conduct without honor and without shame of a Snopes. Mr. Faulkner knows how hard the human condition is for mankind to maintain. When economics is allowed to take its course, the result is the poor-white family in *As I Lay Dying*, who can hold to their human obligations only at the cost of tremendous effort. When nature is allowed to take its course, as it can be perhaps even more easily in the South than elsewhere, the result is a Snopes, who only in outward shape is a man. It is this knowledge, won out of a myth, that gives Faulkner's words weight, even when he speaks to those outside of his region. He is one of its serious writers. There are others. Of all of them I think it can be said that when they damn the South, they are damning man's inhumanity, and when they praise it, they are but praising the humane tradition.

The two most conspicuous failures in American letters of recent years have been Thomas Wolfe and Hart Crane. What the one in his novels, the other in his poems, meant to write about was the greatness of America. As a theme, it was in the air when they began writing, and if they could have written of it, they should have done so. Both had gifts in abundance; both shared "the breath released" of a new world, a world of the machine whose accomplishments, great as they were, were as nothing to its promises of progress; both had access, almost at will, to that secret source of energy we call genius. America is great, in many ways; but the consciousness they had of a country which had spread across a continent in a grandeur of covetousness was scarcely a myth. The "greatness of America" was merely a particular phase of the myth of progress. To accept it was to limit moral criticism. To go contrary to it was something that Crane, once he had conceived *The Bridge*, was unwilling to do. And yet he found not much for his poem which was positive and concrete to celebrate. He had, I have been told by those who knew him, night after night crossed Brooklyn Bridge, prompted by impetuous needs, as personal as love and sleep, so that before he began to make of it a poem, it had become for him, not merely a complex of the engineer's skill, but a symbol of man's undaunted desire. But his faith was arbitrary and forced. He tried to believe in the greatness of America, and when, as a myth, it failed him, he attempted to make myths of his own. And that, I am inclined to think, is something no one man can do. Crane failed.

In working with the same myth, Thomas Wolfe did give, as no other American writer has done in prose, a sense, proud, lonely, exhilarating, of the immensity of the country. With his prodigious appetite for experience, Wolfe did record, so far as one not participating could, one after another, American scenes. His characters are huge, and they are American. But of moral grandeur there is none. Indeed, as the depression deepened, Wolfe grew more and more distressed. He could no longer consent to the "greatness of America"; for it was impossible any longer to hold to the myth of progress. Progress, of course, exists; and as long as science remains free, it can probably be counted on to continue. But progress as a be-all and end-all, progress as a word to give meaning to increasingly restless and more and more meaningless activities, that progress had suddenly stopped. And Wolfe was thrown back on man's capacity to endure suffering, both the suffering which he has brought on himself and the suffering with which others, willing or unwilling, have afflicted him. What else he could have done, had he lived longer, can only be conjectured. At present, it must be said that, for all his concern with myths, he did not and, working as he did, could not find a meaning for *Of Time and the River.*

The Saturday Review of Literature: July 22, 1939

THE SORROWS OF THOMAS WOLFE

I

THOMAS WOLFE is dead. And that big work which he was prepared to write, which was to have gone to six long volumes and covered in the course of its narrative the years between 1781 and 1933, with a cast of characters whose numbers would have run into the hundreds, will never be finished. The title which he had chosen for it, *Of Time and the River*, had already been allowed to appear on the second volume. There its application is not altogether clear; how appropriate it would have been to the work as a whole we can only conjecture. No work of such magnitude has been projected by another of his generation in America; Wolfe's imagination, it appears, could conceive on no smaller scale. He was, he confesses, devoted to chance; he had no constant control over his faculties; but his fecundity was nothing less than prodigious. He had, moreover, a tenacity which must, but for his dying, have carried him through to the end.

Dying, he left behind him a mass of manuscript; how much of it can be published there is now no knowing. Wolfe was the most wasteful of writers.

His aim was to set down America as far as it can belong to the experience of one man. Wolfe came early on what was for him the one available truth about this continent—that it was contained in himself. There was no America which could not be made out—mountains, rivers, trains, cities, people—in the memory of an American. If the contours were misty, then they must be made clear. It was in flight from a certain experience of America, as unhappy as it had been apparently sterile—it was in Paris, in an alien land, that Wolfe first understood with hate and with love the horror and the wonder of his native country. He had crossed the seas from West to East only to come upon the North Carolina hills where he had been born. "I found out," he says, "during those years that the way to discover one's own country was to leave it; that the way to find America was to find it in one's own heart, one's memory and one's spirit, and in a foreign land. I think I may say that I discovered America during those years abroad out of my very need of her."

This is not an uncommon experience, but what made it rewarding in Wolfe's case was that his memory was anything but common. He could—and it is the source of what is most authentic in his talents —displace the present so completely by the past that its sights and sounds all but destroyed surrounding circumstance. He then lost the sense of time. For Wolfe, sitting at a table on a terrace in Paris, contained within himself not only the America he had known; he also held, within his body, both his parents. They were there, not only in his memory, but more portentously in the make-up of his mind. They loomed so enormous to him that their shadows fell across the Atlantic, their shade was on the café table under which he stretched his long American legs.

"The quality of my memory," he said in his little book, *The Story of a Novel,* "is characterized, I believe, in a more than ordinary degree by the intensity of its sense impressions, its power to evoke and bring back the odors, sounds, colors, shapes and feel of things with concrete vividness." That is true. But readers of Wolfe will remember that the mother of Eugene Gant was afflicted with what is known as total recall. Her interminable narratives were the despair of her family. Wolfe could no more than Eliza Gant suppress any detail, no matter how irrelevant; indeed, it was impossible for him to feel that any detail was irrelevant to his purpose. The readers of *Look Homeward, Angel* will also remember that Eugene's father had a gift, unrivalled among his associates, of vigorous utterance. Nobody, they said, can tie a knot in the tail of the English language like old W. O. But the elder Gant's speech, for all that it can on occasion sputter into fiery intensity, more often than not runs off into a home-spun rhetoric. It sounds strong, but it has very little connection with any outer reality and is meaningless, except in so far as it serves to convey his rage and frustration. We cannot avoid supposing that Wolfe drew these two characters after his own parents. At the time he began writing *Look Homeward, Angel,* he stood far enough apart from them to use the endlessness of Eliza's unheard discourses, the exaggerated violence of old Gant's objurgations, for comic effect. He makes father and mother into something at once larger and less than human. But in his own case, he could not, at least so long as he was at his writing, restrain either the course of his recollections or their outcome in words. He wrote as a man possessed. Whatever was in his memory must be set down—not merely because he was Eliza's son, but because the secret end of all his writing was expiation—and it must be set down in words to which he constantly seems to be attaching more meaning than they can properly own. It was as though he were aware that his novel would have no meaning that could not be found in the words. The meaning of a novel should be in its structure. But in Wolfe's novel, as far as it has gone, it is impossible to discover any structure at all.

II

It is impossible to say what Wolfe's position in American letters would have been had he lived to bring his work to completion. At the moment he stands very high in the estimation both of the critics and of the common reader. From the time of *Look Homeward, Angel*, he was regarded, and rightly, as a young man of incomparable promise. *Of Time and the River* seemed to many to have borne out that promise and, since its faults were taken as due merely to an excess of fecundity, it was met with praise as though it were the consummation of all Wolfe's talents. Yet the faults are fundamental. The force of Wolfe's talents is indubitable; yet he did not find for that novel, nor do I believe he could ever have found, a structure of form which would have been capable of giving shape and meaning to his emotional experience. He was not without intelligence; but he could not trust his intelligence, since for him to do so would have been to succumb to conscience. And it was conscience, with its convictions of guilt, that he was continually trying to elude.

His position as an artist is very like that of Hart Crane. Crane was born in 1899, Wolfe in 1900, so that they were almost of an age. Both had what we must call genius; both conceived that genius had been given them that they might celebrate, the one in poetry, the other in prose, the greatness of their country. But Wolfe no more than Crane was able to give any other coherence to his work than that which comes from the personal quality of his writing. And he found, as Crane did before him, that the America he longed to celebrate did not exist. He could record, and none better, its sights, its sounds and its odors, as they can be caught in a moment of time; he could try, as the poet of *The Bridge* did, to absorb that moment and endow it with the permanence of a myth. But he could not create a continuous America. He could not, for all that he was prepared to cover one hundred and fifty of its years, conceive its history. He can record what comes to his sensibility, but he cannot give us the continuity of experience. Everything for Wolfe is in the moment; he can so try to impress us with the immensity of the moment that it will take on some sort of transcendental meaning. But what that meaning is, escapes him, as it does us. And once it has passed from his mind, he can do nothing but recall another moment, which as it descends into his memory seems always about to deliver itself, by a miracle, of some tremendous import.

Both Crane and Wolfe belonged to a world that is indeed living from moment to moment. And it is because they voice its breakdown in the consciousness of continuity that they have significance for it.

Of the two, Wolfe, I should say, was the more aware of his plight. He was, he tells us, while writing *Of Time and the River*, tormented by a dream in which the sense of guilt was associated with the forgetting of time. "I was unable to sleep, unable to subdue the tumult of these creative energies, and, as a result of this condition, for three years I prowled the streets, explored the swarming web of the million-footed city and came to know it as I had never done before. . . . Moreover, in this endless quest and prowling of the night through the great web and jungle of the city, I saw, lived, felt and experienced the full weight of that horrible human calamity. [The time was that of the bottom of the depression, when Wolfe was living in Brooklyn.] And from it all has come, as a final deposit, a burning memory, a certain evidence of the fortitude of man, his ability to suffer and somehow survive. And it is for this reason now that I think I shall always remember this black period with a kind of joy that I could not at that time have believed possible, for it was during this time that I lived my life through to a first completion, and through the suffering and labor of my own life came to share those qualities in the lives of the people around me."

This passage is one of extreme interest, not only for what it tells us of Wolfe at this time, but for the promise it contains of an emotional maturity. For as far as Wolfe had carried the history of Eugene Gant, he was dealing with a young man whose isolation from his fellow men was almost complete. Eugene, and we must suppose the young Wolfe, was incarcerated in his own sensibility. Locked in his cell, he awaits the coming of every moment, as though it would bring the turning of a releasing key. He waits like Ugolino, when he woke uncertain because of his dream and heard not the opening but the closing of the lock. There is no release. And the place of Wolfe's confinement, no less than that of Ugolino, deserves to be called Famine.

It can be said of Wolfe, as Allen Tate has said of Hart Crane, that he was playing a game in which any move was possible, because none was compulsory. There is no idea which would serve as discipline to the event. For what Wolfe tells us was the idea that furiously pursued him during the composition of *Of Time and the River*, the search for a father, can scarcely be said to appear in the novel, or else it is so incidentally that it seems to no purpose. It does not certainly, as the same search on the part of Stephen Dedalus does in *Ulysses*, prepare a point toward which the whole narrative moves. There was nothing indeed in Wolfe's upbringing to make discipline acceptable to him. He acts always as though his own capacity for feeling, for anguished hope and continual frustration, was what made him superior, as no doubt, along with his romantic propensity for expression, it was. But he was wrong in assuming that those who accept any form of discipline are therefore lacking in vigor. He apparently did not understand that there are those who might say with Yeats, "I could recover if I shrieked my heart's agony," and yet like him are dumb "from human dignity." And his failure to understand was due to no fault of the intelligence, but to lack of love. The Gant family always strikes us, with its howls of rage, its loud hah-hahs of hate and derision, as something less than human. And Eugene is a Gant. While in his case we are ready to admit that genius is a law unto itself, we have every right to demand that it discover its own law.

Again like Crane, Wolfe failed to see that at the present time so extreme a manifestation of individualism could not but be morbid. Both came too late into a world too mechanic; they lacked a wilderness and constantly tried to create one as wild as their hearts. It was all very well for them, since both were in the way of being poets, to start out to proclaim the grandeur of America. Such a task seemed superb. But both were led at last, on proud romantic feet, to Brooklyn. And what they found there they abhorred.

They represent, each in his way, a culmination of the romantic spirit in America. There was in both a tremendous desire to impose the will on experience. Wolfe had no uncommon will. And Crane's was strong enough to lead him deliberately to death by drowning. For Wolfe the rewards of experience were always such that he was turned back upon himself. Isolated in his sensations, there was no way out. He continually sought for a door, and there was really none, or only one, the door of death.

III

The intellectual labor of the artist is properly confined to the perception of relations. The conscience of the craftsman must see that these relations are so presented that, in spite of all complications, they are ultimately clear. It is one of the conditions of art that they cannot be abstractly stated, but must be presented to the senses.

What we have at the center of all Wolfe's writing is a single character, and it was certainly the aim of that writing to present this character in all his manifold contacts with the world of our time. Eugene has, we are told, the craving of a Faust to know all experience, to be able to record all the races and all the social classes which may be said to exist in America. Actually, Eugene's experience is not confined to America.

But when we actually come to consider Eugene closely, we see that, once he is beyond the overwhelming presence of his family, his contacts with other people are all casual. The perfect experience for Eugene is to see someone in the throes of an emotion which he can imagine, but in which he has no responsible part. From one train, he sees people passing in another train, which is moving at a faster speed than his own.

"And they looked at one another for a moment, they passed and vanished and were gone forever, yet it seemed to him that he had known these people, that he knew them far better than the people in his own train, and that, having met them for an instant under immense and timeless skies, as they were hurled across the continent to a thousand destinations, they had met, passed, vanished, yet would remember this forever. And he thought the people in the two trains felt this, also; slowly they passed each other now, and their mouths smiled and their eyes grew friendly, but he thought there was some sorrow and regret in what they felt. For having lived together as strangers in the immense and swarming city, they had now met upon the everlasting earth, hurled past each other for a moment between two points of time upon the shining rails; never to meet, to speak, to know each other any more, and the briefness of their days, the destiny of man, was in that instant greeting and farewell."

He sees from a train a boy trying to decide to go after a girl; wandering the streets of New York, he sees death come to four men; through one of his students at the university, he comes in contact with an old Jewess wailing a son dead for a year. Each of these moments is completely done; most of them, indeed, overwrought. From the country seen from a train he derives "a wild and solemn joy

THE SORROWS OF THOMAS WOLFE

—the sense of nameless hope, impossible desire, and man's tragic brevity." He reacts to most circumstances, it must seem to us, excessively. But to men and women he does not really answer. The old Jewess's grief fills him "with horror, anger, a sense of cruelty, disgust, and pity." The passion aroused returns to himself. And it is precisely because his passions cannot attain their object, and in one person know peace, that he turns in rage and desire toward the millions. There is in Eugene every emotion you wish but one; there is no love.

The most striking passages in Wolfe's novels always represent these moments of comprehension. For a moment, but a moment only, there is a sudden release of compassion, when some aspect of suffering and bewildered humanity is seized, when the other's emotion is in a timeless completion known. Then the moment passes, and compassion fails. For Eugene Gant, the only satisfactory relationship with another human creature is one which can have no continuity. For the boy at the street corner, seen in the indecision of youthful lust, he has only understanding and pity; the train from which he looks moves on and nothing more is required of Eugene. But if he should approach that same boy on the street, if he should come close enough to overhear him, he would hear only the defilement of language, words which would awaken in him only hate and disgust. He would himself become lonely, strange and cruel. For emotions such as these, unless they can be used with the responsibility of the artist, must remain a torment to the man.

The only human relationship which endures is that of the child to his family. And that is inescapable: once having been, it cannot cease to be. His father is still his father, though dying; and his brother Ben, though dead, remains his brother. He loves and he hates and knows why no more than the poet he quotes. What he does know is that love has been forbidden him.

The only contemporary literary influence on Wolfe which was at all strong was that of Joyce. I shall consider it here only to note that while we know that Joyce could only have created Stephen Dedalus out of the conflicts of his own youth, we never think of Stephen simply as the young Joyce, any more than we think of Hamlet as Shakespeare. He is a creation. But in Wolfe's novels it is impossible to feel that the central figure has any existence apart from the author. He is called Eugene Gant, but that does not deceive any one for a moment; he is, beyond all doubt, Thomas Wolfe. There is, however, one important distinction to be made between them, and one which we should not allow ourselves to forget: Eugene Gant is always younger, by at least ten years, than Thomas Wolfe.

Wolfe described *Of Time and the River* as being devoted to "the period of wandering and hunger in a man's youth." And in it we are meant to take Eugene as every young man. The following volume would, Wolfe said, declare "a period of greater certitude, which would be dominated by a single passion." That, however, still remains to be seen. So far, Eugene has shown no capacity as a lover, except in casual contact with whores. When for a moment he convinces himself that he is in love with Ann, who is a nice simple conventional girl from Boston, he can only shriek at her and call her a bitch and a whore, which she certainly is not. The one contact which lasts for any time—leaving aside the blood ties which bind him to the Pentlands, his mother's people, and the Gants—is that with Starwick. Starwick is the only friend he makes in his two years at Harvard, and in Paris, some years later, he still regards his friendship with Starwick as the most valuable he has ever known.

It ends when he discovers that Starwick is a homosexual. And it has usually been assumed that the violence and bitterness with which it ends are due to disillusionment; the sudden turn in Eugene's affections for the young man may well be taken as a natural reaction to his learning, first that Ann is in love with Starwick, and only a little later how hopelessly deep is Starwick's infatuation with the young tough he has picked up, by apparent chance, one night in a Paris bar. But that is, I think, to take too simple a view of the affair. There is more to it than that. What we have been told about Starwick from his first appearance in the book is that, despite a certain affectation and oddity of manner, he is, as Eugene is not, a person capable of loving and being loved. What is suddenly revealed in Paris is that for him, too, love is a thing the world has forbidden. In Starwick's face Eugene sees his own fate. Just as in his brother Ben's complaint at his neglect, he had looked back through another's sight at his own neglected childhood and in his brother's death fore-mourned his own, so now, when he beats Starwick's head against the wall, he is but raging against his own frustration and despair.

In his father's yard, among the tombstones, has stood for years a marble angel. Old Gant curses it, all hope he thinks lost that he will ever get his money back for it. It stands a magnificent reminder of the time when as a boy, with winged ambition, he had wanted to be not merely a stonecutter but a sculptor. Then, unexpectedly a customer comes for it. The one symbol of the divine in the workshop is sold to adorn the grave of a prostitute; what the boy might have been the man lets go for such a purpose. It cannot be said that Thomas Wolfe ever sold his angel. But the faults of the artist are all of them traceable to the failures of the man. He achieved probably the utmost intensity of which incoherent writing is capable; he proved that an art founded solely on the individual, however strong his will, however vivid his sensations, cannot be sound, or whole, or even passionate, in a world such as ours, in which "the integrity of the individual consciousness has been broken down." How far it has broken down, I do not believe he ever knew, yet all that he did is made of its fragments.

The Kenyon Review: Winter, 1939

THE POETRY OF A. E. HOUSMAN

I

NOW THAT THE *Collected Poems* are out, we have all we shall ever know of A. E. Housman's poetry. The long silence that followed *A Shropshire Lad* was broken by Housman himself in 1922, when he brought out his *Last Poems* while, as he said, he was still there to see them through the press. He died in 1936. And later that same year *More Poems* were published by Laurence Housman, who after a little decided that he could, without violating the wish of his older brother that nothing be printed after his death that was not up to the average level of what had already appeared, produce twenty-eight *Additional Poems*. Their number is now thirty-three, three of them rescued from old magazines, two from the poet's papers. To these have been appended three translations from the Greek, made long ago for an anthology of odes from the Greek dramatists. The remaining manuscripts and notes have been destroyed. The way in which Housman's poetry has been published is marked throughout by his passion for distinction, his craving to be famous, his equally strong and perverse dislike of being known.

The posthumous poems will not much change the estimation in which Housman has been held. They are work worthy of that proud mind. The *Additional Poems*, while they increase the sum of his poetry, add no poetic quality that was not there before. This they could hardly do, for it is apparent from the list of dates, incomplete as it is, which Laurence Housman has allowed to be included in the present volume, that they were composed along with the poems we already know. Some of them are contemporaneous with *A Shropshire Lad*; the latest, as far as anyone knows, is from 1925. What they do is to let us see the poet plain. Now that we have his poetry whole, we know what his personal plight was, and that is bound to affect our reading of all the poems. To know "Oh, who is that young sinner with the handcuffs on his wrist?" is to know something that we should have known all along about those culprits of *A Shropshire Lad*. We have known and long known those hanged boys who hear the stroke of eight from the clock in the tower on the market place and never hear the stroke of nine. We know now for what crime all of them have been condemned. We have known when the noose went round their necks, but not whose head stood above the rope. They have many names and all have one name. Their features are not beyond recognition. The head is A. E. Housman's.

Romantic poetry as Housman received it was in need of correction. He corrected it. The romantic conflict of man against society, of man against immutable laws is still there, but presented by a man who had the classic craftsman's respect for both himself and his craft. The form is concise and accurate; but, for all their lightness, his poems never lose the sense of earth; for all their grace, they are tough enough to sustain a considerable irony. The limits within which Housman was able to feel at all were strict, but within them he felt intensely, and both strictness and intensity are in his verse.

His style has in it nothing strange. It is not unconventional; it is extremely careful never to affront conventional ideas of what a poetic style should be. The truth was quite strange enough. Poetry that pardons the poet nothing less than the truth, once the truth is assured, pardons him everything. The passion for truth was in Housman. He could, in his poetry, condemn himself as contemporary opinion—in the very year *A Shropshire Lad* was written—had condemned Wilde. When almost all others had abandoned him, Housman sent Wilde a copy of *A Shropshire Lad* to prison; Wilde's answer was *A Ballad of Reading Gaol*. But it was not only on account of the poet that Housman had to consider prison; there was someone else, whom he had known more closely, confined. His death is recorded in *The Isle of Portland*. Housman could go beyond imprisonment; not once, but many times, he sent his culprit straight to the scaffold. For whatever was will and conscience in Housman was conservative. It was on will that his career was founded and it was continued with a conscience as scrupulous as it was churlish, so that he could end, Kennedy Professor of Latin at Cambridge, all honors at his disposal and all declined. He was quite ready, if not willing, in his career as in his style, to conform outwardly to convention. For both career and style are masks.

"While I was at the Patent Office I read a great deal of Greek and Latin at the British Museum of an evening. While at University College, which is not residential, I lived alone in lodgings in the environs of London. *A Shropshire Lad* was written at Byron Cottage, 17 North Road, Highgate, where I lived from 1886 to 1905."

This, as it stands, is honest enough; but, as so often happens in what Housman wrote, behind the straightforward statement there is much that is not said. In 1892, Housman had been able to return to that academic career from which he had been uncomplainingly banished ten years before, when, at Oxford, he had failed to obtain honors in the Final School of *Literae Hummaniores*. Alone he had done it. His gifts that were to make him the most formidable Latinist in England had never been in doubt, not even as a boy, when he had been the terror of his classical masters lest he should ask them some questions they were not prepared to answer. By his studies published in learned reviews, he had made himself known as he was willing to be known, as a scholar with that minute and accurate knowledge of the classical tongues which, as he said, affords Latin professors their only excuse for existing. He was not yet the great scholar he was to become, but the greatness of his qualities had been recognized wherever men cared for these things and, what is perhaps more important, he had himself already correctly appraised them.

About this time something happened to Housman that was not in accord with his will. What that was, there is no way of knowing, or even when it happened, unless from his poetry. *A Shropshire Lad* includes no poem written before 1890; the greater part of it was written in the first half of 1895. Whatever that experience was, whether he had been prepared for it at Oxford, as there seems some reason to suppose, or whether it came to him unexpectedly in London, it was profound and fatal. It was followed, as we know, by great emotional perturbation. It left Housman a poet. "And I think that to transfuse emotion—not to transmit thought but to set up in the reader's sense a vibration corresponding to what was felt by the writer—is the peculiar function of poetry." Alfred Housman in 1895 was thirty-six years of age.

II

No matter where we open Housman's poems, we are almost sure to be struck with how young are those who suffer in them, how brief and sure their suffering—its course predictable, since all has been known before:

> These, in the day when heaven was falling,
> The hour when earth's foundations fled,
> Followed their mercenary calling
> And took their wages and are dead.

THE POETRY OF A. E. HOUSMAN

Their shoulders held the sky suspended;
They stood, and earth's foundations stay;
What God abandoned, these defended,
And saved the sum of things for pay.

Whatever the occasion that gave rise to them, these moving lines can scarcely be read without bringing to mind the part played by the professional soldiers of the British Army in the retreat from Mons. They are called, however, simply *Epitaph on an Army of Mercenaries*, and, as they stand, are as applicable to the soldiers of some desperate and remote army in some forgotten war of antiquity as they are to the men of 1914. Here, a particular situation has produced a tragic emotion; whatever is lacking we can supply, so that the event behind the lines is adequate to the emotion. But this is not always so in Housman. If—to follow Joyce's excellent and convenient definitions —pity is present in poetry whenever what is grave and constant in human sufferings is united with the human sufferer; terror, whenever what is grave and constant in human sufferings is united with the secret cause, then pity and terror should scarcely be lacking from anything that Housman wrote. And pity and terror do not lack in this noble and completely successful poem. And yet, in Housman's poetry as a whole, something is lacking. Despite an apparent clarity such that almost any poem seems ready to deliver its meaning at once, there is always something that is not clear, something not brought into the open, something that is left in doubt. Housman knew very well what he was doing. He could always put himself in the reader's place. You must, he wrote his brother, "consider how, and at what stage, that man of sorrows is to find out what it is all about. You are behind the scenes and know all the data; but he knows only what you tell him." What Housman told the reader is clear. But there is much that he would not, and while he lived could not, tell him. Of the suffering we have no doubt, but something, it seems, has been suppressed that it is essential to know of the particular situation of the human sufferer. There is an emotion here that is unaccounted for. It is apparently united to the secret cause.

Ay, look: high heaven and earth ail from the prime foundation;
All thoughts to rive the heart are here, and all are vain:
Horror and scorn and hate and fear and indignation—
Oh why did I awake? When shall I sleep again?

There is much here that is moving; but again the essential is not evident. Sophocles also believed that a man's best fate would be

141

never to be born and that, failing this, it was best for him to perish young. But Sophocles' pessimism does not, as Housman's seems to do, exist in a void.

The passion of the lad on the scaffold is made appallingly present to us; but for what crime he is being punished is not, in any of the poems in which he occurs, made clear. What had he done, that other lad who lay dead, never to rise, never to stir forth free, to be sent to the island where

> Black towers above the Portland light
> The felon-quarried stone?

Or those lads so in love with the grave, why are they so attracted to that unfeeling solitude? It is not enough to blame the primal fault. Death has its attraction, and it is possible for a poet to put it in a moral framework so that we know, not only how strong it is, but its motivation. Yeats has done it, not once, but many times. But in Housman we move so rapidly from the personal situation to an impersonal despair that we cannot but feel that something has been left out. What has been left out is his personal plight, which did not find a perfect solution in poetry and probably could not, so long as no place could be found for it in any moral scheme of which Housman's mind could approve. The facts are clear; the meaning is not. "Even when poetry has a meaning, as it usually has, it may be inadvisable to draw it out," Housman wrote. "Perfect understanding will sometimes extinguish pleasure."

It is possible that Housman did not want his meaning drawn out; but about that I am not certain. Perfect understanding of his poems depends upon knowledge of his personal plight, for until that is known, the emotion must seem in excess of its object. Now that we know from the posthumous poems what that plight was, all slips into place. The despair is explained; the scholar's abandonment of Propertius for Manilius; the reticence that at last seemed to fix his mouth in a perpetual snarl; the churlish silence which made the poet who had written the poems which above all others in our time have been loved into the least lovely of men. There is point to his philosophy. And we are at last in a position to understand the special pathos of A Shropshire Lad.

III

What Housman did in A Shropshire Lad was not to create an object of desire. That he had found, presumably in London, and none can doubt the intensity, the reality, the impossibility of his love. What he did was to make himself into a proper lover, or at least into one of an appropriate age, and to create in a country called Shropshire conditions where that love—without ceasing to be what it was—could come into its own. He became young, but with such a youth as he had never known. The hands which for almost twenty years had scarcely left their Greek and Latin texts, were put to the plow. He was a young yeoman, complete with an ancestry, which Housman made up, perhaps without knowing it, since he seems presently to have persuaded himself that it was his own. The heart of the youth was his, the temper was his own, and, what is most remarkable, the voice he found for him had the vibration of very youth.

The country of *A Shropshire Lad* is so created that it is with surprise that we learn, not only that Housman was not native to Shropshire, but that he had seldom been there. But once we begin to think about it, we see, not only that no such countryside exists in England, but that there could have been none like it in the last century. It is a country that belongs to the dead. What was important to Housman about Shropshire was that it lay on the western horizon of the Worcestershire in which his own boyhood was passed. The West has long been in popular imagination where the dead dwell, and, at the very time that Housman was writing, English soldiers did not die—they went West.

> Comrade, look not on the west:
> 'Twill have the heart out of your breast;
> 'Twill take your thoughts and sink them far,
> Leagues beyond the sunset bar.

It is underworld. And to Housman, with his mind on the classical poets, it is probable that the West is identified, not only with their underworld of the nerveless dead, but also with a classical world, long dead, in which loves such as his would not have found all the laws of God and man against them:

> Look not in my eyes, for fear
> They mirror true the sight I see,
> And there you find your face too clear
> And love it and be lost like me.
> One the long nights through must lie
> Spent in star-defeated sighs,
> But why should you as well as I
> Perish? gaze not in my eyes.

If we love at all, it is because our bodies, if not we, anticipate death for us. But in this poem of Housman's it is to be noticed that the loved one can, like the lover, love himself and that if he should once be attainted by that desire, he would perish. In the two lovers identity of desire is possible, but the identification of love with death is prompt and precise. Just as in A la Recherche du Temps Perdu, Proust's narrator has never such conviction of completely possessing Albertine as when he sits motionless by her side and looks at her lost in sleep, so, in Housman's poetry, there is no complete consummation of desire until the lad he loves lies dead. The body that lust demanded must be all bone and contemplation before he is finished with fear and condemnation. Even then, Housman cannot delude himself into believing that any love, least of all a love like his, can long survive on the contemplative satisfactions of the grave.

> Crossing alone the nighted ferry
> With the one coin for fee,
> Whom, on the wharf of Lethe waiting,
> Count you to find? Not me.
>
> The brisk fond lackey to fetch and carry,
> The true, sick-hearted slave,
> Expect him not in the just city
> And free land of the grave.

To Housman, all loves are frustrate or faithless. The best a girl can do is to listen to a boy's lies and follow him into the leafy wood; the best the boy can do there is not work her ill. The conception is, of course, prejudiced. Still, what Housman sets down is not so far from the actual conditions under which love is made in youth. The youth Housman reverted to was an imaginary one, his charm is factitious, and yet because he is so often true to the imagination, he seems to speak, not merely for himself, but for all who are, or have ever been, young. What we should know from our own responses to Housman's poetry, if we have not already learned it more explicitly from Proust's prose, is that such desire as his, while it differs from others in its object, is most painfully distinguished from them by the brevity of time in which it is possible, even as unrequited desire. The youth's garland is always briefer than a girl's. And it is this constant present and inescapable pressure of time that constitutes the special poignancy of Housman's poetry.

But if his personal plight is responsible for much of the poignancy of the emotions that went to the making of Housman's poetry, it also placed serious limitations on his emotions. And what nature had not limited, Housman himself thwarted. He is the poet of the end of an age in England, and he is the best poet that could be produced at the end, as he is probably, in England, the purest poet of the whole age. His range is small. We have only to look largely at poetry to see that there is an honesty, a humanity, that simply is not in Housman, any more than it was in the world that made him. What was left in that world was enough for him to perceive how impossible is the achievement of all desire, how vain the search for honor and happiness, and yet what pathos, what beauty, what grandeur even, man releases in their vain pursuit.

Poetry: June, 1940

*FINNEGANS WAKE**

I

ALL THAT JAMES JOYCE has written is of a piece, for the material with which he has had to work has not been added to since he went into exile thirty-five years ago. *Finnegans Wake*, in so far as it had to do with the world of observation, is made up of memories of Dublin. The men and women in it are, no less than those of his first book of stories, Dubliners. But they have long inhabited a city which scarcely exists apart from Joyce's mind. Their Dublin is the one the young Joyce knew, but no one who now went to the capital of Mr. De Valera could wholly find it. So much has changed in the real city and more perhaps in the remembered city. Joyce's memory is remarkable, but his sight was always dim, and for most of the years he has been out of Ireland he has been almost blind. Little has come in from the outside to alter what he recalls, and yet all has been changed, even those aspects of Dublin which we should expect least to change.

> riverrun, past Eve and Adam's, from swerve of shore to bend of bay, brings us by a commodius vicus of recirculation back to Howth Castle and Environs.

This, the opening sentence of *Finnegans Wake*, can be read at least in two ways. It is true that the River Liffey coming into Dublin passes a church called Adam's and Eve's on the outskirts of the city: its course at last brings it to the sea past Howth Head. But the sentence also says that if we start with the first woman and man and follow the course of time, which runs like a river through history, we shall be brought at last to a contemporary city which might as well as not be Dublin. There are other implications here to be ob-

---

* This study first appeared in the *Southern Review* of Winter, 1940. Bishop intended to include it in his projected volume of essays. He had revised it with this end in view and had written a new section that dealt with the prankquean episode. These changes and additions have been made and some obvious errors corrected.

served if we are trying to give a temporal meaning to this statement. For Joyce in this opening sentence not only informs us that his work is a timeless history, such as the seventeenth-century philosopher Giambattista Vico dreamed might be written, but he also warns us that we must be prepared to accept Vico's theory that the course of history is circular and that an end is always also a beginning. Vicus is not only the Latin form of the Italian's name, it is in Latin a street of houses, and there is in one of the suburbs of Dublin a Vico Street; commodius is not only commodious, but also Commodus, for we have now reached that stage in our history which is characterized by the abuse of luxury, and which corresponds to that state of civilization in Rome which saw the appearance of Commodus. There are perhaps still other ways to read this sentence, with which Joyce begins his book, but which itself has no beginning. It is enough for the moment to say that it not only clearly announces what *Finnegans Wake* is about, but that its very ambiguity forces us to consider how ambiguous are the relations of time and space, which is one of the important themes of this "strangest dream that was ever half dreampt." Every word is, as the physicists would say, a time-space event.

The Dubliners in this dream have little left them but the night-life of the mind and of the mind of a man who has long lived, and not only at night, almost in darkness. The Dublin in which Joyce came to young manhood had a place in space. But can one say that of the Dublin of his exile? And yet the one is the other, preserved and enriched in time. Dublin was always for Joyce a place of sounds; it is now composed only of voices, whose speech, even as they speak, becomes something more and less than common communication. Even those aspects of it which one would expect least to change, like the river Liffey that flows through it, have undergone a change which we would hardly expect to happen except in sleep. As in the oldest myths, they have acquired voices. The Liffey is much more than the Liffey; it is "gossipaceous" Anna Livia Plurabelle. It is one river and it is all rivers, and as we shall presently discover much more than a river. However unconsciously these changes in his material may have occurred, Joyce has remarkably rendered them conscious. I have been told that the start of the present work was when, peering at a photograph of Howth Head on a postcard, he saw the promontory changing in his dim sight into the shape of a sleeping man. That man is the sleeper of *Finnegans Wake*.

II

Joyce from the start was a poet; but in *Dubliners*, and through the *Portrait of the Artist as a Young Man*, his prose is submitted to the strictest discipline of Flaubert. He was still, when he wrote these two books, so close to his material that the realistic method is adequate to his demands. Where he surpasses any other follower of Flaubert, and indeed Flaubert himself, is in the range of his prose, which he can on occasion bring close to the conditions of music, without ever allowing it to destroy the conventions of realism. For Joyce is heir not only to the great realistic tradition of the nineteenth century; he inherited as well the opposition to it. In *Ulysses* realism was carried much further than anyone had then carried it, though, considered as a narrative of real happenings, it contained nothing that was not implicit in the principles Flaubert had laid down. That book was painful because of the intensity with which each moment in the eighteen hours of its action was recorded; it was difficult because upon his narrative Joyce has imposed a great weight of symbolic meaning.

The symbolic element was very slight in the *Portrait*; Stephen, with his statement, *I will not serve*, is referred to Satan; he is also, at least in one scene, the greater prophet whom Cranly as John the Baptist precedes. He has been named Stephen in premonition that he will be the protomartyr of the new revelation; he is the son of Dedalus, the artificer who first wrought wings for man. In *Ulysses*, though it was often painful to follow the realistic narrative, it was not hard, if one read and remembered every word. What was hard to make out, what in fact no one commentator ever did make out, were the very complicated meanings which Joyce had seen as implied in the meeting of Stephen Dedalus and Leopold Bloom.

In *Finnegans Wake* it is the realistic element that is difficult to make out. Almost anything, Joyce says, can happen at night, and as to just what is happening throughout this long night we are deliberately left uncertain. On the other hand, the symbolic meanings, though they are many and complicated, and though the way of writing "Doublecrossing twofold truths and devising tingling tailwords" is so devious as to put the reader often in doubt, are certainly not impossible to follow. There are any number of passages that I am unable to elucidate; there are references so personal that they will be nothing to anyone but Joyce; there are others so remote that not one in a thousand will understand them. But darkness, and even pointlessness, are within Joyce's intention. "A hundred cares, a tithe of troubles," cries the Liffey, the river of life, as it is about to be lost and merged with the sea, "and is there one who understands me? One in a thousand years of the nights?" This is man's history, and it must proceed in obscurity. But at last day dawns. And though at the end of the book the impression of any particular life in it may be dim, we should not be unaware of what Joyce conceives to be the truth of his history.

In *Finnegans Wake* Joyce has made an almost complete break with the Flaubertian tradition. When portions of the book began appearing in *Transition* and elsewhere, under the title of *Work in Progress*, most readers assumed that the new book would take up where *Ulysses* had left off. Until then the last thing of Joyce's anybody had read was Molly Bloom's monologue, in which the mind of a woman was presented in a form almost as free from logic as a dream. And when it became apparent that one of the characters in *Finnegans Wake* was asleep, it was naturally assumed that it was the meanderings of his thought under the oppression of sleep that were being presented. The language in which it was written seemed to have been invented admirably to present the night life of the mind. And so it is. But if *Finnegans Wake* is taken to be as a whole the dramatic projection of all that passes through one man, now soundly, now fitfully sleeping, and once or twice starting into momentary wakefulness, it soon becomes not only unintelligible, but artistically impossible. Humphrey Chimpden Earwicker is not a person in the Flaubertian sense, though occasionally he appears as one. He is not an individual whom a dream is constantly transforming into someone else. He is an individual who must not be considered apart from the universal. His transformations are the essence of his being, since everything in the book, including the words in which it is written, are constantly in the process of becoming something else. He can be sought on the realistic level, as can every other personage in the book; for if he could not be found there we should not be concerned with his history. The common man includes all history; he is what he is because of all heroes and saints. What was, is. The divine, the heroic past is his human, all too human present. His is a spiritual night, not merely the night of Dublin. And Dublin is now Purgatory, as in *Ulysses* it was Hell.

III

Present in *Finnegans Wake* is a simple situation which, involving as it does a slight but irremediable change in human emotions, might have made the basis for another such story as those that appeared in *Dubliners*. Humphrey Chimpden Earwicker is the proprietor of a pub, The Bristol, in Dublin, somewhere between Phoenix Park and the River Liffey, close to the former village of Chapelizod, which is reputed to be the birthplace of Iseult. He is a man well on in his fifties, married, and the father of a daughter in her teens, Isobel, and of two younger sons, the twins Jerry and Kevin. He and his wife, who shares his bed, have come to the age where all the passion they once felt for each other has turned toward their children. Save for the fact that *Finnegans Wake* could scarcely have been written save by an aging man, one could imagine that this story, told in Joyce's early manner, might well have taken its place beside that poignant little masterpiece, *The Dead*. But Joyce in *Ulysses* was already leaving the conventions of naturalism behind him. How far he has since departed from them may be indicated by examining the episode of the prankquean, which is not only short enough to be quoted in its entirety, but interesting as the first exposition of what is to be the dominant disturbance of Earwicker's dream.

"It was of a night, late, lang time agone, in an auldstane eld, when Adam was delvin and his madameen spinning watersilts, when mulk mountynotty man was everybully and the first leal ribberrobber that ever had her ainway everybuddy to his lovesaking eyes and everybilly lived alove with everybiddy else, and Jarl van Hoother had his burnt head high up in his lamphouse, laying cold hands on himself. And his two little jiminies, cousins of ourn, Tristopher and Hilary, were kickaheeling their dummy on the oil cloth flure of his homerigh, castle and earthenhouse. And, be dermot, who come to the keep of his inn only the niece-of-his-in-law, the prankquean. And the prankquean pulled a rosy one and made her wit foreninst the dour. And she lit up and fireland was ablaze. And spoke she to the dour in her petty perusienne: Mark the Wans, why do I am alook alike a poss of porterpease? And that was how the skirtmisshes began. But the dour handworded her grace in dootch nossow: Shut! So her grace o'malice kidsnapped up the jiminy Tristopher and into the shandy westerness she rain, rain, rain. And Jarl van Hoother warlessed after her with soft dovesgall: Stop deef stop come back to my earin stop. But she swaradid to him: Unlikelihud. And there was a brannewail that same sabboath night of falling angles somewhere in Erio. And the prankquean went for her forty years' walk in Tourlemonde and she washed the blessings of the lovespots off the jiminy with soap sulliver suddles and she had her four owlers masters for to tauch him his tickles and she converted him to the onesure allgood and he became a luderman. So then she started to rain and to rain and, be redtom, she was back again at Jarl van Hoother's in a brace of samers and the jiminy with her in her pinafrond, lace at night, at another time. And where did she come but to the bar of his bristolry. And Jarl von Hoother had his baretholobruised heels drowned in his cellarmalt, shaking warm hands with himself and the jimminy Hilary and the dummy in their first infancy were below on the tearshcct, wringing and coughing, like brodar and histher. And the prankquean nipped a paly one and lit up again and redcocks flew flackering from the hillcombs. And she made her wilter before the wicked, saying: Mark the Twy, why do I am alook alike two poss of porterpease? And: Shut! says the wicked, handwording her madesty. So her madesty a 'forethought set down a jiminy and took up a jiminy and all the lilipath ways to Woeman's Land she rain, rain, rain. And Jarl von Hoother bleethered atter her with a loud finegale: Stop domb stop come back with my earring stop. But the prankquean swaradid: Am liking it. And there was a wild old grannewwail that laurency night of starshootings somewhere in Erio. And the prankqucan went for her forty years' walk in Turnlemeem and she punched the curses of cromcruwell with the nail of a top into the jiminy and she had her four larksical monitrix to touch him his tears and she provorted him to the onecertain allsecure and he became a tristian. So then she started raining, raining, and in a pair of changers, be dom ter, she was back again at Jarl von Hoother's and the Larryhill with her under her abromette. And why would she halt at all if not by the ward of his mansionhom of another nice lace for the third charm? And Jarl von Hoother had his hurricane hips up to his pantrybox, ruminating in his holdfour stomachs (Dare! O dare!), and the jimminy Toughertrees and the dummy were belove on the watercloth, kissing and spitting, and roguing and poghning like knavepaltry and naivebride and in their second infancy. And the prankquean picked a blank and lit out and the valleys lay twinkling. And she made her wittest in front of the arkway of trihump, asking: Mark the Tris, why do I am alook alike three poss of porter pease? But that was how the skirtmishes endupped. For like the campbells acoming with a fork lance of lightning, Jarl von Hoother Boanerges himself, the old terror of the dames, came hip hop handihap out through the pikeopened arkway of his three shuttoned castles, in his broadginger hat and his civic cholar and his allabuff hemmed and his bullbraggin soxangloves and his ladbroke breeks and his cattegut bandolair and his furframed panuncular cumbottes like a rudd yellan gruebleen orangeman in his violet indigonation, to the whole length of the strength of his bowman's bill. And he clopped his rude hand to his eacy hitch and he ordurd and his thick spch spck for her to

shut up shop, dappy. And the duppy shot the shutter clup (Perkod-
huskurunbarggruauyagokgorlayorgromgremmitghundhurthrumathuna-
radidillifaititillibumullunukkunun!) And they all drank free. For one
man in his armour was a fat match always for any girls under shurts.
And that was the first peace of illiterative porthery in all the flamend
floody flatuous world. How kirssy the tiler made a sweet unclose to
the Narwhealian captol. Saw fore shalt thou sea. Betoun ye and be.
The prankquean was to hold her dummyship and the jimminies was
to keep the peacewave and van Hoother was to git the wind up. Thus
the hearsomeness of the burger felicitates the whole of the polis."

It is a rare reader who, when he first encounters this passage,
will be able to make heads or tails of it. Like much that happens in
dreams, it has no apparent sense; or rather it appears to have some
sense that both haunts and eludes us, like a dream that we cannot forget on waking. The words are blurred as by sleep, so that even their
sound is vague and unfamiliar; the sleeper's hearing is distressingly
indistinct; he is thwarted even in his speech so that at times he
stutters. Yet, when we come back to the story of the prankquean,
after having been through the whole book, it is clear that it contains
the most important elements of the situation which lies beneath the
sleeper's anguish. For by now we have grown used to those symbols
which lie upon his mind, like lowering clouds upon a promontory,
concealing the outlines. It is not impossible to recognize the various
persons that appear to him, though, as is the way in dreams, all have
disguised themselves, even to their names.

Earwicker is himself at first Howth Head, that bold promontory
at the entrance to Dublin harbor. His wife is first seen as Eve (madameen) to his Adam and as the River Liffey (spinning watersilts),
which under Howth Head flows into the sea. He then, without ceasing
to be the promontory with its lighthouse, washed by cold waves (laying cold hands on himself) is incarnate as the Earl of Howth. Since
Earwicker is by name and origin Danish—as indeed is Dublin itself—
it is proper that his title should take a Danish form, Jarl van Hoother.
(Later in the book, page 414, this title becomes Mr van Howten,
which allows us to identify the van Houtens in the letter, to which I
shall presently refer, as Earwicker's family.) The two boys are no
longer connected with the divine twins, the Dioscuri, sons of God,
and the name they wore while still worshipped in Vico's heroic age,
the Gemini, has been corrupted to the shape of the vulgar oath, By
Jiminy! They are the jiminies. Since Earwicker is throughout his dream
assailed by thoughts of incest, the ties of blood have been loosened;
they have ceased to be his sons and become mere "cousins of ourn."

Their actual names, under which they have already been obscurely introduced, have also been altered; one is called Tristopher, while the other, to preserve that contrast which always characterizes them, is made Hilary, that is, the cheerful one, as opposed to the sadness which is implicit in the first syllable of Tristram, which has been combined with the last two syllables of Christopher. The daughter is the prankquean.

It has been pointed out by Mr. Harry Levin that there is in her story a reference to a Princess of Connaught, Grace O'Malley, who was denied the hospitality of Howth Castle one day, as she was returning from a visit to Queen Elizabeth, and in retaliation kidnapped one of the children of the Lord of the Castle. This is undoubtedly true, as calling the prankquean "her grace o'Malice" makes clear. But this, like the other details derived from Irish history, is significant only as it serves to furnish the allegory. The oath "be dermot" refers to Dermot MacMurrough, the King of Leinster, who was responsible for the introduction of English rule into Ireland. He, too, was implicated in a famous abduction, when, without love, he carried away Eva, the wife of O'Ruarc. Hence it is not inappropriate that his name be used here. The oaths uttered at each subsequent appearance of the prankquean are, of course, anagrams of "be dermot."

The time of the tale is said to be that of Adam and Eve. It begins in that age of lost innocence when all loves were permitted and "everybilly lived alove with everybiddy else," a time beyond history, toward which the sleeper in his dream has retreated. But the Fall has occurred, as we are made aware by the statement that Adam was delvin—that is, both delving and devilling. Even in the dream, the sense of guilt persists and makes itself felt whenever those desires which sleep has released bring the sleeper up against one of those taboos around which society is built.

The prankquean asks her riddle, snatches up one of the boys and, running away with him, returns to her condition of the rain that replenishes the river. The kidnapping is obviously an allegorical rendering of the father's fear that life will bear his sons away from him; but there is also indicated a jealous fear that the mother, who is life renewed in the person of her daughter, will deprive him of their love. The passage will bear a still further and more devious interpretation, which is that the father is afraid of his desire to himself become the abductor of his daughter.

The prankquean takes the child out into the world and, with the aid of the four old men, who have long outlived their lives as men, succeeds in turning him into a man. At her second appearance, Earwicker still wears his title of Earl of Howth; but he has resumed his ordinary place behind the bar of The Bristol. She again asks her riddle, sets down the stolen twin and makes off with the other where the father cannot follow. At the first asking, there was a report of the war in heaven and of the anger of God, in the wail that accompanies the fall of the disobedient angels; at the second asking, it is the stars that shoot from their places and the divine remonstrance seems to be recognized as a superstition and an old granny's tale. It is to be noticed that during the time of their absence, the nature of the twins is interchanged. At the third asking of the riddle, the Lord of Howth has recovered his aspect as a promontory, with storms all about him, displaying lightning about his head and—in one of those words composed each of a hundred letters which throughout *Finnegans Wake* signify thunder, the sound of God's anger—manifests himself as a god. Peace is restored to the household as soon as he makes evident his authority.

According to Vico, the beginnings of religion are to be sought in fear of the godhead, as made known to man through the flashing of lightning and the sound of thunder. It was because of this fear of a force that could strike anywhere under the sky that men first began to refrain from enacting their brutish lusts in the face of heaven—*contenando la loro libidine bestiale di exercitarla in faccia del cielo*. Thence arose the institution of marriage, which meant the holding to one woman throughout life. It is interesting to note that Joyce's own fear of thunder was extreme and that, according to the account of his most intimate friends, he could not work in peace unless his whole family was with him under one roof. As we near the close of the episode of the prankquean, the sleeping Earwicker, who has been lying immobile as a promontory, moves and at once becomes a giant and so an enemy of the gods. Then he himself assumes the attributes of a god. Now this, more or less, is what Joyce has done in conceiving his timeless history. Not only is conscious being outside of time the essence of any god, it is also true that Joyce's relation to Earwicker is not the ordinary one of author to character, but that of creator to his creature. This stout Dubliner, between fifty-odd and fifty-seven years of age, has no real existence outside the mind of his maker.

If in the beginning, it was fear of the gods that first led man to restrict his appetites and in particular to avoid complete nakedness, homosexuality and incest—which remained privileges of the classical gods—he has now become his own divinity and himself prevents the acting out of forbidden desires. Though much is permitted in dreams that would not be allowed when awake, yet, even in sleep, conscience still operates and will not let everything be done or even thought openly and without shame.

In the dream, the names of the two sons of Earwicker have been altered, while the name of his daughter has been obliterated. In her passive aspect, she is the dummy, who is represented as being engaged, now with one, now with the other of her brothers, on the floor in the innocent love-play of children in their first infancy. Actually, Earwicker's daughter is no longer a child and the boys, who are as yet children, are advanced in the course of the dream to the age of men. The words that describe the love-play cease to be innocent. The second twin becomes a tristian, while the first receives the appellation Toughertrees, which not only carries a suggestion of increased sexual vitality and vigor, but also in its last syllable repeats with lengthened vowel the first syllable of Tristram. Tristram is the guise which the sleeper always assumes as a lover; for the moment he has identified himself with his sons, in whom his own youth is renewed. He not only lives, but, in his imagination, loves again through them. The prankquean calls him Mark, after herself having been brought in as "only the niece-of-his-in-law," which would be a correct description of the relationship, if only Iseult of Ireland had been married, not to him, but to her lover Tristram. Mark of Cornwall was the uncle of Tristram.

The riddle which the prankquean puts to him has the sound of "A pint of porter, please," a request that Earwicker must constantly have heard across the bar of The Bristol, imposed upon the sound of "Why do I look alike as two peas in a pod?" The sense of the riddle is, of course, "Why do I, your daughter, look as much like my mother at the age when she first stirred your love as two peas in a pod?" The daughter is the rain which, falling on the sources of the Liffey, in time becomes merged with the river. The daughter is Iseult of the Fair Hair, Mark's Queen, but a quean of pranks with Tristram; the mother of Iseult of the White Hand, whom Tristram married without love on his part, to be jealously guarded and at last destroyed by her love. So strong is the power of words on the sleeper, he is constantly confusing the two Iseults. At the third asking of the riddle, he is addressed by the prankquean as Mark the Tris; it would seem to follow from what has gone before that he is merely being called Mark the Third. But he at once takes alarm. Mark the husband is changing into Tristram the lover. The Freudian censor at once intervenes with orders to bring the episode to a close. Jarl von Hoother adds Boanerges, the son of thunder, to his title and himself takes on the rôle of the angry god. The sound of thunder is heard, everyone resumes his natural place and civic peace is restored.

Now what in all this has become of the Earwickers? Even when we have come to the end of this long, this all but unending, night and learned all that Joyce chooses to reveal about them, is anything more clear about them than that, as he says, "from the poign of fun where I am now crying to arrive you at they are on allfore as foibleminded as you can feel they are fablebodied"? Joyce never completely forgets his humble Dublin family, any more than, for all his pride, he was able through the long years of his exile to forget Dublin. But their bodies are so often and so fabulously transformed that at last we look to them only for such truth as may be contained in fables. Before taking off on a flight wider and bolder than any even Dedalus conceived, the old artificer has made sure of Irish ground under his feet. This much remains of that conscience which once made Joyce the most scrupulous of realists: that he has discovered or fabricated and placed among the actual circumstances with which his Dubliners are familiar some justification for the elements that go to make up his immense meditation on human fate. We start off in Phoenix Park, only to find ourselves in the Garden of Eden, where the Fall has just been reënacted. Even an orange peel will suffice to recall the forbidden tree and that first disobedience which was to lead to the redemption of mankind. And we are admonished: "Weeping thou shouldst not be but that divine scheming ever adoring be." This is not Earwicker stuttering in his sleep. The voice is Joyce's. But the *felix culpa* are Saint Augustine's words.

What has happened here is that Joyce has entered that "strange dark cavern of speculation," of which he already was aware as a young man, but from which he withdrew, feeling that the hour had not yet come. Just as *Ulysses* was originally planned as a short story for *Dubliners*, so *Finnegans Wake* was adumbrated at a time when Joyce was writing *A Portrait of an Artist as a Young Man* in a prose as delicate and clear as it was disciplined. Even then, Stephen Dedalus longed to let the consciousness of language slip from his mind. Already he chafed to know that all the crises and victories and secessions of history had been passed on to him in trite words in a language he could not call his own. He wanted to move among dead heaps of words and force the bones to speak. He could not forgive his countrymen for discarding their own speech and adopting that of their conquerors. We must assume that Joyce is speaking for himself as a young man, when he tells how Stephen frets in the shadow of the English language. But he was not yet ready for his present task. He had first to master English in a way no living Englishman had done. After *Ulysses,* his conscience was clear; he would now write an English that was "nat a language in any sinse of the world." He would make a language on which logic had no claim, where "the possible was the improbable and the improbable was the inevitable." So, it would belong only to him and Ireland and the night.

IV

The structure of *Finnegans Wake* has been taken from the *Scienza Nuova* of Giambattista Vico, a seventeenth century Neapolitan philosopher. The extent to which Joyce has drawn on Vico is made clear by Mr. Samuel Beckett in an essay in *Our Examination Round His Factification for Incamination of Work in Progress,* originally published ten years ago by Shakespeare and Company in Paris, and recently reprinted in this country. Much of this book was clearly prompted by Joyce himself, and, while not all the essays are of equal value, some of them are indispensable to an understanding of *Finnegans Wake.* And of these Mr. Beckett's, on the influence of Vico, Bruno and Dante on Joyce, is one.

According to Vico, every society must go through three ages, those of the gods, of heroes and of men. In the beginning was the thunder, which was god; men dwelt in rush-lit caves. It is religion that first set men on the path toward civilization. Cities are built; despotism becomes primitive feudalism, and this, as it advances, becomes democracy. Each age, as it degenerates, generates the following age; the seeds of corruption are the beginning of birth. At last democracy is anarchy, and it is this age which we have now reached, foreseen by Vico as a time of interdestruction. It is a confused age of transition, in which all falls apart and nothing holds. Then the hero returns, and another civilization starts a new barbarism. A new society can only rise as the Phoenix does from the ashes of the old.

Now it will be seen from this all too brief account that in Vico's philosophy the progress of history is circular. The progress in Joyce's work is cyclical. It begins in the middle of a sentence and ends on a sentence which does not end. *Finnegans Wake* is in four parts, which correspond to Vico's three ages, and a fourth in which all begins again. But these parts have other correspondences; each is given over to a quarter of the night, and the division into four also applies not only to society, but at the same time to the life of any man, all of which he timelessly knows in sleep. "A good clap, a fore wedding, a bad wake, tell hell's well." The divisions are variously given and insistently repeated in *Finnegans Wake*, but the briefest and perhaps most convenient to keep in mind while reading is that of "harrying, marrying, burying and binding." But as Mr. Beckett has warned us, it will not do to look for neat identifications. Each part of *Finnegans Wake* is dominated by one of these themes and in the order I have named, but it is not devoted to it. The circular form is one that seems to be especially sympathetic to the Irish mind, for many of the Irish fairy tales proceed in a circle, like the story of Oisin, where we are brought at the end back to the beginning. But in *Finnegans Wake* progress is not one cycle. There are countless epicycles. It seems to be essential to Joyce's conception that his work should be everywhere at its goal, that goal being what Vico called Providence—which in this book is the timeless consciousness of human history that once belonged to God.

Not only does the book as a whole show history as persisting "through intermittences of sullum fulminance, sollemn nuptialism, sallem sepulture and providential divining," but, just as the whole history of man may be contained in one man's history, so a single incident may discover a complete cycle. The letter which the hen scratches up from the dump, from among the fragments of orange peel, seems when we first read it to be merely a parody of any family letter.

"Dear whom it proceded to mention Maggy well & allathome's health well only the hate turned the mild on the van Houtens and the general's elections with the lovely face of some born gentleman with a beautiful present of wedding cakes for dear thankyou Chriesty and with grand funferall of poor Father Michael don't forget unto life's & Muggy well how are you Maggy & hopes soon to hear well & must now close it with fondest to the twoinns with four crosskrisses for holy paul holey corner holipoli whollyisland pee ess from (locust may eat all but this sign shall they never) affectionate largelooking tache of tch."

But looked at a little more closely it will be found to pass through the same four periods of history as *Finnegans Wake*. The letter originates, so we are told, from Boston (Mass.). That is to say, it is a message from another world. The dump on which it is found is also "a fatal midden or chip factory," the source of our knowledge of prehistory. The orange peel has been brought there from the East, from which is derived our traditional spiritual wisdom. The twins who are mentioned are two actual little boys, in the family around which all human history must revolve; but they will appear through the book as the opposing spirits of light and dark; they are Lucifer and Michael, and they assume other forms. And the four old men, who act throughout as a sort of chorus, are nonsensically introduced. They, too, will come in again and again, in their actual form as "four dear old heladies" from whom age has taken all but the memories of manhood, but also as the four Evangelists, the four points of the compass, the four master waves of Ireland, the four ancient Irish kingdoms, Leinster, Munster, Connaught and Ulster. The elaborately comic gloss on the letter—"with its studious omission of year number and era name from the date"—make it clear that Joyce is presenting it as a description of the timeless history he is writing in *Finnegans Wake*. But it is not until we come to Part III, where Shaun is brought in as a postman, that we begin to understand that what Joyce is saying is that the common sensual man does bear a message, a message from another world, but he no more knows what it means than the Postman knows what is contained in the missive he carries, but must not read. Human history is like a letter in "an everyday looking stamped envelope. Has anyone ever sufficiently looked at it?"

Though all that man has thought about himself in the past is nonsense, and though what we think of ourselves will in time seem no less nonsensical, nevertheless, the truth about man is in his history. To interpret it we must look to Shem the Penman. His name is a corruption of Jim the Penman, a forger in an old comedy that used to be played in Dublin, but under that name I think we shall find that Joyce has introduced himself into *Finnegans Wake*, just as in the *Portrait* and *Ulysses* he is brought in as Stephen Dedalus. There is more than a touch about Shem of Swift, for he too has existed in the past to live again in the present; but his career, which is as grossly and outrageously recounted as though he were some invention of Rabelais, is close enough to that of Joyce to allow his identification with the still "insufficiently malestimated notesnatcher." "He had to see life foully. And there were three men in him." And it is these men, Shaun, Jaun, Yawn, who being three are also one, for they compose a human trinity, that are consigned to death in Part III of the book, which is concerned with burial. But they are at the last moment resurrected, and presumably it is Shem, the writer, who is responsible for restoring the ordinary sensual man to life.

In considering a single turn of the wheel, I have been obliged also to follow its motion forward. It is this cyclical form of the book which perhaps more than anything else makes *Finnegans Wake* so exasperatingly difficult to read, and which, without more space than anyone can demand, makes it all but impossible for the commentator to convey what it is about. Joyce's own scrutiny of the letter, in the pages which follow its transcription, reveals much more than I have been able to set down here. And the form of the book as a whole may be reflected, not only as here in a paragraph, but in a sentence. To a degree that has probably never before been attained in prose, the form is content. "The lightning look, the birding cry, awe from the grave, everflowing on the times." Here the four periods of a man's life are indicated in the meaning of the words. But words are also harried, as once the gods harried men; words which have never existed before are brought into being; a word may be buried as Peter is buried in Patrick in the second paragraph on page one, and married, as when the name of the patron saint of Ireland is wedded to the peatrick, which is one of the curses of Ireland; and by all these means words that were dead are brought again to life.

V

"O tell me all about Anna Livia! I want to hear all about Anna Livia. Well, you know Anna Livia? Yes, of course, we all know Anna Livia. Tell me all. Tell me now. You'll die when you hear."

Thus begins the wonderful chapter about Anna Livia, the fifth in the first part of *Finnegans Wake*, which would contain the most beautiful writing Joyce has ever done, were it not exceeded by the passages where the river once more merges with the sea. For, as in *Ulysses*, nothing surpasses the last words of Molly Bloom, which are given over to an affirmation of the awe and abundance of life apart from our thoughts of it, so, in the new book, the surest triumphs of Joyce's poetry are reserved for the celebration of that river which is all rivers, which is the river of life and the river of lives. She is time, the stream which man enters to become history.

"Waiwhou was the first thurever burst? . . . She sid herself she hardly knows whoun the annals her graveller was, a dynast of Leinster, a wolf of the sea, or what he did or how blyth she played or how, when, why, where and who offon he jumpnad her." She appears first and last, simply as the river, as the man who plays against her is seen first as a promontory. In her initials we recognize the Semitic root A.L.P., from which comes the name of the river Aleph, the first letter of the Hebrew alphabet, and the corresponding Greek letter Alpha. She is the beginning of all things. As Anna, she is the great mother; as Livia, she contains all histories; as Plurabelle, she combines all women. The Liffey is filled by its confluent rivulets. She is Iseult-la-Belle, and therefore, according to legend, a princess of Leinster; (the first man's name to be mentioned is that of Tristram, the violator from out the sea, who is one hero of the medieval romance with whom the minstrel himself can be identified, since he is not only a warrior but a musician). She is all women who have ever been loved. She is also the young girl who will become a nun. She is Isobel, the daughter in that household around which so much of the book revolves. And there are various suggestions that the emotions which rise in the sleeping Earwicker for the girl are of an incestuous kind. This, on one level, is admitting what may be true, but what only the unconscious mind will admit, that the passion of parent for child has a sexual component. But it will not do to stop there. For considerations of history demand that we remember that incest, being an abuse of luxury, is one of the characteristics of the age to which the man belongs, who as a contemporary had best be called Here Comes Everybody, since even in his contemporary aspect he is not always H. C. Earwicker. He is also Humme, the Cheapener, Esc. and worthy of the name, being "humile, commune and ensectuous from his nature." And in the past he has had many names, one of them being Tiberius. On the natural level, the incestuous attraction of daughter to father is readily understood. For Anna Livia was not always a river. She was first a cloud. "I could have stayed up there for always only. It's something fails us. First we feel. Then we fall." But the seacloud, from which the rain falls, has itself come out of the sea. And it is to her father, the sea, that the river at last returns.

"And it's old and old it's sad and old it's sad and weary I go back to you, my cold father, my cold mad father, my cold mad feary father, till the near sight of the mere size of him, the moyles and moyles of it, moananoaning, makes me seasilt saltsick and I rush, my only, into your arms. I see them rising." And at the end of the passage, which concludes the long night, we know the resurrection. "Till thousands thec. Lps. The keys to. Given! A way a lone a last a loved a long the"

The keys here are those of heaven, and they go back a long way to the beginning of the book, where we found Saint Peter concealed in an Irish peat-rick. Though these are Christian symbols, they need not be taken only as Christian symbols. The fall of man leads to the resurrection. But for the happy fault of Augustine, there would be no promise of unending life. There are many ways to read this passage and the amazing thing is that, no matter how we read it, it is still true. It is, in the profoundest sense, poetry, and therefore true, interpret the fall how you will. It is true nightly when, in darkness, we fall asleep, that we expect to wake again in the morning light. The mind, which has grown too abstract, is returned in sleep to primitive levels of consciousness, and being returned is restored. And the process is repeated on a more conscious plane whenever a poem is created.

Anna Livia is the most astounding creation in *Finnegans Wake*. The man who is History to her Time has as many metamorphoses as she. Indeed, he has more. But we are usually aware when he changes from one person to another. So, too, the four master waves of Ireland change into four old men and then, a little later, are waves again. But we do not see Anna Livia change from being a river into being a woman. She is always both, as she is also Ireland, as she is always Time, which, always flowing, is ever returning unchangeable, but never without change. She is such a mythological creature as, were she not there, I should have said the modern mind could not make.

VI

Even a timeless history has to be concerned with time, so that all the way through *Finnegans Wake* we are never quite allowed to forget Anna Livia Plurabelle, even though there may be only a lilt in the rhythm of a phrase to remind us of her presence. The book is all about the man whose initials, when they are H.C.E., stand for Here Comes Everybody.

The complaint has been made that Joyce delays too long before he tells us anything about him. There is a realistic basis for everything in *Finnegans Wake*. But this non-day diary is more than half over before we learn very much about the actual contemporary character of the dreamer. Joyce has a devious mind, and in *Ulysses* we had to learn his propensity for concealing certain things, which, once we have come on them, seemed to offer no reason for concealment. But in the matter of structure, no one could be more conscientious. And if Joyce delays telling us about the real man, it is certainly because what is universal in man is more important than what is individual. The past that every man bears is greater than his present, and the proportion is preserved. The Garden of Eden was the scene of the first fall of man, as Phoenix Park in Dublin is the background for the later, so it is impossible to say that one existed before the other. The one was, and both are.

And if Earwicker first appears, not as a man at all, but as Howth Head, that is certainly because Joyce wanted us first to know that he has the permanence of a promontory. He is present in the title of the book and in the first passages devoted to the fall as Finnegan. Tim Finnegan was an Irish hod-carrier who, in popular ballad, fell from a ladder and was laid out as dead. At his wake, the watchers, after drinking take to fighting. A whiskey bottle is thrown, breaks, and some of the whiskey—in Erse, the water of life—falls on the corpse, who promptly starts up as lively as ever to reproach the watchers for supposing him dead. This man of "hod, cement and edifices" is the builder of civilizations. His fall from the ladder becomes the type of all the falls, the fall of Lucifer from heaven, the fall of man in the Garden of Eden, the fall of Earwicker in Phoenix Park. His revival is a typical resurrection. For Finnegan becomes Finn again: the historical hero of Ireland, Finn MacCool. Finn is the fairhaired, the Finn Gall, the fair stranger, the Danish invader who was the founder of Dublin. The first citizen of Dublin must be a Dane. We are told of H. C. Earwicker that he has come, a lifetime ago, out of the sea to Ireland. When he first comes before us he wears the symbolic name of three barbaric kings, Haroun Childeric Eggeberth. His present name is fabulously accounted for; he has fallen in his estate, his occupation is a low one, he is supposed, from his appearance before his present king with a flower pot on a pole, to have been hunting earwigs. This is an ignoble sport, as opposed to the hunting of the fox, in which the King is engaged. (This whole incident we discover is derived from a picture of John Peel in the pub of Roderick O'Connor, "the last uncrowing king of Ireland.")

But the earwig is more particularly attached to Humphrey Chimpden Earwicker, who for an ironic moment is presented in his name of Persse O'Reilly, which is a version of the French word for earwig, *perce-oreille*. The European earwig is, like Haroun Al Raschid, a nocturnal creature. It has wings but almost no one has ever seen it fly. And with it as it goes, it carries its own dead, just as H.C.E. bears through his long night the whole dead past of mankind.

The work progresses from the Fall to the Resurrection. We do not know why Finnegan fell from the ladder; we do not know what it is that Earwicker has done in Phoenix Park. We only know that what occurred there was an abuse of luxury, and that as the result of his deed he is in fear of the retribution of the authorities. Earwicker may have accosted some Grenadiers, he may have annoyed some chambermaids, or all his guilty feelings may come out of his passion for his children, whom he has impiously procreated and around whom, in the dream, many of his erotic fancies play. But whatever he did is connected with what Adam did in the Garden of Eden. We do not know what caused the Fall. "It's something fails us," says Anna Livia, and it is she who has the last word. "First we feel. Then we fall." Traditionally the fall is associated with awareness of the gods and the waking of those sexual powers which are man's means to immortality, which is a privilege of the gods; so that even the proper use of those powers brings with it no less punishment than the knowledge of death. The proper use is one, the perverse uses are many. Joyce considers all sorts of falls, and while he never commits himself to any one explanation, there are occasions where he seems to arrive at the conclusion that the original fall was not that of man, but of the angels, those pure intellectual essences, who could live only through pride.

What Joyce seems to be saying here is that, though we reject the Christian interpretation of the Fall, the fall remains to be accounted for. What has in one age been taken as the profoundest truth, in another appears nonsense, but, despite the nonsensical aspect of all that man has thought of himself, his life is not without sense. Humpty Dumpty is more than a nursery rhyme; behind it is a cosmological myth: the earth tumbling out of chaos; within it is a biological fact: the creation of new life. The truth about man is not to be found in his thought, but in his history. So the writing in *Finnegans Wake* moves incessantly through nonsense to poetry. The content always shows in the form, and when successful it is the form. It has been pointed out that what Joyce is doing here with words is what all poets have always done, and in particular what Shakespeare does throughout his latest plays: employ a sort of pun to make a compressed metaphor. But Joyce carries this process much further than Shakespeare did, and at the same times writes a work which is meant to be read, as the *Divine Comedy* is, not on one but on many levels. Dante told Can Grande that his poem could be interpreted in four ways. I am not sure that the four would exhaust the number of ways in which *Finnegans Wake* may be read.

All this places an almost intolerable burden on the reader, no matter how patient he may be—and Joyce admonishes him to patience—no matter how accustomed he may be to literature that has departed from realism. For there is nothing in the form that Joyce has adopted to force him to stop at one point rather than another further on. Once the presentness of the past has been admitted there is no saying how much of the past is to be adumbrated in any one contemporary event. Once it has been allowed that all is in a state not of being but becoming, words with the rest, there is nowhere that a man like Joyce, with his incomparable mastery over words, is compelled to stop. And there can be little doubt that he has manipulated his text to its harm. The various published versions of the Anna Livia Plurabelle chapter show that, in continuing to superimpose new meanings on what he had written, he has not so much added to the life of it as, by disturbing the rhythm, taken away some of the life it had.

And yet Joyce's form has served him well. For when we have come to the end of *Finnegans Wake*, we know that here is the past and the future of mankind. It is a history which restores religion and accords with science. Indeed, for the first time a poet has created for us a world which outwardly agrees with contemporary physicists, as inwardly it confirms the psychologists of our time. And yet it is so created that we cannot escape the impression that it came into being, not through derivation from what others have found, Joyce being almost blind and largely cut off from other sources of knowledge, but through contemplation alone. His mind in some ways resembles the medieval mind; but the world he has imagined is our own. *Finnegans Wake* is probably the most exasperating book ever written; but as a consideration of our knowledge and as an exploration into the unknown it is worthy of the great comic poet who wrote *Ulysses*.

The Southern Review: Winter, 1940

THE ARTS IN AMERICA*

TO SPEAK ON the future of anything whatsoever is to take on, not only the prerogatives of a prophet, but the risks. And the risk of a prophet is always that he may be dishonored by events.

So many of the true prophets have seemed on their appearance to see no more, but less, than the public. Tiresias came before Oedipus blind, led by a boy, unable to see the steps before him. But what Tiresias could see, his great eyes opened on the night, was how the past impenetrated the present and the impulsion it gave. Seeing the direction of events, he could have foretold, had he been willing, their outcome. For what was about to be was implicit in what had been. The future of the arts in America is contained in their present. If it can be clearly seen, if it were possible to perceive what has brought us to the actual hour, we should know as much as it is necessary for us to know about the future. For not being professional prophets like Tiresias, not living, as he did, out of time, where past and present are one, what we really want to know is what the blind Theban had to depend on an ignorant boy to tell him. We need to know the next step.

I shall begin with the simple conviction that the future of the arts is in America.

That is, of course, when you come down to it a statement about the present. Tiresias's boy knew the next step, not because he was accustomed to the stairs of the palace, but because he had the confidence of his own vigor. He was certainly not unaware of infection about him in the city. But, being young and as yet intact in that stricken air, he went forward, slowed indeed by the prophet's hand on his shoulder, but undeterred by his awful predictions. His own future awaited him. He may have been—as a Theban, must have been—affected by the ruin of the royal house. But there is no reason to believe, granted the chance of youth, that he failed to survive it.

* Delivered as a lecture at Kenyon College, February 17, 1941.

THE ARTS IN AMERICA

We cannot ourselves ignore that we live in an infected time. It was some twenty years ago that Paul Valéry wrote as the first sentence to an essay that has since become famous: "*Nous autres, civilisations, nous savons maintenant que nous sommes mortelles.*" As a European, he knew that Europe, like all the civilizations that had gone before it, was mortal. And that sentence was written, not on the morrow of a defeat, but of a victory.

"We have heard tell," Valéry went on to say, "of whole worlds that have disappeared, of empires that have foundered with all their men and all their engines; gone straight down to the inexplorable bottom of the centuries, with their gods and their laws, their academies and their sciences, both pure and applied, with their grammars, their dictionaries, their classics, their romantics and their symbolists, their critics and the critics of their critics. We have seen through the profound depths of history the phantoms of immense ships, which had once borne wealth and intelligence. . . . And we see now that the abyss of history is big enough for everybody. We feel that a civilization has the same fragility as a life. The circumstances which would send the works of Baudelaire and of Keats to join the works of Menander are not in the least inconceivable: they are in the daily papers."

In the Europe between 1919, when these lines were first printed, and 1939, which saw the beginning of another war, it was impossible to escape the conviction that centuries were hastening to their end. The whole order which had come into existence with the Renaissance was falling apart, and not merely the economic order that had sustained it. Capitalism was failing, not so much because of exploitations too cruel to be borne, as because of an impotence even more impossible to support. As long as it had represented an order, however great the injustices, the inequalities, it entailed, even those who profited least by it had been willing to put up with it. But it was no longer in itself an order or the sustenance of an order. It was complete disorder. The workers were no longer being exploited by their employers as they had once been; they were nevertheless being robbed right and left and they were being robbed by the governments, now of the Right, now of the Left, which they had helped to put into power. They were being stripped of their pay and deprived, not once, but time after time, of the savings of their labors, by the very governments they would presently be called on to defend. The result was an immense disquietude. Men hoped, denied, doubted and came back to a single conviction: that, as long as they escaped death, they were alive. There was no other certainty than that prompted by the perishing body. For in Europe, the mind stood like Tiresias in Thebes, seeing only too clearly what was coming and must come, impotent save to predict disaster, unwilling to speak openly and clearly what none wanted to hear. Picasso's paintings had more and more the appearance of nightmares; his canvases were alive with terrible inhuman presences. Chirico painted immense deserted squares, oppressed by shadows coming from no source that one could see, incongruous and confused ruins, which no one else could see until the bombs began to fall from the air on living cities and to create the disordered debris he had foreseen. Stravinsky, who had once written the *Rites of Spring*, composed music in which one could hear multitudes calling on a no longer worshipped god and mourning the death of empires as they marched. Joyce, immersed himself in a blind night, conceived a night-speech in which to predict the end of the domination of England, that great European power, and at the end of his age-long night, a dawn, another beginning for Ireland, which has never really been a part of Europe.

In the meanwhile, the statesmen of Europe went blindly on their course, knowing neither what had brought them into the world nor to what end they went, believing neither in destiny nor in their own decisions; protesting, like Mr. MacDonald, their constant innocence; attesting, like Mr. Baldwin, their constant complacency; incapable of seeing what was before them, since they were unwilling to recognize their own crimes behind them. At last, when they called on their young men to fight, they sent them out to defend with their lives a civilization whose life was as fragile as their own.

What will come out of this war I know no more than the next man. I know what I hope and I know what I fear. I also know that so far it is not my side that has won.

And yet, it seems to me quite impossible that the Germans should establish their New Order on the continent of Europe by any means at their disposal. An ordered society is recognized, not by the presence, but by the absence of weapons. Take away from the German armies of occupation their tanks, their bombers, their machine guns, and they cease to exist. The fiction behind their force is not one which the conquered can accept, for it is founded on a faith that the Germans are a superior race. Their effective superiority consists in this, that they really do desire to dominate the continent of Europe, while no one else does, and that to attain that domination they have been willing to cast off those scruples with which for centuries men have surrounded their acts. Those scruples are not, as the Communists would have us believe and the Fascists have been only too ready to believe, mere bourgeois prejudices. They are the conditions for action which men long ago created in order to believe in their own worth and dignity. They are not constant, they change, but they must always be there, and only an age of disarray and distrust would have thought of discarding them. To trust to the act only is the distinction of a barbarian, and in persuading his young men of the purity of their destructive acts, Hitler has destroyed for them the human condition.

The tragedy of Europe is that it could no more than Oedipus escape the consequences of its past. It could at last neither ignore nor undo them. There had been a time long before when Europe, too, had been asked the question, *What is man?*, and its answer was brave, ingenious, generous and noble. The eyes of Europe have now been put out.

A tyrant as inhuman as Creon stands in the place and power of the blind. The war, however, may be a long one, and the Germans in all their history have never won a long war. But if the war is prolonged, it is almost certain that it will leave behind it a Europe as exhausted as was Germany itself after the Thirty Years War. But without waiting for the outcome, or even attempting to predict it, it is possible even now to say that the center of Western culture is no longer in Europe. It is in America. It is we who are the arbiters of its future and its immense responsibilities are ours.

The future of the arts is in America.

For only here can the intelligence pursue its inquiries without hindrance from the State and publish its discoveries unmolested by authority. Freedom, to be sure, is not the same for the artist as for the ordinary man. For neither is it the right to do as he pleases, for no man has that right; rather for any man it is the right to determine the terms on which he is willing to survive. What the artist has that the ordinary man has not is another means of survival—his work; but within his work he must still have freedom to choose or to reject the conditions of his survival. On this continent it can still be sought, in this country it can still be found. And to these shores have lately come many of the most remarkable minds that Europe has produced in our generation. Not all of them have come of their own choice; but all who have chosen have come in the conviction that here is the last refuge which a world disordered by war and distracted by tyranny affords for labors such as theirs.

The presence amongst us of these European writers, scholars, artists, composers, is a fact. It may be for us as significant a fact as the coming to Italy of the Byzantine scholars, after the capture of their ancient and civilized capital by Turkish hordes. The comparison is worth pondering. As far as I know, the Byzantine exiles did little on their own account after coming to Italy. But for the Italians their presence, the knowledge they brought with them, were enormously fecundating.

Cut off from Europe, Americans have been turned as never before to their own resources. That is natural. That is good. An increased curiosity may discover riches which, if not new, may seem so, which, if not as great as we would like them, are still ours. We can now say, "I owe no man anything; what I have is my own and I am proud of it." That is to be expected. There is a richness in America of which none can see the end.

Nothing could be more natural than that we should, at such a time as this, ransack our native past as though it were an ancestral attic, raising the lids of old leather trunks with the hair still on them, shaking off the disguising dust and bringing to light, with all the surprise and pleasure of discovery, much that we had forgotten existed: stone-age arrowheads and shirts cut in imitation of the savage's buckskin, yellowed pamphlets devoted to the establishment of liberty in this country, handbills for lost and won elections, uniforms with tarnished gold braid, peacefully folded, pretty bedquilts and quaint portraits painted by itinerant talent, folk art as crude as it is fascinating.

It is perfectly proper that, thrown back on our own resources, we should reckon our own strength and return to neglected possessions we had half forgotten were there. These things are precious and they are ours; but because they belong to past Americans, they are pathetic. They have, it may be, their own value; but they also have a sentimental value. The danger is not, I think, so much that we may add one to the other and so overrate them; it is that, fascinated by the particularity of our native heritage, we may forget that as part of the West we own a longer heritage.

And that is where, I presume to think, the European exiles may come in; they will not, if I may judge from what I have seen, so much tame our enthusiasm as correct our judgment. There is at present in America a distinct tendency to bring all art down to the level of folk art and judge it from that standpoint. I have recently seen, for instance, a critical account of the architecture of Rhode Island which ascribes to some of the early cotton mills quite undiscernible virtues, in order to assert their one indubitable virtue, which is that they were American.

For to tell the truth, folk art is all very well in its way, but its way is limited. And Americans have only exceeded those limits in the arts when, not ignoring Europe, they have come to a proper understanding of their relation to Europe. In the eighteenth century that relation was intuitively grasped and consciously understood, not only by those who gave form to our state, but by those who produced our only formal architecture. They were separated from Europe in space, but continuous with Europe in time. They were contributors to the one civilization they knew; it was not conceivable that they could belong to any other.

What the architects did was to produce local variations on a style that held its own from the Danube to the headwaters of all the eastward-flowing streams of America. As long as a style is living, there is no such thing; there are only variations on that style. And how local these variations were can be seen by observing the changes that occur in the dwellings between Concord and Plymouth, between the story-and-a-half houses of Virginia and the raised cottages of Louisiana. All that was done belonged to a tradition which Americans shared with Europeans. It did not belong to Europe; it belonged to the eighteenth century.

It was not the Atlantic that separated Americans from the European tradition, but the woods of the Old West. Even so, they came to the edge of the woods, aware of all the centuries they brought with them. It was only after the pioneer had gone a long time in that green twilight, where a man could march all day and never see the sun, that he left behind him, not merely the little settlements, in the clearings; he left behind him his age. In contact with the savage, he became the contemporary of the Choctaw and the Cherokee.

The American went West, and as long as he went West, nothing was impossible to his mind. It was only when, having come on the Pacific coast to the last confine of the West, it was only when he turned back toward the East, that uncertainty began to show in his gait, uneasiness in his eyes. Franklin at the Court of Versailles, John Adams at the Court of St. James, had had no sense of inferiority. On the contrary they felt themselves, without any conceit, to be of more worth, as men and as Americans, than any they saw around them. But Mark Twain called himself an Innocent Abroad, and innocence is not the word for what was a sense of inadequacy. His reaction was the common one throughout the predatory period of the Gilded Age and perhaps later, since it certainly appears in those who with the resignation of the deluded and deceived put their signatures to the Treaty of Versailles.

Nowhere was this inadequacy so felt as in the arts. So strong, indeed, was this feeling that when a great artist did appear in America there was nothing to do about it but, as in the case of Herman Melville, to pretend he did not exist, or, as in the case of Henry James, to declare that he was not an American but a European.

In the uncertainty of their relation to Europe, Americans are somewhat like the Russians. A geographer might admit Russia to Europe, though he would probably add that for him Europe itself is only a peninsula projecting from the great continent of Asia. The rulers of Russia, from Peter the Great to Lenin, have tried with great courage and with great cruelty to include Russia in Europe; they have planned, as they thought, for the future; but neither thought nor ruthlessness can eliminate Byzantium from the Russian past. A Russian can only pretend to be a European, but the pretense at times has pleased him. The American, separated by the Atlantic from Europe, has preferred to think he has nothing to do with Europeans. He has—as his history on frequent occasions has reminded him, for his history, since he has had one, is continuous with theirs. Their immense past is ours. And that past is now confided to us, because we alone can prolong it into the future.

What will be the future of the arts in America I do not know. But I do know that whatever is done must by its vigor, by its novelty, by whatever there is in it that transcends the past, satisfy demands that have been created by the past. "No poet, no artist of any art," T. S. Eliot has said, "has his complete meaning alone. His significance, his appreciation is the appreciation of his relation to the dead poets and artists. You cannot value him alone; you must set him, for contrast and comparison, among the dead. I mean this as a principle of aesthetic, not merely historical, criticism." This statement, which seemed to us so illuminating when it first appeared in *The Sacred Wood*, still stands. But the twenty years that have passed since then have somewhat altered its implications.

For twenty years ago it was in Europe that the centers of our civilization were to be found. The feeling of inferiority which then so often afflicted the American as artist, in so far as it was a consequence merely of his being an American, is to be attributed to his knowing that he was remote from them. For it is in these centers that, in each art, the tradition can best be acquired and with it an intenser consciousness of one's own time. The contacts of a capital can mean many things to a young man, but none more important than this. Twenty years ago there were many capitals in the world, but in only one was it possible to know the extreme moment of time. And that was Paris.

But Paris is now silent and, as it were, in exile. The actual center of Western culture is no longer in Europe. It is here. That, I believe, admits little question. The question is, can we provide that conscious center which the culture demands?

THE ARTS IN AMERICA

On the continent of Europe, France was the arbiter of the arts and of all the attributes of civilization, from the moment when that civilization, which is ours, first began to take form, appearing dimly at first, like sculptures on a cathedral emerging from the long night, misty saints and kings attenuated in stone, crude in the false dawn, full of force and fear, and, only as the dawn gains, acquiring clarity and grace, until, in the full rush of morning, all are distinguished by light, and we see that the foreboding on the faces of the prophets has been exchanged on the faces of the angels for felicity and the knowledge of joy. That position France has maintained, with remarkable continuity, down to our own day, in spite of every sort of peril, of outward dangers and inner convulsions. We may well ask, why? For if we must now say of France, not that she is, but that she was, if at the moment her proud position appears lost, lost for a long time, if not irrevocably lost, we must still ask why for so many centuries France was able to establish the criteria by which all manifestations of civilization have ultimately to be tested and judged. There were so many changes in those centuries that it is useless to seek in any one of them the solution; we must look to what in France changed least in that time. And that was her geographical situation. Her borders were now extended, now retracted, by war; her coast line has been altered and realtered by conquest. But always France has stood between the North and the South, always France has from her shores been aware of the Mediterranean and of northern seas. She has had, in order to survive—or perhaps I should say, simply in order to be— to admit the claims of two rival conceptions or civilizations and continuously to mediate between them. It was owing to her own fine and luminous genius itself, it may be, a reflection of the actual light—that she was able to consider both, to control both, to bring both into a single and harmonious whole.

In no other country of Western Europe are the people of so many and such disparate racial strains. France alone has made them French. But men also make the country that makes them, and at every crucial moment of her history, down to the latest, those whose will can be felt in the destiny of France—Charlemagne and Joan of Arc, Louis XI and Louis XIV, the Revolutionary Assembly and Napoleon—all worked for the unity of France. Even Poincaré had no other end. And when the government was no longer able to conserve that unity, but rather, alike by its decrees and by its indecisions, encouraged division, France fell.

So in French art, the human experience from which it is derived is exceeding rich and varied; but what distinguishes it from the art of all other countries is its passion for form. In France, the artist was allowed the utmost possible freedom in the choice of his material; he was praised in the end in proportion to his ability to unite force and form.

The task to which France set herself eleven centuries ago and which she has only now abandoned under her conquerors, was to transmit the Mediterranean tradition to the North. Nowhere was one more conscious of living in the present than in France, and yet there the present was continuously enriched by the past, and not the past of France only, but by a classical past which the French contrived to reconcile with their own. For, in insisting upon a logical structure, upon balance and grace, the French never forgot that these qualities, which we associate with classical art, actually are those of the living body at its perfection, the body which we derive from a remoter past than that of Greece.

What does this mean to Americans? It means that we must find a way to reconcile our own past with the vast past of Western civilization. The time is one of danger. But I for one am not perturbed by the dangers I shall encounter as an American. I am dismayed by the dangerous changes that may come to Western civilization and in the end destroy its continuity.

We must be Americans; but as artists we must remember that, before America was, we were men. Not all, as we have discovered, in our own past is usable, and certainly there will be much in an alien and ancient past which we can neither save nor use. No one man can answer for all as to what should be saved, for what is valuable to one man will not appear so to another. But certainly for all of us should be saved all the answers to that question which the Sphinx so long ago put to Oedipus, What is man? We know from all those over whom time has closed like a sea that he is a creature of time and that, though the answers are many and various, the last is not yet.

The Kenyon Review: Spring, 1941

POETRY AND PAINTING *

I SHALL BEGIN this essay by quoting a passage from one of the *Reactionary Essays on Poetry and Ideas* by Allen Tate. He is speaking of the confusion which results when the common center of experience, out of which the separate arts achieve their special formal solutions, disappears. Then the arts, deprived of their proper sustenance, begin to live one on another. "Painting," he says, "tries to be music; poetry leans upon painting; all the arts 'strive toward the condition of music'; till at last seeing the mathematical structure of music, the arts become geometrical and abstract, and destroy themselves."

The passage occurs in an essay on my own poetry. And it is because Mr. Tate feels, quite rightly, that in some of my poems I lean very far toward the painters, finding in an art not theirs solutions which are possibly proper only to them, that he has asked me here this evening. There may have been malice in his invitation. He may have asked me here only to witness my confusion. But the confusion is not mine alone. It has perhaps always existed. It was present, we know, in the mid-eighteenth century, when Gotthold Lessing wrote his famous essay on the limits of painting and poetry, which he called the *Laokoon*. The distinction that Lessing made still seems to hold good. It would still seem to be sound to say that succession in time is the sphere of the poet, as space is that of the painter. And yet, paradoxically enough, it is with that movement in the arts which Lessing did something to initiate that the confusion becomes serious. I do not want to make too much of Lessing. There is a tendency among critics to play up their predecessors; in order to increase the prestige of criticism; they ascribe to the critics of the past a power for creation which in all probability they never had. However, Lessing was in at the beginning of a movement of which we have not yet seen the end. And it is worth considering his position for a moment,

* This essay was read as a lecture under the auspices of the Creative Arts Program at Princeton University, January 29, 1940.

175

if we are to understand why the clarity of his distinction between poetry and painting should have been followed by a century in which these arts are confused as they had not been before in the history of the West.

Now one of the reasons why Lessing, whose distinctions are so clear, gave rise through his influence to such confusion is that he was, as any of his contemporaries would have been, interested in the means which each art employed in what he called its imitations, only in so far as they limited the artist in his choice of subjects. It was possible for him, in the eighteenth century, consumed as he was by admiration for the Greeks and Romans, to take the means for granted. We cannot. And more, we know that for the artist the assumption of limitations is the beginning of liberation and that, in the complete work of art, while we always know what the means are, we never know what the end is. I can say how Shakespeare wrote *Full Fathom Five*. I cannot possibly tell you what he wrote. All I can say is that it is poetry. I can make out from the canvas, stroke by stroke, how Cézanne painted, but if I were to tell you that what he had painted was some apples and a tablecloth, you would know that I had said nothing.

The art of poetry is, like that of music, made manifest in a control of time. The poet has words to work with, and words are his only sounds; it is by controlling their sequence in time that he seems to control time; it is upon their sensuous disposition that he must depend to convey a sense of duration. A painter is known by his spatial power. What he does when he applies paint to canvas is to create, from what was without depth, an illusion of enduring space. Only a moment in any action can be shown within that space. What goes before and after that moment in time, which must be seen in space, can at most be imagined.

Let us go back before the great modern confusion to see what happens in that space. I am going to take the painting of a battle, which is all action, one of the several paintings which Paolo Uccello made of the Rout of San Romano, that one which is now in the National Gallery in London—or was before it was buried against air raids—and which is reproduced in Thomas Craven's *Treasury of Art Masterpieces*. The horsemen press in from the left with their lances lifted, under white banners tormented by the wind. The white charger of the turbaned swordsman in the foreground rears, snorting in the delight of battle. The lance of the fantastically helmeted Florentine is already lowered to meet the oncoming Siennese. At the right, the fighters on each side are hacking at one another, with swords, across their horses' heads. On a far hillside can be seen, beyond the fray, foot soldiers, and above them on the hill, made small by distance, two more horsemen. The moment the painter has chosen to depict is that of first contact between the Florentines and the Siennese, a moment all action, a moment composed in space of many actions, and yet, in point of time, but a moment. The motion of the warriors is motionless, the plunging of the horses arrested. What has been is, and, in what is actually seen, what is about to be is foreseen. The spatial imitation of a moment (and that is all the Rout of San Romano is) is still an imagination of time.

We cannot ignore time in a painting, and particularly we cannot ignore it in Paolo Uccello. For Uccello it was who introduced perspective into European painting, and perspective is the means which allows the painter to include in his composition the consciousness of time; for it is by means of perspective that we see the distance one from another of objects in space; and all distance, like astronomical distance, may be expressed as time. But, however great the temporal element, it has been converted in Uccello's composition into terms of space. That is why the Rout of San Romano is one of the truly great paintings of the European tradition. The opposing bodies of men and horses are not pitted against each other merely in battle; they are here opponents in space. The lifting and lowering of lances, the raising and breaking of swords, all those movements which in life could not have achieved their meaning unless in time, are here brought into spatial relations, and create their meaning by simply being. And all are under complete control. Since their aim is to kill, all these movements, were they living, would be violent. The impression they convey is one of absolute calm. Man has been added to nature. The order of art has been imposed on human disorder.

In Paolo Uccello's battle we have the actions of time set before us as a complex of space. The poet who wishes to present a battle should have no trouble in rendering the succession of actions. But a battle must take place somewhere.

And one might suppose that Shakespeare could show us how it is done. The difficulty is really to find a battle in Shakespeare's plays. It would seem that nothing would be easier, for we carry away from his plays the impression that they resound from beginning to end with the conflict of arms, so long a reverberation do words like Philippi, Agincourt and Bosworth leave in our ears. But when you go through the plays, looking for the poet's equivalent to the painter's Rout of San Romano, you discover that the poet was almost as wary of fighting as his Falstaff. He is at times forced on the very field, but when he gets there, he, as likely as not, pretends like Falstaff that he has slaughtered his bravest enemy, while actually he has merely gone through the motions of fighting. His failure is not one of valor; for he does not fall. He is simply discreet enough to know that real battles are always fought in real space and that an imaginary battle must take place in imaginary space. He can imagine space, but his danger, since he was a dramatic poet, was that the space he had imagined could be confounded, at what ridiculous risk he knew, with the real stage on which his actors stood, hacking at one another with the theatre's harmless swords.

> O! for a Muse of fire, that would ascend
> The brightest heaven of invention;
> A kingdom for a stage, princes to act
> And monarchs to behold the swelling scene.
> Then should the warlike Harry, like himself,
> Assume the port of Mars; and at his heels,
> Leash'd in like hounds, should famine, sword, and fire
> Crouch for employment. But pardon, gentles all,
> The flat unraised spirits that have dar'd
> On this unworthy scaffold to bring forth
> So great an object: can this cockpit hold
> The vasty fields of France? Or may we cram
> Within this wooden O the very casques
> That did affright the air at Agincourt?

Obviously not. All that the cockpit ever held was a company of actors and all that ever did affright the air in that wooden O were the words of the poet. What then does Shakespeare do? Since he can't put the battle of Agincourt on the stage, he diverts the interest to something he can show. Agincourt was one of the most interesting battles ever fought. But while it is being prepared for, while it is being forced into conclusion, the attention is centered on the relation between the sovereign and subject. Not only was this profoundly interesting to Shakespeare—and presumably to his audience—but it was a relation which could perfectly be shown in a succession of scenes, which present now one aspect, now another, but which never, even in the sum, exceed the possibilities of the stage.

The poet, though his art is one of time, cannot get away from space. For our minds are so made that space is a necessary concept. The greatest expanse of space which Shakespeare ever attempted to put on the stage is in *Antony and Cleopatra*, where, if we but listen to the words, we shall hear the tramplings of armies over three continents. But it is a space that we hear; it comes to us in names, and if we see a plain before Actium, it is only in the mind's eye. Of the battle itself we have only the noise of a sea-fight and then a short report in which we are told how Cleopatra fled:

> She once being loof'd,
> The noble ruin of her magic, Antony,
> Claps on his sea-wing, and like a doting mallard,
> Leaving the fight in height, flies after her.
> I never saw an action of such shame;
> Experience, manhood, honour, ne'er before
> Did violate so itself.

The action at Actium becomes the act of Antony; the issue of the battle has already been decided where for the poet decision is possible: in Antony's violation of his own manhood. And that being the work of time, it is perfectly possible for the poet to handle it, his medium being words and his art being so to control them that they create by their sensuous succession an illusion of time.

What conclusions are we to draw from this? The poet of *Antony and Cleopatra* has not been limited, in staging that ancient tragedy, to a sequence of actions in time. Shakespeare's subject demanded that his actions range over the whole of the known and subjugated world, and we may suspect that what attracted Shakespeare to that particular tragedy at a time when, as a poet, he must have been conscious as never before of his powers, was its spaciousness. Certainly beyond any other of his plays *Antony and Cleopatra* is conceived in space and charged with the emotions which arise from its contemplation. He is limited by his means, for verses are only articulate sounds, which must so follow one another that they create time in a sensuous flow, which, unlike time itself, is under the control of the poet. He is not limited in his subject. The battle, which we should expect, had Lessing been as sound as he seemed on the limits of poetry and painting (since a battle is composed of nothing but actions successive in time), to have been a most appropriate subject for the poet, has actually been presented much more successfully by the painter as a conflict of bodies immobilized in space. What we are concerned with in Shakespeare's play is what is happening to Antony, and Actium is only a point in the long process, whose significance, since Antony is a living man, only time can let out. And Shakespeare was not at a loss when it came to making the life of Antony, which, in so far as it is history, belongs to the past, into the continuous present which is poetry. His means is verse. Shakespeare, I think it is safe to say, was not much interested in action for its own sake, but no poetry was ever written in which more happens, for in no other does so much more happen within the words in a given moment of time. A great deal also happens in the Rout of San Romano, but what counts is not the conflict or armies which prompted the painter, but the use of their lineaments and colors to control space. The exhilaration and the calm which is produced by art is due to the sense it gives of release from the conditions of living, not by its denying those concepts without which life is to us inconceivable, but by controlling them. Only through the means of art can the conviction. be created that man controls time and space. It is in the means of art, then, that we must look for its end.

Lessing's contention that each art is at its best where its power is least to be disputed is doubtless still sound. Each artist is limited by his means, but in those limitations is the source of his power. Why not then, asked Picasso, make the means the end? The power of the painter is shown only in his ordering of space. Why should he not then limit himself to paintings in which the spatial relations should be apparent, in which indeed nothing else should appear? When all is said and done, the subject signifies nothing, the subject is merely a pretext; why not then discard the subject, or if the subject refuses to disappear, let its own life dissolve so that nothing is left but living form?

An Impressionist like Monet had devoted his long life to preserving in pigment the changing appearance of an hour. And Impressionism, conscious of the moment of mutability, had at last, as Lhote said, committed plastic suicide and been drowned like Ophelia among the water-lilies which are the last great work of Monet's age. Picasso for a time at least sought nothing else but form, for nothing in art is permanent but form.

If we look at such a painting of Picasso's as *The Three Musicians* we cannot but be aware that in this canvas space has been superbly created. The whole composition seems to have been made up of surfaces which, like those of plane geometry, are without a third dimension, and yet the illusion of depth is there. If we look closely we can see how it has been produced, by color and by lines, though no one line leads us more than a little way. There is in the painting nothing that we should ordinarily call perspective; there is at most only a primitive approach to it. To find anything that is so nearly a pure creation of space, we should have to go back to Paolo Uccello.

POETRY AND PAINTING

In the *Rout of San Romano* the perspective is still primitive, though for not the same reason as in the work of Picasso. Picasso greatly admires Uccello and would probably admit that his art has been influenced by the Italian. And it is almost certain that we would not now find so much satisfaction in the *Rout of San Romano*, if we had never seen a Picasso. For the art of the present can contribute to the art of the past. History is not a one-way road. But it will not do to allow this contrary traffic to confuse us. The artist of one century can never repeat the art of another.

Paolo Uccello replaced a visible world, where all was disorder, with a world of sensuous form and color, where all is disposed according to some invisible source of order. Pablo Picasso projects an invisible world, in which all is disorder, with a world of abstract form and color, where all is arranged according to some purely material order. Man is so made that he cannot conceive the world except as time and space. But there is a great difference in the world of Italy in the fifteenth century, when time seemed to have been conquered by a dream of eternity, and our own world, in which we suppose a conquest of space through material, not to say mechanical means.

That abstract painting was incomplete was soon clear, but what it lacked, what Picasso had so lately and with absolute logic eliminated, was not clear. At least it was not clear to anybody that counted, until Chirico brought back perspective. But he did not bring back the elaborate perspective that had been lost. The aim was no longer *trompe d'oeil*, but in Cocteau's perfect phrase, *trompe d'esprit*. And it was to be tricked in exactly the way we are tricked in dreams into believing that what is past is present. Picasso had also painted much from memory: his harlequins, his guitars, his three musicians all are memories of Spain when he was a young man. But Chirico's recollections have something of the quality of hallucination; his paintings are excursions into a childhood spent, for all his Italian parentage, in Greece. There is, of course, a difference between painting an object or a person remembered and attempting to paint memory itself. Picasso is sound and sane; Chirico is a man under compulsion and perhaps a little mad; Salvador Dali simulates paranoia. But the point is not there; the point is that the contemporary mind cannot pretend that it is without the consciousness of time. But when time reappeared in the early paintings of Dali it was most self-conscious. It came back marked on those marvellous limp watches in a painting called *The Persistence of Memory*. And not only has Dali restored perspective. He uses it with a skill that is nothing short of ostentation.

The presumption is that perspective was brought back into

painting to satisfy an emotional need. Certainly those empty squares with their arcades in shadow, those streets deserted of all but statues of Chirico, or the immense plains of Dali, where small muscled shapes of men cast disproportionate shadows, are sources of disquietude. I cannot altogether say why they trouble us. But it is not at all necessary for the purpose that I should. I merely want to suggest that the moment a painter insists upon his third dimension of perspective, he has already introduced a fourth, which is time. And when time appears in a painting, it comes somewhat as the messenger in a Greek play comes, not by chance, but as an instrument of necessity.

I have stayed long over the painters, because it is more difficult to discern the temporal element in painting than it is to discover why the poets have never been able to get along without the concept of space.

> Here is no water but only rock
> Rock and no water and the sandy road
> The road winding above among the mountains
> Which are mountains of rock without water
> If there were water we should stop and drink
> Amongst the rock one cannot stop or think. . . .

This is the Dali desert before Dali. In this passage from *The Waste Land*, images of space do occur, but successively and not as they would in one of Dali's paintings: simultaneously. And the dry rocks and the sandy road winding toward the mountains where there is still no water are but symbols of a spiritual drought, due to the disappearance of faith in the truth of Christianity, which is itself a disaster of time. The early poems of Eliot are often situated with great care in space. In *Sweeney Among the Nightingales* Apeneck Sweeney, that extraordinary sensual man, is found in a Parisian dive; but for a moment we are also allowed to see him standing on the great earth itself:

> The circles of the stormy moon
> Slide westward toward the River Plate. . . .

It is an earth still dark with the tragic blood of Agamemnon:

> The nightingales are singing near
> The Convent of the Sacred Heart,

POETRY AND PAINTING

And sang within the bloody wood
When Agamemnon cried aloud,
And let their liquid siftings fall
To stain the stiff dishonoured shroud.

On Sweeney's sordid surroundings the poet suddenly intrudes with the terror of time.

The pure poet is one for whom a poetic solution is possible for any problem which his life imposes upon him. A pure painter is likewise one for whom the solution of any problem is in painting. Shakespeare is such a poet; Uccello, such a painter. Once the problem is solved, it no longer exists as a problem; it is present in the solution, but solely as a force, as a tension. The public is interested in problems; it is seldom interested in the solution; it is seldom interested in art.

The ultimate question concerning any work of art is out of how deep a life does it come. But the question that must first be asked is whether it has a life of its own. And the life of art is in its form. There have been poets among the painters. Chirico is one. There have been poets who not only leaned on the painters, but picked their pockets and stole their palettes as well. Baudelaire was one. But Chirico does not write verse, while in Baudelaire all his colors have their correspondences in sound.

When all the arts strive toward the condition of music, painting becomes abstract and poetry attempts to live on its own technical resources. This is behaving like the child who copies the answers from the back pages of his arithmetic book without having consulted the problem. But that behavior is at the moment unlikely. Today the artist is more like the child who from his schoolroom desk looks first at the window beyond which lies life with all its turmoil and play, and then at the enclosing walls and the door that is slow in opening. In the meanwhile the problem waits, unsolved, but not insoluble. But the problem is one which demands to be solved on its own terms, not those of the playground or the street.

It is the mind that imposes these conceptions of time and space. It is his art that confines the poets to the conventions of time, as it is the art of the painter that holds him to a conventional space. The mind is free; but it is the mind of a condemned man.

The Sewanee Review: Spring, 1945

PAINTERS

THE PAINTER AND THE DYNAMO:
FERNAND LÉGER

I T IS VERY difficult for an American to attend seriously to the new Aesthetics of the Machine. The sound of riveting is too loud in his ears for him to hear the manifestoes with any distinctness. Besides, the Italians, who are most eloquent on the subject, seem to write very badly and to employ too many classical allusions. Signor Enrico Prampolini appears to have turned to the Machine chiefly as a substitute for Ovid's *Metamorphoses*; Signor Marinetti, in his now almost forgotten manifesto, could find no better comparison for a racing automobile than the Victory of Samothrace.

It is only fitting that Futurism, with its insistence on the aesthetic possibilities of mechanical forms and speed, should have originated in Italy—a nation which, lacking coal, is not in the slightest danger of becoming industrially powerful. Besides, if, as the modern artist assumes, the Renaissance was not so much a new birth as a luxurious decay, destroying the free invention of the artist and substituting sentimental description for the delighted employment of color and form, it is Italy that is most encumbered by the dead and magnificent *Rinascimento*. Living among museums, the Italians regard our factories with an almost mystical sentimentalism; knee-deep in the dust of the past, they are consumed of nostalgia for the present. The result is that their work exhibits the exact opposite of the fine qualities of a machine—it is loose in structure, uselessly distorted, sentimentally soft.

Yet to deny the right of the artist to avail himself of the plastic elements introduced into modern life by machinery is absurd. It is impossible to say at a given point that all the possible means of aesthetic expression have been used, and that no new element is to be admitted. The plastic elements of machinery exist, like any other, to be used by the painter as a means to his own ends.

But, if a painting is to present the aesthetic equivalent of a machine, it is only reasonable to ask that it should preserve the admirable qualities of the machine. That is to say, it should be hard, assertive, unsentimental, and organized with the utmost economy. Instead of disorder, there should be order. These are exactly the qualities to be found in the paintings of Fernand Léger. If the locomotive and the turbine have aesthetic values, they will be justified in his canvases, or not at all.

For, as he himself has said, "If an artist is to achieve power and intensity, if he wishes to equal in his work the beautiful objects which industry creates daily, he, too, must concern himself with geometric problems, the relation of volumes, the relation of lines, both curved and straight, and the relation of colors. We are no longer Impressionists at the mercy of a subject, of an instinct, or a brush. We must organize our canvases like any other man in a life organized in the intellectual order; that is to say, we must employ the utmost knowledge of the means at our disposal in order to obtain the maximum result."

In all this, there is no effort to advance mechanical forms at the expense of any other. There are other stops to his recorders; and if one is to pluck out the heart of his mystery it will be found rather in his desire to live completely in his age. That time he sees set off from the past chiefly by the violence of its contrasts and by the dominance of the mechanical element. For not only has machinery altered the visual aspect of things, broken surfaces into contrasting fragments, multiplied and sharpened angles, executed whole cities on a geometric design; it has profoundly altered human values. It has introduced a new ideal of perfection in human conduct, an ideal of no motion lost, of no wasted effort; a mechanical ideal under which the soldier becomes a number on a tag, the workman a mere unit of production, the sentient man a device to be used, unsentimentally, like any other cog or wheel.

We have, therefore, in Léger's canvases not only propellers and turbines painted for sheer pleasure in their own beauty, but a constant play of invention which in its way also celebrates a mechanical age. When the machines are beautiful in themselves, when the subject has its own beauty, it is set down with only so much play of the fancy as will redeem the canvas from monotony. Otherwise, such liberties are taken as the fine painters of the past have always taken with their subjects, before the search for similitude and sentimental description set in, at the end of the eighteenth century.

Fernand Léger, we see, turned originally to machinery to avoid the distortion of the human form, believing that mechanical forms were more readily adaptable to a geometrical pattern. But now, when men and women appear in his canvases, they take on a mechanical air, so far have they been changed in his eyes by the industrial order of things.

"All my paintings are composed by arranging plastic contrasts: by the opposition of flat to modelled surfaces, the opposition of pure and characteristic color to neutral tones. I only utilize the visual values of the moment. We live in an epoch of contrasts, and I wish to live at the height of my epoch." After the mechanical element, it is the orchestration of contrary and strongly opposing values which provides Léger with the greatest excitement. His interest is aroused not alone by the sharp lines of a gaudy billboard cutting the soft green of a landscape, the stiff black lines of the men against the delicate colors and flowing textures of women; he has seen also, during the war and the questionable peace that has followed it, the incessant brutal shock of life and death in hourly contact. The approximate date of any canvas may be determined by its use of contrary values. The influence of Cézanne is evident in the paintings made ten years ago—in the drifting of the colors, the blurring of contours, in a certain smokiness in the pervading air. From that time there has been a continual progress toward a harder line, a cruder, clearer color, a more violent juxtaposition of curves and angles, of grey against vivid tones.

This sense of surprise through contrast is a continuous element of modern art: it is to be seen in the alternation of the present and the past, the confusion of languages in Ezra Pound's *Eight Cantos*; in T. S. Eliot's *The Waste Land*, with its lack of transitions and the simultaneous presentation of present-day London and the legendary world of the Fisher King; and in, say, the Episode of the Sirens in James Joyce's *Ulysses*, where the distinction is lost between actual events and the phantasmagoria of the drunken mind. In the paintings of Fernand Léger fantastic colors are applied to forms derived from the apparent world, and machines, streets and geometrical buildings alternate with patterns of pure invention. And always there is the surprise of color used arbitrarily to heighten contrast or simply to fulfil the need of untrammeled imagination. Cylindrical forms are modelled in a single color—from the darkest of rich blues so thin that it is perceived as grey—and accentuated by a flat background in a dull blood color or crude yellow; behind the wheels and pistons are other, purely subjective designs, derived from the painter's brain and only in the composition related to the forms of the objective world.

There is a distinction of aim between those paintings like the

Mother and Child, exhibited at the Salon d'Automne, and the abstract panels which occupied the place of honor at the Salon des Indépendants. The former exist for their own sake; in them the painter has attempted to isolate and intensify his most personal qualities and every means possible is used toward that end—arrangement of contrasts, multiplication in variety, violent color and assertive form. In the latter, which are painted in fresco tradition, everything is relative. They are intended to be used in relation to architectural designs, on the façades of buildings or the walls of railway stations, relieving the dead surfaces with the delicate colors of a child's paint box and with unobtrusive forms. Strictly impersonal, they have, intentionally, none but a decorative value. The composed canvases are to force themselves upon us with the rude insistence of the *Sacre du Printemps* of Stravinsky. But these subdued arrangements of paler color are a distraction and a quiet compensation for the shrieking of the locomotive and the grinding of the wheels, modernity's discordant clamors.

If I have dwelt overlong on the "ideas" from which these paintings proceed, it is only because they are at present the most successful attempts to authenticate these ideas through color and form. There is no suspicion of description, either sentimental or cerebral, in Léger's art. It depends for its interest purely upon its intensity as plastic expression; its value lies not in its subject matter, but in the way in which that subject matter is combined with a subjective vision. Like nearly all the significant works of the contemporary spirit, it moves halfway between reality and an unreal dream. His streets are filled with familiar forms and unknown colors; his pistons slide not in factories but among fantastical shapes of the mind.

These paintings have a contemporaneous interest. And yet, almost inevitably, they remind me of certain Italian primitives in the Accademia at Venice, paintings on wood, where there is to be found a similar strictness in arrangement, the same insistence on geometrical form and definite line, the same invented color and bold delight in placing moth-green on fuchsia pink, glistening white against profound blue. If by contrast the paintings of Léger seem immeasurably brutal and hard, it is to be remembered that the Italians were impelled by the necessity of relating the figures of peasant life to the sweet mystery of the medieval Church; the problem of the modern is to adjust the individual man to the mechanical forces which surround him. And the conflict of the body and the spirit had not the bitterness, the utter mercilessness, which marks the struggle between our flesh and nerves with the machine.   *Vanity Fair: August, 1923*

THE PASSION OF PABLO PICASSO

I

THERE IS NO painter who has so spontaneously and so profoundly reflected his age as Pablo Picasso. Having made that statement, it may be well to say as precisely as possible what is his age.

For it is a curious characteristic of ours that we tend to apply the word age to shorter and shorter periods. Our extreme consciousness of time is perhaps a concomitant of our extreme precariousness. Nowhere is there stability. Those that have the power are not sure, nor are we. That we may live at all in our thought, we must try to live historically— to see the present as though it were already the past. In order that our living may not be utterly without significance, we must try to regard ourselves, as it were, posthumously.

In the last years of the nineteenth century, Pablo Picasso, then not yet twenty, wandered the streets of Madrid until, as one who saw him there said, the city entered into him through the soles of his feet. He paced the pavements as though he were proceeding through a nightmare; the very porches of the churches, where beggars gathered nightly to sleep, became suspicious in his eyes. He was a young painter, mad about Goya. Goya had had to paint in a sort of darkness, in which only he could see, living as he did between the fading light of the eighteenth century and the dawn of the nineteenth. It is impossible to say when Picasso first discerned that he was another destined to live out his life between two ages. What he knew then was that he could paint. And he was even then, walking at night in a city that has always lived much at night, preparing himself to be the painter of a transitional period. He would paint it as a Spaniard in exile, on the slopes of Montmartre remembering Madrid, on Montparnasse remembering the trivial and the sad, the light and the shade. In another country he would paint it as a Spaniard who had known Toledo, the city of El Greco, with its haunting vision of terrible reality. His Spain would always contain both a Goya and an El Greco. But his world would be our world.

Any attempt, even when made by an historian writing long afterward, to fix exact dates to a movement in the arts, must to some extent be arbitrary. What sets one generation of men apart from another is to be sought in the forms through which they record their emotions. It is impossible to perceive the moment when one sort of sensibility changes into another. For the change is imperceptible until it is expressed, and the first efforts toward expression are necessarily groping. But this much can be said, which was not always clear: that the decade that came to an end with the war and the decade that followed are, so far as the arts are concerned, essentially one period. All those manifestations of the arts which are associated with the years after the war in Europe, and which are commonly supposed to have taken shape from its confusions, actually began long before the war. The *Sacre du Printemps* was publicly performed in Paris in 1913; one portion of the ballet had occurred to Stravinsky in a dream much earlier. *Ulysses* was published in 1922; but the writing of it had consumed eight years, and long before 1914 Joyce had seen—not foreseen—the disintegration of the individual consciousness. The earliest paintings of Picasso, those done around the turn of the century, are in a decadent tradition. There is nothing very remarkable about them except the virtuosity they show, the self-confidence even in the midst of influences, and the virility which could not but be Picasso's own. Interest in his work begins with the Blue Period, which may be considered to extend from 1901 to 1904. But neither then, nor in the Pink Period which immediately followed, is there a complete break with tradition. The earliest Cubist paintings still repose solidly upon the experiments of Cézanne. It was not, indeed, until the Cubist movement was well under way that the possibility occurred and the necessity appeared of making a clean start in painting. "It may be," as Jean Cocteau has said, "that the first days of that astonishing undertaking were, like the days of childhood, days of play. They quickly became school days." The influence of African sculpture on Picasso first appears in the composition of *Demoiselles d'Avignon*. It belongs to 1906. That year and the following year, he carried still further the use of sculptural planes which the Negro fetishes had suggested to him. The first phase of Cubism may be said to run from 1908 to 1913. So that the beginnings of the age of which Picasso is the painter must be sought at least ten years before the Armistice.

The first attempts at Cubist painting, even when made by a Picasso, now look to us rather thin. We may say that they were the means of passing a bad moment in painting. They imply a certain courage and a certain contempt both for the moment and the means of getting round it. Or we may continue Cocteau's metaphor and see in them a school whose instruction would allow something much stronger to be done later. But historically they have this importance: they represent a complete break in sensibility. That shattering of surfaces into planes was significant, and we know now that something more was implied than that, in Paris, a few painters of the advance guard had decided to discard a tradition which had come down to them from the Renaissance. When the old forms go, they go all along the line. And when the old arrangements of power go, there is war.

We may hear now in Stravinsky a Cassandra announcing destruction. But the old Countess de Pourtalès, who was in her box on the opening night of the *Sacre du Printemps*, only thought she was being insulted and loudly declared that it was the first time anyone had ever dared do such a thing to her in public. She rose to go. The Countess has been much derided for her attitude. I think she was right. For neither she nor her world would ever again be what it was before that evening, when such terrible rhythms were loosed. For what are all those youths on the stage who tread and do not advance? What are they but a presentation before the event of all the young who, trenched in earth, were soon to be restored to emotions so old, so primitive, that the longest memory had forgotten them? And music and mythical ballet seem to predict the very form warfare was to take, when the utmost possible movement behind the lines failed to move the long strategic deadlock within them. Of course, nothing is more probable than that Stravinsky, when he started to compose the *Sacre*, was conscious only that the forms which had until recently served men in music were suddenly no longer available for us. He was not concerned with war. If the artist seems to have any skill in the future, it is simply because he must be more attentive than the rest to what is happening. He knows, not what is about to happen, but, before anybody else, what is happening.

It would be presumptuous to put an end to the age of Picasso. We cannot, certainly, after the paintings prompted by the Spanish Civil War, after his still more recent pictures, put an end to Pablo Picasso. The convulsions of the last ten years have profoundly affected our attitude toward the arts. It is not so sure that there has been a corresponding change in the arts themselves. The content has changed. But in the case of Picasso it has not changed very much. For the content belongs to the man, who, young or with youth long past, remains much the same. It is the form that reflects the age.

What he paints may tell us something of what the painter is; it is the way in which he paints that will tell us what we are. For Picasso, the great period of passionate experimentation is over. The passion remains.

II

Picasso came to Paris in 1901, when he was nineteen; to follow him from that time until 1932 is to be present at a series of beginnings. And this is the more remarkable, for Picasso at nineteen was already a competent painter and was little more than twenty when he achieved a completely individual manner. Nothing presents a greater danger for the creative artist than to be always starting again; it is proof of Picasso's power and abundance that he surmounted it. His was perilous painting, by a Spaniard constantly rebellious. Discontent with the accomplished, each new canvas brought him all the risks of creation, for each meant to him a movement toward the unknown. His draftsmanship would have been great at any time. Inventive as the age in which he has lived, he has kept the Spanish awareness of a reality superior to the senses. He has imitated nature, not in her forms, but in her processes, and his fecundity, like hers, involves and does not hesitate before waste.

The content of such painting cannot but have its importance. And yet very little has been made of it. Ramon Gomez de la Serna is one of the few who have attempted to appraise Picasso's human values. It is natural that this should be so. For one thing, his painting is, like all that is most austere in modern art, obscure; and because it constantly changes, it is necessary before each new canvas to make the whole effort of comprehension. Also, at the time Picasso was coming into his fame, it was the thing to say that a painter's form was all that counted. The aesthetic emotion was the only one proper to feel before a painting, and if it was a good painting, no other was possible. Human emotion was out. This was not only the fashionable thing to say; it was also, for a while, a necessary thing to say. But this is no longer so. Picasso has long been accepted, and so have his methods. And we can now see that for a painter of his sort, there is no choice; he cannot, even if he would, exclude his emotions as a man from his painting.

It begins with a sorrowful and pitiful humanity. Other painters have turned to harlequins and acrobats because they could show the body in action; possibly, too, they liked the pretty costumes of the circus and the pacing horses. But Picasso made his mountebanks into an image of man. He was himself both harlequin and acrobat; but his pity is the more profound for being impersonal.

They are homeless and wandering, these families of his: drawn by starving horses over a land not theirs, outcasts that belong to no country, who own only the weather in any land where they pass. When young, they are lithe; when mature, strong; when old, they miserably sag. They live in a chill blast and balance their pathetic bodies on rolling globes. And pathetic is their fecundity.

The persons of the Blue Period suffer an intense loneliness. They have come, as Apollinaire has well said, to their end and are surprised that this blue is not the horizon. They sit in sunk attitudes before empty tables, they caress aged crows with starved hands. But again and again we are asked to look at the family, which represents, if you will, time passing through the human frame. Women look with distressed eyes at plates where there is only one portion; the boys' eyes dream. There is an early group in Picasso's greenish blue: a man and a woman, naked and embraced, who answer with timorous confidence the distracted stare of the gaunt mother beside them who holds in her arms a child. It is called *Life*. On the stones behind the group is shown the single figure's desperation of loneliness, the young woman and the man in the despairing comfort of love. Then there are those dolichocephalic adolescents, whose skulls seem made to contain suffering, not thought. In the Pink Period are naked boys. Puberty has not yet come on their bodies, but already they may be seen carrying babies on their shoulders. It is worth remarking how often Picasso attaches the child to the male; he stands protecting this creature of his loins, while the woman unconcernedly looks away, combing her hair, intent only upon herself.

The poor are portrayed, but only because it is in a beggar that pride is most astonishing. Man is a sad merry-andrew, with hawk's bells on his fool's cap. His suffering is deeper than his thought. There is protest here, but it is against irremediable, not social, ills. The point of it is directed against fecundity, that is to say, against life itself.

III

Picasso was born in Malaga of a Basque father and an Italian mother; his childhood was passed in Barcelona; after several years on his own in Madrid, he came to Paris. The strongest influence in painting was then from the Impressionists. "Among the several sins I have been accused of committing," Picasso has said, "none is more false than that I have as the principal objective of my work the spirit of research. When I paint, my object is to show what I have found and not what I sought." It was precisely the spirit of research that animated the late Impressionists and particularly the Pointillists who were then in full force. They proclaimed that they approached their canvases with the exact seriousness with which an experimental scientist enters his laboratory. They emulated the physicists in their play with light, as later such Surrealists as Salvator Dali were to set themselves the task of rivalling the psychologists in their revelations of the secret places of the mind. Picasso turned the painters to contemplating the mystery of their own craft.

The cry in Paris went from Pointillists to *Les Fauves*. They, no less than their predecessors, were concerned with what passed before their senses, but now the forms of things were distorted to project a personal vision. Whether the contented sensuality of the French painters was for Picasso an occasion for revolt is hard to say. It is certain that he now subdued his color, which is the flesh of painting, returning with Spanish fondness to the skeleton. The blue and rose gave way to grey and brown. His line, which had been baroque and elongated, he now made stern as a geometer's, and soon broken. When he showed bodies it was not now in love, or even in hunger; they were dissolved in planes, as later they would deliquesce in death. He advanced time. He sought what was permanent and not, as the French had long done, the changing appearance of an hour. He conceived new arrangements of space in painting and set his attention not on the object before him, nor on his own sensuousness, but on the relations between them.

His style is given a painter by his age. But in Picasso's case it was not given spontaneously; it was arrived at through endless experimentation. Derain and Vlaminck had brought to his attention the African sculptures of the Trocadéro, and for some time he and his friends had been collecting fetishes like these, so profoundly disturbing, so obviously and yet mysteriously sexual. Hideous they were, and yet so contrived in polished planes that they achieved a strange formal beauty. Picasso now turned to them, seeking, it may be, in their primitive emotion an answer to the theories of the Post-Impressionists. He overturned their reasoning, as he had rejected their sensuousness. The answer was Cubism. It was a Spanish expatriate's protest against Paris.

Or rather this was Picasso's Cubism. For though he has sometimes been credited with its invention, it is probable that the movement would have proceeded without him. Braque had already brought back from the South of France that landscape to which the word was first applied. And though he may have heard hints in Aix-en-Provence which led him to his manner, his compositions seem both as to color and to form to derive rather from the geometric fields of his own Ile-de-France. And before the word *Cubism* was invented, Fernand Léger, working alone in one of the popular quarters of Paris, had begun his search for a formula which would allow him truly to paint the life around him.

And Cubism as a whole takes off clearly from Post-Impressionism. The painters had behind them Cézanne's laborious experiments; they had before them a modern city. And unlike Aix-en-Provence, Paris, at least where it was cheap enough for a painter to live, was ugly and uncomfortable, vicious, vulgar and disorderly. They had to accept it. And it seemed to them, as it has since seemed to many other people, that it should be made acceptable to the mind. They thought that what was needed to make industrial civilization more endurable was to create through art a new attitude toward its smokestacks and dynamos, its migrations of motor cars and its swarms of misshapen men. When they looked out of their studio windows, it was upon a conglomeration of angles; when they looked down into the streets, it was upon moving multitudes. Paris, so many of whose stones had stood for centuries, had acquired a dynamic meaning. That was the only apparent meaning of a modern city—motion. And perhaps it had no other.

And indeed there were many who, instructed by the early Cubists, did attain at moments to a contemplative calm about the machines and the factory workers and saw them in terms of pure color and significant form. But it meant ignoring every humane emotion. This was quite an effort and almost nobody, even among the painters, was able to keep it up. Most of the early Cubists, like Metzinger—and he was one of the most successful in carrying out their program—have disappeared. Only Léger, who is a sort of *paysan de Paris* and has an enormous and utterly unaffected appetite for modern urban life, was really happy in these concepts. His paintings are in complete accord with his emotions and hence are crudely and dynamically alive. The men and women who arrive on his canvases have calmly assimilated the dynamo; their eyes are as blank as factory walls; their hair pours like molten metal; their limbs are rounded like pipes and they have, we know, automatic minds. They have a symbolic existence, nameless as the members of a French corporation; they compose indeed, with a strange humility, a sort of *société anonyme*. But they have ceased to be men and women. Braque, too, has remained from these times, because he was always apart from the movement. For all that his painting is abstract, it comes from the earth and is enriched by it.

It was Picasso's desire to make a *tabula rasa* of painting and start, not where the Impressionists left off, but in lowly stride with those unknown carvers of the African West Coast. And his study of Dahomey masks, of the figures of magical black fecundity from the Kingdom of Benin, was to have the most important consequences, not only for himself, but for the painting of his time. Placing the art of savages, traditional and profound, above the all too conscious art of his contemporaries, Picasso was to be led in the course of time to his Surrealist paintings and at last to his paintings of sleep. And from his understanding of their formality, the principles were derived of abstract art.

The generation of painters that matured around 1900 was the first that had ever had seriously to regard the art of the whole world. It was no longer a question of escaping, as Gaugin had done, to some remote island where the natives, untouched by civilization, still held some secret of life which was no longer accessible to the civilized. Picasso stayed in Paris and crossed the city on a bus to the Trocadéro. Nevertheless, he made a long voyage. For to accept, to truly accept, the art of the savages exposed there in the Ethnographical Museum was to discard much that Europe had held sound for centuries. The European tradition was, to be sure, on the decline. Manet was doubtless the last painter to receive it without unnatural effort and to carry it on as though it were his own true inheritance. Negro sculpture was only one of the primitive forms of art that had to be considered. But once it had been recognized, it became necessary to ask, "What is art?" and to find an answer which would do, not only for modern painting but for Greek archaic statues as well, for the recumbent figures on Etruscan tombs and the animal-faced deities of Egypt, for Roman mosaics and for the painting of a hundred peoples who had known no perspective. Obviously, what was true in art was what was everywhere and at all times true. The mystery of painting was in the craft.

What was true in art was the means by which the aesthetic emotion was produced. There was no longer any end. Picasso made the means the end.

That was at least disposing of the problem. Picasso is a man of prodigious intelligence—which is not to say that he has much in common with the Parisian intellectuals. They had taken away his subject matter. They had told him while standing in admiration before his paintings that they belonged in a museum. His art was grave, tragic and aware; it depicted a poor and suffering humanity.

It was idealistic in a world where ideals were not to be thought of. For some years of exile in Paris, Picasso's painting had remained Spanish. It was to continue so.

In turning to abstract painting, Picasso abandoned those suspicious characters he had found under the church porches in Madrid. He wandered about the streets of Montmartre, picking up objects that were equally suspect: old strips of wallpaper from demolished buildings, newspapers too old for reading, cigar-boxes, metal painted to look like wood, odd bits of junk that the ragman had rejected. If the subject no longer counted, then he would make these his subject. He pasted them on his canvas, arranging them and adding that medium in which so many lovely and noble things had been imagined and set down, giving his scraps an equal virtue with paint. Perhaps one way to escape materialistic theories was to accept the most abject materials. He sharpened his skill to endow them with that superior reality which is to be recognized in the angels, the mad kings and the dead nobles of El Greco. In the objects assembled on a café table he found his own *Approach to Toledo*.

For such a painter as Picasso there is no escape from the subject. Pure painting is shown by Matisse, whose sensuality is so inclusive that it embraces anything the sun shines on, whose sensibility is so fine that it can translate the sunlight itself. But in Picasso there is something of the strenuousness of the ascetic; he is attached to form with an intellectual passion. And much of that anguish which pursues him is due to his failure to find a subject equal to his passion. And if we ask what that passion is, there can be but one answer: it is to prevent death, both in the sense of running before it and arresting its destruction.

We find him returning again and again, and often it would seem secretly, to subjects that have a profounder meaning than can be found in their colors and contours. No one knows better than Picasso what meaning can be in color and contour. But certainly the most moving of his abstract paintings are those in which harlequins, guitars and the three musicians are set before us in a sinister reality. These are memories of Madrid. And they have that disturbing quality which belongs to dreams in which the mind recovers some hardly remembered anguish. These guitars like torsos of nude women, these players of bagpipes and stringed instruments in some forbidden comedy, these harlequins whose sad shapes are, no less than their costumes, cut out of lozenges, are arrangements of space, magnificent in the mastery. But they are something more. For there is an art beyond the art of such painters as Matisse, who introduces an order into what is most disorderly about us, our sensuous life, and who therefore deserves all our moral admiration. There are those who, for lack of another word, must be called poets. These enable us to contemplate the spectacle of human destiny with passion and with calm. We see, and are moved, it may be profoundly moved; but we are serene. These are the painters we place among the great. Of these Pablo Picasso was endowed to be one.

The great women of the Roman period are colored like the earth; yet they are calm. Their crude hands have dug, they have known love, their loins have labored; yet they are serene. They belong to our race and are more human. When they set out on those huge, those all too solid feet, it will be toward eternity.

The immediate occasion for these paintings was a trip to Rome, where Picasso was much impressed by the heroic statues and the few remaining paintings of the Imperial Age. But that was an accident. What is most interesting about these paintings is that they represent a considerable change in Picasso's attitude toward creatures born of this earth. What private circumstances caused this alteration in his emotions, we have no right to enquire. But we can see that it is by accepting their human destiny that these great women have become so like goddesses.

There was a time of some serenity, after the war, after his marriage, after the birth of his son, when Picasso, having attached himself to the oldest tradition in painting which we can properly call ours, could hold that whatever was most permanent in mankind was also what had most of heroism and of grace. To the same time, and also derived from studies in Italy, the country of his mother, belong those painted drawings, the *Lovers*, the *Blue Veil*, the *Resting Acrobat*. They have a pure loveliness not to be found elsewhere in Picasso's work. His serenity did not last.

'Afterwards come abstract horrors, angular creations with nightmare eyes. Afterwards come men and women, apparently taken from the beach at Antibes under a strong sun and a clear blue sky. But they are not men and women. They are merciless constructions of clay and bone, who sit in the sun, on the sand, and amorously assault one another with thrusting tongues in gaping mouths. Theirs are copulations such as mathematicians might dream, for they perform in pure space. Though, living, they act, yet they are shown as they will be when death is done with them.

Influenced by the remarkable exposition of Byzantine art held in Paris in 1931 are brilliant figures, colored like stained glass and, since they are disposed in complicated black circles, like glass in lead, suggesting saints' windows in some chapel of irreligion. Still compressed into almost circular shape are the many women who sleep, alone or accompanied only by their own shapes in mirrors. And in at least one of the paintings of the Spanish war, some men have been rendered who strangely resemble those women in sleep: an outer cruelty has been shown as an inner pain.

Picasso is a man of tremendous vitality, an artist of perhaps incomparable fecundity. But even he, when we survey his work as a whole, seems frantic, exasperated, and fearfully abstracted. The age he has painted has attempted to avoid enervation by repairing to lost sources of life. It has turned from the mechanical to the brutal, from a thought long removed from life and ineffectual to the unconscious and the unknown. It has abandoned the way of reason for the older ways of sleep and sex and blood. When Picasso thought to leave behind him the theories of the Post-Impressionists and to recover from the African sculptors their primitive force, he was not only reversing what European painting had done up until that time, he was also doing the exact opposite of what the savage sculptors had done. They had changed formless and obscure emotions into formal wood and bronze. They had moved through an art—doubtless conceived as magic—to control what else had been mere impulse. They had modified nature in order to control it. They had created order where before there was none. It is little to be wondered at that the record of the age should end, as does Picasso's own, with war.

1933

MANET AND THE MIDDLE CLASS

I T COMES AS SOMEWHAT of a surprise to learn from the catalogue of the Manet exposition which has been held throughout the summer months at the Musée de l'Orangerie that this is the first show of the great Impressionist's paintings since 1884, when he was posthumously honored by the Ecole Nationale des Beaux Arts. In his lifetime, Manet, irritated by the official attitude toward his work, did arrange a one-man show in a sort of wooden gallery, set up at the corner of the Avenue de l'Alma and the Avenue Montaigne, just across the river from the Champs de Mars where, a few weeks earlier, the Exposition Universelle of 1867 had been opened by the Emperor. The recent show did not lack for official patronage; the Committee of Honor included not only the President of the Council of Ministers but every member of the government with the remotest connection with the arts; M. Paul Valéry, who is in the way of becoming the recognized poet of the Republic, presided over the Committee of Organization and prefaced the catalogue with a charming and penetrating essay, *Triomphe de Manet*.

The show itself, though it contains much that is loaned from private collections and foreign galleries, affords no particular occasion for a reëstimate of Manet. There are many paintings here which are unfamiliar, but they only confirm the impression made by those masterpieces which belong to the government and which have long been known in the Luxembourg and the Louvre. And that impression is excellently put by that motto which Manet, playing on his own name, half in fun and yet seriously confirmed by the judgment of the most competent of his critical contemporaries, made his own: *Manet et Manebit*.

And because Manet does remain and no doubt will continue to remain one of the most admirable, one of the few still admired, artists of his time, it may be pertinent to inquire what his relations with that time were. Or, since this would take us too far, it might be better to insist merely upon the relation of the artist to the dominant taste of his day.

We recognize, and if we did not, the critics from the extreme Left would certainly cry it to us, that an artist cannot escape coming, in some measure, under the influence of the dominant class of his age. But how this influence works is obviously a much more complicated question than the Marxists would have us believe. In the eighteenth century, the sensibility of French artists seems to have accorded perfectly with that of the aristocracy—this in spite of their parental origin, which was frequently low. We find them wrangling with their patrons over payment, but there is little or no dispute in taste. Now, the eighteenth century was, at least on its higher levels, rational, licentious and sentimental, qualities all of them which forbid poetry and diminish painting, which must repose upon an ordered sensuality. On the other hand, we find that all the minor arts, those which cannot possibly exist without a patron—dressmaking, cabinetry, the painting of decorative panels and screens (and even the portraiture of the eighteenth century always suggests that its purpose was to adorn a wall and give meaning to a molding), domestic architecture and gardening with its attendant sculpture, these along with such social activities as letter-writing and the composition of memoirs, political treatises, satires and moral tales— remarkably flourished. And all found a manner which has probably not been surpassed. For what we call a period style is the result of a collaboration between the artists and the ruling classes; but only when their nerve-ends coincide can such a style come into being.

But in Manet's generation there was, instead of accord, only antagonism between the artists and those who dominated society. Since 1830, the class that had once been middle sat securely on top; itself a product of change, yet strangely distrustful of life, it violently resented any recognition in painting of those very changes which its own advent to power had helped to bring about. Too timid to acknowledge its real taste—for if the middle class does not admire hideousness, it can certainly stand having a great deal of it around—it was self-conscious in front of art and, as so often happens in the second generation of those who have come up in the world, over-refined. Manet was early known and soon notorious. "*Vous voilà aussi bien connu que Garabaldi,*" said Degas to him maliciously after the scandal broke over the *Olympia*. He was regarded as a bohemian, and insolent—very possibly because he painted the pleasures and distractions of the bourgeoisie, who could not understand how anyone could bring all the seriousness of great art to painting the barmaid at the Folies Bergères or so brood over the portrait of a prostitute that it would express the essential poetry of her candid nakedness and bestial presence.

Yet Manet himself was of sound bourgeois stock, the son of an honorable magistrate. And living amid hatred and hooted as few men of his worth have ever been (for, let it be remembered, the hideousness of his paint and the intolerable vulgarity of his subjects), he dreamed, as his friend Zola well knew, of "success such as can be known in Paris, with compliments from women and being received with adulation in salons, of a luxurious life and galloping amid the acclamations of the multitude." Constantly rebuffed, he continued sending his canvases to the Salon in a desire for official recognition; he painted, sustained only by artists and writers as lonely as himself. It is significant, I think, that so many of his finest paintings are of creatures essentially alone, even when, as with the adolescent in *Breakfast in the Studio*, the barmaid of the Folies Bergères, the dark-browed seated woman in *The Balcony*, there are other figures in the background.

The men and women he depended on were indeed the best of his generation: Degas, Renoir, Pissarro and the finely talented Berthe Morisot; Gautier, Huysmans, Zola, Mallarmé and above all Baudelaire.* And at the time Manet was painting, there was no other human sustenance for an artist. But that he was equally well understood by all, even in that distinguished group, is questionable. The admiration of Baudelaire, with whom Manet had so many spiritual correspondences, must have been as grateful as it was just; but Zola, who had done a good deal of propaganda for the painter, said, a few weeks after Manet's death, that his value to posterity would be that of a precursor and that he had left behind him little but sketches and nothing accomplished. The younger painters condemned him as timid, because he sought a living form and would not follow to their logical limits the principles of the aesthetic revolution which they, with less talent and more ardor, had espoused.

Manet et manebit. A hundred years after his birth and nearly a half century since his death, Manet remains as an example of how much can be accomplished in the teeth of the dominant class. There is danger in such loneliness, as we well know, who have seen how difficult, how more and more "closed," the art of men who work

* It is undoubtedly these men whom we should think of when we speak of taste in the nineteenth century, for they alone made a choice, generous or severe, among the materials which the age offered their senses and imaginations. The middle class made none, but grasped indiscriminately whatever came to it, rejecting only the best, which they could not use.

apart from the world may become. But to return to the question proposed earlier in this essay, and granting that it cannot be finally and briefly answered, we can at least see that Manet's position, uncomfortable as it must have· been, was more fortunate than that of the eighteenth-century painters who lived in favor and had only to accord their palettes to the taste of the most civilized society the centuries of modern Europe have known.

1937

MOVING PICTURES

THE MOVIES AS AN ART:
"THE LAST LAUGH"

C RITIC: I have just seen *The Last Laugh*. It is, if I am not mistaken, the first film of Carl Mayer's to be exhibited in this country since his famous *Cabinet of Doctor Caligari*. And, like that somewhat morbid film, *The Last Laugh* offers me a good deal of support in my opinion that the movies, if not yet an art in any decent meaning of the word, are already capable of providing one with aesthetic sensations. In other words, the movies may, at almost any minute now, take their place among the fine arts—just as the ballet has recently done, after having been for centuries no more than a gawdy and insipid spectacle composed by dancing masters who did not deserve to rank above animal trainers or any other manner of travelling mountebanks. I won't assert that the people chiefly responsible for the mass of the moving pictures annually released in this country are in the same class. I prefer rather to make my point that all that is needed, if the movies are actually to become an art, is for some magnate to discover another Diaghilev, a new Massine, whose genius is for cinematography instead of choreography, place a few millions at their disposal—and the trick is done.

SCENARIO WRITER: I seem to have heard something of the sort before.

CRITIC: You mean that "the movies are an art." I dare say you have. But the statement has been made for the most part by people who had no right to make it. When it has not been made by press agents, a race of meretricious hacks who exist, very much as the barbers did in the days when Ramilly wigs were worn, solely through their ability to make their masters look impressive before the world, it has been made by persons who, if more scrupulous, were also more timid, and through their timidity have missed the mark. They have based their claim on the proximity of the movies to the drama, to the novel, to life, to archeology, in fact on everything but the right thing. The one claim of the movies to being an art is that they are able, or should be able, to give us a paraphrase of life through move-

ment and light, so ordered and so controlled that the emotions produced shall depend less on what is shown upon the screen than on the
way in which it is shown. In other words, before I am willing to
allow that the cinema is a separate art, I must be convinced that it is
capable of providing me with aesthetic sensations quite different from
those I am accustomed to receive from any of the existing arts. As I
just said, I am convinced that it is; and *The Last Laugh* has very considerably fortified that conviction.

SCENARIO WRITER: Very possibly you are right. But as long as I
am dependent upon the moving pictures for my living, I hope that
they will continue to be what they are, thank God, at present: a
highly profitable industry. But why do you speak of *The Last Laugh*
as being Carl Mayer's. On the program he is credited only with having
written the story. The picture was directed by F. W. Murnau and
photographed by Carl Freund. I can assure you out of my own experience that the author is the least important person in the making of a
film.

CRITIC: That is doubtless true out in Hollywood. It may even be
true in general in Berlin. However, I think I am right in attributing
more of *The Last Laugh* to the influence of Carl Mayer than would
in the ordinary film be attributable to the author of the fable from
which it was derived. For one thing, his story is not separable from
the film: it is the film. The simple, poignant and not very extraordinary story of the old porter of a great modern hotel, who, merely
because he has grown old, loses his job, and with it his ability to front
life benignly and in liveried pride—anyone might have conceived it,
but I can't think of anyone else who could have presented it so effectively solely through *moving pictures*. I was convinced after seeing
the *Cabinet of Doctor Caligari* that Mayer had a clear and intelligent
idea of what the moving picture should be; after looking at some
hundreds of films since then, I am inclined to believe that he is alone
in his knowledge. Of course, anyone who cared to consider, say for a
week, just what those two words—"moving pictures"—mean might
very well arrive independently at the same position which Mayer
reached some years ago. It is perfectly obvious that what the moving
pictures should be is just that—moving pictures and nothing more.
And that, as it happens, is exactly what *The Last Laugh* is: it has no
titles and needs none; the occasional inserts are legitimate since they
are seen, or at least supposed to be seen, not directly by the spectators,
but through the eyes of one or another of the characters of the film.

SCENARIO WRITER: Come! Don't be too hard on us—or I shall
begin to suspect that what really annoys you about the people who are

responsible for the American films is that they are making a great deal of money out of productions which, judged by your literary standards, are worthless. After all, whether we are dealing with a novel, a play or a film, the story's the essential thing. (I am old-fashioned enough to like competence; even in a novel, however modern, I insist upon plot and characters.) As far as the movies go, anything which will add to its clarity and significance is legitimate. To concoct a film without titles is only a stunt. It seems to me that I remember Charles Ray having done it some years ago. Naturally none of you critics even so much as took the trouble to see it. Of course, if his name had been Karl Strahl and his film imported—! Then, no doubt, and only then, would you and your friends have gone into a high state of excitement over it. However, to come back to my point: the story's the thing. *The Last Laugh* is extraordinarily interesting technically. But technique, in the movies as in the novel, is of secondary importance. The story of *The Last Laugh*, for all its sentimentality, is too slight to make for popularity. As a matter of fact, it is not a story at all—but simply an episode.

CRITIC: Well, call it that if you will—the final episode in the life of a backstairs King Lear—for that is what Emil Jannings makes of the part of the imperious old porter. It is, as Jannings plays it, a fine, almost tragic thing. The character of the old man is realized through a succession of minute and entirely realistic touches—there is an amazing completeness to his portrait—but with a sense of freedom usually quite lacking in actors of the naturalistic school. Before he has done with his old porter, Jannings has made him something more than a person, pompous with white curled sidewhiskers, magnificent in his gold-braided overcoat, utterly abject in his white jacket of a lavatory attendant: his porter becomes an image of the pretentiousness of the old male, sustained by the circumstance which he had once had the energy to create around him, pathetically declining and foolishly bewildered when his livery, his high position (in the servant world) are taken away from him. He is, as I say, a backstairs King Lear. And the fairytale ending—that happy ending so maliciously tacked on at the end—does nothing to destroy the impression that has already been made of a degraded old man left helpless, and deserted by his mind, rotting away in an underground washroom. That impression, I say, is no more destroyed by what follows, amusing and fantastic as it is, than a sense of King Lear's suffering is obliterated by reading *The Winter's Tale*—which is also an absurd and delicious fairy story.

SCENARIO WRITER: Aren't you laying it on thick? Mr. Griffith's press agent used to call him the Marlowe of the Movies, but I don't think anyone has the effrontery to call himself the Shakespeare of the Screen.

CRITIC: I am comparing two effects, not two men. Carl Mayer, had he gone into literature would probably be regarded, now as an imitator of Hoffman, now as a smaller German Maupassant, depending upon whether you considered him as the author of *Caligari* or of *The Last Laugh*. But the point is that he has gone into the movies, as the phrase is, and he has brought to the moving pictures a certain consciousness of his medium which, so far as I can see, no one else has hitherto shown.

SCENARIO WRITER: You mean that he has shown the producers how to tell a story on the screen without having recourse to titles? But that, as I have implied, has already been done. Chaplin's pictures —I mention him since you don't seem to be familiar with the work of Charles Ray—are virtually without titles. For the most part, they are there simply as chapter headings or as supplementary gags thrown in for the sake of an extra laugh. And there are others who scarcely depend upon titles to put their story across.

CRITIC: As a matter of fact I am familiar enough with the work of Charles Ray. He is one of the few people in America with a genuine aptitude for the screen. And he is a talented actor, just as, let us say, Booth Tarkington is a talented writer. But—and in this he is also like Mr. Tarkington—his intelligence is immature, and he does not quite understand the medium with which he works. Whatever he does that is fine, is done by a kind of simple instinct, rare enough no doubt, but still not quite the thing one most wants to see.

SCENARIO WRITER: And what is that, please?

CRITIC: A fine and deliberate consciousness of what effects may be got from the camera and the ability to combine them toward an aesthetic end. As to what those effects are I think we had best define them negatively: they are those effects which would be less telling if they were produced in some other way or by some other means. Whenever you see something done on the screen which would be less significant, or, better still, unimaginable, in a narrative or on the stage—then, I think, you can say that you have pure cinema. There are endless examples in the later films of Douglas Fairbanks—another person with a very genuine sense of the cinema—while Chaplin frequently does things practically unimaginable in a novel. There is, for instance, nothing in *Easy Street* which I can easily think of as being intelligible, much less effective, if told in words. In *The Last Laugh*, on the other hand, there is nothing which could not be carried over, without great loss, into a short story; but it is also true that there is not a single incident in the course of the film which would not lose something of significance by being translated into words. The cinematographic quality may not be as high as in the best of Chaplin or Fairbanks, but it is continuous. The descent of the old man in the lavatory for the first time is told, exactly as it should be told, through movement; there is no question but that the appropriate emotion is there and that it is conveyed by the sight of an old man, his stature fallen, his arm dwindled at his side, mumbling and unkempt, shuffling down a flight of stairs; words could perhaps convey that emotion just as well, but they would have done it very differently.

SCENARIO WRITER: But if the cinematographic effects, as you call them, in *The Last Laugh* are not superior to those in the American films, why do you consider it so much better than *The Thief of Bagdad* or *Easy Street?*

CRITIC: I don't. I only insist that it shows more clearly than either of the pictures you have mentioned the direction in which the movies must go if they are to become a separate art. Its cinematographic effects may not be so ingenious as those of Fairbanks or in so high a vein of comic poetry as the best of Chaplin, but at least they are continuous. There is nothing there that does not belong in a moving picture. And the whole is consciously directed toward an aesthetic end. It has a continuous rhythm, very beautifully controlled. For this, I suppose, the director is chiefly responsible. There are innumerable instances to show that the tempo has been consciously varied from moment to moment. I need only cite one of the scenes in the restaurant to which the poor old man repairs after inheriting his millions from the fantastic Mexican who is kind enough to die in his arms in the lavatory. As the camera sweeps along the line of assistants to the maître d'hôtel, we are shown first a man sharpening knives with broad slow strokes, and immediately afterward a little man intensely jagging with a very short and almost vertical knife at a piece of pastry. It is a small point but indicative of the attitude the makers of *The Last Laugh* have had toward their film. I have seen bits of movement in American films which were infinitely more moving; but I cannot escape the conviction that they got there by accident. Some of the best of them have occurred in the news reels.

SCENARIO WRITER: But what about Chaplin? There is certainly a definite rhythm to Chaplin himself—

CRITIC: Certainly from the beginning of Chaplin's second period there is in every picture he has produced a continuous movement, which begins with the first image cast on the screen and does not end until the final darkness. It was T. S. Eliot who first pointed out that

Chaplin had succeeded in imparting to his films a rhythm quite other than the rhythm of life, and that in this he was alone. But in a Chaplin film the movement, I am inclined to think, is confined to the actors, in especial to one actor, Charlie Chaplin himself. In *The Last Laugh* the characteristic rhythm pervades the whole: not only the lonely figure of Jannings, but the walls, the doors, the elevator; everything moves, and the movement of every object is so controlled that it falls naturally and easily into the movement of the whole. I suppose the obvious thing here would be to compare the film to a musical composition, but I had rather not do so; in the long run it would only confuse the issue. For we are not dealing with sound but with a succession of visual images; the rhythm of a film is to be comprehended not by the ear, even the unsensual ear, but by the eye. And we are unaccustomed, so to speak, to hearing with our eyes.

SCENARIO WRITER: I should say that we are. However, suppose I grant your point that a moving picture should show a continuous movement from first to last, and that its rhythms, if less marked than those of music, should be at least sufficiently stressed to make it clear that the director has aimed at something more than a haphazard reproduction of gesticulating actors. What then? Chaplin has all that.

CRITIC: Yes, but there is one other respect in which *The Last Laugh* marks a distinct advance on anything that Chaplin has yet done. You have probably noticed that the newspaper critics almost always comment on the poor quality of Chaplin's photography. That is, I suspect, simply their way of saying that Chaplin is singularly unaware of the necessity in a film for that quality which in a painting is called, or used to be called, composition. His pictures are ugly; there is no other term for them; and their ugliness has nothing to do with the sordidness of his favorite backgrounds or his own distressing costumes; rather it is due to his inattention to a decent massing of lights and shadows. Now, whoever has been responsible for this part of *The Last Laugh* has been continuously aware that, in a film, he is painting with rapid and constantly shifting shafts of light. His moving picture is constructed not, strictly speaking, in black and white, but with varying intensities of shadow and with varieties of light. There are innumerable scenes taken through windows and glass doors—the best of them through the revolving doors of the hotel or through the transparent panels of the descending elevator—simply because glass, particularly glass in motion, gives a very definite quality to the light it reflects. The producers have been conscious that their picture, like any other picture, must, if it is to have aesthetic significance, be "composed"; they have also known that theirs was a moving picture and that its composition must be dynamic and not as in a painting static. I don't think they have always succeeded; indeed I should say that they have failed more often than not in imposing significant form on each momentary rectangle. But at least they have seen the necessity of paying some attention to the relation of the lines and masses of the background to each other and to the living figures which move against them. In Caligari, they saw very clearly that a moving picture must be a dynamic composition, but in that picture they made the mistake of trying to compose in black and white. It was a modern painting in continuous motion. In The Last Laugh they have realized that they are dealing not with black and white at all, but with light and shadow. In Caligari, in order to control their effects, they painted sunlight streaking across the floor from a window painted white; in other words, they tried to do with the camera what can be much better done with a brush. In the present instance, they have relied upon the camera. The Last Laugh is pure photography, not imitation painting. And whatever aesthetic emotions it arouses are not musical nor pictorial, but something quite different. I suppose that we should have to call them cinematographical—at least until someone suggests a less ungainly word.

SCENARIO WRITER: What you have to say is very interesting. But I don't think, frankly, that I can afford to bother my head about the aesthetic possibilities of the movies. Suppose we succeeded in making every film a pure aesthetic spectacle—how many people would be aware of it? Yourself, perhaps, and a half dozen others. It would hardly pay for the time and labor involved.

CRITIC: There you are quite wrong. Aesthetic sensations are the common property of the human race—except, perhaps, for the half-educated—to which class I am afraid most of your patrons belong. However, excess of education over intelligence has not prevented what for some perverse reason you call the movie audiences from appreciating every one of the qualities I have praised whenever they occurred. Chaplin, who has rhythm beyond comparison with all his competitors, they adore; and Douglas Fairbanks, who understands more clearly than any other American what opportunities the camera affords in contradistinction to the stage, has not, so far as I have heard, lacked for popularity. No, the truth is that the producers are unforgivably stupid in the matter: witness their attempts to imitate The Covered Wagon. They seem to have thought that all that was necessary to emulate its success was to have a scenario based on a fifth-rate novel by Emerson Hough, to lay the scene in the West before the Civil War, to employ one or another of the mediocre actors who assisted in making that spectacle, and to encourage a sturdy kind of patriotism. They failed to realize that what made *The Covered Wagon* thrilling was something that had nothing to do with the asinine story and little with the setting: it was the *movement* of those wagons. Their progress over the grave of the dead old women; their slow crawling across the prairie; above all, that unforgettable descent into the gully— these were the things to which the public responded, and their response, however little they may have been capable of analyzing it, was due to nothing but the aesthetic significance of those lumbering wagons which seemed, at least to me, to move for the sake of pure movement. No, you are quite wrong, and your wrong-headedness has, I am glad to say, cost you millions.

SCENARIO WRITER: Thanks awfully. I must be getting back to the studio; I shall lose something less than a million if I stay here, but still a week's pay is a week's pay. And I am afraid I see not the least chance of using any of your ideas in my present scenario. However, I'll think about them. They may be of some use to me.

CRITIC: I doubt it. They are hardly worth your bothering about.

SCENARIO WRITER (*moving uneasily in his chair*): Just a moment. To a mind broken down by movie captions, I find this argument a trifle confusing. Could you tell me, in the very simplest of words, just why you think this picture of earth-shaking importance?

CRITIC: To diagram the matter then, I feel that this is a fine picture, first because it is a simple and human story told without recourse to any Roman orgies, fashion parades, and other gaudy nonsense; second because the acting is a great deal better than usual, the people act like real people and look like real people, and the performance of Emil Jannings is masterful; and thirdly because the producers have made a beautiful thing of the film, in the direction, in the settings and—this is most important—in the photography.

Vanity Fair: June, 1925

SEX APPEAL IN THE MOVIES

"**S**EX APPEAL," that peculiar attribute, which permits certain players to move their admirers more agreeably, as well as more directly, than would be possible by any display of their mere talents, is, as everyone knows, most highly thought of in the movies. Possibly it has always been so; but just now, under the influence of a stage successfully libertine, the moving picture producers and their agents seem to be more than ever keenly on the lookout for it. For, as it happens, it is not a particularly common commodity. And, if not actually valued above talent, at least it appears to be regarded as a sounder investment.

It needed the tremendous popular success of *Variety* to bring Emil Jannings to America, despite the fact that he had again and again, over a period of ten years, shown himself the ablest character actor of the screen; Lya da Putti had only to make a single appearance in support of Jannings to gain an American contract. Yet no one could have thought her more than a passable actress, however wisely cast in *Variety*; nor particularly beautiful, however heavily her feminine quality was underlined, first as the dancing girl, then as the acrobat. The most that could be said for her was that she carried, from start to tragic finish, the obvious suggestion of a rôle entirely sensual. But that, it seems, is quite enough for any ordinary producer with an eye to the box-office. Talent is, after all, so variable a thing, and depends for its success upon expert collaboration. Jannings himself was helpless in the face of the confused Italian direction, the bad photography, the inept scenario of *Quo Vadis?* Whereas the appeal of sex can be felt through the flimsiest story; it creates its own drama. The spectators themselves collaborate to make the play a success, and supply whatever imagination the scenarists lacked.

I do not by any means wish to deny the uses of "sex appeal." It has its legitimate place on the screen as on the stage—*Variety* is a capital instance of a film which would have fallen apart had its heroine been less obviously attractive. Still, one cannot help won-

dering whether, considering it for the moment purely as a commodity, the producers are not putting entirely too much money on
it. (I have in mind a number of actresses—it would be impolite to
name them—who have recently been advanced; they must be thought
of as having "sex appeal," so conspicuously do they lack every other
quality that would make them desirable on the screen.) For, if the
erotic spectacle is almost always a success with the public (even
when disguised under so formidable a title as Dante's *Inferno*), the
participants in these shows find short favor: their lives at best are
brief. As for the actors, the actresses, who have kept their place in
the sun of popularity over a period of years, it is difficult to find even
one who owes anything to "sex appeal." On the contrary, it would
seem that most of them hold the public, the vast public of the moving pictures, largely through their ability to project characters whose
sexual life is not more complicated than that of a child.

Take first the comedians. Into the life of that brisk, efficient and
perplexed young man whom Harold Lloyd presents always, sex hardly
enters with more force than it does into the Yale curriculum. There
are young women in his films, but they are at the end of the difficulties, not the cause of them. As for that witless youth who is the
Buster Keaton of the films, he is the forlorn adolescent who has long
since decided that all feminine favors are beyond *his* hope and de-
serving. So, in *Go West!*, when offered a choice (he himself is too
modest to realize that a choice is there) between his grateful employer's only daughter and a faithful affectionate cow, he chooses the
cow. Granted that this is burleque, it is successful largely because it
is completely in character. The world which Chaplin creates around
him—and he alone of all the actors of the screen actually arrives at
creating a separate world—is seen through even younger eyes. It is the
remembered world of a child little if any older than the Kid—who
has played in the streets of London, poor, starveling, dreaming at
windows, continually haunted by the presence of huge policemen.
So much is Chaplin at core the child that he can assume the manners
of one or the other sex without offense; can endeavor—when he
arrives late for work in *Pay Day*—to placate his irate boss by coyly
advancing and offering him a lily, or, as in *The Pawnbroker*, awk-
wardly crack his employer over the head with a stepladder that is
much too big for him to handle. The love scenes in the Chaplin films
take place in the mind of a small boy; the girls who appear remain
mysterious and remote. The episode in *The Gold Rush* where he
waits in vain for the pretty ladies to come to his party began badly
enough; instead of being poignant, it was merely mawkish; it was

saved at the end only by Chaplin's slipping, more or less unconsciously, into his proper character and playing out the imaginings of
a child. The situations which Chaplin meets are, of course, more
familiar to an adult's world than to that of a child; but therein lies part
of their incongruity. They are dealt with logically, but with that terrible direct logic which almost alone children are capable of putting
into action. Even when, as in *Pay Day* and one or two other films of
his middle period, he is represented as married, it is easy to see that
his relations with his wife are simply those of a resourceful and
capricious little boy doing his best to arrange things amicably
with a severe parent whom no persuasion of the intelligence can
reach.

Mary Pickford, too, is not without her childishness, but she
differs from Chaplin in having a common mind. Her feet are those
of a *comédienne*, but she lacks the comic imagination. Nevertheless,
she and Douglas Fairbanks—it is not merely because they happen to
be married that Doug and Mary are constantly coupled in the popular
imagination—have succeeded as no others in projecting the dearest
emotions of the American people in regard to the relations between
the sexes. Those emotions are, to be sure, comparatively immature.
It is not for nothing that Miss Pickford has been compelled to retain
those blond curls. Her attitude toward the opposite sex, even when
her rôle would seem to call for something older, is that of a healthy,
humorous, but by no means unsentimental girl of thirteen toward
the boys of the neighborhood. She rags them unmercifully, and they
adore her for it. Douglas Fairbanks is her male complement—the boy
in his earliest teens. He is the screen equivalent of that age when the
sexual impulse is felt chiefly as prompting to imaginary adventures.
He sees himself now as a pirate, now as a knight under Richard the
Lion-Heart, now the prince in an Arabian fairy tale. But always he is
romantic and chivalrous, fighting against odds, rescuing pallid and
helpless heroines. More prosaically, he represents that self-conscious
age when boys affect to be indifferent to girls and to despise them;
actually, of course, they are continually showing off before them. And
it is not difficult to see in the marvelous leaps of Fairbanks, his scaling
of impossible walls and plunging into impassable streams, the equivalent of the first tentative, largely unconscious approaches of the adolescent to the opposite sex.

It is impossible here to go through the whole list of screen stars
who have kept the favor of the fans over a period of five years or
more. Not that the list is so long—particularly if one subtracts all
those who, like Thomas Meighan, are now kept alive only by the

memory of past performances and increasingly strong doses of publicity. But to analyze a new star is not always to discover another element of the mass mind. Come at once to Valentino. Let it be said at once that Valentino's popularity in the last years of his life was considerably less than would have been supposed by one who regarded his career for the first time when indecent mobs were clamoring around his bier. But let that pass. His career was a brief one, briefer than the number of its years would show. But surely no one ever so violently captured the imagination of the movie fans as did the handsome young Julio of *The Four Horsemen of the Apocalypse*. His discovery was an accident; he was chosen, not because of his looks, much less because of his ability, but because the director thought he approximated the young Argentine wastrel in character. Within the year, a dozen young men, dark-complexioned and with something of the Latin air—including at least one East-Side Jew, who for the purpose had assumed an ancient and aristocratic Spanish name—had persuaded as many producers to put them before the public as rivals of Valentino. Most of them were as handsome, but none of them had his animality or grace, not one of them could convey, with his brazen expertness, the same impression of desire. Here, certainly, it would seem, was "sex appeal"—and with a new persuasion!

Naturally it was assumed that the chief appeal of the new actor was to his feminine admirers. The newspapermen who reported the excitement attendant upon Valentino's death and funeral acted on this assumption. Their accounts were filled with the pictures of hysterical young women and weeping old women patiently standing in the rain. The photographs made at the time tell, however, quite a different story. Eight out of ten of the faces which waited before the hospital, and later before the funeral parlors where Valentino lay dead, are those of young men and boys.

The explanation of this is neither difficult nor strange. It simply depends upon the obvious fact that the figures of the screen are not flesh and blood, but mechanical shadows. They are not the men and women of the stage, and it is impossible that those who stare at them through the darkness should react to them as if they were. They move in silence, and to the accompaniment of a music that is hardly ever distinctly heard. In consequence, it is possible for the spectator of the movies to identify himself with the actor to an extent unknown in the theater. And since this is so, it is but natural that the strongest reactions of the movie fan should always be toward his own rather than the opposite sex. It is young girls who fill up the greater part of

Gloria Swanson's correspondence, and, of those who waited outside when Valentino lay dead, probably the greater number had at one time or another seen themselves as the Sheik.

The New Republic: November 16, 1927

A FILM OF JEAN COCTEAU

THE JEAN COCTEAU film *Blood of a Poet* has at last been released to the public, after a delay of some two years, due, so it is said, to the objections of one of the aristocratic ladies whom the poet, unknown to herself, had cast for a part that was too like a caricature of her class. Her resentments caused the third episode to be done over, with the result that the American acrobat Barbette (born in Trick, Texas, and trained as a young cowboy) is now playing the rôle, in a blond wig and with an accurate androgynous glitter.

The photography is nothing remarkable and the registration of sound indistinct, so that many of the words, spoken by Cocteau himself as commentator, are lost. But in *Blood of a Poet* there remains a concentration of imagination, a mingling of myth and commonplace, a sense of mystery apprehended by a clear and analytic mind, that set it apart and make it one of the most interesting of modern films. The material is morbid, but the film is not. There are faults of taste, as in most of Cocteau's literary productions; like them, it uses symbol and upon what is perhaps the least personal of mediums imposes a lyric style.

In essence, *Blood of a Poet* is a metaphysical autobiography. We are shown first the outer world: two factory chimneys that rise higher and higher into the sky and then collapse in fragments and fire. Then there is the turning of a knob, while two rather lengthy captions divulge the intent of the poet and a dedication to the memory of Pisanello, Piero della Francesca and Paolo Uccello, makers of blazons and riddles, is thrown on the screen. Behind the door, whose knob turns, is the poet of the film, a dark, handsome young man, naked but for a pair of ordinary trousers, turned up over his calves and held by a belt pointed with Cocteau's signature, the star. There is also a star inscribed against the scar on his back. His hair is black, but for the moment is artificially whitened by an eighteenth-century tie-wig. He draws on paper a face—eyes, nose and then mouth.

The mouth comes alive and speaks. There is the repeated knock at the door, and the poet is terrified. Before opening the door, he erases with his hand the one living thing in the drawing. It is the visitor who in horror first sees that the mouth of the drawing has come off on the artist's hand. He thrusts it through a broken window into the air, he attempts to wash it away in water. It stays. The one real thing he has created is now a part of him. Left alone, the poet throws off his wig—in other words, his false eighteenth-century hair.

In his poor room is a statue, a woman, beautiful and of classical aspect, but dead in stone and her arms broken short. This is, of course, a symbol of the poet's art. Embraced, she, too, comes alive and speaks. A warning is heard, saying that whoever embraces a statue is in danger of becoming one. This theme, as we shall see, is repeated in the last episode.

His Muse (to name her as Cocteau has already done in his drawings) tells the poet to plunge into the looking-glass. The glass is solid, reflecting his body and sounding when he strikes it. The Muse urges, "Try!" And he plunges, the mirror splashing behind him like water. This concludes the first episode, which obviously presents the poet's relation to his own work and to the classical tradition of poetry, which, like Cocteau's Muse, is only a broken statue until brought to life.

The second episode has to do with the poet's discovery of himself, above all the recognition of his especial weaknesses. He disappears through the mirror to enter the hidden recesses of himself. "You come," says the voice, "passing through the mirror, to the Hôtel des Folies Dramatiques." The poet is in the lonely long corridor of numbered doors and walls from which the paper has been torn. He stops before the room numbered 19; outside the door have been placed a pair of worn black men's shoes. He peers through the keyhole to see a Mexican shot down by rifles in front of a rock, on which a little image of the Madonna stands. Image and man fall together. The scene is reënacted; the Mexican rises to be shot again, the Madonna again falls from the rock. In the next room, the poet sees a shadow of hands on the ceiling and the infinitely delicate filling of an opium pipe; then, directly against the keyhole, a huge human eye. These, we are told, are the Mysteries of China. The third chamber holds Lessons of Flight, a piece of symbolism already familiar to readers of Cocteau's poems. A child, harnessed in bells, is driven by a hard-faced black-dressed woman with a whip, first to the mantelpiece, then halfway up the wall. Finally, to the child's pleasure and the consternation of her governess, she is seen, her flight held from going higher only by the ceiling. The fourth chamber is that in which the Hermaphrodites make love. In this scene, Cocteau ingeniously recalls Aristophanes' fable of the divided sexes, as narrated in the *Banquet*. One of the figures is always unreal, an outline in white on a black ground; the other has a head, then, to the sound of a pistol shot, first an arm, then a living leg. Thus, we are shown in the second episode, through symbols, the poet's vulnerability, his power to be wounded to death, along with whatever he holds most sacred, and to revive only to be brought again to death; Cocteau's private vice of opium; the poet's need of both courage and art if he would fly above the crowd; and the impossibility for him of satisfying love. When he has accepted all these, the conditions of his living, the Muse (who has by now acquired arms) thrusts a revolver into a sort of white wire abstraction of Cocteau's own head, dangling in front of the film poet. He takes it and applies it to his temple, fires; at once his head is crowned with a burden of laurel leaves and his brow profusely bleeds.

The third episode, in part derived from a similar scene in *Les Enfants Terribles*, concerns the poet and his relation to the living world about him. There is a snowball fight between schoolboys; apparently the scene is a courtyard covered with theatrical snow. The building behind is baroque; from two of the upper windows balconies depend. A statue in the courtyard is demolished by the snowballs of the children (presumably, the sculptured figure is a poet of the past); one of the boys becomes a target for the others. He is perhaps thirteen years of age. He is hurt only when a slightly older boy, toward whom he has already manifested his love, encloses a stone in snow and hurls it at him. He falls in the snow and bleeds from the mouth. His antagonist bends over him, a dark brutal boy's face, and slowly displays his tongue.

The thirteen-year-old boy has fallen close to the table where the poet sits playing cards with his Muse. Both are in evening dress. The balconies have become theatre boxes, filled with an aristocratic and fashionable audience. "If you have not," warns the Muse, "the ace of hearts, you are lost." The poet draws the card from the jacket of the dead boy. It is from the hurts of love, the wounds of his own childhood (for the bleeding boy is also the poet), that the artist derives his feeling for the suffering of others. Then from the building (we are told it is an empty house), down the snowy horseshoe staircase, comes a naked black youth, or, for so it is intended, an archangel. On his back are the wings and the skeleton of an insect, reminiscent of African sculptures. He covers the dead child's face and then slowly takes from the poet's hand the one card he must have. The poet draws a revolver from inside his coat, from above his heart, and hands it to the Muse.

She destroys him. The boxes applaud. The Muse is now metamorphosed; she acquires long black gloves, her hair becomes like sculptured hair, her eyes turn to the enamelled eyes of Greek gods. Once more, she is inhuman.

The fourth episode is devoted to the poet's fame. He is dead. His Muse enters what can only be a hall of the Academy, to stand between busts of illustrious dead poets. Then she walks attended by a sacrificial bull, over whose back and flanks are displayed maps of all the countries of the world. Only the bull's horns are seen, and they become a lyre. Then the Muse withdraws, in one hand the instrument of music, and, balancing it, the globe. She is last seen, herself lying dead, a creature of stone.

The film ends with the factory towers collapsing in fire.

One can hardly say that Cocteau has mastered the medium; it would be amazing if he had. He has nevertheless drawn unsuspected possibilities from it. There are moments, particularly during the metamorphoses of sculptured forms into life, that have a strange and hallucinating beauty. The symbols, which many have found obscure, should not be so to anyone familiar with Cocteau's poems. He has already used most of them in verse; what he intends by their arrangement in the film should be clear. The use he makes of them is exciting, for with them he has created an atmosphere that is less fantastical than metaphysical. The direction is that of a poet's intelligence.

Cocteau is, more than the poet, that rare thing the dilettante of genius. The word is just now in disrepute, and unjustly so; for the dilettante stands between two worlds. In him, the sensibility of the aristocrat meets the sensibility of the artist, and he is aware as neither alone can be of the particular color of his time. Historically, the dilettantes have had much to do with the creation of the style of any period. Horace Walpole, on Strawberry Hill, recognized those changes which were to bring about the romantic revival while the poets were still at their heroic couplets. Madame de Pompadour and her brother, Marigny, brought about that change of taste to which Louis XVI was later to attach his name. And Cocteau has had an influence on the last decade out of all proportion to his talents. He now affects to despise his fashionable world of snobs; but he derives more of his power from it than from that other and purer sphere in which he mingles with Picasso and Stravinsky. He has touched every art (and cultivated most of the vices) of his time; he has brought to the cinema all the qualities of the genial amateur. The blood of the poet, however, still streams from the stock of the higher French bourgeoisie.

The film with which this is most readily compared is Bunuel's

Chien Andalou. But Bunuel was really concerned, as James Joyce is in his *Work in Progress,* with the tortured mind of a man in sleep. The sequence of events had no logic; the conjunction of objects was as strange as in a nightmare; and Bunuel's success was that he created, as no other medium could possibly have done, the very anguish of a man ridden by the most dreadful of nightmares. He was violently sadistic, with a peculiarly Spanish insistence on death and its corruptions. Cocteau, on the other hand, is all French in his lucidity as in his cruel sensitiveness. ("He looks," said a friend to me some years ago, "like an exposed nerve.") He has dealt, not with sleep, or even with dreaming, but with a mind intensely awake. His subject is really that old French subject, *La Gloire;* he has seen the possibilities of the moving camera to present its metamorphoses: both the changes the poet must undergo to attain it and the altering forms his fame will take, living and dead.

1932

NOVELISTS
OF THE
TWENTIES

THREE BRILLIANT YOUNG NOVELISTS

(*The Beautiful and Damned*, BY F. SCOTT FITZGERALD; *The Beginning of Wisdom*, BY STEPHEN VINCENT BENÉT; *Three Soldiers*, BY JOHN DOS PASSOS)

T HE YEARS following the war in America have been remarkable for the rise in popular and critical estimation of a small group of novelists, who represent a revolt against the silliness and complacency of commercialized literature. Although Mr. Floyd Dell, the youngest among them, approaches thirty-five, they have been commonly referred to as the younger American novelists, the reviewers believing, no doubt, that any worthy who had not hitherto reached their notice must be young. Most of them are, alas, middle-aged; one or two, perhaps, prematurely old, grayed by their years of obscure toil. There are, however, three young American writers each of whom is publishing a book this fall who cannot be overlooked by anyone interested in delivering the American novel from the Philistines. The sum of their ages is seventy-two years; each is a graduate of one of the Eastern universities; each is trying to find some other solution to life than that offered by Dr. Frank Crane and Dr. Henry Van Dyke.

Francis Scott Fitzgerald is a Princetonian; Stephen Vincent Benét, Yale '19; John Dos Passos, Harvard '17. Being myself a graduate of Princeton (present at all reunions in orange-and-black costume), I will first consider Mr. Fitzgerald.

Mr. Fitzgerald's novel *The Beautiful and Damned* is to run serially in the *Metropolitan* and later to be published by Scribner's. It concerns the disintegration of a young man who, at the age of twenty-six, has put away all illusions but one; this last illusion is a Fitzgerald flapper of the now famous type—hair honey-colored and bobbed, mouth rose-colored and profane. The minor characters are exhibits of popular stupidities—a reformer, a theosophist, a movie director— burlesque masks behind which may occasionally be seen a shadowy figure with the eyes and lips of Mr. H. L. Mencken.

The humorous portions of the book are exceedingly good, perhaps the best thing Mr. Fitzgerald has done. The satire is deftly and wittily handled, but in spite of the left-handed happy ending the book does not achieve the irony which the author has clearly intended; its mood is rather one of first cynicism.

But, as with *This Side of Paradise*, the most interesting thing about Mr. Fitzgerald's book is Mr. Fitzgerald. He has already created about himself a legend. In New York, I have heard hints, and from Paris, stories which it would be discourteous and useless for me to repeat. The true stories about Fitzgerald are always published under his own name. He has the rare faculty of being able to experience romantic and ingenuous emotions and a half hour later regard them with satiric detachment. He has an amazing grasp of the superficialities of the men and women about him, but he has not yet a profound understanding of their motives, either intellectual or passionate. Even with his famous flapper, he has as yet failed to show that hard intelligence, that intricate emotional equipment upon which her charm depends, so that Gloria, the beautiful and damned lady of his imaginings, remains a little inexplicable, a pretty, vulgar shadow of her prototype. But the book should allay the fears of anyone who has had fears for Mr. Fitzgerald's ultimate commercialization which appeared imminent after *Flappers and Philosophers*. It is an honest record of one of the most interesting minds of his generation.

Stephen Vincent Benét has already published three volumes of verse, *Five Men and Pompey*, *Young Adventure*, and *Heavens and Earth*. If *The Beginning of Wisdom* is his first novel, it is certainly not his last, for *Jean Huguenot* is already completed and a third novel is in preparation—all this at twenty-three.

The Beginning of Wisdom is a picaresque novel of a young man who successively encounters God, country and Yale. Mr. Benét treats Yale as something he remembers rather than as something lived through by his characters. He has, too, been a little too well-bred about it, for all his jibes at the pious athletes and the impeccable parlor snakes. The only way to make literary material out of one's youthful experiences is to be shameless about one's self and ruthless with one's friends. Mr. Benét has concealed nearly everything about himself except his opinions, and what he has had to say about his friends has been said with wreaths tied with Yale blue ribbons. The unfortunate part about it is that no one at that age particularly minds being made stock of. Fitzgerald made a Princetonian figure in my image and thrust it so full of witty arrows that it resembled St. Sebastian about as much as it did me. I was undeniably flattered. Mr. Benét has visualized Yale, but he has not dramatized it. The only incident which has a present air has not to do with the college at all but with the daughter of a dilapidated dentist of New Haven. Amorously entangled, the hero marries her. A few weeks later she dies. Clearly, they order these things better at Yale. In Princeton such adventures seldom end in marriage, and when they do, the women live on forever.

Mr. Benét is a much better novelist when not retracking too closely his own footsteps, and throughout he has the courage and skill to write beautifully. He has so rare a skill with color, so unlimited an invention of metaphor, such humorous delight in the externals of things, so brave a fantasy, that he occasionally forgets that the chief business of the novelist is not to describe character but to show it in action. I am not quite sure what is intended by the beginning of wisdom—but it is certainly not the fear of the Lord. For a while, the hero seems to look toward beauty and arrogance and irony for direction in all things, but in the end he marries a girl who has been with the Y.M.C.A. in France and returns with strange ideas of "service and sanity through service."

Where are the eagles and the trumpets?
Buried beneath some snow-deep Alps.

Fitzgerald, Benét and Dos Passos belong to the generation which suffered the actual indignities of war. In each of these novels we will find an approach to the war quite other than that found in the soldier stories which three years ago begauded our magazines.

It is perhaps no mere coincidence that all our better known war stories were written by women: *Humoresque* by Fanny Hurst, the rhythms of Grand Street reduced to a violin solo—a tribute to sacrifice paid with a wreath of white carnations left over from Mother's Day; *England to America* by the Montague lady with three names— *Hands Across the Sea*, annotated for New England spinsters; Edna Ferber's homely romances—sugared doughnuts served on a service flag; the Sergeant Gray stories of Mary Roberts Rinehart—accurate information on the routine of a division headquarters troop dispensed through a detective story technique. At all events, it was the feminine attitude toward war which found popular favor in the troublous years from 1917 to 1919. The contributions of the older men writers we will pass over in silence. The younger men were either driving ambulances or doing squads right. Later came a revulsion toward war stories of any kind, possibly because readers were a little ashamed of the cheapness of their inflated emotions. Mr. Fitzgerald, when he wrote his first novel, judiciously omitted any actual references to the army, but both in his present volume and in Mr. Benét's there is unashamed treatment of life in the American forces. Mr. Fitzgerald served nearly two years as an officer in the regular army. He now takes occasion to deliver a merciless satire on the stupidity and pompousness of West Pointers and the discipline of training camps. His satire is as rapid as target practice on a rifle range and bitter in the mouth as sand blown over a parade ground.

Mr. Benét's experiences were likewise Cis-Atlantic. Book VII of his novel, written with the impudent buoyance of the early days of the officers' training camps, includes a series of portraits—officers, men, artillery horses, and guns—and one conversation of most unsoldierlike speech on immortality. No less than the Yale section it shows Mr. Benét's tendency to treat incident visually instead of dramatically. But it also shows with what skill and humor he can evoke physical details.

Seeing how these two studies of army life stand out by sheer honesty from previous attempts, it is difficult to speak calmly of John Dos Passos' *Three Soldiers*. However viewed, whether as a novel or as a document, it is so good that I am tempted to topple from my critical perch and go up and down the street with banners and drums.

Here, once and for all, is the very stuff and breath of that strange thing which was the American Army of 1917–1919. The burdensome discipline of the training camps, the unutterable boredom of billets and hospitals, the filth and terror of fight, the dizziness and gay abandon of spring in Paris. He has evoked the American soldier, alive and individual, for all the effort to press him into a mould, a young man with the helpless lovable charm of a child and the uncontrolled viciousness of an animal. His speech is here, with its unceasing obscenity and its hatred of affectation.

Three Soldiers is a story of Fuselli, an Italian of the second generation from San Francisco, eager to adapt himself and to get on in the army; of Chrisfield, a wild-angered lovable boy from an Indiana farm, and of the Eastern John Andrews, insurgent in thought and passion, but outwardly tamed. The background is filled with figures—officers, soldiers, French peasants, Y.M.C.A. workers, cocottes, Parisian aristocrats. I know of no American novel of this generation in which so many minor characters, each unforgettable and perfectly placed, appear and disappear without confusion. Mr. Dos Passos, realizing that two of his principals at least were unusual characters going toward unusual fates, has contrived to silence criticism by placing against his protagonists, in each crucial moment, an ordinary soldier with quite normal reactions. Despite the technical difficulties of carrying three major characters the book has the firm structure of steel.

If it were only that *Three Soldiers* is the first completed and competent novel of the American Army, it would deserve great praise; but it is more than that, for, in Mr. Dos Passos' hands, the army becomes a symbol of all the systems by which men attempt to crush their fellows and add to the already unbearable agony of life. Here is more than an honest record of young men's lives: here are the tears of things, the shadows of the old strong unpitying gods lying across the paths of men; anger and hate and dust are here, and laughter and the manly love of comrades, and at the end, resignation and despair, the return of a bloody and hateful thing done in an autumn wood, the beautiful proud gesture of a man going down in defeat before life. And this is why I say that John Dos Passos is a genius.

Vanity Fair: October, 1921

THE DISTRUST OF IDEAS

(D. H. LAWRENCE AND SHERWOOD ANDERSON)

D. H. LAWRENCE remains the most interesting of that group of English novelists which arose around 1910 and has since proved so remarkable for its brilliant limitations. The rest are, by now, neatly appraised, their defects noted, their places assigned with a fair degree of accord and with as much justice as is possible to the contemporary critic. But there is no such agreement in the case of Lawrence, and therein lies a part of his interest. Miss Rebecca West, whose mordant criticism has fallen haplessly on so many fair young heads, grants him genius in the highest sense, but finds him less clever than herself.

Mr. H. L. Mencken dismisses *Psychoanalysis and the Unconscious* as an "effective if unwitting *reductio ad absurdum* of the current doctrine that Lawrence is a profound thinker. His book is not merely bad; it is downright childish." The voices might be multiplied, either of extreme praise or extreme blame. In the meanwhile, Lawrence sits in Italy, brooding upon another and darker turmoil.

Why should this wide divergence of opinion exist? Well, first there is Lawrence's preoccupation with physical love, which serves to frighten many, and, it should probably be added, disposes others unduly in his favor. Then, too, his talent, being an original and unrestrained one, is not readily measured by predetermined standards. *The Lost Girl* may, perhaps, be considered as a study of manners, treating of certain very credible middle-class English people of the midlands, and a roving band of alien vaudeville performers. But to approach *Women in Love* as a realistic study of manners, is to have the book crumble at one's touch. Moreover, his work is extremely uneven; *The Trespasser* is one of the shoddiest novels I have ever read; *The Rainbow*, dull and turgid in places, has scene after scene of all but overwhelming beauty. But I believe that the real reason Lawrence fares so badly at the hands of certain excellent critics, such as Mr. Mencken, for example, is that these critics are interested only in the ideas of an intellectual aristocracy and, inversely, in the stupidities of the mob. Lawrence's approach both to life and his art is essentially emotional; his understanding comes of having remembered all that his imagination and intuition discerned while under the subjection of emotion. That is to say, Lawrence is, at his best, a poet, even in his novels.

Lawrence has seen, or thinks that he has seen, the disintegration of all those ideas which sustained and fired the best minds in the nineteenth century. He has watched the decay of the Victorian ideals of social equality, of human brotherhood and Christian love; the catch-cries of the modern intellectual find him deaf and skeptic. But where another man might have fallen into a sterile despair, Lawrence remains unperturbed. He has probably never been really interested either in ideas or ideals. His concern is with "the amazingly difficult and vital business of human relationships," and particularly with those relationships which are ultimately sensual. He is like those modern sculptors who, feeling that civilization has reached its last refinement, and that there is no more work left for observation to do, have gone back to the crude beginnings of stone carving to learn again the essentials of their art from Assyrian friezes and the crudely stylized sculptures of West Africa. In *Women in Love* he deliberately introduces this parallel, for in Halliday's flat there are wood carvings from Africa, one of a naked woman, crouched in a strange posture, distorted by pain.

There Gerald "saw vividly with his spirit the gray forward stretching face of the Negro woman, African and tense, abstracted in utter physical stress. It was a terrible face, void, peaked, abstracted almost into meaninglessness by the weight of sensation beneath.

" 'Why is it art?' Gerald asked, shocked, resentful.

THE DISTRUST OF IDEAS

" 'It conveys a complete truth,' said Birkin. 'It contains the whole truth of that state, whatever you feel about it.'

" 'But you can't call it high art,' said Gerald.

" 'High! There are centuries and hundreds of centuries of development in the straight line behind that carving; it is an awful pitch of culture, of a definite sort. . . . Pure culture in sensation, culture in a physical consciousness, really ultimate physical consciousness, mindless, utterly sensual.' "

In his purest form Lawrence's art is not unlike this savage carving. He is evidently a man of tremendous capacities for emotion, variously sensitive to nervous impressions. He has brooded over his own intimate relationships and carefully observed the processes of his own sex life. He has read Freud and has availed himself of the knowledge Freud has liberated, using it, not as a substitute for thinking, but to corroborate his own broodings. Love to him is not the laughing golden-haired Anadyomene, but the dark and terrible Cybele, the many-breasted Earth Mother, mutilating her votaries. The struggle in which almost every one of his characters is most deeply involved is to come to fulfilment through love, without losing identity as an individual. And Lawrence invests this struggle with tragic possibilities.

I do not mean to imply that this is all there is to Lawrence, for he has a varied and fecund genius, but I have indicated what seems to me the essential core. The sun of his wisdom is this: that it would be the wisest of actions for a man to put aside his wisdom, as if it were a shabby stifling garment, and in nakedness to touch and close with the dark vindictive life of the earth, and that better even than this it would be if mankind were utterly destroyed and only the older inhuman world were left. This attitude receives its fullest expression in his poems, in those poems which are not written in accordance with his absurdly inadequate theory of poetry, and in *Women in Love* where his philosophy is everywhere explicit.

Women in Love is indeed an attempt to get at first principles through the medium of a novel. The incidents are chosen, not to hurry the course of the story, not to allow the characters to display, of their own accord, those gestures which are typical of them as individuals and as members of a certain class of English society, but as symbols of the obscure emotions, the unconscious desires, to which they are subjected as men and women. Although both Ursula and Gudrun were remembered from the earlier history of the Brangwens, I could not until halfway through *Women in Love* tell them apart, except by Gudrun's notoriously gay stockings—whose colors are like an inventory of the rainbow, and which deserve a full chapter in the *His-*

tory of Hosiery, whenever the book comes to be written. The young men seem to differ only in their varying degrees of pure maleness. I am accustomed to the novelist, who describes only the clothes and masks of his characters; I was unprepared for Lawrence's stripping his figures, not only of their clothes, but even of a little of their skins. They are left too naked for recognition.

The incidents themselves are imagined to body forth Lawrence's thought or to externalize by a gesture the sensations and desires, the unconscious hatreds and strivings of the characters. When Hermione, an English lady, at one point comes up behind her flagging lover and stands over him in rigid ecstasy, to crash down on his head with a ball of lapis lazuli, stunning him and driving him half-dazed from the house; when the man, leaving the house, goes directly to a wet hillside and there strips and sits down in blissful nakedness among the primroses, it is more or less clear what Lawrence means to say. As an account of the behavior of people at an English country house, it is at least fantastic. Yet Lawrence is perfectly capable of inventing action for his characters which is credible and at the same time a complete symbol, as, for example, in that passage in *The Rainbow* when all the wayward approach of first love, the timid longing of the boy and the sure eluding flight of the girl, all the inner rhythm of their crossplay, are brought beautifully before the eyes by means of that moonlit marching back and forth among the fallen shocks of wheat and the silver clashing of the sheaves, heaped under the moon. *Women in Love* is a strangely interesting book, because Lawrence's philosophy is interesting; it is an unsatisfactory novel because that philosophy is set forth explicitly. The thought of a novelist should be implicit in his novel, in order that his men and women should seem to move of their own accord, or at the command of necessity beyond the control of the man who writes.

In *The Rainbow* and in *Sons and Lovers* Lawrence did incorporate all his sensibility, his understanding and his vision of beauty without obtruding unduly upon his characters, albeit both novels are largely composed of recollections of his own childhood and young manhood. In *The Lost Girl*, the treatment is even more objective, and by attaching himself to a less intimate problem he has gained an unwonted humor. James Houghton, the elegant hypocritical draper, fantastically dreaming in lustrous silks and flimsy poplins, letting his shop fall into an empty decay while trying to impose on the miners' wives "creations" designed for princesses; Mr. May, the pink stout gentleman, slightly down at the heels, who has brought from America some prodigious schemes for making money; Madame Rochard and the four young men of her Red Indian troupe—these and the inhabitants of Woodhouse are set down with an unusually gay detachment. The theme of the book is that of the odd unmarried and unmarriageable daughter of a middle-class English household, in search of an amiable husband of her own station. Through the first half of the book the lost girl remains an ordinary creature, confronted with a commonplace problem, whose uneasiness is set down accurately and a little amusedly. But at the end, married to a low-caste Italian and brought into an ancient savage life, among the filthy peasants of the mountains south of Rome, she too is touched by a cruel pathos.

Lawrence cannot elude the cruelty of things nor the seriousness of the combat. Even in *Sea and Sardinia*, an account of his voyage from Sicily to this island beyond the net of European civilization, there is scarcely a moment of calm. It is a remarkable "travel book," this account of the Mediterranean, and the tall coasts of Italy, of the hard and primitive island of Sardinia, of the peasants, still clinging implacably to a medieval individualism, the men proudly dressed in the old magpie motley, black and white, the women in stiff spreading dresses of mauve and vermilion like Velasquez princesses—remarkable because of the unflagging sensitiveness and the sly observations. But it is never serene. There is always a torment stirred by what people are and are not; there is always the old pagan terror of places, as if Etna were, as he says, a mistress "low, white, witch-like under heaven—with her strange winds prowling round like Circe's panthers, some black, some white."

It is serenity which one misses most in Lawrence, serenity and intellectual control of his material. He is never, save at moments, entirely satisfactory. One wearies of the emotionalism, the welter of words, the disorder and the turmoil. He is the typical English genius, beautiful and profound, fragmentary, touching and absurd.

Sherwood Anderson alone among the Americans seems to bear a resemblance to Lawrence. When I first read *Out of Nowhere Into Nothing*, as it appeared serially in the *Dial*, I thought to have detected the influence of Lawrence on Anderson's phrasing. But this is slight, if indeed it exists. They are alike rather in their mode of apprehending certain things. If Lawrence has influenced Anderson, it is by confirming the American in his own discoveries. Both are interested in searching out what men hide from the world, in probing under worm-riddled floors and ransacking blind attics. In *The Triumph of the Egg*, Anderson is more than ever concerned with those private struggles of the soul in which Lawrence's interest also lies; but where in Lawrence this struggle is almost always between the cruel aloofness of the male and the tender, devastating pervasiveness of the woman, in Anderson it is between some dream of impossible loveliness, which the dreamer wishes to attach to the body of the beloved, and the inane fecundity of life. Always in this new book of his, it is the blind insistent instinct of life for endless recreation which triumphs over the dreamer. This is, I take it, the meaning of the title.

Anderson, like Lawrence, understands the physical ecstasy and contentment that would come of belonging utterly to the dark rich life of the earth and moving with the ancient rhythms of light and dark, of green and sterile seasons, of dayrise and nightfall. "That would have been sweetest of all things," he says, "—to sway like the tops of young trees when a wind blew, to give himself as the grey weeds in a sunburned field gave themselves to the influence of passing shadows, changing color constantly, becoming every moment something new, to live in life and in death too, always to live, to be unafraid of life, to let it flow through his body, to let the blood flow through his body, not to struggle, to offer no resistance, to dance."

He has, too, a sympathy with the simple unthinking life of the African Negro and is stirred strangely by the remembered songs their timid, degenerate descendants sing, songs of defiance and hate and relentless love. He shares with Lawrence a mythopoeic faculty, which peoples the darkness with forgotten devils and inhuman ghosts. But where the Englishman piles words upon words, approximating his meaning by a rich welter of words, Anderson is so sparing in statement as to be almost inarticulate. There is at times in his books an unbelievable and glamorous beauty, but it is the beauty of things seen with delight or known in an intensity of emotion, haltingly recovered and scarcely set down in words.

I have emphasized these qualities in Anderson, because, in casually grouping him with the newer American realists, the critics have largely ignored them. Even in those two earliest books of his, *Marching Men* and *Windy McPherson's Son*, there was no question of his powers of observation, his sincerity, his understanding of American types. He was one of the first to describe accurately and without sentimentality the dreary and monotonous towns of the Middle West and the dwellers in those towns—old grey-headed men, thwarted and disgruntled, bragging of fine deeds that had never been done; silent, pale, stoop-shouldered women, strutting young louts, awkward boys with unuttered longings. In *Winesburg, Ohio*, such a town is always in the background. In this series of short stories, loosely held together by the figure of the boyish reporter, Anderson seemed finally to have found his form. With *Poor White*, he returned to the novel to tell the story of another town, one of the tiny agricultural towns of Ohio, which between the boyhood of the protagonist and his middle age grows into a manufacturing city, another Dayton or Youngstown. Excellent in most respects as it is, the book does not achieve form. There is a constant confusion in the element of time, which always seems to give Anderson trouble; and in an attempt to carry a sense of multitude, he continually follows his minor characters into blind alleys from which there is a difficult return.

In *The Triumph of the Egg*, Anderson again reverts to the short story, and he has gained considerably in artistry since last touching the more restricted forms. He is here more nearly the subtle and facile craftsman than he has ever been before. He will always perhaps labor breathlessly with words; there is still a choppiness in movement, a confusion in the time element. His characters are, more than elsewhere, reduced to a few essential gestures. But there is here, and in clearer form, all that passionate imagination which from the first marked him apart from the other American realists. The first and last stories in this volume are as fine as anything which has come out of this movement.

I Want to Know Why is a tale told by a Kentucky boy of fifteen, a boy for whom all the glamor of life is concentrated on the racetracks, the paddocks and the thoroughbreds. "It's lovely," he says; "the horses are sweaty and nervous and shine and the men come out and smoke cigars and look at them and the trainers are there and the owners, and your heart thumps so you can hardly breathe." He aches with inexplicable longing and delight but to look at Sunstreak, a stallion that "is like a girl you think about sometimes, and never see," and, because the trainer shares the boy's understanding of the horse, he reaches out toward the trainer in warm, boyish adoration. Then, through a lighted window, leaning across a rosebush, he sees the trainer go into a ramshackle evil-smelling farmhouse, and brag among drunken men after the races, and kiss a tall red-headed woman, with a hard, ugly mouth. He sees the man's eyes shine, just as they had shone when the stallion was running. Suddenly he hates the man, and the glamor of the courses is lost and the goodly smell of the air is gone. The egg has triumphed.

In *Out of Nowhere into Nothing* there is a young woman who has seen in her girlhood, going down a marble stairway, bright youths and maidens and old men, noble and serene. Having fallen in love with her employer, a man with a wife and two children—she is a stenographer in Chicago—she returns to her native village to draw advice from her mother. She turns to her mother with her secret, thinking "what a strange beautiful thing it would be if the mothers could suddenly sing to their daughters, if out of the darkness and silence of old women, a song should come." And her mother's answer is that there is no such thing as love. "Men only hurt women. They can't help wanting to hurt women. The thing they call love doesn't exist. It's a lie. Life is dirty."

In both these stories there is this conflict between the desire of the young for a seen or imagined beauty, and the cruel ugliness of life and the meaningless need for perpetuating it. Anderson hates the village, not so much for its dreariness, its repressions, its hideousness, but because it has the power to stop the longing stuttering cry of the villagers who dream of something that is not and "run through the night seeking some lost, some hidden and half forgotten loveliness." One suspects that Anderson's own mind is very like one of these grey towns, and that in it, as in these towns, there is a conflict, and that out of that conflict his books are made.

Vanity Fair: December, 1921

THE MODERNISM OF MR. CABELL

I HAVE NO DESIRE to rediscover James Branch Cabell, though to do so is now so customary as almost to amount to a profession. Mr. Cabell must by now be a little wary whenever a figure of stoutness with eagle eyes approaches, lest he prove another Cortez. From the days of Percival Pollard, who greeted *The Eagle's Shadow*, Mr. Cabell's first volume, admiringly, they have been at it, champions as various as Mark Twain, Theodore Roosevelt and Hugh Walpole, who have stood momently with trumpets before one or another entrance to the Cabellian gardens, blowing praises. And before one gate, Mr. Sumner of the Society for the Suppression of Vice still stands, a self-righteous angel with an unwavering flaming sword, lest any venture in to delight in the art of the topiarist and the gross features of the garden god. *Hunc lucum tibi dedico consecroque Priape!* And even he must, I suppose, be reckoned among the discoverers.

THE MODERNISM OF MR. CABELL

Mr. Cabell has never lacked for judicious praise, no, not in all those many times drawn out years, when one by one he was adding to his bookshelf the precursors of *Jurgen*, without appreciable increase in his royalties. Yet always there seems a glint of pitying generosity in the eyes of his admirers. He is regarded a little wistfully, as though he were a graceful anachronism, a beautiful trifler with romance at a time when all right-minded novelists were about their proper business of social criticism. He is hailed as a perfect craftsman in romance, with the afterthought that romance is probably an outworn mode.

And Mr. Cabell has himself contributed to this impression that he is but raising ghosts from crumbled tombs: ghosts of brave ingenuous boys who had their one hour of wholehearted love before the inevadable compromises came with time; ghostly impeccable girls in a trailing shimmer of silken stuff, their hair antiquely coiffed and frosty with gold in a light that never was from star or sun; centaurs, witches and devils; flawless queens of Troy and Provence, queens indefatigably perverse, with crowns of coral on their heads; and other creatures of a past which has no record on the clock. He has credited his volumes to one and another medieval person, to Nicolas de Caen and such imaginary scribes. He has, in *Beyond Life*, where more than elsewhere his views on life and letters are made explicit, expressed his evident misprision of realism and other modern modes of literature. He has not hesitated to point out that while books written according to the realistic formula have a certain contemporary value, they are not much read after the author's death. And even more in life than in art he holds with romance.

And yet granted that Cabell stands clear of all modern cliques, he is not without his points of contact with the modernists. If he has steeped himself in the literature of Provence and pre-Renaissance Italy, why so has Ezra Pound, who has instigated several modern movements and is not generally regarded as a reactionary. If he has dehumanized his actors in an effort to make them conform more completely to a general human experience, he is in this at one with Gordon Craig, who is usually spoken of as belonging to the future. If he has endeavored to deal with the realities behind the object rather than with the readily observed facts, I understand that the expressionists have a similar aim.

Nor in retiring to his library at Dunbarton Grange has Mr. Cabell so completely cut himself off from American life as he would have us believe. His tales of present-day Virginia do, it is true, deal with a scene where every gentleman is armigerous, and it is still possible to find a Robert Etheridge Townsend subscribing somewhat boyishly to the code of gallantry and a Colonel Musgrave directing his life according to a Virginian conception of chivalry. But a man cannot well rid himself of his first twenty years, and the Virginia of Mr. Cabell's youth presents a scene which has little in common with the raucous vigor of Chicago or the pretentious commercialism of New York. It is rather a land where the twentieth century followed too closely upon the heels of the eighteenth, where decay set in before the first fine strength of the pioneer was wasted, a land gracefully faded, intellectually moribund. It was but necessary that Mr. Cabell, in order not to starve, should turn to neglected books and legends already written in impeccable speech. And yet there is ample proof in his writings of his power of appraisal in the world of actual happenings. Consider, for example, that satire of the popular mind and the doings of public officers during the recent international conflict, in *Jurgen*, where the scene is laid in Hell, whose religion is patriotism and whose government an enlightened democracy. Compare the estimate of an ex-president in *The Cream of the Jest* with Mr. E. A. Robinson's poem on Roosevelt written on a similar occasion, and it will be seen how far Mr. Cabell's skepticism passes that of the New England poet, who, for all his pessimism, behind every cloud still finds a wan exhalation shining.

It is in his style that he seems most to savor of antiquation. For Mr. Cabell is much given to rhetoric, not only that fine rhetoric which results from a character's viewing himself dramatically, but also that vicious rhetoric which consists of vague and sonorous sentiment added merely for general impressiveness. And this style, whose cadences are built upon the elaborate periods of an earlier prose, rather than on the rise and fall of the conversational voice, comes a little artificially to modern ears, which, for no particularly good reason, prefer an illusion of speech.

It is the inflexibility of his style which is responsible for most of Mr. Cabell's failures: this and the thinness of his visual imagination, which too often refuses to find incidents and details to body forth the thought. In this connection it is interesting to remember that it is Christopher Marlowe to whom Mr. Cabell constantly turns as the perfect type of the poet. And while no one could possibly deny that Marlowe is, by sheer genius, in the first order of the English poets, surpassing even Shakespeare in the violence and splendor of his imagination, it must be admitted that the blank verse of his best period is singularly inflexible, that he is magnificently given to rhetoric and that he failed to find any adequate occupation for his titanic personages. Which is not to suggest that Mr. Cabell is another Marlowe, but rather that he has found a consolation for his own shortcomings in that most glorious failure among English poets. Yet when he comes to reread *Jurgen*, where for once his imagination teems with incident, and no sounding phrase goes wandering without its thought, I do not think Mr. Cabell will have need for comfort.

Vanity Fair: March, 1922

INCORRECT ENGLISH

(*The Enormous Room* by E. E. Cummings)

"THE SUPREME test of a book," Ezra Pound says somewhere, "is that we should feel some unusual intelligence working behind the words. I have expressly written here not 'intellect' but 'intelligence.' There is no intelligence without emotion." And the first thing which one would like to say of *The Enormous Room* of E. E. Cummings is that it is intelligent. Behind the disordered, elaborated and frequently beautiful play and interplay of words, one is conscious of a sensitive, pitying and ironic mind, and of varied and intensely felt emotions. In bare outline, the book is the record of three months spent in a French prison for political spies and suspects; but, though one cannot well doubt a single related fact, so evident is the necessity for honesty, *The Enormous Room* is hardly to be taken as a document, another account of indignities and injustices endured and now to be told. It is rather a presentation of emotions, the tale of "the long and difficult way" through which a young man had to come before he could discover the richness of life at its poorest. A loose analogy with the *Pilgrim's Progress* is preserved, and at the end are the Delectable Mountains who are none other than a gypsy, a Negro thief, a none-too-honest Pole and a poor abject creature named Surplice.

The simple facts are these: Cummings and his friend B. were, in October, 1917, serving with the Norton Harjes Ambulance as members of a Sanitary Section affiliated with the French Army. An overzealous French censor decided that B.'s letters betrayed dangerous if not revolutionary opinions; Cummings and his friend were arrested as suspicious characters and despatched to a miserable and unspeakably filthy detention camp, there to await at the autumn's end the commission which was to send B. to Précigné for the duration of the war and to allow Cummings his liberty. I will leave it to others to comment on the justice and wisdom of this arrangement. It need only be said that Cummings never permits himself either a shriek or a whine throughout the length of the book. What he has to say concerning the greatness and goodness of the French Government in permitting him to live at La Ferté is spoken very quietly, now with a gentle contempt and now with a terrible controlled indignation. There are moments of self-pity when he looks firmly at his fellow prisoners to stem his own misery; there are times when his very gentleness seems the effort of a mind trembling upon hysteria.

"And his ghastly and toylike wizened and minute arm would try to make a pass at their lofty lives," he says, speaking of a crippled, impotently indignant little Belgian, whom, with an irony perhaps not unconscious, he calls the Machine-Fixer—for his talk with the little man is almost always on those machines by which peoples are governed. Then follows this passage which will indicate as well as any this vein beautifully incisive and ironic of Cummings:

> O gouvernement français, I think it was not very clever of you to put this terrible doll in La Ferté; I should have left him in Belgium with his little doll-wife if I had been you; for when governments are found dead there is always a little doll on top of them, pulling and tweaking with his little hands to get back the microscopic knife which sticks firmly in the quiet meat of their hearts.

The emotional and visual memory are closely balanced; Mr. Cummings can recall with a full nervous exactitude the look and feel of the scene; he can elaborate with precision the emotions of a given moment. To be able to do both these things is rarer than it would seem, and to show how the sensuous and emotional are fused in his mind I cite those sentences in which the Wanderer is introduced.

Not that he always succeeds in bringing out his effects; there are passages enough where the main thought is outthundered by the overtones, where adjectives and nouns break from his control in a verbal bedlam. Yet when the subject is one of essential importance to his narration he can and does build up a scene, a character intensely and imaginatively alive. Celina confronting le Directeur, the chapters named for Jean le Nègre, the Wanderer and Surplice represent Cummings at his best, and that best seems to me to give him a definite claim to be considered among the important living American writers. I doubt if any other could have informed physical squalor, beastliness and degradation with so splendid a spiritual irradiance.

So far as I am concerned, the trouble with *The Enormous Room* is exactly that which is to be found in practically all the experimental prose in America, which is simply that not enough time has been taken to bring the form to completion.

The Enormous Room is written in a gamey personal idiom which moves in one direction toward a highly organized, rhythmic prose, and in the other toward the last crudities of the vernacular. Cummings' vocabulary shows equally the dustiness of the dictionary and the muck of the street. His interest in extending the limits of prose is obvious. He is quite willing to employ an adverb to modify a noun— "three very formerly and even once bonnets"—or another noun —"softnesses eyes"—and he has not hesitated to use words not commonly accepted in print. If Cummings needs a defense for having done so, it is provided for him in Havelock Ellis' essay on Zola in *Affirmations*. I have neither the desire nor the ability to add anything to what is said there.

LILIES THAT FESTER

(*Young People's Pride* by Stephen Vincent Benét)

Myron, qui paene animas hominum ferarumque
aere comprehenderat, non invenit heredem.
G. Petronius Arbiter

O LIVER CROWE, Amory Blaine and Leopold Bloom were all engaged in the advertising industry; here their resemblance ceases. If Mr. Benét has ever come in contact with the art of Mr. James Joyce, *Young People's Pride* shows no trace of it. The influence of Mr. Fitzgerald has departed; the influence of the magazines which have influenced Mr. Fitzgerald is still to be detected.

I am not attempting to be clever, for I have observed that one is under no compulsion to be clever in the S4N. I wish quite seriously, indeed solemnly, to point out what I believe to be Mr. Benét's most annoying failure. Mr. Joyce and Mr. Fitzgerald, different as they are in temper, differing widely as they do in the results obtained, have this in common: both were brought up in a Catholic tradition and are acquainted with the doctrine of Original Sin. Both, in presenting characters quite obviously derived from their own youth, make no attempt to slur over the more odious and ridiculous features. But Mr. Benét, who is, I suppose, of Protestant upbringing and hence unaware of the value of the confessional, presents his characters as if they had no share in the Fall of Man. It is occasionally suggested that they have a few "modern" faults—but these only make them the more charming. Oliver Crowe's shoes do not conform to quite the latest model, but that is only because his really fine qualities are not appreciated at the aforementioned advertising agency. His vision is myopic, his pyjamas are striped; but the idea that these could render him ridiculous, even at the moment when (honorably and with the full sanction of Church and State) he is about to fulfill his functions as a male—I take it that's what he's doing when the book ends—is hastily scouted. Ted Billett is no Perceval; once, it is true, he followed the Grail—if you allow Miss Weston's rather nasty and doubtless pedantic interpretation of the real symbolism of the Lance and the Cup—but that was a long time ago and in another country. Besides, even if the wench is not dead, he is very honorably ashamed of himself and ready, indeed willing, to assume that it was all the result of the war's taking him so young and still unmarried beyond the influence of Yale and Elinor. And so on, even to Mary Ellen's cute habit of taking off her drawers in public. It is not that Mr. Benét lacks all vision; it is that he has chosen to see through glasses rosily. It is not that he has no sense of proportion; it is that he has been too conscious of an audience to whom that "essential strength and sickness of the human soul" which it is the business of literature to present would be unpardonably offensive.

Plot Number 1—we are dealing with the novel—exhibits certain invariable features: two persons usually of the same age, but always differing in sex, come together in the early pages of the book; the desire to see them married is incited in the reader; circumstances arise which, however trivial they may appear, are sufficient to keep the amorous ones apart until the fourth chapter from the end; thereabouts, the papers are found to have been forged, the bastard is proved the legitimate heir to the estates of the grandduke, the heroine finds that the hero did telephone after all, the supposed libertine is discovered to have visited the bawdy house under circumstances so extraordinary that moral judgment must be suspended, kind hearts receive an influx of Norman blood; and the final chapters are scented with orange blossoms. *Pride and Prejudice*, probably the most successful treatment of this plot in English, contains also a second pair of lovers, whose vicissitudes parallel those of the first, and whose ultimate happiness depends no little on the machinations of Elizabeth Bennett and her noble pursuer.

The only difficulty this plot presents is to find circumstances which will keep the lovers apart for at least two hundred pages. Mr. Benét has found, or thought to have found, his complication in *Young People's Pride*. This was a happy hunch. How a young American of no means, embarrassed by a university education and its attendant ideals, is to attain to marriage before his youth is gone is a problem of some social importance. Oliver is frequent and Ted is common enough in the early twenties; both their morals and manners offer considerable interest to the detached observer. But, just as in *The Beginning of Wisdom* Mr. Benét threw away an excellent theme (What will be the result of an enduring marriage between a sensitive Yale student and the daughter of a decayed dentist of neither breeding nor social importance?) for no theme at all, so here he wanders from *Young People's Pride* to write a lot of claptrap about a middle-aged businessman—presented as a patchwork of the presswork of paid publicity agents—and his mistress, who is shown reading Dickens, although she would seem to have acquired irony from the pages of Mr. Cabell. In Ollie's case the American Express Company—Lordy, bless the American Express!—appears suddenly as a *deus ex machina*; Nancy's pride is softened by her mother's unintentional revelation of the missing telephone call. Ted, who is embarrassed not so much by his lack of funds as by the painful recollection of a bit of belly-bumping done long since on the slopes of Montmartre, is saved at the last minute by Oliver's mendaciously laying down his virginity for his friend. In all charity, it cannot be said that either problem has been approached, much less solved.

In rapidity, sprightliness and in the presentation of the actual scene, the book is a gain on *The Beginning of Wisdom*. The construction is far better, but not yet good enough for me to be especially grateful for it. The style shows every evidence that Mr. Benét did not consider his book worth writing.

When I say that Mr. Benét's style is bad, I do not mean that it is bad as Mr. Rupert Hughes' style is bad; it has that peculiar and utterly disheartening badness of a man who can write and is at present using only a twentieth of his talent. It has the quite awful vulgarity, not of a dance in the two-a-day, but of a dance done by a greyhound. Consider the following passage:

"It was Nancy just as some of her clothes were Nancy, soft clear blues and first apple-blossom pinks, the colors of a hardy garden that has no need for the phoenix-colors of a poppy, because it has passed a boy's necessity for talking at the top of his voice in scarlet and can hold in one shaped fastidious petal, faint-flushed with a single trembling of one serene living dye, all the colors the wise mind knows and the soul released into its ecstasy has taken for its body invisible, its body of delight most spotless, as lightning takes bright body of rapture and agony from the light clear pallor that softens a sky to night."

That is: Nancy's handwriting is like Nancy, who is like her clothes, which are like the colors of a hardy garden, which are not like the colors of the poppy (which is like the phoenix), nor yet like the boy who must speak at the top of his voice, which top of the voice is like scarlet in the color scale, and so on to that last terrible crib from *Tristram of Lyonesse*, which has nothing whatsoever to do with the subject. No one without a rare gift for metaphor could have written that passage, but when metaphor is employed to get as far as possible from what one wants to say, it is time to weep.

And when one comes on, "He stepped back with a gesture of *defeat* but his *feet* gripped the floor," and remembers that it was written by a poet, there seems nothing to do but agree with the New York *Times* that the book tells a truth as old as the race. I have not seen the review, only that one sentence quoted in an advertisement, but I take it that the ancient truth is none other than this: You can't make a sow's ear out of a silk purse.

Young People's Pride fails because it is constantly pretending to be something it is not: it pretends to be a study of manners in America in the third decade of the twentieth century; its main episode belongs to the cloak-and-dagger romance; it pretends, by its elaborate sentence structure, its allusions and its imagery, to be better written than the average serial of the higher-priced magazines—it is not. It is not that Mr. Benét displays no talent for the novel; there is evidence enough that he might, slowly and laboriously, have written a creditable history of manners, or, by stuffing his ears with cotton, have produced an excellent romance of a new and difficult kind. But he must choose where he wishes to abide. If again he descends from the Ivory Tower to the level of the street, he had better leave his romantic baggage behind; else, when his editors arrive by appointment at the foot of the stairs, they may find him squashed under a trunk of Spanish leather and all the unimaginable trappings spread out on the muddy floor.

S4N: 1923

JOHN O'HARA*

JOHN O'HARA, though he is not prop-
erly speaking one of the Younger Generation (he was fifteen at the
time of the Armistice), shows in his novels something of the conclusion of its history.

O'Hara has been affected by both Hemingway and Fitzgerald,
though the influence is not particularly literary. According to a passage
in his writing which may be taken as autobiographical, he read them
at that impressionable age when all reading tends to become an
imaginary extension of experience. His world, as we see it in his novels,
is that of the Younger Generation, no longer so young, but still sustaining a fiction of youth. It has been supplemented by those who were
boys and girls when the soldier's pole had fallen and who, at bars,
are level now with men.

It is a world of country clubs and speakeasies, manufactured in
Detroit, where, in the 1920's, the frontier took its last stand and for a
time paid tremendous dividends, for though there was less of nature
to exploit, there was more of humankind. It runs, this world, as it has
been said the motors of the future will do, on alcohol. We are in
the prosperity of Mr. Coolidge, the depression of Mr. Hoover.

Here are the loves of Fitzgerald turned into quick adulteries on
the seats of parked cars or in the apartments of Park Avenue, the
freedoms that have run to perversions, lost happinesses and lives mechanized out of all meaning. That consciousness of death which
pervades so much of Hemingway's writing has here become that *goût
du suicide* which gave a special savor to the decade. It is fitting that
the Appointment in Samara should be kept in a garage; Death could
not come more appropriately than in the fumes of a running motor.
In Hemingway, the emotions that are not there are a silence under-
lying all sound, a lack which, once felt, constantly gives poignancy to
the whole. But in the world of John O'Hara, these emotions are not
even missed. His plots have a mechanical perfection, which well they
may, for nothing from within moves these people. They merely react,

* This was originally printed as the last section of *The Missing All*, but
Bishop's notes for a volume of his collected essays show that he intended to drop
it—for the reason, no doubt, that, tagged on like a postscript, it impaired the
symmetry of the piece. It is, however, worth including here at the end of these
notes on the twenties.

like Behaviorists' dogs, to certain stimuli; they have appetites, they come into heat, they suffer from sex as from a last disagreement of nature. One imagines their emotional connections as having been put through by the telephone operator of Butterfield-8. It is a mere matter of putting in and taking out plugs. The rest is conversation. For when, as in his latest novel, O'Hara would give us a human emotion, the episode falls flat; any affair which involves love is nothing more than a schoolboy recollection. It does not, in this world cannot, exist.

It is the world of the Younger Generation played out to the doom. These are the lost people: they are below moral condemnation. *The Missing All* is no longer missed.

Virginia Quarterly Review: Winter, 1937

NOVELISTS
OF THE
SOUTH

WAR AND NO PEACE
(Gone with the Wind BY MARGARET MITCHELL)

MISS MARGARET MITCHELL has
adapted the picaresque novel to her own purposes, presenting in
Gone with the Wind a rogue's-eye view of the Civil War and Reconstruction. But since the unscrupulous rascal who must traditionally
form the center of such a novel is not only a young woman, but also
—at least by virtue of her upbringing—a Georgia lady, adventures
must come to her; she cannot go far out of her way for them. They
come to her in devastating plenty with the war and continue throughout the carpetbag dictatorship.

Scarlett O'Hara is the child of a gently bred Creole mother from
the seacoast and of a riproaring, hard-riding Irishman on the make,
whose stiff head for liquor and sure hand for poker have won him a
large plantation in the Georgia uplands. For the critical uses of the
novelist, therefore, she is well placed; for though she is born to a position in the planter class, she takes after her father and is never completely of it. Besides, this is a new country, red lands rich for cotton,
but only a generation before cleared of Indians. It is constantly
threatened by seedling pine and blackberry brambles and ready to slip
back to wilderness. And Atlanta, where much of the action takes
place, has at this time all the rawness of a frontier town; conventions
appropriate enough to old settlements like Charleston and Savannah
must here appear trivial.

Scarlett, in any case, could not be assimilated. Mean, superstitious
and unsurpassably selfish, only in girlhood does she even superficially
wear the manners of her apparent class; their emotions she never
shares. Any necessity of the spirit is beyond her; the most she knows of
the mind is a low peasant cunning, which values nothing beyond her
own precious skin and the land and money that will allow it not to
perish. To hold the one and procure the other, she kills a thieving
Yankee soldier, robs his corpse, engages in several marriages, buys mills,
exploits convict labor, cheats, and indifferently sends several to their
deaths.

Scarlett is matched with another rogue, her male counterpart, a renegade aristocrat originally from Charleston, as reprehensible as she in morals, but much her superior by reason of his romantically cynical intelligence. Miss Mitchell uses the two of them to assert indirectly the virtues of the society whose destruction they witness. By this device, she has clearly hoped to avoid sentimentality in treating a subject she fears as sentimental. A greater novelist would have had no such dread: Tolstoy is not afraid of Prince André's enthusiasm for the Tsar. And Miss Mitchell is somewhat hampered in the long run by the emotional inadequacy of her heroine, as well as the limitations of her mind. Scarlett undergoes the war, but reacts neither to its pity nor its terror. And she is too stupid to know that there are larger issues involved than her own survival.

Gone with the Wind is one of those thousand-page novels, competent but neither very good nor very sound. The historical background is handled well and with an extraordinary sense of detail. The moral problem is less sure in its treatment. It is this: In a society falling apart, upon what terms can the individual afford to survive? Scarlett wants only to last and takes any terms life offers. Miss Mitchell seems to approve of her persistence. But she also implies that civilization consists precisely in an unwillingness to survive on any terms save those of one's own determining.

The New Republic: July 15, 1936

VANITY FAIR

(In Their Own Image by Hamilton Basso)

M R. BASSO'S new novel In Their Own Image represents an advance on his previous one in that he here declares with unequivocal directness the side he has taken in the social struggle. His disillusionment with the owning classes of Louisiana was evident in Cinnamon Seed, as was his sense of Negro wrongs. But in that book his emotion was transmuted into narrative.

In Their Own Image moves with a stronger rage, employing at times the method of realism, but constantly approaching the simplicity of allegory. It is as though impatience with the fantastic world of winter visitors to Aiken had forced Mr. Basso to speak his mind openly, in a sort of angry declamation scarcely disguised as fictional dialogue, as soon as a glimpse has been had, beyond the terra-cotta dwarf-guarded gates, of the imitation château of the Mayonnaise Queen—with her perfect servants and her silly court of people who, on the substantial base of her fortune, maintain the illusion that they are the aristocracy of America. He does this, as a matter of fact, before that most unimpressive lady even appears. To be sure, she is there throughout, allegorically, as Money; but of the one-time Emma Troy of Rock Center, Illinois, nothing remains to show that she was ever human beyond the fact of her one dull son, married to a nymphomaniac of impeccable ancestry, and her one unhappy daughter, about to be engaged to an imbecile Italian count. That Mr. Basso is morally justified in questioning Emma's right to existence goes without saying; but it is done before he has demonstrated that, as fiction, she exists at all.

It is, of course, part of Mr. Basso's thesis that such people as the rich of Aiken are deprived of reality by their money. But Aiken exists in appalling proximity to Berrytown, a mill village where families of five must be supported on sixty dollars a month, and where a strike will bring in its train pellagra, near-starvation, typhoid, deaths and dismissals. There, life is hopelessly real. But what of the millhands? They, too, except for their class-consciousness, are left somewhat in doubt. Timothy is localized in South Carolina by being made a father from fifteen; he works passionately for a union, provokes an unsuccessful strike. Young Michael appears always with his paint-box, like a saint with the instrument of his martyrdom. But, except allegorically, his painting is not altogether convincing. And his death at the hands of Emma's detectives, being heard only in a secondhand account, is affecting simply as the news item of any similar death would be. It works on emotions that are already there. But it does not create a new emotion.

The truth is, I believe, that in this book Mr. Basso has been in too great a hurry to get on to his opinions. And this has hurt his portrayal of both wastrels and workers. Opinions count in a novel only when they can be conceived in terms of character. If, for one moment, they are felt simply as the author's, then they are not worth a rush. That they are the right opinions will not save him. Besides, they will seem primary, like that mention of politics which, as Stendhal says, coming in the midst of imaginative interests, is like a pistol-shot at a concert, deafening without being emphatic. Mr. Basso is too competent a novelist not to know this, and therefore I think we find him in this book working his way toward a form that will allow him a more immediate clarity. *The New Republic:* May 29, 1938

THE DEATH OF AN ORDER
(*The Fathers* BY ALLEN TATE)

THE QUALITY above all others which has hitherto been evident in Allen Tate's writing is intensity. It is not surprising that in *The Fathers*, his first novel, the characters should convey the impression that they are living in a state of uncommon tension. The prose is straightforward and, sentence by sentence, of the utmost simplicity. Yet the air of the narrative is charged, and behind the words—behind the imaginary narrator, who is rather a simple fellow—we are aware of a mind sharp and intense, clear as to its own situation, yet so caught in difficulties that it seems devious; secure in its own courage and yet in the midst of combat never ignorant of the imminence of defeat. The book is not the work of a native novelist, though it is as much so as, say, *The Scarlet Letter*, since the characters, however obscure the motives of their violence, are nevertheless solid in substance. And yet, *The Fathers* is, like Hawthorne's romance, an allegory of good and evil. A lot of water and blood has flowed since Hawthorne's day, and it is significant that good and evil are now considered in social terms. The problem of *The Fathers* is what constitutes a good society and what part the individual, by his own nature made rebellious to the claims of society, may be expected to play in it.

It may be said that this is not new. Since the novel has been the novel, since, in fact, *The Princess of Clèves*, nothing has been seen so often in its pages as the single person pitted against social laws, to be struck down or confined. But what is new in *The Fathers* is that one man gets away with it. It is the society that is destroyed.

George Posey is the individual and the society that of the Buchans, who are Virginia aristocrats of the several generations extant in the year 1860. Posey shares the same past as those around him; he does not, as Virginians do, regard it as the present. He knows no laws stronger than his own nature; consequently, in 1860, he contains within himself the whole conduct of the future. Nothing confines him, not even his marriage into a circle whose every movement is made in accord with a code. The Buchans have no sense of being restrained; brought up in a school of custom, they conceive that, by acting so as to save their own honor and dignity, they will also, so far as it is in them, serve the State. And they can do no more. Major Buchan is "a

256

true gentleman, disinterested and honorable." Only the confusion of their youth makes his sons any less sure in their decorum. George Posey disrupts them all. We are asked to regard how far this conflict —which may stand for any personal problem—will be influenced by the coming of general catastrophe. Mr. Tate has found—and I should say correctly—that the only effect of war on it will be to hasten the outcome. The Buchans are already consigned to oblivion. The Northern armies will only finish what George Posey has begun. For the Major's son-in-law is the American that was to be against a Virginia already of the past.

Mr. Tate does not sentimentalize his Virginians; he neither flatters nor blames their betrayer. He is caught here, as he has always been, between his dispassionate approval of a society which he believes to be as good as any ever known on this continent and his passionate disappointment in the limitations of the sort of men it produced. Posey fascinates him. He is attracted by the man's unscrupulous energy, by his air of accomplishment. Yet he sees that everything George Posey does is damnable. He knows that he will sell Yellow Jim down the river with no thought that the Negro, who is his own half-brother, is anything more than liquid capital. Indeed the catastrophe of the book is precipitated when what all the characters, however they deny it, have known as a commodity returns to let them know that he, too, is a man. Mr. Tate is not unaware of the conflict in which he is involved. Because he is a poet and because it is as clear in his mind as it is confused in his emotions, he has created out of it, first in his poetry and now in his prose, a dramatic irony, which for intensity is scarcely to be surpassed among his contemporaries.

The New Republic: November 9, 1938

THE VIOLENT COUNTRY
(*The Robber Bridegroom* BY EUDORA WELTY)

"MURDER IS soundless as a spout of blood, as regular and rhythmic as sleep. Many find a skull and a little branching of bones between two floors of leaves. In the sky is a perpetual wheel of buzzards. A circle of bandits counts out gold, with bending shoulders more slaves mount the block and go down, a planter makes a gesture of abundance with his riding whip, a flatboatman falls back from the tavern to the river below with scarcely time for a splash, a rope descends from a tree and curls into a noose. And all around again are the Indians."

Such is the violent country in which Eudora Welty has laid *The Robber Bridegroom*, as it is described by Clement Musgrove, the innocent gullible planter, who stands close to the center of her tale. The scene is that dank primitive forest of Louisiana, some way above New Orleans, between the muddy Mississippi and the old murderous Natchez Trace, which even today, where it lasts, has the appearance of going back to the beginning of time. At the end of the eighteenth century, when it was just beginning to be cut into plantations by Americans coming in before the Spanish had resigned their claims of sovereignty to the French, it must have been a place of fear. To its natural terrors were added, not only the Indians with their scalping knives and tortures, but the white bandits who worked up and down its trails.

It is not difficult to understand how Miss Welty was attracted to it as background for a fairy tale which is, at least in part, a reworking of the plot of the older *Robber Bridegroom*. Out of all Grimm's fairy tales, none more intensely conveys the early terror of the forest. Out of another story of Grimm come Clement's daughter, the fair Rosamond, who is as beautiful as day, and her wicked stepmother, who is as ugly as night. Mike Fink, the fabulously strong flatboatman, is a creature of the folklore of the Lower Mississippi, and so is Little Harp, who carries Big Harp's severed and still speaking head around with him in a trunk, though the Harps had, I believe, an actual historical existence along the Natchez Trace. Jamie Lockhart, the robber bridegroom, is harder to place as to source; at first sight, he might well be what he appears, a New Orleans gentleman, though through the greater part of the story he is a bandit, with his face so thoroughly stained by berry-juice that even Rosamond, though she shares his bed, does not discover his identity. Their relations derive in part from Grimm, though more, I should say, from the myth of Cupid and Psyche.

The fascination of the genuine fairy tale is that it allows us, for a time, to penetrate the minds of our remotest ancestors and to recognize, as we cannot through any other imaginative medium, their terrors and their beliefs. The modern fairy tale cannot do this. It aims at arriving by fantasy at an end which we can accept as sound and true. It will bring together things which mere observation could never find in one place, in order to discover their hidden connection. Since it assumes at the start a suspension of credibility, it must disarm by an air of simplicity and persuade by its charm. And this Miss Welty does. But what her tale adds up to, I cannot be sure. Rosamond and her wicked stepmother are incongruous in Louisiana, and though the dangers, as we well know, were real enough under the live oaks, where the light is drowned and the Spanish moss drifts like seaweed in the submarine shade, we are never made to feel that terror of the forest which is always present in the tale of Grimm.

If Miss Welty meant to establish that our tall tale is our equivalent of the European folk tale, she fails to do so. Her deepest interest in *The Robber Bridegroom* would seem to be in the question of identity. Nothing is what it seems. All bridegrooms, she seems to be saying, are robbers; their love is brought under a mask, and they never call anything by its true name, so that they destroy a woman's faith and their own honor by taking that love which is a woman's right to bestow freely. But, in time, the hurt is healed, and at last the robber bridegroom is seen as a prosperous gentleman of the world. The predatory lover becomes the respectable father of twins, and nothing is easier than the transfer of a bandit into a merchant. This, I take it, is the moral of *The Robber Bridegroom*; but it is to be found in words rather than in the narrative.

The New Republic: November 16, 1942

POETRY
REVIEWS

THE INTELLIGENCE OF POETS

(*Collected Poems* by E. A. ROBINSON; *The Open Sea* by EDGAR LEE
MASTERS; *Poems 1918–21* by EZRA POUND)

IT HAS ALWAYS seemed to me a strange
and regrettable thing that anyone who might be a fine poet should,
even for a little while, pursue another life, though, like Dante at the
moment of his exile, he might be the first counsellor of Florence, like
Villon, a murderer, or like Arthur Rimbaud, a conductor of caravans
into Abyssinia. Above all, I see no reason why poets should be urged
to become prose writers. And yet this is precisely what is constantly
being done, especially when the reviewers are weary of berating poets
for not being politicians, sociologists, or respectable and high-born
gentlemen.

Many poets have, it is true, written wisely and well in prose. In
our time, Yeats in *Per Amica Silentia Lunae* and in *Four Years* and
Masefield in *Gallipoli* have shown that the finest measures of prose
are not beyond them. But the poets are asked not so much that they
should also become masters of prose as that they should write their
verse as if it were prose.

Ford Madox Hueffer in *Thus to Revisit* puts the case for the
prose tradition in verse a little more clearly than the rest. "There is
hardly a poet of today or yesterday who ever, in his matter, his ideas
and his verbal texture, attempts to soar above the level of the intellect
of scarcely adolescent pupils in young ladies' seminaries—hardly a
poet who, in his verse, attempts to render a higher type of mentality
than might be found in a Grimm's fairy tale. Or it might be more just
to say Hans Andersen; for, as far as I can remember, Andersen was
more of the snob than Grimm. . . . Poets, in fact, once they put on
their laurel crowns, divest themselves of every shred of humor, irony
or incisive knowledge of life as it is lived. I can hardly think of anyone
save Heinrich Heine, Browning—and sometimes Christina Rossetti—
who was born since 1790 and did not consider verse-writing as something aloof from life, art, form and language."

Thus Mr. Hueffer. And I immediately began to wonder what

poets Mr. Hueffer is accustomed to read, aside from himself, that verse-writing has become so inane. And, turning the page, I found that his attacks were directed against two suppositious journalists, apparently contemporaries, who had each published a volume of ex-schoolboy verses. Mr. Hueffer's shells then seemed to be aimed at the camp followers and to have fallen among them with no sound but the dropping of duds.

Mr. Hueffer, it is true, is but preparing his way to praise certain poets whom he admires above the academicians and the Georgians. But his remarks are typical of those who wish to attack poetry as the one medium open to the immature, fit only to express ideas which are untrue or else too obvious for expression. All the writer's artillery is usually brought out to slaughter some half-hearted band of amateurs or some mediocre poetaster. When Mr. Yeats vents his hatred of Swinburne's rhetoric, or Mr. Pound assails Milton's vague grandiloquence, they are exercising legitimate critical faculties; but when Mr. Mencken devotes a long essay to the inanity of magazine verse he seems to me to be wasting his efforts.

There is no reason that a poet should not bring to his work a knowledge of life as it is lived in the streets and a spirit of mockery. It is difficult to warble divinely with the tongue in the cheek, but it has been done.

What matters is intensity, and with intensity the poem may survive anything—even archaic language. I do not intend to apologize for emotion; it would be too much like apologizing for the human race. And, happily or not, there is no occasion to explain away any excess emotionalism on the part of the established American poets. Mr. Hueffer's "brandified sentimentalist" does not exist. Ezra Pound, "HD," T. S. Eliot, Edgar Lee Masters, Robert Frost, in part at least belong to the prose tradition. There is not one who, in his verse, loses the least subtlety of his intellect or betrays a dissolute air.

But if there were no other who, having put on his laurel crown, held to his humor, irony and incisive knowledge of life, there would still be Edwin Arlington Robinson. His collected poems show that if he has not always written well, he has at least written wisely. It is charged against Mr. Robinson that he is now employing his idiom independently of his thought. But this at least implies that he has brought his style to such a pitch that he himself is content. He may be pardoned for imitating himself well, when others have done it so badly.

But I do not in the later poems find a perceptible slackening. If some of the sonnets are little more than rhymed mannerisms, there is still Mr. *Flood's Party*, which perhaps will serve as well as anything else to show Mr. Robinson's humor, irony and observation. [The whole of the poem was quoted here.]

Mr. Robinson has from the first written in a style which is at once clear and evasive, stark but indirect. He begins by a direct statement which is no sooner made than qualified, or after a suggestion of dark hints he surprises us with an epigram. Standing before his characters, with one hand he snatches away a mask and with the other casts a veil. His right hand knows perfectly well what his left hand is doing, but there are times when the reader is too confused by the swiftness of his movements to know what has been revealed.

I speak now of those poems in which Robinson has failed of his best, and yet probably no American poet of his generation has maintained such a high level of execution. His method has in part been forced upon him. His terse epigrammatic style is adapted as no other could be to the kind of psychological poetry at which he is aiming, and the uncertainty of his statements are due, not to a trembling of his hand, but to the doubt which exists in his own mind when pronouncing moral judgment. For his interest lies in those men and women who belong neither to success nor to failure. He is a pessimist with whom there remains a doubtful hope. He has eaten his bread alone and knows that it is bitter; he trusts that it may be yet the best nourishment for a man's soul.

Always he seems to stand outside the event. It is for this reason, I believe, that his dramatic monologues are almost inevitably failures. *John Brown*, for example, would be an interesting commentary on the libertarian fanatic, were it delivered by an observer. As an expression of the man's own mind, it scarcely comes off.

One might have thought that after the Victorians there was nothing further to be done to the Arthurian legend but to restore its original violence and barbarous courtesy. Mr. Robinson, however, has taken these famous, but no longer fabulous, lovers, Merlin and Vivien, Launcelot and Guinevere, and made of them men and women afflicted with modern doubt, wearily appraising a world which has fallen to ruins about them. There is in *Launcelot*—which on the whole succeeds better than *Merlin*—no hint of high emprise, of adventurous and courteous passion. The burning of the queen, an incident ignored by all since the earliest chronicles, and her rescue by Launcelot after the lighting of the faggots, is seen not on the spot, but as mirrored in the eyes of the tired and disillusioned king. The two great scenes between the lovers—when Launcelot and Guinevere discover the weariness which has overtaken them, and when they come to their final parting, after Arthur is dead and Guinevere cloistered in a convent—are realized with psychological subtlety, but with a sensuous dimness which renders them all but unreal. Only occasionally passion, more desperate than weary, breaks through, as in that moment when Launcelot, parting from the Queen,

> "Crushed her cold white hands and saw them falling
> Away from him like flowers into a grave."

Mr. Robinson has taken dust and ashes and transmuted them into something which gleams with a pallor not unlike gold. Mr. Masters, in *The Open Sea*, has taken the fine gold of Shakespeare's famous lovers, Antony and Cleopatra, and corroded it with acid. The current of the Spoon River has been turned into the Nile. The Queen of Egypt is seen thus:

> She's twenty-eight, fruit fresh and blushing, most
>   mature and rich;
> She spoke the language of the troglodytes,
> The Medes and others. And when Antony
> Sent for her in Silicia, she took time,
> Ignored his orders, leisurely at last
> Sailed up the Cydnus in a barge whose stern
> Was gilded, and with purple sails.

So looks from Chicago the barge that like a burnished throne burned on the water and the lass unparalleled who so sternly avoided a Roman holiday. Wise enough to outwit the full-fortuned Caesar, she cannot escape Mr. Masters, industriously intent on showing how so noble a lover of liberty as Brutus may find his last imitation in a John Wilkes Booth.

Mr. Masters has, no less than Browning, learned to think in blank verse, and it is by the facile control of his instrument and his unfailing irony that the volume is chiefly distinguished. The failure of Mr. Masters to live up to the *Spoon River Anthology* seems to me to be largely due to his determination to make poetry out of books which he has scarcely read. It is not that fine poetry may not be created out of books and lonely meditation. Tennyson, for example, was an excellent poet until he left the Ivory Tower and went down into the Crystal Palace.

THE INTELLIGENCE OF POETS

The trouble with Mr. Masters is not that he has gone into his library for material, but that he has not stayed there long enough.

Mr. Ezra Pound is not so much a man as a trinity. There is Mr. Pound the poet, Mr. Pound the pedant and Mr. Pound the instigator. The pedant and the author of *Instigations* have frequently of late put the poet out of the house.

I have never doubted that Ezra Pound was a true poet and I do not use the term lightly. *Blandula, Tenulla, Vagula* from the volume called *Lustra* is pure poetry such as has not often been produced in this country.

> What hast thou, O my soul, with paradise?
> Will we not rather, when our freedom's won,
> Get us to some clear place wherein the sun
> Lets drift in on us through the olive leaves
> A liquid glory? If at Sirmio,
> My soul, I meet thee when this life's outrun,
> Will we not find some headland consecrated
> By aery apostles of terrene delight,
> Will not our cult be founded on the waves,
> Clear sapphire, cobalt, cyanine,
> On triune azures, the impalpable
> Mirrors unstill of the eternal change?
>
> Soul, if She meet us there, will any rumor
> Of havens more high and courts desirable
> Lure us beyond the cloudy peak of Riva?

Mr. Pound knows perhaps better than any living American what poetry should be, and he has been justified in turning to the Troubadours, to the Italian poets of the *dolce stile nuovo*, to Catullus and his contemporaries, as models of that precision which, after the vague rhetoric of the Victorians, it was valuable that poetry should regain. One must, in order not to be a parvenu, find a precedent in the past, or in some literature which has developed upon a different tradition than our own. And once a personal idiom is achieved, no one can gainsay the accomplishment. Masefield found his corrective in Chaucer, and Yeats the model he needed for his plays in the Japanese Noh drama. But Mr. Pound has never stayed long enough in one place to build surely, nor has he been able to secure a permanent color by blending his dyes. It is true that, after all the ransacking has been done in the books read, something still remains which is the essential Pound. And it is this Pound, nervous, harassed by modernity and yet loving the Attic grace, the Pierian roses, which brings one again and again to whatever he has written.

His failure to realize his high talent, his inability to create a style always at his service, cannot, I think, be wholly charged against him. He is of those poets who must take their images out of old books or legends of the countryside, who cannot deal with life directly but must transmute it into something strange in their own minds. Had he been content to remain in America, and could he have found here some such material as Yeats found waiting to his hand when he returned to Ireland, he might, I think, have been a poet such as is more than any other needed in this country.

Homage to Sextus Propertius is a learned account of the love affair whose actual history shines through pages of Roman history, the pilferings from classical literature superfluously pasted across it. Thinking perhaps of the excuse which Propertius made to Maecenas for celebrating his own Cynthia rather than the epic wars of Rome, Mr. Pound offers a precedent for devoting himself to a love poem at a time of such worldly tumult. *Moeurs Contemporaines* and the carefully distorted self-portraits published under the guise of *Hugh Selwyn Mauberley* are elliptical, coolly wrought, delicately pointed satires, but there is nothing here so poignant as the poems of T. S. Eliot in a similar genre.

This will perhaps indicate their quality; incidentally it seems a just appraisal on the part of the poet of his own work.

> Turned from the "eau-forte
> Par Jaquemart"
> To the strait head
> Of Messalina:
>
> "His true Penelope
> Was Flaubert,"
> And his tool
> The engraver's.
>
> Firmness,
> Not the full smile,
> His art, but an art
> In profile;

THE INTELLIGENCE OF POETS

> Colorless
> Pier Francesca,
> Pisanello lacking the skill
> To forge Achaia.

Envoi has a lyricism which Mr. Pound seldom permits himself these days, comparable, perhaps, to *La Figlia Che Piange* of Eliot. The final appraisal of the book must, however, depend on the *Six Cantos* with which it concludes. I shall have to learn at least three more languages and read seven years before I shall pretend to recognize all the references, but patchwork of erudition, of phrases in five tongues and paraphrases as it is, it still contains much that is pure poetry. Lines like the following would not be easy to match in contemporary literature:

> The silver mirrors catch the bright stones and flare,
> Dawn, to our waking, drifts in the green cool light . . .

> Bathing the body of nymphs, of nymphs, and Diana,
> Nymphs, white-gathered about her, and the air, air,
> Shaking, air alight with the goddess
> > fanning their hair in the dark,
> Lifting, lifting and waffing:
> Ivory dipping in silver,
> > Shadow'd, o'ershadow'd . . .

> Upon the gilded tower in Ecbatan
> > Lay the god's bride, lay ever
> Waiting the golden rain . . .

> And all that day, another day:
> > Thin husks I had known as men,
> Dry casques of departed locusts
> > speaking a shell of speech. . . .

> The scarlet curtain throws a less scarlet shadow . . .

Vanity Fair: January, 1922

POETS IN PROSE

(*Memoirs of a Midget* by Walter de la Mare, *Rosinante to the Road Again* by John Dos Passos)

I T IS THE CUSTOMARY thing to say of Walter de la Mare that, among the living poets of England, he is most skilled in conditions of magic. But Mr. John Gould Fletcher, with a nice desire to have nothing whatsoever to do with a word associated in his mind with Victorian criticism, would have us believe that all the term means in this connection is that Mr. de la Mare is a better craftsman than most. He will have it that the poet's traffickings have been with the thesaurus, not with demons; that delicate as his ears are, they have not been licked by the dragons.

And yet it seems to me a good deal more apt to refer certain of Mr. de la Mare's qualities to the magician than to the artisan. For is there not, in certain poets, a power to so order words that they become an incantation, producing an effect out of all proportion to their strict meaning?

> Not poppy nor mandragora,
> Nor all the drowsy syrups of the world
> Shall ever medicine thee to that sweet sleep
> Which thou owedst yesterday.

Lines such as these, even when torn from their context, have a portentous sound; the senses are troubled, and it seems that a statement has been made, obscure but of vast and terrible import. There is something here beyond music, though doubtless the effect has been produced by an arrangement of sounds and by the vague associations called up by each word. This power to enchant the intellect and steep it in a vinic drowsiness Mr. de la Mare has, though to be sure in a paler and milder fashion.

> Hear the strange lutes on the green banks
> Ring loud with grief and delight
> Of the dim-silked, dark-haired musicians
> In the brooding silence of night.

There seems no gainsaying that these verses from *Arabia* are unearthly in color, sorcerous in sound. Of course a tremendous amount of water, some blood and a few bottles of laudanum and whiskey have flowed beneath the bridges since the Romantic Movement got under way, and there are now many masters in magic to whom a poet when young may put himself to school; but there is something here beyond craftsmanship and more than an inherited attitude of wonder. The vision has the slow uncertain quality of things seen in a dream, as if it were a recovered recollection of a boy's daydream, brooding over a book of Arabian tales. The commonplace has been made strange, not only through art, but by the green corrosions of time.

At his best—and, like all romanticists, he is seldom at his best—Mr. de la Mare is never far from the mind of a child. Not that he has anything in common with the present cult of naïveté, which presents a sophisticated vision with a crude childish drawing and the colors of a cheap paint box. Rather he brings all the resources of a mature art to the bodying forth of the remembered impressions of his first years, years sensitive to wonder, delighted by the gray curl of a willow leaf or the gilded shining of a bird. Love is a lad with broken wing, Death a mobled shape that moves dimly between twilight and dusk, War no news for a child to hear. Mature experience is a horror to be charmed away by the rattle of foolish bells or by the playing of chamber music. Something has drawn away his vigor, incapacitated his mind to deal with life soundly. Childhood is the only refuge left in a world so gross and so scientifically explored.

In a way, it is a child's world that is presented in the *Memoirs of a Midget*. Miss M. has the separateness, the wonder, the bewilderment, even the petulance of a child, qualities which are preserved for her by her minute size. "My eyes," she says, "dazzled in colors. The smallest marvels of flowers and flies and beetles and pebbles, and the radiance that washed over them, would fill me with a mute pent-up rapture almost unendurable. Butterflies would settle quietly on the hot stones beside me as if to match their raiment against mine. If I proffered my hand, with quivering wings and horns they would uncoil their delicate tongues and quaff from it drops of dew or water. Bees would rest there, the panniers of their thighs laden with pollen; and now and then a wasp, his jaws full of wood or meat. When sunbeetles or ants drew near, they would seem to pause at my whisper, as if hearkening. As if in their remote silence pondering and sharing the world with me." The illusion of a world tinily seen and delicately heard is never for an instant broken. Ordinary human beings appear monstrously gross; their actions are those of stupid brutish giants. A strangeness of vision pervades the whole book; for not only does the Midget keep, in the eyes of the reader, a small unearthly air, but the commonplace men and women around her, being seen from so lowly a height, become unaccountably queer. Even Mr. Anon, the dwarf who tries for the Midget's love and is only a few inches her superior in height, is for her "like one of those strange creatures which thrust themselves out of the sleep world into the mind's wakefulness; vividly, darkly, impress themselves upon consciousness, and then are gone."

But, despite her size, Miss M. is very much the woman. She has the arrogance of a woman who knows herself to be, in her own fragile way, very lovely; she has the pettishness of one who knows she suffers under an insuperable physical disadvantage. With her serpent-like dart, she is remarkably like an old-fashioned spinster; indeed it is difficult to remember that, when her memoirs come to an end, she is very little over twenty.

And yet the passions and troubles of a mature world are for her as remote and unaccountable as if she were a child. Love is a bodiless desire: her own affections are fixed on her landlady's daughter; she looks toward her own dwarfish lover eagerly and without warmth. Death is as bewildering and crazy a terror at twenty-one as when, a child, she had stumbled on the carcass of a dead mole. Young men commit suicide, hopeless or weary of desire; Mr. Bowarter chases after scarlet petticoats and dies beyond the sea; Fanny marries for money: life goes on around her in a remote and mysterious grossness, and no one in her history satisfies his longing.

The heart of Miss M.'s mystery is not to be plucked out; the intention of the book is kept cautiously obscure. But I expect that the Memoirs of a Midget might, mutatis mutandis, serve as an autobiography, and that if the heart of the tiny creature could be found, its measurements would be very like those of Mr. de la Mare.

John Dos Passos is also among the poets. I have been allowed to read the manuscript of A Pushcart at the Curb, his volume of poems which Doran will bring out within the year. His most recently published volume of prose—Rosinante to the Road Again—is in manner and mood more nearly akin to these poems than to Three Soldiers, on which his reputation was made.

Rosinante to the Road Again is, on the surface, a volume of sketches on Spanish life and letters; actually, it is a record of mental adventurings. Two youths, named for convenience Telemachus and Lyaeus, take the road to find if it may be the essential gesture of the

Spaniard, the irreducible quality of Spain. Between the chapters re-counting their search are notes on Ibañez, Antonio Machado and Juan Maragall—poets, the one of Castile, the other of Catalonia; on Benavente and Baroja, and occasionally the account of some Spanish scene written in the first person. Yet even in these apparent interludes the search is never far away. The gesture is variously seen, now as a dancer shining in a golden shawl, now as an ancient Castilian noble-man writing his one unforgettable poem to Death, now as a bucket of dirty water deliberately swung down on their young heads from an alley window. It is seen, too, in the traditionalism of Benavente's plays, in the saints of El Greco aspiring like white flames toward an ecstasy where God is a sublimation of the Spanish soul. The search is after all for that Spain which, shut off by the Pyrenees from mod-ern civilization, presents the most complete contrast to industrial America, where, it is said, men work and rest only that they may work again. And this Spain is early found; the rest is but variations of a theme.

"Before the Revolution, before the Moors, before the Romans, before the dark furtive traders, the Phoenicians, they were much the same, these Iberian village communities. Far away things changed, cities were founded, hard roads built, armies marched and fought and passed away; but in Almorox the foundations of life remained un-changed up to the present. New names and new languages had come. The Virgin had taken over the festivals and rituals of the old earth goddesses, and the deep mystical fervor of devotion. But always remained the love for the place, the strong anarchistic reliance on the individual man, the walking, consciously or not, on the way beaten by generations of men who had tilled and loved and lain in the cherish-ing sun with no feeling of a reality outside of themselves, outside of the bare encompassing hills of their commune, except the God which was the synthesis of their souls and of their lives.

"And predominant in the Iberian mind is the thought *La vida es sueno*: 'Life is a dream.' Only the individual, or that part of life which is in the firm grasp of the individual, is real."

Rosinante to the Road Again is unquestionably better written than *Three Soldiers* or its predecessor, *One Man's Initiation*, whether because of an advance in craftsmanship or because the subject comes more easily to his hand I cannot say. There is a proportion, a subtlety in the placing of accents, in the tale of the youth's wanderings that is clear gain. There is still a touch of the amateur in his treatment of landscape, brought there by too close an adherence to the imagistic method, by assuming that the visual imagination of the reader will be

able to reconstruct the scene from an accumulation of accurately observed detail. In treating landscape the memory—if it is a memory—
is a better source than a suitcase load of notebooks.

Vanity Fair: May, 1922

"INTRODUCING IRONY"
BY MAXWELL BODENHEIM

IN *Introducing Irony* Maxwell Bodenheim
has [like E. E. Cummings in *The Enormous Room*] performed with
violent skill upon English speech, though the charge of impatience
cannot be made against him as against Cummings. He has, since the
beginning of his career some ten years ago, cultivated a small and
quite private garden, where he weds orchids and gilliflowers, sprays the
morning-glories with vitriol, sprinkles the grass with rust, and puts
drugs at the roots of his hydrangeas to turn them blue. When he
pauses in these pursuits, it is to express his contempt for the people
on the highway.

Bodenheim's style is decadent, by which I mean to imply that it
represents the furthest extreme from the classical. There is the decadent insistence on the line above the poem, the word above the line.
But in his decadence he is probably more akin to Poe than to the imitative poets of the nineties. He is to be found at his best in *Seaward
from Mars, Insanity* and *A Simple Account of the Poet's Life. Impul-
sive Dialogue* offers an excellent and dispassionate critique of his own
art. I heartily recommend the book to anyone the least interested in
American poetry.

Vanity Fair: July, 1922

ON TRANSLATING DANTE
(*The Inferno of Dante*, TRANSLATED BY LACY LOCKERT;
The Divine Comedy of Dante Alighieri, TRANSLATED BY
JEFFERSON BUTLER FLETCHER)

THE INTENTION of both Mr. Lockert
and Mr. Fletcher has been to provide, the one for the *Inferno* only,
the other for all three books of the *Divine Comedy*, a new translation

ON TRANSLATING DANTE

which shall keep the movement of Dante's *terza rima* and, by allowing themselves certain liberties of rhyme, to surpass their stricter predecessors in this measure, in accuracy of phrase and in literary distinction. For this purpose, Mr. Fletcher has kept the tercet. Dante's verse, as he quite justly says in his introduction, revolves upon it as an ever-repeated unit. "To reweave his separated words into the ampler and more varied strophes of blank verse would be to alter fundamentally, not only his music and his style, but the very structure of his composition." But to facilitate his task, as well as to relieve the ear unaccustomed to Italian richness and the intricately repeated sounds, he has simply rhymed the first and third line of each tercet. At first, the reader is rather bewildered by this and looks for something to be done about all these unwedded words that wait neglected at the ends of every second line. But once he ceases to listen for rhymes that are not there, the effect is not unpleasant. And Mr. Fletcher's version of Dante's poem can be read with greater ease and rapidity than any other I know. It should serve admirably for anyone who, knowing no Italian, wants to know what the *Divine Comedy* is about or for one who, like myself, reads Italian slowly and will occasionally want to go quickly through one of the books to see its structure as a whole.

Mr. Lockert has made his translation of the *Inferno* in *terza rima*. But, while following the strict scheme of his poet, he has permitted himself the use of false rhymes: *sad, aid, displayed*; of half-rhymes: *visage, rage, sage*. He also uses assonance and once or twice, when it has seemed to him imperative to render the exact sense of an important passage, dropped out a rhyme altogether. There is nothing in this to shock an ear accustomed to the muted rhymes of, say, Mr. Yeats. Moreover, Mr. Lockert has but followed the practice of those who have best written *terza rima* in English; Shelley, for instance, retards or speeds the measure by placing now perfect, now subdued, rhymes. And the very difficulty of the scheme has had a happy influence on the style, has made for concision and dignity—at times, indeed, for grandeur. His *Inferno* is more vigorous than Mr. Fletcher's; it is also more finished.

It may be that the present is propitious for translation of Dante. It is now so difficult to write English verse, and one of the reasons is that we admire the very qualities which the Florentine had in all excellence. Though he could compress the most abstruse thought— and the medieval mind could move in circles as intricate as those it conceived, under the Ptolemaic system, to account for the progress of the planets and the turning of their moons—into a single tercet, it is not, I should say, when the thought is most involved that the translator is most tried. It is rather in those terrible and poignant and intense passages where Dante adds one simple statement to another, and each line in its senses seems almost a conversational commonplace. It is the implications of Francesca's,

> Se fosse amico il Re dell' universo
> Noi pregheremmo Lui per la tua pace,
> Poi che hai pietà del nostro mal perverso . . .

that are tremendous; so simple is her remark that at first we are aware only of the courtesy and pity of it. Then we know that we have heard a damned woman speaking, and that she has acquiesced in her damnation. The effect is terrible.

Now, supposing that the translator has found a modern skill to convey this passage in all its dignity, simplicity and poignancy, he will still have left something unsaid. For in these lines, and as long as Francesca speaks, the verse trembles, moving as the wind moves on which she with her lover is endlessly blown. In this, Dante is unsurpassed; he learned, of course, from Virgil; but where the Latin poet is usually content merely to enforce his description of natural sounds by apt and imitative harmony (a trick Tennyson could learn), Dante, having once told us of the wind, makes us feel throughout Francesca's complaint its rise and fall, though only once does she mention it. Her punishment is forever present—for in hell it is by the wind, as on earth by their desires, that the lovers are afflicted. This is more than the imitation by sound of sense; the very essence of the scene is in the sound.

An even more remarkable instance of this is to be found at the end of the Brunetto Latini canto. Dante, after he has justly placed Brunetto among the sodomites, wishes to assert the moral grandeur of the damned man. His intellect approves what he conceived of as the just judgments of God; with his mind he accepts the moral order as Aquinas and other saints and doctors of the Church had defined it. But Dante, as Blake said of Milton, is of the devil's party whether he knows it or not. He is a poet and as a poet is to be found passionately on the side of the damned. Conscious of the conflict, he uses it for irony, and one of the reasons why the *Inferno* seems to most readers so much more vivid than the *Purgatorio* or the *Paradiso* is because it is only when he is presenting the alienated from God that this irony has full play. (Not, of course, that he ever completely drops it, even in Paradise: his reply to Saint Peter when the latter questions him on his faith is so ironically phrased that the good saint would certainly, had he not long since discarded all human feelings, writhe most uncomfortably.) Now, Dante, having dramatically expressed his astonishment at meeting his friend among those who, unrepentent, were given to sodomitical lusts, goes on to accord him every possible courtesy and respect. He goes beneath Ser Brunetto, listening with reverence. But, not content with this, Dante means to convey that, however low this man may be sunk in the divine scheme of things, he was, and is by all humane values, high. And he chooses for this purpose an image which at first sight will appear grotesque: he says of Brunetto that when he had done speaking,

> Then he turned back; and he appeared like one
> Who on the plain before Verona tries
> For the green mantle; and of those that run
> No loser seemed, but he who gains the prize.

I quote here from Mr. Lockert's translation. This is a clear and almost literal rendering of the Italian. Mr. Fletcher's is better:

> Then round he swung him, and of those seemed one
> Who across country at Verona race
> For the green mantle; and he seemed to run
> As one there gaining and not losing place.

Much of the movement of the original is there; the repetition of "seemed" is correct; the contrast of *gaining* and *losing*, both participles, is clearer; the right emphasis falls on *not*. Probably this is as good a translation as one has the right to hope for. And yet much of the effect of the original is gone. The last line of the canto is

> *Quegli che vince, non colui che perde.*

The verb rather than the participle is an immediate gain in vividness, and more, Dante, knowing that he must weight both *vince* and *perde* as heavily as possible, begins, lines back, to play the *p-v-f* combination, which, as any poet knows, is the most poignant possible; he includes and varies it with a succession of *n* sounds to enforce his *non*. He also, very adroitly, introduces into his image of the race the phrase *per la campagna*, through the open field, and places it so that it brings into the suffocating air of the burning plain a breath of freshness and of spring (the foot-races of Verona were run at Easter). The effect is strong and triumphant: Brunetto is vindicated against the very edicts of God. But the moral force of the passage, as I have tried to make plain, is in the sound. And when for Dante's music another or none is substituted, the sense is no longer the same.

Both Mr. Lockert and Mr. Fletcher have done very well at a task ultimately impossible. Both are aware of the mistakes of earlier translators and, on the whole, have been successful in avoiding on the one hand the false magniloquence of Cary, on the other the abominable flatness of Longfellow. Of the two, Mr. Lockert is the more vivid; his *terza rima* is more satisfactory than Mr. Fletcher's partly rhymed tercets. Mr. Fletcher gains in skill as he proceeds: his *Purgatorio* is better than his *Inferno*; his *Paradiso*, really excellent. But the greatness of Dante the poet remains in the Italian.

The New Republic: December 9, 1931

THE SOCIAL MUSE ONCE MORE

(A letter to the *New Republic*, published in the issue of February 8, 1933)

SIR: Archibald MacLeish's *Invocation to the Social Muse* is an admirable poem. Furthermore, it says something that needed very much to be said at this time when every force, including a fear for his own skin, urges the poet to take political sides. It is too often assumed that if a poet does not mix in politics, he is refusing in some cowardly fashion to face life, and that, if once engaged, he does not take up an extreme position, he is not only a poltroon but an ignoramus. The truth is, a poet has shown enough courage if he can face his own life. And it requires a great ignorance of literary history not to be aware that politics is the besetting sin of poets and one which has done them and their craft more harm than all forms of drunkenness and debauchery put together.

For having yielded to that temptation, the Tuscans suffered exile, the Tudor poets decapitation and the liberal poets of the nineteenth century extinction through rhetoric. Think of what *Paradise Lost* might have been had John Milton not attached himself to the warty Cromwell and wasted the best years of his life! Nor are recent examples more edifying. Louis Aragon has only yielded to his own already excessive love of violence in putting himself at the service of the revolution, and I notice that Yessenin and Mayakovsky found that, once

FINAL DREADING

on the extreme Left, there was no place to go but toward suicide. Nor is it recorded that politics has benefited much by their intrusion.

There is a way for the poet, as there is for the novelist, to write of political events. There is *Coriolanus*, there is *The Possessed*. The one is a dramatic poem, the other a novel. They have no immediate interest. Mr. MacLeish deserves the highest praise for his stand that a poet should attend to his business, which is writing poems, at a time when so many have deserted literature to engage in polemics. For it would be, I think, a mistake to describe the American Communists as engaged in political activity when what they are really doing is indulging themselves in an intellectual coma and letting two other men, both dead, do their thinking for them.

Orgeval, France   John Peale Bishop

FINAL DREADING

(*The Assassins* by FREDERIC PROKOSCH)

MANY IN OUR time have the sense of foreboding. They need not have read Spengler, or for that matter Gibbon; they need only to have seen political disintegration over a great part of Europe—order disturbed in the name of justice and new injustices following immediately on disorder; and—as surely as in a modern city disease must follow on a breaking of the water-drains—all these things accompanied by moral dissolution. Frederic Prokosch is one with a prescience of disaster. *The Assassins* is an impressive first book of poems; not all of them are obviously political; in fact, very few of them are. And yet, the volume as a whole is filled not merely with dread and longing that, as so many revolutionaries suggest, a particular phase of contemporary civilization may be passing, never to return; there is also the knowledge that over vast tracts and long stretches of time all specifically human endeavor may cease, while men themselves, in countless hordes, survive. Whether this country is young enough, remote enough, to escape contagion from "these enormous European fevers" is not certain.

> I gaze from the edge of a vast America
> Toward the three continents twined in a common terror
> Whose creatures still implore their nocturnal heroes
> A phase toward the infinite, then as here; no more.

279

Mr. Prokosch has traveled widely. Africa is the beginning of his vision and the end Asia. For he has gone beyond the falling cities of the West to "the white death of stagnant centuries." (In these poems, as in Melville, white is the color of dread, of destruction, of death.) In his voyages he has seen those peoples who have outlived their time of foreboding only to come to a timeless doom. It is this contact, an experience as imaginative as it is actual, which gives to these poems their immediacy.

In more than one poem, but particularly in "Going Southward," he has set down in a flowing verse, slow but secretly impetuous, steadily mounting, like a torrential stream temporarily halted by a green region of heavy vegetation, the vast supineness of the Asiatics in Siberia, in China, and more especially in India, country of dead cities: the awful surrender of people who, in more than the Spenglerian sense, have passed out of history.

> The great
> Dead cities, secret with weeds, sacred; the great
> Living cities along the land's end, ocean-angered;
>   the dead now conquered
> By roots, moss burning among the moonstones,
>   Buddha the lover
> Smiling serene through the leaves in the cavern.

For this is the secret of the spirituality of Asia: complete surrender; a meaningless submission to a bleak and crowded impermanence; an endless change, but no significant change; an absence of thought and memory. This is the end, it may be, which is to be reached "by the northern road of doing." It is not thus that the Asiatics have come there, but by suffering and exhaustion; yet there is no doubt that this is the promised end.

The poems of *The Assassins* are not all a sensuous record of thoughts on the present state of the world. This is the trouble of a young man and a poetry of desire. In a sick world, love sickens and acquires the sterile qualities of hate; it becomes hostile and escapes into solitary or shared perversions. In the old days, through its power, men felt "their thighs cooled in the old tribal water." They were absorbed into the race, to become one with its past and future. It is here that Mr. Prokosch's poetry is at least clear; phrases are employed whose implications are too private to be understood. It is only when the particular case dissolves into the common that clarity is completely regained. Through love, the poet is aware of humanity, and with that awareness again comes fear, the prescience of a common doom. The absorption into the race is contemporary—that is to say, it is spatial and not immortal.

All this is traced with considerable power. The verse of *The Assassins* is adroit, fluent and remarkably sustained; it is supported by no small sensuous abundance. The images have that timeless quality which Perse achieved in his *Anabase*, which is also a poem of Asia. Mr. Prokosch has, I think, learned much from Perse, but whether directly or through Archibald MacLeish, I cannot say. It is unimportant; for though it is clear that Mr. Prokosch has been to school to several contemporary poets, he has learned his lessons. There may be lines that are slightly reminiscent; there is no poem that is not his own. He is a poet to be watched; he is, even now, a poet to be read.

Poetry: March, 1937

A LITTLE LEGACY

(*Reading the Spirit* BY RICHARD EBERHART)

Loose the baleful lion, snap
The frosty bars down from his cage
And unclasp the virgin pap
Of the white world to his rage.

THE OBVIOUS influence here, as in many of the shorter poems in Richard Eberhart's *Reading the Spirit*, is Blake. And William Blake, for all that he is among the great poets, is also among the worst influences. There is none of us who cannot be instructed by Blake's insight, which is startling, bright, sure and profound; but it is to be doubted if anyone can be taught much by Blake's way of presenting his vision. For while he seems both to declare and in his art to demonstrate a continual departure from discipline, Blake is actually under two disciplines: there is, first, the thing so intensely seen, whether derived from what he would have called innocence or from experience; and, secondly, the strictly disciplined verse of the eighteenth century. From the practice of his predecessors Blake does indeed depart, but his ear has been trained by them. He is not so far from them as to forget them, just as in his drawings he is never really so far from Flaxman; what he adds is inimitable, for it is his own genius. The corresponding influence in Mr. Eberhart's case would appear to be the more or less forgotten Georgian poets; his natural ear is, to say the most, uncertain; and it has been trained in an inept school.

For with Mr. Eberhart, as so often with the Georgians, we never know which way a line is going to fall, whether into a flat prostration of prose, which, like an old lady after an accident, continues discursive, or into some strange contorted shape, which at first glance looks like poetry, and may be, but is poetry that has suffered a serious mishap. One thing seems fairly certain: we can no more trust him than we could most of the Georgians to keep going as he has started. It is not as though there were no gifts. If This Be Love is quite a good poem. And there are many felicitous lines, some that are powerful; but once we have come on them we have no confidence as to what will happen next. Mr. Eberhart's Muse is like a cornered rat, ready to turn any way. There is no direction.

Mr. Eberhart is concerned, very properly, with the place of man in the modern world. The world, though it may never know it, in Mr. Eberhart's poetry comes off a very poor second. What he asserts is a negative, hysterical and sterile individualism:

> The intense quality of desire
> Blasphemes, and is at fault to the core.
> Silence in bitterness is the hardest thing;
> But nobler to ask the fire to burn more,
> If the man can endure, and can sing.
> Even beyond joy and despair are spun
> Unutterable remoteness in the air,
> Intolerable nearness in the sun,
> And the separateness of each man in his lair.

This is not badly said. But it is as far removed as possible from Blake. What that poet thought men and women required was "the lineaments of satisfied desire."

Poetry: June, 1937

THE POEMS OF FORD MADOX FORD
(Collected Poems by FORD MADOX FORD)

THOUGH the Collected Poems of Ford Madox Ford now appear for the first time in an American edition, it is not the first volume of that title to be published. A Preface to Collected Poems, dated 1911, is here reprinted, with some apology for the frivolity of its tone, none for its opinions. This is as it should be. For if it is hard not to resent the patronizing attitude which Mr. Ford then took toward William Butler Yeats, it must be allowed him that, while his own poetic art shows a sure consistent gain down through the war period, there is, from first to last, no essential change in his point of view. In 1914 there was an English edition of Collected Poems, which was reissued in 1916. The present volume gathers together all that Mr. Ford has written in verse, from The Wind's Quest, his first poem, printed in 1891, through Buckshee: Last Poems, finished in Paris only last year. His famous On Heaven, which first appeared in Poetry in 1914, has here its pride of place, and is followed by the equally unforgettable Antwerp. From these two poems we are led, in the familiar Ford manner, back and forth through time until we have covered a career of forty-five years.

Mr. Ford's position as a poet has been somewhat overtopped by his place as a writer of prose. For it has been his fortune—and it is this that has won him, in so many cities and in more than one country, the esteem and affection of many writers younger than he—to insist upon the professional attitude. He has done it by precept and, more importantly, by example. The novelist might, as he so often told us, practice a métier de chien. It was still a métier. And nothing less than a complete consciousness of the craft would do. Of course, he was not alone among his contemporaries in holding that the French had a far finer and fuller sense of what it meant to construct a novel than the English; around the turn of the century there were not a few who spoke and wrote his language and like him followed the cult of conscience, ready at any instant to call upon Flaubert as their only saint. But of them none survive who has proved more constant to that faith; none was ever more devout than Ford Madox Ford.

His approach to the novel is in the French manner. But when it comes to poetry, Mr. Ford would have us believe that he is a man of England. It is a country where, as a living French poet has ob-

283

served, poems grow like grass—that is to say, with apparent ease and an incomparable freshness, secretly sustained by centuries of care. Ford Madox Ford disclaims too profound a concern with poetry, either his own or others'. If, when he starts a novel, he knows from the beginning to the end just how each word is to be placed, he knows— or so he says—practically nothing of how his poems are made. They come to him—a little tune in the head, then words, and then more words, on paper. How should he say if they are good or bad? He has read so little poetry. When he opens the morning paper, it is to turn first to the cricket scores.

This need not really deceive us. Like Congreve, who told Voltaire he did not wish to be visited as a dramatist, Mr. Ford, the poet, prefers to be thought of as among the country gentlemen. Their class, it might be remembered, has made no small contribution to English literature.

Before the War came, Mr. Ford was able to bring to the writing of verse not only the skill and scrupulousness which have distinguished his best novels, but also a good many tricks of his conscious trade. There are, from first to last in his work, poems which have the April spontaneity of grass; but they are not his best poems. At his best, he will be found almost invariably not to have departed too far from his methods in prose. This discourse which is a record of his own emotions and is meant, too, to record the contemporary world; which is so realistic on the surface, so romantic in its depths; which is never so pleased as when adding one discordant passage to another; which slides as smoothly as a *wagon-lit* from place to place, and at dead of night from a known country to one that is strange; which is careless with the years and indifferent to the clock as memory is: where have we encountered it before? The verse has a strong, insistent, uneven beat; the rhymes arrive unexpectedly. But this cosmopolitan speech, whose English slips so readily into a French or a German phrase, which pauses scarcely an instant and with only a touch of superiority before it turns to slang: where did it come from —if not from the prose of Ford Madox Ford? When he began writing verse, it was under those influences which a young Englishman of independent tastes might have been expected to feel just before the close of the last century. They were soon discarded. Mr. Ford's own manner seems to have been rather easily come by; it has been worn since with comfortable assurance, like an old countrycoat of good cut and the best tweed. If at times something in a poem reminds us of one of his contemporaries, that is only because his aim and theirs happen to coincide.

THE POEMS OF FORD MADOX FORD

Mr. Ford's contribution to the poetry of his time was to assist in bringing it nearer to the art of prose. It was, when he did it, a necessary thing to do. There were others: Ezra Pound also knew that if poetry was to live and not die in a living and dying world, it must, in his own phrase, catch up with prose; but none of the others knew so much about prose as Ford Madox Ford did.

It is thus that poetry has always been renewed. Jules Romains, in his recent *Préface à l'Homme Blanc*, reminds us that it was so in France, for as late as his own boyhood the charge he constantly heard leveled against Victor Hugo was one of *prosaïsme*, while in the *lycées* Baudelaire was still referred to as *un prosateur froid et alambiqué*. When the Muse's sandal is bound too strictly, there is nothing for her to do but loosen it and for a time go barefoot. When too much that he sees about him in the world is forbidden to the poet, there is nothing he can do but lay violent hands on the immense matter of prose and seize whatever he thinks he can appropriate.

So little is now forbidden, that it is not altogether easy for us to conceive how difficult this was for an English poet in the decade before the war. Mr. Ford could conclude a poem on the death of Queen Victoria with these straightforward lines:

> A shock,
> A change in the beat of the clock,
> And the ultimate change that we fear feels
> a little less far.

But he had to go through no small amount of rather facile poetizing—

> Keep your brooding sorrows for dewy misty hollows,
> Here's blue sky and lark song, drink the air—

before he could come to:

> This is Charing Cross:
> It is midnight;
> There is a great crowd
> And no light.

And it is precisely because there were difficulties to be surmounted that there remains so much that is tough and enduring in these poems, despite their constant use of not too particular sentiment.

285

They await the lost
They await the lost that shall never leave the dock;
They await the lost that shall never come again
    by the train
To the embraces of all these women with dead faces;
They await the lost who lie dead in trench and
    barrier and foss,
In the dark of the night.
This is Charing Cross; it is past one of the clock;
There is very little light.

There is so much pain.

This gives, as does no other poem, the feel of a great London in the midst of the war. And, more than that, *Antwerp* remains one of the distinguished poems of our time.

Poetry: September, 1937

A DIVERSITY OF OPINIONS

(*Conversation at Midnight* BY EDNA ST. VINCENT MILLAY)

CONVERSATION at *Midnight* is that book which in its original form was, by a remarkable mischance, destroyed by fire and which, through an effort of memory as desperate as it was for long uncertain, has now been recovered. What could not be completely recalled, Miss Millay tells us in her Foreword, has been reconstructed; and some recent poems have been added. It would be interesting to speculate on what has been gained, what lost, in the process. But it would not be profitable. For, once we have granted the poet her conception and allowed these conversations their tone, it is not easy to say how they could have been bettered. But when they are ended, long after midnight, when the shouts of the last quarrel have died down and the last good-night been said, if we are conscious of having been more amused than moved, of having been, in fact, continually diverted and scarcely moved at all, the fault is not in the talk. The fault is in the plan. And that, of course, must have been there from the start.

A DIVERSITY OF OPINIONS

It was, to be sure, a tempting plan, to bring together seven men of almost as many occupations, as unlike in their opinions as in their positions, but all alike in being seriously concerned with the present disorder of the world. The host is Ricardo, who, though the son of a petty Italian nobleman, shows no Fascist adherence, but rather the subtle skepticism and aloof dignity of the aristocratic mind. It is to his house in Tenth Street, New York, that the others come. To no small extent, he is the arbiter of their differences and, more than any other among the characters, he seems to represent the controlling play of the poet's mind. He is, like most of his guests, in his forties. John, the gifted and unsuccessful painter; Pygmalion, a very successful, rather sophisticated, and on the whole obnoxious writer of stories for popular magazines; Carl, who is Communist and poet; Father Anselmo, who is Catholic and musician: all have reached that doubtful age when a man must know, if ever, by what force or reason he lives. Merton, the prosperous stockbroker, is there to represent wealth and the pursuits of the wealthy under capitalism. He is sixty-eight, sufficiently sustained, and not only materially but morally, by the substance of past accomplishments. It may be because he is a product of the past that he is less troubled than the others by present uncertainties. If he cannot be justified by his works, he will be by their profits. And as a matter of fact, he believes, profoundly, in the works. Lucas is twenty-five, in love and unhappy. He is full of contempt for those corrupting words of the contemporary world, which, as in the advertising copy he writes for a little pay, are put between the populace and the objects for which they must be persuaded to give their money. Perhaps because of this, he has less to say than any of the other characters. Or it may be because he alone is young enough to survive on none but animal faith.

For it is in the demand and the desire for faith on the part of man that is found the center of all these conversations. "But you have time," Ricardo says to the priest.

Pascal had time; you all have time
Who have the time to think.
Your Church is built upon a rock of doubt—on three
Denials and a dozen hearts of little faith.

What a man believes, he lives with quietly. They build
No Church upon the daily rising of the sun, who howl not
With terror while the dragon eats the sun.

But of all these men, ironically, it is the capitalist only who seems to be living with becoming quiet on his small faith and a large income.

The talk begins after dinner, harmlessly enough, with a discussion of quail-shooting and the training of hunting dogs. It continues, ranging widely, again and again is interrupted, lightly or angrily, is dropped by one speaker and taken up by another. It can go both high and low, be grave or ribald; it is frequently witty and not very often poetic; it is concise, apparently casual and convincingly masculine. The men, it seems, have little good to say of the women in their absence. On one occasion, Merton, Pygmalion and Lucas take on the rhymes and manner of Ogden Nash to do up the opposite sex, with such farcical force that henceforth it has almost no place in the conversations.

It is to faith they return. And since the speakers are of the contemporary world and have met in New York, it is inevitable that sooner or later they should be involved in what was only a little while ago being proclaimed as a living faith. Carl still holds to Communism and, precisely because he is a Communist, shows himself alert to catch on any conversational hook to hang his undoubting argument. None is so slight, so small, but he can find a way to attach to it a great mass of Marxian doctrine. Possibly he is more fervid than orthodox. But then Merton, the capitalist, is in the room and serves continually to inflame him. The host is obliged to observe:

> It is a pity these communists feel called upon to imbibe
>   not only their morals
> But also their manners, from Marx;
> The grandfather of present-day communism regrettably
>   has stamped his progeny
> Not only (and this only on occasion) with the broad
>   philosophical brow,
> But also with the narrow humorless vanity and the
>   shrill spite
> That marred somewhat his articulation then as now.
>
> He was a talented, intolerant, jealous, nasty old man.

This is a dramatic poem in the limited sense that each of the characters speaks from his own and not directly from the poet's mind. The case for capitalism could hardly be better put than Merton puts it, and the curious thing is that, for all that the Communist tells him that not only he but the system that made him, fattening together, is now "so overweight it can hardly waddle," and promises both an early extinction,

> If you have tears

> For a prehistoric monster prepare to shed them now,
> For it's about to croak,

he leaves us with an impression of august solidity. Certainly he stands up under Carl's onslaught of argument and personal vituperation very much better than Carl's argument withstands the counterattack. Admirable he may not be, but solid Merton seems—and if this is odd in a stockbroker, I can only conclude that he represents not only the accumulated fat of capitalism, but even more the advantages of an undeluded, if somewhat limited, mind. Whereas in Carl delusions have quite taken the place of thought.

Edna St. Vincent Millay has not been known for her lack of sympathy for those in revolt nor has she been silent in her indignation against an unjust and imperfect society. She has, I cannot doubt, put the best case she imaginatively could for Communism. But it would seem, in this year of 1937, that it is no longer possible for one of good will to put up a case for Communism. The argument depends too much on statements which resemble their father, the wish, far more than their mother, the fact.

Nothing could be more tempting than to bring together in a room a group of men and let each speak his heart out. For so the poet can give play to all the opposing opinions which, at any given moment, disturb his mind with claims and counterclaims. But in the end we are left with merely a diversity of opinions, and there is nothing in literature that has less lasting power. This is not the first time the device of Conversation at Midnight has been employed, and there are instances of its use which last. But if I may cite The Courtier in comparison, I think we can see that, though all that the men and women gathered about the Duchess of Urbino have to say has an interest that is more than historical, at least while we are reading Castiglione's account of their conversations, once the book has been long closed, what remains in the mind is not so much what was so eloquently said—no, not even the wonderful discourse on love that only ceased when the candles had turned pale in the dawn—but the emotion with which the author has been able to endow his characters. But they were not only names. They were those whom Castiglione had known, honored, loved, and all or nearly all, when he wrote, were gone in death. Out of all the discussions about the Courtier, nothing stays longer than the passionate and poignant cry: "The Duchess, too, is dead." And it is precisely that feeling for her characters that is lacking in Miss Millay's book. They are dramatized points of view. What they have to say matters, on occasion, no doubt, matters profoundly. But they are all argumentative. And I am inclined to think that even now it is as dangerous to argue in poetry as ever Queen Elizabeth once made it out to be in the presence of princes.

Poetry: November, 1937

THE FEDERAL POETS' NUMBER OF "POETRY"

(A Review of an issue of Poetry—July, 1938— devoted to the work of the Federal Writers' Project)

T HERE IS no such thing as pronouncing final judgment on any poet. For all that he had, while still living, drawn the shroud around his head and closed his eyes for the sculptor to set his simulacrum in death, have we not seen, in our own time, John Donne stir? Three hundred years to the day after he died, I was in Saint Paul's looking for his tomb. I asked any number of men who seemed to belong there where it could be found: no one knew. Donne's statue was beside the altar; the lineaments composed for eternity had, I suppose, changed as stone changes after three centuries. Presumably that was not much. Donne's poetry was, as everyone knows who cares to know such things, undergoing considerable change. It had been discovered to be, not only alive, but subtly and sensually so; the Dean was dead, in fact so utterly dead that the attendants in his own cathedral had not remembered, if they had ever seen, his name under the statue posed on the urn. But the poet was at that moment being made over into a contemporary.

We have had three hundred years to make up our minds about Donne; and we have not yet done so. One thing only is settled: that he was a poet. And Ben Jonson, who thought him "the first poet in the world, in some things," already knew that much.

I have had three days to make up my mind about the poets who appear in the last issue of *Poetry*, chosen from among those who have worked under the Federal Writers' Project. Both the editor and I thought we had so arranged things that I should have the better part of a month to consider this anthology. Because of circumstances which neither of us could control, the July copy of *Poetry* reached me only three days ago. I have, however, read the other anthologies which, in *Direction*, *The New Republic*, and *The New Masses*, have been made from the work of these poets. Some of the names were until then unknown to me. I have done what I could to repair my ignorance. Some of the names which appear in these other collections are not represented in *Poetry*; I shall ignore them in what follows, for, although none of them is unknown, I do not think their omission any great poetic loss. It is at once obvious that the collection in *Poetry* is far and away the best that has been made from the work of the Project poets. I do not say this simply as a compliment to the editors, though it is one. I suspect that if their showing is better than any of the others from the same sources, it is because they were not moved, in the selection, by extraneous considerations, such as the political complexion of the poets. They have admitted both the pallid and the rubicund. They have not thereby made my task any easier. For what I should like to do, what I had hoped to do when I undertook to comment on the collection, which I knew to be made up from poets who were young, was to discern their directions, to make out, if I could, what moved them. So far, I have used the word *poet* as editors use it, for anyone whose work is clearly not prose whom they have decided to publish. I had also hoped, using the word as a moment since I used it for Donne, to find out if there were any poets among them.

Willard Maas, who was one of the editors of the anthology, has told us that "these poets, with few exceptions, have been forced to qualify for relief in order to obtain their present connections with the Federal Writers' Project." He has taken over the official way of putting it, which is a nice way of saying that they had to declare themselves destitute as men before they could receive support as poets. This was humiliating—how humiliating one of the contributors to this collection, Alfred Hayes, has shown in his *In a Home Relief Bureau*, published in *The New Masses*. But to go into the matter of federal aid to poets would not only take me far, it would take me away from the particular task I have set myself. And besides, it has already been dealt with in the July number by those who through experience are more competent to deal with it. On that score let me merely say that the aid was given; that, because it was given, some writing was done that would not have been done without it; and—which is most important in the present state of the world—whatever was written as poetry was written without the imposition of official opinion on the poet. Whatever has been written has been freely written.

These Federal Writers have not only looked on the actual world. They have been caught up in it, no less surely than the conscripted soldier is caught and confined in a uniform. I find none who has not heeded the first part of Mr. MacLeish's counsel to the poet; and there is none who has not, within his powers, tried to create, through poetic statement, a "poetry native to the actual world." Now, all of Mr. MacLeish's essay was stirring, but not all of it was new; and this particular counsel, it seems to me, I have been hearing for some twenty years and more. The fault in that counsel is this: that while it takes courage to look at the actual world, it is a courage that can be found by the will. But to do more than look, to see; to see more than another, and in particular to see more than the journalist sees, or the historian is likely to discover; to see what is dying, what dead, what living, what coming to life—that requires something more than the determination to stare, the resolution and the strength to keep staring. It takes more than speculation in the eyes to see. And yet it is precisely this seeing that is of avail to poetry. And because it is very rare, poetry is rare. In the meanwhile, we do what we can; we use what we have learned of the poetic craft to record what we have to say, or think we have to say. And we console ourself by hoping that it may have a certain value as writing, even though its values may not be those of poetry. And it is also true, as Mr. MacLeish implies, and as I have said elsewhere, that too fine a pursuit of purity, whether in poetry or morals, leads to sterility. There is always the example of Mallarmé to frighten us.

In the matter of craft, I cannot discern much that is new. And this is important; for a genuine advance in craft always means a change in sensibility. I can only conclude that in this respect there has been no great change in the generation of the depression and the preceding one. Let me take, simply for convenience, the first four poems. First, I shall take *A Little Nightmusic* of Alfred Hayes, for although it is not printed first, it can well stand foremost as a point of reference. Mr. Hayes is a Communist poet; he has been associated with the Living Newspaper Theatre; he lives in New York. So that he might be supposed to be in touch with whatever is latest and to represent whatever is most advanced. But listening to his *Little Nightmusic*, it is impossible to hear anything which is politically an advance on T. S. Eliot's *Preludes* and *Rhapsody on a Windy Night*.

I do not know just when these poems of Mr. Eliot's were written, but they are already in the *Ara Vus Prec* volume, which came out in 1919; and I suspect they were written some time before that. I am not saying that Mr. Hayes has nothing of his own: he has; I am merely saying that technically he stands very close to the early Eliot, just as James Daly, in *City*, is doing as a craftsman the sort of thing Cummings was doing fifteen years ago. Mr. Larsson does show an advance, and happily the person on whom he has advanced is himself. He has, I should say, more clearly than most others in the issue, a style; but he has had longer than most of the others to acquire and perfect a style, for he has been writing since the years immediately after the war. And the qualities which his poem on the war in Spain show are exactly those qualities he has always been ready to show, but which now are more admirably displayed than before. He has asked me not to comment on the present poem, which is not here exactly as he would have it; but I must refuse his request, simply because *Compline of the Men of Peace*, with its repetitions and contrasts— the men of peace contrasted with the men of war; the metaphors repeated but altered, like musical phrases transposed into another key—seems to me the best thing he has done. As it stands, it avoids the poet's worst fault, which is diffuseness. And I hope he does nothing to change it, except to remove the special marks of attention which he has placed around the word *Spain*, which needs none.

I have kept back Kenneth Fearing, though he has, and because of his tone, I think rightly, the first place in this anthology. He, more than any of the others, has something new, though it is not altogether easy to say briefly what his technical contribution is. What immediately strikes one is the sense of foreboding, which is conveyed by a series of images so spare that his speech seems almost abstract. Whatever is seen is surely but not clearly seen, for it is scarcely caught sight of before it has dissolved into something else. It is by this means—reminiscent of nightmare—that he convinces us that what he is telling us about, with such hints and indirections, is something that is like an end, and yet may never end. This, surely, is a poetry of the depression. And I should like particularly to note that the quality of the depression is rendered to us not so much by what he says as by his manner of saying it. He does not need the emphasis of capitals. But is it for emphasis that he has used them in this poem? Are they not rather reminders of all those dictates that continually assail us from signboards, which seek to impress by the enormity of their print, while they admonish us that only by doing what they say can we escape the feeling of fear? And all the time the aim of the signboards is to stimulate fear. Who can say that Mr. Fearing's name has not entered his writing? So far, he has been limited to this one effect; but this he carries off extremely well.

What are these poems about? Well, there is no doubt that most of them are concerned with the actual state of the world. They know a world in which there is war and rumor of war. Even Willard Maas's *Journey and Return*, which goes into the country of memory, after recounting much that was desirable, must in the end record:

> And the naked trees in the dark
> Cry out with dreams before we awake
> With machine guns mounted on the window sills.

It is a world in which the actualities are hunger and greed, ignorance and protest, deprivation and doubt. Daring is praised; and the downtrodden are urged to rise. There are those who care; there is the man whose conscience stirs when walking in the lazy air, knowing there has been another raid in Barcelona; there are those who do not care, "those who turn guiltily in their sleep." Mr. Funaroff's tribute *To Federico Garcia Lorca* says what he started out to say. But I cannot but feel that most of the poets of social protest look faint under the weight of their subjects. Their cries are like those we try to make in sleep, when the anguish is real, but sound will not come.

It is because he keeps within his compass, his subject limited, not only to what he knows, but also to what he knows he can do within the range of a country ballad, that Sterling Brown's *The Young Ones* is more effective than, say, *Summons at Night* of Virgil Geddes, or *The End of the World* of Harold Rosenberg.

Mr. Maas is not a poet of protest, nor is Charles Hudeburg; both seem to me poets. Since they are, their work deserves a more careful analysis than I can give it. Mr. Hudeburg seems to me to promise more than any other poet whose name was not known to me before reading these anthologies. But if he is promising, he is also troubling; as in Hart Crane, there are hints in his poems of something held back, of something obscured. And I would rather reserve comment on him until I have seen more of his work. So must I, too, with Kenneth Rexroth, whom I admire, but whose contribution to the Federal Poets' Number I cannot understand nor place in relation to other poems of his I have seen.

I have written more than I intended and said less than I should.

I have had to pass over a number of names simply from lack of space. And even where it has been possible for me to comment on a poet, I do not pretend that I have said the last word—not even that I have said my own last word. And certainly if he is really a poet, the last word will not be mine, but time's.

Poetry: August, 1938

THE MIDNIGHT OF SENSE

(*First Will and Testament* BY KENNETH PATCHEN)

BEYOND any book of poems I have encountered, *First Will and Testament* gives a lively sense of what it is to be a young man in America in a time when, for more of the young than we like to think, living and dying have lost all meaning. Kenneth Patchen is sure of his vocation as a poet, somewhat less sure of his craft. But he is able and eloquent, witty and strong. And what he is trying to do in this book is through poetry to recover meaning.

His is a world in which war is immanent, or rather, is constant. For there is but one war, and it is waged to maintain those modern cities whose only makers, he says, were ambition and avarice. The more people increase in the cities, "the more wicked all of them." He repudiates civilization, and with it not only those who have made it what it is, but those who profess to know how to remake it.

> Those smug saints, whether of church or Stalin,
> Can get off the back of my people and stay off.
> Somebody is supposed to be fighting for somebody
> And Lenin is terribly silent, terribly silent and dead.

He has faith in revolution, but it is remote and less real than his anger, and his anger is without purpose. He does not miss the irony that all these commotions in the outer world are supposed to be for the benefit of somebody. And that somebody might as well be himself. Ours is a country in which for a long time society has been conceived to be centered on the individual; but in attaining an extreme individualism we have lost sight of the real desires of the individual. As stated by Mr. Patchen they seem moderate enough; but if he has won through to the satisfaction of any of them, he owes pathetically small thanks to the nation.

He is of a generation that fears death largely because life has dealt so coldly with it. He speaks for them in Street Corner College, where are the young men who have nothing to do and nowhere to go.

> We manage to have that look that young men have;
> We feel nothing behind our faces, one way or another.

> We shall probably not be quite dead when we die.
> We were never anything all the way; not even soldiers.

It cannot be said that Kenneth Patchen feels nothing. He feels disintegration intensely. But he has not been unaffected by the young men's indifference. And like them he fears death inordinately.

His poetic speech is contemporary and close to the streets; but he has held to nothing he has heard in the streets unless it has its own vigor to recommend it. The form his poems most often take is that of hallucination. They are made up as dreadful dreams are from the remembered happenings of commonplace days. But if the details are realistic and clear, they are arranged by some obscure necessity that is not logic. They add up to a private horror—"And all the rooms of them haunted by war." His affinities are not with Rimbaud, the first master of the literary hallucination, nor with the surrealists who derive from Rimbaud. He is closer to Cummings. For Patchen presents a deliberate derangement, not of the senses, but of the mind. "It is the midnight of sense . . . mind's desolate cave."

The Nation: December 2, 1939

THE POETRY OF MARK VAN DOREN

(Collected Poems, 1922–1938, BY MARK VAN DOREN)

THE Collected Poems of Mark Van Doren show that the poet's manner was formed as soon as he had found his material. The manner is remarkable in that, almost alone among his contemporaries in this country, Mr. Van Doren shows no trace of French influence. He is in the English tradition; his master, we can hardly doubt it, is Dryden. He has the ease of Dryden, as he has the sanity; though he has always clarity, he does not have a comparable radiance. He has his own grace, but does not give that sense of inexhaustible strength which, more than anything else in Dryden, contributes to the impression of manly nobility. Mr. Van Doren is more easily resigned. He has come late to the English tradition, as he is rather belated in coming to his particular New English material. The style he has made for it is properly autumnal and dry. But if we should by any chance be about to complain that it has the dryness of an October cornstalk, it is then we discover, under the dry rustle of the long leaves, the authentic golden grain. Mark Van Doren is extremely prolific; and yet his poetry is presented, amid his verse, with a sparse hand. Nevertheless, it is always there.

The enormous influence of the French poets of the nineteenth century on contemporary American poetry is easily accounted for if we remember that these poets were the first to explore the effects on the sensibility of a civilization in which, with each decade, industry played more and more the predominant part. It cannot be too often said that what the symbolist poets sought was not an escape from the life of their times. What they sought was life; they could only report where it failed. The poetic means which they created to that end corresponded to the exasperation of nerves which accompanied the hunt, the distraction of the mind, the extremity of the heart that came with its failure. There was not one of the great symbolist poets who might not have declared, as the last of them did, that his aim was to write of his race and of reality. That, it is true, is also Mr. Van Doren's intention. It is significant that in adhering to the English tradition, which he has adapted to the use of a modern sensibility with no small skill, he has been constrained to take as his peculiar province a place where industrialism has not apparently penetrated. It has, of course, only in that portion of Connecticut that is Mr. Van Doren's poetic property, it does not look like industrialism. It looks like death.

And yet, having made his choice, how honestly Mark Van Doren has held by it! He is a completely integrated person in an age when all we have known disintegrates. He seems while young to have become accustomed to the fact that his own particular world was already lost. And these things make him not altogether of our time. He is not solitary but remote. The region into which he takes us is one where "Time smiles at us and rests his heels."

His poetry proceeds from the New England air and, like it, is both harsh and delicate. And, like that atmosphere, it lends itself continually to fine perceptions; it has its own clarity, which may perhaps conceal, as the district it celebrates, how intricate its thought really is. Mr. Van Doren's corner of Connecticut may now appear old, harmless, and mad. It was not always so.

For New England is more than a section of the country; it is a peculiar spiritual climate. And it may well be that they will weather it best who, like Mr. Van Doren, were born and nurtured in the Middle West. The native New Englander, if he happens to be a poet, will probably revolt like Cummings against Concord, Cambridge, and all their works. He will escape as rapidly as possible and yet continue to breathe, with full lungs, upon its furthest confines of air. The Middle West was settled by New Englanders who sought less inclement elements and hoped to find an earth not so frugal with her children. Across country they carried a spiritual culture, and the Middle West has no other. It is a soulless region. The Middle Westerner must either be content to get along without a soul and record, as Hemingway has done, all the circumstance of living without an inner life, or he must look elsewhere. It may be that he will return, as Mark Van Doren has done, to New England. The old landscape is still there. Much in Connecticut is permanent. And yet it is a land that men have abandoned. The poet looks at what was once a farm to see a fallen barn whose timbers the rain will soon sink into sod.

> Nothing remains
> Of what it was that made these beams a barn.

This country around West Cornwall was where a man once could say:

> I can go home. I can be my own master.
> I've got a house now, a little patch of corn,
> A plow, and a shed, and a one-eyed mule;
> As ignorant and poor as I was when I was born;
> But I'm my own pauper and I'm my own fool.

That was the self-reliance of the 'sixties. But that was long ago. Now, where there were such men, is

> No corn upon an aged trembling hand.

THE POETRY OF MARK VAN DOREN

To look for the genius of the place is to find, in a poem appropriately
called *Spirit,*

> A straight old woman, tall and very pale,
> Moving from room to room of a musty house
> No voice is ever heard in.

It is a land, not only abandoned by its men, but of men abandoned
by their gods. (Mr. Van Doren's *American Mythology* is not about
gods, but about folkways, which he calls by the names of gods.) It
is a land of death and resignation to the approach of death by way
of a dragged-out living, which is no longer desperate and scarcely
tragic, which is, in fact, no longer much of anything.

That Mr. Van Doren loves this land almost every page of his
bears witness. Though he is without romantic illusions about it, he
finds in these hills somehow his proper surroundings. He makes
them the landscape of his spirit. It is the land of his poetry. Out
of it he has made much, for it is his by choice. He comes there to
write his *Winter Diary,* and it is a charming account, in most skilful
couplets, of a cold season spent there with his family, playing at being
snowbound. For it is play. The snow that falls is real. But the Van
Dorens, not being farmers, not being cut off whenever they like from
escape, only pretend to be confined by the long cold. Yet it is for
them, as for the reader, a pleasant pretense.

When so much has been given of New England, it seems ungrateful to ask for more. But what is lacking here is something that
went out of the region long ago and whose loss was set down with
incomparable intensity by another poet who was completely aware
of what had gone.

> The missing All prevented me
> From missing minor things.
> If nothing larger than a World's
> Departure from a hinge,
> Or Sun's extinction be observed,
> 'Twas not so large that I
> Could lift my forehead from my work
> For curiosity.

That is the authentic New England note, not self-reliance, which
before and after Emerson could be carried away, but the soul sufficient
to itself. That is the note. But we can scarcely blame Mr. Van Doren

that he has come too late into the country to hear it. For none since Emily Dickinson has heard it. It is no longer there.

The capacity for tragic action, which is continually present in Emily Dickinson's verse, is gone. And the strain of loss is over. What is left has assured Mark Van Doren a singular tranquillity and enabled him to write his elegies of New England.

The Nation: December 23, 1939

CHAINPOEMS AND SURREALISM

(An introduction to the "Chainpoems" by various *Hands* published in *New Directions in Prose and Poetry, 1940*)

CHARLES HENRY FORD'S account of how these poems were written is so complete that they scarcely need another introduction. He has himself done what he asked me to do. But now that they are presented, I cannot but wonder why it occurred to him and his companions in the craft to do them at all, and why, having undertaken them, the world being what it is, their compositions should have turned out as they have.

For more than a year we have seen in a continuous advance of devastation an army long prepared and disciplined to the death. And I cannot but ask why, in this year of 1940, in the midst of a war in which the conquerors have left nothing conceivable to chance, in which the exact methods have been adopted to promote a brutal triumph, why should so many poets have collaborated on a work from which discipline has been deliberately discarded and which, if it is to succeed, can only do so by the happiest of hazards?

A chainpoem, Mr. Ford tells us, is an intellectual sport. That is to say, it is, to begin with, simply another one of those games which people with a poetic apprehension of words have long liked to play. I remember the game to which A. E. Housman was addicted as a boy and at which he was wonderfully adept. It consists in being given a longish list of incongruous words, all of which must promptly be put into a poem which shall not be without congruity. This was the game that Lewis Galantière taught me and night after night we played it the winter I was living in the Rue de la Rochefoucauld. Nobody ever wanted to go to bed, because all night the taxis would be going with increasing noise as they lost speed up the steep street, past the police station that was always awake, toward the *Grand Duc* or on toward the Place Pigalle. Then there were the *bouts rimés* that were made with another poet named Ford. Ford Madox Ford used to collect more people than he had chairs in that high apartment of his in the Rue Vaugirard. They sat, half of them on the floor, looking up to receive from Ford the sheets he had prepared. He passed among them, his moustaches dripping like a sea-god's, his breath as heavy as though he had just risen from the waves. When each of us had his rhyme scheme—taken always from one of Shakespeare's sonnets—Ford would leave us and we would hear, from a small room across the hall, his unhesitant typewriter. Presently he would be back, very pleased with himself that he had within the allotted time turned out two sonnets to the one anybody else had been able to write. His indeed sounded as though they had been ghost-written —by some Pre-Raphaelite ghost, haunting him from childhood. They were faultless in form and as he read them more or less aloud, in a voice that was always on the point of being lost to silence, with an air of depreciation that was meant to precede our applause, they also seemed to make impeccable sense.

In these games, the test of skill was provided by the necessity of giving to what was really nonsense an appearance of sense. For these were intellectual sports that had come down to us from the nineteenth century, and it was part of the fun in nineteenth-century nonsense that it could pretend to endow whatever was most preposterous with a logical structure. It was an unreal escape from reality. The solid masonry was always there; the bars were unbroken, the laws enforced; but in the meanwhile the walls of the prison could be adorned with the most fantastic landscapes.

Now this is not what is happening to the chainpoems here. As far as I can make out, what the writers have planned is not their own escape but that of their words. It is the words that have been set at liberty, like a prisoner's bird through the bars of his window. From that moment, their flight is their own. If the words have a purpose, if they have a destination, it is no longer the poet's but their own. They are free, not merely to sing, for that they could do in prison. They are free, not merely to sing, but, in André Breton's phrase, to make love.

What has led poets to want to write like this? The surrealist approach presupposes that words have a life of their own, that, if allowed to combine spontaneously, they will in time disclose a meaning, even though no meaning has been imposed on them by the poet. What if the combinations they make look at first sight like nonsense? Has not Freud taught us that what looks like nonsense is often portentous with meaning? When the motion of the words is no longer dictated by the conscious mind, then the unconscious takes over and enforces its decrees.

But to write poetry is not to conduct an experiment in psychology. And in practice what the surrealist poet does is to drain words of their power to denote in order to allow their powers of connotation more apparent play. We see the beginning of this sort of thing in Poe and Rimbaud. *Ulalume* is a surrealist poem if there ever was one, and Rimbaud in the famous sonnet on the vowels insisted on the power, not only of words, but of those letters which are the symbols of the essential sound of each syllable to evoke sonorous and disparate images.

> I, pourpres, sang craché, rire des lèvres belles
> Dans la colère ou les ivresses pénitentes.

Mallarmé, moreover, had his part in preparing the present movement by his insistence that the position of each word is no less important than the meaning, in determining the meaning of the statement of which it is a part.

> Tel qu'en Lui-même enfin l'éternité le change.

Alter the position of a single word in this line and the meaning is no longer the same. What a word means is the sum of its history. And so much contemporary effort has been expended in destroying history that it would be a wonder if words were allowed to go unscathed and still encumbered by their past.

> This lunar beauty
> Has no history
> Is complete and early;
> If beauty later
> Bear any feature
> It had a lover
> And is another.

In much contemporary poetry the words are used as though they had no past, nor need they, in their present identity, expect a future.

The pleasures of recognition are sacrificed, as in much contemporary painting, to make more certain the pleasures of surprise. It was Guillaume Apollinaire who first used the word *surréalisme*, and it was Apollinaire who wrote, with Georges de Chirico in his mind, "In order to depict what is modern in its fatal character, of all resources surprise is the most modern on which one can depend."

It is not difficult to see in the present attitude of poets, who work with words, the influence of painters, whose medium is pigment. For the revolution that occurred in painting a little after the turn of the century took its departure from the desire, not so much to reproduce life as to create it on the canvas. The painters consciously began, before the politicians, to substitute the means for the end. Matisse once painted a vase of blue flowers against a white and blue brocade. It is a representation of still-life, but the colors are in another sense living; they are not still, but vibrant with a life of their own. That they chanced momentarily to be imprisoned in petals and patterned cloth is nothing, now that they have been released in pigments. We discover in the Matisse painting relations between the various blues which, so far as we are concerned, simply were not there until he had displayed them in paint. In Picasso's painting of the ram's head and the shells, it is a relation in form that is disclosed between the volutes of the beast's horns and the coiled shells. But to the whites he had seen in both, an arbitrary black has been added and, for the sake of surprise, or perhaps as a spontaneous assertion of the painter's authority over these natural forms, a succession of blues. The colors have combined to make something that was not before the painter's eyes.

Words are like pigments in this, that they also have their sensuous qualities. And it was supposed, if they were given play and allowed uncontrolled to combine, that in these combinations new relations would be disclosed. The words released from conscious control were to be abandoned to the compulsions of the unconscious. Any word that the poet uses was once a part of the common speech, but at the moment of composition he has but one place from which he can produce the words he needs for his poem. And that is his own skull. It was assumed that the words which, unprovoked by the will, emerged and the way in which they combined would, somehow, reveal something of the source from which they came: those troubled depths that lie below the surface of the conscious mind. And it might be they would come not so much from any one man's mind as from a memory common to us all.

That may be. But the unconscious, so far as we have been allowed to perceive it in poetry, is not in itself very interesting. What is interesting in a work of art is to have what it offers to the conscious mind brought completely under control and made subject at once to a sensuous discipline and a moral order. *Oedipus Rex* is, after all these centuries, interesting. Our interest in the Saint Theresa of *Four Saints in Three Acts*, once we have got over our delighted surprise at Miss Stein's ingenuity in displaying her split personality on the stage, is soon exhausted. Nor has Hart Crane lasted as might have been expected, and yet he was, without meaning to be, the best poet of his time who can be called surrealist. For all his astonishing felicity with words cannot hide his failure in content. A poet's best phrases are almost always spontaneous, but spontaneity will never account for a poem.

For the aim of poetry is at the whole man. The surrealists, in surrendering the intellectual potency of the word, have lessened their own power. They have done so, no doubt, in distrust of the intellect and in sound protest against the abuse of abstract language. Their poetry is a protest against those who would rather not remember that words are combinations of sound as well as means of conveying ideas. They have themselves not forgotten that words are symbols and like all symbols cannot be too strictly limited in their significance. They know that, though the past history of any word can be learned from the dictionary, its present is best discovered through poetry.

It is a necessary protest, but like so many protests, costly to those who make it. For it is the responsibility of the poet to be aware of every aspect of the speech he uses, and to use less than the whole word is to aim at less than the whole man. But it is precisely by playing up, now one, now another aspect of the language that poetry advances.

THE MUSE AT THE MICROPHONE

(*Air Raid*: A Verse Play for Radio and *America Was Promises* by Archibald MacLeish)

"THE SITUATION of radio is the situation of poetry backwards. If poetry is an art without an audience, radio is an audience without an art." So Archibald MacLeish wrote to

THE MUSE AT THE MICROPHONE

James Angleton in a letter published last summer in *Furioso*. For a poet to allow his lines to be printed on so small a scale as that provided by the magazines of verse is to look for few readers or none. He is certain to find there no reader but himself. The audience which rightfully belongs to poetry and which surely can be brought to listen to simple, sensuous and passionate speech is elsewhere. *Air Raid* is addressed to that immense audience which nightly hears the news broadcast. It presents through commentary and scene an imaginary event, but one all too probable in the contemporary world, the bombing of a hill town on the border of an unnamed country, the massacre of women and children. It is not quite accurate to call it, as has been done, a verse play for radio. Rather, it is the poetic equivalent of a report from the scene of a catastrophe.

T. S. Eliot wrote long ago, in his essay on *The Possibilities of a Poetic Drama*, of the advantage to the poet who wishes to reach a large audience of taking over an existing form, not merely because it was there, ready for his use, but because his audience had already accepted its conventions. "To have, given into one's hands, a crude form, capable of indefinite refinement, and to be the person to see the possibilities"—no words could better describe than Eliot's the fortunate position in which MacLeish found himself writing *Air Raid*. His Announcer does nothing that any announcer might not do. At the same time, he is subtly translated in such a way that he carries out the part of the Messenger in a Greek play. The women from the tenement of the town are now heard singly and now they combine into a Chorus. They, too, do nothing strange. But to his form MacLeish has brought the consciousness of a poet. And, having taken it from others, he has been able to concentrate almost the whole of his effort on finding an appropriate verse for the form.

For his verse there can be only praise. It is formal without being forced; it is elaborate and yet, if well spoken, should seem perfectly natural. It was, from all accounts, effective on the air. I have heard it only on the records. If it seems better read than heard, that is the fault, not of the poet, but of his players.

When war comes, it comes now to women. MacLeish has already said, in many of his poems, what he now allows one of his women in *Air Raid* to say, that life is more truly itself for them than it is for men. But they live unconsciously until told by a man what their lives are. The young woman lying beside her lover implores him to say that what they are living in that moment is happiness. "How can a woman know that the world is good? She can't tell. She can't and be a woman." But he only implores the moment to stay. Below in the courtyard the women chatter, neither knowing what is in store for them nor wanting to know. They are a nation without history,

> the ancient nation
> Settled in the seasons of this earth as
> Leaves are and oblivious as leaves.

It is against them—against life—that war now comes. And it comes by no apparent will of men. The Announcer says of the planes over the town:

> They move like tools not men;
> You'd say there were no men;
> You'd say they had no will but the
> Will of motor on metal . . .

The implications go beyond war. The enemy is mechanical, and the living are always its victims.

Air Raid is true. It is not tragic. For, in taking consciousness away from his women, the author has denied them the possibility of tragedy. Where there is no awareness, nothing is tragic. There is no one in the play who can both acknowledge and sustain defeat. So that, at the end, it is as depressing as a catastrophe. It is depressing as poetry has no right to be.

The conflict out of which all that is most moving in MacLeish's poetry has come is a conflict between silence and sound—between a sensuous sound and a spiritual silence. It is a conflict that lies at the heart of the age, and, because this is so, MacLeish is a poet important to the age. For him the report of the senses has always been lively in the extreme. But they cannot prevent his asking the most pressing questions, and when no answer comes he knows he is in at a death of the spirit. He would deny that death if he could. He likes to end his poems on a question, for, as long as his question is in the air, he can put off silence. In *America Was Promises* he attempts himself to supply an answer, to speak to Americans, as he believes the "speaking dead" would, were they, as he is, alive. But the answer when it comes fails to dissipate the silence. For all that it is delivered on a high pitch, it fails to convince us that what was once living is not now dead.

For this new poem MacLeish elaborates a form which he first worked out in *Public Speech*. But public speech, even when made by a poet, demands ready solutions; it must point the way to action. Yet action is scarcely the way out of this conflict. It can be resolved, if at all, only through poetry.

The Nation: February 3, 1940

THE UNCONSTRAINING VOICE

(Another Time by W. H. Auden)

THE AIM of W. H. Auden in his poetry is toward a complete speech, in which whatever is pertinent to his purpose at the moment may be said. He will not, like the capital in one of his poems in *Another Time*, hide away the appalling in unlighted streets. A poet would do well to consider himself "a dark disordered city"—the image occurs in a poem on Matthew Arnold—to be explored until all its ways are known and he has become

> Familiar with each square and boulevard and slum
> And found in the disorder a whole world to praise.

Auden's powers have been expended on increasing the possibilities of the language; his interest in the form his poems take is slight. He stands as far as he can from such a poet as Paul Valéry, for whom a poem is something to be constructed, word by word, until at last it is there, a complete composition. From that point, it is outside the poet and must make its own way in the world. What it has to say is then no concern of his, though he has weighed the consequence of every word. What Auden has to say is very much his concern. He can be, and often is, remarkably complacent with mere communication. Valéry, the descendant of Baudelaire and the disciple of Mallarmé, tells us there was a time when he had no other aim than to recover from music what belonged to poetry. Auden's intent is to give poetry the range of prose, so that it may again become, though not in the constraining sense that Arnold meant, a criticism of life.

Since Baudelaire it has been assumed that poets, if they are to advance their art, must move now in one, now in another, direction.

Whenever they have concluded that they must add to their material resources from the contemporary world, they have had no choice but to encroach on the province of prose. When, on the other hand, they have been most concerned with the feelings and emotions called into being by that world, they have, not always consciously, come closer to the condition of music. It is not an accident that Auden, in this volume, follows a sonnet, *The Novelist*, after a page with another, *The Composer*.

Poets, he says, "amaze us like a thunderstorm." But the novelist, "encased in talent like a uniform,"

> Must struggle out of his boyish gift and learn
> How to be plain and awkward, how to be
> One after whom none think it worth to turn.
>
> For, to achieve his lightest wish, he must
> Become the whole of boredom, subject to
> Vulgar complaints like love, among the Just
>
> Be just, among the Filthy filthy too,
> And in his own weak person, if he can,
> Must suffer dully all the wrongs of man.

It is probably not too much to say that Auden is here presenting the novelist with his own problem. His own boyish gifts were prodigious. But poets who have only their natural grace and power to depend on as poets have a way of dying young. Or else they are forced into solitude. Like Arnold, they become their own jailers. They become like A. E. Housman, who deliberately chose the dry-as-dust and, growing old, "Kept tears like dirty postcards in a drawer." What Auden hopes to learn from the novelist is obviously nothing technical, but a greater humility toward living creatures and a humbler attitude toward his own craft.

To the composer alone belongs a pure art. But it is beyond his power to say that an existence is wrong.

> Rummaging into his living, the poet fetches
> The images out that hurt and connect.

It is clear that Auden has made his choice. It is not at all clear that a choice is necessary between sense and structure.

THE UNCONSTRAINING VOICE

The pure poet, as Auden has recently had occasion to write in an extraordinarily interesting review, is not one like Valéry but one like Shakespeare. He is one who rejects nothing that life offers him, for there is nothing living that he cannot translate into poetry. Shakespeare could face any problem, for there is none to which he cannot propose a poetic solution. And that is the only solution we have a right to expect from a poet. But there has been none since Shakespeare who has had his unlimited choice. It is not the appalling in the contemporary world that limits the poet; that he can face. What causes him to falter is that our consciousness of it has become increasingly abstract.

Within the limits of possible choice, no living poet of England has acted more brilliantly or more poignantly than Auden. In the midst of much that is trivial, much that is careless, much that is interesting, but whose interest might as well have been conveyed in prose, we are aware again and again, in this book as in every other that he has written, of that miracle which Coleridge thought might be wrought in poetry "simply by one man's feeling a thing more poignantly or more clearly than anyone had felt it before." What Auden feels is something that could scarcely have been felt so clearly before: a disorder of the spirit inseparable from the dissolution of the social order to which he belongs.

What Auden brought to poetry was a new sensibility; his poems are a record of what has hurt and sustained that sensibility. Possibly because the modern man's sense of estrangement from nature is in him particularly strong, he has been able to set his personality against civilization in much the same way as the romantic poets of the last century were able to dramatize themselves against a natural world. The consciousness of the contemporary civilized world is constant in whatever Auden writes. It is in him like a sensation of cold— "winter for earth, and us"—the coldness his in the winter that is England.

> But in that child the rhetorician's lie
> Burst like a pipe: the cold had made him a poet.

The poems in *Another Time* derive in part from Europe, and these have a density that none of those composed since he came to America have. An American influence is obvious in a number of the lighter poems, with their rhythms taken from blues and popular ballads. It is probable that the decision to come to America indicates a change in Auden more significant for his poetry than anything that has happened to him since he got here. It is a heartening rather than a hope, not so much an overthrowing of negation and despair as a certainty of the means, not so small, of affirmation he has against them.

> All I have is a voice
> To undo the folded lie,
> The romantic lie in the brain
> Of the sensual man-in-the-street
> And the lie of Authority
> Whose buildings grope the sky:
> There is no such thing as the State
> And no one exists alone;
> Hunger allows no choice
> To the citizen or the police;
> We must love one another or die.

The Nation: April 6, 1940

THE HAMLET OF L. MACNEICE

(Autumn Journal BY LOUIS MacNEICE)

AUTUMN is the time when trees cast their leaves; *Autumn Journal* is the record of a man trying to cast his past from him. But it is not so easy for a man as for a tree to shed the summer, and though at the end the season has changed and in Spain he sees the white plane trees bone-naked and thinks he sees the issues plain, he is still encumbered by the past. He has made an honest and determined effort to stand forth as bare as he can in the wintry weather. He is disillusioned, but he cannot entirely discard heredity and upbringing. He is still a British oak, not a Spanish plane tree. And the oak is a tree that holds its leaves long after they are sere, discolored, dead.

The autumn which his journal covers is that of 1938. It was a time for examining everything that had brought the English to that pass where, in September of that year, there was nothing for them to do but "To squander principle in panic and self-deception," and let the Czechs go down without fighting. MacNeice feels that his having been born in Ireland gives him an edge on the sentimental English. And perhaps that is why he can put down these reactions after Mr. Chamberlain had appeased Herr Hitler:

> But once again
> The crisis is put off and things look better
> And we feel negotiation is not vain—
> Save my skin and damn my conscience.
> And negotiation wins,
> If you can call it winning,
> And here we are—just as before—safe in our skins;
> Glory to God for Munich.

But by the time he reaches Spain he wants to have done with his complacent and "cynical admission of frustration." In Spain he sees what may be the future of England. But that is a perception that cuts two ways.

> The cocks crow in Barcelona
> Where clocks are few to strike the hour;
> Is it the heart's reveille or the sour
> Reproach of Simon Peter?

He does not know. In the midst of remorse he has still that sense, which continually afflicts him, of spiritual sloth, of desire for defeat. Spain that was once a great empire, powerful in its possessions, is now a small poor country, at the mercy of greater powers. And to be no more than Spain may be the fate of Britain. But whatever their losses, the Spanish have not lost the essential desire for life that is so much more than the mere keeping alive. And the England that passes before us in these pages is an England whose possessions are still many, but whose people give hardly a sign of life.

For those who have inherited a dead culture, with all its burden of living without love an existence that no one loves, to die and lie under a respectable inscription might be a solution. It is not the solution MacNeice is after, though he considers it with sympathy. When a man has repudiated his inheritance, to be or not to be is more than ever the question. The properties of *Autumn Journal* are as up to date as can be; there is not much in the poem that is not contemporary, and that little is given a contemporary setting. The mood, too, may be of our time. But it has, for all that it changes, always a counterpart in one or another of Hamlet's soliloquies.

MacNeice's Hamlet is as given to self-accusation as the original. He is all hesitation and doubt; he has come, not from Wittenberg, but from Oxford, and the one advantage, as he explains, of having been to the University of Oxford is that you can never afterward "believe anything that anyone says." He wants to commit some action that will redeem his will, and yet is unable to arrive at anything in which he can wholeheartedly believe. He is as irresolute as Shakespeare's prince, but it is impossible to imagine him, even in the rashness of a moment, stabbing Mr. Chamberlain, who for him plays the part of Polonius. He can wake up knowing that "The bloody frontier converges on our beds," yet do no more about it than Hamlet did after seeing the soldiers of Fortinbras. The one act recorded of him, outside of those strictly necessary for his existence, is going down to Oxford to help win an election, which is promptly lost. He does get rid of his Ophelia, but simply by the process of letting time erase her from his mind. There is a Ghost in his cast. To be accurate, there are many ghosts in the *Journal*; the soldiers of the last war are brought on, hordes of ghastly apparitions; and they have their effect, which is to increase his ineffectualness. But there is one ghost who pervades the whole poem and prompts its action, and that is· the buried majesty of England.

But MacNeice as Hamlet is definitely post-Prufrock, and, besides, is a contemporary of Auden's. He has been influenced by Auden as, I have no doubt, Auden has been influenced by him. But in *Autumn Journal* MacNeice shows that he is not the same sort of poet as Auden. Auden is the poet of the tortured sensibility and at his best has an intensity that MacNeice cannot attain. MacNeice is the ordinary sensual man with an extraordinary endowment for poetic speech. When Auden falls off, he can fall very far indeed; when MacNeice fails to write poetry, he still commands a wholesome racy English. Nobody expects a poem as long as *Autumn Journal* to be all poetry; the alloy that MacNeice uses is solid, even when it seems to have been insufficiently worked. For if the speech in MacNeice is strong, the verse is frequently very weak. He pretends, whenever he has occasion to mention them, to depreciate the wisdom of the classical writers, whose works he must teach for a living. But it is probably because he has them to fall back on that, when he ceases to be a poet, he is still as sound as he is. In his approach to his material and in the shape he has given it, he may have found an example in the Horace of the *Satires*. But it is a Horace whom he has first taken care to bring down to his own level. He despises pumice. For MacNeice has too much of that special post-war conception of honesty to believe it desirable to revise. That would be to return to the past.

SPIRIT AND SENSE

(*This Is Our Own* BY MARIE DE L. WELCH; *A Turning Wind* BY MURIEL RUKEYSER; *Song in the Meadow* BY ELIZABETH MADOX ROBERTS)

THE IMPRESSION conveyed by *This Is Our Own* is not unlike that of trying to carry on a conversation with someone who is taking care of a child. Miss Welch comments on the animals and their ways and points out in nature what a child might not see unless it were brought to its notice. She shows how grass burns brown in summer, grows green in autumn. She tells the story of how Adam, naming the beasts, came with surprise on Eve. She is cheery and harassed. There are little counsels to courage and a constant demonstration of the obvious. What she has to say to an adult listener seems under the circumstances almost an interruption, though when there is a chance she displays both charm and sagacity. That something of the child should remain in a poet is, we have been told, good; but that poetry should be addressed with such blithe confidence to what is most childish in the reader is not so recommendable.

Where Miss Welch's poetry is confined by its own simplicity, the sophistication of Miss Rukeyser's allows her no restraint. She has gone over America, a crude country "whose form is unquietness"; West she has gone, then South,

> seeing the distance of false capes ahead
> feeling the tide-following and turning wind traveling farther
>
> under abrasive weather, to the bronzy river,
> the rust, the brown, the terrible dead swamps,
> the hanging moss the color of all the hanged.

And having covered the continent, she is stayed by neither coast. She knows of China and, in *A Turning Wind*, crosses the Atlantic and sweeps, insatiably curious, through a decayed Europe, past England, toward Spain, noting as she goes both the living and the dead. But though she follows the prevailing currents of the air, there is little in Miss Rukeyser to suggest a natural force. Her poetry is put together and expertly welded, after the latest models: a product indeed of skill, but even more of an ambitious will. It is primarily a means of getting about; it might be the propeller of a plane that makes this sound of the wind. This is, perhaps, as it must be. For Miss Rukeyser, in more ways than one, reminds us of what Gide said of Aldous Huxley: she is intelligent, but all her problems lie outside her. She must go to meet them, for otherwise she would miss all emotion.

Her life is in her eyes, the light in them disillusioned. Her powers of observation are remarkable. In line after line she has shown with what alertness and acuteness she can survey the contemporary scene. The lines accumulate, like a tourist's postcards, but what they add up to we never know. The moment of proof—to use her own phrase— never comes. The meaning is missing. Miss Rukeyser's poetry proceeds from the intelligence and is itself unintelligible. And this, in a poet, almost always means one thing: that the emotion has not been adequate to the experience.

In the first of her elegies, *Rotten Lake*, there is but comment on a situation that is never created by the poem. It is not impossible to make out what the situation is, for the poem certainly comes out of an experience in love which has proved unhappy and brought, as is so often the case with the young, more disappointment than unhappiness. This is the Rotten Lake, as the river which recurs through the elegy stands for the life of the family which must be left behind when one approaches love "hoping for wonders." But neither river nor lake is a symbol. They are simply words substituted for other words. For though Miss Rukeyser is aware that symbols may become "sources of power," she believes in them only as a student might— that is to say, with the mind. She does not believe in them sensuously. The consequence is that they have in her writing no imaginative reality. If we contrast her practice with that of Yeats, who was, as we know from his prose, often skeptical of his symbols intellectually and yet, when he came to write his poems, always believed in them as we believe in the body of a person we love, we can understand why, with all her gifts, Miss Rukeyser succeeds in writing, not poetry, but only a sort of ambitious and cryptic rhetoric.

314

SPIRIT AND SENSE

Today the whole world impinges on the mind, and Miss Rukeyser's poems, being products of mind and will, can in an abstract way encompass the world. Miss Roberts has, apparently, never left her grandmother's chair. She is more limited in her material and in her own right much richer than either of the other two poets I have discussed. She is countrified and conscious, her countryside real and her consciousness rarefied. She has rendered as no one before her has done the sights and sounds and smells of the particular portion of the border South which she inhabits. It is a land richly endowed and constantly "renewed in the giving." Her poetry is like it, proudly provincial, composed of local recollections, its battles old and local, while through it runs as through that region the sound of old hymns and older ballads. Miss Roberts delights in her sensuous knowledge and no more trusts what is known through the senses than Bishop Berkeley did.

> I draw my sight in when I sleep
> I gather back my word and call.
> I take my senses from the air
> And wind them in a little ball.
>
> I curl them in a lonely ball
> And wind them in a lonely mesh.
> I fold it over with my dream
> And wind it round and round with flesh.

If there is something here of the oddity of a distinguished mind in a remote setting, there is also the touch of a hand which, itself slight, exquisite and skilled, can take up nothing without knowing that it has long been worn and warmed by common hands. Miss Roberts writes as though she had never been out of Kentucky nor needed to look beyond its borders, having found within them life enough for endless meditation. Kentucky is a state where living had, certainly down to Miss Roberts' childhood, an uncommon continuity. And it is scarcely to be doubted that much of what she writes is made up of childish memories and even of things that happened before her day. *Song in the Meadow* has the feel of an older America than any now extant, I am afraid, even in her own Kentucky. Even there the world penetrates, not merely to the mind but to the senses. Corbin the cobbler has many smells on him—leather, tanbark, rosin, turpentine—but one of them comes from the way he was gassed in the Argonne. Yet that penetration, threatening as it is, has only strengthened her conviction that politics, like poetry, is all the better for beginning with something small—like people.

> One man cannot make a song.
> One man cannot make a state.

> A theory, a Plan, a technique, is not a state.
> A technique established by a tyrant is not a state.
> Thus: it will never be a state.

> States are made as songs are made.

Miss Roberts is certain that if you want to know what man is, you can start anywhere. She has started at home. "You can never escape God's great flood. Death is only a part of it. You can never escape God's great flood." Miss Roberts has not escaped it. But neither has she been submerged by it. She has simply made her choice for high ground, where she is in no danger of being drowned.

The Nation: July 20, 1940

PORTRAIT IN PAPER

(*One Part Love* BY BABETTE DEUTSCH)

B ABETTE DEUTSCH'S poems bear about the same relation to poetry that book reviewing does to criticism. They are brisk, brittle, competent and, above all, timely. The book reviewer, though he may handle more books than the critic, though he takes them up and puts them down with the same appearance of authority, though he may on occasion show great critical acuteness, can never forget that what he writes is going into print alongside the news of the day. He cannot forget the competition of the front page. Miss Deutsch, when she sits down to write a poem, presumably looks into her heart, to write of what she finds there. But she can never quite see what she has found. For everything comes to her through a blur of headlines. She is diverted. She is unable to concentrate either on the horrors of the outer world or on the domestic situation of the heart. She may achieve moving passages, but her poetry is not sustained. She is too distracted to concentrate on the exigencies of a poem.

But just as Picasso in his *papiers collés* period, out of fragments of the most disparate material—a bit of a musical score, scraps of wallpaper from demolished houses, squares of workmen's sandpaper, old newspapers—could put together, adding paint where it was strictly necessary, a composition that was at the same time a portrait, so *One Part Love* does carry a certain conviction as a self-portrait. The fragments are here; we have only to put them together to see a woman of decent discernment, who in the midst of a friend's porcelain and fine furniture can come out fearlessly for revolution, whose feeling for the friendless goes out in a glance. The sympathy for the empty, the sick and the cold, for all those whose courage is worn and whose peace is gone, is genuine, but being, without will, it ends in a glance. She announces the coming of violence in a brave voice and solidarity with the suffering in a strong voice; but, having more melancholy than rage, she knows that, when doom comes, it will be as dingy as decay in a street of brownstone houses, to which "Tomorrow will come, naturally, like death"; and, when she stops speaking, she knows she is as lonely as ever. Her distress is that of a seamstress who would have more trust in her own skill if she had more confidence in her material. Miss Deutsch does not really trust poetry. Every effect is scattered, but that in the end produces a certain effect, which is that of a document on the depression. This is a portrait which, like the *papiers collés*, already dates; but it has a certain period value.

The Nation: July 27, 1940

THE POET AS AN AMERICAN

(*West Walking Yankee* by HENRY CHAPIN; *Poems and Portraits* by CHRISTOPHER LA FARGE; *Collected Poems of Kenneth Fearing*)

MR. CHAPIN'S *West Walking Yankee* is a romance of the American pioneer written no more romantically than common sense will permit. His early voyagers are occasionally made to use a speech as high and ponderous as their galleons, but for the most part the narration is as plain and salty as their sailors. In the first section of his book, there are, very properly, passages reminiscent of Elizabethan poetry. But before the seventeenth century is out, the tone is lowered, and the style neatly carries the transition to the eighteenth century, when the colonial speech becomes for the first time clearly marked as American. And again it changes after the first settlers have crossed the mountains, corresponding to a change in the character of the Americans, who, the seaboard left behind them, coveted a continent and, setting out across the plains, came, still unsatisfied, to the sight of the Pacific.

All these changes, so conscientiously set down, do not prevent a certain monotony. Mr. Chapin, following his pioneers across the country, has kept, whatever the period, close to the vanguard. And one trapper, one Conestoga wagon, is very like another. The migration which began with the voyages of discovery and ended only when there was no further land to the westward would seem to be of epic proportions. But in spite of Mr. Chapin's poetic rendering, the events remain immense and prosaic. West Walking Yankee is not an epic. In part, this is the poet's fault, for, though he has noted the motives that impelled the pioneers westward, he has not dramatized them. But in part, it must be admitted, failure is implicit in the material. It contains too many anti-climaxes. We are, with the pioneers, continually setting out for the Land of Promise, and wherever that may be, as one of Mr. Chapin's characters remarks, it "certainly ain't Pittsburgh." And it is with Pittsburgh that we are left.

It is with the panning of gold in California that Mr. Chapin brings the West Walking Yankee to a stop. His long effort of two hundred years to escape the consequences of pride and greed in others ends in his succumbing, all but natural pride lost, to the consequences of his own greed. Though Mr. Chapin draws a moral from this, he does not point up its irony; he gives us this episode as he has told the rest of the story, with matter-of-fact honesty, but without indignation, without severity.

Mr. La Farge's *Poems and Portraits* are mostly made up of personal and pastoral loves. His private emotions, though they have had to be recollected in a time without tranquillity, seem to have been tranquil enough. His stream, strictly contained, has known only "petty torrents." It is as an American that he is troubled; it is the rivers of America, no longer at flood, whose subsiding most disturbs him.

> We are the children whose lips have tasted the alkaline,
>   bitter
> Water of stagnant liberty.

THE POET AS AN AMERICAN

He is aware of his country, of its past and its present, and aware, too, that in its future lies his fortune. He is indeed so thoroughly an American that he feels no need to be "tempestuous in his statement of it."

In one of his poems, Mr. La Farge puts together as many of the discordant elements that make his America as he can think of, the silly and the sound: Emily Post and Chief Justice Marshall, the hot dog and the sagebrush, the Texas longhorn and Saint Cecilia's Ball. But though something happens as the result of these juxtapositions, the essential for poetry does not happen. The relation that makes it possible to bring all these people and things together on the page is that they are American. It is true; we accept it because it is true, and that is all there is to it. But Mr. La Farge has none of that unpredictable vision which brings separated things together in a way that continues to move us and disturb us.

It is precisely this "madness of vision" that makes practically everything that Kenneth Fearing writes exciting and gives it that disturbing quality that belongs to poetry. He sees red, and what he sees of the "gray, hungry, envious millions" which since the depression are more than ever a part of America has made him mad in the popular sense of the word. In the other, he is only apparently so.

> These, however, are merely close-ups.
> At a distance these eyes and faces and arms,
> Maimed in the expiation of living, scarred in payment
> exacted through knife, hunger, silence, exhaustion, regret,
> Melt into an ordered design, strange and significant,
> and not without peace.

The madness, we begin to see, is in the movement of the images, in which Mr. Fearing has caught something of the meaningless rapidity with which the modern world impinges on the mind.

Mr. Fearing is a poet who can compete in excitement with the journalists and surpass them in that his words have a speed equal to his impressions. He at times seems too closely in competition with them, so rapidly does he pass from a personal anguish to a cold impersonal dismay. What saves him is that, in his approach to what he sees, "hatred and pity are exactly mixed." He is a product of the depression and somewhat limited to its mood. In his America is more despair than hope, and even hope is ominous. But it is a country in which, while he disclaims his ability to bring miracles to pass, he

319

knows that miracles still occur; where even that mercenary and corrupt fortune-teller—to whom he gives the last word—facing the clients on whose credulity she preys, must still admit

That always I feel another hand, not mine, has drawn and turned the card to find some incredible ace.

The Nation: October 12, 1940

A CATHOLIC POET

(Weep and Prepare BY RAYMOND E. F. LARSSON)

RAYMOND LARSSON'S way of writing derives initially from that of Ezra Pound:

we sighed
, crossing the Piazza, sunwise
toward light, the sun, the column (the fish—
, the fish-speckled light on the tide the tide the
sails riding, riding wide, riding the wind
in wind against isle, against island): ai! ai!

It is easy to recognize the connection between this and

Diana,
Nymphs, white-gathered about her, and the air, air,
Shaking, air alight with the goddess

and the rest of the beautiful passage from *Canto IV*. Perfect in sound as this is, it is obvious that Pound has repeated the word "air" to convey the movement of light about the body of the goddess. And her radiant image remains. With Larsson, the images are soon dissolved into words. They are chosen, not so much because they have imposed themselves on his senses or been dictated by his mind as because they correspond to a mood. And presently they become merely themes for the variations of an elaborate and extraordinarily fluent verse, in which he has brought his writing as near as any of his contemporaries to the condition of music. His repetitions are musical. He has made his skill his own. And in his most recent poems he no longer reminds us, as he once did, now of Cummings and now of Pound.

Composed over a period of fifteen years, the poems of *Weep and Prepare* record a continuous experience. Since not all of them are dated and Larsson has not arranged them in the order of their composition, it is not possible to say clearly by what stages he has come from an abject despair of the world to a faith that consoles by presupposing the failure of the world. The character of that experience is, however, clear. Its end was already in the beginning. For in those years which we thought of as postwar, in the midst of the jazz bands, Larsson was aware of hands pierced by the nails of the crucifixion. Henceforward, he has little choice; he is impelled toward conversion. For if a man believes that

> the unseeing eye
> of man makes sightless
> light

he must look elsewhere for vision. If the men of peace can offer nothing against war but prayer, then pray they must. For one of Larsson's disposition, there can scarcely have been anywhere to turn but to that cross where agony has the shape of a Man.

The actual world continues to intrude upon his consciousness, but it is not much with him. It never was. His grasp upon it was never strong. It cannot have been altogether hard to let go.

The most that a profane critic can say of the experience recorded in these poems is that it is convincing. Larsson persuades us to believe in his belief. But what we stick at in most religious poetry is not the beliefs but the emotions. In poetry, we can readily suspend our judgment as to the poet's beliefs; we cannot but appraise his emotions. And it is very seldom that we are convinced that what is said to have been felt in devotional poetry was really felt. When we are, as in Donne and Villon, we may get poetry of great intensity and power. But such poets are rare. And in both Donne and Villon, what is impure in their devotions serves as an alloy to strengthen their verse. It is Donne's knowledge of the "condensed dust" that gives such density to his divine poems. Even with death before him, in the extremity of his cry to God to recreate him after death, he recalls that "being sacrilegiously Half wasted with youth's fires, of pride and lust," and, remembering, is not less of a man and more of a poet.

It is really very hard for a poet to be a Christian. For though we think of so many of the great poets as having been religious, the realms of poetry and religion are not the same. The essential relation to Christianity is that of man to eternity, while in poetry the relation that must always appear is that of man to time. And for one whose purpose it is to assert human values, it is not always easy to accept the moral values which the Church, seeing beyond time, places on human conduct. Poetry does not see beyond tomorrow and tomorrow. What is mortal cannot but deplore, and must often protest, the edicts of an eternal justice, so that great religious poetry is constantly close to blasphemy. It is a danger which Dante eludes only by being dramatic; Baudelaire and Blake did not avoid it; on the contrary, they were deliberately drawn toward it.

It is not, I should say, a risk for Larsson. His virtues are the Christian ones, of which the first is humility. His will is simple and his heart contrite. He has not the vigor of the great religious poets, nor, though he knows the discovery of death in the seed, their overwhelming sense of mortality. He has a subtle sadness, which is moving, but might be more so if he had not so soon cast off the times in which we live for the timelessness of a saint's contemplation.

The New Republic: October 21, 1940

MUSICIAN AS POET

(The Gap of Brightness BY F. R. HIGGINS)

FREDERICK ROBERT HIGGINS was much with Yeats in the last years and appears from the latter's correspondence to have been his favorite among the Irish poets younger by a generation than he. Yeats trusted his instinct for poetry and learned from his knowledge of folk music; and Higgins, in turn, learned something of his own craft from Yeats. They were not, however, much alike. The younger man shared nothing of Yeats's concern with philosophy and has not, as is so often true with musicians, a comparable feeling for the music that can be made only with words. He is closer, perhaps, to Synge.

IMPASSIONED NICENESS

Higgins has a folk quality that is genuine but not consistent. He can catch in his lines the rhythms, not merely of Irish speech, but of poetry written in Irish; he cannot hold them uninterruptedly. What he aims at is the boldness he attributes to Ferguson, who

> saw the heavenly horse,
> Pegasus, harnessed to that hearse—
> Damn it, he cut the traces!

His phrases are knotty, vigorous, humorous, and not without a high imagination that suddenly, for a moment, allows some familiar commonplace object to be seen in a rare intense light. That moment is the gap of brightness. It soon dims. For if Higgins has force, he has not a driving force; he lacks the compelling passion to carry through what was well begun to an accomplished end. There are some finished poems; but more often than not the poet seems to suffer that peculiar affliction of the Irish when not sustained by a fanatic heart—the unaccountable failure of emotion in mid-course. While it stays, he stands, like his own blackthorn in flower, "flaunting out the fierceness." When it is gone, nothing is left him but loneliness and rage. The blackthorn, its flowers and green days gone, can be turned into a cudgel.

The Nation: October 26, 1940

IMPASSIONED NICENESS

(*Pattern of a Day* by ROBERT HILLYER)

ROBERT HILLYER'S poems come to us covered with honors. *In Time of Mistrust* was delivered at the College of William and Mary for the one-hundredth anniversary of the founding of that learned society Phi Beta Kappa. *In a Quiet Country House at Night* was read as Phi Beta Kappa poem at Goucher College. So much academic attention is seldom paid to a poet who has not safely arrived. Mr. Hillyer won the Pulitzer Prize for Poetry in 1934. And yet, in his present volume, he seems not so much like a poet who has safely arrived as like a man who has never departed from safety.

323

Mr. Hillyer says that his attitude toward the world is modeled on that of Samuel Johnson.

> By niceness impassioned,
> His mood, like his tense,
> Was fantasy fashioned
> From strict common sense.

There are indeed points of resemblance. It has been said of Dr. Johnson that the virtue he had invariably before his imagination was his own; Mr. Hillyer is quite consistently engaged with his own merits. His poems are often didactic in intent but so personal in their complacency and conceit that it is improbable they will persuade anyone to follow his counsel. Common sense was good in the eighteenth century and ought to be in ours. But Dr. Johnson's poetic manners were already somewhat antiquated in his own day; they would scarcely carry over into ours, even though someone with the facility in verse of Mr. Hillyer attempted—as he has not—to revive them. He comes closer to our own age. He writes not as an Augustan poet but as one who intended to contribute to the Georgian anthologies. He combines a more or less conventional poetic idiom with a more or less careless colloquialism. It is the mood, not the tense, of Dr. Johnson he aspires to.

The trouble with the common-sense attitude for a poet is that to adopt it is to ignore the tragic complications of life. In Mr. Hillyer's case, it is hard not to believe that it has meant ignoring life itself, unless we are to consider that a man

> With a checkbook before him
> And schedules to bore him

is at the center and core of being. He is serenely closed in his "temperate dominion," with not only his checkbook but his conscience before him and, like a good New Englander, with both scrupulously in order. "I know," he says, "my temptations will never begin." He is aware of getting on in years, but also of getting on nicely. His *Pattern of a Day* is to die the academic death daily, between eight o'clock in the morning and midnight. Sometimes then, snow or storm without, doubts assail him and the sense of mortality. But not for long; for no doubt could long survive in the presence of such complacency. Indifferent to everything but his private peace, he still, after midnight, has moments when he knows it is a false peace. They are soon dismissed for the calm of sleep. Surely this is the very reverse of Dr. Johnson, who was impassioned, but not always for nicety, who knew only transient calm and none which for more than a moment could for him "lull the sense of woe."

The Nation: November 23, 1940

SHAFTS OF SPEECH

(*Make Bright the Arrows* by EDNA ST. VINCENT MILLAY)

IN THE FIELD which she first chose for herself Edna St. Vincent Millay was excellent. And her excellence was almost always in exact proportion to the closeness with which she worked to the classical tradition. That tradition had come to her affected by the practice of poets in English for over three centuries; she was not unaware of it at the source. Of the Latin lyric poets, she had the clarity and the grace; she used only such words as anybody might use, but with a personal precision, so that even her slightest poems have often an epigrammatic charm. The one conspicuous artifice in her writing was the verse itself.

I do not know how consciously this was done. But I do remember that at the time she was coming into her own, Catullus was all the cry. Certainly the speech she sought was as direct and fervent as his. Miss Millay's poetry had a romantic import, and through much of it there runs a conflict with whatever was unjust and outworn in the social conventions of the time. She does not write as a romantic, and as a poet she is at her best when most conventional. Many of her images seem to come to her from other poets; actually she has taken them out of the public domain and by long familiarity made them her own. A comparison with Catullus can only be carried so far. Catullus is a poet of the first order, and in place of his male imagination there is, in Miss Millay's poetry, not an imagination, but a feminine sensibility. Her amatory poems share certain qualities with those of Catullus, of which the first, I should say, is an outrageous honesty. But they sound much more as though they had come from one of Catullus's naughty girls. She has used Lesbia's name as though it were her own. And she is like the Latin poets in this, that, in accounting for the conduct of lovers, she can turn, in little more than a line, from a light disparagement of love to a sudden, grave and deferential praise. Her levity has often been imitated; what none of her imitators knew was her sense of the austereness of passion.

> illa, siqua alia, viderunt luce marinas
> mortales oculis nudato corpore Nymphas
> nutricum tenus exstantes e gurgite cano.

Her nymphs rise from colder seas than any Catullus disclosed to mortal eyes and scatter when they are seen, half submerged and half in light cold spray from the coasts of Maine.

Miss Millay was at her best in her love poems. In *Make Bright the Arrows* she is writing what—since war is an extension of politics—can be called political poems. In them she is not at her best. She has often written beautifully, but she was never very sure of her style. Though in the present volume there are lines that recall the old grace and precision, the recollection is dim. And, for the most part, the book simply is not "written" at all. For what is there to say of lines like these:

> Not France, not England's what's involved,
> Not we—there's something to be solved
> Of grave concern to free men all:
> Can Freedom stand? Must Freedom fall?

This sort of thing might get by at a public meeting. But on the printed page it simply will not stand.

One of the difficulties of making poetry out of politics is that whatever concerns politics is bound to be a matter of controversy, while no poetic statement that can be controverted is worth anything. The conviction that lies behind it may be one which we should like to see overthrown, but the poetic statement must be one which, despite our opinions, we cannot but accept. I can accept most of the convictions that lie behind what her publishers call Miss Millay's *Notebooks of 1940*, for they are already my own. I can accept her dismay at the fall of Belgium, Holland and France, for that I shared. But I cannot accept her poetic statement either of her convictions or of her dismay. For that would be to accept a counterfeit coin merely because it has a proper head of liberty stamped on it. The weight still is not there.

Poetry such as Miss Millay has written owes little to imaginative insight; it depends, therefore, on a minute accuracy in the statement

of emotion. That we have the right to demand of her. In urging us
to make bright the arrows, she has weapons in mind. It is only the
martial arrows she has sharpened here. The arrows of Apollo lie
neglected, tarnished, blunt.

The Nation: December 7, 1940

THE TALK OF EZRA POUND

(*Cantos LII-LXXI* by Ezra Pound)

"THERE IS no other poetry like the *Cantos*
in English. And there is none quite so simple in form." So Allen
Tate has written, and then added of Ezra Pound: "The secret of his
form is this: conversation." To take this view of the *Cantos* is very
valuable, for no other explains so well the power of Pound's allusions.
The formal approach is conversational; the secret of the form is
another matter and as yet hidden in the recesses of Pound's mind.
Say, then, that what we have is talk, talk of men and of arms, of men
who fought and got the credit for it, and of those who also fought,
as desperately and as bravely fought, and got no name for it: the
companions of Ulysses who did not hear how sweetly the sirens sang
and for all their pains had only the recollection of ear-wax and of
pulling at the oars.

> And they wanted to know what we talked about?
> "*de litteris et de armis, praestantibus ingeniis,*
> Both of ancient times and our own; books, arms
> And men of unusual genius
> Both of ancient times and our own, in short the
>   usual subjects
> Of conversation between intelligent men."

An epic, Pound has said, "is a poem containing history." His
poem, which slowly attains the length of an epic, contains a great
deal of history—not the text of the historians, but only so much of
history, of ancient times and our own, as may agreeably enter the
conversation of intelligent men. For in good conversation the text
must not enter; only a bore would think of bringing it in. What is
best in conversation is the marginal comment, the text itself being
taken for granted among the listeners. At most a complete anecdote
may be introduced, because it is pertinent or simply because at the

moment it seems amusing; a singularly happy or telling phrase may be quoted, a document or a translation of a poem brought out and shown; the rest is all illustration, personal exposition and interpretation—and, in Pound's case, imaginative marginalia.

The new *Cantos* are longer-winded than any that have gone before. Chinese history is sustained as a subject through the first ten *Cantos* of the present volume; through the rest the character and career of John Adams are under consideration. All depends here upon allusion; not to know the text of Pound's talk is to miss most of the points he is making. The *Cantos* are not imaginative as they once were. And yet to read them is to hear again the old talk in the Rue Notre-Dame-des-Champs, in the studio back of the courtyard, under the high window that cast no shadow until twilight, with Pound lolling in his homemade armchair, with an air of weariness, like a strong man worn out by the stupidities of the world, his mind un-wearied, his soul unbelieving but still his own. Pound has his own particular *hubris*, his pride, not lofty like that of Capaneus, to whom he once compared himself, but still unpersuadable, not to be put down. "There's not a wheel," he once said to me, "can go low enough to crush me." Out of his rut he utters his defiance, not against the gods, for there are no longer gods to defy, but against the great of this world, against the powerful who have put "money-lust above the pleasures of the senses."

There was always something about Pound of the sailor returned to tell of the strange sights he had seen, airing as he talked the strange tongues he had learned; but the limpness of the long body in the chair betrayed that it was not from actual seas he had come. The mind was his Mediterranean, whose shores are alive with antiquity, above whose islands the clouds still seem to rise in mythopoeic shapes. There history accumulates and none can quite escape the presence of the past, which strikes, like light from a wall, at the passer-by. Outside, as we talked, was Paris and that present which has now become a past.

That was the winter of 1922–23, when I was trying to read the Provençal poets, word by word, with the aid of an incomplete dictionary. And Pound told me how he, as a young man, had pondered over one word whose meaning he could not make out or find any-where, and how at last someone had told him that there was one man in Europe who would know if anybody did, and how he had set out and crossed half of Germany to find old Lévy, all for that one word. I heard the story then; it is now set down in its place in the *Cantos*. And I remember one night after dinner, when the Beaune was finished and we had begun on the brandy, that I told Pound the story of the British and the god-damned Portagoose. And that, too, is now in the *Cantos*, and the word, which was a corruption of soldiers in the last war, has become a permanent part of the Pound vocabulary, so that it now appears even when it is with the seventeenth-century Chinese that the Portuguese have to do.

> And the Portagoose king sent an envoy
> and they cured Kang Hi with wine from the Canaries
> w'ich putt 'em up a jot higher.

It is hard to get the point of the spelling in the last line, as it is to understand why John Adams of Braintree should from time to time drop into the drawl of a West which did not exist in his day. It is hard, that is, when we receive the words from the printed page; and yet it is precisely the deformation of the words on the page that brings back for me the unforgettable voice, so determined in the midst of Europe not to lose its native accent that it constantly assumed a speech which might well pass for American among Europeans, but which, to a compatriot's ear, belonged to no America that ever was.

In those lines I hear the talk, impatient and unwearied, polyglot and full of queer quirks, surprising and in the long run consistent, either wonderfully right or preposterously wrong, always generous and always limited.

It was limited, no matter who the listener, to what Pound was interested in. I remember once discussing with him those passages in the *Divine Comedy* which are in themselves so dull that I could only conceive that Dante had brought them in because they in some way contributed to the structure of his poem. "Wa'al," said Pound, "they may not interest you. But I think you can be sure that Dante put nothing into the *Divine Comedy* that did not interest him."

Now the same thing can be said of Pound's *Cantos*. Nothing is there that has not at some time interested Pound, and it is probably vain to look for any other reason for its being there. The complexity of the poem is due to the complexity of a contemporary mind; and so is its incoherence. He has long been interested in Chinese civilization; he is now, like everybody else, interested in what constitutes good government. His account of China, covering all the dynasties, from the first, which is more or less mythical, down to the Manchus, is constructed so as to set forth Pound's distinction between good governments and bad. His John Adams is presented as "the clearest head in Congress," as

the man who at certain points
made us
at certain points
saved us
by fairness, honesty and straight moving.

Adams is also presented as a man who at certain points was in complete accord with Ezra Pound.

Pound has recently been credited with being a Fascist. It is true that he continues to live in Italy and that he has spoken with more toleration of Mussolini than I, for one, would have expected. But no man can be a consistent admirer of Fascism who holds John Adams in admiration. And that Pound clearly does.

Whether he is speaking of Chinese emperors or of Adams and his contemporaries, Pound sees the misuse of money on the part of the governors as the root of most of the evils with which the governed are afflicted. It is not only on the opening page but throughout these *Cantos* that he pleads for an understanding of the true base of credit—that is, "the abundance of nature/with the whole folk behind it." Somewhere behind the poet is Major Douglas. How sound Pound's position may be as an exponent of Social Credit, I cannot say; what can be said is that his concentration on economics has simplified his morality, which was already a little too simple, while his concern with the money-lust of others has caused him, as a poet, to neglect the pleasures of the senses. He announced some years ago that he was thinking of giving up poetry in order to write economics. He has not given up his poetic method. In these *Cantos* the poet has compromised with the economist; it is a proof of Pound's superb versatility that the poet comes out as well as he does.

The Nation: December 21, 1940

A GEORGIAN POET

(Poems 1930–1940 by Edmund Blunden)

IT HAS been said of the Georgian poets that they turned to the countryside for subjects because, with their limited poetic equipment, there was nowhere else for them to go. But it might also be thought that by an unconscious premonition they went to find the one England they could love, before they were called on to defend all England. Of these, Edmund Blunden was one of the best, for he was, beyond any possibility of a choice, a pastoral poet. His first poems appeared in 1914; his present poems are like a recollection of that time. Since then the English countryside has diminished and, if now threatened by another war, has never for the poet ceased to be haunted by the dead battalions of the last war. But if his poems are haunted, they are not haunting; they are mild and comforting, not exhilarating. They are well made, but the freshness that once pervaded them has somehow gone. The volume might very properly have been brought to a close by the elegy on King George V. For it is, even though only now published, Georgian poetry.

The Nation: February 15, 1941

ENGLAND AND POETRY
(Poetry and the Modern World by David Daiches)

POETRY and the Modern World is, so far as I know, the first attempt to give a consistent account of poetry in England between 1900 and 1939 and as such is quite a remarkable achievement. The method which Mr. Daiches has adopted requires that he consider the changing attitudes of the poets toward the various traditions of their art and the meaning of their accomplishment in its relation to the contemporary world. His book begins with a cursory survey and, on the whole, a conventional estimate of the Victorians; for Mr. Daiches is not so much interested in their worth as poets as in whether or not they were able to come to terms with their age. In either case, they were to have their followers, and it becomes the critic's task to trace their influence, whether, like Tennyson, they can be conceived as having accepted the world they had to live in, or whether, like Hopkins, they remained secretly cloistered from it. Mr. Daiches begins with the nineteenth century at the flood in order to discuss its overflow into the twentieth century.

For the waters did not all recede at once. There were pools that lingered, in which the Georgian poets were content to contemplate the reflected calm of an English countryside, the twilit reflections of an English sky. Actually, the romantic contribution to English poetry was pretty complete by the close of the century. Nothing much was left of the tradition that had come down from the Romantics and been transmitted by the Victorians but its readers. For there is this to be said of the poets who had accepted that century which still wears an English name: they had made for themselves an audience. What is more, they had trained it in what to expect from poetry. If the Georgians found an audience, it was one the Victorians had made. They had not, perhaps, much to offer, but what they had was acceptable. The thirst of the reader for poetry was less than it had been. But his taste had not changed. He preferred the dregs of something to which he was accustomed to a new drink. The poets that came after the war could do little to assuage him.

They walked in the Waste Land, and the living water they had to offer had been brought from far off. It was strange. The English found it unpalatable and bitter.

The young English poets who emerged in the late twenties and early thirties of this century found themselves without an audience. They formed a group, but about them was a void across which their words did not go. "The disintegration of the audience for poetry—one aspect of the breakdown of common value criteria and the dispersion of public belief that we have several times referred to—" says Mr. Daiches, "meant that the poet was now faced with a very difficult decision: for whom was he going to write? The problems of determining an attitude and finding an audience are not really distinct; once you have decided on the former, you will find that the latter has been decided for you." Presumably what Mr. Daiches means here is, that if the poet is capable of communicating socially relevant truths, he will secure an audience. And his truths will be relevant if his attitude is, as it should be, integrated and sound.

The rest of the book is taken up with an account of how the generation of Auden, Spender and C. Day Lewis faced these problems. And it is according to their success in solving them that Mr. Daiches accords his praise. This places him in the predicament of having to put C. Day Lewis before Spender and Auden.

For C. Day Lewis has done what Mr. Daiches would have a young poet do. He set out to understand the English tradition and interpret it in such a way that it would seem, not death, but life. It was too bad that his critic has to note that the writing throughout *Transitional Poem* is "somewhat loose, even at times sloppy." He proceeded to sing "in vigorous and triumphant language the flight of two English aviators from their own island to Australia." It was too bad that he did not see the irony of their taking off in "a tiny, obsolete machine." In the early 1930's, C. Day Lewis was full of confidence and revolutionary optimism. It was too bad that, before the decade was over, these had to go, giving way to bitter foreboding. It is really too bad for Mr. Daiches that he has constructed his book in such a way that it must come to its climax in a poet who is the very summing-up of mediocrity. For a poet, whatever he may do as a man, does not solve problems, either his own or the world's. What he does is to provide a resolution in poetry for problems which neither he nor the world can solve.

But to put it as I have done is not altogether fair to Mr. Daiches, who, if not a profound critic, is a careful one, whose judgment, so long as he is dealing with his own countrymen, is usually discriminating, often of an extreme accuracy and always admirably set down. His discussion of the poetry of D. H. Lawrence, for instance, is excellent. "Lawrence's intensity and impatience led him to construct his poetry in such a way that the poem concludes at the point where most writers begin—with the achievement of an interpretation of the phenomena which are being described." This statement, with what follows, accounts as well as anything I have ever seen for Lawrence's power as a poet and the failure of that power in poetry. And who else has put so nicely into one sentence what ailed the poets who once appeared in Edward Marsh's anthologies? "With the Georgians the attitude was just sufficient to cover the subject matter."

Throughout the poetry whose history he is writing, Mr. Daiches is prepared to make us see the change in the conception of the poet's function: from the age of Tennyson, when, perhaps to Tennyson's undoing, the poet was conceived as having a public function; through the succeeding period, represented in England by Housman and Hopkins, when the poet had no choice but to stand alone, all values for him dissolved but those of his art, all pride renounced save in his own integrity; then, after Eliot, after Yeats, the attempt of the younger left-wing poets to return to England and as poets to play a part in the modern world. And these changes in the poet's conception of his relation to the world correspond to as many attitudes on the part of the poet toward his art. "There are thus," says Mr. Daiches, "three groups—those who met the problem by limitation of the existing tradition, those who met it by going back to an older, long abandoned tradition and those who tried to create a new tradition." This is an interesting and serviceable scheme. But it will be noticed that the words are so weighted that all of Mr. Daiches's favors are bound to fall to the younger poets.

Now one can understand that the young poets of the left wing, eager for action, should have turned away from what seemed to them in Eliot pessimistic conversatism and in Yeats a cold inhumanity. But the critic whose concern is with poetry and not with programs for action cannot do so with impunity. The fault in Mr. Daiches's scheme is that it does not properly accommodate either Yeats or Eliot. But then it is in the nature of schemes that they do not readily accept the great.

The word *tradition* occurs on almost every page of *Poetry and the Modern World*. But I am not sure that Mr. Daiches has pondered long enough on *The Sacred Wood* to have quite grasped the new meaning that Eliot gave that word. Or it may be that, as he half confesses, he is as an Englishman made uncomfortable by what seems to him Eliot's self-consciousness about the tradition. There is, he says, something "monstrously artificial" about it. One either has a tradition or one has not; and if one has it, one does not talk or even think too much about it. Pound, who arrived in London some years before Eliot, had seen before him that English poetry was in a sad state of depletion and that the old unconscious approach to literature would no longer do. Eliot, with his pitiless lucidity, introduced some order into Pound's discoveries and then went beyond Pound. He saw not only the exhaustion of English poetry; he saw also the essential horror of the life-as-habit into which the unconscious traditionalism of the Englishman had led him.

> A crowd flowed over London Bridge, so many,
> I had not thought death had undone so many.

It was precisely that element of consciousness toward the tradition that Eliot introduced that later was to enable Auden to return to a purely English tradition and find there what none before Eliot would have found.

Poetry: July, 1941

ON TRANSLATING POETS

(*Three Spanish American Poets* TRANSLATED BY LLOYD MALLAN, MARY AND C. V. WICKER AND JOSEPH LEONARD GRUCCI)

WHAT IS the excuse for translating a poem? Is not a poem by definition something that cannot be translated? Every word is immutable; every sound, once it has been brought into a poetic order, is immovable. Every language, like every land, has its own genius. I recall Elinor Wylie's words on turning Latin into English:

> Alembics turn to stranger things
> Strange things, but never while we live
> Shall magic turn this bronze that sings
> To singing water in a sieve.

Elinor Wylie, as I recall it, wrote those lines only after spending some time trying to do what she had to admit in the end could not be done. And I have spent some time, over a period of twenty years, trying to turn, now Latin lines, now lines written in some speech derived from the Latin, into an English that could be read without displeasure and without distrust. I ought to have some excuse for an activity whose aim I have felt impelled to put down in these negative terms.

The positive gain for the translator is that he keeps his pencil sharp. There are times with all of us when we are dull, when there is nothing within which wants to come out, and yet when, uneasy with idleness, we need to write, if only to keep the hand in. Translation is an excellent exercise; it is a test, I believe, which tries less the knowledge of the foreign speech than of our own. The limits of English cannot be accurately determined until we have ventured beyond its borders. We can compute our wealth at home the better for having been abroad. And we who use a northern speech must from time to time emerge from the cold mists which still cling to it and permeate it for the clear view of seas under the sun and the sharp outlines of southern shores.

But it is useless to pretend that the translator does not always hope against hope to have something to show for his pains.

There are two ways of going about translation of poetry. The first, which was followed with more or less skill, with more or less success, through most of past centuries, presupposes that the translator can have no other aim than to produce an English poem. He will boldly seize whatever he wants from the original, plunder the lines, discarding what is of no use to him. He will approach his undertaking as the Renaissance pope—whose name at least was barbarous—did the monuments of an older Rome, regarding them as easy quarries for contemporary palaces. This was, to name only one successful example, the method of Ben Jonson when he wrote "Drink to me only with thine eyes." He rifled two Greek poems to make one in English. But he did make a poem.

This approach was perfectly natural to the Renaissance mind and indeed as late as the eighteenth century seems to have been a congenial one. To us it seems high-handed. We ask greater respect for the original and admire a translation in the degree to which it reproduces its essential qualities in another language. We ask, if not the impossible, at least the unlikely, if we also demand that the translation be a poem in its own right. Luck counts for a great deal. If we can at once find the right rhymes and our invention is otherwise lucky, we may come out with something that neither betrays the original nor discredits the English speech. The case of Ezra Pound comes to mind. Pound was, it cannot be denied, and should not, even now, be forgotten, a poet of distinction, fertile in imagination, wasteful of his fecundity; he was also, at one time, a translator who surpassed in vigor any of his contemporaries. His translations can still be read for their own sake; but he has taken great and unabashed liberties. He has declared his admiration for the Renaissance translators, and his practice is perhaps closer to theirs than we would be willing to admit. Nevertheless, Pound's aim thirty years ago was what I think must be our aim—to make available to readers in English what would otherwise be inaccessible to them and to write nothing which will cause the translator to sound as though it were English that to him was the alien speech.

These thoughts have been, if not provoked—for I have long held them—at least brought to the front of my mind by the publication of *Three Spanish American Poets*. The three poets are the Mexican Carlos Pellicer, translated by Mary and C. V. Wicker, the Chilean Pablo Neruda, translated by Joseph Leonard Grucci, and the Ecuadorian Jorge Carrera Andrade, translated by Lloyd Mallan. All three richly deserve to be known in this country, for they are among the most gifted poets of the Spanish-speaking countries to the south of us. They belong all of them to a generation which, following that of Rubén Darío, has so remarkably varied and reinvigorated poetry in Spanish America. Darío was their forerunner as a discoverer of America; but they have gone on, their spiritual independence declared, to explore the continent first sensuously and then poetically.

What to us gives a poignant value to this poetry is that it is unmistakably contemporary and yet is the product of men who have not been, as poets in all other countries of the West have so long and desperately been, cut off from the common life. They have an abundance to show, rich, and sustained by a sap that does not fail, for nothing has happened to sever the stem which in turn goes down to undisturbed roots. To Pellicer, his own table spreads, on any Sunday, sights and savors

> as impressive
> as a monument to the heroes
> of any nation.

But he knows that even amid all his tropical splendor

> The passions
> grow until they die of grief.

Neruda is bitter, ironic, desperate even; he has accepted the material world as completely as Whitman did, but his is a world in which it is all too easy to weary of being a man.

> I walk, passing offices and orthopedic shops
> and yards where there are clothes hanging on a wire,
> drawers, towels and shirts that weep
> slow dirty tears.

Jorge Carrera Andrade looks with eyes of a singular and tender innocence on a world which once was full of a great hope, but where "we are slave-traders in our own lives," a world which has now succumbed to its own guilt and can now only expiate through war the destruction of tenderness and hope.

The selection from each of these poets, though in no case long, is, I should say, sufficient to show their qualities. The translations vary, both in felicity and accuracy. It would be easy to disagree with a number of readings, to cite passages which cannot be altogether accepted as English, words which deliberately or unconsciously belie the Spanish. I know well what difficulties await the translator of these poets, all of whom have learned that compression, so admirably suited to Spanish—a language which like Latin is most eloquent when a few words must do the work of many—which among modern poets is first found in Mallarmé. In them, too, one word is often offered to convey a whole and sometimes complicated metaphor. I have worked over that stanza in *Islands Without Name* whose last two lines are:

> en la noche de cuero y de pupila
> y de ataúd y de alga.

337

This Mr. Mallan renders as

> in night of eyeball and raven
> of seaweed and coffin.

But *cuervos* is raven, not *cuero*, which is literally leather. What the poet intended here—I have his own word for it—are certain physical, and for the most part tactile, sensations, which night produces, on such sea-islands as the poem celebrates without naming them. The night is dark, thick, obscure, and hence like leather; through this night eyes stare and strain, becoming all pupil, and yet not penetrating it. There is no issue for the sight, and hence the darkness is felt close and inescapable as a coffin. But it is still a sea-night and the man caught in it feels it clinging to him cold as seaweed. I am no Spanish scholar, indeed I have but a brief knowledge of the language, but I should say that something has been done in these lines which could not be so well done, if done at all, except in Spanish. A spiritual reality has been conveyed by the mere mention of four things, none of them seen, but all carnally felt.

So we are led back to the Spanish. And that, it seems, is the most useful service translation can render. It is possible to aim at more and achieve less. Except where there is long and familiar acquaintance with a language, I, for one, am grateful for a trot.

Poetry: May, 1943

THE CAGED SYBIL

(*New Poems*, 1943: *An Anthology of British and American Verse*
EDITED BY OSCAR WILLIAMS)

O SCAR WILLIAMS, in compiling his book of *New Poems*, 1943, has been extraordinarily successful in achieving what he set out to do, if that was, as I take it, to present the most interesting poems written within the year in the English language. Occasionally he has gone beyond this limit of time: Allen Tate's *More Sonnets at Christmas*, which celebrate the last occurrence of that holiday, are preceded by the earlier and now well-known *Sonnets at Christmas* written ten years ago. Though I recognize several other poems from having seen them before, there are, so far as I am able to discern, none, with the exception I have noted, which has not been done in an awareness of a world at war. A considerable number of the poems are here published for the first time. The volume is made up in large part from the work of established poets whose worth has been approved by their contemporaries, but there is also a generous selection from young poets whose talents as yet exceed their reputations. The range, among Americans, is from Robert Frost, who was born in 1875, to Dunstan Thompson, who did not see the light of day until 1918; among the British, from Edith Sitwell and Herbert Read, who have long been known in this country, to Alex Comfort, who at twenty-three years of age makes here his first appearance in an American volume.

The choice, then, is wide; and Mr. Williams's taste seems to me sufficiently sound to allow the volume to be taken as indicative of the present state of the poetic mind. Statements on dust-covers are notoriously untrustworthy, since they are designed, not to describe a book, but to sell it. In this instance, however, I may be permitted to start with the publisher's blurb, which declares that the poems included in the anthology have been chosen because they deal with realities and then goes on to say that the book is essentially one of war poetry. The editor is then quoted: "It is the work of poets who have intensely felt the fact of war."

The standard of the book is high, because most of the poets represented do deal with their own realities. And that they have intensely felt the fact of war may be assumed, since no one could well live in the world today and avoid either fact or feeling. But it is remarkable, considering the wide range of the anthologist's choice, how little war poetry he has managed to get between his covers. The blurb at least makes it clear that whatever he found is here. But it is quite as clear from the pages that, however intensely his contributors may have felt as men and women, as poets they have for the most part neither cared nor dared to write as if the war were their main concern. They are like Dante's angel, who, opening the gate on that portion of Hell where the violent are, looked as though he were moved by quite other cares than those around him.

Very early in the book—the poets are arranged alphabetically by name—amid the scattered brilliance of George Barker's phrases, there is a reference to the Austrian corporal "At whose word once, from Europe to the sky, Suddenly everyone everywhere began to die." But it is a phrase among a hundred others. William Empson asks to be told again "about Europe and her pains." But we have gone one-third of the way through the three hundred pages before, in David Gascoyne's *A Wartime Dawn*, there is a clear mention of a specific event, the invasion of Norway, and even here futile battles off a bitter coast are merely numbered among the circumstances of a return from the blankness of sleep to the consciousness of one more day of a world at war. The first poems by an Englishman unmistakably devoted to the war are C. Day Lewis's *Word Over All* and *Reconciliation*; the first by an American is Marianne Moore's *In Distrust of Merits*, which seems to me much the best poem about the war yet written in this country. And yet, when I expressed this opinion to Miss Moore recently, her response was that she had been relieved, at the outbreak of hostilities, to know that she would not be required to write a war poem.

At this point we are halfway through the anthology, and what I have said about the first half is not invalidated by the second, in which there are only two outstanding poems which I am quite sure have the present war for their central theme: Allen Tate's *Ode to Our Young Proconsuls of the Air* and *Jubilo*. And even then I am uncertain about the second. The war certainly provided the occasion for the poem, but the center of interest is perhaps rather in the disarray of a world which has been able to find no release save in the outrage and carnage of overwhelming war.

How are we to explain this reluctance of poets who are among the most serious of our time to bring the war into the foreground of their thought? The more serious they are, the more they would seem to be determined to use the gifts with which they have been endowed, the talents they have trained, to discover some other issue from the disorder of the times than the destructive one which the world of action, willingly or not, has desperately accepted. Of course, when a man's country is in danger, he will do what he can to defend it. But he will do this as a man, because it is the part of a man. As a poet, he has other responsibilities and other compulsions. He wants a principle of coherence and asks of his thought, which provides none, only that he might address it as Donne once did his God: "Thou hast contracted thine immensity, and shut thyselfe within Syllables and accepted a blame from us."

Then, too, being under the compulsion to tell the truth, the poet is bound to be wary of any knowledge he has not won in his own right. Most of the poets here represented have been, for one reason or another, excluded from combat, and those who are of an age and condition to do the fighting are still too taken up with their own brief youth, whose brevity now becomes especially poignant, to have assimilated their military experience. Miss Moore's poem succeeds because, while by no means unaware of those who are "fighting in deserts and caves, one by one, in battalions and squadrons," she finds the heart of her matter in her own responsibility for their having to fight: "There never was a war that was not inward." And it is because she has essentially restricted herself to this inward war, which she knows as no one else does, that she has written a poem profoundly personal and at every point precise.

It may be, too, that the poets neglect war because the theme is to them outworn. When peace was proclaimed after the last war, the poets had no ease, and between the laying down and the taking up of arms, they took it as their responsibility to tell of a world which was like Trimalchio's Sybil, who, when the little boys questioned her in her cage, wanted only to die. It was only twenty-one years ago that T. S. Eliot, with that curious genius of his own for taking over passages from other writers and resetting them so that they acquire quite another meaning than the author intended and take on in the reader's eye a new glint and brilliance, seized on those lines from the *Satyricon* and, placing them before *The Waste Land*, gave them a tragic import. In Petronius the passage has a comic intent, for the Sybil is brought in to point up Trimalchio's ignorance and boastfulness. Yet the meaning which Mr. Eliot found there must always have been in the words. What was, by the time he used them, a learned reference became, beyond any other one phrase, an expression of his own and a generation's disease. Mr. Eliot's desperation, he has been careful to tell us, was his own affair. Nevertheless, what he said about the world was recognized by anyone who could read poetry as true. One might escape his conclusions, which were singularly inconclusive, and reject his solutions, which solved none but his personal problems; but one could escape his premises only at the risk of rejecting the truth. The poetic situation is still very much what he found it; at bottom, it has not greatly changed since Baudelaire. To write now of war, when for so long nothing has promised peace, would be to write of events which, though the accompanying heroism and devastation exceed anything that could have been imagined, have already occurred in the imagination. Their moral import has already been set down.

The Nation: October 16, 1943

MISCELLANEOUS
ARTICLES

A HUMANISTIC CRITIC

(Men Seen BY PAUL ROSENFELD)

MEN SEEN, Paul Rosenfeld's latest collection of critical essays, is presented frankly as a miscellany. The various essays have not, as in *Port of New York*, been remolded to give a formal shape to the book nor have the subjects been chosen as illustrative of a single tendency in American life. On the contrary, these are figures from eight literatures: the twenty-four novelists, critics, and poets included in the title are so divergent in aim, so disparate in quality, that their presence in a single volume would seem to signify nothing unless Mr. Rosenfeld's sensitiveness to the most varied impressions, the generosity of his mind, his passionate interest in every manifestation of the creative spirit of his time. There is no effort to diminish the differences between these writers; rather his aim has been to reproduce, in pigments of his own, the very color of each and his prevailing mood. And they are judged in the end, not by a literary standard, nor even, it would seem, always by their literary accomplishment, but by the extent to which they suggest the possibility of a "life completely used, exercised to the fullness of its capacity for tragedy and for delight, and deprived by death of nothing of worth."

This desire to discover among contemporary writers some stay for the mind, "stale and weary in its youth, dissonant, jumbled and out of tune with the eternities as with itself," this preoccupation with an ideal of "lustiest living," not only determines the process of judgment: it has also, though perhaps unconsciously, influenced the critic in the selection of his material; and in the end it is seen to have been strong enough to give to a volume frankly put forward as a miscellany and pretending to no other unity than that of method, something very like a unity of purpose. In any case, though these are literary studies, Mr. Rosenfeld's concern is not entirely with literature. If it were, he could hardly have found a place for Jean Toomer, who as yet remains "a writer experimenting with a style"—a style, I gather, not his own. Nor would he have devoted an essay to Edna Bryner, celebrating merely her fine love of the American forests and her sane attitude on the Woman Question. And yet it may be that Mr. Rosenfeld did well to include both among his *Men Seen.* For the book as a whole represents a continuous search for the poet—not for poetry but the poet—who will "beat the rhythm of his age" and bring to it a new "impulse toward freedom"; who will, like the youth of Isaiah's prophecy, show himself an ensign of the people, and "give the race the direction in which it has to go." And each of the chapters represents a pause in the adventure and a looking around for anyone who might, even momentarily, be mistaken for this poet—or else (with a bludgeon) for such critical scribes as possibly stand in the way of his coming. It is significant that the book opens with a portrait of D'Annunzio.

For aside from the fact that already he dates somewhat, Gabriele D'Annunzio resembles the poet of the critic's search exactly as—if I may borrow an image—a reproduction in plaster resembles its original in marble. That is to say, in everything but authenticity. The episode at Fiume is seen to be of the same stuff as the novels and the poems, theatrical but dispiriting, grandiose and at the same time insignificant. D'Annunzio has moved, as Mr. Rosenfeld would have his poet do, in the world of affairs without ceasing to be a poet; but with him, self-assertion has never quite become self-fulfilment. His bravery of exterior is only an antiquated piece of body armor from Florentine workshops; its burnished surface is intricate with mythologies, the bronze sonorous when struck; but the uncomfortable fact remains that it is, now, empty of life and useless except to curators. D'Annunzio is simply the man who has never felt. And over his head Mr. Rosenfeld sends his cry for the true poet, who will come bringing life abundantly.

But if it is to be doubted that Mr. Rosenfeld's concern is entirely with literature, he is nevertheless an excellent literary critic. By seeing literature constantly against a background of life, he obtains, in regard to literature itself, a completeness of vision hardly to be found in the critic intent only upon formal excellence in writing. There are certain valuations in art which cannot be made by any reference to technical processes, and to prate too long of "significant form" is usually to end in nonsense. For, as Mr. Eliot, a critic whose essential interest in literature cannot be questioned, has remarked, in comparing the characters of Shakespeare with those of Jonson, the difference between Boabdil, say, and Falstaff is not to be explained by a pretty theory of humors, but rather by Shakespeare's "susceptibility to a greater range of emotion, and emotion deeper and more obscure." Mr. Rosenfeld is perhaps less interested in range of emotion than in depth and obscurity. Too intelligent not to be aware of the necessity for structure, too sensitive to ignore any felicity of line, he is ultimately concerned only with one thing; and no "mystery of construction" can ever long divert him from what is always the object of his search: emotion at the core. The advantage of his method appears at once in his essay on Wallace Stevens, a poet whom an aesthetic critic could hardly have placed so boldly and so accurately. Possibly it is not very important that a poet should be "placed"; it may be more to the point to send us to his work with some assurance that there is a particular enjoyment to be derived from it. But this also Mr. Rosenfeld has done.

No doubt something of the particular quality of a work of art disappears under analysis, and it is just this quality which impressionistic criticism is apt to impart. In so far as his labor is one of definition, it is, whenever the subject is worth his pains, admirably performed. And in any case the style is adroitly adapted to the impression he intends to convey. At all times exuberant and warm, it is perhaps too stiff-jointed to be properly called flexible; and yet it passes easily from one manner to another, as in the opening paragraph of the essay on Wallace Stevens:

> Lord, what instruments has he here? Small muffled drums? Plucked wires? The falsetto of an ecstatic eunuch? Upon deliberate examination, it appears Stevens' matter is the perfectly grammatical arrangement of an English vocabulary not too abstract.

Within its own limits, it has almost as great a range as all the writers of the Old Testament put together: it can be rhapsodical and epigrammatic at will; can stop for a grotesque turn or a jolly bit of clowning, and proceed at once to a serious, even a profoundly sad, observation. There is an endless verbal invention and an originality which does not always appear effortless; a tendency—which may also be observed in the popular coinages in this country—to intensify an expression beyond all need, with a gain in vigor and a more considerable loss of accuracy. And it is at times unnecessarily awkward; a fault due, if I am not mistaken, to Mr. Rosenfeld's having a greater sense for the "feel" of words than for their movement. But movement is there, and amazing vitality. The critic hurries on, wrapped in his style as in a cumbersome overcoat, a little ponderously, but certain always just where he is going. And always he arrives, scant of breath it may be, but nevertheless at the exact point for which he started. And in the meanwhile he has passed completely around a subject and seen him, apart from himself, an individual having his own existence.

If he does not come off so well with Joyce and Proust as with, say, D. H. Lawrence, it is less that his sensibilities have failed before works of such magnitude as theirs as that neither *Ulysses* nor *A la Recherche du Temps Perdu* can be understood simply as an emotional experience. Some account must be taken of their structure and of the extent to which the emotions they present are modified by that structure. Both Joyce and Proust, differing widely as they do in other respects, are highly conscious artists deliberately manipulating their material to impersonal ends. And in treating Proust as though he were merely a neurasthenic writing at all hours of the night to still some inner conflict—a description which I suspect would apply rather better to Robert Louis Stevenson than to the creator of Swann —Mr. Rosenfeld has arrived at what seems to me the only serious misinterpretation in the entire volume. "The *recherche du temps perdu* seems therefore to have been an attempt to give the present and the future the fair chance which the backward-flowing libido would deny to it." If Mr. Rosenfeld will reread *A l'Ombre des Jeunes Filles en Fleurs* and read, as he does not yet appear to have done, *La Prisonnière*, I think he will see that it is more profitable to regard Proust as one who as a boy had immersed himself in Plato and was his life long occupied with the relation of the actual world to the real world of memory and desire, than to regard him as a neurotic unable to free himself of a boyish attachment to his mother. In *Ulysses* he has indeed pierced at once to the emotional centre of gravity of the book: the relation between Dedalus and Bloom. He has seen that their relation is essentially a metaphysical one, but, in minding only the direct lines between them, to the neglect of those parallels which Joyce has placed throughout *Ulysses* to establish Bloom's position in regard to Stephen and his own dead son— such, for instance, as the discussion in the library of Shakespeare's relation to Hamnet Shakespeare and to Hamlet—he has failed to give a completely satisfactory account of it. The analysis stops too soon. He has arrived at what appear the most plausible reasons yet found for Joyce's having made Bloom a Jew; but, as he passes them by without comment, I am not quite sure that he himself is aware of his discovery.

It is to Van Wyck Brooks that Mr. Rosenfeld is indebted for his conception of the poet as redeemer of the people, as well as for one or two other ideas which have seriously influenced his criticism—a debt which he has in a previous volume generously acknowledged. Of the two, it is Mr. Rosenfeld's poet who is the more gracious and humane, as he is the more credible. But both, I am inclined to think, enlarge upon the power of even the great poet to influence living, as they certainly overestimate what the poet can accomplish alone. Before there can be a Dante there must be a Saint Thomas Aquinas to precede him. Joyce has resumed the age as we know it; and for other knowledge and a different apprehension of the universe, we shall have to wait upon the scientists. But of one thing at least we may be certain: if the poet does arrive in our time, either in America or elsewhere, Mr. Rosenfeld will be among the first to recognize him and praise him. As for Mr. Brooks, we cannot be so sure. It seems highly probable that he will be too tightly shut in his library, tracking down the literary failures of the last half-century, to be faintly aware of his existence.

The Dial: August, 1925

ANSWERS TO A QUESTIONNAIRE

1 Are you conscious, in your own writing, of the existence of a "usable past"? Is this mostly American? What figures would you designate as elements in it? Would you say, for example, that Henry James's work is more relevant to the present and future of American writing than Walt Whitman's?

(1) I am conscious of a usable past, though whether the use I have made of that consciousness is one of which others can approve is more than I ought to say. In so far as this past is a part of my own memory, it is, of course, American. Because I was born and brought up in a portion of the border South which had had complete experience of Civil War but which had partially escaped Reconstruction, I have had access to an older America than most of my contemporaries. I have known, not through documents, but through sight and touch and smell a way of living that belonged to the early Republic. Indeed, when I remember certain people I have known, old when I was very young, and recall all I have heard them say, it

seems to me that I can stretch, not only my mind, but my body as well, into the eighteenth century. But aside from these recollections, which are important only because they are personal, it can also be said that for me, as for any American, the past of America is as long as that of modern Europe. It should not be forgotten that, though America was settled by Europeans, Europe as we know it could never have come into existence without America. The part played by this country in creating contemporary Europe is too potent to be ignored. The relations between the two continents are immensely complicated. And it is because no man of comparable intelligence has applied himself so assiduously as Henry James to exploring these relations that his work, aside from its great value as art, seems to me important. Walt Whitman's direct expression of Americanism would be of equal value if it were equally convincing. To me Whitman never carries the same conviction when he is being conscious of nothing but that he is an American as when, unconsciously American, he sings of love and death. Then he is a poet, and what he has to say should have quite as much poetic weight for a European as for an American. It is a comfort that America of the mid-nineteenth century produced writers of their stature, but I cannot believe that the work of either Whitman or James is particularly relevant to the future of American writing. The problems which they faced in their time remain, however, in our own: to say what America is and to say what its relation to Europe is.

America is continuous in time with Europe, though separate in space, as Russia is contiguous in space with European civilization but disparate in time. Our remote past is, then, in Europe. This is a matter of some importance. For it means that if we are to seek a consciousness of the continuity of time, we cannot look for it on this continent.

2 Do you think of yourself as writing for a definite audience? If so, how would you describe this audience? Would you say that the audience for serious American writing has grown or contracted in the last ten years?

(2) It is convenient to write for those who you know will read you, as it is to talk only to those who you know will listen to you. I should say that I am conscious of writing for three people: Allen Tate, Edmund Wilson and my wife. I have at one time or another pleased all three. But I have never yet pleased all of them with the same piece of writing.

ANSWERS TO A QUESTIONNAIRE

The audience for serious American writing has certainly grown in the last twenty years. It has probably increased in the last decade. Whether the audience for literary criticism has diminished within that time, I cannot say, but there is no doubt that the space allotted to it by editors has been much reduced. This reflects, so far as the editors of the liberal weeklies are concerned, a real shift of interest, not only on their part, but on that of their readers. For while, in the decade after the war, almost all literary values were in for a revaluation, it is now political and social ideas that are in a state of ferment.

3 Do you place much value on the criticism your work has received? Would you agree that the corruption of the literary supplements by advertising—in the case of the newspapers— and political pressures—in the case of the liberal weeklies—has made serious literary criticism an isolated cult?

(3) Any criticism of a man's work represents at least one reader's reaction, and for that reason, if no other, he must regard it seriously. To speak strictly, there are not many critics whose opinions I place highly, and I know, or think I know, what each of them is worth. And yet I should lie if I did not say that I am always pleased by praise and, out of all proportion, hurt by its opposite.

4 Have you found it possible to make a living by writing the sort of thing you want to, and without the aid of such crutches as teaching and editorial work? Do you think there is any place in our present economic system for literature as a profession?

(4) I have not found it possible to make a living by such writing as I can do. Others have done so. There are no poets among them. At best, the profession of letters under our present economic system is in the extreme precarious. And no one who can possibly avoid it should adopt it.

5 Do you find, in retrospect, that your writing reveals any allegiance to any group, class, organization, region, religion or system of thought, or do you conceive of it as mainly the expression of yourself as an individual?

(5) I have always believed that literature should oppose to any system, no matter how perfectly conceived, the "minute particulars

of mankind." The mind craves nothing so much as a closed system, and the writer's mind is no exception; and yet he should, at whatever cost of violence, constantly set against any system, which at the moment is approved, the spontaneity and variety of life. In no other way can he bring his conscience to rest.

All authentic writing comes from an individual; but a final judgment of it will depend, not on how much individuality it contains, but how much of common humanity.

6 How would you describe the political tendency of American writing as a whole since 1930? How do you feel about it yourself? Are you sympathetic to the current tendency towards what may be called "literary nationalism"—a renewed emphasis, largely uncritical, on the specifically "American" elements in our culture?

(6) The political tendency of writing in America since 1930 has been toward the Left. But the tendency of political writing, from Right to Left, has been toward a redefinition of democracy. I do not believe that Communism is a desirable or a possible aim. I do not believe that it is desirable, for it still holds to the conception of the economic man, from which most of the ills of Capitalism seem to me to rise. I do not believe it possible, for I do not think that Communism is an aim at all. It is beginning, not end. It is the original chaos out of which some social order or other must rise. And since events since 1917 would seem to show that the order which follows an attempt to establish Communism in the contemporary world will conform in greater or less degree to Fascism, I am for continuing our own experiment of another sort. I am not unaware of the difficulties which at present confront our democracy, but I am convinced that they are not insurmountable. I share many of the misgivings as regards democracy which were owned by those who designed our government; but they do not seem to me important compared with the certainty that no other society would do for us at all. Democracy is not a magic word, which we have only to utter to have the rocks fall apart and the robbers' cave open for us, filled with all imaginable riches. It is a way of life which in the future, as in the past, will depend less upon its own virtue than upon ours.

An American writer should find American material richer than any other. But that does not mean it is richer for being American. It may be, in human terms, very poor indeed. The men and women along Tobacco Road are as American as they can be. In Erskine

Caldwell's hands, they became excellent literary creatures. But even in his hands, they remain as men and women appalling in their poverty.

Partisan Review: Summer, 1939

MATTHEW ARNOLD AGAIN *
(*Matthew Arnold* by Lionel Trilling)

On THE dust-cover of Lionel Trilling's book on Matthew Arnold is reproduced the head only from a photograph of the poet. The eyes are cast down and we cannot see what it is that draws them. But as we look at the scarred face, tortured more, it would seem, by certainty than doubt, we cannot but conjecture that the object of its stare is one more occasion for that long contemplation which has left its agony on Arnold's countenance. I became, as I read Mr. Trilling's book, so fascinated by that face, constantly turning back to it, that presently I started a line drawing of it. The hair is curled—"that perpetual miracle of my hair," as Arnold called it—I saw it rising from the sides of the head like the peaks of little horns. I set down the twisted eyebrows, the great virile nose, the strong and sensual mouth. When I had traced the lines that accentuate the coarse cheekbones, I found that what I had drawn so far was the face of a satyr. But the chin was still to come. And the chin was massive and firm. To add the chin was to destroy the effect of all I had done. No, what I had drawn was not a satyr; it was a man

> Never by passion quite possess'd
> And never quite benumb'd by the world's sway.

It was the son of Dr. Arnold of Rugby.

The face on the dust-cover is only a fragment of a photograph which is shown as the frontispiece of the book. When we turn to it, we find that what Arnold is looking at is a dachshund—perhaps that very Geist whose death he recorded in an elegy. The whole thing has been carefully posed to bring out Arnold's love of animals. And

---

* This review was written for *Partisan Review*, but the editors declined to print it.

the dog very oddly dominates the portrait, so that his master appears almost like a kindly Mr. Murdstone. If ever there was a satyr, he has disappeared under folds of heavy broadcloth.

Now, the difference between these two photographs—which are really the same photograph—may be made to stand for the difference between the Arnold who was critic and poet and the Arnold who was to become so acceptable to the academic and the timid mind, the Arnold of "culture," of "the best that is thought and known in the world," the Arnold of "sweetness and light." And yet "sweetness and light" was a phrase that Arnold adopted from that most savage and bitter man, Jonathan Swift. He used it to mean something. Indeed, there is none of the celebrated phrases of Arnold which does not, as he uses it, mean something, and what it means is usually quite clear from the context. It is only when taken away from all that qualifies and reinforces them, that they lose precision. Arnold himself was the first to detach them, Mr. Trilling says, because he thought of them as having an almost magical power. That may be true. But it is also true that Matthew Arnold, for all the clarity with which he wrote, did what he could to make himself an equivocal figure to his contemporaries.

His sister, who was accustomed to sitting with the young Matthew, across from him at the breakfast table, was surprised by *The Strayed Reveller*. She had never supposed that her brother had any such thoughts as his poems revealed. This was the time of the gay waistcoats and of the hair unclipped by English scissors. The secretary of Lord Lansdowne passed for a dandy. Now, the point of the dandy, if he happens also to be a poet, is not in the immaculate attire, but in the imperturbable countenance. That we know from Charles Baudelaire, who could write *Mon Coeur Mis à Nu*, but whose appearances among his contemporaries were celebrated for their dandiacal sobriety. He would show, as he moved among the tables of literary cafés, the simplicity of the English gentleman and above it a head impassively prepared for the guillotine. The middle classes were in power, and the poets, distrusted, had to disguise themselves. They had the choice either by their negligence to show their contempt for middle-class conventions or by their elegance to surpass them. They could pretend to be bohemians, or they could, like the young poet of *The Strayed Reveller*, deliberately stand out as a dandy. Matthew Arnold's friends remarked the constant play of humor over his conversation. His poems were something else again. But there was another alternative, beyond those I have mentioned, for the poet's conduct, one by which Baudelaire was for a moment tempted and to which, it seems to me, Arnold after his father's death succumbed. And that was consciously to accept a middle-class condition. At least it was possible to take on the middle-class conception of what was proper work for a man to do. And Arnold, married, bound himself to a tasked morality. What was hidden seemed abandoned. Of poetry there was little. Last was the Arnold who came to America; he was past sixty and stiff beyond the touch of kindness, the poet concealed and congealed. He disturbed those who came to see him as much by the coarseness of his features as by the British eyeglass and the trousers whose rumpled folds had the momentary approval of Bond Street.

To undertake a life of Matthew Arnold could not but be an ungrateful task. He wanted none written and he took care as he went along to destroy all papers—even those of a purely literary nature. The best he had thought and known was in his books and it was in his books that he would descend to posterity. For the rest, he had learned to prepare a face to meet the faces that he met. Yet he was no Prufrock; he was not timid, and there is no doubt that when he heard the sirens singing, it was not each to each, but directly to him. He sought to silence them and put a stop in the sensual ear.

Mr. Trilling's *Matthew Arnold* is not a biography, but rather an effort to discuss critically the published record of the poet's mind and to relate his thought to the historical and intellectual events of his time. It is the work of a professional scholar and to me, who am none, it seems that Mr. Trilling has consulted all the material available in print that is relevant to his purpose. The amount of his reading is immense; his way of reading seems to me something less than admirable. His book might well be taken as an example of contemporary scholastic criticism in America. We have, there is no doubt about it, a great number of critics in this country, all more or less scholarly, who write very well. But the number of people, scholars or not, who know how to read seems to be constantly diminishing. Mr. Trilling quotes Goethe with apparent approval: "What is really deeply and fundamentally effective—what is truly educative and inspiring, is what remains of a poet when he is translated into prose." Now, it is true that many of Arnold's compositions can readily be translated into prose, for the simple reason that they have never got very far beyond prose. If we contrast *Haworth Churchyard* with a poem of Yeats rather similar both in subject and vocabulary, *In Memory of Eva Gore-Booth and Con Markiewicz*, it is easy to see, though not to explain, how in the case of the Irish poet all the words have been transformed into poetry, whereas in Arnold's recollection of Harriet Martineau and the Brontës, for all the emotion that the words convey, that transformation has not taken place. And yet Arnold was a poet and at his best can only be read as a poet. Mr. Trilling avoids the best. He is timid with poetry whose sense is implicit, even when, as in *Sohrab and Rustum*, he has divined that sense. He is not happy until he has brought back the poetic idea into the realm of abstract ideas. He must, for instance, by a quotation, connect the last stanza of *Morality* with Hegel, though, as he admits, it is probable that Arnold never read the German philosopher. Now, that is no way to read poetry. Unless we are prepared to grant that the poet's criticism of life—to use Arnold's phrase—is important in its own right, we had much better leave him alone.

Of quotations there is no end. There are indeed so many that I can only conclude that Mr. Trilling's scholarship must provide him with a very restful sort of activity. He writes a book the way Tom Sawyer white-washed the fence. Whenever he can find somebody else to do his work for him, he lets him do it. He seems to prefer any opinion to his own.

In place of the conventional Arnold, he gives us one that is vastly more complicated. But his Matthew Arnold to the last is dim. Having assembled the material for an important study, he has completed it in a way which will, I suppose, win the approval of professional scholars. He has known the long range and the industrious search of the Swiftian bees, but, unlike them, he has produced neither honey nor wax. He has failed to furnish us with "the two noblest of things, whch are sweetness and light."   1939

A ROMANTIC GENIUS

(*Audubon's America* EDITED BY DONALD CULROSS PEATTIE)

I T WAS AUDUBON'S ambition, in making his portraits of American birds, to show them in action and in their natural habitat. He could not do this alone. He brought to the painting of birds such aptitude, passion and patience as may well be called genius, but his training both in science and art was limited. The backgrounds he left, for the most part, to another. Joseph Mason, that "amiable boy" whom Audubon found in Ohio, at the age of thirteen, and took with him on the voyage down the Mississippi, did the marvelous flowers, leaves and fruit in the earlier prints, where they often surpass in precision and felicity the rendering of the birds. The landscapes in the prints of the middle period are by George Lehman. And later there were other collaborators. After *The Birds of America* came *The Quadrupeds of America*; by then Audubon's powers were diminishing, and he allowed his son, John Woodhouse Audubon, to paint nearly half of the larger plates for that work.

In *Audubon's America*, Donald Culross Peattie has supplied a background for the ornithologist himself and, on occasion, substituted for him. Just as in such a group as that of the Carolina parrots, which is here reproduced, every significant aspect of that perished bird is shown with great vivacity and charm, so Mr. Peattie has neglected nothing we need to know about Jean-Jacques Audubon. Audubon, for instance, gave several accounts of his beginnings, which agree in nothing save that he was born in the New World. Mr. Peattie dispels any mystery that still attaches to his origin, admitting what is uncertain, but dismissing that recent rumor that he was really the lost Dauphin by the simple remark that Louis XVII had deformed ears and Audubon had not. The main narrative is Audubon's own, made up of selections from all his work, with particular attention to that portion of it which has hitherto been neglected or not easily accessible. While Mr. Peattie gives Audubon the benefit of every doubt, he lets nothing dubious get by without comment. What he wants is that we should see the whole man in all his wide range and accomplishment. And in *Audubon's America* we do see him, in action and in his natural habitat, which was the American wilderness of the heroic age.

However, since Audubon has already had as much acclaim as he deserves as an ornithologist and painter, it is rather as a writer that he is here presented. Audubon wrote voluminously. He kept journals on his travels, he was an untiring correspondent, and some at least of his notes and letters have come down to us untouched. He also wrote to sell, and what he wrote sold, though only after it had passed through the hands of one or another of four editors. Born on the coast of what is now the Republic of Haiti, the illegitimate son of a lieutenant in the French navy and of a Creole mother whose name may be conjectured but is not certainly known, the boy who was first called Fougère was brought up in France. He was eighteen when he returned to America; twenty-two when he set out for Kentucky. He was assimilated to the wilderness as perhaps only one who, deliberately and after the age of fifteen, had adopted the first two names of Jean-Jacques Rousseau could have been. He never quite acquired its speech. When, after his voyage down the Mississippi, he celebrated his arrival in New Orleans with a hangover, his sufferings are recorded with a French accent: "I retired to the Keel Boat; with a bad head Hake occasioned by drinking some Wine." He had then been in this country eighteen years. Yet not all the revision Audubon's prose had to undergo could destroy its vividness. His America had other writers and some better than he, but no other among his contemporaries, not even Catlin, covered so much of the continent. What he saw he set down; if his ear was poor, his sight was remarkable. He is a romantic, at least when young; but the romantic vagueness is dissipated by the accuracy of the hunter, by the discipline of the draftsman.

Audubon is the most famous of the early American ornithologists. He was by no means the first in the field. His immediate rival was Alexander Wilson, whose *American Ornithology* preceded *The Birds of America* and the *Ornithological Biographies* by some years. But Wilson's drawings, compared to Audubon's, are merely laborious. And, besides, the little Paisley weaver, with his pathetic look and pace of a peddler, with his solitary flute from which at night he drew his sad Scottish airs, seems misplaced in the wilderness. Audubon belonged to it. Superficially, at least, he is like it; romantic and brutal; he shares its honest hopes and its irresponsibility in movement; he could enjoy its rough humor and tell its tall tales. He impressed his contemporaries as the perfect woodsman. He could hold his own with all sorts of men: with the slave-owners of the Deep South in their houses and runaway slaves in the swamps; with the young braggarts on the flatboats of the Mississippi and the pale malarial squatters beyond it. He could handle that odd fish Rafinesque, when he came out to see him in Kentucky, and fought bats, stark naked, with his host's Cremona violin. He could save himself in that lonely log cabin on the Upper Mississippi, where he watched all preparations being made to murder him, down to the whetting of the knife.

But if Audubon was generous in his sympathies and mingled with ease with other men, he was always set apart from them by his one passionate purpose. His emotions depend on it, and as it advances or is thwarted, he is elated or despondent. He was long poor and always vain and touchy; he had a sharp tongue, and most of his friendships broke up in quarrels. He did not so much belong to the wilderness as in his imagination the wilderness belonged to him. That is the source of his power and sensitiveness, his grace and intensity. It is also the source of his attraction and what is disproportionate in his fame.

There had been so many paintings of American birds before his. It is easy to find fault with them, to say that they are overwrought, that only rarely can living birds be seen so tense with excitement as he habitually depicted them. And yet they are inimitable. Audubon's birds convey the wonder with which they were seen in life, and something of the light of that morning world still clings to them so that the brilliance of their plumage is increased and an excessive wildness is in their gaze. And the prints, taken with the writings that were intended to accompany them, form a record fascinating and incomplete, partial and authentic, of that America whose wild abundance vanished even as Audubon looked at it. There is hunting still in America, but no longer do men live by the black bear and the buffalo. No longer are stacks of grain covered by Carolina parrots. No one will ever again, watching the October sky, wait to see, as Audubon saw, great flocks of Whooping Cranes gradually descend from on high and prepare to alight on the earth. "With necks outstretched and long bony legs extended behind, they proceed, supported by wings white as snow but tipped with jet, until, arriving over the great savannah, they wheel their circling flight and slowly approach the ground, on which, with half-closed wings and outstretched feet, they alight, running for a few steps to break the force of their descent." The America of Audubon affects the imagination like a myth. But for such accurate glimpses into it as this, we might almost believe it was a myth and had never been.

The New Republic: November 11, 1940

GEORGES SIMENON

(*Maigret to the Rescue* by Georges Simenon)

I N THE OLD DAYS in Paris there was a friend of mine who could not sleep without reading for an hour or so. Often at night he would come back alone to his apartment to find there nothing he had not already read and would go out again in search of a book, whose print could be put between him and the day's disquiet, any book, to distract his mind so that he could sleep. Now, the only places in Paris where books could be bought at a late hour were the railroad stations. One night, in the dimly lit stall of the Gare Saint-Lazare, on the shelf of *romans policiers* in their lurid covers, he came on a book by Georges Simenon. He went off with *Monsieur Gallet, Décédé*, and the next night found *Le Pendu de Saint-Pholien*; a month later there was a third, for it was at intervals of one month that the volumes devoted to the adventures of Maigret appeared. It was at this point that he passed the books on to me, with the enthusiastic announcement that there had been nothing so original in detective fiction since Sherlock Holmes was carried to the immortals in a hansom cab.

I must say that it took more than one volume to overcome my distrust. I am no great reader of detective tales, but even I knew that in France they belong to the lower depths of literature. Nothing lower was allowed to be sold in the railroad stations. And yet Simenon's originality was at once obvious to me, and it was not long before I discovered that he was a serious writer, serious in a way that Conan Doyle could never have dreamed of being.

To be sure, his detective is not startlingly original. Simenon, when he made him, might have gone round to the Quai des Orfèvres and taken the first member of the Police Judiciaire he happened to run into as model. Outwardly, there is nothing much to distinguish Maigret from any professional detective under the Third Republic. He smokes a pipe and drinks a fair amount of beer. He lives, appropriately enough, in the République quarter with an Alsatian wife, who, as one might expect of a good housewife from that region, makes excellent *quiches*. Maigret is trustworthy. He is a heavy-set man; but more important is the impression he gives—to use words which Simenon applies not to him but to another character—"of a sort of stability, both physical and moral, that is positively staggering." His nerves are sensitive, as they must be, but sound; he is sure of his skill, and only rarely is his self-assurance exaggerated. About all that Simenon has done to turn a professional detective into Maigret is to make him into a decent man. He is a capable paid servant of the Third Republic. But there are times when he seems much more than that, when, with his comprehending pity and his patience in applying power, Maigret comes close to being what was best, what was most human, in the Third Republic.

Simenon's originality consists in this, that, in the thirty volumes which he has written about the adventures of Maigret, he has created a form of detective fiction into which real characters can enter. For, if his detective is convincing, his criminals are credible. They are the same small people who used to be reported in the *faits divers* of the Paris newspapers, as having run foul of the police. They are those provincials whose crimes were ignored in Paris save by the police. In Simenon's novels they are simply brought closer and made comprehensible. Their crimes, most of them, arise out of the sordidness of living and are only remotely provoked by passion. They may have come about—and this is the most frequent situation—through the necessity to shore up some small threatened position, some meager and dismal security, too hardly won to be let go for a scruple. In *The Flemish Shop*, which is one of the two stories translated here, murder is committed to prevent the son of the house from compromising his future by marriage to a factory girl, whom he loves just enough to have got her with child. In *The Guingette by the Seine*, the other story, crime occurs as the result of an escapade which, as it turned out, was not the escape it promised to be from the inexorable dullness of existence on a thousand francs a month. Simenon's are almost always middle-class crimes.

French literature has always been more conscious of its own conventions than any other literature. The story goes that Georges Simenon began by writing four straight novels and, only when he was convinced that these were failures, turned to the detective novel. But having done so, he is nothing if not scrupulous in observing its conventions. He does not, as so many British and American writers of detective stories do when they get a little above themselves, mix his genres. As long as Simenon holds to Maigret, he continues to write *roman policiers*, and now that he has dropped his policeman, he still holds to that most valuable literary convention of the detective story —that is, the story itself, which, simply because they considered it to be a literary convention, was discarded by most serious French writers of fiction after Maupassant.

As a form, the detective story is partial to cardboard characters and notoriously fatal to any real emotion. There does not seem to be any good reason why this should be so, unless it is that the readers of detective stories demand not to be moved. In the novel as we ordinarily know it, the high point is reached when the protagonist realizes his own predicament. In the detective novel the high point is reached when the predicament in which the criminal has involved himself as the result of his crime is recognized by another, the detective, who is usually hostile and always menacing. Hence the criminal, as well as all those suspected of the crime or concerned with it, must be created from the outside. But to a countryman of Maupassant's there should be nothing formidable about creating a character, first by presenting him in his social background and then by detaching him from it by his own speech and actions. And whatever difficulty there is in introducing real creatures into a detective story, Simenon has got round by devising for Maigret the theory that it is never the criminal who is caught by the police, but the man. What he waits for is the "human fissure," when the criminal cracks and the man who committed the crime is revealed in all his human strength and weakness.

Simenon begins by reminding us, both in his gifts and his limitations, of Maupassant. When he tells a story, it is done with a conscious skill and at the same time it seems to have been prompted by some inner compulsion, as though to tell stories were a necessary activity of his being. His characters have until recently been created like those of Maupassant from outside; but they belong not to a France which had just known the Franco-Prussian War, but to a France between two wars, between a defeat of the Germans and a defeat by the Germans. And the air they breathe is alive with an immense disquietude, which increases as Simenon goes on, until in the latest of his novels to reach this country, *Malempin*, which was printed just ten days before the Germans invaded his country, the atmosphere is heavy with helplessness and tense with dread. It is a simple little story, but as sinister in its implications as anything ever written by Julian Green. War is not mentioned, and I cannot remember much mention of politics in Simenon. Yet the position of the people in his novels is, in a small way, the position of France in the world. They are trying, as France was between Versailles and Munich, to maintain a situation beyond their means. To outward appearance they are sound, but as I reread Simenon it seems to me that it is not altogether because the detective story demands such devices that the outward show of his characters is so deceiving.

The New Republic: March 10, 1941

362

APHORISMS
AND NOTES

POETRY IS AN ART

A POEM is such an arrangement of words that their real qualities are not obscured by those which have been arbitrarily assigned to them.

A poem is such an arrangement of statements that the arbitrary pauses take precedence over the real pauses.*

By the real qualities of a word I mean those which belong to it by the mere fact of its being a word, its sound, length, weight and accent, and also those which, by virtue of its history, have become attached to it. By the arbitrary qualities of a word I mean those which etymology and current usage assign to it.

A poem necessarily consists of a sequence of statements. Into these the poet introduces certain pauses, which occur at regular or at irregular intervals. These may or may not coincide with those pauses which the sense of his statements would dictate; but at all events they take precedence over them.

That verse is most interesting in which the beat of the sentence runs counter to the beat of the verse; but in order to make sure of this, the beat of the verse must be constantly felt.

The late Amy Lowell, in her free verse, based on what she called cadence, allowed her logical pauses to coincide with and to supersede her poetic pauses. As soon as the novelty wore off, it was seen that her verse had absolutely no interest whatsoever.

* The first two aphorisms here appear in a slightly different form in *The Infanta's Ribbon.*

CLASSICISM WITHOUT A TOGA

To LEAD, no longer to follow. To lead where? Where but to joy and glory? Not my glory. To the joy that is rightfully man's and the glory of what is not man.

To invent a new music, for new instruments will be required to witness this joy.

The classic poet does not suffer. Man suffers: only as a man can the poet suffer.

The classic poet is not himself. He assumes a mask in order to speak. Behind the mask is a naked man.

The mask may have contorted features, comic, tragic, or merely grotesque. Behind the mask, the poet's mouth moves to inform the mask with speech. For the mask has no voice.

The purpose of the mask is to dehumanize the voice that proceeds out of its mouth.

I am not the poet. I is the mask.

DICTION

ANY WORD may be used in a poem, provided it is resolved in the poem.
The abstract word:

> Come, thou mortal wretch,
> With thy sharp teeth this knot intrinsicate
> Of life at once untie.

> Do hold discourse with the incorporal air.

DICTION

The vulgar word:

And that worse itch between the thighs.

Scientific words: More difficult, but always possible. Cf. Donne, Marvell, Laforgue, Eliot:

In ephemerides.

The only requisite is that the music should be insisted on in phrases where the abstract word intrudes:

Circumscribed a golden grin.

In general, however, one must avoid any word too far removed from the vocabulary of the ordinary well-spoken man. Excessively technical words tend to take on a comic overtone. Cf. Eliot, where this is deliberate. To be strictly avoided: all words of the political speaker and the editorial writer, not because they are vulgar, but because they are inexact and usually cover up indolence, ignorance and presumption. The use of such a word as *dialectic* (in the jargon of the radicals) is an excuse for not thinking honestly. This, incidentally, is the real objection to Marxism. Marx himself was a great and often profound thinker: his disciples (1) introduce a further and usually false simplification, (2) obtrude variations, often false, on the text. However, MacLeish's use of *dialectic materialism* is correct, since it is dramatically employed. It is no longer his own term, but the terminology of his character.

Country words, dialect. No difficulty, provided they do not interrupt the prevailing mood of the poem.

Urban dialect. Perfectly good, if it is really used by the people and is not the quickly passing invention of newspaper writers, vaudeville and stage personages. In that case, it will soon stale.

Eliot has used cockney to write a fragment of sordid tragedy. Cummings has used the street speech of New York for whimsical and satiric purposes.

Practically speaking, I believe we have all the words we need. There is no necessity (as there was twenty-five years ago) to increase the poetic vocabulary. The problem still remains of how not to use words already too loaded with personal meaning by other poets. For example: Yeats's image, norm, pern, gyre.

The English language, like some women, desires and requires that a certain violence be used on it before it will fully yield its beauty. But, forced, it will respond with advances of its own.

English is a mulatress; hence sensuous beyond either of its parents.

Color is the vision of the north; brilliance the color of the south.

The power of English speech can be brought out by restricting one's self to the use of Anglo-Saxon words; but not its splendor.

Very few poets have ever used English as English. Shakespeare, Coleridge, Blake. Perhaps Keats.

English has a northern and a southern province. The poet should live on the border and in his progress should continually step back and forth between the two. On that border is, as a matter of fact, the only place where he can live. The poet is the crooked man who walked a crooked mile.

American English largely a deterioration of English English. But the English of England has also deteriorated: in many places and among certain classes, its state is far worse in England than in America. Galsworthy is a live man speaking the language of ghosts. Spender and Auden are sick men speaking the language of the sanitarium. Their speech has the febrile, rapid, allusive quality of rocking-chairs on the front porch of an institution for the cure of what? Civilization, perhaps.

American English has more vigor than English English. But much less accuracy.

Office of the poet: *Donner un sens plus pur aux mots de la tribu.*

The accuracy of the poet is not that of a man sticking a pin in a pinhole already there. It is the accuracy of an archer who hits a butt so far that it cannot be clearly seen, in a high wind.

There is always an element of chance in the poet's hitting his

word. The true poet has luck. However, all poets are allowed a second
try if they want it.

THE SUBJECT

T̲HE POET does not explain. He illuminates.
All poetry has political consequences. But who changed Victorian England—Mrs. Browning with her outcries against industrialism, Hood with his *Song of the Shirt*, Tennyson with his exposure of the meanness of the middle classes? No, the Pre-Raphaelites, who, in writing of a state of being as far as possible removed from Victorian England, made that realm unendurable, ultimately uninhabitable.

Poetry works its cures almost as slowly as nature.

All poetry is philosophical. None deliberately so.

Poetry is complete. It is at once the lover, the beloved and the act of love continually being consummated, forever consummated.

Whenever in doubt about any quality of poetry, remember this image.

Subjects to be avoided by the poet: anything that can be understood by a newspaperman.

Secret of success (writing as a career): treat of nothing not already known to newspapermen.

OBSCURITY

C̲ONCEPTS clearly and explicitly expressed are thereby condemned to death. The question then becomes: How long can they be kept alive in the death-house? Some have been known to be given reprieve after reprieve. Others, by disguising themselves, have been able to escape—for a time.

Mathematics is an attempt to [construct] a system of deathless statements which shall also be explicit. All that it creates is a series of symbols unintelligible except to the initiated.

Music is mathematics rendered intelligible to the whole man.

The obscurity of Rimbaud largely disappears if we look through the windows of certain sordid hotels in Belgium.

In Rimbaud's poetry, what begins as a sexual predicament ends as a spiritual problem. Compare the two versions of *Loin des oiseaux, loin des troupeaux, des villageoises.*

It was not poetry that Rimbaud rejected, but two poets, himself and Verlaine.

Any poet may appear obscure to one who has not learned what his speech includes, what his silences intend.

The blank margins at the side of the page are part of the poem.

But the contemporary poet, having learned the value of silence, almost at once began to depend too much upon his blanks, upon what was not in his poem rather than upon what was there that could be transferred to the printed page. He is full of hints and innuendoes. But a disproportion remains between the reference and the thing referred to.

There is an intimate connection between modern universal literacy and the obscurity of modern literature.

Obscurity becomes frequently a matter of decency.

But the prowess of a poet is not to be judged by the size and the thickness of his fig-leaf.

Failure of surrealism: The unconscious is exciting but not interesting. The conscious is interesting but not exciting. It is the passage from the unconscious to the conscious that is both exciting and interesting. The chimaera must be seized at the moment she rushes from the cave. Dissect the chimaera in the cave and you have only an incongruous collection of feathers, bones, viscera, a tongue uprooted from the gullet, eyes torn from the sockets and some surprising objects which can only be dubiously catalogued as sexual in shape and probably in purpose.

Giorgio de Chirico's childhood was spent in Greece, where every day he saw his mother seated by the Aegean, knitting, among the broken columns of the remote ancestral world. But were we not all of us brought up among the divine shards of Greece? In my childhood, Bullfinch lay on the school-desk in the backroom.

Americans are said to rejoice because their landscapes contain no satyrs, their history no saints.

Salvador Dali's hallucinations are deliberately provoked. To understand his symbols one needs only to analyze them. His castrated boy is wistful, not awful, troubling as a case history. They at once disappear as symbols and leave behind certain observable facts, accessible to a scientist. What remains moving are his perspectives.

The most beautiful youth on the Sistine roof holds a horn of abundance overflowing with monstrous acorns. One grasps their meaning at first glance; but their significance is not so soon exhausted.

Symbols do not die. They become innocuous, useless and at last ornamental, like an antiquated bronze cannon in a park where children and pigeons play.

The poet is explicit at his peril.

The artist is a child in two respects only. He is innocent and he is cruel.

Liberalism becomes vegetarianism.

371

Debauchery is useful to the artist only in that it allows him to feel that he has come to an end.

Trotsky is hateful, not because he is a revolutionist (though most revolutionists, being compounded of hatred, are hateful), but because he is for us what Voltaire was for Baudelaire: the antipoet.

Love is both means and end. So is poetry.

Debauchery is useful to the artist as a form of spiritual exercise—also because it enables him to resist more serious temptations.

The essential problem of living for the artist: to subject himself to enough disturbance to incite creation and to attain the serenity necessary for creation.

Poems have been written on the top of Ben Nevis in a thunder shower. But no good poems.

The inciting cause of a poem is merely the witch-hazel fork: it serves only to disclose secret waters, discover secret springs until then hidden.

My dreams: A statue of the garden god in a tempest of sybilline leaves.

Every poet over twenty-five must live with a critic. He must not go to bed with him.

Some poets employ their critics as ghost writers. In the end, the ghost strangles the critic while he is asleep.

Truth is beauty, beauty is truth. How to understand this: Man is the measure of all things.

Whatever is satisfying to man in the light of his whole previous experience is, while it lasts, true.

That is true which seems to conform at any given moment to the whole previous experience of man. That is beautiful which conforms to his present state of spiritual grace and his permanent physical structure.

OBSCURITY

The prose-writer writing prose writes in paragraphs. When the poet writes prose he writes in sentences.

When the poet thinks he has written a paragraph, he has actually written a strophe. Cf. Pound.

Lately, however, poets have taken to writing paragraphs in verse, which they mistake for strophes. Cf. myself.

Mozart is the classical poet par excellence. No other speaks with such assurance.

Matter is essentially rebellious; the poet pretends it is only coy.

Poetry as propaganda: a female impersonator.

Contribution of the Chicago school: literature as a competitor of the front page.

Poetry is a joining of those things which nature has sundered.

When the poet sets up as a prophet, he is very liable to place an undue emphasis on the brasses of his orchestra and drop the drums.

Poetry should descend from singing, rather than rise from speech.

The poem comes inevitably to its end, but the poet does not reach a logical conclusion.

Apollo has a bisexual countenance. The vigor and daring of the poet should be employed at the moment of conception. The elaboration should be carried out with delicacy. The male should engender, the female complete, the poem.

The weak artist attempts to make up for a flaccid and meagre conception by being very slapdash in his treatment later.

An artist of feeble imagination nearly always employs bold brush strokes. Chase.

Art is not sacred—any more than religion is.

Beethoven was shocked at Mozart's treating a scandalous subject. It was, he said, an affront to the sacredness of art.

That is why Beethoven, no more than Milton, is among the great artists. They are more humble and more bemired.

The only way to insure purity to one's art is that which insures purity to one's body: by embracing sterility. All one can do is to open one's arms to purity. It may come; it will not stay.

Nothing should ever be dedicated except monuments to the dead.

Critics are scavengers. One of the critic's duties is to keep the streets clean.

If the critic mounts the soapbox, the garbage remains in the streets.

Obscurity may be either a fig-leaf or a face-veil. Or a hood.

Obscurity should be worn for decency. It is not necessary to cover the head.

Critics are dissectors and scavengers.

The critic should never touch anything until it is accomplished.

The critic should on no account say what should be written. What he should say is this: "I find that these works have been written and from their particulars I have been able to deduce the following general laws (of their being)."

Why is art necessary to complete living? Why is the sun necessary to any living at all?

The critic would like the artist to treat those subjects in which he (the critic) is interested. When the artist does not do so, the critic is obliged to feel superior to the artist.

My imitation of other poets is in part a desire not to be myself.

OBSCURITY

It is also due, in part, to the provincial's fear of lagging on his time.

To fear nothing and despise nothing—especially the commonplace.

The personality of a poet is, probably, a by-product of his fame. In attempting to exploit it, he is apt, oh, very apt, to acquire spiritual pride—in art as in religion the worst of sins. Genius is a long training in submission.

The office of the poet under capitalism is not to combat capitalism, but to sustain the desire of life and the dignity of death, both of which capitalism continually destroys.

The poet does not clench his fists: he has other employment for his fingers.

The poet is a product of a border country, of the mixed race and the misalliance. He is a man between two ages. His art is an attempt to recover a civil status and to reconstruct the calendar and bury it in accord with the seasons.

Poetry and propaganda: Propaganda is aimed always at a group, actual or potential; it strives to affect men through what they have in common. Poetry answers a common purpose, appeals to man where he is most alone and most silent.

Life, liberty and the pursuit of happiness! Incompatibles! Liberty is beyond happiness. Only those who are aware they have left happiness behind can hope for liberty.

The poet can do nothing about offering the people economic freedom. Much less can he actually give it to them. The freedom he offers is not of this world.

The ancient purity and the coming freedom! They can be known; they cannot be secured.

The speech of poetry is directed at the whole man.

Each generation has to carry on its own work, while settling the parental estate.

APHORISMS AND NOTES

The only living difference between one generation and another is sensibility.

Style belongs to the age, his manner to the poet.

What is permanent in poetry depends upon what is permanent in man: his bodily structure.

A poem has unity of content when it is concerned throughout its length with a single relation.

A poem has unity of form when, after arousing in the reader a desire to have something happen (in the poem), it satisfies that desire in such a way that the reader is surprised but not resentful.

One of the uses of a metrical pattern is to secure a succession of surprises, all the while avoiding shock.

Modern poetry frequently confuses the necessity for surprise with a need to shock. The reader is pleased when he is surprised; the poet, when he is shocked.

Form does not grow out of the material, though a given material may immediately suggest an appropriate form.

The truth of the matter is the novel in its great period (when this was depends upon what race we are at the moment discussing) had more form than the poems of the same period.

The form of an age does not reflect the conditions of the age, political, social, economical; but the state of its sensibility. And its conception of man's place in relation to the universe. These also affect politics, etc., so that it will later be possible to trace a resemblance between the forms they assume and those the poetry of the period assumes.

Over the Elizabethan tragedies and the discoverers and piratical adventurers, one word: Unknown.

The instinct toward art is profoundly, essentially conservative; the technique of art is profoundly revolutionary.

OBSCURITY

Propaganda is a criticism of life by ideas; literature, a criticism of ideas by life.

The intellectual labor of the artist is properly confined to the perception of relations. The conscience of the craftsman must see that these relations are so presented that, in spite of all complications, they are ultimately clear. It is one of the conditions of art that they cannot be abstractly stated, but must be presented to the senses.

It was unfortunate that every goal we sought should have turned out to be a gaol.

America is continuous in time with Europe, though separate in space. Russia is contiguous in space with European civilization, but disparate in time.

If we are to seek a consciousnes of the continuity of time on this continent, we must look for it, not among men, but in those desert rocks that hid the bones of the dinosaurs.

The mind craves nothing so much as a closed system, and the writer's mind is no exception; and yet he should, at whatever cost of violence, constantly set against any system which at the moment is approved the spontaneity and variety of life.

All authentic writing comes from an individual; but a final judg ment of it will depend, not on how much individuality it contains, but how much of common humanity.

More than once, I have tried, like all my friends, to shut myself within a system, in order that I might preach at my ease. But a system is a sort of damnation, which drives us perpetually to abjuration; we must be forever inventing another, and this continual fatigue is a cruel punishment. And yet, always, my system was so beautiful, large, spacious, clear and comfortable and everywhere smooth to the touch; at least, it seemed so to me. And yet always something spontaneous and unexpected, out of the fulness and universality of life, arose to give the lie to my knowledge, that childish old maid, the deplorable daughter of Utopia. I could change or extend my criterion as much as I wanted, always it was too slow to catch up with the infinite variety of man. It ran without stopping after beauty, so various in color and in form, dying in the infinite spirals of life.

In order to escape from the horror of these philosophical apostasies, I proudly resigned myself to modesty; I became content to feel. I took refuge in an unassailable innocence. And there my philosophical conscience found its rest.

Sainte-Beuve relates that Napoleon one day said, when somebody was spoken of in his presence as a charlatan: "Charlatan as much as you please; but where is there not charlatanism?" "Yes," answers Sainte-Beuve, "in politics, in the art of governing mankind, that is perhaps true. But in the order of thought, in art, the glory, the external honor is that charlatanism shall find no entrance; herein lies the inviolableness of that noble portion of man's being."

Actually, it is much more difficult to take into consideration all the imagined history of mankind than to attempt to explain existing phenomena by a theory of history which is probably accurate enough in its analysis of industrial society, but is hopeless to help us once we go even as far as the machine of Marly, which was, and is still, used, not to turn men toward an enervating and for them profitless labor, but to make fountains play in light and air. To come from the Marxists to these men is like leaving a schoolroom where a bigoted and impotent teacher lectures on and on, into a world where there is a more than pedantic violence, but also love and birth and death.

No, the escape theory will not do. The effort to conceive the present as a continuous past will add to, not decrease, the burden. And though these men went to the well of the past, it was to draw living water.

There seems to be a confusion here. On the one hand, a consternation which came from the recognition of the existing spread of savagery, and on the other a willing, a grateful return to primitive ways of thought and feeling. But this confusion is in part resolved as we consider that civilization owes its existence to the accumulated memory of the race. And that memory was failing. Under the impact of the physical sciences, men's minds were growing shorter and shorter. In America, the tendency was marked to consider that no experience was valuable which preceded the invention of the internal-combustion machine. All before Ford was pre-history. There was no mystery in the machine, and therefore for an age which was more and more dominated, not by tangible machines, for their place even in the most modern of countries is small, but by the concept of the machine, all sense of the mysteriousness of life was gone. There was little in heaven and nothing on earth which could not soon be accounted for. But this certainty was secured by limiting the time under consideration. A sociologist, investigating the criminal, invariably finds him to have been conditioned by his environment—that is, by the space within which he had his being in boyhood; his history must not go back beyond his parents' marriage, or at most is allowed to extend to an alcoholic grandfather.

At this point it becomes imperative to restore memory—if necessary, since only here and there does it persist in the Western world, to re-create it. This is a labor of the imagination, though the materials may be derived from the anthropologist and the archeologist. As Stravinsky has said, in connection with his borrowings from Pergolesi for his *Pulcinella*, it is only those whose life overflows that can hope to make the dead live again.

TIME AND ART

WIIAT IS the relation of an artist to the time in which he lives?

I. *The Recorder.*

It is possible to go to the artist to increase our knowledge and amplify our experience. He is in any time present as the sensitive and intuitive observer. The Satyricon. *In Our Time. Education Sentimentale.* Tanagra figurines. Abraham (Hieronymus?) Bosch.

We immediately recognize that the minor artist is the more complete observer, that if we wish to know the manners and customs of any time, it is not to the creator that we will attend.

Music: Strauss waltzes, Gershwin.

Somehow in these men we are aware that while the age is mirrored, its significance is not to be found.

II. *The Creator.*

What the creator is not:

Aware of the triviality of most observers—those critics and intellectuals who are, or suppose themselves to be, conscious of what is serious and significant in the age, desire that the artist should concern himself with whatever seems to them important. From a historian of manners, he is urged to become a social historian.

It is a matter of amazement to many that Jane Austen does not once mention the Napoleonic wars.

In our own time, the artist has constantly been urged to concern himself with those forces which are at strife, to show a world dying and a world being born. Or, say, the struggle between Individualism and Collectivism, Marx vs. Jefferson. Nothing is of so great moment, and for an artist to concern himself with anything less is to convict himself of triviality or fiddling in the flames of a world conflagration.

Not only must the artist treat of this struggle, but he must, perforce, ally himself with one or another side. Willingly, or unwittingly, he is either for life or for property, either deliberately communist, or unintentionally fascist. He should openly commit himself, and, having done so, his art must become an aid to action, an instrument of battle.

Those in the past who have not kept aloof. The example of Dante, Milton, Beethoven, David, André Chénier.

Those in the present who have participated: Dos Passos, Diego Rivera, the Russian poets and musicians, Salvador Dali, Gide, Malraux.

Objections to this point of view.

Big subjects make little works. The Jewish grandiosity. *Paradise Lost*. With good intentions one makes bad art.

Art as communication: To the individual, not to the crowd. Each hears alone, whereas in oratory, propaganda, etc., the communication is to what is shared.

How art affects action: Its static quality. To be and not be overcome. To feel, to comprehend, to be. If this leads to action, the artist is irresponsible. Rousseau and Robespierre. *The Possessed*. The idea in its pure state and the idea in action.

TIME AND ART

Art affects the sensibility. Sensibility as the one living change between generations. Why a century is a comprehensible division of time: extent of *living* memory.

Form vs. matter. Form becomes important when a real change of sensibility takes place.

Art is concrete. Hence it is difficult for it to express those relationships which are of use to the general, the statesman, the revolutionist, the sociologist. These relations belong variously to the historian, the economist, the technologian.

We are aware in dealing with great art that it deals with other relationships. Its connection with time is not that of the journalist nor of the historian. Its values are very distinctly not the same.

III. *Art and Time.*

What, then, is the relation of the artist to his time? The question as yet unanswered.

Let us consider what time is, or rather what the consciousness of time is.

The purpose of life is to continue. Biological time as seen by the primitive. Cf. the Southern Negro.

The purpose of human life is consciousness. This consciousness takes the form of an apprehension of time and space, which in turn brings a desire to escape from time and space.

Consciousness of time. Science. Ancient astronomy, modern physics. Abstruseness of the modern definition, mathematical formula. Poetic equivalent of this; human time and universal time not the same. Shakespeare.

Escape from time. Ecstasy. The saint, desire to be deified. Lovers and drunkards. The general. Battle ecstasy, but the general sees all phases in a single moment. The intellectual escape.

The artistic escape: Fixing the moment. Permanence of the artistic monument. Gibbon and the statue of Eugenius. Gregorian chant.

We are led now to a third way in which time must be perceived: Institutional time.

1. Earth time. Seasons, changes; but decay so slow as to be scarcely perceptible, at all events much slower than

2. Human time. The growth and decay of the body, the impermanence of thought and emotion.

3. State time. All human institutions subject to growth and decay. The State.

CONSIDERATION OF STATE TIME

The condition of the State determines how men think and feel. Ultimately this depends upon economic conditions. Marx. Spengler. Discussion and criticism of. Examples. Platonism. Neo-Platonism. But the State is a complex—its economy only one element determining its growth and decay. The economic man an abstraction with which the artist cannot deal. He must take the whole man. Gregorian chant. Bach and Mozart.

The artist has also his own institution, or rather his technique. How he must face the condition of his art when he finds it. Example. Condition depends [on] the whole mind of man. Bach again. Rise of polyphonic music. Baroque conception of State. Social position of artist. Prince and composer. His predecessors. Content of Bach. Baroque conception of time, Suite Anglaise. Same as Andrew Marvell's. Cf. Newton. But Bach goes beyond time: the spiritual problem of the age as discovered by Bach. Contrast Beethoven. Bach the purer. Why? Because he restricts himself to his specific problem, with which the artist is qualified to deal. Beethoven looks like Saint Just. Went out of his field. But also because Bach inherited his technique. That technique he developed. Mozart and the rococo. Competence still there. But Beethoven had to create his own competence.

ENGLISH AND AMERICAN STYLE

WHAT IS THE difference? Huge subject.

1. No such thing as English style as there is a classic French style. There is a period style in English.

Nevertheless certain persistent characteristics. Lack of grammar. Latin foundation. Anglo-Saxon and Latin elements. Must always be. Alternation.

American English has shown this. Take care of sound and sense will take care of itself.

The quincunx of heaven. In the fall the war was always there. We cannot dedicate, we cannot consecrate, we cannot hallow. A rat crept softly through the vegetation.

2. This traditional character always modified by sensibilities of each generation—spoken language.

What spoken American language is. Against Mencken. A modification and to some extent a disintegration, a debasement of the language. Not like Synge. Same thing happening in France. Romains, Céline.

3. Postwar style: Speed. Non-logical associations. Freud and the automobile. *Les Lauriers Sont Coupés,* Joyce.

Attempt to make a style out of the spoken speech. Joyce, parody of spoken style.

Stein, a rhythmic beat. Repetitions. *Three Lives.* Influence of Flaubert. The word *table.* Sherwood Anderson.

Faults of these two writers.

From Joyce: Cummings; Dos Passos; Faulkner; the proletarian writers; Edward Dahlberg; the aim to produce a style that will not falsify the material.

From Stein: Hemingway: the hardboiled school.

Outside influences; mostly French: Rimbaud and the ellipsis; Laforgue: ironic contrast between the sentimental and the sordid; past and present, etc.: Eliot.

Books of the postwar period: *The Enormous Room, The Great Gatsby,* (Eliot), Hemingway, Anderson, decadent writing.

SOME INFLUENCES IN MODERN LITERATURE *

I

POEL'S suggestion; talk of celebrities I have met. Anecdote of Lytton Strachey. Portrait of: inordinate length of neck; appeared tall and was not; squeaky voice; brown beard. Bennett: lions in front of New York Library; soft tucked shirt, bulging like a man; hair en brosse; rather surly expression, as though he had just eaten a zebra and it was too much for him. Siegfried Sassoon, the war poet: morose at the top of the stairs, looking as if he were determined to nurse his own solitude; when seen [at close range], a glittering cast in his eye, like a person insane on one subject and only one, but that filled his mind most of the time. American English ladies, Oxford students. Strachey in cab?

Subject of talk. Why the modern novel has the shape it has. In particular, the influence of three people on that form: Gertrude Stein, James Joyce, André Gide. So in a way I shall be talking about celebrities.

Why the novel is what it is.

A middle-class art form. Appears first with rising middle class. In England first. Aristocratic forms of writing: romance and poetry.

Being middle-class, it is concerned with things.

Attitude toward action moral. These characteristics at once appear in Defoe. Moll Flanders, a moral reprobate, who is a pickpocket. Robinson Crusoe, accent on comfort from things. Sinclair Lewis.

But the middle class also the revolutionary class. Invented a dynamic economic system, necessitating change in every generation. Insensibly the novel becomes social history. Two types: Tea table—

* These were evidently notes for a lecture.

which studies a small group; historical panorama: Scott. The two combined more or less in Dickens and Thackeray. The nineteenth century completes the triumph of the middle class and with it of the novel. We even have novels in verse: *Aurora Leigh, Lucille, The Ring and the Book, Enoch Arden.* Material with which the novel deals is changing material. Poetry permanent.

The weakness of the novel. Due to middle-class origin, has no form. Morality the middle class substitute. Artistically, the dynamic quality secured by a moving plot. Dickens. Unimportance of the plot: cannot remember in what novels his characters are.

Novel not only temporary, nor contemporary. Flaubert and Hemingway. *In our time.* Poetry which is permanent. MacLeish.

France. The one country which in the nineteenth century retained an interest in form. The social forms of the aristocracy taken over by rising middle class.

Stendhal purifies plot, makes the psychology the dominant interest. Flaubert insists on form.

What the problem of form is: First, to make the reader believe in what is happening; second, to preserve his interest; third, to make him feel that the action is significant.

II

State of novel at beginning of century: Serious novelists had agreed that credibility depended on the author's keeping in background. Characters must appear to move of themselves. Not to be explained as Thackeray explained *Vanity Fair.* Ibsen had shown that the most subtle motives could be presented in action by the use of symbols.

Now, while the novelist reported what the characters said and did, he still obtruded, discreetly and as quietly as a good butler, in order to investigate what was behind their actions. He moved around a little like a butler among the guests at a party, from this and that said and done piecing together and explaining his story. Or at worst he was like the ghostly butler Peter Quint in *The Turn of the Screw.* He went into people's bedrooms and into their minds and reported what was going on.

Joyce: portrait of: declined gentility. Pictures not true. Ruddy complexion in the bloom of health. But looks tired always. A man exhausted by his work. Difficulty of communicating. Has increased this by his blindness, eyes always weak, but probably neurotic. Hitler. Drinks only white wine; must have family about him when he writes. Sings, Irish tenor. Mrs. J. never forgiven him. Afraid of height and thunder.

What Joyce did to novel. Form: investigation of one mind in *Portrait*; sordidness and ecstasy. Told more than any writer up to that time about the development of a certain type, Hamlet, in modern dress. Stephen Dedalus. Proud as Lucifer. Style changes to record different periods of his life.

Ulysses carries this much further: three minds presented in their entirety. Different style, vocabulary, rhythm, images, etc., for each. Stephen in a poet's phrases, jumbled with theology from St. Thomas Aquinas.

Bloom the scientific but uneducated mind. Molly the inert, fecund matter out of which all life comes, but which is as yet intellectually unconscious, though with a desire for conscious purpose.

Technically: The minds no longer described, but presented. Interior monologue. Objection to: The will cannot function: Elegiac effect.

How we are introduced to characters in *Ulysses*. Tell no more about them than a person first meeting them would know. Joyce's belief that ordinary life is exciting enough. Birth, death, eating, digesting, thinking.

Movement in Joyce. Cf. Proust. The novel almost static. Twenty-four hours. Nothing much happens. An expanded anecdote. Bloom meets Dedalus. Cf. *Dubliners*. A small event which will profoundly alter people's lives thereafter. In a sense, the story is after the story. Yet the book is full of verbal movement. Collision of atoms. Like a table seen by a modern physicist. A table moved from one side of a room to another. The room will never be quite the same. In the meanwhile, the most intense activity goes on.

Influence on style. Sound. *Stately, plump Buck Mulligan came*

386

from the stairhead. No movement on Mulligan's part. But the words move; to an attentive ear something exciting has happened. Hemingway's *In the fall the war was always there, but we did not go to it any more.* Conscientiousness. Obscenity.

Gertrude Stein: An American Jewess. Long abroad. Royalty in exile. No major domo to tell you how often to kneel. Not enough genuflections. Hemingway, influence on. Gertrude always right. Her jealousy of. Astute woman of McKinley period.

Her weakness. No material. Person to whom their personal experiences do not serve. An emotional invalid. Sees things as we all see walkers when rising for the first time from bed.

What she thinks she is doing: making writing have implicit sense instead of explicit. Take care of the sound and the sense will take care of itself. Gertrude takes care of not only sound but the weight, smell, color and potential energy of the word. Not nonsense, strictly speaking, but in much of it useless to look for sense.

Pigeons on the grass, alas.

Her influence. *Three lives.* Style adapted to minds of her characters. Three servant girls. Cf. *Un Coeur Simple.* Servant confuses Holy Ghost and parrot. A symbol. But style is Flaubert's best. Miss Stein makes story of *Melanchtha* use only words Melanchtha would use. Enormous influence of this. Formal prose made from ordinary speech. First thing you notice is repetition of words. Contrary to accepted English style.

Gertrude's later development of this. Repeats words to make patterns. Cf. Cubist painting. I believe she misunderstood just what they had done. A dislocation of the grammar of speech. Hemingway. Used repetition to link one sentence to another, for musical effect. His fine ear. Characters in *Autobiography* speak like Hemingway's. I believe this a complete invention of Hemingway's. It is not the way either of them talks. Or anybody else, for that matter.

American style as opposed to English. Hergesheimer. Obvious that such a style by its false elegance betrays the subject. Rise of the hardboiled style. Comes primarily from Gertrude Stein. Miss Stein is rather hardboiled, like a politician of the Mark Hanna school. Hemingway not a bit hardboiled. A sensitive and apprehensive man, who cultivates the stoical virtues of the American Indian but has never adopted them. Except for hunting.

In art the human mind moves but does not advance; there is in any form a development, necessary, inevitable, but not necessarily an improvement.

Art moves but does not advance; it develops but does not always improve. *Moll Flanders* one of the great English novels, perhaps the greatest.

The aristocrat is content to be known by his actions; but the bourgeois wants to be recognized by his intentions. His actions are usually very bad. And Moll Flanders was a pickpocket, an adulteress, a murderer and guilty of incest, yet Defoe makes you feel she was essentially a good woman.

PORTRAITS
OF PLACES

PRINCETON *

I

PRINCETON University was founded in 1746 as a Presbyterian college and is now one of the most desired and desirable places in America in which to loiter through four years of one's youth. This establishment of a place whence good Calvinists should go forth—laymen if need be, divines if possible—was, from the first, doomed to failure. Calvinism requires a clear and mountainous air; Princeton is set near slow streams, and the air is always either softly damp or suave with sunlight. Although the trustees desperately made Jonathan Edwards president of the college, he could do nothing against the indulgent climate. It is evident that the cause was early lost, for the younger Aaron Burr, the first graduate to rise to distinction, destroyed a village virgin at sixteen and shot Alexander Hamilton when a little more mature. I drag in these somewhat doubtful details because it is my conviction that the University of Princeton is what it is largely on account of its site. Had it been left to Elizabeth(town), New Jersey, and named, as was originally intended, for Governor Belcher, its history and character might be quite otherwise.

This quiet leafy New Jersey town, continuously troubled by the sound of bells, still keeps a sense of its past. In Nassau Hall the Continental Congress sat in threatened assembly, and behind the secondhand furniture shops of Witherspoon Street are the graves of a half dozen Signers. All but the most indifferent students are aware that a barren acre of cornland to the east of the town is the battlefield of Princeton. It is the privilege of certain towns to mumble over their past. Edinburgh, for example, wears its age proudly and obviously; little of London, except to the bearers of Baedekers, seems older than the Crystal Palace or the Albert Memorial.

Princeton is older than the rocks upon which it sits, perhaps be-

* This essay was written for a series, published in the *Smart Set*, called *The Higher Learning in America*.

391

cause it needs but four years to establish a precedent in antiquity, so that, since the middle of the eighteenth century, forty generations of youths, each with its stiff customs and cries of revolt, have passed through the town on their way to middle age and mediocrity.

Tom D'Invilliers, the poetic feeder to the epigrammatic hero of *This Side of Paradise*, was aware of this when, with Amory Blaine, he crossed the campus on their last night before leaving for the war: "What we leave is more than this one class; it's the whole heritage of youth. We're just one generation—we are breaking all the links that seemed to bind us to top-booted and high-stocked generations. We've walked arm and arm with Burr and Light Horse Harry Lee through half these deep blue nights."

The campus accepts this tradition and attempts an air of even greater age by borrowing an architecture of Oxonian medievalism. It is the fashion just now among intellectuals to decry this imitation of the English collegiate Gothic. But the only endurable form of American architecture is the ferro-concrete skyscraper, which in such a village would be ridiculous. Colonial Georgian is American only by virtue of its early importation. Besides, it has already been used in its two adaptable forms at Harvard and the University of Virginia. No, J am unfortunately fond of the grave beauty of these towers and spires trembling upward, intricately labored and grey; of these grey quadrangles and deep slate roofs, at night hooding under dormer windows' solitary lights, the slate only less luminous and blue than the sky uplifted above it; of Seventy-Nine stately, in red brick, and Holder, enclosing with cloisters and arches a square of sunlight and sod. . . .

Here it is possible that the student should believe himself in a rich current of life. Here no dreamer in his ivory tower, no drunkard, driveling and about to pass out under the table, is farther removed from actuality than the sophomore sunning his white-flanneled legs in front of the soda-shops on Nassau Street. The trains that pass three miles away, plying between New York and Philadelphia, loaded with bankers, clergymen, fertilizer agents, Italian immigrants and cigar drummers, are only so many swift blurs trailing a long foam of smoky cloud across a wash of summer green. Life outside exists—for weekends and eventually for more troublesome purposes—but there is no immediate reason to bother about it. After four years, the undergraduate becomes so studiously lackadaisical, so imperturbably serene, that a young Princeton alumnus looks little better to him than a bank president or a United States senator.

For during these four years he will have heard an affirmation of the older aristocratic tradition—such as it was—of the Middle States, that barbarous gentility, that insistence on honor and physical courage, which America as a whole scarcely preserved after the eighteenth century. He will have found life more nicely adjusted than he is likely to find it again in his youth, and he will have had leisure in which to adjust himself after the turbulence of adolescence. During these years he will, according to his measure, acquire a more gracious conduct: the puritan will be forced toward tolerance, the philistine will become less raucous. And some will find the pathetic beauty of the wisdom of dead men and come with the fervor of contemporary discovery upon the books of those who have written beautifully of themselves.

Cut off from the present, it is possible to stare with a wild surmise at the past. In New York and Chicago, Dr. Johnson must remain a rather shadowy corpulence, ghostily closeted in bookstores. In Princeton his too solid flesh becomes as substantial as Mr. Chesterton's. Even Tiberius descends from the monstrous and tragic cloud in which Tacitus has enveloped him and dwindles to a studious and able administrator quite as credible as, say, the Honorable Josephus Daniels. Dante may be found at the end of a dreary term in Italian. And the young Swinburne, flamboyant and incarnate, with tossing red hair and wobbly knees, emerges from the Chancellor Green Library with the 1866 volume in his tiny hands.

The campus, already aloof, becomes the more circumscribed because of a lack of girls in Princeton. There are some few, but they are hedged about or wear flat-heeled shoes or serve epigrams with cucumber sandwiches or—but enough. Of course, every once in a while some unwary student returns from vacation sad-eyed and engaged, and, in my generation, there was likewise a society known as the Grousing Club, from whose adventures Fitzgerald drew heavily in his thesis on petting. But in ordinary times the ordinary student contents himself as best he can with masculine society and regards proms and houseparties as something of a nuisance.

Trenton is near by, but bad form. Except for a few undiscriminating freshmen, who ride by trolley on Saturday nights to dance with rouged but chaste shopgirls, the place does not exist. New York and Philadelphia are possible, both socially and by reason of the Pennsylvania Railroad. One mournful professor recently told me that everyone spent the week-end in Princeton except the students. Certainly these absences are more frequent than before Prohibition, when the Saturday night drinking-parties at the Nass afforded passable amusement. Then, at least, week-ends were not talked about, whether one went to Philadelphia for the Assembly or to New York for more ribald amusement.

II

What shall be said of the Princeton social system and the upperclass clubs, of which so many bitter and uninteresting things have been said already? The clubs have been called undemocratic, as if a goosestep method should be applied to choosing one's friends. They have been assailed as snobbish, when many a poor but honest student has found that neither poverty nor honesty could keep visitations of upperclassmen and election committees from his door. It has been said that they accustom the undergraduate to a too luxurious manner of living. Even this is, I am afraid, a fiction, for, if the architecture is at times pretentious, the food is unfortunately simple and wholesome —and it is to be remembered that the clubs are, first and last, eating clubs.

No, the trouble with the clubs is that, once in them, they matter so little after having seemed to matter so much. During the first two years even quite sane students look upon these formidable buildings on Prospect Street as having the awesomeness of the College of Cardinals and as bearing the hereditary privileges of the stalls of the Knights of the Garter. The President of Ivy—the most ancient of the clubs—is regarded more enviously than the President of the University, the Captain of the football team, the Governor of the State or the Prince of Wales. But once the elections are over, it is difficult for even the election committees to maintain their fervor.

These elections are held in the spring term of sophomore year, usually the first week in March. Invitations are sent out to a limited number of sophomores, who move among their own class, sounding out their friends and desirable acquaintances. A day or so later the bicker begins, and committees of upperclassmen from each club are free to approach the sophomores. The campus takes on an air of Old Home Week in a faintly alcoholic Bedlam. Juniors and seniors harass and harangue the amorphous sections; names are brought up to be blackballed or passed. Eventually—no one ever knows quite how—the sections are formed and signed up. The delirium ends, and the sophomore starts self-consciously to cultivate these bosom friends of a week's standing or, in loneliness and it may be with heartburnings, broods over his failure to realize himself.

Many an arrival at this season has based his success on brilliantine and a gift for silence. For at times it seems as if nothing matters much but that a man bear an agreeable person and maintain with slightly mature modifications the standards of prep school. Any extreme in habiliment, pleasures or opinions is apt to be characterized as "running it out," and to "run it out" is to lose all chance of social distinction. Talking too loudly at Commons, an undue concern over the souls of unconverted Chinese, drinking more liquor than can be held quietly and steadily, dressing too dowdily or too flamboyantly, the display of more money than necessary for maintenance on a plane with one's peers—all these are "running it out" and wooing damnation. I knew one able youth who barely got into a club on the ninth ballot because his legs were bowed so that he walked like a sailor in a heavy gale. Another sank far below his hopes after boasting too loudly and complacently of his goings-on in New York. Still another failed altogether because he wore pale yellow shirts and was near-sighted.

These somewhat naïve standards may be violated on occasion by the politician or the big man, but to the mere individualist they will be applied with contempt and intolerance. There are certain activities—all of them extra-curriculum—which have a recognized social value, though what a man does counts rather less at Princeton than elsewhere, certainly less than at Yale. Most influential are those sports which play to large crowds—football, baseball, track and crew. Closet athletics, such as wrestling and the parallel bars, are almost a disadvantage.

Outside of athletics, the most powerful organization is the Triangle Club, an unwieldy and smart assemblage, which each year tours a dozen cities, presenting a musical comedy written, book and music, by the undergraduates on a lively but slightly antiquated model. The English Dramatic Association, with a record of Elizabethan Comedies, Molière and Shaw, is looked on askance, and the more recent Théâtre Intime regarded as a little queer.

Of the publications, the Daily Princetonian is received, journalism being, as readers of the New York Times know, a highly reputable pursuit. The Nassau Literary Magazine suffers from its pretentious title, although literature is admitted in the curriculum. The Philadelphia Society, which is only the Y.M.C.A. in a Brooks suit, is socially and politically powerful. There is more to be said on this subject, but this should be enough to give a hint of the undergraduate's mind at the midpoint of his career.

Yet I do not wish to cry down the clubs. They are pleasant enough places in which to loll over a second cigarette at breakfast, with the sun striping the cloth and the bell for your nine-ten class, which you are quite conscious you are cutting, ringing outside. And dinner is crowded but intimate, with amiable kidding from the professional jesters and all the amenities of youth save wine. After dinner, the idlers saunter toward the movies, and a few will, for an hour, lean across the fire or, in warmer weather, stare wistfully into the blue emptiness of evening, as if youth were immutable and time had stopped. If the judgments on which the elections are based are immature, it is that the sophomores are themselves immature, the average age being but nineteen. The periodical revolts are raised not, as the leaders suppose, against the clubs, but against the intolerance of the young and youth's contempt for all that do not walk after their own way, whether because of some austerity of soul or weak ankles.

Once the division into clubs is made, it is largely ignored. Many of the idols of sophomore year are discovered to have not only clay feet but clay heads as well. The Secretary of the Triangle Club fails to be elected president; the promising athlete becomes ineligible. And a new valuation begins, based more on the individual and less on powerful friends. In the meanwhile, the junior has probably discovered that Princeton is a university and gives himself, somewhat belatedly, to such education as may be had in the two years that remain.

For it is unfortunately true that the first two years are spent on studies so general and elementary that they might well have been completed in preparatory school. Despite the fact that the entrance requirements of Princeton are as high as those of any university in the country, the average boy at entrance is little better than literate.

This is not the place to go into the defects of our educational system, but it is idle to rail at the universities for their lack of accomplishment while the average American boy of eighteen remains so hopelessly untrained and uninformed. The sole pretense of the preparatory schools seem to be (1) that they prepare their charges for college entrance exams, which is true and the beginning of their inadequacy; and (2) that they build character, which means that they uphold a sweet and serious ideal deriving somewhat from Tennyson's death-mask of the Victorian Prince Consort and somewhat from the most unselfish of the Boy Scouts. But I don't know that anything can be done about it, so long as we keep up a pretense of universal education.

At the beginning of the junior year, the student is free to choose a department in which henceforth he concentrates his energies. History and Economics gather the fairest crowds, with English and the Romance languages holding those who hope for an easy two years or who believe that Princeton can best be appreciated by following beautiful letters. Science, mathematics and the ancient languages keep only small and serious groups.

During these last two years the ends of education are directed toward upholding the humanities and establishing a more intimate relation between student and instructor. This last is done chiefly through the preceptorials, small and conversational groups, which supplement the more formal lectures. The aim of the faculty now becomes, in theory at least, the inculcation of that form of education so abhorred by H. G. Wells, for Princeton does not attempt to make good citizens, but to create a respect for ideas and to make the student aware how intolerably men have suffered that beauty and wisdom might have form. Education is conceived as being quite as useless as a drawing by Da Vinci, and as having nothing to do with training a man to vote intelligently for Democratic congressmen or to become a more earnest member of the Christian Endeavor Society. There is a certain amount of social service hocus-pocus extant on the campus, and occasionally revivalists appear with theatrical gestures and voices like Dunsany gods, but they do little harm and represent a compromise rather than an aim.

These things are goodly and well enough for the average undergraduate, but the exceptional boy will not come off so happily. If he does not flunk out—which he is more than likely to do through indifference or boredom—he will waste most of his time, unless he discovers a more intimate relation with the faculty than the classroom allows or contemptuously devotes himself to reading outside his courses.

III

My first view of the Princeton faculty was in the autumn of 1913. I had been herded along with some four hundred other freshmen into the seats of Marquand Chapel—a hideous brownstone building, recently burned, to the rich delight of all those who care more for Christian architecture than for Christian instruction. My legs were lost in bulky corduroy trousers; my somewhat skimpy shoulders were evident under a tight black jersey. A black skullcap (the sole remaining vestige of this once compulsory uniform) fidgeted between my knees.

An old man, rosy as a stained-glass prophet and only a little less severe, flapped by in a gown of black.

"That's St. Peter, the sexton," whispered an informed freshman.

The organ began—an orgulous roll—and the academic procession passed slowly down the aisle beside me: gowns of voluminous black, hooded with orange, sapphire and crimson; the pale robes of the Doctors of Oxford and Cambridge, the rich proud reds of the Académie Française: mortar boards and beef-eater caps of crushed velvet, brilliant or black.

Presently they were seated in semi-lunar tiers in the chancel, and a speech began, tactful with platitudes. But I did not hear it. I was intent on the aspect of these grave, serene and reverend scholars; philosophers grown old in the pursuit of Truth, mathematicians entranced by the dizzying splendor of numbers, humanists who dined nightly with Lucretius, Erasmus, Pico della Mirandola and Sir Thomas More. I came out of the chapel still dazed by the sight of these noble creatures and was told to run home by bawdy sophomores eager for horsing.

Have I given you, gentle and credulous reader, a true impression of the Princeton faculty? The question is obviously rhetorical. I have not. I have looked on many academic processions since that day and have never been able to see more than a number of bored elderly gents, tricked out in cotton wrappers, black with an occasional gaudy streamer or color, worn over their everyday Kuppenheimers.

But if the faculty is not, as I supposed in my credulous eagerness, a noble body of rapt scholars, neither is it exclusively composed of the kind of professors made famous by their own published platitudes and the satires of intelligent critics. Most of them are old boys with a weakness for pedantry. They play golf in knickerbockers and are not more than ordinarily absentminded. If they are in their craft disinclined to face facts, their conversation is more full of good sense than is the average businessman's of their years. They lead, indeed, a cloistered life, and many of them are as chaste as the very gargoyles on their scholastic cells. They are jealous of their privileges and regard a doctor's thesis as the only substitute for an initiatory vow in their cult. But they are not moralists using the arrows of Apollo to point a Sunday text. If they deplore the text of Petronius Arbiter, it is not because of the horrible decay of Roman morals, but because of the decadence of Neronian Latin and the mutilations of the manuscript.

There are, of course, this being America, moral enthusiasts and pallid respectabilities who deplore the vagabondage, the thyrsus-twirling and harlot-hunting of the poets they pore over, and who would be mightily disturbed "should their Catullus walk that way." I have not forgotten that lecture where an hour was spent trying to bring the late Percy Bysshe Shelley safely into the Anglican Church.

But neither have I forgotten that the wisest of the English faculty are as anxious that the student escape the dominance of the Victorian tradition as Mr. Ezra Pound might be in their place.

For beyond the pedants and the prudes there are still a few wise and gracious individuals, who are more than pedagogues and—on occasion—less than scholars. They do not write moral essays for the *Atlantic Monthly* nor contribute to the Sunday edition of the *New York Times*, having little in common with the box-office hokum professor, that crabbed and senile androgyne who rushes weekly into print to uphold his little store of dogma and to deplore with recent sorrow the death of Elizabeth Browning and Thomas Carlyle. Neither are they erudite non-intelligences, chattering over marginalia, useless phantoms in a noisy and passionate world. They are, rather, quiet-mannered gentlemen, urbane and skeptical, content to uphold the dignity of the scholar in an age without dignity and crassly uneducated. Sometimes I feel that they are all that is permanent in Princeton, when I return and find that all the men who were young with me are gone. Much of the grave charm of the place is due them, and I had rather the elms of McCosh Walk were cut down and burned away than that a single one of them should move from his chair.

*   *   *   *

After four years at Princeton, what remains beyond a piece of black-printed parchment, waxed and tabbed with a colored string? What beyond the recollection of Sage Tower, misty and strange, standing like a gray alchemist over October's gold; of the days of the big games, with broad orange banners over the towers and the gay, opulent, easy-going crowds come down in motors or by train; of my own small room in Witherspoon with books, dingily red and brown, or with golden blazonries, and the portrait of Georg Gyze, wistfully serene; of rolling marbles down the declining floor to bump against a lecturer who had droned overlong; of examination rooms, intense, hot and cigaretteless? What beyond the recollection of torchlight processions, the "whoop 'er up" song and the gargoyles creeping out into the crimson glare; of drunken students drilling imaginary squads under midnight windows; of the mid-year prom and the gymnasium diaphanous in streamers of apple-green and pink; of arriving drunk at the Phi Beta Kappa dinner and passing out before the roast; of students leaving a little sorrowfully and without illusion for the war, after farewell parties which began on Perrier Jouet '93 and ended on Great Western; of Holder Court under a descrescent moon, softened by snow as by age, startled by the sudden sound of revelling footsteps under the arches?

What remains beyond these and other such recollections? Well, not much, to be frank: a few friends whom time has proved, men with whom I have shared many things and who are after my own kind; a few books I should not otherwise have read; a smattering of Italian and the ability to pronounce Middle English passably well. But it is enough. If I had a son who was an ordinarily healthy, not too intelligent youth I should certainly send him to Princeton. But if ever I find myself the father of an extraordinary youth I shall not send him to college at all. I shall lock him up in a library until he is old enough to go to Paris.

The Smart Set: November, 1921

RHAPSODY OVER A COFFEE CUP

IN THE GRABEN the Holy Trinity soars from the market-place on clouds of solid marble: the Son, stripped to bronze, graceful as some lesser divinity, with shoulders of sunbeaten gold, bears aloft the triumphant cross; God the Father, bearded in bronze, one divine bright thigh hung over the globe, sits on a broad bottom contemplating his potence; the Holy Spirit descends in the form of a white stone dove. Saints and angels, cribbed from Perugino and despoiled of their colors, stand below in androgynous adoration. The imperial donor kneels at the base in the stiff posture of a figure on a tomb, offering praises for the deliverance of Vienna from the plague of 1393. Putti ascend and descend indifferently, mute in stone.

But here in the Stadtpark one sits at tables painted a light green and regards the Pavilion. The sunlight is strained through leaves, the grass is green as in spring, the gravel appears newly washed by the rain. The orchestra plays, and waiters bring from afar coffee and pale and raspberry tinted ices. The heavy brown liquor is sweetened and covered with a foam of cream. A newsboy with a close-cropped scurvy head edges his muddy-fringed and overpatched raggedness between the tables. On a bench under the linden trees, a square kerchief over the strings of her greasy hair, her brown hide wrinkled like a wrung-out scrubbing cloth, an old peasant sits heeding the violins. The American lady at my left, with the face like an unfortunate horse and the two agile palms, explains to her French companions that New York rises from the sea on clouds and the skyscrapers soar through forty flights of steel and concrete to achieve their name.

In Saint Stephen's, to the right of the altar, is the tomb of Rudolph IV, Duke of Austria. About the base, crocodiles with the dugs of bitches give suck to their crawling young, and dogs with the long lean tails of hairless rats commit obscenities among themselves. Armored reptiles are worried by hounds with webbed feet;

lizards thrust their whiskered snouts under the tails of wingless griffins. All the grotesquery of some fourteenth-century and very German Callot is there, carved from the brain to adorn the rest of a Hapsburg.

On the steps of the bookstore opposite sits, and for three days now has sat, a young man with a brown-speckled, not unhandsome face, nursing his poverty. He neither moves nor begs, but sits, turning on passers-by his dark hurt look, his dirty wool socks sliding over his cracked and leaky shoes.

In a small hotel in the Mariahilferstrasse a diminutive English lady sits among her Baedekers. Last year she travelled through Spain with a courier, and saw Cordoba of the Moors and the bull-fighting at Madrid. This year she is touring the Tyrol, second class, with a handbag bought in Regent Street, an umbrella and an Italian grammar. She carries her meagre lunch in a reticule; her one regret is that the tea on the Austrian trains is invariably sweetened and her doctors have forbidden her sugar. Her hat is not what it was at all, and her rain-proof, in covering her tiny body, reveals her British soul. She wears two pairs of stockings, one of cotton and one of wool, to protect her from the insects. Her watch is secured to her purse by a safety-pin, and her pince-nez is forever on the point of falling. "There are so many Beauty Spots here," she says, "and now that I have seen all on the upper route, I shall return to Innsbruck by the lower, spending a day or two in each place. I shall never come back here again, and I know I could never again do it so cheaply. And there is so much to see in Vienna. I have a great fondness for pictures: I once spent two years in London just to do the museums and the galleries. If only my son were here I should be walking on clouds." Next winter she will spend in Florence in a pension near the Pitti Palace. She is well past the changes of the moon; they may yet build her tomb in the sands of Abyssinia. One remembers Lady Hester Stanhope and nods respectfully to the spirit of the British Empire.

But to the Stadtpark (here there being no tea) she will not come, as now this female buffoonery comes with the massive pomp of a pachyderm. Stiffened by an armor of stays, she trails the gravel with voluminous silks, twenty years old and the color of dead leaves. She lifts the nose of a Tiberius and surveys, unseeingly, the rabble; the emergence of her ponderous chin from the tulle folds of her boa is an event. Her veil of blond lace does not conceal the preciousness of her earrings. The Oberkellner comes tilting. Behind her trails an obscure washed-out girl. her paid companion—Lunisequa attending the moon.

RHAPSODY OVER A COFFEE CUP

The orchestra plays Lehar; the young Viennese exquisite with his too-tight coat and his absurdly loose trousers leans on his cane and imagines himself another Anatol. A one-legged beggar in a grimy grey uniform of the Austrian Infantry hobbles at the edge of the crowd, receiving nearly valueless banknotes in a lousy cap. The music melts on the ear like some delicious rose-tinted ice on the tongue. The headwaiter's formerly satin lapels are creased and shiny like black leather.

In the Josefsplatz, before the old palace of the Hapsburgs, Joseph II, the unrenowned son of Maria Theresa, rides a slow-pacing horse, laureled in black bronze—an Austrian imitation of a French imitation of a Roman Emperor. And the old palace is dingy and fine, with the sombre air of a fortress. But the new Hofburg of Francis Joseph turns in a semilune of white marble, shouldering a hundred columns. In the centre is a grandiose portico with a balustrade, where his gracious and imperial majesty was accustomed to display himself to his subjects. (The roadway is overgrown with clumps of grass, and in the entrance hall under the portico are packing-boxes, where food was lately handed to a bread-line. But of that no matter.) It was the last project of a reign devoted almost entirely to building and the adornment of existing buildings with superfluous statues. This pink-faced old man with the kindly sidewhiskers razed the walls of the inner city, erected showy palaces, baroque theatres, Grecian parliament buildings, Gothic cathedrals, museums and innumerable fountains. He had a touch of the Roman passion for aqueducts and deflected the course of the Danube. He employed whole schools of sculptors, who filled the roofs of the city with athletes, centaurs, muses and victorious four-steeded chariots. He supplied the public squares with horse-trainers, generals and symbolic figures representing the four rivers of Austria. He made Vienna the third capital in Europe.

And yet, O Francis Joseph, Caesar and heir of all the tyrannies of the Hapsburgs, was it for the glory of Vienna that you spent so many taxes and put to labor so many men or for the easement of your own heart? Your Empress was assassinated, and your son died a not very noble death, alone. The Emperor Maximilian could not stand long against the Mexican wall after the bullets of the greasers, and the Archduke Ferdinand was, quaintly enough, murdered at Sarajevo. Augustus Caesar found Rome a city of brick and left it marble; and his daughter Julia committed adultery with a provincial.

John J. McNulty in a new straw hat and a slick business-suit stands outside the Grand Hotel and orders a taxi. His bullneck grows thicker and his pink hair bristles, and the sidewalk is astonished.

Mr. McNulty prides himself that he can go anywhere in Europe and get anything he wants by shouting loudly enough and tipping lavishly enough. And why should he not shout loudly—is not man above all the other vertebrates? And why should he not tip lavishly—did he not this morning receive 53,000 kronen for every one of his good American dollars? He has just lunched on *pâté de foi gras, filet de boeuf Bordelaise, pommes frites, savarin* and Emmentaler; his bill, including a bottle of Château Palugyay, coffee and a cognac, amounted almost to two dollars. Now he would like a taxi and roars for it, and the sidewalk is mildly astonished.

In a not unfashionable street just beyond the Inner Stadt, lives a colonel of the late Imperial Army with his wife, his mother and his two small sons. They are now obliged to rent their available rooms, even to the former dining-room, to passing foreigners. They employ one maid. Gretel is thirty-three; already she begins to call herself old; yet she will laugh or weep on the slightest provocation, like a child. Once an American lady offered to pay her passage to New York, but she could not well leave her mother, who, at seventy-two, cannot hope much longer to support herself by washing clothes. Gretel's most luxurious memory is of a year spent in a public hospital; nothing pleases her more than to find someone to whom she can show her wound, counting the stitches. She rises at five, shines eighteen pairs of shoes, prepares the breakfasts of the guests, makes the beds and cleans the rooms, chops the wood for the fires, does the household laundry and assists with the cooking. For this she receives 20,000 kronen a month. When her last red apron wore out, she could not afford a new one. Lest she lose caste, for it is essential that aprons shall be red, she bought a white one and dyed it. The pound of sugar which she bought yesterday for her mother cost 31,000 kronen. At night she sleeps on a cot, in a room too poor to let even to the most impecunious guests.

The orchestra in the Pavilion begins a waltz of Strauss's. The peasant girl with the crimson square over her gay flowered dress regards the exquisite with amorous slyness. The two American undergraduates, who came to Vienna seeking a cheaper Paris, absorb the table next to the elegant young Egyptian with the swart and pustular face. The sunlight turns the gendarme's sword to the thinnest of rapiers; the scarlet tabs of his collar add to the shoddiness of his uniform. On the gravel-walk beyond the circle of tables stand a man and a woman and a child, listening to the music. The woman's face has the vacuity of despair; the countenance of the man suffers stolidly, hopelessly, uncomprehendingly; the child's look has grown petulant with continued denials. Their expressions do not alter nor do their eyes move, as they stand listening to the pretty music, sweet and gay as a colored ice, faintly stirring as the cream-coated coffee, light as the shadow of a cloud.

Vienna, 1922   *The New Republic:* December 13, 1922

NEW ORLEANS: DECATUR STREET

A BLANK SUN stares down at Decatur Street. The sky is high and, as always here, shows clouds which, strangely, do not affect the intensity of light. The air hangs heavy, with no perceptible stir, except that occasionally there is a strong odor from the docks, where coffee is being unloaded from boats of Brazil.

This is the Vieux Carré of New Orleans, with houses that date from the docks, where coffee is being unloaded from boats of Brazil. shutters opening on narrow galleries. All have fine railings: festoons of cast-iron grapes and black twining leaves are looped along a second story with wet wash; formal intricacies of the early eighteen hundreds project over the pavement signs of Jax and Regal Beer. Under the galleries, Decatur Street garishly rots in the sun. In the afternoon, the dubious barbershops, red-striped and fly-specked, are not drowsier than the riverfront saloons. But at night the latter waken with sinister entertainment. An eleven-year-old boy, his face racked by sleeplessness (he is said to support a mother and four younger children), sings to the music of a hammered piano On the Isle of Capri, with the mechanical gestures of a suffering doll. Monotonous jazz is provided by Negroes, liquor by bars; sailors come here from the ends of the world, the girls mostly from the hill-country of the surrounding states. They are not called hostesses, for they order these things more directly in the South; after Prohibition, there was never any hint that the saloon would not return. The darkness of backrooms is alive, on a good night, with crowded shapes of love in the making.

Painted invitations outside saloons are for seamen: "Sink Your Hook in Here." Doorways opening on tobacco-colored corridors advertise "Rooms for Spanish and Filipino Sailors," with prices from fifteen to fifty cents. Popeye and the native pirate, Jean Lafitte, lend their names to places of amusement. Blank's Place declares that it is "Famous from Coast to Coast." Inside, it has between bar and backrooms the usual white lattice, inscribed "Tables for Ladies" and surmounted by seven white stars each inscribed with a girl's name—Doris, Nora, Edna, Dorothy, Helen, Marie, Mary Ann. New Orleans is a Southern port, and in this aspect resembles an American Marseilles, expurgated, it is true, from time to time, for this is, after all, America. The latest purge, which was begun something over a year ago, came as a result of the controversy between the late Huey Long and the city government of New Orleans. The underworld, which was with the state dictator almost to a man, quite faithfully believed, as long as he was alive, that once the Hillbilly Napoleon was triumphant and the last remnants of the Bourbon regime were destroyed, everything would be wide open again. Huey is dead by assassination. And his interdiction stands against the famous old district, through which generations of great Creole ladies drove on their way to the opera. It closed most of the houses and all of the shutters. It also overcrowded the waterfront.

The French Market begins with the Creole Café du Monde, which also allows itself to be known as the Original Coffee Stand. It looks, beyond the corner of Decatur Street, at the only baroque square in this America. In Jackson Square the general on horseback, uprearing in bronze, is surrounded by a staff—in constant attendance —of bench-warmers, panhandlers and river bums. They look across a green luxuriance of tropical vegetation to a waste of railroad-tracks and the great warehouses on the docks. The Mississippi runs below them, a swift, deep, yellow, muddy flood. Nowhere, not even at New Orleans, did the Americans of the last century know how to put their waterways to any but commercial uses. Water traffic is always pleasant to watch: white paddle-boat ferries, the unloadings from the tropics to the concrete docks. But the Mississippi is romantic only to the mind; here it is an ugly river, in its lower stretches between levees, the only ugly river I remember ever to have seen in America.

Once, if we may judge by the small model in the Cabildo, the old Halle des Boucheries of the French Market must have looked extraordinarily like a primitive Greek temple, on squat columns, all the space under the roof open to the air. Progress in the nineteenth century half enclosed the arcades with bathroom tiles, without thereby increasing the cleanliness, half screened them with wire, to accumulate more dirt, and painted the almost hidden pillars a dull oxblood red. A still more progressive twentieth century proposes to demolish it altogether and replace it by something not less sightly and a little more sanitary. This should not be hard. But the proposed change is resented by all who remember it in some happier romantic stage before the war, when Choctaw women sold herbs and sassafras-bark from grass-woven baskets and Negresses in tropically gay chignons dispensed hot drip-coffee with a flavor of chicory.

The sheds beyond have, also, I am told, parts from the past; but all that can be seen of them is a haphazard construction of time, more patched than repaired. Outside, a drowsiness of Southern sun falls on a grey man asleep on a chicken-coop. His dishevelled socks are grey above his cut shoes, his forlorn hat pulled over his eyes. An old Negro sits bent in a witless doze over his cart, in a somnolence only less deep than that of his donkey dozing in the shafts. Sleep pervades the market; at any hour of the day or night one finds Negroes in blue jeans stretched on sacks and lost to the world, or shelved in twos and threes on high-piled crates. Cajun boys curl in their carts to snore on beds of kale and cabbage; snoozing farmers dangle their legs over dropped backboards, undisturbed by the crap game in the next truck.

The booths are Sicilian, hung with red peppers, draped with garlic, piled with fruit, trayed with vegetables, fresh and dried herbs. A huge man, fat as Silenus, daintily binds bunches for soup, while his wife quarters cabbages, ties smaller bundles of thyme, parsley, green onions, small hot peppers and sweet pimientos to season gumbos. Another Italian with white mustache, smiling fiercely from a tanned face, offers jars of green filé powder, unground allspice, pickled onions in vinegar. Carts and trucks flank the sidewalk; one walks through crates of curled parsley, scallions piled with ice, wagon-loads of spinach with tender mauve stalks, moist baskets of crisp kale; sacks of white onions in oyster-white fishnet, pink onions in sacks of old rose; piles of eggplant with purple reflections, white garlic and long sea-green leeks with shredded roots, grey-white like witches' hair. Boxes of artichokes fit their leaves into a complicated pattern. Trucks from Happy Jack, Boothville and Buras have unloaded their oranges; a long red truck is selling cabbages, green peppers, squashes long and curled like the trumpets of Jericho. There is a more than Jordaens profusion, an abundance more glittering in color than Pourbus. A blue truck stands in sunlight, Negroes clambering over its sides, seven men in faded jeans, washing-blue overalls; the last over is a mulatto in a sweater of pure sapphire. A mangy cat steps across a roadway of crushed oranges and powdered oyster-shells.

Two women pick wood from the waste between market and railroad-tracks; three slum-boys quarrel among the stands over the division of five rotting oranges. Here, as elsewhere, penury in a land of abundance. From their covered wagons of unsold produce two Cajun lads look out with an air of hopeless poverty. On this narrow but rich alluvial soil, accumulated through a million years of flood, the new Sicilian survives; the older stock of whatever race, whatever color, diminishes toward starvation.

In the fish-market, a black man huge as an executioner hacks the meat of snapping-turtles from giant shells. Red-snappers, rose-scaled, lie beside the slender silver-foil Spanish mackerel and pompano from the Gulf of Mexico. Lake trout from Pontchartrain are tied together by strips of palmetto; carried on nappy heads, great round baskets of crabs go by, bedded in Spanish moss. Vast piles of shrimps, transparent shells from Barataria, are cooled under shovels of crushed ice. In their wire confines, the mahogany-red crawfish are in constant crawling motion; the monster swamp frogs squat under continual streams of water.

Once again on the sidewalk of Decatur Street, I am offered for sale a short-eared owl. And without turning my head, as the owl in his cage of withes is amazingly able to do until he blinks painfully between his shoulders, looking backward, I find myself listening to a conversation between a Negro man and two women: "This nigger wanted to commit suicide. But then *he* come in and found him. And then *he* got mixed up and pretty near killed *hisself*." I remember the old superstition that no black man ever does away with himself. The man's voice is soft, high, uncomplaining, almost gay. His speech is confusing until I make out that the dead man is always "that nigger" and that the live one is simply "he." " 'Cause they was good alcohol and they was wood alcohol. See? And the bottles was mixed up and he pretty near got a swallow of bad alcohol. They was that great big demijohn of creosote, and that nigger just turned it up and drank. He wanted to die, see? That nigger, he wanted to die. And then when he felt the pains in his stummock, he began hollenin', 'Lordy, Lordy! Get me sumpin' quick! I didn't mean to do it.' But he did, see? That nigger wanted to die. And he did. They give him some milk. And he drunk too much of it. Then he didn't even talk any more, he had such cramps, but he was sufferin' with his eyes. That was when *he* come in and almost killed hisself mixin' up that bad alcohol. It scared him when he seed him on that bed. He was sufferin' so it upset him sumpin' awful. And he got that bad alcohol. But that other nigger, he wanted to die."

The owl had quite closed his eyes. And looking up, at the corner, in the bright sunlight, I saw a sign, "Poor Boy Sandwich: Grande Dame Coffee: J. Battistella." At the moment, it seemed to me to resume much of Louisiana: a neon sign, unlit in the sun, ending with an Italian name.

The New Yorker: November 30, 1935

MR. ROCKEFELLER'S OTHER CITY

AS LATE AS FIVE YEARS ago a visitor to Williamsburg, Virginia, might have discovered a town which had not lost its eighteenth-century aspect. On the hot August day that I was there in 1930, the Duke of Gloucester Street, magnificently wide, drowsed deep in summer shade. The sun glittered on service stations and scattered leaves fell on concrete roadways. Yet Williamsburg had saved something of the air of a provincial capital. On shady side streets the past survived in a great number of private houses. Modest for the most part, they still wore that fine distinction with which the eighteenth century knew how to endow white clapboard and steep roof spaced by dormer windows. Many of them took the story-and-a-half shape which older Virginians used to say was first imposed on them by the taxes of Queen Anne. The formal gardens were gone, but here and there remained a stray crape myrtle, a tree of dogwood.

Williamsburg had once been the seat of royal authority over a vast domain, for the Colony of Virginia, in claims at least, extended to the Mississippi. But of evidences of the power of its governors there were but two extant five years ago: a Powder Magazine and a Public Gaol. Of the governors themselves nothing was to be seen but an effigy of the Baron de Botetourt, elegant in moss-soiled marble. This, the only statue ever erected by Virginians to one of the King's officers, stood under an arch of elms on the old campus of William and Mary College and faced toward the Duke of Gloucester Street. The perspective was long. Down the central green ran a row of electric poles. It looked all too much like the main street in any small Southern college-town. Where the cupola of the Capitol should have risen at the east end of the vista, there was only a waste of land, recently excavated and revealing some foundation stones, for safekeeping reinforced with concrete by the Association for the Preservation of Virginia Antiquities. The Capitol had been twice destroyed by fire—the first building in 1747, its successor in 1832.

Of the Governor's Palace of Colonial days there was left only the approaching green, in the dry year of 1930 a parched expanse of grass, oaks and catalpas. But on the site of the Palace I found a young man with small, intent face and pince-nez, who was pointed out to me as a Boston architect, a member of Mr. Rockefeller's advance guard.

One would have supposed there was no use looking for the Raleigh Tavern, which had burned to the ground in 1859. In the days of its Colonial grandeur, the tavern had been two things: a place where arriving governors were received, where distinguished visitors, such as the Emperor of the Cherokees and his nobles and attendants, were entertained, and where, during the Assembly, the best balls were held; also the place where the upper-class revolutionaries repaired when the British governor, Lord Botetourt, shut them out of the Capitol. (Before it burned down, the tavern had sunk to the level of an academy for young ladies.) Yet in 1930 the Raleigh Tavern, or something amazingly like it, was once more on the Duke of Gloucester Street. A restoration stood on a corner where only a short time before two stores had hidden the long-forgotten foundations. The tavern was freshly painted. A sign posted the name of the contractors who had rebuilt it. The antique face-bricks on chimneys were pointed with oyster-shell mortar, the roof-shingles were of asbestos fibre and cement, fabricated to age like cedar. It was appallingly new.

Five years ago the past had to be looked for in Williamsburg. It was everywhere, impoverished or improved. It was in Bruton Parish Churchyard among quiet tombs. But it had to be looked for. Whereas no one could have overlooked the cohorts of Mr. Rockefeller, who had undertaken to restore the Colonial capital. They, too, were everywhere.

At the beginning of the eighteenth century, the government of His Majesty's Colony and Dominion of Virginia had been moved from Jamestown, after the statehouse there had twice burned, to the Middle Plantation, which was renamed Williamsburg, in honor of that sinister widower, William III of England. Jamestown had never been a proper seat for authority, located as it was on a small peninsula, susceptible to fire, malaria and rebellion. In 1699, an Act of Council decreed that a Capitol should be built in Williamsburg and a town laid out, "suitable for the accomodation and entertainment of a Considerable number of persons." A College endowed by the King and the late Queen was already established there.

Williamsburg was the first planned city in the Western World. The Governor, Sir Francis Nicholson, laid out his tiny capital grandiosely. The main thoroughfare, starting at the College, proceeded with double roadways and a wide green to the Capitol, almost a mile away. In the first design, the streets beyond formed a "W" and "M," but Governor Nicholson promptly dropped the plan when King William died. He hastened to name his long street after the Duke of Gloucester, the eldest son of Queen Anne, but only partially filled in the gullies that crossed it. He was himself content with two side streets, which he named Francis and Nicholson.

As an approach to his Palace, a later governor, Spotswood, laid out a green of noble proportions, at right angles to the Duke of Gloucester Street and meeting it midway between College and Capitol. Under his administration (1710–1722), the Palace itself was completed and surrounded with intricate gardens of box, terraces, ornamental waters and all the dependencies needed to support a great house of the period. As other official buildings were added to the town, each was brought into the general and formal design.

Yet, even in its golden age, Williamsburg was a small town. A prodigious number of coaches crowded its sandy roads, but the population, including the not very numerous slaves, scarcely touched two thousand. It was the centre for the Tidewater region, whose four great muddy rivers rolled rich with tobacco toward the Chesapeake. But the planters were in Williamsburg less for business than for pleasure and politics. Taverns and ordinaries sprang up for their convenience. In 1716, a theatre, the first in America, opened its doors to them for a performance of *The Merchant of Venice*. On the King's Birth-Night, the Governor set off illuminations above the green, and on occasion four hundred guests sat down for supper under the crystal lights of the Palace. The Raleigh Tavern added the Daphne to the Apollo Room, where the young Jefferson danced half the night with his Belinda.

In 1752, James Carter was selling Fresh Drugs at The Unicorn's Horn. Some arts and crafts were practiced, but Williamsburg was not a mercantile town, nor could it have been, for it was exactly midway between rivers. All the commerce of the Virginia of that period went by waterways; English ships rode the estuaries and docked far up the James, York, Rappahannock and Potomac at private landings. The planters discouraged roads; in the first place, they were an expense, and in the second, they brought in undesirable people. As long as the Tidewater grew tobacco, the one market for the one money crop was London.

The end came abruptly in 1779, when the state government was moved westward. The American Republic had first taken shape in the speeches in the Williamsburg Capitol, in the talk of the taverns.

But the discarded capital never recovered from the victory at York-town. The decline of the surrounding plantations had begun two decades before; labor was scarce and tobacco a voracious plant. Noth-ing had been done to replenish the soil, and it was fast returning to wilderness. Soon nothing would show what the city had been but a few columned derelicts of grandeur.

Today, in contrast to five years ago, the eighteenth century is obvious on everything in Williamsburg but the clock and the calendar. Presently you begin to doubt them. From a cupola at one end of the Duke of Gloucester Street, against a blue sky flies a British flag of 1705. A counterpart of the first Capitol, completed in that year, has arisen from its foundation stones, but it may be said to rest quite as heavily on the two hundred documents that dictated the restoration. The rounded towers of rose-and-grey glazed brick look like those of an elegant fort. Within, means have been found to restore those former "capacious Apartments, so well adapted to all the weighty purposes of Government," as Governor Gooch described them after the fire of 1747. I could find nothing lacking, as far as I was able to compare rooms and records, but a Turkey-work carpet for the table in the Council Chamber and the two chamber pots which Mr. Audr. Byrd was sent to buy for the House of Burgesses. The carpet, I am told, will be supplied. Queen Anne's portrait is displayed on the walls, her arms, still quartering France, blazoned on the cupola. Curiously and appropriately, her motto is "Semper Eadem."

Gone today from the Duke of Gloucester Street the row of electric poles of five years ago, gone the concrete roadways. It was only a little over ten years ago that the city fathers decided to make the street over into a modern improved highway, which would for the first time in history run in a mathematically straight line. The taxpayers of Williamsburg sigh when they remember those perfectly straight curbstones bordered by level sidewalks, those two beautiful concrete roadways, the bonds for the building of which have not yet been amortized.

The appearance now of the Duke of Gloucester Street is that of an old gravel road, without its authentic dust and mud. A good wear-ing surface and solid foundations have been provided for motorists. The grading now wobbles as it did in Colonial times (as indicated by old tree roots). Under the Rockefeller restoration, the gullies Sir Francis Nicholson neglected to fill in at the very beginning of the eighteenth century are once more perceptible. Even the sidewalks waver as they pass watering troughs, hitching posts and mounting blocks. The lampposts, of antique design, are lighted by electricity.

I was in Williamsburg after the main buildings of the restoration had been opened to public inspection, but before the last of the old stores had disappeared from the Duke of Gloucester Street. The Campus O.K. Shoe Shop had a sign in its window that said simply "Moving." So did Lapidov, The New York Tailor. Their false Western store-fronts, painted nobody knew when a dirty brown or grey with oxblood trim, looked more than ever derelict. But beyond Colonial Street, a small white shield discreetly announced the presence of the Great Atlantic & Pacific Tea Company, and Georgian bay windows and rose brick enclosed the College Beauty Shop, the Williams Barber Shop and Rose's 5, 10 and 25 ct. Store. The three buildings in the ancient yard of the College of William and Mary, by special sanction of the state authorities, have been included in the Rockefeller scheme. Any morning now you may see the students cross their seventeenth-century campus, pass by the eighteenth-century effigy of Lord Botetourt, and enter the restoration façade of the Capitol Luncheonette to partake of an old Southern breakfast of hot dogs and Coca-Cola.

Throughout the town the worst depredations of time have been repaired, the worst accretions of modernity—which here, I take it, begins with the death of Thomas Jefferson—carted away. Three hundred and fourteen pieces of property have been acquired and corporations set up to care for them; four hundred and forty-two buildings demolished; seventeen others and the enormous portico of the First Baptist Church (circa 1850) shifted from sight; eighty-seven buildings obliterated by fire or the outrages of two conquests have been rebuilt; sixty-nine restored; twenty-five period shops cover two blocks. The one man capable of baking grey-glazed bricks by hand has been discovered. There has been no official opening of the restored city. Some smaller taverns and other buildings are still to be built on old foundation-stones; research into the town's past will continue indefinitely. But in its broad outlines, Williamsburg has probably been brought as near to its condition before 1779 as love, labor and elaborate deduction can do it. Only a native ghost would be likely to find the flaws.

The original impulse came from Dr. W. A. R. Goodwin, who first came to Williamsburg, as rector of Bruton Parish Church, in 1901. It is not without significance that his first meeting with his later patron was at a banquet of the Phi Beta Kappa Society in New York, or that it was the sesquicentennial celebration of the learned society in 1926 that first brought Mr. John D. Rockefeller, Jr., to Williamsburg, its birthplace. His consent to back Dr. Goodwin's project was not given at once. When it came, it was to prove felicitous in more ways than financial, for Mr. Rockefeller, it will be remembered, had already had considerable experience with the reconstruction of the past at Versailles.

His first care was to set up a Department of Research and Record, a Division of Archeological Investigation. Under them, the dust of Williamsburg was sifted as though it were another Pompeii. The past was brought up in a sieve, twenty-five tons of it, all material for deduction. An account of the reconstruction of the Raleigh Tavern reads like a vastly superior detective story. Forgotten foundations gave up measurements of walls. A marble fragment in the cellar bloomed, by logical processes, into the fleur-de-pêche mantel of the Apollo Room. The Venetian blinds are similar to ones known to have been sold in Williamsburg by Joshua Kendall in 1770. A broken bit of china has been turned by Wedgwood into a whole eighteenth-century set. The business ledger of Humphrey Harwood, recovered from an attic, supplied evidence for whitewashing the interior plaster walls. Import manifestoes, invoices and advertisements have brought to light not only the colors but the ingredients with which to paint other walls sea-green or fig-blue.

Even the winter holly, the yellow jasmine of spring, have to produce Colonial credentials before they are allowed to come to berry or flower. The pattern of box in the Governor's knot garden can be vouched for by the Bodelian librarian. A hundred gardens of the period in Virginia, the Carolinas and Maryland have been searched, photographed and measured, as many more have given up their neglected box trees, a mile and a quarter of them, to take root here. Over one of the Governor's gates now climbs a rose which was in the ground when Cornwallis marched unwarily into the Peninsula. But not, however, that ground.

The result is not what you might think. Not at all. Behind gates guarded by the Lion and the Unicorn, the Governor's Palace has an unexpectedly splendor. It is strangely and uncannily alive. The demands of the archeologists have given the architects a boldness and invention lacking in most reconstructions from a dead period. The stands to hold your wig in the powder-rooms, the real live nigger mammy in the kitchen to explain the antiquated culinary contraptions, are rather disturbingly quaint. The rooms smell not of orrisroot but freshly of varnish and paint. Just the same, you presently begin to feel like an Alice who has stepped, not through the looking-glass, but into a Wollaston portrait.

The most valuable document for the restoration, an unknown

Frenchman's map of 1782, was known to exist in Williamsburg, but to supplement it every possible and improbable source of information has been ransacked, from the British War Records Offices to the Vatican, from the Huntington Library in California to the great Spanish library at Seville. Not a stone, literally, has been left unturned to insure accuracy. And there are some stones that have been turned a good many times.

The Christopher Wren Building, one of the original buildings of the College of William and Mary, was the first to be restored under the Rockefeller regime. The work was almost completed when a research worker wired from the Bodelian Library at Oxford the discovery of a copper-plate engraving which showed dormer windows of a slightly different disposition. The roof was promptly ripped apart, the windows made right. Hardly were they in when somebody else ran down a letter written in 1705 by a master of the grammar school who had talked with the survivors of the first of the three fires suffered by the building. He records the escape of students and masters down a central stairway. No one had ever heard of a central stairway in Sir Christopher's design. But there it was. Out went the centre of the building and in went the stairs.

This was, of course, all very well, putting its dust preciously through a sieve, but Williamsburg is not another Pompeii. Its citizens had not been consumed. On the contrary, they were living, not a few of them, in the very houses wanted for restoration. They were quite ready to have them done over. They were not at all averse to having electric lights installed. And, as everyone confessed, it would be pleasant to see all the houses in Williamsburg painted at the same time—it had never happened before. But the citizens did not want to move. Their ancestors, in many cases, had been living in these very houses when George Mason, in his Bill of Rights, came out quite clearly for life, liberty and the right to acquire and possess property.

Dr. Goodwin quietly obtained some places in his own name. As soon as it was known that Mr. Rockefeller was in the background, a system of "life tenures" was devised. Under this, the property was bought, restored and then reconveyed to the seller for the rest of his life, with no rent and usually with no cost for repairs, taxes or insurance. Colonial Williamsburg, Inc., holds the title to all buildings whose use can be called educational, such as the Governor's Palace and the Capitol. Williamsburg Restoration, Inc., owns all others—dwellings, stores, everything for which rent can be charged. The distinction has been made, presumably, with taxes in mind. All properties bought by the Restoration are owned outright, whether subject to "life tenure" or not. Less than ten per cent of the restored area is now in private hands.

Even more difficult were the shop-owners. Demolition awaited them. There is one man whose father and grandfather kept a little store just where he is keeping it today. Why should he sell out to Mr. Rockefeller? He has always lived there. He doesn't want to move. And he seems to have no desire to become rich. Granted he has been offered twice what the place is worth—what is that to him? And if you ask his opinion, he prefers the Duke of Gloucester Street the way it was before the gravel and before the concrete—with six inches of dust in drought and six inches of mud after rain. He is still holding out. But at last account he was planning a private restoration of his own. The Western front of his store is coming off; he will restore the gable of 1800. The Williamsburgers will tell you that he belongs to a disgruntled minority.

Williamsburg is the most ambitious attempt yet made to re-create the American past. All that research can do has been done. The aim of the restoration has been not simply to furbish up an old town but to restore the actual life of eighteenth-century Virginia. As to how successful this has been, I can answer for only one person. I believe I understand the Colonial planters the better for Mr. Rockefeller's effort. They represented a complicated and amiable culture. The rich retained an aristocratic sense of responsibility toward society. Not many were poor, none were hungry. It was a culture that lacked, as far as I can make out, only two things to make it completely satisfactory—leaven for the spirit, fertilizer for the fields. As for the planters themselves, there is but one place in Williamsburg where they can be found. In the walled yard of Bruton Parish Church, their armigerous tombs, and those of their always more numerous consorts, preserve the only authentic eighteenth century. They have not been restored.

The New Yorker: January 11, 1936

NEWPORT AND THE ROBBER BARONESSES

THE SEASON at Newport runs through July and August; in summer the colony is in occupation. Then the streets of the old town have a forsaken air. Here and there they show a faded and forgotten elegance; in the midst of maritime sordidness, an old Market House, yellow brick with pilasters of a dubious white. The waterfront is animated; three Yacht Clubs are open; the harbor is filled with pleasure-craft. Occasionally in summer the navy appears in force and half a hundred or more battleships, cruisers, destroyers and base-ships lie at anchor in the wider water of Narragansett Bay. Crowds come for the yacht races; the International Yacht Race two years ago dropped three million dollars into Newport pockets. Thames Street is long and there are hang-outs for sailors; every alley leads to a wharf.

But as the old town rises from the bay, it seems rather like something remembered than something that actually exists. In these steep streets is a recollection of a period of native affluence. On the highest ground of the ridge, in a shade of fern-leaf beech and half-concealed under a coat of drab paint, is a small domed structure with a portico in the purest classical style. This is the Redwood Library, the successor to that Philosophical Society which Bishop Berkeley promoted here and the last outpost that can be said to belong to the town. The Casino announces the summer resort. Rhode Island narrows and the colony begins.

It extends on both sides of Bellevue Avenue, increasing in ostentation as it approaches the sea. Every cottage (that name is a last concession to modesty) is the rival, prodigiously rich, of every other. The island before it comes to an end spreads out in broad promontories. The colony spreads with it, covering all the cliffs to the south, until the rocks stand over the Atlantic.

Roughly, the colony has the shape of a blunt-toed shoe, kicking backward toward Newport Beach, where the populace is allowed to bathe. Bailey's Beach is under the heel and naturally protected by it.

418

But in the season it is even more strictly kept by a guard in gold-braided uniform.

Newport is to New England what Charleston is to the South. Both are ports that have lost most of their commerce; their strategic position remains to attract the navy. In both, the period of native wealth goes gack to the eighteenth century. Charleston before the Revolution was the richest city in the two Americas north of Lima; Newport acquired wealth, leisure and the comforts of philosophy on the good old triangular trade, whose other two points were in the Caribbean and on the West Coast of Africa, and whose three sides were molasses, rum and Negroes. Molasses from Jamaica was discharged on the Long Wharf and promptly distilled to New England rum. The rum went out again, shiploads of casks, to be exchanged on the African coast for even more tightly packed cargoes of slaves. The blacks, or as many of them as survived the rigors of the Middle Passage, were sold in the West Indies. More molasses was picked up on the way home, and the traffic went on. The profits were prodigious. The foreign trade of Newport surpassed that of New York. The social prestige of the shipowners was recognized through the colonies.

Newport is in Rhode Island and hence in New England. But it long ago turned its back on both and looked south.

The coast is rockbound and not stern; the cliffs are broken in many places to include beaches. The surrounding waters are brilliantly blue, the winds are blown from the Gulf Stream, the climate is salubrious and mild. Early in the eighteenth century, the Southerners discovered Newport as a summer resort.

The English planters of Jamaica and Antigua sent their families here to escape the heat of the tropics and the deadly malarial fevers. The South Carolinians came and found their own rhododendrons growing wild and, across the bay in South County, plantations worked like their own with slaves. The social customs were much like those they had left behind. Newport was worldly and tolerant. The town was founded by Antinomians, whose sect should have been a convenient one for a slave-trader, for it discredited the moral law as a means to salvation. But most of the shipowners with wealth were comfortably ensconced in the Anglican faith. The Charlestonians were as much at home in Trinity Church as they would have been in their own Saint Michael's; the interior was somewhat austere, but each of the pews was enclosed like a gentleman's closet for meditation. And here, as in their own city, visitors from Charleston might have found a learned and honored colony of Spanish and Portuguese Jews. The Enlightenment was not unknown here. The arts were cultivated, and at least two artists of some distinction produced: Gilbert Stuart, the painter, and Peter Harrison, in point of time the first of American architects.

Newport, like Charleston, was occupied by British troops during the Revolution. A thousand houses were destroyed, and half the population departed. Then came the French occupation.

Today in Newport, as in South Carolina, there are old families who live diminished in most things, but not in pride. They have had to live in the presence of great wealth, not theirs. The Newporter is less romantic than the Charlestonian. Still the two understand each other perfectly. Only here in this colder air the wistfulness of Charleston turns to reserve.

The Revolution stopped the trade of Newport. After 1808, the traffic in slaves was forbidden and passed to Bristol. Newport had always been more scrupulous than her neighbors about smuggling; most of her sailors now went into the navy. All New England knew hard times as a result of the War of 1812, and the long depression of the 1820's followed. From 1815 to 1828, not a house was built between Brenton's Point and Coddington Cove. Newport was ruined.

Then someone had the idea of opening a boarding-house to attract summer visitors. It was successful, and presently there were others, each a little more pretentious than the last. The Brimley House changed its name to the Bellevue, and what had been Jew Street became Bellevue Avenue. Captain Hazard added a tea-house to the Perry House and as a particular attraction set bath-houses on wheels along the beach at Easton's Point. Then two native Rhode Islanders, who had sojourned for a while in New York, returned with some very interesting notions of promoting Newport as a watering place. The whole country was fulfilling the promises of Jacksonian democracy in the terms of land speculation. Newporters altered their old houses to suit newcomers and moved out. The farmers began converting their fields into summer estates.

But the story of Newport as a summer capital of New York society does not begin until Mrs. August Belmont deserted Staten Island and, returning to her native town, built By-the-Sea. This was the first of the great estates, with an entrance on Bellevue Avenue and an outlook across the cliffs toward the ocean. To one side of the big frame-house was adjoined a porte-cochère; the roof pointed toward heaven from every peak with fancy lightning-rods. Mrs. Belmont's coming was a portent. For in her own imposing person she united the three elements out of which a rich summer colony at Newport could be precipitated. She was the daughter of Commodore Matthew Perry, who had opened Japan and given the old sea-port a brief hope that its foreign trade might revive. She belonged, therefore, to one of the patrician families of Newport, and it was in the name of Newport that she passed on all arrivals in the summer colony. Behind her, too, was one of the most distinguished traditions of the American navy, and she was prepared to carry the prowess of the Perrys on the high seas into high society. Her commands were issued as from a quarter-deck. And no one got by unless she approved of them. Among other things, she insisted that the navy must have its social due. And to this day, the officers from the Naval War College and the Naval Training Station have the entrance to Bellevue Avenue and dominate what is left of Newport socially in the winter. Most important of all, Mrs. Belmont represented New York money.

The Charleston influence, which had lasted through the 1850's, was done for. It was not competitive. But after the Civil War, competition was something more than the life of trade. It was the principle of life. The American continent was conceived as one vast grab-bag; the grabbing was wild, the prizes were supposed to be endless. Anyone, so it appeared, might come out with a railroad, a silver mine or a couple of dozen congressmen; they might not seem worth holding, but you had only to apply a little pressure and they dropped into your hand the richest resources of the country. A society whose wealth was based on a waste of its natural resources could hardly object to a Society whose aim was a proud wastefulness. The Gilded Age had begun. Newport was to be its bright particular spangle.

It is now the thing to call the men who dominated that age the Robber Barons, as though they were a predatory race apart from the smaller more scrupulous men on whom they preyed. Unfortunately for us, all their traits are American. What they represented was the final culmination of the old squatter ideal, which had belonged to America since the first frontier was crossed. They had simply staked out the biggest claims and were ready to hold them against all comers, including the government. They were what every man on the make—and in the Gilded Age, what American wasn't?—would wish to be. To call them the Robber Barons is unwittingly to play their game. Though there was not one of them who, to begin with, looked like old Giovanni of the Black Band, they presently began seeing themselves as Medicean. It needed time to improve the resemblance. It took almost twenty years, even in the imagination, to transform these magnified squatters into Magnificoes.

It was a game, playing at Kings and Queens. Since males were not very conspicuous in the summer colony at Newport, it here resolved itself into playing at Queens. At one time, there were four, as in a pack of cards: Mrs. Stuyvesant Fish, Mrs. Astor, Mrs. Herman Oelrichs, Mrs. Oliver Belmont. This being America, it was, like all games, played very hard. A game familiar to most children, it was played with the complete mercilessness which children are only too apt to display, but with an extravagance of which a child could only dream.

Along Bellevue Avenue can be found almost as many châteaux as in the whole valley of the Loire. Sometimes they imitate with a certain chilliness the voluptuous architecture of the Valois. But at Newport there is no French reign neglected, from Francois I through Louis XVI. (The Oliver Belmonts were the most antiquated, being Gothic à la Musée de Cluny.) Nor are any of the provinces of the French crown overlooked: turrets of Normandy look down on the flat roofs of Provence; and across the next hedge lies Italy. The Breakers resembles one of those palaces which Italian architects built in the late seventeenth century for German princelings. Obviously, no architecture has much meaning that is not wedded to the landscape, as the Wittelsbachs knew and apparently the Vanderbilts did not, for here one looks in vain for the baroque gardens, the interminable perspectives of clipped yews and statues, the long basins of water that melt into the horizon. The Breakers is loot, stuck on a cliff. A short lawn runs straight to the Rhode Island rocks and thence to the sea. The last point in the game of playing Queen came in the imitation of a Queen's playing: at Newport, as at Versailles, there is a miniature Swiss Village.

Newport was a summer capital. A seaside resort could be more strictly controlled than a great city like New York. And here society's high command laid out the winter campaigns, sitting in open conclave on the Casino terrace, white gloves to the elbow, with parasols and enormous flopping feather hats, lace at the wrists and throats. Laces dragged behind them when they rose. Battles were prepared that would not be actively fought for months. In the evening, intent on strategy, down the great staircases the petticoats trailed, circled with cupids strumming lyres of pure gold, embroidered in true-love knots and seed-pearl doves. It was still August, but the snobbish massacres of December had already been decided.

If you could get by at Newport, you were quite sure of New York. But how? That is a question which must have puzzled a good many who had spent a vast amount of time on it, not to speak of pouring out the money. Money was almost a requisite, but money alone was not enough. Horses could carry some quite a way. But as far as one can make out at this late date, nothing counted more than the ability to entertain lavishly and well. That, of course, meant no mean outlay. It was nothing at Newport to set aside $200,000 for the season, and if you were not quite sure of yourself, it was wise to add $100,000 more. The plate must be of gold, the wines irreproachable, the butler ducal and the cook acquired from some prince's household. Ultimately, whether you got in or not depended upon one or another of the Queens, and their decisions, like those of Queen Elizabeth, seem to have depended half the time on nothing but whim.

You were taken up and that settled it. Or you were dropped and left Newport. There was a saying that if you could bathe at Bailey's Beach, you could swim anywhere in society. Once passed by the gold-braided gateman there and you had the privilege, denied to the vulgar, of seeing Mrs. Oliver Belmont go down to the sea in a full-skirted bathing-costume and a large green umbrella, Mr. Van Alen in the surf, complete with monocle and a white straw hat, or, stretched on the sands, the legs of Mr. Harry Lehr, which were said to surpass any chorus girl's. With this privilege, you had arrived.

But not unless you were close to the high command could you afford to be rude. To be really in was to be very sure of yourself and there was but one way to show it. To be supremely sure was to be superbly ill-mannered. Proust's friend, Robert de Montesquiou, found Mrs. Astor "nonchalante et froide." But those who terrified everyone else had their own tyrants to endure; even the most intrepid had one place where they were afraid. That was the butler's pantry. Those English servants had the most dreadful eyes and never missed a breach of etiquette. "Just as you wish, Madame," Morton would say to Mrs. Fish, "but I assure you it is not done in the best English households." Morton (for an account of whose habits I am indebted to Mrs. Harry Lehr) was not the only one who had acquired, "through much aristocratic service, a fine taste in wines." He was uncommonly drunk one day and sassed his mistress through a lunch that he thought too large. He was dismissed. But before he left, knowing that Mrs. Fish was giving a formal party the following evening, he sat down on the pantry floor and unscrewed the entire gold service. It took two men from Tiffany's, hastily summoned by telegraph, to put it together again.

It was magnificent foolery which should have taken in nobody. But Russian Grand Dukes were impressed by the lavishness of the outlay at Newport, and throughout the Gilded Age there were

Americans who succumbed to their own pretenses. Buckingham Palace was imitated at Elm Court. It is true, however, that no one at Newport ever went quite so far as Mr. Robert W. Garret, at one time President of the Baltimore and Ohio Railroad, and later, so he thought, the Prince of Wales. His house had to be kept filled with supers to represent court officials, gentlemen-in-waiting, ministers, ambassadors. An expert from London regulated the correctness of all this mad procedure, as well as passing on details of costume and regimental uniforms. Mr. Garret once wore the full regalia of a British Field Marshal to receive Harry Lehr, which he did standing, under the impression that it was the German Crown Prince who was calling. Lehr, to keep things going, spoke with a German accent. Mr. Garret eventually departed for a realm where princes and commoners meet in silent equality, and it was only then that his wife, sanely remarried, arrived in Newport to become a part of the summer colony. But he might have served as a dangerous example.

Newport was touched with a common madness. Children are seldom, and then only briefly, persuaded by their own pretenses; and there are times when the cottagers appeared terribly like irresponsible children. They wanted to be amused. The dinner at Mrs. Stuyvesant Fish's when the guest of honor turned out to be a monkey in tails, is sinister until you remember that bringing a monkey to the table is just the sort of thing to delight the humor of a child. Mrs. Fish was not a child. But it may be that simply because they were Americans, the dowagers of Newport could only think of amusement in childish terms. Playing at royalty was fun for a while, but it soon got to be an appalling bore. That was where Ward MacAllister and Harry Lehr came in. They could always think of something new to do.

Both were Southern. Ward MacAllister had spent his summers as a boy at Newport. He had flown kites over that deep chasm in the rocks called Purgatory; he had occasionally been indulged with a picnic at Paradise. When, as a man, he returned to become a member of Mrs. Belmont's colony, he revived these wild dissipations of the ten-year-old. He bought a farm and there gave a barn dance, with sheaves of wheat and stacks of corn in the background, pumpkins hanging gaily from the rafters. Everybody romped till midnight. Mrs. Belmont had to abandon her dinners and give barn dances. Mr. MacAllister at once advanced to a clambake. Not even the rain could spoil it, for the host promptly produced from hampers enough Shaker capes to cover all the ladies. He gave picnics on the rocks, picnics on boats. When these palled, he had the table laid in his garden at Bayside Farm; dinner was served at six o'clock, and there were favors for every one of the guests. He was also fond of phaetons, when driven by pretty girls, with stiff footmen beside them.

Ward MacAllister was a serious snob; his spare moments he devoted to books on heraldry and ceremonial. He could always be counted on for an off-hand opinion on court customs. He had a grave face and cultivated an appearance of Napoleon III. Harry Lehr saw Ludwig II as his spiritual counterpart. But he looked nothing at all like the Bavarian; his photographs show him as being very much like a Gibson man carved out of a potato.

He took up, as he said, where Ward MacAllister left off. Extravagance greatly increased. Lehr loved luxury as only those can who have known poverty in youth. There were no barn dances now, but Harvest Festivals. There were *Fêtes des Roses*, with the guests walking under showers of roses, among walls entirely hung with crimson roses. But still the guests had to be amused. So when the last rose had fallen and been kicked underfoot, the next thing was a rowdy imitation of Coney Island. There were dinners of two hundred covers, with a footman behind every four chairs, followed by coconut-shies, rifle-ranges and tents with fortune-tellers. There were cotillion dinners, all the favors set with jewels; garden fêtes which concluded with vaudeville performances. There was a ball surrounded by a circus, complete with freaks, peanuts and pink lemonade. Lehr contributed laughter, a little too high, but still laughter, and that was the one thing, apparently, which Newport could not buy. He made, it is said, every woman he talked to feel at her most attractive. Attractive, one wonders, to whom? Over Lehr's bed was hung a portrait of the wasp-waisted Duc de Loyeuse, mignon of Henry III. Lehr amused Newport.

But the curious thing is that whenever Newport was out to be amused, it turned American. No matter how much money was spent, no matter how magnificent the service, Newport always ended up doing what any common Americans would have done.

When, a few years before the war, the Lehrs went to Paris to live, the glitter was gone from the Gilded Age. Then, a short time after the war, Lehr suddenly began to resemble his Ludwig II: his mind was impaired. Before he died, Elsa Maxwell had taken up where he left off. But her place was not at Newport. Another generation had discovered other Casinos than the one on Bellevue Avenue and had deserted Bailey's Beach for more attractive *plages* at San Sebastián, Deauville and along the Riviera. Besides, Miss Maxwell had reversed Lehr's rôle as jester; she was teaching royalty to behave like American children.

Suddenly one turns back in admiration to the shipowners. They trafficked in human flesh, but at least they grew up. And they created on these rocky ridges a certain civilization, brief but native and something of a sport, like the fern-leaf beech, which grows nowhere but here. When they built, it was in the style of their age, yet in a manner peculiar to the shores of Narragansett Bay. Their dwellings aimed only at propriety; their public edifices aspired no higher than a substantial dignity. If they have grandeur, it is because they are right, and not because they are pretentious. It was possible for Peter Harrison to go from Newport to London and there build Blenheim House. What still stands of his work in Newport is admirably simple on the outside. The interiors are an intellectual delight. All is serene, right, and not because they are pretentious. It was possible for Peter England at its best, for their surpassing quality is that chastity which is the outcome of spiritual fastidiousness. The Atlantic did not cut America off from Europe; only the Alleghanies did. The later fortunes of Newport were really on the frontier. The wealth of the shipowners was also of the New World, but they lived naturally in the European tradition, without thinking about it one way or the other. But in the Gilded Age, Europe was lost as a tradition to be lived and had become loot to be acquired. The Newporters were at home nowhere.

1936

FALL RIVER: MILL-TOWN

FALL RIVER is probably known to most New Yorkers as the other terminal of the Fall River Line. The harbor is locked now in ice. For four days no boat has come into the frozen waters of the bay.

The city is built on a great granite ridge rising abruptly to a height above the eastern shore of the Taunton River and the harbor where it flows into Mount Hope Bay. There is, looking down, a more than winter silence on the waters. The gulls flash white in the air. But here there is no feeling of a port. Fall River is a mill-town, inescapably a mill-town, one that before the depression was the largest manufactory of cotton-goods in America. The docks but served the mills. The Fall River Line first sent its boats to New York at the behest of the Bordens and those few other families, allied to them by marriage and like them descendants of original settlers, from whom the early and powerful mill-owners were drawn. Bales of raw cotton were brought to them by water. At night the wharves were busy, while their laborers stacked high the products of their looms to be loaded on the morning boat.

From my guide-book I learn that the first Richard Borden came from England in 1635. A little later are these sentences: "The earliest conquerors of the soil have here established an unconquerable domain based on industrial force more potent and more lasting than the sword. The four million spindles of Fall River whirl at their command and are served by imported labor." *The Handbook of New England*, from which these ringing statements are taken, is dated 1921. The combination of machinery and operatives too new to the land of the free to be anything but docile could seem even then to the mill-owners, as to their eloquent spokesman, irresistible. It had worked for one hundred and ten years. Why not forever? The earliest laborers were of native stock, mostly girls; but with the print works and the power looms came weavers from Lancashire and Scotland; from 1843 on, the famine-stricken Irish; after the Civil War, French

427

Canadians. Whenever any of these had been long enough on the ground to protest their rights and to organize for resistance, as soon as the complaint became even mildly loud against reducing wages below the level of subsistence, others could always be brought in to take their places at the looms. The latest were the Portuguese from the Azores, who, after 1910, were imported by the thousands. Of course, all that time the mills were expanding, more and more labor was demanded. The older immigrants, some of them, were moving up into the middle class. But as long as there was impoverishment and overpopulation in the Old World, there could be no lack of operatives, and while they lasted, there seemed no reason why the brave new world of Fall River should not go on felicitously forever.

But you have only to be here a few hours to discover that, at least so far as the mill-workers are concerned, in Fall River the depression began in 1921. (The owners would perhaps date it from 1940.) It has lasted fifteen years. It is now only an accident of cold if the boats cannot come into the harbor. The docks are empty.

The poor creep about the streets in covering only less miserable than nakedness; their clothes have already lasted a long time; they are patched and cared for, for they must last a long time yet. The men's hair is shaggy; they do not look at you nor do their eyes avoid you; they are apparently looking at nothing. Their faces have a long custom of sadness. Although a third of the people of Fall River are on relief, you will not in the course of the day, walking its streets, see many of them. And unless you accost them, they will not speak to you. When they do, it is without complaint. It is strange in a city so large to encounter such silence.

Streets are everywhere steep. The sidewalks are covered with a snow that has melted long enough to acquire a crust of soot, and congealed again in icy shapes of footprints. From Main Street to the waterfront, the descent is precipitous.

Leave that thoroughfare at the corner where the Five and Ten Cent Store exposes its wares through the plate-glass of an Italian Renaissance façade: a block or two below, the Quequechan River issues from its passage underground. It is a small stream, yellow as stable water, as frothing over rocks it pours turbulently down a granitic chasm. These are the falling waters that gave Fall River a name. They also provided it with a destiny. On a bank of snow stands the roofless ruin of a stone-built mill.

Above the escarpment of Fall River, on an upland to the east, lies a long chain of fresh-water lakes. Fed by perennial springs and dammed, their one outlet is this stream. The whole course of the

Quequechan River is only two miles; its fall within the last half mile is a hundred and twenty-seven feet. It was the presence of this powerful mill-stream falling so close to an excellent harbor that first set going the mills along the Fall River. For a long time, it was their one source of power; steam took its place, and is now superseded by electricity. The waters of the Quequechan are used only in processing and for this purpose are carried by conduits under the town. But the mills still stand on its banks.

Cotton mills follow its course: empty brick walls, windows broken by small boys' stones. The iron gates of their yards are locked and overhung with strands of barbed wire. Side streets cut across the slope, endless silence of tenements of workless workers. In spite of inactive chimneys, in the sharp winter sunlight, the air has a taste of smoke.

At the bottom of the descent, almost at the water's edge, stands a gaunt stone belfry tower. In front of the steep roof is a clock stopped at two minutes past six; above it a flagless flagpole. The date is 1868; below the carved figures, draped across the tower, spreads a wide painted cloth: For Sale. The mill to which this tower once provided entrance has stone walls based on a sort of false arcade, simulated in low relief. The roof is crowded with red ventilators rising like great angry crested birds. A huge metal sign is swung across the sky. This was the American Printing Company. When six subsidiary mills had been added to it, all making cheap cotton goods, printing percales, it was the largest in America. When Number 2 was completed in brick, in 1889, Mr. M. C. D. Borden gave a magnificent dinner to businessmen of Fall River and New York on the *Priscilla* of the Fall River Line. As a final gesture that night, he bestowed $100,000 on the charities of his native town. The last of these mills, Number 7, was built in 1906.

Alongside the original mill are railroad-tracks. There a grinning, grizzled, rather handsome man is packing and loading discarded machinery. Within the car are steel shaftings, shored in their cases against moving. "They are going South," he says, "but I don't know where. But somewhere South. No. 7 over there I shipped to China." He grinned. No. 7 is one of the blackened brick buildings above the Quequechan. "I shipped that out before the war. It was the latest of their buildings, too. My son-in-law he told me he was motoring through Texas and saw some machinery he was sure come out of No. 5. But No. 7," he said, grinning again, "that went to China." We talk a little longer. "I'm the only man in Fall River," he says, "that's not afraid of losing his job. It's a hell of a job, out in the cold all the time. I'm out in the rain and snow. But I got work here for the next twenty years. I been shipping machinery out of here ever since before the war. And all the way to China." I can't make out what his grin implies. It may be only cold. And I look across the Taunton River at the snow-covered farms and feathery woods, soft and brown as a partridge's breast. They are remote, and not only because the river is wide; they seem, like the winter landscapes in the prints of Currier and Ives, to belong to another America that is very far away in time. Then, thinking of the great granite ridge behind me, I remember a statement out of Marx: that only sterile soils are favorable to the full development of industry.

I have often motored through Fall River, on my way elsewhere, passing through the city by that long street which without apparent irony is called Pleasant Street. It follows, more or less, the course of the now subterranean Quequechan River. Here there is every opportunity to buy cheap goods cheaply. S. Greenberg offers New and College Misfit Clothing; here there are Profit-Sharing Sales on Rubbers, Going-out-of-Business Sales, Unexpected-Notice-of-Departure Sales. Here the New York garment-makers have crept in to occupy corners of abandoned cotton-mills. It has always seemed to me the most desolate street in America. For if Fall River is an industrial city like any other in New England, it has a dark forbidding quality all its own. For one thing, there are eleven long miles of it. Nowhere else are the factories so like prisons; even from the outside, those stark granite walls appear inescapable. They oppress one like a doom, and so it is: an industrial doom, in which we are all involved, even though, as fast as the traffic will allow us, we attempt to escape from its portentous presence.

Those ledges of granite rock, over which went the slow crawl of the last continental glacier, denuding them of soil, are grimy now with a century of chimneys. The tenements of the workers form endless perspectives declining with the hills or unevenly following the course of the ridge. They are frame-houses with porches, gable-roofs, bay windows. They are like American dwellings anywhere, but for the darkness of their paint. Their walls are a dark brown with a purplish cast, more rarely a deep leaden grey. Built to contain one family to a floor, they may in Polish and Portuguese side-streets hold five.

But go to the Highlands, where the mill-owners built—along Rock Street—you will find, except for a few houses of the last decade and one or two left over from the Federal period, the same sombre hue, Their houses, too, are dark. They have more space. They have an excellent view over Mount Hope Bay. This is known as Mortgage Hill.

The house on Second Street in which Mr. Andrew Borden was so atrociously done to death while taking a nap on the parlor sofa, and his wife hacked down while changing bedclothes upstairs, still stands. No doubt it has gone down socially, but has long since recovered its gloomy chocolate-colored respectability. (It is a typical abode of the dominant class.) From the roof rises a tower like something out of a Gothic tale; the portico in front projects from one of its dusky pillars a sign: Piano Studio; the cornice is surmounted by high elaborate cast-iron ornaments. There is little space to the grounds, and there was even less before the garage, in 1892 a stable, was torn down in recent years. Between the partitions was found concealed a discolored axe, presumably the weapon of the crime, so mysteriously absent at the time of the trial of Miss Lizzie Borden for the murder of her father and stepmother. But the stains on the blade were too old; no one could say what they were. The police of Fall River still remember that crime, because on that hot August morning on which it occurred the whole force was out of town on a picnic, and they haven't dared take such a holiday since.

This is the first time I have lingered in Fall River. As I become more familiar with it, its aspect no longer appears so forbidding. I see more, but I also hear more. It may be that they are so much more alive than the city; it may be that curiosity overcomes emotion. Their fate is frightening; but these people are nothing if not calm. I talk to an old Irish dock-worker, who has come back to Massachusetts in order, with his approaching seventy years, to get in on the state pension for the aged. "Then," he says, telling me of the wanderings and excitement of his young days, "I was the happiest boy alive!" I talk to a man in his late forties, whom I find waiting in the hall of the building where city relief is dispensed; he has worked for thirty years in the mills, where he was placed by his father, a French Canadian, as bobbin boy at fourteen. "To tell you the truth, I can't see any reason to go on living." I talk to a Greek restaurant-keeper, who has been in Fall River since the age of nine. "I tell you this is heaven compared to the Peloponnesus. There's plenty to eat in America. And everybody always has money. Why, even a man out of work, he always has a quarter in his pocket." I talk to mill-owners. The Fall River they have known is dying. They all know that; they do not delude themselves. They do not complain, unless against the government. What impresses me about all these people is their courage: all of them, even the mill-worker, have found a resolution to outlast despair. Things, they say quietly, are better than they were a year ago.

Of the one hundred and ten mills which were in operation fifteen years ago, Fall River has already lost half; five of these were closed only last year. In 1921, its population consisted of 26,000 Americans, most of whom are still here; but of the 107,000 who at that time were still considered foreign (though some of them had been in this country more than two generations), there remain 26,000 French Canadians, 23,000 Portuguese, 18,000 British, 9,000 Irish, 6,000 Poles, 2,000 Italians. Once the mills of Fall River employed 25,000 operatives; now they employ 10,000.

The making of textiles remains the largest single industry in New England. If Fall River has suffered more than most industrial towns in this region, it is simply because it was committed almost entirely to the manufacture of cotton-goods. Its history is a history of that industry; its faults are those inherent in a method of production that must continually expand. Thus, it would seem to be a complete vindication of the correctness of the analysis which Marx made of capitalistic production in the middle of the last century, in so far as Marx's conclusions are based on what he had actually seen and learned, and are not an attempt to pull from the machine that most remarkable of all gods, which he called historic necessity.

Fall River was during its great period devoted to the making of cotton-goods of the cheaper sort. (Finer prints were made in New Bedford.) These goods could only be made and profitably put on the market if labor costs were held to the lowest possible level. The war advanced wages artificially; even before the war, the South was beginning to industrialize, and this at a time when the industry had already reached the desirable limits of expansion. It was not, however, until 1924 that Southern competition was disastrously felt; because of climatic conditions, the mill-worker in South Carolina could be kept alive more cheaply than he could on the cold barren ridge over Mount Hope Bay. And since the South was in an earlier stage of industrialization, the workers could be exploited there as they no longer were in Massachusetts. From the standpoint of the mill-owners, who must sell their products profitably or go under, there was overproduction. One third of the spindles in America could be destroyed and the market could still be supplied. Inexorably, it is in New England that these spindles are being destroyed or stilled. Besides, there has now appeared in the market in which Fall River must sell, the Japanese competitor who can buy cotton from Brazil more cheaply than anybody can buy American cotton with its price artificially raised, and whose labor is cheaper even than the hills of Tennessee can supply. The mills that survive in Fall River now make fine or semi-fine fabrics, taking advantage of the superior skill of their operatives; and have improved their technical processes. That has, of course, led to some technological unemployment. Within the last fifteen years, one out of four weavers has been rendered superfluous; in other crafts, the displacement is not so great.

Putting it simply, Fall River represents a phase of industrialism that has passed, but whose passing is accompanied by great human agony; it can also show instances of that later form of industrial production which Mr. Lewis Mumford calls neotechnic and from whose appearance in this world he derives great hope. I wish Mr. Mumford well. But I do not ask him to go to Fall River. It is true that the neotechnic machines are lodged in paleotechnic walls. In others words, the new automatic machines inhabit the same old mills. And the mills still look like prisons, though very clean prisons, with gay red-lead fire-escapes. Ventilation and light are alike artificial; the old windows are still there but the common light of day is subdued by white blinds and an even white radiance of electricity prevails. Each room has its humidity regulated automatically, but both temperature and the degree of moisture are determined by the needs of the yarn and not by those of the workers. These, to be sure, are few.

You may see bales of raw cotton brought in, cleaned of all the waste the gin has left behind, nits, seeds, bits of leaf—the lint eliminated; the cotton separated according to length of fibre to within one sixteenth of an inch. You may see cotton from different sources doubled—that is to say, mixed to insure evenness of grade; rolled into "laps"; taken from the picker by cards; combed and the last waste brushed off the combs; emerge as a broad filmy "web"; rolled through a trumpet into slivers; again doubled; the fibres, now all of one length, laid parallel by the drawing frame; put through the intricate process known as roving, which is essentially one of attenuating and twisting the fibres into a fragile yarn. You may see this yarn again twisted until the requisite strength is attained, then wound on spools and dressed with a "size" of potato starch and Japanese wax; then spread into sheets and wound on beams; drawn into the harness of the looms (the harnesses control the movement of the warp-yarn, while the shuttle throws the fill-yarn across; the weave will be more or less complicated, according to the number of harnesses); finally, woven into a fabric. All this takes place with scarcely the touch of a hand unless the yarn breaks. (I believe the latest machines actually repair breaks in the thread; but these I have not seen in Fall River, and I am told they are not in use here.) The operatives do not, the most of them, work; they tend the machines to see that *they* work. In the long process, there is still some human intervention; the machines are not perfect; nor are they as pretty as their photographs. But it is quite possible to look the entire length of the weaving-rooms, down rows of automatic looms, all throwing their shuttles across the warp, all weaving like mad, and not see a man anywhere. No, nor woman either, as Hamlet remarked on a different occasion.

What these machines portend, I do not pretend to say. I only know that, in the yard of this very mill, all day the unemployed wait. I know that all around is Fall River, and that there the old ghosts of mill-owners are lively yet: Holder Borden, who discovered the speed-up when he saw, in 1827, that if the boys, at twenty-five cents, carried the usual eleven o'clock drink of rum to the male weavers, who were worth a dollar fifteen, instead of allowing the men to leave their looms and come and get it, the mill would make money; Philip Borden, who, not content with being at his mill with the workers from 6 A.M., made a practice of peeping in between 9 P.M. and 3 A.M. to see what the night-shift was doing. I think I had better leave the last word on them to my good friend who keeps the Bijou Restaurant. He said it in Greek. "What is that?" I asked. "It's an Athenian proverb. It means, They accomplished and they fell."   1936 or 1937

WORLD'S FAIR NOTES

I

ENTER THE WORLD'S FAIR from your train, and alongside and aloft are banners: *Science* is inscribed on a deep blue field, the sun scattering red and orange rays, while yellow stars shine on an orange earth, washed by exactly three blue waves; *Art* is not named, but shows on a pale blue ground a composition in the manner of Picasso around 1920, the cutout profile of a woman combined with palette, columns and T-square. All are crudely brilliant. The crowd moves over the wide wooden floor. If under the flags, close to the railing, you stop to look down, you will see a remnant of the original marsh, thick slime and green springing grass, from which all else has been at one time redeemed. "From Dumps to Glory" is the phrase of the guide-book.

Before me lies the World of Tomorrow.

The World of Tomorrow is in sunlight. It looks very gay, if only temporarily gay. It is indeed temporary, and perhaps that is why it looks so gay. Gay, certainly, is the Fountain of the Atom, which stands at the entrance to the Fair, the first of innumerable fountains. The shaft of structural glass that rises from the center is green, and green, too, seems the water that plays over it and splashes the surrounding ceramic creatures.. Those standing can be taken as the four elements of antiquity: a winged armless youth for fire, and three maidens, green, maroon, blue and terra-cotta for the others. Below, about the basin are the spirits of modern energy, children in shape, but most preciously endowed, as anyone can see, the boys amazingly alert, the girls happily cavorting in their separate play. It is all very gay, in an innocent way. But I suppose if you want to look for it, there is instruction even in the fountain. There is in most things at the Fair. But not all of them are so gay. Not all of them are so innocent.

At first glance the city before you seems to have been contrived of nothing more solid than paper. Only on closer approach is it seen that the World of Tomorrow, constructed on steel, has a surface of stucco. Many of the walls are blank. Monotony has been avoided by a carefully considered scheme of color, imposed upon all contributors to the Fair, beginning with the Trylon and Perisphere at the center, which alone are pure white, and spreading outward, deepening as it goes. On Constitution Mall, for instance, the color used turns from rose to dark burgundy. The background, however, remains throughout one or another off-white, which is further varied by murals and by sculptural groups of white plaster, which stand out at night from an illumination like a haze of gold. And the continuous stretch of stucco is altered and accented by other structural materials, marble and metals—aluminum, stainless steel and chromium—and glass. Glass is more often than not used to reflect light, rather than to admit it—for that would have meant a loss of wall-space within the buildings as well as an increase of heat in summer.

Except in the division set apart for the States, no traditional architecture has been permitted. All the other buildings may be alleged to be functional in character, but since the only function of a building at a fair is to contain exhibits, the word here has a meaning that is frequently nothing short of fantastical. The Hall of Marine Transportation rises from what was once the Flushing Meadows like the prow of an ocean liner from the shallow sea. The Aviation Building, perhaps inevitably, took on the shape of a hangar. But these are exceptions. Not many of the architects have so confused functionalism with symbolism. Some of the symbols at the Fair are pretty odd, and some are pretty silly, like those two structures which rise from the Communication Center and which, I am told, represent the positive and negative charges of electricity. Their shape, I suppose, has been suggested by electrodes, but actually they look like nothing so much as two elongated box-kites, covered with red and white striped paper and set on end. If they have a function, it is simply to be tall.

Such accents are necessary in a fair whose buildings as a whole have been deliberately kept low. Some of them are certainly no part of the general design. Roma sits against the sky, a helmeted goddess of marble, holding her spear and orb, above the Italian pavilion. By some chance, I always seemed to be seeing her through a waving row of British flags. The Soviet Worker is also very tall; he is almost too tall, and he is certainly too big for the shaft that sustains him above the U.S.S.R. pavilion. I saw him first through flags, ranged around a quadrangle, of the baseball teams in the major leagues. Not all of the contrasts at the Fair are intentional. Some of the happiest are not.

Whether the architecture of the World's Fair will have the lasting effect on Americans that the classic buildings of the Chicago Fair of 1893 had on their fathers cannot be now determined. It cannot but affect their sensibilities, and in the long run it will probably make the International Style more acceptable to them. That style was first made available to the public at the Exposition of Decorative Arts in Paris in 1925; it was carried out with greater competence at the Paris Exposition of 1937. The New York World's Fair has not the originality of the one nor is it quite as achieved as the other. But it will probably do more than either to spread a method of building which has developed not without logic from providing a habitation for the machine to preparing proper housing for man. The World's Fair is really the work of engineers—and so is modern architecture—but of engineers who have acquired an artistic conscience that does not always counsel them well. The closer this art to pure engineering, the finer its forms. So that I cannot but suspect it is not architecture at all. It is more than a matter of nomenclature. At the same time it must be admitted that a fine piece of engineering, such as the General Motors Building, is infinitely to be preferred to the dead imitation of what was once a fine art.

II

Officially, the World's Fair was planned to celebrate the one hundred and fiftieth anniversary of George Washington's inauguration as first President of the United States in the City of New York. The date was convenient. But the sponsors could have found some other historical event to commemorate if they had had to.

A statue of Washington stands at the head of Constitution Mall, looking toward the Lagoon of Nations and beyond to the foreign pavilions and at last to another Federal Hall, erected by the government he founded. He is on the grand scale, his proportions heroic, his substance plaster. He is on much too grand a scale for his surroundings. He disturbs the statues in the basin before him, delightful and moving figures who skim the water beneath them. He is clothed as they are not. Never before have so many charming and completely naked creatures of sculpture been offered to the American sight. It is possible to measure by the forgotten fig-leaves the distance we have come since 1893, when the Chicago Fair exposed its own Greek slave of Hiram Powers; to say nothing of the distance from 1789.

Washington's place is before the Trylon and the Perisphere. They are supposed to mean something. And, as almost anyone will point out to you, they are sexual symbols. The Perisphere is a huge globe, its white surface already streaked by rain; it contains within its shell a panorama in miniature of some imaginary city of the future, which is reached by the longest escalator in the world. The Trylon is a three-sided obelisk. Whatever it was intended to look like, it resembles nothing so much as an extremely attenuated Washington's Monument. That is an unconscious propriety.

The Fair takes the historical view. The spectator is constantly being asked to consider something or other à travers les ages, a way of looking which we are accustomed to think of as natural to the French but which, until recently, has been strange to Americans. The World of Tomorrow has one eye on the day before yesterday and the other on the present. Throughout there is an awareness that the political structure bequeathed to us by Washington has passed dangers, and has more to pass, from the age of power that came in with the industrial revolution. There is also the awareness of dangers that press upon us from more recent revolutions, whose aim is political power. The Fair is in no small part devoted to showing man's conquest over nature; it cannot help but show that there is a desperate contest on as to how the spoils shall be divided. Industry is on the defensive. And so is democracy. Washington stands in impressive calm. But those of us who can move about on two legs will discover in every one of the foreign pavilions before him an effort to win his (and our) favor. Behind Washington's imperturbable back are the great industrial exhibits. And there the powerful industries are engaged, no less than the foreign powers, in persuading Americans. Ford, General Motors and General Electric are spreading propaganda no less than England, Italy and the U.S.S.R. I name but three of each, but there are many more. Money has been spent and is being spent; art and science have been called to aid. It is reputed that General Motors put over five million dollars in their show, and the French no less in theirs.

III

The Union of Soviet Socialist Republics has thrown a great semi-circle of white marble about a courtyard paved with colored stones. The sweep culminates on each side in a solid block; the front of one is adorned with a disproportionate head of Stalin, the other with an equally large, equally realistic, head of Lenin. Below each is carved a bit of speech. Between these two blocks is a forecourt, beyond which rises a shaft of porphyry and Gasgan marble. There the Soviet worker in aluminum overalls holds a red star.

When I was at the Fair, only an antechamber to the Soviet pavilion was open. But a considerable propaganda was already being spread there, under the forbidding statues of Kalinin and Molotov. Copies of the new Constitution were lying about and a very jiggly little movie was being run off in daylight, showing the joy of the workers over its adoption. Their pictures were interrupted at intervals for an official declaration whose intent was to prove that the U.S.S.R. is a democracy. As propaganda it was—shall I say?—somewhat primary. It was aimed clearly at people who believe what they are told or who already believe what they are about to be officially told.

The effect of the whole is like that of a tomb, one of those impressive tombs which in almost every country after the last war were erected about an Unknown Soldier. No man is buried under the flagstones of the courtyard; and yet I am not so sure that there is not something dead there. It is a hope that lies dead.

The entrance to the Italian Pavilion is between two colonnaded porches. Rising about it, with continual setbacks, is a tower, which forms a pedestal for the statue of Roma, seated in state. Below her feet falls a sheet of water, which still falling forms stairs, then again flows in a sheet. A pool is at the base of the monument. "*L'Italie emmerdante le monde,*" was the comment of a French friend of mine, who went with me to visit the pavilion.

The impression inside is one of perfect order. Long quotations from Mussolini's speeches are on the wall, signed now simply M. The M also appears in relief, surmounted by carved eagles. And the statue of Mussolini does look like a mammoth Napoleon, but a Napoleon dressed for the Campaign. The King of Italy at the far end of the hall has his eyes popped wide open, but for some reason his stare appears blind.

There are a great many statues, some reproductions from the antique, but more from contemporary sculptors. These are all of young men and of boys approaching military age; they stand in Donatello poses, but with something added in the way of swagger, which is, I suppose, due to the suggestions of Fascism. There is a most interesting use of *collage*. Mussolini has obviously gathered together his best artists and put them to work on propaganda for his state. They have worked so well that anyone might, if he took every statement literally, come away with the notion that Mussolini had created not only modern Italy, but ancient Rome as well. However, except in the division devoted to the interests of tourists, all the statements have been left in the Italian. It seems as though all this propaganda were aimed, not at all Americans, but only at those of

Italian birth or ancestry. Perhaps the others were assumed to be immune.

The Italian Pavilion does not convey an impression of Italy, but merely of Mussolini's idea of Italy. The smell of Italy is simply not there; there is, in fact, no smell of anything human. The French Pavilion, on the other hand, is France, and quite effortlessly so. It is as though the French could do nothing else, having decided on a pavilion at the Fair, but transport thither as much of France as they could and build a French casino to hold it. For that is what their building is, a perfectly good casino, which takes full advantage of a position that, if it is not the best at the Fair, is adroitly made to seem so.

The French, of course, want our friendship. They begin by assuming that they have it, for in their propaganda they simply trace the course of the connections between France and America, from the time of the War of the American Revolution down through the War of 1914–1918. This has been done by transferring all the significant documents, treaties and so on, engravings of such men, on the one side, as Benjamin Franklin and, on the other, as Vergennes, Voltaire and Rousseau, to glass, and illuminating them. The engravings are followed at the proper time by photographs. Mallarmé and Baudelaire are exposed along with Edgar Allan Poe. Pershing is seen descending from transport to dock in France in 1917. The American troops advance at Cantigny. The method is simple, ingenious and rapid. And because it is not overdone, it is exceedingly effective.

The British Pavilion is not Great Britain, as the French casino is France. It is British in the same way a great British liner is; whatever else it carries, it will also convey a sense of the awe and majesty of the British Empire. The British here present themselves as the creators of our own liberties: an authentic Magna Carta is shown, as well as a great many other documents which carry the history of political freedom and protection of individual rights. The two arts upon which they have most relied to put themselves over on Americans are the art of the court painter—there is a Coronation of King George VI—and, of all things, the art of heraldry. For the British do not forget their own former greatness. If it is surprising to find whole walls blazoned with coats-of-arms, it is somewhat disarming to discover that they are not, after the Middle Ages, those of great nobles, but those of truly great men. And, for whatever it is worth to Americans, the lineage of our own George Washington has been traced from King John and from nine of the barons whose signatures are on Magna Carta.

After all these pavilions of nations who want nothing of us but love and admiration, it is rather a shock to enter the Swedish Pavilion and find it frankly commercial. The Swedes, apparently, do not expect to have to fight, and, if they do, they do not expect us to defend them. They have things to sell. But among them is not, so far as I could make out, the Swedish way of life. They make mention of it, in their pavilion, but they make no exaggerated claims for it. They also show some enlarged photographs of young Swedes on the outside, which makes the walls look like billboards. Their pavilion is comfortable and apparently a great commercial success. Like most things which are designed only for comfort and commerce it is very, very ugly.

IV

Art has been put to the uses of propaganda at the Fair to an extent which I can only barely indicate. It proves most effective the closer it approaches, at least in method, the work of those artists in our time who have been truly creators. Mussolini's compositions of disparate photographs pasted together are good, not because of what he has to say, but because whoever did them learned his *collage* in a good school and because, as Jean Cocteau long ago showed, classical materials lend themselves admirably to *collage*. The Soviet Worker is bad, not because of what Soviet workers are, but because it is done by a sculptor badly trained in a bad tradition.

Now, it is not without interest that those paintings in Art of the United States Today which can be included under propaganda are, with one or two exceptions, poor as paintings and also poor as propaganda. Here the artists were on their own. The lithographs, wood-cuts, and drawings of social protest are frequently good.

The exhibit in the Contemporary Arts Building was brought together merely to show that painting is being done all over America and is no longer, as it once was, restricted to a few centers. It is excellently shown. But since there are some eight hundred works of art exposed there, I can make but the most general comments. One is the lack of surface in the paintings. And this must come from the fact that those destined to paint do not, when young, if they are Americans, see enough paintings. What they see, if the passion is in them, are reproductions, which can give everything about a picture but its paint. The pleasure in pigment they never know. One of the rare paintings of social protest in the show which is good is by Georg Grosz. Grosz made his reputation in Germany with line drawings, whose satire was as bitter as any that came out of the post-war decade anywhere. Only since his coming to America has he taken up oils. But there is no doubting his passion for pigment. His painting has a surface; it is unmistakably painting. And that is what most American art is not.

I do not see any inherent impossibility in an artist's taking directions from a contemporary patron. There never was in the past. But he must be able to see in the conditions laid down for him an artistic problem which he is to overcome. Let his difficulties be made for him, as once the Church laid down infinite prescriptions for the painting of each saint it ordered and in time paid for. But let the solution be his own. The trouble with art in the United States today is not that it is discouraged. It is rather that it is overencouraged and undernourished.

V

The great industries have, as princes once did, called art to their aid. The mobile mural in the Ford building should be seen, as should the gold and aluminum murals painted on black bakelite and continued in reflections on a gilded ceiling, in that room of the General Motors building where the Diesel engine is displayed and the transparent motor car, its body of plexiglas and its inner workings of chromium plate on stainless steel. But industry, which at the Fair is most consciously on the defensive, depends less on its patronage of art than on its alliance with science to persuade the public to its side. It is always possible, as in the magnification of the copper atom, that the exposition of a scientific concept, when carried out in copper and glass, will have the surprise and formal beauty of a work of art.

Industry does, of course, depend upon applications of scientific knowledge, and, in putting its case, it not only places foremost its interest in scientific discovery, but does it in such a way as to insinuate that it is no less disinterested than the research worker in the laboratory. Steinmetz Hall has been built solely to repeat one of the great inventor's experiments—that of man-made lightning. Industry, apparently, exists only to convert science to the service of mankind. There is scarcely a suggestion that anybody has anything to sell.

The Ford Exposition is there to show "the far-reaching benefits which thirty-five years of productive activity by a great industrial organization have brought to American life." In other words, it is there to instruct the public in the ideas of the founder of the company and make it accept his solution of industrial problems. The Ford

Exposition is concentrated on Henry Ford as certainly as the Italian Pavilion is centered on Benito Mussolini. It is only when you go outside and see Ford cars, yellow, pale blue and red, pretty as toys and with apparently as little purpose, running up and down the spiral ramp that has been called the Road of Tomorrow that you remember that the man has cars to sell.

The Highway and Horizons Exhibit of General Motors is quite the handsomest thing at the World's Fair. Once you enter it, you are already in the brave new world of 1960. Sink into one of those soft deep-moving chairs, with the soft insinuating voice at your ear—for every chair is wired for sound—and be carried through an artificial day and through an artificial night, as though high in air above a vast stretch of the earth's area, with towns and cities, rivers and lakes, industrial plants in full operation, forests, farms and steep snow-topped mountains, all connected by the most perfectly planned and perfectly constructed roads, and you will feel like nothing so much as one of Aldous Huxley's babies, just out of the bottle, already being conditioned for a future in which everything, including yourself, will be under the most perfect control.

VI

As I walk through the Court of States, it is clear to me that they are not here as sovereigns under one sovereignty. The political structure of many States within one State no longer corresponds to reality. They are merely geographical divisions in one country and they have nothing to offer, here at the Fair, but their natural attractions. As States, they have nothing to say. A reproduction of Independence Hall looks across a long lagoon toward a copy of Jefferson's Rotunda at the University of Virginia. In the World of Tomorrow they have been allowed to remember their past.

The States were once in the position of great nobles in regard to the King, when he was merely first among his peers. They have now sunk to the place of courtiers in an advanced monarchy, who crowd the royal palace, beggars of benefices, falling over one another for favors, each intent upon getting his share of corrupt privileges. Only in talk do they recall their past rights.

Their place in the scheme of things has been taken by the great industries. These are still powerful enough to stand opposed to the power of the Federal Government. If the Civil War was, as has been said, the second American Revolution, we are now advanced into another, which one day may well be called the Third American

Revolution. Only this is not, any more than the war in Europe, a civil war of blood but of nerves. There can be no more doubt that the industries, under the American conception of society, are in the right in 1939 than there was that the States about to secede in 1860 were, under the American Constitution, strictly within their rights. But they, like the Southern States then—or, for that matter, like the European democracies now—have great faults to pay. Here, in the World of Tomorrow, industry may be seen on the defensive. It is attempting, by every persuasion, to gain people to its side. But the real question is whether the industries have time on their side. And that can be answered only in the real world of tomorrow.

The Kenyon Review: Summer, 1939

THE SOUTH REVISITED *

I

SUPPOSE you come down the continent, as I have done, coming from Cape Cod, coming remotely from Nausset Beach, that long desolation of sand which the Atlantic has bounded with dunes, a stretch where no shell survives the incessant turmoil of the beached sea, where Thoreau once stood and declared that all America was west. West it is, America, at least in the imagination; and yet that is not the course determined. You will cross states, not as men did when they were moving gradually and impetuously from the seaboard to subdue the wilderness and ravage and settle the immensity of America. You will follow not the old trails, the irregular passages westward, but, like migrants seeking the sun, since this is the autumn season, straightways southward. However, the course is not in the air, but on concrete highways. And Delaware is still the East; but in the first small town of Maryland, the South is already there, to be seen in a street whose shade would anywhere else seem excessive, in a girl sweeping a porch, in an old negro drooping half-sleep over the board of his wagon, to which is attached a drowsy and equally immobile mule.

To cross the border is for me to proceed into the landscape of boyhood and youth. In this country I was reared, and the very smells have an air of memory; there is no other land in the world where the late summer ripens so redolently with sun, where in fall orchards dispel so rich an odor of misty fruit. The fields are rolling; the hills, instead of confining the view, lead it on through fold after fold of fading blue, increasing the distance. It is a land that has been loved, and not only by me; all that have lived here have had the feel of this earth. I talk to a blind man. It is the Blue Ridge whose sight he most regrets. "I miss just being able to ride out and look at those hills." But Tidewater Virginia is already strange, a land abandoned by time, largely despoiled by the voracity of the tobacco-plant, returning in

* This piece and the two that follow were never worked into final shape.

445

many places to a wilderness of scrub-oak and dwarf pine. And the strangeness is increased by two encounters: a chance hyena being driven in a lonely cage over a sandy road; two boys dragging a raft ashore from a small inland lake, surrounded by the degradation of a poverty-stricken settlement. They and their parents are the last of the Chickahominy Indians.

State lines are real. I suppose I had never considered this before, but I can only say that, coming south, I was struck always at the change both in land and inhabitants that confronts the traveler as soon as he goes from one political division to another. In the passage from North to South Carolina, even the sky changes, becomes more spacious, and the clouds accumulate in the high heavens with the slow dignity, with the arrogance almost, of a Charleston planter. The division is as distinct as that between the French provinces, which are still realities of contour and custom, though the first emperor long ago cut them up into convenient administrative units. Napoleon meant to complete the work of time and the kings and destroy the old historical, partially racial, groupings. He did not quite succeed. And even the Third Republic has not been able to give any but a political meaning to the departments. To pass from Virginia to North Carolina is to remember the passage from the rich country of the Lyonnais to the dull baked plains of the Dauphiné. There is another and beautiful North Carolina, but I do not see it; I am in the coastal plain. I must take Mr. Thomas Wolfe's word for the vigorous imagination, the argumentative virtues of the men of Old Catawba. The North Carolinians I see remind me only of William Byrd's account of their ancestors in the early eighteenth century. And, as I pass the thinly populated plains, the meagre cotton-patches, the poor cabins and untended garden-plots, the comparison returns to the Dauphiné, that province from which the heir to the throne might take his title, but which never seems to have belonged either to the old domain of France nor yet to Provence. That ancient kingdom comes suddenly in plane trees dappling white roads; at Montélimar we are all at once in the old Roman world. Not quite so suddenly are you in the Deep South of America; it is announced by scattered cotton-patches; you are aware of it in the first live oaks, in the swamps haunted by stilted blue herons, hanging with Spanish moss, in the rivers of burnt umber, colored by the clay. Cheraw is a prelude to Charleston, but in the old part there is first the sense of a complete accommodation of the Southerner to his climate. About the Battery is a noble architecture, double galleries the length of the house, which is presented to an enclosed garden, access to the street being through a postern door in a projecting wall. There is that ostentation of privacy amid shade which the world over belongs to hot climates.

Savannah approaches through a land as monotonous as Provence. Its early nineteenth-century squares interlinked by shaded streets revive an impression of Nîmes with its summer gardens, where Louis XV remolded in stone the balustrades above the intricate shape of the Roman pool. (Incidentally, I wonder if Mr. Lewis Mumford, who is so interested in city-planning, has ever, even on the grandiose blueprints of the future, seen anything finer as an urban conception than this part of Savannah. It is as admirable as the long streets of slipshod cribhouses, slatternly Negro slums, through which one arrives at the center, are disgraceful.) The first glimpse of the Gulf of Mexico comes as blue as the Mediterranean, though seen not through gaps of the Maritime Alps but across piney barrens. But not even that most mythical of seas could show a beach so dazzling in loveliness as that crescent of white sand and sun beyond Pensacola, outlined by dunes, so that there is no sight save toward the brilliant expanse of water, whose lucid greens deepen and waver to darkest blue, then fade under the sun to blinding azure. Marseilles is encountered at New Orleans, at least along the riverfront, a port of the extreme South opening upon an alien and still more Southern world. Cargoes and vice, the dusky and olive-skinned faces, in this case of African and Sicilian stevedore, and cranes grappling boatloads of bananas; open markets reeking with savors of the sea; drowsy and flyspecked barbershops in the hot afternoon, sinister and mechanically musical saloons at midnight, all combine to set Decatur Street in mind beside the Cannebière.

But let me not insist too strongly on this comparison, though on the road it was spontaneous. Now, it is enough to say that in every country there is a South which feels itself alien to the North. Sorrentines will tell you that Italy begins at Rome and goes north; I have known a Gascon gardener who after years in the Ile-de-France would let no one call him a Frenchman. And long after the Confederacy is lost in the national archives and the last old lady has forgotten in the grave that this was conquered territory, there will still be, regardless of the government, a deep division between the states that grow cotton and those which first manufactured it into cloth. A people are the result of race and climate, though one be mixed and the other variable in its seasons; men are the sum of their memories, the makers as well as the victims of economic systems.

The road from New England to the mouth of the Mississippi has often been taken, and it is not that great distance which I wish here again to traverse. Rather I should like to mark a little the differences between the upper South in which I was born and the Deep South into which I have come. It is for the first time. And I have but first impressions: the country is vast and varied; the very atmosphere seems more heavily saturated, just as there are evidences of greater if vanished wealth, the poor-whites poorer, the Negroes blacker and more primitive. It is with difficulty that I understand the small black street-boys of Charleston when they propose to dance for my pennies. Any morning one may awake in New Orleans to find the cook in a state of terror, having stepped over a voodoo charm left for her on the back-door sill by the laundress.

It is no longer a land of moderate contours, hills gently rolling to receive and beneficently retain the rain; but flat, with pine barrens, sandy plains, or else rank with swamps, as dense in vegetation as the prehistoric forest. Even in the soil there is that constant meridional contrast presented by poor unfertile stretches which seem about to last forever when suddenly they change into an excessive richness of alluvial deposit. It is a land where Protestantism becomes abased, belonging, as it does, as a code, to cold climates. But it also, in Louisiana, provides the rare instance in America of a country dominated by Catholicism, and not that puritanic Catholicism which here and there has been brought in by Irish peasants, but the rich and humane Catholicism of France.

Yes, the distinction is there between the Upper and Lower South—immediately sensed. I also remember a conversation with Allen Tate, in which he put it as his opinion that, even at the time of the War between the States, the latent antagonism was so strong between the two sections that, even with the Confederacy victorious, they must have broken apart into disparate and perhaps separately governed regions.

II

The difference is first one of climate. In the Virginias, four seasons with more or less accuracy quarter the year. But in Louisiana, winter is hardly more than a suspension of summer. Frost may be sure, but snow is rare, and when, once in a generation, it lies long and deep enough to mold into snowballs, little boys will carry them to school and ask the teacher to preserve them in glass. In January camellias will begin to bloom: petals so precisely whorled, so painted in color, that they recall those porcelain flowers with which the gardeners of Louis XIV pricked the parterres of the Grand Trianon to make them gay all winter long for the old age of the king.

It is to the climate that must be attributed, in no small part, the increased respect for politeness, a greater attention to formal manners. And this is as it should be: in a climate as enervating as this, where it is comparatively easy to make a mere living, there is no natural discipline to insure decency, such as is derived from Connecticut snows or the sea off Cape Cod. One simply cannot let down. Some artifice must be imposed on conduct. No characteristic of the South has been so endlessly satirized; it has been shown, not only as provincial, pretentious or silly, which it often is, but as something much worse. The planter who is such a perfect gentleman in the parlor can be a perfect reprobate once he has stepped down the stairs under the Roman portico. Where there is a supremacy of manners over morals, there is apt to be a disparity between them. And sometimes this is appalling. Long before the modern novelists, a half century indeed before Mrs. Stowe, Crèvecoeur had seen, in a swamp near Charleston, a Negro suspended in a cage, his eyes picked out by birds of prey, his cheekbones bare, left to expire of thirst and tormenting insects. The man had killed the overseer of the plantation and was confined thus to expiate his crime.

There is, then, the increased summer, the long heated air, which ripens citrus fruits, which once enriched Carolinians with indigo, which later grew and still grows cotton, rice and sugar-cane. That is, between the Upper and Lower South there is a difference in space; there is also, I suspect, a difference in time. Maryland and Virginia were settled a whole generation before the establishment of the Bank of England. Economy was a land economy; it could be nothing else. Though the Virginia planters were quick to discover that they had in tobacco what today must be called a money-crop, since their accumulations made them the first capitalists in the country, nevertheless it also happens to be well known that even the richest of them seldom had the feel of money in their hands. Credit, I dare say, there was; but I have never come across any such instances of its abuse.

The tale of cotton has been so often told that there may seem to be little to add to it. Nevertheless, in enforcing the contrast between the Upper and Lower South, I may perhaps be permitted one or two comments on it. The holdings in the border states were always comparatively small: Mr. Wertenbaker has made it clear that even in the seventeenth century the great landlords were few. Virginia society had as models the English country gentleman and the yeoman (who, though then dwindling in his native land, thought to revive his estate in the new). Possibly the Scotch crofter should be included. The land had to be fought for before it was cleared, it was sometimes paid for in personal blood, often in money; sometimes it was granted for military services. Often, of course, it was sold. But the possibilities of credit, the continual American curse, were limited. And the land was there to be lived on, once acquired, and hence conserved; only later was its profit considered. There was, to be sure, a money-crop, and the first in America; but tobacco which created the Tidewater aristocracy (as well as a good many smaller people) at length despoiled the land and destroyed its owners.

These things are, of course, relative; but I think in general it is true that the planters of the Lower South lived on a far grander scale than anything that the Peninsula or the Piedmont could show. Their lands became immense domains, whose crop, whether cotton, rice or cane, could be—in fact, must be—turned into money, whether coin or credit. Where had they come from, these vast estates? Well, I think that almost the first glance reveals that, so large, so magnificently dominated, they came out of the tills of banks, out of the money-drawers of lenders. Swamps went down before credit, forests were felled by speculators; cotton and blacks amazingly spread over territory lately and forcibly deserted by the Cherokee.

That is certainly one of the distinctions between the border states and those of the Gulf. These were settled much later, and in that time the possibilities of credit had been continually enlarged. To be sure, there is something in the bright and optimistic air of the continent that abuses confidence and lightheartedly mortgages the future. Did not the town of Plymouth find itself at the end of King Philip's War pledged for an amount more than double the total holdings of the colony? Commodities were exchanged; tobacco-leaf was shipped to England, useful and luxurious objects returned, minus the factor's double commission.

In Louisiana, the beginnings seem to have been very much the same: the wild swamp had to be cleared before it could be settled, the pine tree felled. Grants from the government, royal or colonial, often had still to be paid for in blood until the Indians were dispelled. The Creole plantations along the river were modest and conservative undertakings. But by the time the Americans came in, the way was clear for money. Royal Street was lined with banks, and out of their tills came forth bills of sale from the earlier owners, titles to vast domains, possibly uncleared but soon to be cultivated; from the cashiers' caged windows were shoved out boatloads of darkies, buck niggers and corn-fed negresses, machines perfected in Africa for use in this sun, and capable, amazingly, of reproducing themselves in all their parts. We are now in the nineteenth century. No longer is the land there to be lived on (with profit a later, if perfectly proper, consideration), to be used, but also to be conserved as a form of wealth more nearly permanent than any other. No, the age is one of speculation. Gamblers are not all on the river, nor, at Natchez, under the hill. The plantations on both sides of the Mississippi changed hands, passing into money and back again; there was as yet no boll weevil, the wilful degeneration of the sugar-cane was not evident until very late in the period; credit was easy to come at, and so were markets.

Possibly I exaggerate; there was more attempt at permanence in the Lower South, more movement in the Upper, than I have allowed for in this contrast. Tidewater Virginia was early worn out; even before the war there were efforts made in the warmer states toward a more varied agriculture. Still, the point is there: the Lower South was soon committed to a capitalist agriculture. Its economy is based still on the money-crop. How disastrous this has with time proved, readers of a recent symposium, *Culture in the South*, will know. Failing that book, they may, of course, read the daily papers.

III

The culture of the Deep South after 1830 was, I am convinced, far more commercial than it is commonly credited with being. The plantation was dependent upon this factor. And this, along with first the presence, and then the recollection and débris of slavery, which seems to have numbed the critical sense and not a little destroyed the realistic sense of politics, may have contributed to the failure of the governing classes accurately and effectively to rule. The rise of Huey Long has all but overthrown the last remaining stronghold of Bourbon government in the South, which even Long's opponents admit to have been about as corrupt as it was ineffectual. The event was, if you will, delayed. The Senator from Louisiana is in not a few respects like Andrew Jackson; in politics he has displayed the same perseverance, skill and energy that Jackson devoted to his military exploits; he lacks Jackson's bodily courage, but not his indiscretion, his quarrelsomeness, his perversity. His sense of strategy is superb; his information on his enemy before every battle, complete. He is, I believe, uninterested in money, except in so far as it can be used to promote his power. If, like Jackson, he succeeds in achieving a revolution through the ballot-box, it is his economic ignorance that will undo him. And one had only to go under the Hill to discover with what extreme of frontier violence, gaming fever and untutored lust they were neighbored.

Why, then, was this not another Pittsburgh? The answer is to be found, I think, in the greater continuity of life in the South. The humane tradition was stronger. And how strong it was is shown in the architecture. In this region, as I say, the planters came comparatively late; but they were still able to build dwellings, harmonious with human dignity, when this art had been lost in the rest of the Western world. And it is a living art, for it is in complete accord with the climate. And I think that in the recent talk of the functional character of architecture, it has been too often forgotten that the first function of a house is to shelter from the weather. And its second is to express the social status, not the individual taste, of the owner. The long double-galleried houses of Charleston were, I am told, derived in the first instance from a similar type of architecture in the Barbadoes. The plantation-house of Louisiana, enclosed in double rows of columns, can be shown, in a model of the Government House in the Cabildo, where it is still in transition, to have been devised out of the French manor-house with the hip-roof and small dormers. The Americans added magnificence. and in the raised cottage— elevated originally from fear of occasional floods and constant damp —created the last and loveliest instance of the classical revival. That architecture is gone in the decline of the class that created it, for it is essentially a social art. Already in 1857, Belle Grove shows an opulent decadence; the pink-washed walls, the unbalanced adornment are as depraved as a Grand Duke's villa at Nice. And it has had, nowhere in America, a successor. For the skyscraper, all that is called functional architecture, is not architecture at all but a branch of engineering, thrilling when pure and purged of all mediocre reminiscence of art, impersonal as a modern battlefield, an expression merely of the control of modern science over matter, marvellous but inhumane.

But that there was more vitality in this class than they are commonly given credit for is manifest in their survival. For survive they did, though depleted, not only by the war waged in order to commit the country to industry, but even that ten-year period of dictatorship of the proletariat, under the Republican party, known as Reconstruction. (Though, it may here be said, these are subjects as rarely referred to in the Deep South as is heard there, among the survivors of this class, what is known as a Southern accent. The speech of the Battery at Charleston is as distinct as that of Beacon Street; there is no more drawl in the Boston Club of New Orleans than there is in the Somerset Club of Boston.) With the confiscation and freedom of slaves succeeded an arrangement of labor, including blacks and whites, not unlike that of the colonies of Italy in the second century, when agricultural slavery was likewise on the point of being turned into serfdom. The impetus in both cases was provided by poverty and helplessness before taxes. The position of the share-cropper is hardly better than that of the serf—in some respects worse, for he is not, unfortunately for his family, permanently attached to the land. And his slovenliness, his poor knowledge of farming, his indifference to anything beyond a bare subsistence for himself and, if it is not too much trouble, his children, make him a destructive and unprofitable agent for the planter. As one of the larger members of his class, a man of energy, conscience and, as it happens, considerable capital, said to me, walking over land beyond the Fausse Rivière, "This plantation supports a hundred and seventy-five families; every one of them gets a living out of it except me."

The war of 1861–1865 was, of course, a civil war, though, for some reason which I have never been able to discover, Southerners object to its being called one. Dr. Charles Beard has already referred to it as a revolution and was, I believe, the first to do so. But I do not think even yet it has been made clear how many points it has in common with the Russian Revolution. One only I should like to comment on; but it is one that can be strongly recommended to the study of our modern enthusiastic revolutionists. It is comparatively easy to overthrow political power: that requires, as Napoleon said, an idea and bayonets, or, to modernize the armament, machine guns; and it is still easy forcibly to seize the discarded power. But to substitute for one working economic arrangement by another is another matter altogether. The Southern economy cannot perhaps be called a system; but, on a basis of slavery, and at the cost of justice, it did, more or less, work. Destroyed, it was followed, not by a superior system, industrial rather than feudal, free and not slave, but by no system at all. Industrialism did, of course, eventually invade the South and conquered no small part of it. But whether John Brown or even Thaddeus Stevens would regard Gastonia as a cause for rejoicing, I have, not being in communication with the dead, no way of knowing. Just so, the Bolsheviks in a few months succeeded to the political power of the departed Czar. But, for all the grandiosity of their plans and the correctness of their Marxist principles, no single account can yet give them credit after nearly twenty years of rule, most of it absolute, of endowing the U.S.S.R. with anything that can be called an economic system, socialist or otherwise. These things, it must be said, are ordered better in France.

IV

It is always difficult in speaking of the South not to seem to prefer the terms of the past, even when the real concern is the present. This country is backward; there are customs and attitudes that persist here which have long disappeared elsewhere; or, to put the matter in a more favorable phrase, one can say that in the Deep South, more than anywhere else in America, better than in many parts of Europe, the humane tradition of living has outlasted the many attacks upon it. I am not pretending that there are not Southerners who do let us down, or that, when they do, the results are pretty awful. I am not forgetting either Senator Bilbo or Senator Long. But even among the hill-billies there is continuity of a sort, a conservation of the ways of the first pioneers. It is too often ignored that in the South, scarcely less than in the West, there are remnants of an early frontier, unaltered, save in so far as the slovenliness of the frontiersman, his ruthless destruction of forest and game, his bad tillage of soil never understood, have mutilated his background and diminished his sustenance.

I have had but a glimpse of the Charleston drawing-room, shaded from the afternoon light, still golden in the street below, the walls showing the subdued colors of Audubon's mocking-birds in formal and terrified flight about the huge coils and darting head of a black snake—the plate composed from sketches made by the ornithologist on an ancestral plantation. I know that the forms of society are carefully preserved there, that the conversation is cultivated and aware. And yet I have the impression of something wistful in the charm, even in the force, of the Charlestonian. It is a little as though one had strayed into some legitimist sect who are determined, perhaps, not so much to restore the present heirs of the Bourbons as to commemorate the martyrdom of Louis XIV with an appropriate emotion. It is not snobbery that one finds here, but an overwhelming sense of an immense and heavy heritage. And I am obliged to notice that both Mr. DuBose Heyward and Mrs. Peterkin, at least as literary figures, prefer to consort with the colored race, whether of city or remote country, rather than admit the existence of that huge, sprawling, tawdry expanse, white but vulgar, that is Charleston beyond Broad Street.

Though I am told that the youngest generation in New Orleans is not entirely uncorrupted, I have nowhere else in America seen such polite ease among youngsters. The influence of the Carnival balls is potent; their fantastical prodigality is more than a spectacle and the courts of the mock kings and queens are not all a travesty; for they provide something of a center to the social life of the whole year, though they begin with Twelfth Night and are over with Mardi Gras, and, for all that they lack seriousness and even sobriety, they do succeed in imposing a code on their followers. Now that the old French Opera is gone, it is the balls more than anything else which give New Orleans its living and delightful air of a provincial capital. They are, of course, Creole in origin. But if French is still frequently heard, conversation in New Orleans is essentially Southern; where there is wit, it is not, as usually in France, dictated by vanity; the desire is not to startle but to please. Domestic difficulties are not among the common topics, nor loss of money, nor even mishaps on the golf-course; politics may be, but the discussion of it will have a certain aloofness and will lack, amazingly to one recently from the East, the rancorousness of the opinionated intellectual, the fatuousness of the businessman to whom politics has ever been a variation on his one theme of personal interests. Comment on an emotional situation will be, as in the mid-century Natchez of Mr. Stark Young, oblique rather than straight. This last may lead at times to an alarming vagueness. But the Southerner at his best, like the French at their worst, has always known at least what manners were for, that they are not intended, as the Westerner with his broad handclasp and easy salutation supposes, to bring people together out of a loneliness as wide as the prairies, but to keep them comfortably apart, to preserve between them and you whatever distance is necessary both for their integrity and yours.

The families with French names have still a formidable unity. And it is perhaps the French sense of tradition that gives to social gatherings in New Orleans a meaning that, as far as I am aware, has been lost elsewhere, and that not only in American cities. For they are, as they should be everywhere, a school of manners. This demands a mingling of generations. While in the other American cities with which I am familiar it is customary rigorously to separate those of various ages, it is by no means uncommon in New Orleans to find seventy-seven in conversation with seventeen. And this is as it should be. The young should not be admitted to society until they are prepared to adopt the conventions and behavior of adults. . . .

1939

WEST VIRGINIA

THE STATE of West Virginia lies in part in the Allegheny Plateau and in part in the great Appalachian Valley. The land that lies between the Blue Ridge and the Alleghenies is extremely fertile and favorable to small farms and orchards. The mountains make meagre farming; once the trees are cut down, the slopes plowed and planted to corn, they are soon denuded of soil. Often after three years they are washed to a barren clay. But the rivers that drain toward the West are themselves sources of power, and under the poor ground lie even richer sources of power: coal, petroleum, natural gas.

This natural division is reflected in the lives of the people. The first settlers came into West Virginia in defiance of the restrictions placed on their westward advance by a timid and parsimonious British government and indifferent to the grants already made of this land to great proprietors like Lord Fairfax. Scarcely were they established beyond the Blue Ridge before they were divided in the common speech as Cohees and Tuckahoes. And this division persists. The people of the mountains have always been Westerners. In the beginning they belonged to the Old West, that wilderness in which the pioneer spirit of America first came into being. In West Virginia much of the Old West is still in existence; its ways and customs still hold among the mountaineers. A laggard time has left them almost exactly what their ancestors were; they have the same speech and sing the same songs, scarcely altered in two hundred years. They are as fiercely loyal and as desperately lazy, their laziness being a concomitant of their pride. They are distrustful of all outsiders, but, once they have placed you and know exactly who you are, will offer you whatever their poverty affords in the way of hospitality. And their poverty, where they have held to the ways of their ancestors, is permanent. It has made them brutal and kept them ignorant. They are careless of human life and extraordinarily considerate of human dignity, and they value their apartness as a means of preserving it. They are slow in changing, even when they have become miners. Because of the mines, much of their country has been taken over and exploited. And one of the consequences of the existence of coal in the Western part of the state has been to attach it to the industrial Middle West. But the people of the Eastern panhandle, for all that they have long been separated politically from Virginia, remain, socially and economically, inseparably Virginian.

The first settlers in the Shenandoah Valley were Germans. Led by the Baron Joist Heidt, in 1730, they crossed the Potomac at what was soon to be called the Packing Horse Ford and, climbing the steep southern bank, looked about them and saw that the country was good. There that company stayed. There they built their log cabins, probably the earliest to be set up on American soil. Some of them still stand in the older streets of Shepperdstown, their hewn logs colored by time, their chinks filled with white plaster, and still strong against the weather. It was not for a generation or more that the settlers of English descent began to build cabins out of hand-hewn logs, in imitation of the Germans. Nor was this all they learned from these refugees from Moravia and the Palatinate.

The valley into which these Germans had come lies between two ridges of strangely blue hills. Underneath are caves, arched upon limestone and hollowed by a continual dripping. The dissolution of the stone has kept sweet a soil already rich. Before the coming of the Germans, the Indians had known that herds of buffalo and elk could be lured into this long valley by burning it over each autumn to keep the growth low. Here they hunted, Indians from as far north as the Lakes, from as far south as the Carolinas. The coming of the settlers was as fiercely contested here as anywhere in the country. The Germans penetrated the valley as far as the western gaps, followed after a few years by Scotch-Irish and English. These fought the Indians as they went, raid being answered by punitive raid, until 1775, when, after the battle of Point Pleasant, the savages were driven beyond the western mountains. In that battle, my great-great-grandfather, Charles Edward Cameron, fought and his brother Hugh died.

Their father had escaped to Virginia with a price on his head, after the defeat of the Young Pretender, Charles Edward Stuart, at the battle of Culloden, in 1745. The Scotch Highlanders sought the mountains, and it is not difficult, even today, to trace their influence on the West Virginia mountaineers. For their famous feuds descend clearly from the clan warfare of Scotland. The Scotch-Irish came in even greater numbers—a solid people, stubborn and sturdy, good pioneers, because they were in the first instance good fighters.

Their most distinguished son in this region was to be Stonewall Jackson, who could show in action not only their sober qualities but that imaginative brilliance which occasionally appears among them. The English were not important in western Virginia until about 1760, when the rich land along the four Tidewater rivers began to be worn out from a century of cultivation of tobacco. The British in the eighteenth century knew only how to exploit land, not how to conserve its productivity. Where, as in much of the Shenandoah Valley, they were willing to learn from the descendants of German peasants, they prospered; where, as in most of the mountainous country, they had only their own stubborn ignorance to depend on, they soon destroyed the possibilities of the land and either moved on or sank into a prolific poverty. Those of English stock did, however, impose their own conceptions of government on the country, and, in the more prosperous portions of the valley, something of their sense of social structure. Burrells, Bassetts, Washingtons, Harrisons, Peytons, Byrds, the great landholding families of the Tidewater, sent their sons to take up land which Virginia claimed but to which Lord Fairfax, through his grandmother, Lady Culpepper, held an hereditary title. It was this dispute over property rights that brought many of them, and the Washingtons in particular, to the side of the Revolution.

The conflict which had existed between the coast and the backcountry was thus brought into western Virginia. The eastern counties had the power and the prestige; they were wealthy, aristocratic and slaveholding; the western counties were poor and democratic, and neither had nor wanted slaves. They had every reason to distrust the government of the commonwealth, which had failed to defend them when they needed defense, which now took their full share of taxes and in return gave them neither roads nor schools. A petition had been presented to Congress as early as 1776 that a separate state be created for them.

This situation was seized on in 1861. The formation of the State of West Virginia is, as far as I know, the first instance of the method used by Hitler in the Sudeten. Strategically, West Virginia occupied in the Civil War much the position toward the Union that Czechoslovakia held in 1938 toward Germany. Someone in the North saw this; no one in the South did. Had the Confederate leaders grasped the importance, first, of that portion of the state which is contiguous with the Middle West, and, second, of the Baltimore and Ohio Railroad, which could readily have been cut at Harpers Ferry, they might have gained the military advantage. As it was, they soon lost the state and a hostile wedge was driven into the Confederacy.

West Virginia-saw plenty of the war. It escaped Reconstruction. As a consequence, those portions of the state which were truly Virginian became, if anything, more so after the Civil War. The pattern of society, which had been established there in the eighteenth century, was scarcely disturbed and remained more or less intact until my childhood. Passions engendered by the Civil War increased the division within the state. Besides, with the development of coal mining, the western counties turned inevitably toward the industrial Middle West.

The West Virginian had never found he could look to his state government for consideration and care. And he had learned to look out for his own rights and to protect his own independence. Mountaineers, he had declared, were always freemen. It was doubtless this distrust of government that allowed him, even with a state of his own, to lose control of it. The mine-owners became the government. And resistance to their power was construed as rebellion against the state. In the early twenties, some guards at a mine having been shot, sixty miners were brought to trial, not merely for murder but for treason and conspiracy as well. Since that time, however, the unions have steadily increased in power.

Though the story of West Virginia is, to my mind, essentially a story of a continuous but constantly changing struggle for power, between sections, between different conceptions of society, and between classes in an accepted society, it need not be told in abstract terms. For power is not an abstraction, and every struggle brings forth its protagonists. Nor does the region lack characters. I can name here only a few who have at some time been a part of the state's history.

Andrew Lewis, the Indian fighter and Revolutionary general; Horatio Gates, who conspired to deprive Washington of his position as commander of the Continental Army; his friend, General Charles Lee, that brilliant and eccentric soldier-of-fortune; Samuel Washington, who equalled Henry VIII in the number of his marriages; Bushrod Washington, the justice of the Supreme Court, who built Claymont before inheriting Mount Vernon; the abolitionist John Brown; Stonewall Jackson; James M. Mason, Jr., who devoted his life to solving the problem of the Virginia debt (the original of the grandfather in my novel Act of Darkness). . . .

1940

459

CAPE COD

CAPE COD is in the sea; you feel its presence even before you come into sight of it, as you do in Provence; and indeed the country, low and uneven, with its scattered growth of windswept pines, is not unlike the country around Fréjus. There is, relatively speaking, the same sense of a long adaptation on the earth; the land has been lived with; the houses belong to it as they do in no other part of America I have seen.

Every other person you meet will tell you that Sir Christopher Wren sent over three designs for Cape cottages and that these have been faithfully followed and varied through two centuries. This is quite possible; such passage of designs was common at the time. But certainly the oldest standing houses on the Cape are older than Wren; the one-and-a-half stories are very similar to those in parts of Virginia, where I have always understood that the fashion was instituted by the taxes of Queen Anne. There are white painted cottages here very similar to the Mary Washington house in Fredericksburg.

Yet, as I say, they belong to the land; the grey shingles have been weathered in a sea-air; the long sloping roof at the back is against the north wind, and the front doors to the south, open as they are to friendliness, are protected. In their low shapes they are like maritime trees, bent and twisted by the salt winds.

The churches, for the most part, are blank in front, desperately plain; only the spires, seen above trees, are delicate and fine. That of Sandwich, rising from a circle of small columns, is, particularly when seen across water and included in elms, of an especial grace. As far as the churches themselves go, the best is at Wellfleet, built 1852.

The air is moist and mild; in the early summer sun, strongly aromatic with bay, pine, sassafras; at all times, subdued by the wash of the Gulf Stream. At Woods Hole, the sea-water is found to be filled with tropical infusoria, and all along this southern coast the water is ten to fifteen degrees warmer than on the bay side.

The softness of the air accounts in part for the temperament of the people. The children here are calm; there is not that nervousness which belongs to the rest of America. It is to be remembered that even the Cape Indians were, compared to those on the mainland, of a mild disposition, gentle and unrevengeful. . . .

STORIES

PORPHYRIO, THE DELICATE PRINCE

OR

The Martyrdom of Cupid

A Rococo Comedy

Sed mellitos verborum globulos et omnia
dicta factaque quasi papavere et sesamo
sparsa.. . . .

I

THE YOUNG PRINCE stepped shiveringly down the cold stone steps of his bathwell. There he held a swift palaver with the water, turning its blue-green smoothness to froth; splashing, between gasps, he sang:

> "Le sette donzelle della reina
> sono vestita ciascuna di colori
> di foglie verdi e di fiori
> ricamati sul color di mattina."

Emerging, he nodded to his two Moroccan pages, who stood, with sidelong glances, in the doorway, awaiting his wet nakedness. The blacker of the two rubbed him dry, briskly; the other enviously extended a long blue-sapphire dressing gown. The Prince stood staring futilely at the painting of the northern ceiling: Danaë on her tower bed lying open to the divine bright-falling rain; and the sunlight moved about him as he stood. With a sniffle he slipped his arms into the silky sleeves and went toward his bedroom; his gown, ungirdled, trailed blue clouds on the reflecting floor. The pages followed slowly, with sidelong looks and the muted clicks and hisses of their barbarous tongue.

The Prince was eighteen years old and commonly awoke hungry. So his breakfast was brought him immediately and served on a little table: a plate of blue-purple plums, the frosty bloom still on their blue smooth skins, and afterwards an omelet of pigeons' eggs flavored with chives and coffee poured from silver into Venetian glass. This breakfast was looked on with disfavor by the antique members of the court, who remembered sternly the vigor of the Prince his father, who from his youth up had been satisfied with a sop of crusty bread in a pot of warmed ale. Neither did they altogether approve of his African pages, Babu and Agadu, those two black ephebes whose shiny round foreheads and crinkled earwool were crested with glistening turbans and cerulean heron plumes, whose speech was like the spluttering of a wet log on the fire. The Prince had chosen them because of his habit of talking aloud when in private, and, since neither Babu nor Agadu had as yet shown any intelligence in Italian, which was the language the Prince commonly thought in, or in French, which he used in all subjects relating to cookery, fashion and the military, or in Latin, which noble and thoughtful language he found indispensable in all discussions of rhetoric, philosophy, prosody and anatomy, refused to let them go. He had found them adroit in attending to his person, and their own jargon sufficed between themselves so well that they seemed quite content with their lot. What they said to each other the Prince thought it impertinent to inquire. His only compromise with his critics was to advance the hour of his breakfast so that even the lapis lazuli bowl of Falernian wine, into which he trailed his fingers after the fruit, and the pretty napkin, with which he wiped the edges of his mouth after the eggs, should have disappeared before the First Gentleman of the Bedchamber came to wake him in the accustomed manner.

It was now time for the first entry, and, the breakfast being ended, the Prince lay down once more on the great bed and closed his eyes, while Agadu drew a dark damask over his feet. He knew that the old gentleman enjoyed waking him according to the ancient usage, and besides he had no sense of humor. The door opened as if aware of the personage it was about to admit, and the Marquis Verdastro entered on lacquered heels; sidling to the bedside, he gravely swabbed the Prince's neck and cheeks with *eau de vie*. Porphyrio opened his eyes as though astonished at the length of the Marquis's nose and the many little hairs in his nostrils; leapt from the bed and inquired of the weather; seated himself in time to receive the morning courtesies of the princely uncles and great-uncles, who with the ministers and a cardinal or two streamed into the bright air of the bedroom. Scarcely had the mumble of their compliments subsided, when a second assemblage, only less brilliant than the first, entered through the guarded doors: courtiers in favor, distant relatives, an archbishop and two barbers. It was, when one considers the size of the Prince's domains, a magnificent and polished company; their names, degrees and exploits had been fit material for an epic poet; indeed the court of Porphyrio might well have found its Campens had not all the poets of the time been exclusively concerned with imitations of the Tuscan lyric.

The barbers advanced with bowls of lather, towels of wool and Spanish razors. The Prince, whose cheek was so smooth that he might without her annoyance have pressed it against the cheek of Isabella dei Rigogliosi, who was but fifteen and of such incredibly ancient blood on both sides that she could, without looking, distinguish the sex of a butterfly lighting on her hand, nevertheless submitted daily to the ministrations of his barbers, thinking it beneath his dignity not to support a beard. Meanwhile a wholly delightful informality prevailed; the Marquis Giallatesta moved among the company relating whatever gossip he had composed since dinner the night before; no one objected, for the old man was troubled with insomnia and his stories were more often malicious than ribald. It was only when the butt of his wit laughed too uproariously, as was the case this morning with the Cardinal Candela, that anyone suspected them of being true. The Prince heard all this scandal from under the lather and hot towels, and heard his guests' laughter; but himself, he did not laugh. Whatever gifts had been given him, laughter was denied; even his smile was like an angel's, sad and rather distracted.

The barbers put away their razors and the ceremonious habiliment of the Prince began. The First Gentleman of the Bedchamber and the Master of the Wardrobe took each a sleeve of his dressing gown and, loosening it from the shoulder, made a silky screen of sapphire between the modest youth and the stares of the company. With the assistance of his two pages, whom, because they were black, he regarded no more than his monkey, he drew on a shirt thinly white and of silk and his scarcely magenta trunkhose, and adjusted the silvered codpiece with its tassels of bullion. Then Babu brought his shoes and Agadu his belted tunic—black damask corded with silver, lifted stiffly by plaited folds from the rump, lined and unexpectedly slashed with a color of coral.

The dressing gown was lowered to the sound of Ah!, and someone brought the traditional mirror; the Africans, advancing from behind, held each a flambeau; and the Prince nodded approvingly to his toilet.

When the order of the day had been read in a bright almost extinct voice, the Prince was handed his gloves, and the Cardinal pronounced the *Quaesumus, deus omnipotens*—less hastily than one would have expected from so lofty an ecclesiastic. Rising from their knees, the company departed.

Left alone, the Prince called quickly for his monkey Satannino, an agile hairy homunculus, whose most embarrassing acts could never be construed as discreditable to the human race.

II

Porphyrio looked into the profundity of Satannino's face and thought of Death; of his father's death, when for six months he had dressed only in black and eaten nothing but black foodstuffs—ripe olives, caviar, truffles, mushrooms and the like—and had no drink but the *vino nero* of the peasants. Softly he stroked Satannino's soft-grey ruff and thought of Love. Closing his eyes, he thought of love: of lovely girls in a silken haze embroidered in violets and olive leaves, amorously moving through a wooded sunlight; the versicolored folds closed on the rounded thighs and pointed the delightful kneecaps; quietly they moved in translucent gauze through slight changes of the wind. And he thought of Atalanta and the love which she, a virgin, showed for Meleager; of Selvaggia and the courteous Tolosan lady under the Golden Roof; of Fiammetta and the song in the *Decameron* which begins: *Io mi son giovinetta, e volentieri M'allegro e canto en la stagion novella, Merzè d'amore e de' dolci pensieri.* His hand slid over the monkey's sleek back and slipped closely, smoothly, joint by joint of the spine, to the long slow tail. And he thought of the Princess of the Isles, whom he was presently to wed—not plainly, as he had imagined the others, but in a confused splendor, a pale-gold glamor, walking delicately under the trees. But he did see clearly that her lips were moist and of the red color of wild strawberries bitten in two. Taut with pleasure at the thought of her amiability, he followed the Princess through the woods; then they ascended together a stair with a marble balustrade, which led them to a pavement of colored stone, where there was a little fountain playing by itself; there the Princess departed, seeming to vanish into a pavilion, whose doors locked, clicked behind her.

He had scarcely composed himself after the surprise of her departure when Babu entered on tiptoe to remind him that his advisers were awaiting an audience in the Chamber of the Little Council. Smoothing his hair, he put on his gloves, asked for a new scented handkerchief and hurried toward the paneled closet.

Lightly he entered, unannounced, and found his ministers: the

Cardinal Candela, leaning his yellow melancholy head against the back of an armchair, his feet crushing a cushion which matched his slippers; the Count Pantaleone, the Minister of the Treasury, stiffly erect on a narrow uncarved seat of olive wood; and Ser Petronio degli Epuloni, his Minister of Pleasure, lolling gallantly on the window sill. They rose as he entered, with compliments.

"Ah," said the Prince, as he took his place as near as possible to the fire—for the morning was chill for May—"was there ever a ruler so happy in his counsellors as I? You, my lord Cardinal, have succeeded where the more handsome Pico della Mirandola failed. A Minister of State who has reconciled Plato with the Church Fathers, who believes in the unity of the soul and the possibility of reducing all known systems of thought to one—who could be more useful to a prince so often involved in diplomatic difficulties as I? My Lord Treasurer, a mathematician of such brilliance that he is able to compute the state expenses to a centesimo, by merely driving from the palace to the barracks and back again; to adjust the year's taxes with a nice justice, simply by standing for an hour or two in the public square and gazing intently at a peasant or so and several money-lenders! And you, Ser Petronio, have, I am sure, a most charming acquaintance among zanies and mountebanks."

"Sire," said the Cardinal, "it was you who chose us." And he plucked at his voluminous carmine robes with pointed nails.

"I admit," said the Prince, "that my admiration for elaborate thought is extreme, my delight in symmetry knows no diminution. It is perhaps a fault. But then I learned Greek at such an early age. It is not everyone who touches Plato at thirteen.

"But your masque—?"

The Cardinal was still engaging in his huge labor of confuting the *Philosophumena* of Hippolytus, Bishop of Portus, of which he alone among Italians possessed all ten books.

"It advances. I am planning to conclude with Attis drinking hemlock, St. Paul being wounded in the thigh by a wild boar, and Socrates submitting to circumcision. Throughout I maintain, with many learned and I hope graceful digressions, that all wise men have at all times held the same set of beliefs and that there is no heresy but ignorance. But it grows a little long for the stage."

"And you, my Lord Pantaleone, have you no late discoveries, no comets, stars or constellations? Is there no news of Orion and his sextuple sun, is there no susurrus in the schools of Saturn?"

The Count Pantaleone, a brown withering of a man, with greasy white sidelocks viridescent at the ends, shook out the folds of his tunic, thin and the color of dead leaves, and turned his ear to the wind.

"Alas, I have nothing to do now but to imagine comets and plot their phantasmal courses and times of return. I long ago worked out all the problems our decadent age presents, and with these eyes of mine I can no longer hope to see anything remarkable in the heavens. Once I planned a solar system, which I thought a great improvement on the one we inhabit, especially as regards climate, but the mathematics involved kept me from sleep five nights and brought on a cough. Now I must content myself with a comet, or at most two, every evening after a meagre supper and a flask of wine."

"We are come," said the Cardinal, "to discuss the marriage of Your Highness to the Princess of the Isles."

"Oh!" said the Prince, moving away from the fire.

And the Cardinal proceeded windily to advise the marriage, not only for the Alliance's sake, but also on account of the fairness of the Princess and the amorous disposition of the Prince. For Love, the Cardinal explained characteristically and with an admirable display of erudition, is not opposed to Marriage nor Marriage to Love. They are not, as commonly supposed, dissonant but consonant. They correspond in much the same way that the women wailing over the body of Adonis answer to the women weeping at the foot of the Cross.

"I have no doubt," added the Minister of the Treasury, "that your Highness is covetousness itself for the Princess's beauty. However, the dowry must be paid at once and in gold. Otherwise, there is not the slightest use in your providing yourself with heirs; unless nature has changed her custom in these matters, you will be bankrupt before they have time to be born."

The Minister of Pleasure pressed a prodigious ruff and a shoulder of rose-madder against the diapered window-panes; below in the courtyard a very comical scene was being enacted between a three-legged man and a protuberant peasant wench.

Porphyrio was advised that the Ambassadors of the Isles were expected presently. Whereupon the Cardinal and the Count departed.

Porphyrio felt the cruelty of these bloodless old men like a cold wind snuffing at his shins. He had been glad to have taken the Princess clad only in a rough nut-stained shift; but he remembered that he did not like the feel of coarse stuffs.

Ser Petronio regretfully left the window sill. A swart man, his black thick hair curved to a peak at the center of his forehead, his beard, stiffened with wax, bristled most at the black point beneath his chin; he assumed a laborious elegance. Tumbling the ordered vermilion folds of his cape, he demanded only that he might be allowed to entertain the expected ambassadors.

"Perhaps," he continued, "I have found something which Your Highness will find not unworthy of laughter. A troupe of comedians lately discovered on the border—"

Ser Petronio's thought was without irony; his laughter, like an earthquake, subterranean and profound. He could not understand why the Prince retired, saddened and amazed, from the spectacles he provided for his amusement. Not only had he hired the most skilful performers of his day; he had, night long and night after night, hunted through high memoirs and old piles of histories, hoping always to find some risible thing enjoyed once by dead princes and now forgotten by the mountebanks. But not even the procession of dwarfs which had so diverted Frederick, Prince of Naples, nor the wedding of the hunchbacks, which had so much amused Piero del Tolomei, had brought more than a wavering and terrified smile from the Prince.

"You may do what you like for the Ambassadors," replied Porphyrio. "But tell me, Ser Petronio, you who laugh so often and so loudly, what pleasure do men have in seeing dwarfs and deformities? Why do they like to see dignity brought down and the wise made ridiculous? What do all your clowns but display some horrible distortion of their bodies, pretend lunacy or drunkenness or else some dreadful pain? What do your comedians but break all symmetry and with wild wit destroy love and beauty and the love of love?

"I have seen my father throw back his head and laugh until all the wrinkles in his chin had mounted into his cheeks over things which were to me unspeakably coarse or cruel or vile. (And I am not an unpious son.) I have seen wiser men than I snicker and grow raucous, and ladies so kind-hearted that they could refuse their lovers nothing smile with their teeth apart at ribaldries and sad buffooneries, and, strangest of all, I have seen the gravest of them laugh out when Tragedy entered showing an auspicious face, when they saw beauty distorted, desire grown stale, and vast illusions topple like burning towers. Tell me, Ser Petronio, tell me, why do men laugh? Most of all, why did these serious men laugh, turning their decent countenances into lewd grimaces, dropping their jaws until you could see what teeth they lacked?"

The Minister twisted his mouth a little, remembering Porphyrio's father and how unceasingly he had been amused by cuckolding old and hopelessly obese burghers, in tripping up priests when, masked and disguised, they hurried with heads down through the dark streets, in watching the more comely culprits whipped in the prison yard at high noon. His forehead wrinkled, his eyebrows rose, his nose became a fox's, his mouth pouted, his hands turned ineffectually on his wrists.

"I hardly know," he said, "except that such things are funny." The Prince exhaled a little sigh.

"Perhaps then—Ser Petronio, you are a gallant and courteous man, and have, I know, the gentle heart. What is Love like?"

The older man was silent for a moment, almost thoughtful.

"Love," he appropriately quoted, "Love and the gentle heart are one same thing, as the sage in his saying sagely says. All that the poets have said of Love is true," he added, "but it is well to remember that they wrote before the event. In action, it is brutal, soporific, sudorific, rapid and mephitic; sometimes in the young it is also strongly carminative."

III

With vicious eyes and pointed ivory cane, the first Ambassador paused before a portrait.

"Ah, that look of a sleepy kestrel perched in an intensity of sun!"

"Elisabetta Giallatesta," explained Ser Petronio in a voice lowered for scandal. "The daughter of an ancient Roman house, she came here at seventeen, the fifth bride of the nineteenth Prince, Alessandro IX. Her preference was for pages and she could endure no lover after his beard was noticeable in the light. Only the undowned cheek and the thyroid cartilage developed: a brief combination. She died an old lady surrounded by a large retinue of boys who followed her to the grave mourning in yellow and black, thc ancestral colors of the Giallatesta. Her palace I've heard was in a continual uproar. She died regretting that she could not live long enough to enjoy the charms of one especially pleasing little page who was then but twelve years of age."

Porphyrio, at the far end of the gallery, one knee bent, leaned against the wall.

"Love," said the second Ambassador, "is a variant of avarice. The old are misers of fair flesh, and the young spendthrifts. And both are miserable, the one because he gets no good of his hoard-ings—"

"And this," said Ser Petronio, "is the Prince Alessandro himself. He used always to celebrate his wedding nights on the Golden Staircase, in remembrance of his own too early taking-off by one of his mother's aides, whom he met by design on the backstairs. They say that, as he lay on his deathbed, the priests had to be hoisted from the courtyard and brought in through the window of his bedroom, with cords and pulleys, lest, hearing once more the creaking of the steps, he should die unrepentant. But the story is doubtless untrue."

"—And the other sighs and yawns that his treasure slips so quickly through his fingers," continued the second Ambassador. "But anything may be affirmed of Love if only at the same time the opposite is also declared to be true. After the twelve labors of the Sun, Hercules made of it the last test of vigor. And the chaste hermits, who with mortifications starved and shrunk to yellow age in the burning deserts of the Thebaïd, also made of it a trial of strength. The blind man will get no more good of it than the man who has had his nose cut off will enjoy his food. And yet lovers willingly make themselves blind in a dark chamber. Profoundly animal—"

"Ah," said the other Ambassador, "the delicate head exactly poised on the just curving throat! The points of the hair gilded and straying in the wind! The glaucous eyes and the troubled gaze, the pretty nose upcurved and repeating the throat's curve!"

"That," answered the Minister of Pleasure, "is the Duchess Pasiphaë, painted in her youth. I can, unfortunately, by no means believe that the historians have been quite fair to her, but the story goes that for a long time she secretly desired to emulate her famous namesake and even travelled as far as Nîmes and into Spain to see the bullfights. She was only turned aside by hearing from her maid, a country girl, who in the time of her peasantry had seen many things not commonly regarded from the windows of palaces, of the swift and brutal duration of the taurine embrace. Whereupon, she took for her uses a young and husky groom who carried about him a thick strawy odor of stables. You may see him, on a small scale, in the painting: lolling upon the terrace, a bullskin over one shoulder, the bull's head falling across his bovine breast."

"—But instinct has no more part in it than hunger had in the skill of Trimalchio's cook when, on one platter, he served the entire zodiac, edible constellations to the number of twelve."

"I am very grateful to you," said the Prince, "but have you noticed the portrait of my grandfather, whose nose was said to be the longest in Italy?"

They left the gallery for the tennis court, where the Prince, contrary to the custom, played a very poor game.

That evening the Ambassadors assembled in the Hall of the Centaurs. Aloft they sat, their fed bellies softly heaving; and the carved arms of the chairs curved out in claws; the burnished beams of the ceiling shone, descended and burned in the candle-flames, rose and darkening were dulled in shadow. The Centaurs heaved their huge horse-flanks among the guests at the wedding feast, their long curled fetlocks worked in a dull thread, the color of faded blood. Centaurs lifted their odd feet stiffly, paced in a steady file between the embroidered trees, bows pulled taut, their shoulders hunched, the notch of the plumed arrow hard by the ear. The Prince, young, pale in the torchlight, tasted his melancholy, twisting his neck till his shoulder was close to his ear.

The performance of the clowns began.

A gross fellow, large-eared, slanted across the platform, a salver of glasses tilted. Dressed as a wine-pourer, the zany shifted his platter of wineglasses, making dreadful perpendiculars. His feet, large wooden feet, protruded stiffly; his arms described crude angles with the deformed body. Hardly the glasses fled toward the floor, hardly stopped; the abrupt figure tottered, lengthened, tottered, stretched, tottered, tottered, sank, fell, with a resounding sound of tinkling glass.

The zany began again with his tray of unbroken glasses; swayed, a scarecrow in an unfelt wind, falling fell; rose and swayed, about to fall and not falling; fell; rose and fell; rose and fell; rose.

The Prince turned to an approaching courtier and demanded a cushion to be placed under his sadly bruised buttocks.

The second zany, his small face blackened with a smudge of burnt wood, disclosed his mouth, an enormous red-ripe fig oozing seeds between pressed hands; his eyes glinted in his black face like Babu's when he was afraid. Hurriedly he crossed the stage, a travesty of motion. His fists closed upon his cheeks and his voice, derisively epicene, rose upon the air. Sliding, he turned; slid, spreading his legs, on his long feet; made of his body an inverted T, all the while shrieking and baying to the sound of pounded brass. He thrust out his shoes, twisting his feet, all the while making new and preposterous angles; turned with more violent shrieks in more epileptic dances; spread sprawling, spreading sprawled and suddenly rose in an intense vertical effort, howling.

Porphyrio, feeling an elaborate pain through all his thighs, his knee-joints and hip-joints, turned to an inattentive courtier in order to demand a hot bath and an oil-rub after the performance. But his voice was so hoarse from the song he had just heard that his request was inaudible, and the young fop only kept on applauding.

PORPHYRIO, THE DELICATE PRINCE

A eunuch strutted across the stage. A woman's red chevelure covered his scanty head; a woman's gown fell in silk folds over his pretended bosom and increased hips. Her companion, a frail homunculus, plied her with prepared questions, to which she replied in the raucous voice of an ancient and besotted baggage. The Prince heard this wit of the narrow streets with displeasure. The unaccustomed accent of the alleys fell disagreeably on his ears. The confusion of sexes filled him with apprehension. The last jest, delivered in a quite unintelligible argot, gave way to a clamor of applause.

Porphyrio carefully slipped his hand into his tunic to make sure that there was no new accumulation of fat over his breast muscles. Still only half reassured, he withdrew into a minute and scarcely lighted closet adjacent to the Hall of the Centaurs. There he remained for some time and only returned to the Hall after consuming the better part of a bottle of wine, lately arrived from the South.

The curtains closed on the last dancer. Sighing, he rejoined the delighted Ambassadors, who complimented Porphyrio on his Minister of Pleasure and Petronio on his clowns.

They remained for a long time in the Hall. The Ambassadors were silent, thinking on the dowry they had promised to send with the Princess. Silently they sipped their wine and wondered who it was that had cajoled them into paying so large a sum and at once. The Count Pantaleone twirled his glass under the torchlight and saw the golden globules spinning on the glass's rim as if they had been tiny worlds revolving about an unformed sun. The Cardinal Candela drained liqueurs from a constantly replenished thimble and meditated on the thoughts of the drunken Alcibiades. Ser Petronio chuckled in the midst of his wine and, choking, sent a tart scarlet spray into the face of the wineboy. The pages yawned and felt their legs fail with numbness from the draft that moved along the floor.

The Prince drank nervously. And as he drank, the Centaurs on the tapestried walls reared hugely over the fallen Lapithae, and violent horse-hoofs plunged among the torsos. Over the disordered banquet the bride screamed, her arms thrust outward and her long hair outspread; the bulky Centaur lifted her high above the tables; the bearded face opened in a lusty shout; the blood of his forearm ran down, staining her unwounded thigh; upreared on unshod hoofs, the laughing Centaur bore her away from the marriage feast. The night wore down.

Before going to bed, the Prince went first into a little closet to regard his one piece of Gothic sculpture; two monks copied from the Cathedral of St. Julien in Maine. He did not like the art of medieval

France and only studied it when, as now, he felt he had drunk too much. One look at the grotesque four-legged figure usually served to relieve him of his superfluous wine. Tonight was no exception, and when he closed the closet-door, he was quite sober though still a little queasy.

The morning of the wedding arrived. The noble families spread blazoned cloths from their windows and hung their balconies with ancestral colors.

Girls walked arm in arm down the thoroughfares, hoping to be kissed by the Princess's guardsmen. Young boys for the first time sneaked into the wineshops.

Brisk cavalcades trotted with clatter over the cobbles, their lances at rest, violet gonfalons bickering behind them in the wind of their moving.

Three murderers, seven pickpockets and a blasphemer were released from the prison at sunrise, and the choirboys of the Cathedral were awakened early.

The air was clear as the tears of a child. Before the palace and in the broad squares the princely banners of violet and silver drooped slowly.

The Prince remained a long time in his bath, which was filled not with water but with a distillation of wood-violets especially diluted by the Court Perfumer. Emerging at last like a dawdling wind from a garden, he was rubbed dry on a towel offered for the occasion by the Guild of Wood Merchants; and his toenails were pared with a knife presented by the Lord Mayor of Toledo. An hour was consumed dressing his hair and a splendid ritual accompanied his robing; each piece passed from noble to nobler hands until at last the princely fingers themselves drew on the ivory-silk hose, the violet doublet. The Prince was trembling when he put on his white leather pumps (with low silver heels) and the hat of crushed violet (starting into an ostrich feather), and violently trembling when at last he drew on his mantle, which enclosed him like a silver sheath. But he collected himself driving to the church, for suddenly it came to him that this was the twenty-second day of June and, consequently, one of the longest days, if not the longest, of the year.

The old coach swayed on its silver axletree as it passed slowly over the identical route which had once been used by Caligula Caesar on the way to one of his imperial auctions.

The Prince gravely saluted a multitude of reflections in the glass windows and wondered who had first thought of putting plumes on the heads of horses.

476

PORPHYRIO, THE DELICATE PRINCE

The diamond collar of St. Mirabel glittered in the sunlight and the purple cordon of the Order of the Cherubim grew more rich in the shadow.

When he passed the Flower Market, a young girl fainted in a basket. When he passed the Convent, the Mother Superior ordained the next day as a day of fasting and penitence. When he passed the Corner of the Orb, a mendicant friar began selling special dispensations for venial sins. When he passed the bridge, a second coach, inverted, accompanied him in the water.

During the procession the Prince thought mostly about nothing at all, so that when he arrived at the church porch, he felt quite careless and only recovered his astonishment when, at the high altar, lifting his head, he beheld his bride. The Princess was dressed in white as became her state, and all her hair was over her shoulders and over it a thin veil spread a silken haze, a mist diminishing the morning of her tresses.

Seeing her, the Prince was astonished, for neither his memory nor his desire had been enough to hold her beauty in its completeness and he marvelled that one hour should bring together such loveliness as hers and his lustihood. The Archbishop, seeing her, had all but laid down his crozier and his mitre at her feet; and the thurifers felt the first down bristling suddenly on their cheeks and in an instant left their childhood behind them. The choristers sang more sweetly, regretting for her sake the sweetness of their voices, and the stone cherubs, which but a moment before had been only wings and heads, fluttered and elongated into bodies.

The ceremony, Christian and royal, was tedious.

As they galloped back to the palace, the guards once more elevated their lances, and the crowd imagined that the color of the Prince's doublet had passed to ultraviolet and that his mantle gleamed with an unprecedented splendor.

The wedding-feast was fastidious and bountiful, an endless cortège of courses, from which the Princess selected a lark in aspic and three olives, the Prince a paté of pheasant and some raspberries in sour cream.

The afternoon was spent on the four balconies of the palace, responding to the people.

When the evening had come, the Prince, partly to pass the time and partly because he disliked Gothic art (not only was the Cathedral a relic of the twelfth century, but the Archbishop himself and his service had changed nothing since the Middle Ages), had a second ceremony performed in the palace after the classic fashion, the bride wearing yellow shoes and a wreath of marjoram over her still loosened hair. The chamber was windy with a light of torches, and there were youths and maidens of gentle blood who sang while three instruments improvised an epithalamic music. When the evening star had actually arisen and was to be seen by anyone near the window, they sang the verses of Catullus as well as they could, and the bride was brought to the chamber door. "*Hymen o Hymenaee*," they sang, "*ades o Hymenaee*," and the Princess closed the door against the paranymphs. After a decent interval the Prince followed her on tiptoe, smiling.

And the night came and the moon arose; and the palace slept, all but the guards, who paced, paced over the flagstones, up and down the steps of stone, unresting.

The halls had long been vacant and the windows bare of light when a new guard, passing under Porphyrio's bedroom, stopped and looked up; listened, hearing from the Prince, leaning on the night, long and long, bitter passionless laughter.

But because he was new and unacquainted with matters at the court, he did not think it worth while reporting to the Corporal of the Guard when the latter came to relieve him.

Playboy: First Quarter, 1923

HOW BRAKESPEARE FELL IN LOVE WITH
A LADY WHO HAD BEEN DEAD
FOR SOME TIME *

B RAKESPEARE sat humped on one of
the gates of a stableyard in a new pair of long trousers. Harry was
perched above him on a fence-post. They were waiting to see a young
stallion put for the first time to a mare.

Virginia is a country of moribund customs, dating from another
age. Thus, though slavery had been for some time officially abolished,
it was still usual in certain families to assign to each child shortly after
it was born a slave of the same age and sex, to serve first as a convenient playmate and later to be trained as a body-servant. Harry,
however, was unruly, and Mr. More O'Brien had decided to put him
to work in the fields. His Christian name had not been acquired at
baptism and his surname, Harris, was not, strictly speaking, a pat-
ronymic. Familiarly known as that black bastard of a Harry, not even
his mother, who had long since disappeared, could have said whether
it was a just appellation. The relations between the two boys had
never been those of equals; at first one might have thought that
Harry was the superior, for not only did he sleep in the groom's
quarters, but was quicker physically and had the black aptitude for
imitativeness. But he had now reached the age when the mind of
the Negro tends to retrograde instead of advancing. It was Brakespeare,
therefore, who was now the older, although he had but fifteen years
while Harry was approaching seventeen. It was just as well that this
shift had occurred; otherwise Brakespeare would very likely have
dropped him.

For the intimacy between the two boys depended only upon
their being close to one age. It had been allowed to continue unmolested, for it was inconceivable to Mr. Brakespeare's Southern mind
that the manners of one of his descendants could be corrupted by a

* Chapter VII of an unpublished novel called *The Huntsmen Are Up in
America*, which was finished in 1926. See Introduction.

black; had Harry been white and of obscure origin, it would have been seen to that he kept another distance, if indeed he had not been carefully forbidden the place. As for Brakespeare, he was glad enough to have the Negro as a companion, for Harry, merely because he was young, could wade a little way into that sea into which Brakespeare must, without him, have plunged alone.

The mare had already been brought out and stood, haltered and held by a burly black groom, in one corner of the yard. The checkered brick walls of the stables were mild with shadows; the slate roofs, moist from a shower, reflected only the necks of the pigeons that wheeled above them and settled noisily among the gutters and under the glittering vanes. A steel-wire fence stretched a taut net of light against the air. And from the musky yard the odors of spring arose with a difference: earth loosened by warmth; musty straw; the pungent steam of foaming puddles; fresh horse droppings, ammoniac in their smell; the stale smell of stalls newly cleaned; salt sweat and the sniff of leather harness, itself like the reek of sweat and rut.

A lean black stripling came running out of the stables, the young studhorse trotting behind him, a shining bay with waxed flanks. Animation by Brandywine out of Quatrefoil.

Genealogy of horses. On a field gules, a charger trippant, regardant, proper. Azure, a charger, rampant, gardant, proper, the tongue and vaillance sable. Jessant of a mare sable. Supporters: two equerries, sable, bearing batons, proper, pomades. Brakespeare eagerly watched the blazoning of these successive heraldic symbols on the brick walls and the blue sky.

"It seems to me," he said, as things were approaching a climax, "that it's all very badly arranged."

Harry answered without turning his eyes.

"Those boys know what they are doing."

"But what do they have to interfere so much for?" Brakespeare was curious. And he still had left a good deal of confidence in Harry's knowledge.

"They have to keep him from tearing up that mare's back, don't they? They know what they are doing. Don't you worry about them."

When the mare had been led away, Brakespeare dropped to the ground.

"I've something to do," he announced.

Harry regarded the trembling of the young stallion indifferently.

When Brakespeare entered his grandfather's house, he knew what he meant to ask, in case he found him at home. He therefore formulated the question in his own mind—without, of course, the least intention of putting it to Mr. Brakespeare. That would have required a courage he did not, at fifteen, possess. Walking into his study, he was relieved to find it empty.

He looked over the books on the table. Under the glass paperweight, he saw, distorted by the crystal, the key to the desk, a single key, small, a curlicued thing of brass—for it was only necessary to unlock and open the middle drawer in order to release all the others. He removed it from its apparent hiding-place and held it for a moment between his thumb and forefinger as firmly as though he meant to use it. Then he put it back. It was too bad; there were undoubtedly things in those drawers which he would like very much to see. He turned toward the door, walking with quiet breath; stopped. The afternoon was pouring through the open windows. It was April, and the day was clear.

Out of a golden cloud slowly a woman's body took form. A solid block of blond light carved into hips and thighs, ripe breasts and darling loins. The beautiful erect head, the body untired: Danaë erect with striding thigh, untired by the incessant falling of the golden rain. The high pointed breasts, ripe pulp of gilded fruit, were tasted and sweetly tasted. A nakedness, strange, not known before nor remembered when the eyes were closed. A nakedness, lost through surfeit, fading into a golden drift along dead canals, into a dust of water under the color of morning that slowly comes up from beyond Malamocco, to the east of Venice. Lost through surfeit, marvellously regained.

The boy's life somehow continued, though his breath was lost. He did not move, his feet were on the floor—and yet he was like a person going on tiptoe.

Before him a young woman stood, leaving a Venetian boudoir. One thigh was advanced, one heel had left the floor. A sombre air obscured the pale and sea-green panels, their clear outlines lost in a twist and curl of shells. In the shadow a table, the color of coral-rose, supporting a plate of fruit, imported by sea. The slender body was painted as though it stood in another light than that offered by the room; one would have said that the distinct naked flesh was caught in the reflection of a mirror of bronze (beyond the vision of the painter). The face was turned almost full, the eyes looked out without surprise, serene in their voluptuousness; the fabulous red hair was drawn back from the face and threaded with pearls, in the manner of princesses of the blood masquerading as sea divinities. The belly, haunches and breast were held in equipoise. She had turned in the moment of her departure to take a pomegranate from the plate held to her; in her hands the fruit became a petrified flame. The Negro page was there only to heighten her pallor and offer her fruits; his plumes and coral vest were submerged as surely as though he had been painted under the lagoon. The whole had an air of discreet sensuality which belongs to dying and luxurious aristocracies. The moist air, which had begun by softening, had ended by rotting the moldings; the beauty of the body had been bared for the last time, or for the last time before death. The portrait had kept its eighteenth-century frame, a broken border of extinguished gold.

Brakespeare presently subdued his agitation; but he was no longer quite the same person who, a half hour before, had walked into the room. He was like a nebula, vaguely luminous and shifting, which, under the influence of some near attraction, gathers its center and becomes a star.

His grandfather, coming down the stairs unheard, surprised the boy before the portrait.

The old gentleman was, however, a good deal more embarrassed than his grandson. With a flustered gesture, he picked up the black curtain which had fallen to the floor, shook out its shabby folds and carefully covered the canvas from view.

"Someone might come in," he muttered, and then more loudly added: "What are you doing here? Who asked you—?"

Brakespeare made himself slight in the great armchair beyond the table. Not that he was afraid; he found himself small, but suddenly complete, and in some new way strangely unassailable.

"You were not supposed to have seen that—still, I dare say, no great harm has been done. You are old enough—how old are you? I never can remember. But you are not to tell your father, you understand. You are old enough for that, surely." Mr. Brakespeare leaned into the hall and called the servant.

The painting was carried upstairs. Brakespeare listened carefully to learn by the sound of the Negro's footsteps into which room it was being carried. Then he left the house.

The incident at the pool had added a certain precision to his imagination and so far hastened its maturity. But he had not till now been able to reconcile what he definitely knew with what he as yet only vaguely desired. The image which had been lately before his eyes was distinct enough to satisfy the requirements of his mind; beautiful enough to support the evidence of the poets; naked enough to remind him of the changed processes of his blood.

Crossing the lawn, he met Harry, who proposed that they should go to the island for a swim. Brakespeare refused on the ground that he was still too cold. He wanted to be alone; he was ashamed, not of his experience, but that it should have made him feel so unutterably sad.

That night, he undressed before the long mirror. For the first time he felt he was able to criticize his own body with intelligence. And turning to his bed, he understood why the row of gilded angels, despite their sweet faces and bending curls, had always displeased him.

All his notions of beauty had been disturbed. Was it any wonder, then, that his sleep was slight. Before morning he dreamed of Alessandrina: in the place of the Negro page of the painting, he saw Harry, smaller than life and darker. Or was it Harry? It seemed to him that somewhere in the dream he heard his name pronounced.

In the morning he had his lessons. They were long. In the afternoon he went to his grandfather's. Mr. Brakespeare, assured of the boy's discretion, unsuspicious, delighted that he was at last showing an interest in his ancestors, permitted himself hours of loquacity.

The painting, Brakespeare found out, was that portrait of Alessandrina Cigogna which the first Urquart had brought to Virginia, from Venice. She had entertained him there, most intimately, it seems. Nothing was said of how Mr. Brakespeare himself had got hold of the portrait.

"Clarence Urquart had followed the old Pretender into Italy. A fervent Jacobite, he thought the only way to make up for having been but a boy at the time of the Rebellion of 1715 was, as soon as he came of age and into his estates, to sell them and follow after James in order to attend him in his exile. It was Alessandrina, I believe, who first persuaded him that it was all up with the Stuarts; anyone else could have told him as much years before he was born; but she only got round to it when she began to tire of him. That, at least, is my conclusion; for when she tired of her lovers, she tired with a violence and was clever beyond words in devising ways to be rid of them. Since he couldn't go back to England, he came—reluctantly, I suppose—to America. He must have had a pretty time of it after he arrived—wearing out his winters in Norfolk, trying to bring up his children as Catholics. But, at that, he probably got off better than most—unless you think the backwaters of some dead lagoon better for him, at least, than the backwoods of Virginia—and received this painting as a present at parting.

"I cannot tell you much of the painter—apparently an unknown contemporary of Longhi. He had a pretty facility with stuffs and surfaces. His flesh is luscious, if you like, and I believe a little in the manner of the great Venetians. From what I have been told, I should say that he was a sort of Venetian Boucher, just as Longhi was a more bizarre and less poetic Watteau. But that, so far as I am concerned, is mere repetition. I don't pretend to know anything about painting. I like a good likeness, if it happens to be a historical personage; beyond that I am indifferent."

Finding Brakespeare so intent a listener, the old man developed new ideas of the boy's intelligence. It is worth remarking that he never again spoke to him quite as a child. And he presently permitted him the run of the house.

However, at the end of several days, he found himself annoyed at the frequency of the boy's questions. Conversation, at least his conversation, should be allowed to proceed without interruption; if anyone else was allowed to talk, how could he properly direct his own thought? Plagued by this too narrow interest in a Venetian courtesan —for once the euphemism seemed to him justified—at the expense of more generous characters, he decided to dispose of Alessandrina by giving the boy everything he had written concerning her and the Venetian episode in the life of Clarence Urquart. Brakespeare, however, indicated that he thought it would be safer not to entrust him with both manuscripts at one time.

Mr. Brakespeare put a portfolio into his hands.

"Bring it back tomorrow," he said severely, "and take care that you don't lose any of the sheets. I stitched the covers myself, and it's not very well done."

"Did you write it?" Brakespeare asked simply. The cover was labeled: *Appendix H.*

"Not entirely. You may call as much of it as you like a translation."

The boy moved toward the door.

Outside, he walked slowly, inspecting the covers. Looking up, he saw, over the laurel-hedge, his grandfather staring at him through the windowpanes. The sun was on the panes, so that the old man seemed to be staring at him blindly out of a golden cloud. The boy started off on a lope which did not slow down until he had reached his own bedroom, where he coiled himself on the shining brocade and began at once to read.

Although at the age of fifteen Alessandrina Cicogna had not been generally seen, she was already remarkable among Venetians for her quiet and sumptuous beauty. Her family possessed the two most beautiful pearls in Venice, a stagnant palace of the Grand Canal, the privileges of their descent from one of the Doges, and scarcely any other fortune. She was married just as she was entering her sixteenth year to Count Monza, a vindictive, vain and ridiculous person, the heir of a rich Bolognese family who had come up to Venice in his youth to enjoy the distractions of the Carnival and found the city so agreeable to his tastes that he had stayed on from year to year, most indulgently, only returning to Bologna to attend the funerals of his noble connections and to collect his rents and legacies. Micro- cephalous, with the distinction of a great nose and pompous neck, he yet appeared to advantage in a mask and was commonly considered possible as a husband. On the day of her wedding Alessandrina wept; but whether her tears came from the chill modesty of a virgin or more warmly from chagrin at the uncomeliness of her bridegroom, was a matter of opinion and afforded some conjecture; long afterwards she herself said that she must have wept for the affront done her pride in offering her to one not born a Venetian.

The first year of her married life was not over when Alessandrina discovered that three of her maids were with child; a little after her first anniversary she came on her husband embracing a fourth behind an inadequate screen. Annoyed by this unwarranted interference in her domestic arrangements—she had already noticed a slackness in her service, and her morning chocolate was frequently cold—she de- termined on revenge in kind. Unfortunately, she selected as a com- panion in its accomplishment her quick and handsome cousin, Ippo- lito Venier, a youth as noble as herself and so naturally gifted for venery that the Countess would soon have found herself at the dis- posal of her emotions had not the Venetian state, for reasons of its own, seen fit to remove her lover under a decree of permanent exile.

Disconsolate, Alessandrina sought consolation. What had begun in intellectual pride and for the sake of revenge was continued for its own sake and without thought of her husband. She showed an ever- increasing zest in variety. It began to look as though the Countess was bent on transferring all the names in the Libro d'Oro to her small and most intimate diaries. This was not due to natural inconstance; rather she was faithless through fate. Her second gallant was attached in an untimely hour to the Ambassador to Portugal; the third had the mis- fortune to murder his uncle after a game of faro; another, who was but seventeen, was kidnapped by a fleshly Cardinal on his way to Rome; the fifth, whom she had chosen for his length of nose, fell into the canal when drunk and was not recovered until the following morning, during which brief interval his nose had been eaten away. Those that followed were as unfortunate in circumstance as brief in their attendance.

The Count Monza fancied himself a logical man with a nice sense of justice. When his vanity finally admitted what all Venice had been ready to believe at the first rumor of scandal, he smiled cuckoldly, and said: "Allora, sorpasso tutti i veniziani, anche nobilissimi; le famiglie ducali non portano mai che un corno supro lo stemma, di qui innanzi ho il gran privilegio di portarne due." The next day he gathered together his wife's meagre dowry, placed it in her hands, and with a politeness which does him credit, ordered her from under his roof. He descended with her to the gondola, saw to the arrangement of her private chests and boxes in the barges, stood at last among the lights of the linkboys while her black gondola, mirrored on the black waters in reflections of sulphur, disappeared on the canal. The next day he saw to it that she was enrolled among the twelve thousand prostitutes of the city; the expense of enregistration he paid and undertook to pay the taxes which the Most Serene Republic, since it had lost the East, imposed upon this traffic. The necessary papers were carried to her by one of the servants she had lately commanded.

"The Countess," her husband wrote, "has shown so marked a disposition to change her lovers on the least occasion that I can but wish her in a position to indulge her humor to the utmost without offense to the proprieties and my honor. Her present fortune, increased by presents, which will, I am sure, be handsome, should give her a roof over her head. With discreet administration, she may even survive without suffering into old age. At least she will be spared certain troubles—as disembarrassing herself of her gallants once she is tired of them. Indeed, I doubt if she will find many now who will ask two successive nights for her favors; the most bothersome will hardly last a fortnight."

The Countess accepted his gambit as though it had been the fool's mate. She acquired a palace on a discreet canal and painted her own arms on the gondola poles. There she lived like any other great Venetian lady, only she was supported by her admirers, by those she chose to admire her, not her husband. Alessandrina was, in many respects, a conservative of manners.

Alessandrina was, like her century, urbane, witty with elegance, reasonable and discreet. She had as an Italian inheritance from an earlier generation that fondness for grandeur which appears alike in the stage decorations of Bebbiena and in those solid simulacra of clouds which are the finest achievement of baroque architecture. But this she allowed to appear only in the extravagances of her dress and the conceits of her cookery. It never occurred to her that the sentiments which her beauty aroused in men partook of the divine; it was enough that they should not through custom become stale.

It was therefore that she planned that marvelous series of bedrooms. She knew that beauty, to be continuously perceived, must retain its power to surprise. And, as though she had learned her art in the baroque school, she aimed to seduce through astonishment. There was one high chamber of the Renaissance, and in the center a bed of burnished wood broad as a barge, covered with deep brocades —a gilded bewilderment of carved petals and jutting buds that climbed along the four turned pillars to the carved roof, whence the elaborate reflections gave her flesh the gold colour of figures in a Giorgone landscape, her eyes their profound serenity, her hair points of flame. There was a paneled room with a fragile couch, painted an apricot color, with flat loops of leaves, in which she became as rosy as a shepherdess in an elegant pastoral. In a room with tiny mirrors, there was a bed of Venetian green, with a plumed baldaquin, hung with curtains of blue satin and greenish blue, where her beauty became so white that one could see the blue veins under her skin, and the black velvet band at her neck made her look as though she had been gracefully decapitated in a powdered wig hung with little bows and rosebuds. There was another room with wider mirrors, which, when she received there and the lights were on, revived all that Giulio Romano had ever imagined of love, the clear mirrors, mirroring the opposite mirror, so endlessly mirrored their own diminishing surfaces and images. There was a room made entirely of Capodimonte china, where the porcelain bedstead, curtained in perhaps magenta, gave her the lustre of a fine figurine and dabs of carmine on the cheeks and lips. There were other rooms with other beds. The last was a cell like a nun's, with narrow blue plaster walls and one stern pallet set under an arch; it was here that she took last leave of her friends.

The pride of the Countess was that of an aristocrat, not of an angel. Had she lived before time, she had doubtless looked on Lucifer as a foolish and inconsiderate angel. Living when she did, she never lost an opportunity to ridicule the rebellious and all who complained of the arrangements of a wise and beneficent Deity. Reason had placed its limitations on the senses, and if there was a desperateness in her love, it was brought by a presentiment of death. And in the Venice of the eighteenth century she was much sought after; a city which stank with the odour of decomposed magnificence, where the revellers of the Carnival went shrouded in black and looked out through the sockets of their bone-white masks with the eyes of skeletons, could not well ignore her. For it seemed, almost, as if she had succeeded, at last, in bringing love to its proper pitch. With her wit she destroyed its metaphysical pretensions, with her taste she overcame its grossness, with the inventiveness of her mind she relieved its intolerable tedium. She resolved the discords of the treble and the bass, and reduced its violent and uneven rhythms, with which men had once striven in vain to produce a divine symphony, to the small and ordered proportions of a pleasant chamber music.

It was through no lack of seriousness that Alessandrina treated love as a form of social intercourse, like dining or any other. She often said that it was through dining, no less than through love, eloquence and the exercise of the rational faculties, that man distinguished himself from the lower animals. She gave as much thought to the entertainment when she had many guests as when she had only one; though there was but one dining-room, her dinners were as formal and various as her ways of making love. In neither case did she overlook the necessity for some sort of artificial intoxication; her winecellars were replete with rare vintages. Young English lords, traveling on the Continent, became courteous, eloquent even, over her Ronciglione, Chiarella di Calabria and the Greek wines from Samos; the Abbé de Bernis, on one occasion, swooned from excess of expectation before he could be served from a dish of figpeckers which had been brought in by an old and very slow servant; and cardinals were sometimes seen, gorging beyond discretion, to carry away the dessert in their napkins.

She was not rapacious; she put the matter quite simply, very nearly anticipating a later sentiment: men must love and women must live. She left all matters of money to be carried on by her major-domo, a scrupulous man who was thought to be either a Turk or a Jew by birth and was certainly a eunuch through later transactions. She was, she said, far too generous by nature ever to touch money. She did, it is true, occasionally permit herself an unprofitable diversion, just as a great actress will sometimes find amusement in playing charades before her friends. The most celebrated of these was her affair with the comedian Sacchi; it was not typical.

The Count Monza, seeing all that was most gallant in Venice and even princes from the most distant provinces gathered at the Countess's waterstair, boasted that this was the same woman he had chased from his bed when she was still young. He seemed to take a certain pride in calling attention to his ridiculous position. He had failed in his revenge, but was not properly ashamed of it. Alessandrina saw that he must be crushed into silence, must be made to suffer, if possible, from jealousy. Now it was quite obvious that the Count could not be made jealous of a hundred lovers, for jealousy, like desire, disappears in a crowd; she must somehow create in the Count's mind the illusion that he alone had the right to her favors and at the same time prevent him from ever entering into the possession of her beauty. It was a matter requiring some subtlety.

She sent for Antonio Sacchi and put her plan before him. Sacchi was the true creator of Truffaldino, that wittier cousin of Pantaleone, the latest addition to the characters of the old *commedia dell' arte*, for the comic dramatists of the time simply indicated his scenes by writing, *Entra Truffaldino—Esce Truffaldino*, and left the rest to his own invention. Inimitable as a mimic, delighting in his own facility, Sacchi found the part the Countess had assigned him in her comedy exactly suited to his genius.

They waited until the Countess had been informed by her spies that the Count was expected at the theatre. She appeared in her loge just before the fall of the first curtain. At the beginning of the entr'acte, the Count turned instinctively to see what bloods would come to ply their courtesies. He raised his lorgnette. Alessandrina was alone in her box. The crimson doors at the end of the box opened, and he saw his own self enter and, coming forward, kiss her lifted hand. He saw himself sit down beside her, move the gilded chair, smile, then raising his lorgnette ogle the pit with an identical gesture. There could be no doubt about it. The Count Monza was familiar enough with his own visage: the powdered tiewig with the one streak of reddish hair, the great nose, the rose-wattled neck falling in folds over the neckcloth. The figure smiled and tittered as he would have done, and with ludicrous ease. Every detail was reproduced with the ample proportions of a caricature. He was astounded and aroused. He plucked at his solid thighs. The play began again, and the apparition disappeared. But it appeared again at the end of the act, and when the Countess left the box, left with her.

From now on the Countess was never seen in public without Sacchi. The Count fell into a rage of annoyance, then, as with repetition the thing gained on his mind, into a trouble of desire. He listened, eavesdropping, to the scandalmongers, who pretended to be shocked that the Countess should, of all people, choose the Count as an *amant de coeur*; he sat fascinated with the thought of the favors which he had unknowingly enjoyed, favors, it seemed, quite beyond common. But when he was again alone, he felt nothing but jealousy— jealousy for his own body which could perform such delicious feats without his knowledge. He hired an assassin to put an end to his troublesome impostor, but hesitated at the last moment lest he should fall into the sin of self-murder. He consulted a cabalist but was afraid to act too definitely on his somewhat obscure advice. He went abroad in a new mask of white parchment of grotesque size and a peculiar shape. The other assumed a similar disguisement, even more grotesque, and was still recognizable by his gait, like a swan's.

After a period of violent depression, the Count came on dull despair and at times believed himself dead. When somewhat later he did actually die, it was found that he had practically exhausted his fortune in payments for the masses which had already been said for the repose of his soul.

The Countess had begun delighting in the comedy and ended by being pleased with the comedian. She sometimes referred to it as a moral episode, designed for the instruction of the young.

The fame of Alessandrina had long since passed the confines of the Venetian Republic. Which is not remarkable, when one considers how well she had succeeded in being gay without being callous, how prettily she had maintained her dignity in a thousand difficult positions, how wisely she had restrained the pretensions of love. Catherine of Russia, aware of her own grossness, used always to write to her for advice whenever her amorous affairs became too complicated for her own comprehension. The Duchess of Kingston praised her with envy. And James III of England, during his wandering exile, presented her with the Order of the Garter; she was the only woman who ever in public wore its insignia where it was intended to be worn.

Her career was brought to an end by an attack of smallpox which left her constitution unimpaired but also unrecognizable. The last two decades of her life are not so satisfactory, for she seemed to be quite unable to make up her mind whether to become a bluestocking or simply a pious old lady. After having been induced to give up a goodly portion of her wealth for the restoration of decayed convents, the importation of miraculous fragments from saintly cadavers exhumed in the Indies, the baptism of abandoned infants, and the beatification of the holy Ortensia, a Sicilian nun whose credentials of holiness she afterwards came seriously to doubt, she gathered her forces together and devoted the rest of her life to combating those romantical sentiments which she saw with a withered eye were gradually coming into fashion with the young. It was true that she had always distrusted unkempt passion and violent lyricism, that she thought excessive sensibility indecent and saw nothing charming in suicide; but the maliciousness of her attack was rather the result of her having frequently seen Rousseau when as a young man he was attached to the French Embassy and found him a mean silly fellow, of no presence and suspect habits.

Dying, she ordered herself dressed once more in a court dress of cloth of silver, spreading voluminously from the pointed waist, spangled with lace looped from silver rosebuds. The straight stays prevented its falling at the shoulders and leaving bare the shrunken breasts. The powdered hair was brought low to cover the ears which for a long time had been too large. "God," she said, "will appreciate my mundanity."

TOADSTOOLS ARE POISON

BEYOND THE WINDOW sill was the grape-arbor, and the sky looked cold. And the grape-vines climbed from the ground, twisting a hairy bark. Few leaves were left on the lattice and they were brown; bunches of grapes, dwarfed, had dried. Along the top of the arbor the sparrows gathered in drooping rows, sitting cold.

When I stood up, I could see over the sill. I waited while Ginny cooked my supper. And I could see across the garden to the fence and the alley, and then another fence and the alley, and then another fence with whitewashed points and Mrs. Gage's garden and, beyond, the roof of the Rainleys' house. That was where Alice lived. They had a red roof. And though they lived in town they had two cows.

I used to see their cows coming home. But when it was cold, they stayed at home. And I would go down with Alice to the stable to look at them. There was a dry smell of hay when you stepped into the dark, and when you crossed the light that came from the left, you could count the dust. Then Alice would lift me up and I would see the cows in their dark stalls, chewing and moving and looking meanly with big eyes. I held tight to Alice's arms, afraid of their horns. And then Scott would come and bring more fodder on a pitchfork and throw it in to the cows.

He was a little nigger and very old. His clothes were old. His black felt hat had no brim and he pulled it on the back of his head; two holes were cut in the crown. His hair was grey, and he wore on his chin a little beard like a goat's, but crinkled, for after all he was black. He was shrivelled and black and dried up like those bunches of grapes that stayed on the vines after the leaves were fallen or brown. One eye had been bored by a cow's horn and was blue and blind. The other bulged and could see, the ball bloodshot and strained.

When he came in with the cows' supper, when he came to the stalls with fodder, I saw his pitchfork. The tines were long and, in the dark stable, shining. There was dust in the slanting line of sun. He made me afraid. And I held Alice's hand. He wore blue jeans, but, pitching the fodder, wore besides an old black broadcloth vest and coat.

I was waiting for my supper. I do not know when I began listening, but soon it was dark in the kitchen. John Harris came in, tramping on the back porch before he opened the door. And Ginny said, "I can't hardly see to cook supper." There were still the sparrows on the grape-arbor, sitting cold. But when Ellie Lee lit the gas, it was darker outside.

John slapped Ellie Lee and she giggled and said, "Go on!" And Ginny said, "I don't know how in the name o' th' Lord you speck me to get supper an' you-all carrying on like 'at."

Ellie said, "Is it time for me to fix that chile's table?" She didn't mind when John hurt her. She only laughed. Ginny was the one that minded.

But she laughed, too, when John asked about how I was growing. They all laughed. And Ginny said, "You'll be a big boy afore we-all know it."

John washed his hands at the sink, and on the towel behind the door dried them. And I sat down at my table, and Ellie sat on another chair across from me and watched me eat. Hers was a big chair and mine just the right size.

"Yessa. He went right in de drugstore and ast Mr. Huff. He says, 'I want some Rough-on-Rats.'"

"Poor Sister Scott," said Ginny. "I certainly do feel sorry for her."

"He says, 'My house is jes' overrun with rats, jes' as big as life,' he says, and Mr. Huff sole it to him."

"Who'd 'a' thought it?" said Ginny. "He took on sumpin' awful at the funeral. He went on jes' like a crazy man. All de way out to de grabeyard."

"Who buried her, Miss Ginny?"

"We did, Sister Ellie. She was a Galilean Fisherman. Same as me."

When Ginny went to funerals, she wore a black dress that had been my mother's and her gold-rimmed spectacles and a purple silk scarf that wound over her shoulder and went down to her waist. She was laced very tight and my mother said that was what made her sick all the time, but Ginny said it was a strange man had walked three times around the house and put a spell on her. Her scarf had a fringe and letters of gold.

"And paid right up. She had a real nice fune'al," said Ginny. "She was always kind o' poorly, Sister Scott was. So I never thought nothing about it."

"Was you there, Miss Ginny?"

"Yes'm, Sister Ellie. We was all dere. All de Galilean Fishermen went wid 'er to de grabeyard. I walked all de way out and back."

"You want some more milk-toast?" Ellie asked me.

"Yes."

"Yes, what?"

"Yes, please."

"You got some more milk-toast, Miss Ginny?"

"I reckon if he's a good boy I got some mo' for 'im."

"He give 't to her in de coffee," John said. "And she drunk it down and never knowed they was poison in it."

I ate my milk toast. I was not naughty. I did not spill.

"Why do they call him Pleas, Ginny?"

" 'Cause dat's his name. His name's Pleasant, but dey jes' calls him Pleas. His name's Pleas Scott."

There was a steel comb on the shelf and a mirror beside the door, and John bent to it to part his crispy hair.

"He knowed how to pleasure himself with the women," John said, "and always did." He stopped to laugh.

"He always was an ornery nigger," said Ginny.

"What's he get now?" asked Ellie.

"I got some nice prunes for 'im ef he's a good boy. What d'you say?"

"Please, Ginny." She gave me the prunes.

"Poor Sister Scott," said Ginny. "She was always complaining. I reckon she must 'a' suffered pretty much the way I do. Seems like Pleas might 'a' waited till the good Lord was ready to take her."

John said, "He mussa got tired waitin'."

"Yes," said Ginny. "He always was an ornery nigger. An' there's sumpun else he gone get tired of afore he's through. He gonna get mighty tired o' dat jail."

Ellie untied my bib, and I folded it in two. "This way!" she said and helped me fold it along the other wrinkle. "You think they'll hang him?"

"Sure, he's a black man," said John. "They got him in jail now. Behind the bars. Mr. Huff's done testified ag'inst him. He done swore he sol' him de poison."

I pondered over what I had heard. Poison I knew, although it was winter.

It had rained and then the rain had stopped, and when we ran out of the house and down the porch steps, we saw that it was sunny

494

on the grass. We played. It was my birthday. And there were many children to play. High up in the maple leaves there was still a sound of rain, and when we came into the hollow of shade under the trees, it was wet there and green. Water played, running out of the hydrant. And the grass all around had put up its umbrellas.

Clumps of umbrellas. All tiny and white, each with a top and little white handle. I plucked one and lifted it; the smell was not nice. Then all the children took one, all through the grass where the rain was still twinkling. And we paraded. We held umbrellas between us and the sun.

Then Alice came running to tell me to put it down. "Toadstools are poison. You mustn't touch them. If you taste one, you will die. You mustn't ever touch them. If you do, it will make you sick."

"Why don't you touch one and be sick?" I asked her.

"Put them down. You all must put them down. They are toadstools."

Then my mother came and called us in. We went in slowly. In the dining-room was a party and a cake with candles. And they told me to blow out the candles.

Three candles for three years and one to grow.

I blew and blew hard. And while we were at the party, it rained again.

I heard them every evening, while I waited for my supper and John came in and wiped his black bony hands on the towel and it was dark in the kitchen till Ellie lit the gas; I heard them. And sometimes, too, coming into the parlor, I heard them. My mother would see me there and say, "Come speak to Mrs. Cole." And then, "Run, now, and play." But I could still hear them.

Pleas I did not know. But Scott I knew. I had seen him in the stable. And I had seen him coming past our alley, driving the Rainleys' cows. It was cold now, and he did not come any more. So I knew he must be in jail.

He was a crooked little man. He walked with a goatee and one eye lifeless and blue. And he walked straight into the drugstore. (Sometimes I let him stop outside on the pavement and look at the red and blue and green jars shining in the window. But not always.) I saw Pleas Scott go into the drugstore and lean across the counter, leaning on the counter with his elbow. He had on a black broadcloth suit and a boiled shirt, washed and stiffened but not starched. He leaned toward Mr. Huff—his lifeless eye was toward the store and he looked through his bulging brown eye that was bloodshot and strained at Mr. Huff. He said, "I want Rough-on-Rats. I want it to kill rats." Mr. Huff was scared. But he told him all about the rats. There was no one else in the drugstore. He was a little man with thin pale hair. And at last he was so scared that he went behind the glass screen and brought out a square paper package that said, "Rough-on-Rats" and handed it to him. He put down his money, and Mr. Huff put it in the cash drawer which shut with a bell. And Pleas went home and watched his wife get supper. He sat in a rocking chair. He rocked fast. And when his wife said, "Supper's ready," he said, "Look out there!" She looked out the window and, while she wasn't looking, he put the poison into her coffee. Then they sat down to the table. He drank his coffee and watched her all the time she drank hers.

His wife I could never see. She was just a colored woman who complained a great deal and drank rat poison in her coffee. I saw her pour it out from her cup to the saucer and let it cool, and Pleas was watching her all the time, leaning across the table, with his blind and his big red bulging bloodshot eye.

Ellie Lee was a good girl. My mother said she was. She kept me from going past the cellar door when it was open. It was dark there, the stairs were steep, and the Buggaman was down there. She was a yellow girl and could read and write. She taught me my letters. I could read them from my blocks. She used to take a block with her when we went for a walk, so she could show the other nurses how I could read.

Now we only took one walk. Sometimes we started another way, but always we came home past the jail. The windows were high, and there were iron bars. Sometimes we saw a Negro man behind the bars. But it was never Scott. We walked in the afternoon, after my nap.

But that day we went upstairs right after my breakfast and she pulled my arm going up the stairs. She hurried me so she made me cry, and my mother came to the foot of the stairs and said, "What's the matter, Ellie?"

"I don't know'm. He jes' contrary as anything this morning."

"Go with Ellie," said my mother.

But my feet couldn't go fast enough. She jerked my arm. And all the time I was in the bathroom she kept coming and saying, "Ain't you done yit? I wish you'd hurry up. We ain't never gonna git there."

My arm wouldn't go into my coat. She hurt me. "If you don't stop bothering me, I'm gonna call the Buggaman. 'Cause he's right there." And I heard him growling. I couldn't see him. I couldn't tell where he was. But I heard him and I put the other arm in my coat. Ellie pushed on my hat and said, "There!"

And we went down the stairs and along the hall and into the kitchen, where Ellie took her hat and coat. "I'm going, Miss Ginny," she said.

"I'll be prayin'," said Ginny. "I'll be prayin' to the good Lord for him. He's a sinner, but we all knowed him. So I'll be prayin'."

Ellie had on her hat and put on her coat while we crossed the porch. She still held my hand and we hurried on. John Harris was waiting for us at the back gate, the little gate, which only one of us could go through at a time.

When we were in the alley, Ellie said, "Here, take 'is chile." And when I was in his arms, I could see over the fence and into our garden; I could see over the points of the whitewashed fence into Mrs. Gage's garden. There was a Negro man pushing a plow. He went very slowly; the earth curled back and fell and crumbled. It was shiny where the plow had cut it, as though the steel had rubbed off on the earth.

We came out on the sidewalk and John Harris put me down. Ellie took my hand and made me run while she walked and John Harris walked beside her. She didn't say anything while we went, and all the time we went downtown.

Mrs. Hunt's rocking-chair was on her porch but it rocked alone and the door was shut and all the shutters were shut on the house. Mr. Hunt was in his blacksmith shop. There were many people while we were going past, and Ellie would not let me stay. I remembered Mr. Hunt deep behind his open doors in the dark splashing sparks from a red fire.

There were more people. They were on the sidewalk and all in the street and even under the white wall. Ellie had to go slowly. She held me by the hand. We went between the people. She spoke to somebody and laughed. Then she put me in front of her and pressed, and the whole crowd pressed. And against us again, pressed. Her hands were on my shoulders, and she pushed me by a pair of muddy legs and past an apron. We squeezed out on the long grey stone that was the curb.

I couldn't see Ellie. But above me she laughed and said, "I never thought we'd get here."

"I guess 'twasn't but one nigger wasn't in no hurry to git here dis mawnin'."

"No, he warn't in no hurry." They laughed.

497

"Where is it?"

"It right dere. Right where you lookin'."

"Is dat it?"

"Dat's it?"

"Never knowed it'd look like dat."

"Dat's it all right."

I clung to Ellie's apron. It was fresh and white and still smelled damp. I said, "I want to see."

So Ellie held me up, and I looked at the windows of the jail. It was dark behind the bars of the windows. I could see the panes, but I couldn't see Pleas Scott.

The jail was brick. And beyond it was a high wall of whitewashed stones. There were little grasses that grew there. They slept between the stones, seeded and brown. All winter they slept.

"There!" she said. "You see?"

There were colored boys on the roof that looked down behind the wall. They held on with their hands, and their legs clambered down the roof. They were staring at something that was like a swing, with a rope. And beyond was a catalpa tree.

"There! You done seed!" She put me down. The crowd pressed and pushed us back from the curb. I was down among legs, corduroy legs and blue-jeans, and black skirts and aprons. And I wondered why it was women had laps and men didn't and men had long legs. And above me and all around me, I could hear the hum of their voices and far out into the street, calls, "Hy there, Lucy," and "Look out there, boy, they'll be gittin' you next," and hoots and shoves and, in the shoves, shrieks and a shrill girl and giggles. I couldn't see. I could smell. I was lost and held close to Ellie.

Then the clock struck and there was a hush. It struck from the courthouse and was a long time striking. I could feel the niggers straining. Ellie's hands were on my shoulders.

I heard Ellie whisper, "He comin'! He comin'!" I heard the crowd hushing. I heard them a long time when they were making no noise. Then somewhere a man began talking the way they do when they read. The niggers breathed. They did not move.

Ellie shook like she was cold. And she held me hard. She pulled my coat tight and it came against my throat, and hurt.

Then the crowd moved and opened their mouths. The woman in front of me went down on her knees. And I heard "Amen!"

I wanted to see and turned my head to Ellie. She was smiling like something hurt her and looking straight ahead. John Harris was behind her. His face was very black, and there was sweat on his cheeks.

He held her, his arms coming round from behind her, and gripped on her arms. And she still looked away with that look like a smile. She shook like she was cold.

I wanted to go. But Ellie would not hear. The woman in the gutter moaned, and the crowd was moving away. She bowed back and forth. "O Jesus!" she moaned, "O Jesus!" And Ellie took my hand. We left the woman in the gutter.

We did not go home the way we came. John Harris was not with us. We went alone.

I said, "What did they do?" And Ellie said, "They done hung Pleas Scott." And I said, "What for did they?" And she said, "He was a bad man." And I said, "Did it hurt him?" And she said, "I reckon so." And I said, "Why?" And she said, "Don't ast so many questions." We went slowly. Ellie walked tired.

We were going by the Rainleys'. I saw the back-gate. Then I said, "Is Scott dead, Ellie?" And she answered, "Yes." I wondered did it hurt to be dead. A dead bird squints his eyes and holds his claws shrivelled on his breast. He can not fly any more. I never saw a dead horse.

And the gate opened and its hinges swung, and Scott came out. Ellie spoke to him. And he asked her, and she said, "Yes, I was there." He had on his old hat with the holes in it and his old black coat. He had a basket in one hand that sagged on the side. He shook his head, squinting the eyelid. Then he looked at me with his fierce red eye. And he could see.

I held to Ellie's apron. I did not want to hear what he said. "He didn't seem to mind. He behaved just like he was lookin' at what was going on." That was Ellie's voice. Scott said something about the Lord.

And when he was gone, I took Ellie's hand and said, "Why can he walk?"

"What you talkin' 'bout, chile?"

I ran beside her. "If he's dead," I said, "why can he walk?"

"But that's Scott, honey. That ain't him. It was Pleas Scott they hung."

"Of course, I know that's Scott," I said. "But why does he squint his eye if he's not dead? Why does he, why?"

But Ellie wouldn't answer me. She only said, "He's not dead." That wasn't what I wanted to know.

The North American Review: June, 1932

I

THE DOOR OPENED with a slow precision, very slowly at first, then with a sudden, still timid resolution swung wide. A colored man emerged. The door closed softly again.

"Mr. Wanhope—" The Negro had on a canvas apron. Around him the room swept in grand proportions. Between pilasters the walls rose, curving to form a perfect oval at the cornice. All was ample, all was white and austere.

"Mr. Wanhope!" He could not make out if the man in the low chair was asleep. He came closer.

"Those boys out there again."

The paper that had been held in slack hands suddenly crackled.

"You black scoundrel!" Like a fire from stirred ashes, Wanhope's eyes leapt under his grey tufted eyebrows. "What are you bothering me about?"

The Negro shuffled backward a step or two. He was not really afraid of the old gentleman. He wanted to take himself away from that noise.

"I just thought you might like to know, Mr. Wanhope."

"Know what?"

"It's those boys. They out in the backyard. They come climbin' all over yo' arbor. An' now they done eatin' yo' Seckel pears."

"Drive 'em away, Sam. What do think I keep you for? Drive 'em away!"

"Yes, sir, Mr. Wanhope." Sam moved a little further toward the door. "Yes, sir."

"Well, what are you standing there for?"

From concealed corners light came into the room; subdued by arches, the early afternoon of August was here no more than a sober glow. The chair Wanhope sat in was the utmost the mid-century could grant to comfort. It was all curves and carvings, wadded and tufted, and like nothing else in the room. Elsewhere the furniture stood with the staid dignity of the English Regency.

The Negro was small and gnarled. "I don' think they go for me. They common boys."

"Call the police. What do I pay taxes for? Tell me, do you know what I pay taxes for? Then I'll tell you. Do I get the police when I want them? No! What do I get? Schools!" He heaved himself out of his chair as though he were a man of great bulk. His breathing was heavy. "It's this damn fool education, that's what it is. What do they teach 'em in these public schools? To trespass on other people's property. And I pay for it." He shouted at Sam as though he had been an assembly.

The Negro fidgeted uneasily. Then Wanhope looked at him. "Get out!"°

Philip Wanhope was tall rather than large. His complexion was, like his sisters', naturally florid; but in his case it had been saturated until above the cheekbones the color was more than crimson. He imported his own pipes of Madeira, and in the eighties was one of the last three members of the Pomham Club who did so. He was dressed in a Norfolk jacket of a rough pale tweed, a costume which his contemporaries among the manufacturing gentry of Rhode Island regarded as outlandish. The impression he made on them was of something bucolic and at the same time sinister. Men at the club liked to talk to him; they were not so sure they liked Wanhope. His voice was very loud; the look in his grey eyes was disquieting; and to be overheard in conversation with him was a little like being caught consulting an old goat.

In the eighties of the last century, the backyards of Providence had still a carefully tended country aspect. Behind Felicity Street the arbors ran continuous, and boys, once they had climbed the first, could pass from one to another, when grapes were ripe, feeding on Niagara, Catawba and Concord sweetness. That summer the arbors hung in green profusion, but the bunches were small and hard. The earliest vines had only begun to ripen. The pilfering boys, Wanhope knew, would have dropped to the ground.

"After my pears—" He had lived so many years alone, he was scarcely aware that he was talking aloud.

He passed through one of the arches to the window it concealed. It showed a small corner of the grape-arbor, the pear-trees not at all. Yet he leaned through the open space under the sash to shout:

"I'll pay fifty per cent taxes to support jails, but not one cent for schools. You hear me? Not one cent for schools!"

What Wanhope could see was the party fence that divided his backyard from that of his sisters. As he caught sight of the tall, close, whitewashed palings which cut him off from them, he was appeased. He almost smiled. And the goatish look came back to his face.

II

The tradition of the younger son of noble parentage who came to America in the seventeenth century—or at latest in the first half of the eighteenth—seeking his fortune, perhaps to find it, but at all events to leave a great name to his descendants, we must usually regard as suspect. There were undoubtedly some young men in the American colonies whose names were very old; but there cannot ever have been very many of them. For why, we must ask, when the privileges of the aristocracy were still unassailed, should anyone, even in the rashness of youth, forego position and influence for the very uncertain advantages of adventure in the wilderness? Those on top in the Old World did not come easily to the levelling of the New. The great colonial families, we know, were usually people who started with some means; but they were for the most part of unmistakable middle-class origin. They were on the make. Their place was in America.

However, it happened that several aristocratic English families did send sons over to New England to take their share in the textile industry. This was well after the Revolution. George III was in his dotage when the first Wanhope set foot on these shores, descending from a packet to the docks at Providence. He was tall, spare, approaching forty. As many Englishmen are apt to do to Americans, he appeared stupid when he was not. Edmund Wanhope drove in a caleche about the Narragansett Plantations (the name remaining from an imaginary project that in all clsc had been abandoned), with an eye as obviously unseeing as his grandfather had used in his youth on the Grand Tour. Yet, just as the grandfather, then a young man, had returned to England with gods in the hold, bronzes from Herculaneum and some late, though fine, marbles from the outlying Greek isles, Mr. Wanhope came back to the Bay House at Providence with options on three mill-streams in the back-country. He promptly acquired full rights in one of them, a small river, running strong and steep in its descent. Presently he was importing skilled weavers from Lancashire.

The grandfather was the Earl of Urchinfield. And behind him ancestors stretched, in the male line alone, each more and more misty, until the last dissolved in Saxon myths. The Wanhopes were pre-Conquest.

AN ARISTOCRAT

Because he was not mean in his manners as were most of the native mill-owners, Mr. Wanhope was given credit for a magnanimity he did not possess. Providence supposed that he had come out to America prepared to sacrifice his own labors in order to sustain ancestral estates in England. It was not so. He was on his own; he had seen a chance and taken it; his profits, when they did not go back into the mill, he used to maintain himself in what he conceived as the only proper state for a gentleman. As soon as his means allowed, he never considered any other. He was as hard as any manufacturer among them; but the fact that he did not impose on himself the same privations to which he put his workmen, as did his competitors in Fall River, just across the Massachusetts line, nor like them live in meager gloom, in houses as like as possible to the millhands' tenements, set Edmund Wanhope apart. He was thought to be richer than he was. Since he kept his own counsel, any rumor about him was good. Occasionally his sister, a great lady married to an Irish marquess, imposing in figure as she was outrageous in tongue, would descend on him. It was commonly supposed that her visits had no other purpose than to carry away from Rhode Island enormous sums.

There was always a Lord Urchinfield in England. He might change, but at no time did he lack for heirs. The possibility of the title's devolving upon Edmund was remote. Still, Wanhope was a name to pass on.

The mill-owner married a lady of New England, who as promptly as the proprieties permitted bore him a son. Edmund outlived him. He had married late and lived to be nearly ninety. He would train his grandson Philip to take over the mill. But at home he remained what he had always been, a gentleman of eighteenth-century England who chanced to survive until he learned by telegraph that James K. Polk had been nominated for President of the United States. The transition from Norfolk to the Narragansett Plantations had not been for the man of forty less easy than for his contemporaries in England to pass from the reign of George III to the riots under William IV and the reforms of Victoria. In his great old age, when his face, in spite of the wrinkles in the all but wasted flesh, acquired an intense and almost spiritual purity of gaze, he reverted more and more to the speech and, as far as decrepitude would allow, to the habits of his youth. After dinner, when the cloth had been removed, young Philip sat late at table with him. The Madeira was a concession to Rhode Island; but, once having adopted this custom, he continued it long after most of the natives of the country had ceased to serve wine altogether. He taught the boy to drink it as though it were

Port. For, from the day when Philip, then sixteen, entered Brown, his grandfather made a great to-do about treating him as a man of the world. When, as sometimes happened, the lad drank more Madeira than he could hold and still stand, Edmund had him carried upstairs. He would then finish his own glass. When the servants were out of the way, he would find Philip laid on his bed, where he tucked him in, as though he had been a sleeping child.

His granddaughters, Agatha and Georgina, Philip's sisters, he left, with an indifference that was like an ignorance of their existence, entirely to the care of their mother. Now that he was old, he liked his daughter-in-law less than ever. The girls grew up under his roof and were gawkily fitted to a spare gentility. Both were tall, their complexions were bright; otherwise they were unremarkable. They were products of New England, and yet belonged to that state which more than any other in the region has a generous air. They were not unread; their innocence had a fatiguing complacency. Their mother had instructed them in no vice but avarice, which she inculcated under the virtuous name of thrift. Secure in their position, they were taught fine sewing and along with it a sense of responsibility toward the poor; but pity, being a quality of the imagination, was unknown to them.

Their mother kept them, as far as the great house allowed, away from their grandfather's voice, which more and more, as senility screeched it, indulged in scurrilities and worse, unsuited to their gentle ears. Since she could not keep them entirely out of its sound, she told them they simply must not hear what their grandfather, now quite lost in schoolboy memories, muttered about those lovely gracious walls. "Men," she said, "are like that." Since this particular old man clung to life after she had gone out of the house for good, Agatha and Georgina had some years which they spent almost entirely in bedrooms without windows on Felicity Street.

III

Litigation began almost with the old man's death. Agatha and Georgina would have the small house, which had been built for their father at the time of his marriage. It was next the one from which they traipsed, voluminous in mourning, pointing stiff bonnets and flapping veils of windy black. They made their departure as soon as grandfather could be said to have spent a decent interval in the grave. They left early one morning, dropping their keys noisily as they went past the console in the hall. The tenants, who until then had occupied the small white house, having no lease, were dispossessed.

Philip was left to his grandeur. Philip was a bad lot. They were not quite sure just what particular badness his was, but he had been spoiled, and they knew, somewhere below their consciousness, that sooner or later he would compromise them if they stayed. He had not asked them to stay. Far from it. On the contrary, they had heard his obstreperous laughter, when, coming downstairs unaware on the day they were to move, he had found their bandboxes piled in the entrance hall under the black-glazed amphorae.

They were glad to be leaving the great house. It was too lofty, too bare. They would no longer have to keep their eyes lowered to their plates throughout meals, lest, raising them, they should disconcertingly stray toward that mythological god, whoever he was, who stood unabashed before them, bare in his niche. Then, too, it would be a satisfaction, at last, to live like everyone else, in a house with windows that looked out on Felicity Street. They would be able to see everything that went on, without more effort than it needed to lean from their rockers. For they would have rocking chairs. So long they had wanted one apiece. And they had already planned little curtains for the windows.

For the house in which their grandfather Wanhope had lived and died presented to the elms, which through the sunlight shook out their long shadows against colonnade and walls, a blind brilliance. Constructed during the classic revival, it was an Oedipus among houses, Providence the Colonnus of its exile. No light pierced that noble front.

The house was Philip's. The grandfather had left it to him. But even if the will had not been precise as to its disposition, Agatha and Georgina would readily have consented to his having it. It was too tragic for their taste. The little house was modest and more suitable for two maiden ladies. For, though they were but twenty-five and twenty-seven at this time, it was already rather more than probable that they would bear the name of Wanhope the rest of their lives. Once, as young girls, they had been fearful lest they should be married for the sake of the money that was coming to them. Now, they were disturbed by the very thought of marriage itself. Their feet were quite large; they no longer wore shoes that were too small for them.

Philip would manage the mill. They supposed him capable. And they would depend on their lawyers to see that they got their just share of income.

The point of contention was the driveway, which ran between the two houses and gave access to the stables behind. Philip claimed it. Anyone could see that it properly went with the big house. But to show that it was his property he proposed to put a fence, a low white picket fence, along his sisters' line, to prevent their using the driveway.

Three holes had been dug for posts. When they woke one morning, three earthy gaps had appeared in their lawn. A lilac bush had been uprooted.

They rushed off at nine o'clock to see their lawyers. This depredation must be stopped. That afternoon, Philip's fence was stayed, but not before eleven white-primed posts stood on the inner side of what Agatha and Georgina believed their line.

A week later, Philip saw two of his posts had been overthrown. Others had been hacked, rather ineffectively, with a hatchet. He haled Agatha and Georgina into court for wilful and malicious damage to property. But his case was weakened rather than helped by his witnesses, who declared that they had seen the two ladies out on the lawn in their nightgowns.

Charge was followed by countercharge. The law added its own complications. The simple and sensible solution, which was the one the grandfather had obviously intended, whereby all three should share the driveway and brother and sisters use the large stables in common, had become impossible. A fence there must be. Upon that, all three were fixed. The point at issue was on whose property the fence should stand, for the ladies were now, like Philip, claiming that the driveway was all theirs.

It was three years before the courts reached a laborious and expensive conclusion. It was that a line should be drawn for the fence-posts down the middle of the driveway. This would, of course, prevent anybody from ever using it again as a passage from Felicity Street to the stables. The sisters were satisfied. The fence was to be erected at Philip's expense. He was also ordered by the court to bear all costs.

Philip took the decision with calm. Felicity Street had been divided, almost as evenly as the driveway was now to be, between the partisans of Philip and those of Agatha and Georgina. They agreed only in finding the controversy deplorable: a family as imposing as the Wanhopes should make at least a show of solidarity. The grandchildren might as well have driven a great gap through the front wall, under the Greek portico, and allowed every passer-by to peer through at their private squabbles. The conflict outraged respectability. But if the sisters' faction was, in an uneasy way, rather pleased at the court's decision, Philip's adherents got what satisfaction they could out of his moral superiority. He had behaved like the aristocrat that he was. No

one, they said, with the court against him, could have shown himself
more perfectly the gentleman.

Philip did not look put out. He drove to the Pomham Club, the
carriage coming all the way round the block to wait for him before the
door. He bowed to acquaintances. He descended on Brown University,
and after several visits, one of them with the President, it was publicly
announced that he had presented his grandfather's editions of the
Latin poets, his collection of eighteenth-century American sermons
to the library.

He watched the holes being dug for the fence-posts. The surface
of the driveway was hard with stones. The work at first went slowly.
When the workmen were sunk below their knees in the ground, he
stood above them, trampling the loose loamy gravel. Though still a
young man, his breath already came thickly. Always tall, it was now
noticed, though perhaps not for the first time, how sinister it was to
find those features, so like an antique goat's, staring at you from such
a height. The posts lay on the ground, new, extremely long and
shaped round. The lumber for the palings, it could be seen even from
the sidewalk, was secondhand.

"This lawsuit has ruined me," he announced. "I can't afford to
put up a new fence."

The workmen talked. But the fence was up, each panel in place,
Philip's side whitewashed, before word got around as to where he had
procured his planks for palings.

Providence had just installed a new and complete sewage system.
And Brown University had at last decided to displace its old outdoor
privy. It had been standing since the beginning of the century when
Philip Wanhope bought it for boards.

" 'The hopes, the fears, of boyhood years,' " he exclaimed as he
casually inspected the interior. And then, as he stopped to read the
inscriptions, " 'The words of love then spoken!' "

It had been carved from one end to the other by generations of
adolescents. The walls were as thickly scrawled as a Latin text with
interlinears cribbed from a trot.

Still humming *Oft in the Stilly Night*, he hurried off to complete
his purchase. This was the side he would expose to his sisters' view.

They ignored his revenge. They even allowed a respectable interval to pass before they applied a first coat of whitewash to the fence.
Gradually, under successive coats, the work of the pencil was more or
less obliterated. But what the pocket-knife had done when it cut into
the wood the thwarted fantasies of the young mind was not so easily
undone. It was merely whitewashed, and still perceptible. Agatha and

Georgina gave no sign that they ever saw that their fence was different from any other. But whether this was innocence or pretense, no one could know.

IV

Philip was still looking at the fence when the Negro returned to report.

"I shooed 'em away." He held his apron in both hands as though he were driving birds from a seeded plot.

"I didn't see them. Where are they?"

"They dropped over the fence into Miss 'Gatha's and Miss 'Gina's backyard."

"I hope they eat all their pears and then die of the belly-ache."

"Those boys ain't eatin' pears, Mr. Wanhope."

"Then what are they doing?"

"Those boys are reading off that fence. They readin' out loud."

"My God," said Philip. "I used to be able to laugh. But now all I can do is to wheeze. And to think I've been waiting twenty years for this, and I can't even laugh."

1937